Perspectives in
Contemporary Criticism

Perspectives in
Contemporary Criticism

A COLLECTION OF RECENT ESSAYS
BY AMERICAN, ENGLISH,
AND EUROPEAN LITERARY CRITICS

edited by / *SHELDON NORMAN GREBSTEIN*
State University of New York at Binghamton

Harper & Row, PUBLISHERS

New York • Evanston • and London

Acknowledgments

I am deeply indebted to Frederick Moyle for the several kinds of help he gave so generously and efficiently in the making of this book, from the performance of the most mechanical tasks to the provision of cogent and perceptive editorial opinion.

I am also grateful to my colleagues at Harpur College for advice and encouragement at one time or another: Carrol Coates, Glenn Burne, John Hagopian, Melvin Seiden, Robert Kroetsch, Mario Di Cesare, and others.

Grateful acknowledgment in the order in which the works appear in the book is made to the following contributors, publishers, and periodicals for permission to reprint the copyrighted material included in this collection:

The Princeton University Press for "Odysseus' Scar," from *Mimesis: The Representation of Reality in Western Literature*, by Erich Auerbach, translated by Willard R. Trask. Copyright 1953 by the Princeton University Press.

Alfred A. Knopf, Inc., for Chapter II from *The Death of Tragedy*, by George Steiner. Copyright © 1961 by George Steiner.

John Henry Raleigh and *The Sewanee Review* for "The English Novel and the Three Kinds of Time," by John Henry Raleigh, from *The Sewanee Review*, Vol. LXIII, No. 3, (Summer 1954). Copyright 1954 by the University of the South.

David Daiches and Oliver & Boyd, Ltd., publishers, for "Religion, Poetry, and the 'Dilemma' of the Modern Writer," from *Literary Essays*, by David Daiches. Copyright 1956 by Oliver & Boyd, Ltd.

The Macmillan Company, M. B. Yeats, and the Macmillan Company of Canada Ltd. for selections from *Collected Poems*, by William Butler Yeats. Copyright 1933 by The Macmillan Company, renewed 1961 by Bertha Georgie Yeats.

New Directions Publishing Corporation, J. M. Dent & Sons Ltd., and the Trustees for the Copyrights of the late Dylan Thomas for a selection from *The Collected Poems*, by Dylan Thomas. Copyright 1939 by New Directions.

Harry Levin and the University Press of Virginia for "Symbolism and Fiction," by Harry Levin. Copyright © 1956 by the University Press of Virginia.

The Bollingen Foundation for "Problems of Poetry," from *The Art of Poetry*, by Paul Valéry, edited by Jackson Matthews, translated by Denise Folliot. Bollingen Series XLV.7, Pantheon Books (1958). Copyright © 1958 by Bollingen Foundation.

Cleanth Brooks and the New York University Press for "Literary Criticism: Poet, Poem, and Reader," by Cleanth Brooks, from *Varieties of Literary Experience*, edited by Stanley Burnshaw. Copyright © 1962 by the New York University Press.

Wayne C. Booth and The University of Chicago Press for "Telling and Showing," from *The Rhetoric of Fiction*, by Wayne C. Booth. Copright © 1961 by The University of Chicago Press.

Howard Nemerov and *The Graduate Journal* for "Composition and Fate in the Short Novel," by Howard Nemerov, from *The Graduate Journal*, Vol. V, No. 2 (Fall 1963). Copyright © 1963 by the Board of Regents of the University of Texas.

Allan Swallow, publisher, for "The Audible Reading of Poetry," from *The Function of Criticism: Problems and Exercises*, by Yvor Winters. Copyright © 1957 by Yvor Winters.

William K. Wimsatt and the University of Kentucky Press for "What to Say About a Poem," from *Hateful Contraries*, by William K. Wimsatt. Copyright © 1965 by the University of Kentucky Press. The original version of this essay was published in *Reports and Speeches of the Eighth Yale Conference on the Teaching of English, April 13 and 14, 1962*, edited by Edward Gordon, Office of Teacher Training, Yale University, 1962. Copyright © 1962 by William K. Wimsatt.

Lionel Trilling and The Viking Press, Inc., for "The Fate of Pleasure," from *Beyond Culture*, by Lionel Trilling. Copyright © 1963 by Lionel Trilling.

The British Book Centre, Inc., for "The Visionary Individualists," from *The Creative Element*, by Stephen Spender. Copyright 1954 by Stephen Spender.

The Macmillan Company, M. B. Yeats, and the Macmillan Company of Canada Ltd. for a selection from *Collected Poems*, by William Butler Yeats. Copyright 1924 by The Macmillan Company, renewed 1952 by Bertha Georgie Yeats.

Harper & Row, Publishers, Incorporated for "The Ideology of Modernism" (pp. 17–46) from *Realism in Our Time* by Georg Lukács. First published in English translation under the title *The Meaning of Contemporary Realism*. Copyright © 1962 by Merlin Press, Ltd.

Harcourt, Brace & World, Inc. and Faber and Faber Ltd. for a selection from "The Cocktail Party," by T. S. Eliot. Copyright 1950 by T. S. Eliot.

The publisher, Horizon Press, for "The Fiction of Anti-Utopia," from *A World More Attractive*, by Irving Howe. Copyright © 1963 by Horizon Press.

Eric Bentley for "The Political Theatre Reconsidered," by Eric Bentley, from *The Kenyon Review*, Vol. XXIII (1961). Copyright © 1961 by Eric Bentley.

Norman N. Holland and *Victorian Studies* for "Psychological Depths and 'Dover Beach,'" by Norman N. Holland, from *Victorian Studies: Supplement*, Vol. IX (September 1965). Copyright © 1965 by Indiana University.

Kenneth Burke and the *Centennial Review of Arts and Sciences*, for "Catharsis: Second View," by Kenneth Burke, from *Centennial Review of Arts and Sciences*, Vol. V (1961). Copyright © 1961 by Michigan State University.

The publisher, Horizon Press, for "The Creative Experience in Poetry," from *The Forms of Things Unknown*, by Herbert Read. Copyright © 1960 by Horizon Press.

The Johns Hopkins Press, publishers, and Elliott Coleman, translator, for "Molière," from *Studies in Human Time*, by Georges Poulet. Copyright © 1956 by the Johns Hopkins Press.

Stein and Day, Publishers, for "The Novel and America," from *Love and Death in the American Novel*, by Leslie A. Fiedler. Copyright © 1960 by Criterion Books. Copyright © 1966 by Stein and Day.

The Michigan State University Press for "The Myth and Ritual Approach to Shakespearean Tragedy," from *The Agony and the Triumph*, by Herbert Weisinger. Copyright © 1964 by the Michigan State University Press.

Francis Fergusson and *The Sewanee Review* for "'Myth' and the Literary Scruple," by Francis Fergusson, from *The Sewanee Review*, Vol. LXIV (1956). Copyright © 1956 by the University of the South.

Columbia University Press, for "The Drunken Boat: The Revolutionary Element in Romanticism," by Northrop Frye, from *Romanticism Reconsidered*, edited by Northrop Frye. Copyright © 1963 by Columbia University Press.

The University of North Carolina Press for "Homo Faber and Poetry," from *The Poet and the Machine*, by Paul Ginestier, translated by Martin B. Friedman. Copyright © 1961 by The University of North Carolina Press.

The Macmillan Company for a selection from *Collected Poems*, by Vachel Lindsay. Copyright 1914 by The Macmillan Company, renewed 1942 by Elizabeth C. Lindsay.

Harcourt, Brace & World, Inc. for "Smoke and Steel" in *Smoke and Steel* by Carl Sandburg. Copyright 1920 by Harcourt, Brace & World, Inc.; copyright 1948 by Carl Sandburg.

Random House, Inc., and Faber and Faber Ltd. for selections from *Ruins and Visions: Poems 1934–1942*, by Stephen Spender. Copyright 1942 by Stephen Spender.

The Macmillan Company for a selection from *Collected Poems*, by Marianne Moore. Copyright 1951 by Marianne Moore.

W. H. Auden for "The Quest Hero," by W. H. Auden, from *Texas Quarterly*, Vol. IV (Winter 1961). Copyright © 1961 by the Board of Regents of the University of Texas.

For My Sons,
Jason and Gary

Contents

Acknowledgments   v

Preface   xv

I. The Historical Critic

Introduction   1

Selected Bibliography   10

ERICH AUERBACH   /   Odysseus' Scar   12

GEORGE STEINER   /   from *The Death of Tragedy*   28

JOHN HENRY RALEIGH   /   The English Novel and the Three Kinds of
Time   42

DAVID DAICHES   /   Religion, Poetry, and the "Dilemma" of the Modern
Writer   50

HARRY LEVIN   /   Symbolism and Fiction   63

II. The Formalist Critic

Introduction   75

Selected Bibliography   84

PAUL VALÉRY   /   Problems of Poetry   87

CLEANTH BROOKS   /   Literary Criticism: Poet, Poem, Reader   96

WAYNE C. BOOTH / Telling and Showing 108

HOWARD NEMEROV / Composition and Fate in the Short Novel 120

YVOR WINTERS / The Audible Reading of Poetry 133

W. K. WIMSATT, JR. / What to Say About a Poem 146

III. *The Sociocultural Critic*

Introduction 161

Selected Bibliography 169

LIONEL TRILLING / The Fate of Pleasure 171

STEPHEN SPENDER / The Visionary Individualists 188

GEORG LUKÁCS / The Ideology of Modernism 202

IRVING HOWE / The Fiction of Anti-Utopia 220

ERIC BENTLEY / The Political Theatre Reconsidered 226

IV. *The Psychological Critic*

Introduction 237

Selected Bibliography 246

NORMAN N. HOLLAND / Psychological Depths and "Dover Beach" 248

KENNETH BURKE / Catharsis: Second View 268

HERBERT READ / The Creative Experience in Poetry 284

GEORGES POULET / Molière 293

LESLIE A. FIEDLER / The Novel and America 299

V. *The Mythopoeic Critic*

Introduction 311

Selected Bibliography 320

HERBERT WEISINGER / The Myth and Ritual Approach to Shakespearean
       Tragedy 322

FRANCIS FERGUSSON / "Myth" and the Literary Scruple 337

NORTHROP FRYE / The Drunken Boat: The Revolutionary Element in Romanticism 345

PAUL GINESTIER / Homo Faber and Poetry 357

W. H. AUDEN / The Quest Hero 370

Index 385

Preface

This book was engendered, like many books, from my own needs and interests and from events in the classroom. As a teacher of contemporary literature and as a person inevitably engaged with the literary criticism that is produced in great quantity and complexity in our time, I increasingly felt the need for a book that would: (1) organize the mass of contemporary critical writing into coherent groups, types, or perspectives; (2) clearly describe the premises and modes of operation of each group; and (3) permit the comparison of one approach with another. For myself and others of similar situation, both amateur and professional, the result of such study and comparison might be not only a deeper understanding of an important aspect of our literary culture but also the opportunity to clarify and further develop our own critical methods.

At the time when this project was conceived and proposed to the publisher, no book of this kind existed. Others have since appeared, and no doubt mine will not be the last. But because literary criticism itself becomes an ever larger and more dynamic endeavor, we must make a continuing attempt at classification and elucidation. Although the formal study of modern literary criticism has a secure place in many curricula, especially that of the advanced student, I deduce from my own experience that the study may sometimes be attended by vagueness and confusion. In short, I hope others may benefit as much from the making of this book as I have; compiling this volume has helped me to gain some perspective, at least temporarily, on the state of contemporary criticism.

In surveying the criticism of the past twenty-five years, I held to a number of constant criteria for the selection of essays to go into this collection. First, I chose the best criticism I could find that would illustrate the types dominant in contemporary practice, what I have called the *historical*, the *formalistic*, the *sociocultural*, the *psychological*, and the *mythopoeic*. Undoubtedly there are essays included that some readers will find disagreeable; however, I question whether any of these selections will be thought dull, trivial, or superficial.

Secondly, I chose essays that to the best of my knowledge have not appeared in comparable collections. That is, the present text aspires to freshness and original-ity, or, at worst, to contemporaneity. The earliest essay reprinted here is that by Paul Valéry, and it was first published in 1938. All the other selections were first published after 1950.

Next, the collection was assembled with an eye toward balance and symmetry. Each critical perspective receives nearly equal space, and there is also a good deal of scope in the treatment of genre and period. Although I usually opted for diversity of topic, in a few cases I deliberately chose essays that overlap and inter-relate. For example, a number of essays discuss tragedy. I fear there may also be a prejudice, despite my attempt to suppress it, in favor of modern literature.

Another of my considerations was to include the work of talented critics of less familiar reputation as well as that of men of general renown. For example, the names of John Henry Raleigh, Norman Holland, Herbert Weisinger, and Paul Ginestier are probably well known only by specialists. Perhaps in this way the book will serve to introduce able critics to a wider audience.

Two additional principles guided my selection. Without pretending to ade-quately represent the range and quality of criticism on the Continent, I neverthe-less wished to include at least a few of the many important critics who have writ-ten in a language other than English. Accordingly, each group of essays contains one selection by a European critic: Erich Auerbach, German; Georg Lukács, Hun-garian; Paul Valéry, Georges Poulet, and Paul Ginestier, French. Secondly, I selected the essays for each group so as to represent the spectrum of opinion within the specific approach, from the emphatic or doctrinaire statement of a particular position at one pole, to the implicit or highly individualistic statement at the other. So, for example, Georg Lukács expresses a much more extreme kind of Sociocultural Criticism than does Lionel Trilling.

In the choice of each selection, my preference has been for those essays that combine both theory and practice, that begin with their critical hypotheses or premises and then proceed to apply them to literary texts. I have generally avoided essays devoted to exhaustive analysis of a single work because I believe that the reader will better comprehend the rationale of a particular critical perspective if he sees it more broadly applied.

Inevitably, an editor's last and keenest lament is for what could not be in-cluded, and this collection makes conspicuous exclusions. Edmund Wilson, T. S. Eliot, Allen Tate, Douglas Bush, John Crowe Ransom, R. S. Crane, William Empson, and R. P. Blackmur are among the distinguished critics whose work is not reprinted here. However, I excluded them not out of ignorance or hostility but simply because essays by others were better fitted to my special design. Fortu-nately the work of these important critics has often been reprinted and is readily available. No reader who wishes to be conversant with contemporary criticism can ignore these eminent names.

Because the essays usually manifest the critical premises of their group or type,

I have kept my introductions to each group brief. In the introductions I offer these materials in due proportion: (1) the sources and recent development of the particular critical type; (2) a discussion of its major precepts as they are advanced in the selections to follow; (3) an assessment of its successes and failures. A selected bibliography is provided after each introduction. Note that the bibliographies stress theoretical statements and analyses of the critical method in question rather than works of applied criticism in that method. I have attempted above all in my introductions to be accurate and impartial. Indeed, I found myself temporarily converted to each critical perspective in turn as I studied it.

A collection of this nature becomes an exceedingly hazardous enterprise for its editor because he must try to impose categories and classifications upon the writing of critics whose subtle intelligences resist hard and fast categorization. For example, exactly where does one place Leslie Fiedler, whose writing is variously and sometimes simultaneously sociocultural, mythopoeic, and psychological? Or Kenneth Burke, whose system is his own integration of virtually all others? Northrop Frye is a distinguished historical scholar-critic as well as a leading mythopoeic critic. Yvor Winters is here listed as a "formalist," yet in his emphatic belief in the moral quality of literature he departs from the formalist's repudiation of extrinsic norms. And so on. I can find no way out of this difficulty except to announce my awareness of it and to restate my intention to represent each type of criticism in its widest range. I make a further effort at correct placement and description of the individual critic's perspective in the brief note that prefaces each essay and identifies its author.

I conclude with this statement of belief: Good criticism depends far less on theoretical systems and formulas than on men. Although each reader will quite naturally find some critical approaches more useful than others to his own needs, no system is inherently superior to those who practice it. Whatever its particular bias and method, when criticism is successful it brings to its reader a sense of heightened understanding, illumination, and appreciation of the literary work, and the success of the criticism depends upon the quality of the critic's mind and the soundness of his taste. If the critic's mind is an instrument of intelligence, learning, sensitivity, and judgment, he will probably succeed regardless of his espousal of a certain method or formula. Intelligence, learning, sensitivity, judgment—inspired by a love for literature—this is the best formula for literary criticism.

SHELDON NORMAN GREBSTEIN

Binghamton, New York
July, 1967

I. The Historical Critic

ERICH AUERBACH

GEORGE STEINER

JOHN HENRY RALEIGH

DAVID DAICHES

HARRY LEVIN

INTRODUCTION

The historical method of literary criticism has been traced into antiquity, but for our purposes it can be said that historical criticism began in the seventeenth and eighteenth centuries with Dryden and Johnson. Dryden believed that every poet in some degree belonged to "an age," and in *An Essay of Dramatic Poesy* (1668) argued from a rationale that was at least in part historical and comparative. Samuel Johnson was fundamentally concerned with literature as the expression of general and unchanging truths, yet he also held that "to judge rightly of the present, we must oppose it to the past."

However, it was not until the nineteenth century that the historical method received explicit and emphatic statement, most notably in the writings of two Frenchmen: Charles Augustin Sainte-Beuve and Hippolyte-Adolphe Taine. Influenced by the growing concern with science characteristic of his time, Sainte-Beuve declared, "What I should like to establish is the natural history of literature." In his applied criticism, Sainte-Beuve consistently employed the biographical approach, seeking to establish the personality of the literary work through the

1

personality of its author. He wrote, "To me, literature—literary production—is not at all distinct or separable from the rest of man and his nature. I can enjoy a work; but it is difficult for me to judge it independently of a knowledge of the man himself. I would readily say, 'Like tree, like fruit [*tel arbre, tel fruit*].' " Taine, in a sense Sainte-Beuve's disciple, went beyond his master in bringing to the study of literature methods originally inspired by the natural sciences, seeking to find in literature a deterministic process of cause and effect. Taine's determinism becomes apparent in the major criteria for literary analysis, which he named in the opening pages of his *History of English Literature* (1863), the criteria of race, moment, and milieu; or, to paraphrase, national character, historical period, and social environment. Taine's approach was also to become one of the sources for the sociocultural method.

The theories of Taine and Sainte-Beuve had enormous influence on the Continent. Indeed, much of the European scholarship and criticism, regardless of the country where it is practiced, is still primarily concerned with the author's "mind" and biography, his historical and social environment, and his literary sources. Not many years after their origins, the theories of Taine and Sainte-Beuve also affected American literary study, which was highly imitative of the European throughout the nineteenth century. From its founding Johns Hopkins University was patterned after German methods of scholarship, and American scholars everywhere emulated German and British literary research as it was exemplified by the work of such German philologists as Bockh and the Grimm brothers and of the English scholars Skeat and Furnivall.

Historical scholarship continued to dominate the serious study of literature in America through the late 1920s, when it first came under attack by the Formalists. During the 1930s the attack increased in urgency and intensity, aided from quite another quarter by the Liberal-Marxist critics. In the 1940s and early 1950s historicism was largely in retreat or on the defensive; however, any announcement of its surrender would have been premature, for by the late 1950s its resurgence had begun. Today, having absorbed some valuable lessons from its antagonists, having redefined its objectives and strategy, and having recruited a number of vigorous young troops to march beside the old guard, it promises to regain its former eminence. One doubts whether it will ever again be said of the new historical critic and his present critical method what Sinclair Lewis declared in his 1930 Nobel Prize speech: "Our American professors like their literature clear, cold, pure, and very dead."

We may deduce from its sources that the central doctrine of the historical criticism, its basic article of faith, is the conviction that no literary work can be approached as though it were complete in itself. Rather, each work must be studied with reference to its dossier, that is, the entire body of information pertinent to it. The historical critic compiles this dossier through his pursuit of one or more of several possible lines of inquiry:

1. He makes certain that he is using a reliable text of the work.

2. He operates with an awareness of the work's language as it would have functioned in the particular time and place of the work's creation.

3. He studies the work in light of the author's life and material circumstances, especially those affecting the composition of the work under scrutiny; he also considers the work within the context of the author's entire career.

4. He compares the author and his work with their predecessors and contemporaries and assesses the influences that might have modified the work; similarly the historical critic will consider the work's own reputation and influence upon other works and writers.

5. He views the work as "of an age," that is, as an expression of the culture in which it was composed, and as a possible reflection of the events and condition of that culture.

6. He locates the work within a literary tradition, convention, mode, or genre, and determines its relationship to other similar works.

Although some of these activities in practice tend to merge or overlap, we can see that no matter what his special interest, the historical critic regards knowledge as essential to the act of criticism. For him, the functions of scholarship are difficult to separate from those of criticism, and even if these functions could be separated, they would remain complementary and integral parts of the same process.

Whether the historical scholar can indeed be distinguished from the historical critic remains a question so hotly debated I hesitate to offer a definition and delimitation of one that would exclude the other. Nevertheless, I believe that scholarship and criticism are distinguishable, at least in their proper emphases and in their relative positions in the process of literary study. Very simply, the scholar provides the facts, the hard data, that the literary critic then applies in his interpretation and judgment of the work. To extend this distinction three further differentiae can be suggested: (1) The scholar is essentially concerned with the meaningful change or flux in the continuity of literature; the critic is most concerned with the similarity and permanence of literary works. (2) The scholar occupies himself with the correct placement and accurate apprehension of the work; the critic occupies himself with the elucidation and evaluation of the work. (3) The scholar concentrates on the origins and genesis of the work; the critic concentrates on the aesthetic nature of the received work. Perhaps the discussion to follow will untangle some of the strands of this knotty problem. For emphasis, I will consider separately each of the several aspects of the historical method already cited.

1. TEXT

The establishment of a reliable text is primarily the activity of the scholar rather than of the critic, although in many cases in which the documentary evidence is indecisive the text that best represents the writer's intention cannot be determined without the exercise of critical acumen and taste. The task of the textual scholar-critic is not complete until the text has been restored and dated and its authorship identified and authenticated. Identification and authentification are, of course, essential in cases of anonymous authorship, doubtful attribution, or collaborative work.

Obviously no trustworthy criticism can be performed upon a corrupt text, yet hilarious and terrifying examples abound of the unwary critic who has labored with great pain and ingenuity to explicate the ambiguities of a word or passage, when, in fact, the ambiguity was the result of a misprint. The textual problem pertains not only to older works but also to modern works as well. To cite but one such example, my colleague John V. Hagopian recently argued that a long-unnoticed error in Hemingway's much-discussed story "A Clean, Well-Lighted Place" was probably responsible for much of the critical uncertainty about the story's theme and characters and by a process of close reading and careful reasoning was able to demonstrate that some lines of dialogue in the story had very likely been printed in the wrong order. His study has resulted in a promise from Hemingway's publisher to correct this error in subsequent printings of the story.[1]

2. LANGUAGE

Here again the activity of the scholar tends to merge with that of the critic, defying sharp differentiation. But to inquire further, we see that the historical approach performs two operations with language, explanation and elucidation. The first task belongs more to the scholar, the second to the critic.

To explain or define the particular meaning of the writer's language in its cultural setting at the moment of its use, the scholar calls upon pertinent documents, sources, and biographical information. For example, in dealing with a passage from Shakespeare we often encounter words that are either no longer current or whose meanings have changed drastically:

> When he himself might his quietus make
> With a bare bodkin? Who would these fardels bear . . . .

And in such instances as these we depend upon the scholar to give us a "translation" of the work's language so that we ourselves can begin to respond critically to it. In short, the scholar employs historical facts in his investigation into the language of the work in order to banish its strangeness. He uses history so that the work's reader may later ignore it.

In the second of his linguistic operations, elucidation, the historical scholar-critic aspires to bring the reader to a full understanding of the language's effect and impact and to reveal to him its manifold allusiveness, its covert meanings,

---

[1] John V. Hagopian, "Tidying Up Hemingway's Clean, Well-Lighted Place," *Studies in Short Fiction*, I (1964), 140–146. Mr. Hagopian tells me that a correct text is now in print.

and its place in linguistic and literary convention. Thus the critic working with an eighteenth-century text must consider the multiple possibilities of meaning in such words as *wit, imagination,* and *nature.* The word *quietus* in the preceding passage from Hamlet's soliloquy could be translated simply as *discharge* or *release,* but it also conveys a whole complex of associations that go beyond *Hamlet* itself into the world-view of its age. The associations are precisely the critic's concern. Eric Auerbach's "Odysseus' Scar"* is an especially apt demonstration of this aspect of the historical critic's method and illustrates Auerbach's keen perceptions into the largeness of implication in particular Biblical words and phrases.

In dealing with the language of the literary work the historical critic therefore assumes a dual responsibility: he must return the present-day reader to the state of linguistic apprehension or awareness of the work's contemporary audience; he must also treat the language as a currently viable medium. This doubleness of language is fundamental to a work's duration in time, part of the secret of both its original and continuing appeal. Furthermore, the language conveys values, the values of its own culture and era, against which we inevitably compare our own. Roy Harvey Pearce, one of the foremost apologists for the new historicism, has said it well: "Studying language, we study history. We study history so that we can study language. . . . Studying history, we study culture. Studying a culture, we study its poetry. Studying its poetry, we study its language. The system is one and whole."

3. BIOGRAPHY

Biographical information, supplied by scholarly research, is among the most valuable kinds of data utilized by the historical critic. Because the historical critic judges the success or failure of the work of art against the context of the author's intention, he seeks out all information that will illuminate that intention. The facts relating to the author's mental and physical condition, his place of residence, his books, the situation of his family, his debts, friends, romantic entanglements, politics—in short, all the writer felt, heard, saw, knew and was as a man—are of possible importance, not in themselves but as they affected the writer's human purposes and ultimately the embodiment of them in his art.

Through the study of the author's life, the critic attempts to grasp what Helen Gardner has called *the habit of his mind;* that is, the writer's characteristic modes of response and patterns of thought, out of which will arise his use of language, selection of theme, and the ideas, forms, symbols, and images that recur in his work. To the critic who approaches the literary work via biography, the single work also becomes richer and more meaningful as it is placed within the sum of a career; and the career, in turn, becomes larger than the sum of the individual works that comprise it. Much European criticism is committed to this position, although not always overtly, so that what often seems the European critic's

* This symbol is used to indicate that the essay appears in this book.

intuition of the work (a personal, even mystical sense) is actually based upon knowledge previously gained through historical study. To the historical critic who openly professes his method, a knowledge of the writer's life and career serves as a safeguard against subjective or eccentric interpretation. The work and the man are inseparable.

Although all readers are naturally and humanly curious about the fellow human who creates a work of art and although the scholar is professionally interested in the writer as a historical person, the critic is fundamentally concerned with the portions of the man's experience that shape his career as a writer. The historical critic finds it more than coincidence that Poe, who lost the women he most loved, his mother, his foster mother, and his wife, came to believe that the death of a beautiful woman was the best subject for poetry. F. Scott Fitzgerald, who at twelve prayed that he would not have to go to the poorhouse, was later in his fiction preoccupied with money and social class. The historical critic seeks out correlations between the writer's life and work not only to get at content but also to illuminate form: Hemingway's terse and objective style reflects his training as a newspaperman; Faulkner's high rhetoric reveals his immersion in the living tradition of Southern eloquence and oratory. David Daiches in "Religion, Poetry, and the 'Dilemma' of the Modern Writer"* employs biographical data in his interpretations of Milton and Yeats; George Steiner in the selection from *The Death of Tragedy** makes frequent reference to the writer's intention; and Harry Levin in "Symbolism and Fiction"* argues that the explication of a writer's symbolism should begin with the known facts of the writer's life and career.

4. REPUTATION AND INFLUENCE

Although the study of a work's or writer's reputation and influence would seem to be more properly the scholar's pursuit than the critic's, the critic may well address himself to such considerations. The critic may raise the question of the writer's reputation both to demonstrate the aesthetic values of the writer's contemporary audience and to illuminate the functioning of our own. For example, when we compare the reception of *Moby Dick* by the audience of its time with that of the twentieth century, we throw light in two directions, backward upon the evolution of American taste and forward upon enduring factors in the work itself.

Similarly, in the critic's treatment of influence, that is, the effect of one writer's work upon another, the critic would not halt his inquiry once the historical fact of influence had been ascertained; he would then proceed to make this fact part of his explication or evaluation. A study of Frank Norris might appropriately be prefaced by a study of Zola, and the relative merits of both writers could be assessed if analogous works such as *Germinal* and *The Octopus* were placed side by side. Moreover, the study of influence need not be limited to a strict chronological cause-effect sequence but may be broadened to become an analysis of confluence, the treatment of similar themes in various times and places by different writers.

5. CULTURE

Central to the whole rationale of historicism is its sense of the past, its concern with the existence in time of the work of art. Lionel Trilling has observed that the artwork partakes of history in three respects: the work itself records historic fact; its own existence is a historical fact; its aesthetic quality, its mystique, is inseparable from its pastness. In contrast to the historical critic, the historian, or the historian of ideas, views the artwork as less important in itself than as a piece of documentary evidence. He uses the work of art to enter or reconstruct an age and a culture; for him the work is primarily an expression of the culture's *zeitgeist* because his main interest is the writing of *geistesgeschichte*. For the historical critic, on the other hand, history culminates in its literary expression; the creation of the artwork is the historic moment.

Just as the critic has a double concern with the language of the literary work, its pastness and its presentness, he is likewise doubly engaged with the values and ideas conveyed in the work. Acting both as relativist and absolutist, he exhibits the civilization's changing values and ideas while at the same time he demonstrates how and why Aeschylus and Chaucer still speak to us. To the historical critic literature is the voice of *humanitas*, and through it he aspires not merely to literacy but to humane literacy.

But if the critic must return to the past to explain the work, he must function in the present to judge it; that is, he must beware of lapsing into what has been called the *genetic fallacy*—the error of mistaking the study of the origins of a literary work for the explanation of its present value. David Daiches has succinctly described the whole problem: "Confusion between origin and value is perhaps the commonest critical error of the present day. Explanation of origin, however, can serve some very fundamental purposes. If we know just what is in the civilization of his time that led the writer to adopt the attitude he did, to shape the work the way he did, to tell this story in this way and no other, then we realize what we may call the logic of the work; we can see what its real principle of unity is; we can see the work as a whole and be sure of seeing the right whole. And only then are we qualified to talk about appreciation and value." It is precisely with this spirit that John Henry Raleigh* links the Victorian attitude with the treatment of time in nineteenth-century novels and then proceeds to contrast these with the twentieth-century attitude and the modern writer's time-sense. Similarly, Erich Auerbach* reveals how the temper of the Greek and the Hebrew is manifested in the style and structure of the masterpieces each civilization produced.

6. CONVENTION

The literary lineage or genealogy of a work, its place in the appropriate tradition or convention of like works, is one of the historical critic's major concerns. Whereas the scholar studies convention with his main emphasis on its origin and status within a given period, the critic views convention as a vital and present force that helps determine literary form. J. V. Cunningham cogently remarked on this point: ". . . a literary form is not simply an external principle of classification of literary works . . . nor is it an Idea. It is rather a principle operative in the production of works. It is a scheme of experience recognized in the tradition and derived from prior works and from the descriptions of those works extant in the tradition. It is, moreover, a scheme that directs the discovery of material and detail and that orders the disposition of the whole. If a literary form is an Idea, it is an idea only in the sense that it is an idea that the reader and writer have of the form." Each writer comes into competition with all others who have worked in the same convention (or form), just as the reader brings to a work of art his memory of all others like it—which, in turn, shapes his expectation of what the work can be. The new work (primarily its form) is thus consciously or unconsciously judged in the light of what has gone before and contests with past works for the reader's response and appreciation. This is in part what T. S. Eliot meant when he said that tradition constantly rearranges itself to make place for the new. Obviously the historical critic needs a sound knowledge of a particular convention before he can apply his taste to a work that falls within it. I like Ihab Hassan's statement of it: "The pressure of tradition is Taste in action."

This awareness of convention and tradition is clearly evident in the essays to follow: Steiner contrasts the open form of Elizabethan drama with that of the medieval and neoclassical; Auerbach alludes to the various epic traditions; Levin discusses the changing modes of symbolism; Raleigh surveys the development of certain new artistic forms and techniques in the novel; Daiches compares the poetic forms of Yeats and Thomas with those of Milton.

Although I have so far described and analyzed the historical method in literary criticism rather than appraised it, I will now summarize some of the important points and proceed to an assessment.

First, to review the troublesome issue of the distinction between historical scholar and historical critic, I would say that the distinction is largely one of degree rather than kind. The scholar studies the facts of the literary work's origins, sources, function as a vehicle for ideas. The critic directs his attention primarily to what might be called the truth of the received work, to the form and significance with which the facts about the work are finally embodied. For example, Lovejoy's *The Great Chain of Being* and Lowes' *The Road to Xanadu* are monuments of historical scholarship and astonishing displays of intelligence and erudition. They could not, however, justly be described as criticism. But my fundamental purpose is not to establish separate and inviolable provinces over which the scholar and critic rule, each remote from the other; on the contrary, my point is that to both historical scholar and historical critic the truth of the work is inseparable from its facts.

The historical approach has been so often and so openly attacked during the past generation that its faults have already been publicly exposed. Its detractors have charged that scholars became more concerned with the process of their studies than the result and that the historical stress on methodology and research not only delayed criticism but even forbade it. It has been pointed out that the exhaustive preliminary investigation of the sources of the literary work often tended to become an end as well as a means, thus lapsing into the genetic fallacy of the confusion between origin and value. It was said that the knowledge about the work tended to become self-sufficient, so that the work itself was ignored or else dismissed with vague, sweeping, impressionistic criticism. It was declared that the historical method tended to debase the literary work and the creative process because biographical data degenerated into gossip and because the study of literary sources and backgrounds degenerated into diluted history or philosophy. Finally, it was charged that the historical method (or *external* or *extrinsic* method, as it has been variously called) heaped so much data and fact upon the literary work that all sense of the work's form, structure, symmetry, and beauty became obscured, that the concentration upon the work's pastness forbade any appreciation of its presentness and forestalled the reader's direct experience of the work itself. Opponents of historicism claim that it even now prevails in the graduate schools and still produces teachers and scholars suspicious of criticism and possibly unfit to practice it.

In rebuttal, defenders of the historical approach assert that the critic's awareness of the work's dossier, compiled by means of exacting scholarship, permits a wholeness and accuracy of response impossible in other critical systems. The historical critic's consciousness of a literary work's place in a sequence of historical, cultural, and literary events enhances his appreciation of the achievement of the individual work. To him the literary work is an organism, having its own identity like any other organism yet also existing as a creature shaped by its environment and not fully intelligible without reference to its environment—which would include its line of descent. The historical critic regards his method as a more reliable means of explication and evaluation of a literary work than the dependence upon an essentially subjective response. He warns against the imminent danger of the critic's exercise of his own ingenuity to the point of eccentricity, a point where the critic replaces the work's author as the creator of its meaning and value. The historical critic aspires above all to achieve in his criticism of literature a fusion of learning and judgment.

Certainly any critical system that has numbered among its recent practitioners such scholar-critics as Erich Auerbach, Harry Levin, E. M. W. Tillyard, Douglas Bush, F. W. Bateson, David Daiches, George Steiner, Ernst Robert Curtius,

John Henry Raleigh, Roger Asselineau, M. H. Abrams, and C. M. Bowra, to name but a few who come readily to mind, recommends itself to our most respectful attention. The historical critics have had their troubles; now, with new insights, techniques, and modes of inquiry, they are perhaps stronger than ever before.

SELECTED BIBLIOGRAPHY

Aldridge, A. O. "Biography in the Interpretation of Poetry," *College English*, XXV (1964), 412–420.

Altick, Richard D. *The Art of Literary Research* (New York, W. W. Norton & Company, Inc., 1963), pp. 3–6, 47–117.

Bowers, Fredson. *Textual and Literary Criticism* (New York, Cambridge University Press, 1959), pp. 1–34.

Bush, Douglas. "Literary Scholarship and Criticism," *Liberal Education*, XLVII (1961), 207–228.

Cunningham, J. V. *Tradition and Poetic Structure* (Denver, Alan Swallow, Publisher, 1960), pp. 59–75, 263–270.

Daiches, David. "Fiction and Civilization," in *The Novel and the Modern World* (Chicago, University of Chicago Press, 1939).

Dougherty, James P. "The Aesthetic and the Intellectual Analyses of Literature," *Journal of Aesthetics and Art Criticism*, XXII (1964), 315–324.

Gardner, Helen. *The Business of Criticism* (Oxford, Clarendon Press, 1959).

Hassan, Ihab. "Criticism as Mimesis," *South Atlantic Quarterly*, LV (1956), 473–486.

Heyl, Bernard. "The Critic's Reasons," *Journal of Aesthetics and Art Criticism*, XVI (1957), 169–179.

Knights, L. C. "On Historical Scholarship and the Interpretation of Shakespeare," *Sewanee Review*, LXIII (1955), 223–240.

Pearce, Roy Harvey. "Historicism Once More," *Kenyon Review*, XX (1958), 554–591.

Pichois, Claude. "L'Histoire Littéraire Traditionelle," *Cahiers de L'Association Internationale des Études Francaises*, No. 16 (March, 1964).

Robertson, D. W., Jr. "Historical Criticism," in Alan S. Downer, ed., *English Institute Essays: 1950* (New York, Columbia University Press, 1951), pp. 3–31.

Spiller, Robert E. "Is Literary History Obsolete?" *College English*, XXIV (1963), 345–351.

Tillotson, Geoffrey. "The Critic and the Dated Text," *Sewanee Review*, LXVIII (1960), 595–602.

Trilling, Lionel. "The Sense of the Past," in *The Liberal Imagination* (Garden City, Doubleday & Co., 1953), pp. 179–193.

Wellek, René, and Austin Warren. *Theory of Literature* (New York, Harcourt, Brace & World, Inc., 1956), pp. 61–124.

Wellek, René. "Literary Theory, Criticism, and History," *Sewanee Review*, LXVIII (1960), 1–19.

Whalley, George. "Scholarship and Criticism," *University of Toronto Quarterly*, XXIX (1959–1960), 33–45.

Williams, Arnold. "Why Literary Scholarship?" *Centennial Review of Arts and Science*, VIII (1964), 278–291.
Wimsatt, W. K., Jr. "History and Criticism: A Problematic Relationship," *PMLA*, LXVI (1951), 21–31.
Wimsatt, W. K., Jr., and Cleanth Brooks. *Literary Criticism: A Short History* (New York, Alfred A. Knopf, Inc., 1957), pp. 522–551.

Erich Auerbach

ODYSSEUS' SCAR

Erich Auerbach, a distinguished German scholar-critic, was dismissed from his university position by the Nazis. He taught for several years in Turkey and then came to America in 1947. He was teaching at Yale University at the time of his death in 1957. This essay is the first chapter in his book *Mimesis: The Representation of Reality in Western Literature* (1946, English translation 1953), a pioneering work in a new kind of historical criticism. Professor Auerbach's other major books available in English are *Scenes from the Drama of European Literature*, *Dante, Poet of the Secular World*, and *Literary Language and Its Public in Late Latin Antiquity*.

Readers of the *Odyssey* will remember the well-prepared and touching scene in book 19, when Odysseus has at last come home, the scene in which the old housekeeper Euryclea, who had been his nurse, recognizes him by a scar on his thigh. The stranger has won Penelope's good will; at his request she tells the housekeeper to wash his feet, which, in all old stories, is the first duty of hospitality toward a tired traveler. Euryclea busies herself fetching water and mixing cold with hot, meanwhile speaking sadly of her absent master, who is probably of the same age as the guest, and who perhaps, like the guest, is even now wandering somewhere, a stranger; and she remarks how astonishingly like him the guest looks. Meanwhile Odysseus, remembering his scar, moves back out of the light; he knows that, despite his efforts to hide his identity, Euryclea will now recognize him, but he wants at least to keep Penelope in ignor-ance. No sooner has the old woman touched the scar than, in her joyous surprise, she lets Odysseus' foot drop into the basin; the water spills over, she is about to cry out her joy; Odysseus restrains her with whispered threats and endearments; she recovers herself and conceals her emotion. Penelope, whose attention Athena's foresight had diverted from the incident, has observed nothing.

All this is scrupulously externalized and narrated in leisurely fashion. The two women express their feelings in copious direct discourse. Feelings though they are, with only a slight admixture of the most general considerations upon human destiny, the syntactical connection between part and part is perfectly clear, no contour is blurred. There is also room and time for orderly, perfectly well-articulated, uniformly illuminated descriptions of implements, ministrations, and gestures; even in the dramatic moment of recogni-

12

talks to Odysseus; Odysseus talks to the suitors when he begins to kill them; Hector and Achilles talk at length, before battle and after; and no speech is so filled with anger or scorn that the particles which express logical and grammatical connections are lacking or out of place. This last observation is true, of course, not only of speeches but of the presentation in general. The separate elements of a phenomenon are most clearly placed in relation to one another; a large number of conjunctions, adverbs, particles, and other syntactical tools, all clearly circumscribed and delicately differentiated in meaning, delimit persons, things, and portions of incidents in respect to one another, and at the same time bring them together in a continuous and ever flexible connection; like the separate phenomena themselves, their relationships—their temporal, local, causal, final, consecutive, comparative, concessive, antithetical, and conditional limitations—are brought to light in perfect fullness; so that a continuous rhythmic procession of phenomena passes by, and never is there a form left fragmentary or half-illuminated, never a lacuna, never a gap, never a glimpse of unplumbed depths.

And this procession of phenomena takes place in the foreground—that is, in a local and temporal present which is absolute. One might think that the many interpolations, the frequent moving back and forth, would create a sort of perspective in time and place; but the Homeric style never gives any such impression. The way in which any impression of perspective is avoided can be clearly observed in the procedure for introducing episodes, a syntactical construction with which every reader of Homer is familiar; it is used in the passage we are considering, but can also be found in cases when the episodes are much shorter. To the word scar (v. 393) there is first attached a relative clause ("which once long ago a boar . . ."), which enlarges into a voluminous syntactical parenthesis; into this an independent sentence unexpectedly intrudes (v. 396: "A god himself gave him . . ."), which quietly disentangles itself from syntactical subordination, until, with verse 399, an equally free syntactical treatment of the new content begins a new present which continues unchallenged until, with verse 467 ("The old woman now touched it . . ."), the scene which had been broken off is resumed. To be sure, in the case of such long episodes as the one we are considering, a purely syntactical connection with the principal theme would hardly have been possible; but a connection with it through perspective would have been all the easier had the content been arranged with that end in view; if, that is, the entire story of the scar had been presented as a recollection which awakens in Odysseus' mind at this particular moment. It would have been perfectly easy to do; the story of the scar had only to be inserted two verses earlier, at the first mention of the word scar, where the motifs "Odysseus" and "recollection" were already at hand. But any such subjectivistic-perspectivistic procedure, creating a foreground and background, resulting in the present lying open to the depths of the past, is entirely foreign to the Homeric style; the Homeric style knows only a foreground, only a uniformly illuminated, uniformly objective present. And so the excursus does not begin until two lines later, when Euryclea has discovered the scar—the possibility for a perspectivistic connection no longer exists, and the story of the wound becomes an independent and exclusive present.

The genius of the Homeric style becomes even more apparent when it is compared with an equally ancient and equally epic style from a different world of forms. I shall attempt this comparison with the account of the sacrifice of Isaac, a homogeneous narrative produced by the so-called Elohist. The King James version translates the opening as follows (Genesis 22: 1): "And it came to pass after these things, that God did tempt Abraham, and said to him, Abraham! and he said, Behold, here I am." Even this opening startles us when we come to it from Homer. Where are the two speakers? We are not told. The reader, however, knows that they are not normally to be found together in one place on earth, that one of them, God, in order to speak to Abraham, must come from somewhere, must enter the earthly realm from some unknown heights or depths. Whence does he come, whence does he call to Abraham? We are not told. He does not come, like Zeus or Poseidon, from the Aethiopians, where he has been enjoying a sacrificial feast. Nor are we told anything of his reasons for tempting Abraham so terribly. He has not, like Zeus, discussed them in set speeches with other gods gathered in council; nor have the deliberations in his own heart been presented to us; unexpected and mysterious, he enters the scene from some unknown height or depth and calls: Abraham! It will at once be said that this is to be explained by the particular concept of God which the Jews held and which was wholly different from that of the Greeks. True enough—but this constitutes no objection. For how is the Jewish concept of God to be explained? Even their earlier God of the desert was not fixed in form and content, and was alone; his lack of form, his lack of local habitation, his singleness, was in the end not only maintained but developed even further in competition with the comparatively far more manifest gods of the surrounding Near Eastern world. The concept of God held by the Jews is less a cause than a symptom of their manner of comprehending and representing things.

This becomes still clearer if we now turn to the other person in the dialogue, to Abraham. Where is he? We do not know. He says, indeed: Here I am—but the Hebrew word means only something like "behold me," and in any case is not meant to indicate the actual place where Abraham is, but a moral position in respect to God, who has called to him— Here am I awaiting thy command. Where he is actually, whether in Beersheba or elsewhere, whether indoors or in the open air, is not stated; it does not interest the narrator, the reader is not informed; and what Abraham was doing when God called to him is left in the same obscurity. To realize the difference, consider Hermes' visit to Calypso, for example, where command, journey, arrival and reception of the visitor, situation and occupation of the person visited, are set forth in many verses; and even on occasions when gods appear suddenly and briefly, whether to help one of their favorites or to deceive or destroy some mortal whom they hate, their bodily forms, and usually the manner of their coming and going, are given in detail. Here, however, God appears without bodily form (yet he "appears"), coming from some unspecified place—we only hear his voice, and that utters nothing but a name, a name without an adjective, without a descriptive epithet for the person spoken to, such as is the rule in every Homeric address; and of Abraham too nothing is made perceptible except the words in which he answers God: *Hinne-ni*, Behold me here—with which, to be sure, a most touching gesture expressive of obedience and readiness is suggested, but it is left to the reader to visualize it. Moreover the two speakers are not on the same level: if we conceive of Abraham in the foreground, where it might be possible to picture him as prostrate or kneeling or bowing with outspread arms or gazing upward, God is not there too: Abraham's words and gestures are directed toward the depths of the picture or upward, but in any case the undetermined, dark place from which the voice comes to him is not in the foreground.

After this opening, God gives his command, and the story itself begins: everyone knows it; it unrolls with no episodes in a few independent sentences whose syntactical connection is of the most rudimentary sort. In this atmosphere it is unthinkable that an implement, a landscape through which the travelers passed, the serving-men, or the ass, should be described, that their origin or desent or material or appearance or usefulness should be set forth in terms of praise; they do not even admit an adjective: they are serving-men, ass, wood, and knife, and nothing else, without an epithet; they are there to serve the end which God has commanded; what in other respects they were, are, or will be, remains in darkness. A journey is made, because God has designated the place where the sacrifice is to be performed; but we are told nothing about the journey except that it took three days, and even that we are told in a mysterious way: Abraham and his followers rose "early in the morning" and "went unto" the place of which God had told him; on the third day he lifted up his eyes and saw the place from afar. That gesture is the only gesture, is indeed the only occurrence during the whole journey, of which we are told; and though its motivation lies in the fact that the place is elevated, its uniqueness still heightens the impression that the journey took place through a vacuum; it is as if, while he traveled on, Abraham had looked neither to the right nor to the left, had

suppressed any sign of life in his followers and himself save only their footfalls.

Thus the journey is like a silent progress through the indeterminate and the contingent, a holding of the breath, a process which has no present, which is inserted, like a blank duration, between what has passed and what lies ahead, and which yet is measured: three days! Three such days positively demand the symbolic interpretation which they later received. They began "early in the morning." But at what time on the third day did Abraham lift up his eyes and see his goal? The text says nothing on the subject. Obviously not "late in the evening," for it seems that there was still time enough to climb the mountain and make the sacrifice. So "early in the morning" is given, not as an indication of time, but for the sake of its ethical significance; it is intended to express the resolution, the promptness, the punctual obedience of the sorely tried Abraham. Bitter to him is the early morning in which he saddles his ass, calls his serving-men and his son Isaac, and sets out; but he obeys, he walks on until the third day, then lifts up his eyes and sees the place. Whence he comes, we do not know, but the goal is clearly stated: Jeruel in the land of Moriah. What place this is meant to indicate is not clear—"Moriah" especially may be a later correction of some other word. But in any case the goal was given, and in any case it is a matter of some sacred spot which was to receive a particular consecration by being connected with Abraham's sacrifice. Just as little as "early in the morning" serves as a temporal indication does "Jeruel in the land of Moriah" serve as a geographical indication; and in both cases alike, the complementary indication is not given, for we know as little of the hour at which Abraham lifted up his eyes as we do of the place from which he set forth—

Jeruel is significant not so much as the goal of an earthly journey, in its geographical relation to other places, as through its special election, through its relation to God, who designated it as the scene of the act, and therefore it must be named.

In the narrative itself, a third chief character appears: Isaac. While God and Abraham, the serving-men, the ass, and the implements are simply named, without mention of any qualities or any other sort of definition, Isaac once receives an appositive; God says, "Take Isaac, thine only son, whom thou lovest." But this is not a characterization of Isaac as a person, apart from his relation to his father and apart from the story; he may be handsome or ugly, intelligent or stupid, tall or short, pleasant or unpleasant—we are not told. Only what we need to know about him as a personage in the action, here and now, is illuminated, so that it may become apparent how terrible Abraham's temptation is, and that God is fully aware of it. By this example of the contrary, we see the significance of the descriptive adjectives and digressions of the Homeric poems; with their indications of the earlier and as it were absolute existence of the persons described, they prevent the reader from concentrating exclusively on a present crisis; even when the most terrible things are occurring, they prevent the establishment of an overwhelming suspense. But here, in the story of Abraham's sacrifice, the overwhelming suspense is present; what Schiller makes the goal of the tragic poet—to rob us of our emotional freedom, to turn our intellectual and spiritual powers (Schiller says "our activity") in one direction, to concentrate them there—is effected in this Biblical narrative, which certainly deserves the epithet epic.

We find the same contrast if we compare the two uses of direct discourse. The personages speak in the Bible story too; but their speech does not serve, as does speech in Homer, to manifest, to externalize thoughts—on the contrary, it serves to indicate thoughts which remain unexpressed. God gives his command in direct discourse, but he leaves his motives and his purpose unexpressed; Abraham, receiving the command, says nothing and does what he has been told to do. The conversation between Abraham and Isaac on the way to the place of sacrifice is only an interruption of the heavy silence and makes it all the more burdensome. The two of them, Isaac carrying the wood and Abraham with fire and a knife, "went together." Hesitantly, Isaac ventures to ask about the ram, and Abraham gives the well-known answer. Then the text repeats: "So they went both of them together." Everything remains unexpressed.

It would be difficult, then, to imagine styles more contrasted than those of these two equally ancient and equally epic texts. On the one hand, externalized, uniformly illuminated phenomena, at a definite time and in a definite place, connected together without lacunae in a perpetual foreground; thoughts and feeling completely expressed; events taking place in leisurely fashion and with very little of suspense. On the other hand, the externalization of only so much of the phenomena as is necessary for the purpose of the narrative, all else left in obscurity; the decisive points of the narrative alone are emphasized, what lies between is nonexistent; time and place are undefined and call for interpretation; thoughts and feeling remain unexpressed, are only suggested by the silence and the fragmentary speeches; the whole, permeated with the most unrelieved suspense and directed toward a single goal (and to that extent far more of a unity), remains mysterious and "fraught with background."

I will discuss this term in some detail,

lest it be misunderstood. I said above that the Homeric style was "of the foreground" because, despite much going back and forth, it yet causes what is momentarily being narrated to give the impression that it is the only present, pure and without perspective. A consideration of the Elohistic text teaches us that our term is capable of a broader and deeper application. It shows that even the separate personages can be represented as possessing "background"; God is always so represented in the Bible, for he is not comprehensible in his presence, as is Zeus; it is always only "something" of him that appears, he always extends into depths. But even the human beings in the Biblical stories have greater depths of time, fate, and consciousness than do the human beings in Homer; although they are nearly always caught up in an event engaging all their faculties, they are not so entirely immersed in its present that they do not remain continually conscious of what has happened to them earlier and elsewhere; their thoughts and feelings have more layers, are more entangled. Abraham's actions are explained not only by what is happening to him at the moment, nor yet only by his character (as Achilles' actions by his courage and his pride, and Odysseus' by his versatility and foresightedness), but by his previous history; he remembers, he is constantly conscious of, what God has promised him and what God has already accomplished for him—his soul is torn between desperate rebellion and hopeful expectation; his silent obedience is multilayered, has background. Such a problematic psychological situation as this is impossible for any of the Homeric heroes, whose destiny is clearly defined and who wake every morning as if it were the first day of their lives: their emotions, though strong, are simple and find expression instantly.

How fraught with background, in comparison, are characters like Saul and David! How entangled and stratified are such human relations as those between David and Absalom, between David and Joab! Any such "background" quality of the psychological situation as that which the story of Absalom's death and its sequel (II Samuel 18 and 19, by the so-called Jahvist) rather suggests than expresses, is unthinkable in Homer. Here we are confronted not merely with the psychological processes of characters whose depth of background is veritably abysmal, but with a purely geographical background too. For David is absent from the battlefield; but the influence of his will and his feelings continues to operate, they affect even Joab in his rebellion and disregard for the consequences of his actions; in the magnificent scene with the two messengers, both the physical and psychological background is fully manifest, though the latter is never expressed. With this, compare, for example, how Achilles, who sends Patroclus first to scout and then into battle, loses almost all "presentness" so long as he is not physically present. But the most important thing is the "multilayeredness" of the individual character; this is hardly to be met with in Homer, or at most in the form of a conscious hesitation between two possible courses of action; otherwise, in Homer, the complexity of the psychological life is shown only in the succession and alternation of emotions; whereas the Jewish writers are able to express the simultaneous existence of various layers of consciousness and the conflict between them.

The Homeric poems, then, though their intellectual, linguistic, and above all syntactical culture appears to be so much more highly developed, are yet comparatively simple in their picture of human beings; and no less so in their relation to the real life which they describe in general. Delight in physical existence is everything to them, and their highest aim is to make that delight perceptible to us. Between battles and passions, adventures and perils, they show us hunts, banquets, palaces and shepherds' cots, athletic contests and washing days—in order that we may see the heroes in their ordinary life, and seeing them so, may take pleasure in their manner of enjoying their savory present, a present which sends strong roots down into social usages, landscape, and daily life. And thus they bewitch us and ingratiate themselves to us until we live with them in the reality of their lives; so long as we are reading or hearing the poems, it does not matter whether we know that all this is only legend, "make-believe." The oft-repeated reproach that Homer is a liar takes nothing from his effectiveness, he does not need to base his story on historical reality, his reality is powerful enough in itself; it ensnares us, weaving its web around us, and that suffices him. And this "real" world into which we are lured, exists for itself, contains nothing but itself; the Homeric poems conceal nothing, they contain no teaching and no secret second meaning. Homer can be analyzed, as we have essayed to do here, but he cannot be interpreted. Later allegorizing trends have tried their arts of interpretation upon him, but to no avail. He resists any such treatment; the interpretations are forced and foreign, they do not crystallize into a unified doctrine. The general considerations which occasionally occur (in our episode, for example, v. 360: that in misfortune men age quickly) reveal a calm acceptance of the basic facts of human existence, but with no compulsion to brood over them, still less any passionate impulse either to rebel against them or to embrace them in an ecstasy of submission.

It is all very different in the Biblical stories. Their aim is not to bewitch the senses, and if nevertheless they produce lively sensory effects, it is only because the moral, religious, and psychological phenomena which are their sole concern are made concrete in the sensible matter of life. But their religious intent involves an absolute claim to historical truth. The story of Abraham and Isaac is not better established than the story of Odysseus, Penelope, and Euryclea; both are legendary. But the Biblical narrator, the Elohist, had to believe in the objective truth of the story of Abraham's sacrifice—the existence of the sacred ordinances of life rested upon the truth of this and similar stories. He had to believe in it passionately; or else (as many rationalistic interpreters believed and perhaps still believe) he had to be a conscious liar—no harmless liar like Homer, who lied to give pleasure, but a political liar with a definite end in view, lying in the interest of a claim to absolute authority.

To me, the rationalistic interpretation seems psychologically absurd; but even if we take it into consideration, the relation of the Elohist to the truth of his story still remains a far more passionate and definite one than is Homer's relation. The Biblical narrator was obliged to write exactly what his belief in the truth of the tradition (or, from the rationalistic standpoint, his interest in the truth of it) demanded of him—in either case, his freedom in creative or representative imagination was severely limited; his activity was perforce reduced to composing an effective version of the pious tradition. What he produced, then, was not primarily oriented toward "realism" (if he succeeded in being realistic, it was merely a means, not an end); it was oriented toward truth. Woe to the man who did not believe it! One can perfectly well entertain historical doubts on the subject of the Trojan War or of Odysseus' wanderings, and still, when reading Homer, feel precisely the effects he sought to produce; but without believing in Abraham's sacrifice, it is impossible to put the narrative of it to the use for which it was written. Indeed, we must go even further. The Bible's claim to truth is not only far more urgent than Homer's, it is tyrannical—it excludes all other claims. The world of the Scripture stories is not satisfied with claiming to be a historically true reality—it insists that it is the only real world, is destined for autocracy. All other scenes, issues, and ordinances have no right to appear independently of it, and it is promised that all of them, the history of all mankind, will be given their due place within its frame, will be subordinated to it. The Scripture stories do not, like Homer's, court our favor, they do not flatter us that they may please us and enchant us—they seek to subject us, and if we refuse to be subjected we are rebels.

Let no one object that this goes too far, that not the stories, but the religious doctrine, raises the claim to absolute authority; because the stories are not, like Homer's, simply narrated "reality." Doctrine and promise are incarnate in them and inseparable from them; for that very reason they are fraught with "background" and mysterious, containing a second, concealed meaning. In the story of Isaac, it is not only God's intervention at the beginning and the end, but even the factual and psychological elements which come between, that are mysterious, merely touched upon, fraught with background; and therefore they require subtle investigation and interpretation, they demand them. Since so much in the story is dark and incomplete, and since the reader knows that God is a hidden God, his effort to interpret it constantly finds something new to feed upon. Doctrine and the search for enlightenment are inextricably connected with the physical side of the narrative—the latter being

more than simple "reality"; indeed they are in constant danger of losing their own reality, as very soon happened when interpretation reached such proportions that the real vanished.

If the text of the Biblical narrative, then, is so greatly in need of interpretation on the basis of its own content, its claim to absolute authority forces it still further in the same direction. Far from seeking, like Homer, merely to make us forget our own reality for a few hours, it seeks to overcome our reality: we are to fit our own life into its world, feel ourselves to be elements in its structure of universal history. This becomes increasingly difficult the further our historical environment is removed from that of the Biblical books; and if these nevertheless maintain their claim to absolute authority, it is inevitable that they themselves be adapted through interpretative transformation. This was for a long time comparatively easy; as late as the European Middle Ages it was possible to represent Biblical events as ordinary phenomena of contemporary life, the methods of interpretation themselves forming the basis for such a treatment. But when, through too great a change in environment and through the awakening of a critical consciousness, this becomes impossible, the Biblical claim to absolute authority is jeopardized; the method of interpretation is scorned and rejected, the Biblical stories become ancient legends, and the doctrine they had contained, now dissevered from them, becomes a disembodied image.

As a result of this claim to absolute authority, the method of interpretation spread to traditions other than the Jewish. The Homeric poems present a definite complex of events whose boundaries in space and time are clearly delimited; before it, beside it, and after it, other complexes of events, which do not depend upon it, can be conceived without conflict and without difficulty. The Old Testament, on the other hand, presents universal history: it begins with the beginning of time, with the creation of the world, and will end with the Last Days, the fulfilling of the Covenant, with which the world will come to an end. Everything else that happens in the world can only be conceived as an element in this sequence; into it everything that is known about the world, or at least everything that touches upon the history of the Jews, must be fitted as an ingredient of the divine plan; and as this too became possible only by interpreting the new material as it poured in, the need for interpretation reaches out beyond the original Jewish-Israelitish realm of reality—for example to Assyrian, Babylonian, Persian, and Roman history; interpretation in a determined direction becomes a general method of comprehending reality; the new and strange world which now comes into view and which, in the form in which it presents itself, proves to be wholly unutilizable within the Jewish religious frame, must be so interpreted that it can find a place there. But this process nearly always also reacts upon the frame, which requires enlarging and modifying. The most striking piece of interpretation of this sort occurred in the first century of the Christian era, in consequence of Paul's mission to the Gentiles: Paul and the Church Fathers reinterpreted the entire Jewish tradition as a succession of figures prognosticating the appearance of Christ, and assigned the Roman Empire its proper place in the divine plan of salvation. Thus while, on the one hand, the reality of the Old Testament presents itself as complete truth with a claim to sole authority, on the other hand that very claim forces it to a constant interpretative change in its own content; for millennia it undergoes an incessant and active development with the life of man in Europe.

The claim of the Old Testament stories to represent universal history, their insistent relation—a relation constantly redefined by conflicts—to a single and hidden God, who yet shows himself and who guides universal history by promise and exaction, gives these stories an entirely different perspective from any the Homeric poems can possess. As a composition, the Old Testament is incomparably less unified than the Homeric poems, it is more obviously pieced together—but the various components all belong to one concept of universal history and its interpretation. If certain elements survived which did not immediately fit in, interpretation took care of them; and so the reader is at every moment aware of the universal religio-historical perspective which gives the individual stories their general meaning and purpose. The greater the separateness and horizontal disconnection of the stories and groups of stories in relation to one another, compared with the *Iliad* and the *Odyssey*, the stronger is their general vertical connection, which holds them all together and which is entirely lacking in Homer. Each of the great figures of the Old Testament, from Adam to the prophets, embodies a moment of this vertical connection. God chose and formed these men to the end of embodying his essence and will—yet choice and formation do not coincide, for the latter proceeds gradually, historically, during the earthly life of him upon whom the choice has fallen. How the process is accomplished, what terrible trials such a formation inflicts, can be seen from our story of Abraham's sacrifice. Herein lies the reason why the great figures of the Old Testament are so much more fully developed, so much more fraught with their own biographical past, so much more distinct as individuals, than are the Homeric heroes. Achilles and Odysseus are splendidly described in many well-ordered words, epithets cling to them, their emotions are constantly displayed in their words and deeds—but they have no development, and their life-histories are clearly set forth once and for all. So little are the Homeric heroes presented as developing or having developed, that most of them—Nestor, Agamemnon, Achilles—appear to be of an age fixed from the very first. Even Odysseus, in whose case the long lapse of time and the many events which occurred offer so much opportunity for biographical development, shows almost nothing of it. Odysseus on his return is exactly the same as he was when he left Ithaca two decades earlier. But what a road, what a fate, lie between the Jacob who cheated his father out of his blessing and the old man whose favorite son has been torn to pieces by a wild beast!—between David the harp player, persecuted by his lord's jealousy, and the old king, surrounded by violent intrigues, whom Abishag the Shunnamite warmed in his bed, and he knew her not! The old man, of whom we know how he has become what he is, is more of an individual than the young man; for it is only during the course of an eventful life that men are differentiated into full individuality; and it is this history of a personality which the Old Testament presents to us as the formation undergone by those whom God has chosen to be examples. Fraught with their development, sometimes even aged to the verge of dissolution, they show a distinct stamp of individuality entirely foreign to the Homeric heroes. Time can touch the latter only outwardly, and even that change is brought to our observation as little as possible; whereas the stern hand of God is ever upon the Old Testament figures; he has not only made them once and for all and chosen them, but he continues to work upon them, bends them and kneads them, and, without destroying them in essence, produces from them

forms which their youth gave no grounds for anticipating. The objection that the biographical element of the Old Testament often springs from the combination of several legendary personages does not apply; for this combination is a part of the development of the text. And how much wider is the pendulum swing of their lives than that of the Homeric heroes! For they are bearers of the divine will, and yet they are fallible, subject to misfortune and humiliation—and in the midst of misfortune and in their humiliation their acts and words reveal the transcendent majesty of God. There is hardly one of them who does not, like Adam, undergo the deepest humiliation—and hardly one who is not deemed worthy of God's personal intervention and personal inspiration. Humiliation and elevation go far deeper and far higher than in Homer, and they belong basically together. The poor beggar Odysseus is only masquerading, but Adam is really cast down, Jacob really a refugee, Joseph really in the pit and then a slave to be bought and sold. But their greatness, rising out of humiliation, is almost superhuman and an image of God's greatness. The reader clearly feels how the extent of the pendulum's swing is connected with the intensity of the personal history—precisely the most extreme circumstances, in which we are immeasurably forsaken and in despair, or immeasurably joyous and exalted, give us, if we survive them, a personal stamp which is recognized as the product of a rich existence, a rich development. And very often, indeed generally, this element of development gives the Old Testament stories a historical character, even when the subject is purely legendary and traditional.

Homer remains within the legendary with all his material, whereas the material of the Old Testament comes closer and closer to history as the narrative proceeds;

in the stories of David the historical report predominates. Here too, much that is legendary still remains, as for example the story of David and Goliath; but much—and the most essential—consists in things which the narrators knew from their own experience or from firsthand testimony. Now the difference between legend and history is in most cases easily perceived by a reasonably experienced reader. It is a difficult matter, requiring careful historical and philological training, to distinguish the true from the synthetic or the biased in a historical presentation; but it is easy to separate the historical from the legendary in general. Their structure is different. Even where the legendary does not immediately betray itself by elements of the miraculous, by the repetition of well-known standard motives, typical patterns and themes, through neglect of clear details of time and place, and the like, it is generally quickly recognizable by its composition. It runs far too smoothly. All cross-currents, all friction, all that is casual, secondary to the main events and themes, everything unresolved, truncated, and uncertain, which confuses the clear progress of the action and the simple orientation of the actors, has disappeared. The historical event which we witness, or learn from the testimony of those who witnessed it, runs much more variously, contradictorily, and confusedly; not until it has produced results in a definite domain are we able, with their help, to classify it to a certain extent; and how often the order to which we think we have attained becomes doubtful again, how often we ask ourselves if the data before us have not led us to a far too simple classification of the original events! Legend arranges its material in a simple and straightforward way; it detaches it from its contemporary historical context, so that the latter will not confuse it; it

knows only clearly outlined men who act from few and simple motives and the continuity of whose feelings and actions remains uninterrupted. In the legends of martyrs, for example, a stiff-necked and fanatical persecutor stands over against an equally stiff-necked and fanatical victim; and a situation so complicated—that is to say, so real and historical—as that in which the "persecutor" Pliny finds himself in his celebrated letter to Trajan on the subject of the Christians, is unfit for legend. And that is still a comparatively simple case. Let the reader think of the history which we are ourselves witnessing; anyone who, for example, evaluates the behavior of individual men and groups of men at the time of the rise of National Socialism in Germany, or the behavior of individual peoples and states before and during the last war, will feel how difficult it is to represent historical themes in general, and how unfit they are for legend; the historical comprises a great number of contradictory motives in each individual, a hesitation and ambiguous groping on the part of groups; only seldom (as in the last war) does a more or less plain situation, comparatively simple to describe, arise, and even such a situation is subject to division below the surface, is indeed almost constantly in danger of losing its simplicity; and the motives of all the interested parties are so complex that the slogans of propaganda can be composed only through the crudest simplification—with the result that friend and foe alike can often employ the same ones. To write history is so difficult that most historians are forced to make concessions to the technique of legend.

It is clear that a large part of the life of David as given in the Bible contains history and not legend. In Absalom's rebellion, for example, or in the scenes from David's last days, the contradictions and crossing of motives both in individuals and in the general action have become so concrete that it is impossible to doubt the historicity of the information conveyed. Now the men who composed the historical parts are often the same who edited the older legends too; their peculiar religious concept of man in history, which we have attempted to describe above, in no way led them to a legendary simplification of events; and so it is only natural that, in the legendary passages of the Old Testament, historical structure is frequently discernible—of course, not in the sense that the traditions are examined as to their credibility according to the methods of scientific criticism; but simply to the extent that the tendency to a smoothing down and harmonizing of events, to a simplification of motives, to a static definition of characters which avoids conflict, vacillation, and development, such as are natural to legendary structure, does not predominate in the Old Testament world of legend. Abraham, Jacob, or even Moses produces a more concrete, direct, and historical impression than the figures of the Homeric world—not because they are better described in terms of sense (the contrary is the case) but because the confused, contradictory multiplicity of events, the psychological and factual cross-purposes, which true history reveals, have not disappeared in the representation but still remain clearly perceptible. In the stories of David, the legendary, which only later scientific criticism makes recognizable as such, imperceptibly passes into the historical; and even in the legendary, the problem of the classification and interpretation of human history is already passionately apprehended —a problem which later shatters the framework of historical composition and completely overruns it with prophecy; thus the Old Testament, in so far as it is concerned with human events, ranges through all three domains: legend, historical reporting, and interpretative historical theology.

Connected with the matters just discussed is the fact that the Greek text seems more limited and more static in respect to the circle of personages involved in the action and to their political activity. In the recognition scene with which we began, there appears, aside from Odysseus and Penelope, the housekeeper Euryclea, a slave whom Odysseus' father Laertes had bought long before. She, like the swineherd Eumaeus, has spent her life in the service of Laertes' family; like Eumaeus, she is closely connected with their fate, she loves them and shares their interests and feelings. But she has no life of her own, no feelings of her own; she has only the life and feelings of her master. Eumaeus too, though he still remembers that he was born a freeman and indeed of a noble house (he was stolen as a boy), has, not only in fact but also in his own feeling, no longer a life of his own, he is entirely involved in the life of his masters. Yet these two characters are the only ones whom Homer brings to life who do not belong to the ruling class. Thus we become conscious of the fact that in the Homeric poems life is enacted only among the ruling class—others appear only in the role of servants to that class. The ruling class is still so strongly patriarchal, and still itself so involved in the daily activities of domestic life, that one is sometimes likely to forget their rank. But they are unmistakably a sort of feudal aristocracy, whose men divide their lives between war, hunting, marketplace councils, and feasting, while the women supervise the maids in the house. As a social picture, this world is completely stable; wars take place only between different groups of the ruling class; nothing ever pushes up from below. In the early stories of the Old Testament the patriarchal condition is dominant too, but since the people involved are individual nomadic or half-nomadic tribal leaders, the social picture gives a much less stable impression; class distinctions are not felt. As soon as the people completely emerges—that is, after the exodus from Egypt—its activity is always discernible, it is often in ferment, it frequently intervenes in events not only as a whole but also in separate groups and through the medium of separate individuals who come forward; the origins of prophecy seem to lie in the irrepressible politico-religious spontaneity of the people. We receive the impression that the movements emerging from the depths of the people of Israel-Judah must have been of a wholly different nature from those even of the later ancient democracies—of a different nature and far more elemental.

With the more profound historicity and the more profound social activity of the Old Testament text, there is connected yet another important distinction from Homer: namely, that a different conception of the elevated style and of the sublime is to be found here. Homer, of course, is not afraid to let the realism of daily life enter into the sublime and tragic; our episode of the scar is an example, we see how the quietly depicted, domestic scene of the foot-washing is incorporated into the pathetic and sublime action of Odysseus' homecoming. From the rule of the separation of styles which was later almost universally accepted and which specified that the realistic depiction of daily life was incompatible with the sublime and had a place only in comedy or, carefully stylized, in idyl—from any such rule Homer is still far removed. And yet he is closer to it than is the Old Testament. For the great and sublime events in the Homeric poems take place

far more exclusively and unmistakably among the members of a ruling class; and these are far more untouched in their heroic elevation than are the Old Testament figures, who can fall much lower in dignity (consider, for example, Adam, Noah, David, Job); and finally, domestic realism, the representation of daily life, remains in Homer in the peaceful realm of the idyllic, whereas, from the very first, in the Old Testament stories, the sublime, tragic, and problematic take shape precisely in the domestic and commonplace: scenes such as those between Cain and Abel, between Noah and his sons, between Abraham, Sarah, and Hagar, between Rebekah, Jacob, and Esau, and so on, are inconceivable in the Homeric style. The entirely different ways of developing conflicts are enough to account for this. In the Old Testament stories the peace of daily life in the house, in the fields, and among the flocks, is undermined by jealousy over election and the promise of a blessing, and complications arise which would be utterly incomprehensible to the Homeric heroes. The latter must have palpable and clearly expressible reasons for their conflicts and enmities, and these work themselves out in free battles; whereas, with the former, the perpetually smouldering jealousy and the connection between the domestic and the spiritual, between the paternal blessing and the divine blessing, lead to daily life being permeated with the stuff of conflict, often with poison. The sublime influence of God here reaches so deeply into the everyday that the two realms of the sublime and the everyday are not only actually unseparated but basically inseparable.

We have compared these two texts, and, with them, the two kinds of style they embody, in order to reach a starting point for an investigation into the literary representation of reality in European culture. The two styles, in their opposition, represent basic types: on the one hand fully externalized description, uniform illumination, uninterrupted connection, free expression, all events in the foreground, displaying unmistakable meanings, few elements of historical development and of psychological perspective; on the other hand, certain parts brought into high relief, others left obscure, abruptness, suggestive influence of the unexpressed, "background" quality, multiplicity of meanings and the need for interpretation, universal-historical claims, development of the concept of the historically becoming, and preoccupation with the problematic.

Homer's realism is, of course, not to be equated with classical-antique realism in general; for the separation of styles, which did not develop until later, permitted no such leisurely and externalized description of everyday happenings; in tragedy especially there was no room for it; furthermore, Greek culture very soon encountered the phenomena of historical becoming and of the "multilayeredness" of the human problem, and dealt with them in its fashion; in Roman realism, finally, new and native concepts are added. We shall go into these later changes in the antique representation of reality when the occasion arises; on the whole, despite them, the basic tendencies of the Homeric style, which we have attempted to work out, remained effective and determinant down into late antiquity.

Since we are using the two styles, the Homeric and the Old Testament, as starting points, we have taken them as finished products, as they appear in the texts; we have disregarded everything that pertains to their origins, and thus have left untouched the question whether their peculiarities were theirs from the beginning or are to be referred wholly or in part to foreign influences. Within the limits of our purpose, a consideration of this question is not necessary; for it is in their full development, which they reached in early times, that the two styles exercised their determining influence upon the representation of reality in European literature.

George Steiner

from THE DEATH OF TRAGEDY

Since the appearance of *Tolstoy or Dostoyevsky: An Essay in the Old Criticism* (1959) and *The Death of Tragedy* (1961), George Steiner has become widely known as both a historical and a sociocultural critic. He is a frequent contributor of reviews and essays on literary and political topics to such periodicals as *Encounter* and *The New York Review of Books*. Steiner teaches at Cambridge University. The present selection is Chapter Two of *The Death of Tragedy*.

The word "tragedy" entered the English language in the later years of the fourteenth century. Chaucer gave a definition of it in the Prologue to the *Monk's Tale:*

Tragedie is to seyn a certeyn storie,
As olde bookes maken us memorie,
Of hym that stood in great properitee,
And is yfallen out of heigh degree
Into myserie, and endeth wrecchedly.

There is no implication of dramatic form. A tragedy is a narrative recounting the life of some ancient or eminent personage who suffered a decline of fortune toward a disastrous end. That is the characteristic medieval definition. Dante observed, in his letter to Can Grande, that tragedy and comedy move in precisely contrary directions. Because its action is that of the soul ascending from shadow to starlight, from fearful doubt to the joy and certitude of grace, Dante entitled his poem a *commedia*. The motion of tragedy is a constant descent from prosperity to suffering and chaos: *exitu est foetida et horribilis.* In Dante, as in Chaucer, there is no inference that the notion of tragedy is particularly related to drama. A misunderstanding of a passage in Livy led medieval commentators to suppose that the plays of Seneca and Terence had been recited by a single narrator, presumably the poet himself. Two Latin tragedies in imitation of Seneca were actually written by Italian scholars as early as 1315 and *c.* 1387, but neither was intended for performance on a stage. Thus the sense of the tragic remained dissociated from that of the theatre. A remark in Erasmus' *Adagia* suggests that even in the sixteenth century classicists still had doubts as to whether Greek and Roman tragedies had ever been intended for dramatic presentation.

Chaucer's definition derives its force from contemporary awareness of sudden reversals of political and dynastic fortune. To the medieval eye, the heavens of state were filled with portentous stars, dazzling in their ascent but fiery in their decline.

28

The fall of great personages from high place (*casus virorum illustrium*) gave to medieval politics their festive and brutal character. Sweeping over men with cruel frequency, the quarrels of princes implicated the lives and fortunes of the entire community. But the rise and fall of him that stood in high degree was the incarnation of the tragic sense for a much deeper reason: it made explicit the universal drama of the fall of man. Lords and captains perished through exceeding ambition, through the hatred and cunning of their adversaries, or by mischance. But even where the moralist could point to a particular crime or occasion of disaster, a more general law was at work. By virtue of original sin, each man was destined to suffer in his own experience, however private or obscure, some part of the tragedy of death. The Monk's lament "in manere of tragedie" begins with Lucifer and Adam, for the prologue to the tragic condition of man is set in Heaven and in the Garden of Eden. There the arrow of creation started on its downward flight. It is in a garden also that the symmetry of divine intent places the act of fortunate reversal. At Gethsemane the arrow changes its course, and the morality play of history alters from tragedy to *commedia*. Finally, and in precise counterpart to the prologue of disobedience, there is the promise of a celestial epilogue where man will be restored to more than his first glory. Of this great parable of God's design, the recital of the tragic destinies of illustrious men are a gloss and a reminder.

The rise of English drama in the Tudor period and its Elizabethan triumph restored to the notion of tragedy the implications of actual dramatic performance. But the images of the tragic estate devised in medieval literature carried over into the language of the theatre. When Fortune abandoned men in medieval allegory, it was with a swift turn of her emblematic wheel. Marlowe preserved this ancient fancy in *The Tragedie of Edward the second*:

> Base fortune, now I see, that in thy wheele
> There is a point, to which when men aspire,
> They tumble headlong downe: that point I touchte,
> And seeing there was no place to mount up higher,
> Why should I greeue at my declining fall?

Mortimer accepts his doom with grim calm. Only a few moments earlier, he had spoken of himself as "Jove's huge tree, And others are but shrubs compared to me." A proud thought, but also an annunciation of disaster, for in medieval iconography trees were dangerously enmeshed with the image of man. They carried the graft of the apple bough from which Adam plucked, and some minute splinter of the desperate consolation of the cross. And it is when they are blasted at the crown, burnt, or wither at the root, that trees are most illustrative of the human condition. In the early Elizabethan tragedy of *Jocasta*, the wheel and the tree are joined together to convey a vision of fatality:

> When she that rules the rolling wheele of chaunce,
> Doth turne aside hir angrie frowning face,
> On him, who erst she deigned to aduance,
> She never leaues to gaulde him with disgrace,
> To tosse and turne his state in euery place,
> Till at the last she hurle him from on high
> And yeld him subject unto miserie:
> And as the braunche that from the roote is reft,
> He never wines like leafe to that he lefte.

As Wagner's *Tannhäuser* reminds us, the withered branch did not lose its grip on the poetic imagination. Drawing on two lines by Thomas Churchyard in that most medieval of Elizabethan poetic narratives, the *Mirror for Magistrates*, Marlowe gave to the image a final splendour. In the epilogue to *The tragicall Historie of Doctor Faustus*, the Chorus matches the tree of Apollo to the burnt vine of the eightieth Psalm:

Cut is the branch that might have growne
   full straight,
And burned is Apolloes Laurel bough
That sometime grew within this learned
   man.

We are asked to regard "his hellish fall" because it holds up a cautionary mirror to the fate of ordinary men. The tragic personage is nobler and closer to the dark springs of life than the average human being. But he is also typical. Otherwise his fall would not be exemplary. This, too, is a medieval conception which retained its vitality in Elizabethan drama. By examples "trewe and olde," Chaucer's Monk would give us warning of pride or soaring ambition. And it is in this light that the authors of *Jocasta* regarded the myth of Oedipus. They saw in it neither a riddle of innocence unjustly hounded nor an echo of some archaic rite of blood and expiation. The play dealt with a clash of representative characters:

Creon is King, the type of Tyranny,
And Oedipus, myrrour of misery.

The glass does not break with the close of the medieval period. We find it still in the mirror which Hamlet bids the players hold up to nature.

Thus the wheel, the branch, and the mirror had their strong life more than two centuries after the tragic fables of Chaucer and Lydgate. Translated into the *coup de théâtre* or the "doctrine of realism," these ancient images still govern our experience of drama. But in the Elizabethan

theatre, the idea of tragedy lost its medieval directness. The word itself assumed values at once more universal and more restricted. With the decline of hope which followed on the early renaissance— the darkening of spirit which separates the vision of man in Marlowe from that of Pico della Mirandola—the sense of the tragic broadened. It reached beyond the fall of individual greatness. A tragic rift, an irreducible core of inhumanity, seemed to lie in the mystery of things. The sense of life is itself shadowed by a feeling of tragedy. We see this in Calvin's account of man's condition no less than in Shakespeare's.

But at the same time, "tragedy" also acquired a special meaning. A poem or prose romance might be called "tragic" by virtue of its theme. Yet it was no longer designated as a "tragedy." The rediscovery of Senecan drama during the 1560's gave to the word clear implications of theatrical form. Henceforth, a "tragedy" is a play dealing with tragic matters. But were all such plays tragedies in the true sense? The conflicts of critical definition appeared nearly from the start. They have never ceased in the history of the western theatre. Already at the very beginning of the seventeenth century there are foreshadowings of the difficulties which preoccupy Racine, Ibsen, and Wagner. Theory had begun to harass the playwright with what Ibsen might have called "the claims of the ideal."

We can date rather precisely the moment at which these claims were first presented. In *Sejanus* (1605), Ben Jonson had written a learned tragedy modelled on Senecan rhetoric and Roman satire. Nevertheless, he found himself compelled to defend certain liberties in the play against the canons of strict neo-classicism:

. . . if it be objected, that what I publish is no true poem, in the strict laws of time, I confess it: as also in the want of a proper chorus; whose habit and mood are such and so difficult, as not any, whom I have seen, since the ancients, no, not they who have most presently affected laws, have yet come in the way of. Nor is it needful, or almost possible in these our times . . . to observe the old state and splendour of dramatic poems, with preservation of any popular delight.

Seven years later, in the preface to *The White Devil*, John Webster made the same apologia. He conceded that he had not produced a "true dramatic poem," meaning by that a play in severe accord with Aristotelian precepts. But he added with confident irony that the fault lay with the public. The Elizabethan and Jacobean audiences had proved themselves unworthy of "the old state and splendour" of tragedy.

These statements arise from the great division of ideals that shaped the history of the European theatre from the late sixteenth century nearly to the time of Ibsen. The neo-classic conception of tragedy had on its side ancient precedent, the force of the Senecan example, and a powerful critical theory. The popular, romantic ideal of drama drew its strength from the actual performance of the Elizabethan playwrights and from the plain fact of theatrical success. The general public cared more for the gusto and variousness of Shakespearean drama than for the noble form of the "true dramatic poem."

Neo-classicism arose with the scholar-poets and critics of the Italian renaissance. It can be traced back to imperfect understanding of Aristotle and Horace, but was given its current shape by the art of Seneca. The neo-classical view found two expositors of genius, Scaliger and Castelvetro. The latter's interpretation of the *Poetics, Poetica d'Aristotele vulgarizata*, proved to be one of the decisive statements in the development of western

taste. It set forth precepts and ideals which have engaged the concern of critics and dramatists from the time of Jonson to that of Claudel and T. S. Eliot. Its principal arguments were carried over to England and given memorable expression in Sidney's *Defense of Poesy*. Sidney's style bestows a seductive nobility on the spinsterish discipline of the neo-Aristotelian view. "The stage," he tells us, "should always represent but one place, and the uttermost time presupposed in it should be, both by Aristotle's precept and common reason, but one day." Observe the direction of Sidney's appeal: to authority and to reason. Neo-classicism always insists on both. Unity of time and place, moreover, are but instruments toward the principal design, which is unity of action. That is the vital centre of the classic ideal. The tragic action must proceed with total coherence and economy. There must be no residue of waste emotion, no energy of language or gesture inconsequential to the final effect. Neo-classic drama, where it accomplishes its purpose, is immensely tight-wrought. It is art by privation; an austere, sparse, yet ceremonious structure of language and bearing leading to the solemnities of heroic death. From this principle of unity all other conventions follow. The tragic and the comic sense of life must be kept severely apart; the true poet will not "match hornpipes and funerals." Tragedy, moreover, is Augustinian; few are elected to its perilous grace. Or as Sidney puts it, one must not thrust in "the clown by head and shoulders to play a part in majestical matters."

But even as he wrote, clowns were asserting their rights on the tragic stage. They perform their comic turns on Faustus' way to damnation. They open the gates to vengeance in *Macbeth* and trade wisdom with Hamlet. Through the long funeral of Lear's reason sounds the hornpipe of the Fool. Sidney ridicules the kind of popular drama "where you shall have Asia of the one side, and Africa of the other, and so many other under-king-doms, that the player, when he cometh in, must ever begin with telling where he is." Yet even before the *Defense of Poesy* had been published, Faustus was soaring through the air

Being seated in a chariot burning bright,
Drawn by the strength of yoaked dragons
neckes.

And below him lay the licentious geography of the Elizabethan theatre, with its instantaneous transitions from Rome to Egypt, and its seacoasts in Bohemia. Sidney argues that it is absurd that a play, which requires a few brief hours to perform, should claim to imitate events which have taken years to come to pass. Nothing of the kind can be cited in "ancient examples," and the "players in Italy," who were the guardians of the neo-classic style, will not allow it. But Shakespearean characters grow old between the acts, and in *The Winter's Tale* some sixteen years go by between the opening discord and the final music.

The Elizabethan playwrights violated every precept of neo-classicism. They broke with the unities, dispensed with the chorus, and combined tragic and comic plots with indiscriminate power. The playhouse of Shakespeare and his contemporaries was *el gran teatro del mundo*. No variety of feeling, no element from the crucible of experience, was alien to its purpose. The Elizabethan and Jacobean dramatists ransacked Seneca. They took from him his rhetoric, his ghosts, his sententious morality, his flair for horror and blood-vengeance; but not the austere, artificial practices of the neo-classic stage. To the genius of Greek tragedy, or rather to its inferior Latin version,

Shakespeare opposed a rival conception of tragic form and a rival magnificence of execution.

Despite massive scholarship, the history of that form remains obscure. There were practical reasons why Marlowe, Kyd, and Shakespeare departed from neo-classic models. A playwright could not make a living by the precepts of Castelvetro. The public resolutely preferred the romance and turmoil of the tragicomedy or the chronicle play. It delighted in clowns, in comic interludes, and in the acrobatics and brutality of physical action. The Elizabethan spectator had strong nerves and demanded that they be played upon. There was hotness of blood in the world around him and he called for it on the stage. "Learned" poets, such as Ben Jonson and Chapman, sought in vain to educate their public to more lofty pleasures. But even if we discount the realities of the popular theatre, it would seem that Shakespeare's genius led him toward "open" rather than "closed" forms of stagecraft. Whereas Dante's vision bends all light rays toward a controlling centre, Shakespeare's sense of the world appears to move outward. He used dramatic forms with marvellous pragmatism, shaping them as the need arose. The real and the fantastic, the tragic and the comic, the noble and the vile, were equally present in his apprehension of life. Thus he required a theatre more irregular and provisional than that of classic tragedy.

But the shape of such plays as *Doctor Faustus*, *Richard II*, *King Lear*, or *Measure for Measure*, represents more than the personal bias of the Elizabethan dramatists. They are a result of the concurrence of ancient and complex energies. Beneath the fact of the development of dramatic blank verse, beneath the Senecan spirit of majestic violence, lay a great inheritance of medieval and popular forms. This is the live undergrowth from which the late sixteenth century draws much of its strength. In Shakespeare's sovereign contempt for limitations of space and time, we recognize the spirit of the mystery cycles which took the world of heaven, earth, and hell for their setting, and the history of man for their temporal scale. The clowns, the wise fools, and the witches of Elizabethan drama carry with them a medieval resonance. Behind the Senecan funerals come the hornpipes of the Morris dancers. And one cannot understand Shakespeare's history plays or his late, dark comedies, without discerning in them a legacy of ritual and symbolic proceeding which goes back to the imaginative wealth of the Middle Ages. How this legacy was transmitted, and how it conjoined with the nervous freedom of the Elizabethan temper, is as yet unclear. But we feel its shaping presence even as late as Jacobean drama. When the new world picture of reason usurped the place of the old tradition in the course of the seventeenth century, the English theatre entered its long decline.

In retrospect, the contrast between the actual work done by the Elizabethan playwrights and the claims put forward by neo-classic critics is overwhelming. The plays of Marlowe, Shakespeare, Middleton, Tourneur, Webster, and Ford are clearly superior to anything produced in the neo-classic vein. But this disparity is, in part, a matter of focus. Our own experience of the dramatic is so largely conditioned by the open, Shakespearean form, that it is difficult for us even to imagine the validity of an alternative tradition. The Elizabethan classicists were no fools. Their arguments were founded on more than the authority of Italian grammarians and the rather tawdry example of Latin tragedy. The neo-classic view expresses a growing perception of the miracle of

Greek drama. This perception was fragmentary. There were few translations of Aeschylus, and the plays of Euripides were known mainly in the versions of Seneca. Renaissance scholars failed to realize, moreover, that Aristotle was a practical critic whose judgements are relevant to Sophocles rather than to the whole of Greek drama (there is no unity of time, for instance, in the *Eumenides*). Nevertheless, the ideals of Sidney and the ambitions of Ben Jonson convey insight into the fact that the tragic imagination owes to the Greek precedent a debt of recognition. Time and again, this insight has mastered the sensibility of western poets. Much of poetic drama, from Milton to Goethe, from Hölderlin to Cocteau, is an attempt to revive the Greek ideal. It is a great and mysterious stroke of fortune that Shakespeare escaped the fascination of the Hellenic. His apparent innocence with respect to more formal classic attainments may account for his majestic ease. It is difficult to imagine what *Hamlet* might have been like had Shakespeare first read the *Oresteia*, and one can only be grateful that the close of *King Lear* shows no conscious awareness of how matters were ordered at Colonus.

The English classicists were not the earliest in the field. Neo-Aristotelian precepts and the Senecan example had already inspired a considerable body of Italian and French drama. Today, only the specialist in theatrical history reads the plays of Trissino and Giraldo Cintio, or Tasso's *Torrismondo*. This neglect extends to Jodelle and Garnier. In the light of Racine, French sixteenth-century tragedy seems an archaic prelude. But this view also is largely one of modern perspective. There is in both these French tragedians a strong music which we shall not hear again, even in the high moments of the classic style. Consider the invocation to death in Jodelle's *Cléopâtre captive* (1552):

Ha Mort, ô douce mort, mort seule gueri-
son
Des esprits oppressés d'une estrange
prison,
Pourquoy souffres tu tant à tes droits faire
tort?
T'avons nous fait offense, ô douce &
douce mort?
Pourquoy n'approches tu, ô Parque trop
tardive?
Pourquoy veux tu souffrir ceste bande
captive,
Qui n'aura pas plustot le don de liberté,
Que cest esprit ne soit par ton dard
écarté?[1]

The voice rises in ornate grief above the lament of the chorus. The lines fall like brocade, but beneath their stiffness we hear the loosening inrush of death: *ô douce & douce mort*. The *Parque trop tardive* is like an allegoric figure arrested in midflight; it is hard to believe that Valéry's eye did not chance on her.

In Garnier's *Marc-Antoine*, a somewhat later play, the same moment is drama-tized. Refusing Charmian's advice that she plead with her conquerors, Cleopatra prepares for the ceremonies of death:

Quel blasme me seroit-ce? hé Dieux!
quelle infamie,
D'avoir esté d'Antoine et son bonh-heur
amie,
Et le survivre mort, contente d'honorer
Un tombeau solitaire, et dessur luy pleu-
rer?
Les races à venir justement pourroyent
dire

Que je l'aurois aimé, seulement pour
l'Empire,
Pour sa seule grandeur, et qu'en adversité
Je l'aurois mechamment pour un autre
quitté.
Semblable à ces oiseaux, qui d'ailes passa-
geres
Arrivent au Printemps des terres estran-
geres,
Et vivent avec nous tandis que les chaleurs
Et leur pasture y sont, puis s'envolent
ailleurs.[2]

The words persuade us by an absence of rhetoric. Cleopatra refers to herself as Anthony's *amie*. In the sixteenth century the erotic connotations of the term were stronger than they are now; but in this quiet, cruel hour the force of friendship is as vital as that of love. Her simile lacks all pretension; she will not be flighty as are the birds. But at the same time, the quick-ening of pace and the cadence of *ailes passageres* directs our imagination to the deathward flight of the soul. The royal hawk on Egypt's crown will open his wings. The values here are not the same as in Corneille or Racine. The characters are shown in a manner which marks a transition from allegory to drama. They tend to live at the surface of language, and the action is one of successive orna-mentations rather than direct progress. But there is in these tragedies a commit-ment of emotion at once more naïve and

---

[1] Ah death, O gentle death, sole remedy
For spirits pinioned in captivity,
Why let your rights be flouted thus?
Did we offend thee, gentle, gentle death?
Why not draw near, O tardy Fate?
Why condescend to our captive state,
Who can no sooner from our bondage part
Than when our souls are stricken with your
dart?

[2] How infamous, ye gods! how much to blame,
Had I loved Anthony and his bright fame
And would survive his death, merely content
To shed a tear by his lone monument.
How justly, then, could future races say
I doted only on his sceptre's sway
And on his might, but when his star sank
down
Had stolen off to find some other man.
Then were I flighty as the birds of spring
Who come from foreign lands on transient
wing
To pasture with us during summer's noon,
But at first winter fly elsewhere again.

more humane than in mature neo-classicism.

Four years after Sidney's death, the Countess of Pembroke translated *Marc-Antoine*. Garnier was the model for Samuel Daniel's *Cleopatra* and Thomas Kyd translated his *Cornélie*, a tragedy dealing with the fall of Pompey. These were closet-dramas written for the enjoyment of a coterie. But they initiated a tradition of formal tragedy which extends into the romantic period. Fulke Greville destroyed one of his political tragedies at the time of the Essex rebellion. The two that survive, *Mustapha* and *Alaham*, have the kind of ornate and intricate solemnity which marks the architecture of the high baroque. They foreshadow the Moorish plays of Dryden and the works of a far more talented aristocrat—Byron's Venetian tragedies and his *Sardanapalus*.

The neo-classic view, moreover, found at least partial expression in the Elizabethan and Jacobean theatre. Chapman and Ben Jonson sought to combine the rival conceptions of learned and popular drama. They were at the same time scholars and men of the living stage. Of all the Elizabethans, Chapman is nearest to Seneca. His vision of human affairs was stoic, and his style had a natural darkness and complication. He entirely accepted the neo-Aristotelian belief in the moral purpose of drama. Authentic tragedy must convey "material instruction, elegant and sententious excitation to virtue, and deflection from her contrary." He shared the feeling of the later Roman historians that high matters of state are rooted in private lust and private ambition. *Bussy d'Ambois* and *The Tragedy of Chabot, Admiral of France* are among the few major political dramas in English literature. In Chapman's conviction that violence breeds violence and that evil will not be mocked, there is something of the lucid grief of Tacitus. Yet simultaneously,

Chapman was striving for success on the popular stage. Hence he gave to the audience its due ration of physical brutality, witchcraft, and amorous intrigue. His ghosts are as bloody as any in the Elizabethan theatre, his murders as frequent. But the stress of conflicting ideals proved too great. There is no unity of design in Chapman's plays. Amid the thickets of rhetoric there are sudden clearings where the grimness of his political vision carries all before it. But no proportion is sustained, as if a severe Palladian threshold gave sudden access to a baroque interior.

Chapman's Latinity is that of the Roman decline. The classicism of Ben Jonson belongs to the high noon of Rome. He is the truest classic in English letters. Other writers have taken from the surface of Latin poetry; Jonson went to the heart. His powers of close, ironic observation, his salty realism, the urbanity and energy of his statement, show how strongly his turn of mind was related to that of Horace. Had Jonson brought to his tragedies the virtues of *Volpone* and *The Silent Woman*, he would have left a body of work classic in spirit yet of a force to rival Shakespeare's. Instead, he resolved to affirm his claims to classic learning and social status. *Sejanus* and *Catiline's Conspiracy* were intended to show that Jonson could use with mastery the erudition and formal conventions of the neo-classic style. Both plays exhibit a sure grasp of the murderous tenor of Roman politics, and there are in each, passages whose excellence resists analysis precisely because Jonson's control was so unobtrusive. One must look to *Coriolanus* to find anything that surpasses the nervous intelligence and contained pressure of the dialogue between Caesar and Catiline:

CAESAR: Come, there was never any great thing yet
         Aspired, but by violence or fraud:

> And he that sticks for folly of a
> conscience
> To reach it—
> CATILINE: Is a good religious fool.
> CAESAR: A superstitious slave, and will die
> beast.
> Good night. You know what Cras-
> sus thinks, and I,
> By this. Prepare your wings as large
> as sails,
> To cut through air, and leave no
> print behind you.
> A serpent, ere he comes to be a
> dragon,
> Does eat a bat; and so must you a
> consul,
> That watches. What you do, do
> quickly, Sergius.

But Jonson's tragedies, like Chapman's, suffer from their divided purpose. They grow unwieldy under the attempt to reconcile neo-classic conventions to the very different conventions of Elizabethan historical drama. *Volpone* is far more "classical" than either of the Roman tragedies. It has the cruel tooth of Roman satire and a perfect discipline of proportion. The edges of feeling are hard-cut, and the characters are seen in the kind of direct, somewhat flattening light which is found also in Roman comedy. No other Elizabethan play is more distant from Shakespeare. It belongs with the lyrics of Matthew Prior and Robert Graves in that small corner of English literature which is genuinely Latin.

Neither Chapman nor Jonson fulfilled Sidney's ideal of the "true dramatic poem." Does this mean that there is no English tragedy in a classic mode to set against the world of Shakespeare? Only one, perhaps. Its preface is a rigorous statement of the neo-classic view:

Tragedy, as it was antiently compos'd, hath been ever held the gravest, moralest, and most profitable of all other Poems: therefore said by *Aristotle* to be of power by raising pity and fear, or terror, to purge the mind of those and such like passions. . . . This is mention'd to vindicate Tragedy from the small esteem, or rather infamy, which in the account of many it undergoes at this day with other common Interludes; hap'ning through the Poets error of intermixing Comic stuff with Tragic sadness and gravity; or introducing trivial and vulgar persons . . . brought in without discretion, corruptly to gratifie the people. . . . they only will best judge who are not unacquainted with *Aeschulus*, *Sophocles*, and *Euripides*, the three Tragic Poets unequall'd yet by any, and the best rule to all who endeavour to write Tragedy.

"Unequalled yet by any"—the words were written sixty-three years after the publication of *King Lear*. The judgement they convey and the tragedy which they introduce are the great counterstatement in English literature to Shakespeare and to all "open" forms of tragic drama.

Samson Agonistes is difficult to get into focus, exactly because it comes so near to making good its presumptions. The work is a special case by virtue of its power and of its intent. English drama has produced nothing else with which it may justly be compared. The organization of the play is nearly static, in the manner of the Aeschylean *Prometheus*; yet there moves through it a great progress toward resolution. Like all Christian tragedy, a notion in itself paradoxical, *Samson Agonistes* is in part a *commedia*. The reality of Samson's death is drastic and irrefutable; but it does not carry the major or the final meaning of the play. As in *Oedipus at Colonus*, the work ends on a note of solemn transfiguration, even of joy. The action proceeds from night-blindness of eye and of spirit to a blindness caused by exceeding light.

In *Samson Agonistes*, Milton accepted the claims of the neo-classic ideal and met them fully. He wrote a tragedy in a modern tongue; he did not even draw on Greek mythology; he strictly observed the unities and used a chorus. But at the same time, he created magnificent theatre.

This assertion should be a commonplace. Performance holds one spellbound, and the merest intelligent reading conveys the formidable excitement of the play. Only an ear deaf to drama could fail to experience, sharp as a whiplash, the hurt and tension of the successive assaults on Samson's bruised integrity. And there is little before Strindberg to match the naked sexual antagonism which flares between Samson and Dalila, "a manifest Serpent by her sting discover'd."

It is through *Samson Agonistes*, more readily perhaps than through archaeology and classical scholarship, that we glimpse the lost totality of Greek drama. Milton's language seems to draw after it the attendant powers of music and the dance. In certain passages the fusion is as complete as it must have been in the choral lyrics of Aeschylus:

But who is this, what thing of Sea or
    Land?
Female of sex it seems,
That so bedeckt, ornate, and gay,
Comes this way sailing
Like a stately Ship
Of Tarsus, bound for th' Isles
Of Javan or Gadier
With all her bravery on, and tackle trim,
Sails fill'd, and streamers waving,
Courted by all the winds that hold them
    play. . . .

No theatre since that of Dionysus had heard like music.

The preface to *Samson Agonistes* drew lines of battle which cut across the history of western drama. After the seventeenth century the writer of tragedy faces a persistent conflict of ideals. Should he adopt the conventions which neo-classicism derived from Aeschylus, Sophocles, and Euripides, or should he turn to the Shakespearean tradition of open drama? This problem of rival modes was in itself a difficult one; but there lay beneath it an even more crucial dilemma. Was it possi-

ble for a modern writer to create tragic drama which would not be hopelessly overshadowed by the achievements of the Greek and the Elizabethan theatre? Could a man write the word "tragedy" across a blank page without hearing at his back the immense presence of the *Oresteia*, of *Oedipus*, of *Hamlet*, and of *King Lear*?

One may argue, as Lessing and the romantics did, that the rigid distinction between the Sophoclean and the Shakespearean vision of tragedy is false. One may assert that the living should not bend under the weight of the dead. But the facts are undeniable. Until the time of Ibsen, Chekhov, and Strindberg, the problem of tragedy is shaped by the divided heritage of the classic and Elizabethan past. The eyes of later poets were riveted to these summits, and their own ambitions were arrested by the mere fact of comparison. Ibsen was to be the first in whom there were fulfilled ideals of tragic form which derived neither from the antique nor the Shakespearean example. And before this could happen, the centre of expressive language had to shift from verse to prose. These great problems of past magnificence and present failure were first posed in the late seventeenth century. With it must begin any inquiry into the condition of modern drama.

It was a period notable for the sharpness of its critical perceptions. Even prior to *Samson Agonistes*, critics saw that drama was riven by contrary ideals. Richard Flecknoe, in his *Short Discourse of the English Stage*, drew the line between Shakespeare and Ben Jonson. Compare them and "you shall see the difference betwixt Nature and Art." This statement is a Pandora's box from which confusion swarmed. "Nature" and "art" trace a maddening pattern across the weave of criticism. At times, art is equated with classical conventions and nature with the open, mixed forms of Shakespearean drama. More often, rival critics proclaim that their own conception of the theatre achieves the freedom of natural fantasy by means of concealed art. No school will wholly relinquish either term.

The subtlest mind brought to bear on these matters was that of Thomas Rymer. He was a critic whose power lay in a deliberate narrowness of taste. He saw deeply, and the questions he asked were those which two centuries of European drama sought to resolve. Even his critique of Shakespeare, which shows Rymer at his greyest, has a certain memorable honesty. By comparison, Voltaire's attack is disingenuous. In his examination of *The Tragedies of the Last Age*, Rymer tries to show that the conventions of classical drama are not artificial limitations, but rather expressions of the natural modes of reason. The forms of Greek tragedy codify the truth of experience and common understanding. The wildness of incident in *King Lear* or the alternance of grief and buffoonery in *Macbeth* are reprehensible not because they violate the precepts of Aristotle, but because they contradict the natural shape of human behaviour. It was the genius and good fortune of Aeschylus, Sophocles, and Euripides to have inherited and moulded a kind of drama whose conventions were at once satisfying in their proportionate formality and concordant with common sense.

Though clearly argued, Rymer's theory is, in fact, founded on equivocations. He began with the prevailing assumption that Greek drama is deliberate art whereas the plays of Shakespeare are spontaneous effusions of natural talent (the "warbling of wood-notes wild"). Upon it he imposed the idea that classical tragedies are realistic whereas Elizabethan dramas are pieces of unbridled fantasy. Note the intricate cross-weaving of critical terms: art is now expressive of common-sense realism,

while nature has been traduced into the realm of the fantastic. Beneath this inversion of traditional critical values, we find hints of a subtle and complicated aesthetics. To Rymer, Greek tragedy is at once formal and realistic. It is natural to the mind because it imitates life when life is in a condition of extreme order. Its "rules" or technical conventions are the means of such imitation; order in action can only be reflected by order in art. Lacking this coherent framework, Shakespeare's naturalism in fact leads to extravagant license and improbability (Lear leaping off Dover Cliff). The bias of Elizabethan drama is that of realism, but the image of life which it enacts is far less real than that put forward by Sophoclean tragedy. In short: true realism is the fruit of intense stylization. These are not Rymer's terms, and it is doubtful whether anyone but Racine fully grasped the paradox on which neo-classical theories were built. But the contrary notions in Rymer's dialectic—art-nature, common sense-imagination, reason-fantasy—were to exercise great influence. They haunt the theory of drama from the age of Dryden to that of Shaw and Brecht.

It is one of Rymer's merits that he did not evade the difficulties inherent in the neo-classic view. Having assumed that Athenian tragedy should be the governing ideal of modern practice, he faced the awkward question of how myths and beliefs central to Greek art could be carried over to a Christian or secular playhouse:

Some would laugh to find me mentioning *Sacrifices*, *Oracles*, and *Goddesses*: old Superstitions, say they, not practicable but more than ridiculous on our Stage. These have not observ'd with what Art *Virgil* has manag'd the Gods of *Homer*, nor with what judgment *Tasso* and *Cowley* employ the heavenly powers in a Christian Poem. The like hints from *Sophocles* and *Euripides* might also be improv'd by modern Tragedians, and something thence devis'd suitable to our Faith and Customes.

The question is more searching than the answer. Again it was Racine who grasped the nettle and perceived that the underlying conventions of neo-classical tragedy are myths emptied of active belief.

Rymer is on firmer ground when he argues that the Sophoclean ideal implies the use of a chorus: "The *Chorus* was the root and original, and is certainly always the most necessary part." He touches here on the essential distinction between the open and the closed theatre. The encircling presence of the chorus is indispensable to certain modes of tragic action; it renders other modes, such as those of Shakespearean drama, impossible. The problem of the chorus will arise continually in European drama. It preoccupied Racine, Schiller, and Yeats; it plays a role in the theatre of Claudel and T. S. Eliot. Rymer, moreover, acutely notes that the intervention of a chorus carries with it the possibility of music drama. The lyric element may undermine the vital force of the spoken word. Choral drama can be a halfway house to opera. Sir Robert Howard, a contemporary of Rymer, regarded this peril as imminent: "Here is the *Opera* . . . farewell *Apollo* and the Muses!" It is a prophetic cry, and we shall hear it again in the age of Wagner and Richard Strauss.

The critical language of Rymer and his contemporaries is no longer that of our own usage. But the controversies in which they engaged are with us still. For since the seventeenth century, the history of drama has been inseparable from that of critical theory. It is to demolish an old theory or prove a new one that many of the most famous of modern dramas have been written. No other literary form has been so burdened with conflicts of definition and purpose. The Athenian and the Elizabethan theatre were innocent of theoretical debate. The *Poetics* are conceived after the fact, and Shakespeare left no manual of style. In the seventeenth century, this innocence and the attendant freedom of imaginative life were forever lost. Henceforth, dramatists become critics and theoreticians. Corneille writes astringent critiques of his own plays; Victor Hugo and Shaw preface their works with programmatic statements and manifestoes. The most important playwrights tend to be those who are also the most articulate of purpose. Dryden, Schiller, Ibsen, Pirandello, Brecht are working within or against explicit theoretic forms. Over all modern drama lies the cast of critical thought. Often it proved too heavy for the underlying structure of imagination. There are many plays since the late seventeenth century more fascinating for the theory they represent than for their art. Diderot, for example, was a third-rate playwright, but his place in dramatic history is of high interest. This dissociation between creative and critical value begins with Dryden. It makes of him the first of the moderns.

His situation was artificial. He was required to restore that national tradition of drama which had been broken by the Cromwellian interlude. At the same time, however, he was compelled to take into account the new fashions and sensibility which the Restoration had brought with it. With the Restoration came a strong neo-classic impulse. Ideas such as those of Rymer were in the ascendant. How, then, could Dryden carry forward from Shakespeare and the Jacobeans? Should the English theatre not look to France from which the court of Charles II had taken so much of its style and colouring? Dryden, who possessed a catholic taste and a critical intelligence of the first rank, was aware of these conflicting claims. He knew that there towered at his back the divided legacy of Sophocles and Shakespeare. To which should he turn in his endeavour to re-establish a national theatre? In seeking to hammer out a compromise solution, Dryden imposed on his own plays a preliminary and concurrent apparatus of criticism. He is the first of the critic-playwrights.

His attempt to reconcile the antique and the Elizabethan ideals led to a complex theory of drama. This theory, moreover, was unstable, and the balance of Dryden's judgement altered perceptibly between the *Essay of Dramatic Poesy* (1668) and the preface to *Troilus and Cressida* (1679). Dryden's point of departure was itself ambiguous. The bias of his own temper, and the example of Tasso and Corneille, inclined him toward a neo-classic observance of dramatic unities. At the same time, however, Dryden was profoundly responsive to the genius of Shakespeare and felt drawn to the richness and bustle of the Elizabethan stage. He thought that he had found in Ben Jonson a *via media*. In contrast to Rymer and Milton, Dryden was prepared to allow a mixture of tragic and comic modes: "A continued gravity keeps the spirit too much bent; we must refresh it sometimes, as we bait in a journey, that we may go on with greater ease." But the type of drama which resulted from this compromise, the heroic play, followed neither Corneille nor Jonson. It is, in fact, a continuation of the romantic tragicomedies of Beaumont and Fletcher and shows the influence of the dramatic masques of the Stuart and Caroline court.

Yet Dryden was clearly dissatisfied with his own work. In the preface to *All for Love* (1678), he seems determined to restore a Shakespearean tradition. The confines of neo-classical drama "are too little for English tragedy; which requires to be built in a larger compass. . . . In my style I have professed to imitate the divine Shakespeare." But only a year later, he again shifted his critical ground. Much of the essay which precedes Dryden's version of *Troilus and Cressida* is a gloss on the *Poetics* according to the strict canons of Boileau and Rymer. Yet in the midst of the argument, we find praise for that most unclassical figure, Caliban. The entire essay is a strenuous attempt to show that Shakespearean drama does accord with Aristotle, and that there is a necessary conformity between Aristotelian "rules" and a just rendition of nature. The inherent instability of such a critical view also affected Dryden's use of verse. He vacillated between a belief in the natural propriety of Shakespearean blank verse and an adherence to the rhymed couplets of the French neo-classical theatre. At times, his arguments end in total confusion. Thus he declared that heroic rhyme was "nearest Nature, as being the noblest kind of modern verse."

These theoretical doubts and conflicting ideals are reflected in Dryden's plays. He wrote for the stage during a period of some thirty years and composed or collaborated in twenty-seven plays. The finest are the comedies—*Marriage à la Mode*, in particular. Dryden had many of the virtues of a great comic writer. He had a quick ear for the social shadings of language. He measured the distance from the centre of conduct to its eccentric verge—a distance that is the classic ground for comedy. He had a robust but tactful insight into the skirmishes of sexual love. *Marriage à la Mode* has the pace and cool intelligence of vintage comedy. By comparison, Sheridan's work is coarse-grained. It is in his treatment of political and tragic motifs that Dryden failed. The heroic plays live best in parody. They are great edifices of rhetoric and flamboyant gesture built on a void of feeling. Where we are moved at all, as in certain scenes of *Aureng-Zebe*, the delight is technical. One marvels at Dryden's ability to sustain in rhymed couplets long flights of passion and fury. Nor are the later, "straight" tragedies satisfactory. The finest are other men's work redone. This is a decisive point. The history of great drama is full of inspired plagiarism. The Elizabethans, in particular, had plundered freely wherever their eyes roamed. But what they took, they took as conquerors, not as borrowers. They mastered and transformed it to their own measure with the proud intent of surpassing what had gone before. In Dryden, this is no longer the case. When he "adapts" *Anthony and Cleopatra*, *Troilus and Cressida*, and *The Tempest*, he does so in complete awareness of the original. He is assuming that the earlier work lives in the remembrance of his public. His own version acts as a critique or variation on a given theme. It is "literary" in the narrow sense. In short, what we have here is pastiche, not re-invention. After the seventeenth century the art of pastiche will play an increasing role in the history of drama. Barren of invention, poets start pouring new sauces over old meats. In dealing with Dryden, we are still worlds away from such miseries as *Mourning Becomes Electra* or Cocteau's *Machine infernale*, but we are on the road.

This does not detract from the virtues of *All for Love*. No other English play after Shakespeare uses blank verse to such advantage. Dryden was a great master of his instrument:

> 'Tis time the World
> Should have a Lord, and know whom to obey.
> We two have kept its homage in suspense,
> And bent the Globe on whose each side we trod,
> Till it was dented inwards: Let him walk

> Alone upon't; I'm weary of my part.
> My Torch is out; and the World stands before me
> Like a black Desert, at th' approach of night.

But behind the grave nobility of these lines, we hear the richer, more close-knit music of Shakespeare's Anthony. Between the two, moreover, there has taken place a perceptible diminution of the pressure of feeling upon language. The effect is that of a skillful transcription for piano of a complete orchestral score. Dryden designated the play as *A Tragedy Written in Imitation of Shakespeare's Style*. Even if he was referring mainly to his use of certain Elizabethan conventions, the touch is ominous. Great theatre is not conceived in imitation.

Dryden saw reality in the light of dramatic encounter and dialectic. In a poem such as *The Hind and the Panther*, we "hear" the thrust and parry of ideas as we do in Ibsen. If Dryden failed to produce plays to match his talent, it is because he was working at a time when the very possibility of serious drama was in doubt. The Athenian and the Elizabethan past threw a lengthening shadow over the future of the dramatic imagination. Dryden was the first of numerous playwrights who found between themselves and the act of theatric invention a psychological barrier. The greatness of past achievement seemed insurmountable. Saintsbury is right when he judges that Dryden never attained that "absolute finality, which makes the reading of all the greatest tragedies, whether Greek or English, a sort of finished chapter of life."

But we may ask in turn: has any tragic dramatist attained such finality since the seventeenth century?

John Henry Raleigh

THE ENGLISH NOVEL AND THE THREE KINDS OF TIME

John Henry Raleigh is Professor of English at the University of California, Berkeley, and has written on nineteenth- and twentieth-century English and American literature. Among his most recent work is a critical study of Eugene O'Neill, which has been highly praised. The present essay first appeared in the *Sewanee Review* in 1954.

It is a truism that both the form and the content of the novel are bound up, more than is the case in any other of the major literary forms, with the dialectic between man and time and/or history. Upon this primordial fulcrum, which leans, in one direction, toward the private, the individual, the subjective and, in another and opposite direction, toward the public, the collective, the objective, the novel rests, achieving grandeur, like all art, only insofar as it maintains an equivocal synthesis, constantly breaking down and knitting together, between these two diametrically different but interacting areas of human experience. "Thus," writes Santayana, "two concomitant yet strangely different streams would seem to compose human life: one the vast cosmic flood of cyclic movements and sudden precipitations, in which man has his part like other animals; and the other, the private little rivulet of images, emotions, and words babbling as we move, and often hidden underground in sleep or forgetfulness." Santayana's aphorism, which sounds like a capsule-description of *Finnegans Wake*, is saying, like *Finnegans Wake*, that human experience is simultaneously a public nightmare and a private dream. And it is precisely this perspectivist observation post over the life of man that the great novelists have commanded, from Cervantes to Joyce. But the exact artistic formulation differs from author to author, and, more importantly, from century to century.

"A nous deux maintenant," says Rastignac (the private dream) to Paris (the public nightmare). This is the classic nineteenth-century formulation of the dialectic between man and time-history: the individual (here conceived of not as a psychic unit but as a whole, socio-biological person) clashing and coalescing with the city (contemporary history). But the twentieth-century purview of Stephen Dedalus includes not only the city and contemporary history but the nightmare of universal time-history as well. So that the major movement in the novel over the last one hundred years consists of a successive radicalizing of the two sides of the antithesis, with the individual becoming more and more a purely psychic entity, finally turning into a literal private dream, and time-history becoming more and more all-embracing until it eventually becomes a literal, public, multi-encompassing nightmare. *Finnegans Wake* formulates the dialectic in terms at once the most minute and grandiose: the ego dreaming on the history of the universe. The basic categories in the two centuries remain the same, but, whereas the nineteenth-century novel filled them out normatively, prosaically, the twentieth-century novel fills them out violently, grotesquely.

It is the purpose of this essay to trace out the broad outlines, using for illustrative material the history of the British novel of the last one hundred years, of this movement from man-social history to ego-universal history, in terms of the differing conceptions of and differing metaphors for the idea of time-history, with final remarks concerning, first, the bearings of these metaphors upon the conventions symbolizing personality and, secondly, the relationships between the idea of man and the idea of time-history.

The Platonic tradition held that time was "the moving image of eternity." This definition, while it may well be philosophically unsound, is just artistically and imaginatively if we grant that Everyman must somehow come to terms with time-history and evolve for it an emotionally satisfying metaphor which then constitutes an emblem of things ultimate. This is one of the things that literature attempts to do. But if we say that the time-sense and the historical-sense of a work of art is "the moving image of eternity" and is, as Spengler and others have held, profoundly axiological, we must still have more precise categories for more specific analysis. The categories most often used, of course, are the time-space antitheses.

Yet to hypostatize time as a discrete entity is to pass over precedent aspects of the problem, for there are, in life and art and anterior to the space-time antithesis, several divergent metaphors for describing time-history itself.

According to the late Nicholas Berdyaev there are three basic categories and symbols for describing time-history (Berdyaev makes no distinction between the time-sense and the historical-sense, taking them both to be specific manifestations of the general attitude toward temporal experience). First, there is cosmic time, which can be symbolized by a circle and which refers to the endless recurrence of things: night following day, season following season, the cycle of birth, growth, and decay; in short the circular character of human and natural experience. Secondly, there is historical time, symbolized by a horizontal line, and referring to the course of nations, civilizations, tribes (i.e., mankind in the mass) through time. Likewise the individual has a linear as well as a circular relationship to time. The line, for man or men, may slant upward, to indicate progress, or downward, to indicate regress. Third, and symbolized by a vertical line, there is existential time, referring to a notion of time somewhat like Bergson's *durée*, only religious or mystical in nature. This concept of existential time is actually an extreme form of individualism, or in Berdyaev's words, "personalism," and presupposes the individual's ability to free himself from either cyclic or historical time. Existential time, in effect, denies the validity of time-history. Historically, this idea of time manifested itself in the apocalyptic tendencies of early Christianity; in secular terms it still survives in certain anarchist doctrines. Popularly, it receives prosaic expression in the old wives' tale about a drowning man's whole life flashing before him in an instant, and, generally, in the common notion that, in all men's psychological experience, time has differing speeds and, at certain critical moments, seems, almost, to stop.

The time-sense of the Victorians was, of course, the linear one, which for twentieth-century man, so accustomed to the idea of "recurrence," seems to be almost equivalent to having no time-sense at all. In fact what appears, for us, to be absent in most Victorian novels—this despite the preoccupation of the nineteenth century with the past—is precisely an acute sense of time and a deep sense of history. And we do not need to go all the way up to Joyce, Proust, and Mann to see the difference between the central Victorians and us in these matters. Hardy and James will do.

In the work of neither Dickens nor Trollope, to take them as our examples, is there any what you might call "metaphysical" concern with time. Both authors, of course, were signally unintellectual and uninterested in such matters. They did use time for a certain shock value, for it was "in time" that the convolutions of plot were unravelled, the hero restored, and so on. But their time convention was vague and loose as compared, for example, to the rigorously observed "continuous present" of the late James. Trollope was given to suspending novel time altogether, by dropping the narrative and candidly predicting future events. In *The Eustace Diamonds* the diamonds at one point mysteriously disappear, as far as most of the characters in the novel are concerned, but Trollope informs the reader thus:

In the mean time, the Eustace diamonds were locked up in a small safe fixed into the wall at the back of a small cellar beneath the establishment of Messrs. Harter and Benjamin, in Minto Lane, in the City. Messrs. Harter and Benjamin always kept a second place of business. Their great shop was at the West End; but they had accommodations in the city.

The chronicler states this at once, as he scorns to keep from his reader any secret that is known to himself.

In other words novel time to Trollope was a joke. Generally he assumed that a convention of time existed and that the essence of his art, along with delineation of character, was temporality and that only by the passage of time would events unfold. But Trollope, like the rest of the Victorians, practiced a narrative method which explicitly allowed the author to see before and after, and hence for him as for God, there was no time and eternity lay spread before him. Thus every so often, banteringly (and Thackeray did the same thing), Trollope told the reader that novel time was his, and the reader's, sport, to be suspended at will, as the novelist desires. With how little seriousness novel time was taken by Trollope and the other Victorians can best be realized by comparing the above novelistic convention, which is not at all uncharacteristic of the Victorians, with the intricate "time-shift" of Ford and Conrad, where time is a cross to bear.

What is also absent in both Trollope and Dickens, and in most of the other Victorians, George Eliot perhaps excepted, particularly in the Jewish passages of *Daniel Deronda*, is a sharp sense of history. Of course practically all of the Victorians, following Scott, wrote historical novels, and, as a rule, failed to recapture and reconstruct a valid representation of the age they were concerned with. Yet their lack of historical sense is not best exemplified by these partial failures, although one might say that they were bound to fail, given their general attitude toward human history. What is absent in the Victorians is that more profound sense of the past (deeper than any fascination for the past as picturesque or the past as more attractive socially, in the fashion that Thackeray was intrigued by the eighteenth century)—the obsession of modern man that the past is continually impinging on the present and assuming the proportions of a nightmare.

The classic Victorian attitude toward history and the attitude which underlay most of its literary conventions is presented most unequivocally by Dickens, whose opinion of his collective heritage was negative, to say the least. Dickens had only pity and contempt for those unfortunates who had been born at other times and in other places than nineteenth-century England (although this is not to imply that he thought that he himself was living in paradise). It is reported that he had, in his library at Gadshill, a set of false backs which purported to be a history of Western civilization and which bore the following general and specific titles: "The Wisdom of our Ancestors—I. Ignorance. II. Superstition. III. The Block. IV. The Stake. V. The Rack. VI. Dirt. VII. Disease." So much for the past.

Turning now to James and Hardy, one finds quite a different situation. Both James and Hardy, in different ways, represent the ingress of temporal and historical preoccupations in the British novel. James was one of the first novelists to take time seriously and to make it an implicit part of his work. Preeminently in James things happen in time. In the typical James novel, meaning a late novel, all the psychic action is seen as the relentless unfolding of time, minute by minute, hour by hour, year by year, within the mind or sensibility of an individual.

History or the sense of the past likewise begins to appear in the novels of James. James, of course, did not have the historical imagination of his friend Henry Adams with its conception of man's past

as a construct of great forces bearing down on the present. Nevertheless, it is history that plays, generally, a major role in the motivation of all James' novels and it is history that became an obsessional preoccupation in his late works. In James' abiding theme—the American in Europe—the sense of the past is one of Europe's most subtle blandishments, something that pierces the soul and makes one laugh and weep simultaneously. Thus Isabel Archer on seeing the Eternal City for the first time:

She had always been fond of history, and here was history in the stones of the street and the atoms of sunshine. She had an imagination that kindled at the mention of great deeds, and wherever she turned some great deed had been acted. These things strongly moved her, but moved her all inwardly. . . . By her own measure she was very happy; she would even have been willing to take these hours for the happiest she was ever to know. The sense of the terrible human past was heavy to her, but that of something altogether contemporary would suddenly give it wings that it could wave in the blue. Her consciousness was so mixed that she scarcely knew where the different parts of it would lead her, and she went about in a repressed ecstasy of contemplation, seeing often in the things she looked at a great deal more than was there, and yet not seeing many of the items enumerated in her Murray.

This sense of the past became successively more acute in James' works and is the explicit and sole concern in some of the late tales and novels. In *The Altar of the Dead* the protagonist perpetually lights candles in commemoration of the dead, or the past; the hero of *The Jolly Corner* symbolically recaptures his own past; and, most bizarrely, Ralph Pendrel of the late unfinished novel *The Sense of the Past* actually changes place with a dead ancestor. And here, in this novel, James gave his most magniloquent testimony to the force of human history:

On the day he disembarked in England he felt himself as never before ranged in that interest [the past], counted on that side of the line. It was to this he had been brought by his desire to remount the stream of time, really to bathe in its upper and more natural waters, to risk even, as he might say, drinking of them. No man, he well believed, could ever so much have wanted to look behind and still behind— to scale the high wall into which the successive years, each a squared block, pile themselves in our rear and look over as nearly as possible with eye of sense into, unless it should be called out of, the vast prison house. . . . If his idea in fine was to recover the lost moment, to feel the stopped pulse, it was to do so as experience, in order to be again consciously that creature that had been, to breathe as he had breathed and feel the pressure he had felt.

In Hardy too time is taken seriously and becomes, in fact, dramatized as a malignant Fate, lying ominously in the future, waiting to strike down humans. Likewise everything in Hardy, natural or human, reverberates with history. The background for Hardy's Wessex series is provided by an immemorial community, the peasantry, who are, in a literal sense, the past, and who surround the main characters with an aura of ancient custom, legend, and myth, and the landscape itself mutely speaks for and of the ages.

But if time and history had become more pressing and more of a concern in the later nineteenth-century novel, they had also become something quite different, in their very nature; and a new set of literary conventions arose to symbolize the new attitudes. Dickens and Trollope were committed, by their unconscious assumptions and by the literary conventions which they inherited, to historical time, or time as a straight line, from the past into the future. In their case the idea of time was tied up with the idea of progress; so that the line of history led upward and receded downward, with the result that one looked forward to a pleasant but indefinite future and shunned a definite but unpleasant past. This attitude—rationalistic, progressive, secular— is, of course, the heritage of the eighteenth century and is known as liberalism. But what is noteworthy about the liberal attitude toward time-history is that, while it is generally confident about the future, it is vague about the concrete content of the future, as compared, say, to a Marxist, a conservative, or a cyclist. The key here is the ending of a novel, which is a specific and concrete manifestation of the general sense of time-history underlying the novel as a whole. At the end of a Dickens novel, for example, the leading characters are briefly projected into the future. But as the late George Orwell said, although the reader is assured of the infinite happiness of all parties, he is never quite sure as to why they are happy or what they are happy at, save that there is a childbirth every year and a Christmas spirit all the time. The assumption about futurity here is that these happy few will continuously but mistily compound their happiness, piling cheer on cheer, for the rest of their mortality. In short, the Victorian convention of the "happy ending" was not simply the result of a solid society wishing to have its sense of the fitness of things reaffirmed, for there is plenty of evidence to prove that the Victorian was anything but the stable and unworried cultural group that it is often supposed to have been. The "happy ending" does make sense if it be regarded as a literary convention metaphorically expressing the Victorian time-sense; i.e., man projected into an imprecise but, nevertheless, happy future. And for the Victorian novelist, before the "happy ending" happened, the substance of things and the material for his novel was a reality composed of an historically-emptied conjunction of the present and the future.

With Hardy and James it is precisely this concept of time and history as a straight line, leading upward, that begins to break down. Hardy's sense of the past is, partially anyway, a metaphorical expression of cosmic time, whose essence is the endless recurrence of things. In *The Return of the Native* an entire cycle of nature takes place, while the humanity in the foreground works itself out into an unhappy and ambiguous ending. Likewise in so many of the other Wessex novels, the one immutable certainty is that nature will continue her ceaseless cycle, no matter what sad fate besets man. As in nature so in man: the only solidity that man possesses is that which he inherits from the past, and Hardy's natives, like Faulkner's negroes, "endure." For the moderns, the civilized, the rationalists, the dependents on a liberalist future, the type who in the Victorian novel had the "happy ending," there is only tragedy, or misery, waiting in the future. In other words the universe of Thomas Hardy has only one certitude, the cyclic character of existence, and only one prop for humans, an allegiance to the past.

James' time-sense was obviously different from Hardy's and is, in effect, a secular version of existential or subjective time. Ralph Pendrel of *The Sense of the Past* literally fulfills Berdyaev's definition of existential time—he escapes from history. Less obvious is the implicit sense of existential time in all of James' late work, where there is no objective reality, and thus no real time, outside of the mind of the individual. Moreover, this internal time, while it flows continuously, does not always move at a constant rate. What happens in James is that time is extricated from history, as, with the clock stopped, James explores, often for pages, the infinity of implications arising from an instantaneous impression, and, in a sense, James' late works constitute a long

essay on the potential infinity of individual psychological moments.

As in the case of the Victorians, the key to Hardy's and James' time-sense is the manner in which each ends his novels. They both wrote "happy endings" but their most characteristic novels end either tragically (Hardy) or ambiguously (James). This is to say that man's future is either dark or unsure. In Hardy and in James, then, simple historical time, built along the idea of progress, is breaking down and cosmic and existential time are becoming the province of the novelist, who is, simultaneously, developing an historical sense and an immortal desire for an immersion in the past. It should be added that with James, at least, the novel is turning away from the objective world of society toward the inner world of the self for its subject matter.

Of Joyce's preoccupation with time-history, nothing need be said. He had, said Wyndham Lewis in paying the highest insult he could think of, a "time-mind." Nor do I propose to unravel the incredibly elaborate time-history structures underlying *Ulysses* and *Finnegans Wake*. For the purpose of this essay, however, *Ulysses* and *Finnegans Wake* may be taken as the uttermost extensions of the movements in the British novel being sketched here. As compared to Hardy, where a cosmic vision of time-history appeared only in regard to nature, the cycles in Joyce are all-inclusive, embracing human experience in its entirety, from personal, to social and natural, to, finally, divine history. As compared to James, where a limited existentialist time is employed at certain times, in Joyce the moment actually becomes infinity. "I hear," thinks Stephen Dedalus, "the ruin of all space, shattered glass and toppling masonry, and time one livid final flame." Thus in *Finnegans Wake* every moment is infinity and everything in history happens in every moment. Existential and cosmic time here coincide, producing a continuous, multileveled present which, by the principle of infinite regress, constantly recapitulates the key events of human and divine history, preeminently the Fall of Man. This concept of time-history could be symbolized in Berdyaev's categories as follows: time-history is a series of concentric circles; at dead center is H.C.E. (Man) who rays out vertical lines of existential being in all directions and through all levels of the cyclic experiences. Joyce has made incommensurables—the circular and the vertical—complement one another.

Likewise the implication for human destiny of the endings of *Ulysses* and *Finnegans Wake* is neither the vague happiness of the Victorians nor the ambiguous tragedy of James and Hardy. Joyce had the concrete circular vision—everything that has happened before will happen all over again—and it is this assumption that makes Joyce's work the true "tower beyond tragedy." At the end of *Ulysses* we know that Bloom will arise the next day and, with slight and unessential differences, will repeat his day-cycle once more. At the end of *Finnegans Wake* the cycle is made even more explicit by the famous broken sentence whose end can be found at the beginning of the book.

At this point the novel has turned from its Victorian standing-ground at a conjunction of the present-future to a conjunction of the past-present; and time-history, formerly a prosaic segment in the life of the city, in the linear image, has become a giant nimbus of exfoliating circles, shot through with existential lines of being.

While the concept and metaphor for time-history were expanded and elaborated, the concept and metaphor for characterology contracted and intensified.

Thus Dickens' eccentrics with their diamond-hard outlines turned, finally, into Joyce's blurred and fluxial egos, into their shadowy archetypal bases. In both the line of expansion and contraction, James' late novels appear to be a critical stage, for here the novel, in matters of character, is narrowing down, simultaneously decreasing the number in the cast of characters and turning away from the world into the self; at the same time there is an elaborate burgeoning of the idea of time-history into a complex metaphor which affords a glimpse of eternity and provides a bizarre vision of life, under which man, now time-obsessed, is, at certain moments, free of time and, at other moments, bears the whole of human history, like a cross, upon his back.

And the case of James points out too the intimate interconnection between these two lines of contraction and expansion, in fact, their cause-and-effect relationship. James' methods and interests led straight to the central convention of the early twentieth-century novel, that is, "the stream of consciousness" or "interior monologue." And this device, while its most obvious function was to body forth the inner life in a fashion impossible within the nineteenth-century novelistic conventions, was also a way of objectifying time-history in a manner unavailable to the Victorians: first it permitted the illusion of a continuous present (the existential), and, second, it permitted by reverie and memory, exploration of the past and the juxtaposition and confounding of past with present (the cosmic). It is only one more step for the individual memory, with which the "stream of consciousness" was initially concerned, to step over into collective memory and thus pass out into history.

Historically this is about what happened, for as the novel turned inward and contemporary history became thinned and abstracted (the late as opposed to the early James, for example), universal history began to emerge. In Thomas Mann's words, "the bourgeois and individual passes over into the mythical and typical." As in the children's fable, one digs a hole in the ground, to turn away from the world, but finally emerges in China, and, as a matter of fact, when one thinks of James' famous pagoda and caravan images or the orientalism of *Finnegans Wake*, the analogy is apt.

What has happened, then, in the novel is that the two sides of the basic antithesis of the novel (the private dream and the public nightmare) have had their respective time-schemes changed. Whereas both once traveled the linear line of historical time, in the twentieth-century novel the individual's time-sense has been, in great part, existentialized and the time-scheme of the universe has been circularized. *Finnegans Wake* carries these twin, complementary movements to their highest and most equivocal pitch, into an area, in fact, where they

are breaking down, one into the other, and where the parallels of development are beginning to curve and cross: a subjectivity, on the side of the individual, so complete, minute, and intense that it is constantly verging into the most broad and representative kind of archetypism; a vision of time-history so elaborate, so all-encompassing, so grandiose that it threatens, continually, to turn into a private, esoteric, mystagogic poem. Yet *Finnegans Wake* achieves the balance between the private and the public, the "perspectivism" which the great novel, since *Don Quixote*, has always achieved, albeit here in a radical, almost desperate fashion. And the success of this equivocal equation is, in great part, due to the organic blend of two kinds of time: the existential being the most extreme form of individualism; the cosmic being the most impersonal and objective way of describing the incessant tick, whose meaning is a circle, that sounds throughout *Finnegans Wake* and in all our ears.

David Daiches

RELIGION, POETRY, AND THE "DILEMMA"
OF THE MODERN WRITER

David Daiches, since 1961 Dean of the School of English and American Studies at the University of Sussex, has also taught at the University of Chicago and at Cornell University. He has written or edited more than two dozen books, including *The Novel in the Modern World* (1939), *Robert Burns* (1950), *Critical Approaches to Literature* (1956), and the notable *A Critical History of English Literature* (1960). The essay here reprinted first appeared in his *Literary Essays* (1956).

Nearly three hundred years ago John Milton, pondering in his age and blindness over the mysteries of human fate and thinking doubtless of the bitter frustrations and disappointments of his own life, put into the mouth of his hero Samson an almost desperate questioning of God's ways with man:

> God of our Fathers, what is man!
> That thou towards him with hand so
>   various,
> Or might I say contrarious,
> Temper'st thy providence through his
>   short course,
> Not evenly, as thou rul'st
> The Angelic orders and inferior creatures
>   mute,
> Irrational and brute.
> Nor do I name of men the common rout,
> That wand'ring loose about
> Grow up and perish, as the summer fly,
> Heads without name no more remem-
>   ber'd,
> But such as thou hast solemnly elected,

> With gifts and graces eminently adorn'd
> To some great work, thy glory,
> And people's safety, which in part they
>   effect:
> Yet toward these, thus dignifi'd, thou oft,
> Amidst thir highth of noon,
> Changest thy countenance and thy hand,
>   with no regard
> Of highest favours past
> From thee on them, or them to thee of
>   service.

The cry is a familiar one in the history of literature. Why do the wicked prosper and the virtuous suffer? It was a very real question for Milton as he sat in darkness and heard the bells ring out the end of all his political hopes, the end of his dream of being the poet and prophet of a new and regenerate England; as he heard the celebrators of the restoration of Charles II,

> The Sons
> Of Belial, flown with insolence and wine,

50

roistering in the streets outside. 'Why standest Thou afar off, O Lord? Why hidest Thou thyself in times of trouble? . . . For the wicked boasteth of his heart's desire, and the covetous vaunteth himself, though he contemn the Lord.' So the Hebrew psalmist had long before asked the same question. It was Job's question, too. 'Behold, I cry out of wrong, but I am not heard: I cry aloud, but there is no justice.' 'Wherefore do the wicked live, become old, yea, are mighty in power?'

This old question of theodicy, of the justice of God, or, if we prefer, of the way in which the universe is organized so far as it affects man, has long been a central theme in literature. The answer is generally given in terms of attitude rather than of logic. Job's problem disappears in a note of wonder—wonder at the grandeur and immensity of creation. The psalmist finds refuge in faith: 'Better is a little that the righteous hath than the abundance of many wicked. . . . For the wicked shall perish, and the enemies of the Lord shall be as the fat of lambs— they shall pass away in smoke, they shall pass away.' The Prometheus of Aeschylus, on the other hand, strikes a note of heroic self-confidence—ἐσορᾷς μ'ὡς ἔκδικα πάσχω 'behold me, how unjust are my sufferings.' These are very different answers to a single question, but they are all *literary* answers rather than philosophical solutions. By this I mean that the answers have force and meaning in virtue of their poetic expression, of the place they take in the myth or fable or situation presented, and of the effectiveness with which they project a mood. Job's solution is no answer if detached from its eloquent expression and paraphrased as a philosophical position. Such a procedure would make Job sound merely pusillanimous, just as it would make the psalmist a naïve self-deceiver and Prometheus a futile exhibitionist. In other words, we see

in earlier literature a religious (or mythological) tradition and a literary tradition mutually supporting each other, each depending on the other for full richness of expression and significance.

Let me try to explain this point more fully by turning again to Milton. We know that the justification of the ways of God to men, the professed theme of *Paradise Lost*, was a major preoccupation of Milton's throughout his life. We see the problem first stated in 'Lycidas,' a poem ostensibly lamenting the death of a young friend who died before he was able to fulfill his promise as poet and teacher but actually concerned with the larger problem of the ambitious idealist in an uncertain and arbitrary world. What is the use of dedicating oneself to a future of service to humanity (in Milton's case, through the writing of poetry 'doctrinal and exemplary to a nation') if one might be cut off at any moment, before even one's period of self-preparation was completed?

> Alas! What boots it with uncessant care
> To tend the homely slighted Shepherd's trade,
> And strictly meditate the thankless Muse?
> Were it not better done as others use,
> To sport with Amaryllis in the shade,
> Or with the tangles of Neaera's hair?

The question is turned this way and that throughout the poem, and every kind of traditional answer suggested before the real answer emerges in the mood and tone of the conclusion:

> Thus sang the uncouth Swain to th' Oaks and rills,
> While the still morn went out with Sandals gray.
> He touch't the tender stops of various Quills,
> With eager thought warbling his Doric lay:
> And now the Sun had stretch'd out all the hills,

And now was dropt into the Western bay;
At last he rose, and twich't his Mantle
  blue:
Tomorrow to fresh Woods, and Pastures
  new.

Like God's answer to Job in the whirl-
wind, this is not a logical disposal of the
problem, but the distillation of a mood in
the light of which the poet is able to carry
on. The quiet sunrise which proclaims a
new day brings a note of humility and
acceptance to the poet, who now describes himself as an 'uncouth swain'—
that is, an unknown or unlearned rustic
—and with that comes the determination
to do what one can while one can, to enjoy such beauty as life grants and to turn
one's hand to what lies to be done without too much speculation on possible
accidents: 'Tomorrow to fresh Woods,
and Pastures new' has the sound both of
peace and of purpose.

When his blindness came, some fifteen
years later, Milton again raised the question of God's justice in so dealing with
him:

When I consider how my light is spent,
  Ere half my days, in this dark world
    and wide,
  And that one Talent which is death to
    hide,
  Lodg'd with me useless, though my
    Soul more bent
To serve therewith my Maker, and present
  My true account, lest he returning
    chide;
  Doth God exact day-labour, light de-
    nied,
  I fondly ask?

But Patience replies, and stills the
poet's questioning with a picture of various services rendered by different men
actively or passively, God being best
served by those 'who best bear his mild
yoke'; and the poem ebbs quietly away

on the concluding line: 'They also serve
who only stand and wait.' Has this answer
vindicated God's justice? No; but it has
projected a mood in the light of which
life seems more interesting, more significant, and more tolerable.

In *Paradise Lost* the justification of the
ways of God to men is developed on a
more deliberate and even grandiose scale.
On the surface Milton, by telling the
story of man's fall in Eden, is showing
that man fell by a deliberate abuse of
his free-will, so that he has himself and
not God to blame, and also pointing out
that God provided a scheme of redemption which would enable those who made
the effort to attain to a state far above
that from which Adam fell. Thus man
deserved what he got by deliberately
doing evil, but God in His mercy brought
good out of evil by the Christian scheme
of redemption. This is the cold, para-
phrasable message of *Paradise Lost*, but it
is neither the true meaning of the poem
nor the real way in which Milton justified
the ways of God to men. The real justification of God's dealings with men lies in
the implicit contrast between the ideal
idleness of the Garden of Eden and the
changing and challenging world of moral
effort and natural beauty which resulted
from the Fall. This argument is presented
obliquely and continuously through mood
and imagery: when the beauty of Eve in
her unfallen state is described in terms
of classical myths which give an atmosphere of ineffable loveliness to the whole
picture we get a sense of values which can
only emerge in the fallen human imagination. The postlapsarian world (to use the
theological term) may lack the bliss of
Eden, with its perpetual spring and its
freedom from the curse of earning one's
daily bread by the sweat of one's brow,
but the procession of the seasons which
was part of the punishment of the Fall

provides some of Milton's most moving imagery, while symbols of rustic labour with its beauty and dignity contradict or at least modify the explicit statement that work was imposed on man as a curse. Even prelapsarian nature, ideal nature before the Fall, can only be made desirable in our eyes in terms drawn from a postlapsarian consciousness, just as good can only be made significant in terms of moral effort against known evil—evil known only in man's fallen state.

The real theme of *Paradise Lost* is man's essential and tragic ambiguity, illustrated in the fact that love is bound up with selfishness (as when Adam follows Eve's example in eating the forbidden apple because he cannot live without her); that good is bound up with evil; that the beauty which adorns the earth as it passes from seed-time to harvest, from the white of winter to the gay colours of spring, is bound up with change, and change, which means growth, also means decay; that the rich pattern of different human civilizations as Milton passes them under review with all the magic of exotic and musical place names and the excitement of geographical discovery was made possible by the curse of Babel; that the dignity and beauty of rustic labour, the basis of some of Milton's finest similes, is the other side of the law which decrees starvation and suffering for those who can find no land or no work. In the personal outburst at the beginning of the third book, what the blind Milton most laments are those sights of seasonal change which resulted from the loss of Eden's perpetual spring:

> Thus with the Year
> Seasons return, but not to me returns
> Day, or the sweet approach of Ev'n or
>   Morn,
> Or sight of vernal bloom, or Summer's
>   Rose,

> Or flocks, or herds, or human face divine;
> But clouds instead, and ever-during dark
> Surrounds me, from the cheerful ways of
>   men
> Cut off. . . .

They are 'the cheerful ways of men' still, in spite of 'the sons of Belial flown with insolence and wine.' And the curse that 'in the sweat of thy face shalt thou eat bread' can make possible the imagery of such lines as these:

> As one who long in populous City pent,
> Where Houses thick and Sewers annoy
>   the Air,
> Forth issuing on a Summer's Morn to
>   breathe
> Among the pleasant Villages and Farms,
> Adjoin'd, from each thing met conceives
>   delight,
> The smell of Grain, or tedded Grass, or
>   Kine,
> Or Dairy, each rural sight, each rural
>   sound. . . .

This is how Milton justifies the ways of God to men—by showing through the emotional pattern of his great poem how everything worth while that we can conceive of is made possible by the results of the Fall. Again, this is not a logical but a poetic solution to his problem, like the solution of *Job* and of the psalmist. A religious tradition and a poetic sensibility co-operated to produce an effect which needed both but which was wholly produced by neither.

In *Samson Agonistes* Milton handled this problem for the last time. Samson the hero was brought pitifully low, apparently deserted by God, and he recovered only to destroy himself with his enemies. Samson's moral recovery is a main theme of the play, but we know from the beginning that there is no going back to the young heroic Samson doing great deeds for his country. He recovers only to die. Is that fair or just on God's part? Is that

the only answer to his great cry: 'God of
our Fathers, what is man!'? No: the real
answer is an aesthetic one; it lies in the
'katharsis' which the tragedy produces.
The chorus sums up the significance of
the action in the well-known conclusion:

His servants he with new acquist
Of true experience from this great event
With peace and consolation hath dismist,
And calm of mind, all passion spent.

This is Milton's interpretation of the
Aristotelian 'katharsis,' the purgation of
the emotions through pity and fear, which
is Aristotle's view of the function of
tragedy. The calm of mind produced by
the tragic 'katharsis' is at the same time
the mood which accepts God's dealings
with men as just. At the end of his life
Milton completely and finally reconciled
religion and aesthetics, the Christian and
the humanist, by justifying the ways of
God to men in terms of a mood distilled
aesthetically by tragedy. What Professor
Douglas Bush has called 'the dilemma of
a sacred poet and a Puritan bred in the
congenial air of Renaissance classicism'
was resolved by applying a classical notion
of the function of tragedy to the solution
of Job's question.

What I am trying to show is that the
interplay between religious and aesthetic
impulses has always been fruitful in literature and that an appreciation of it is
independent of the reader's creed or philosophical system. One could demonstrate
a similar interplay in Dante and Shakespeare as well as in the Greek dramatists.
But I must hasten on, to ask the questions
that we are most concerned with here.
Has the contemporary literary artist anything to learn from this? Has the disintegration of community of belief which
most observers agree to be a characteristic
of our present age altered the situation so
radically that the kind of thing done by
Aeschylus and Dante and Milton—posing

questions suggested by religion and answering them in literary or aesthetic terms
—becomes impossible? Is there an un-
bridgeable gap between the past of literature and the contemporary literary artist?

These are not easy questions to answer,
and they certainly cannot be adequately
answered here. I am all too conscious of
the dangers of facile generalization and
of the ease with which a showy thesis
can be developed by the manipulation of
an arbitrary selection of examples. As I
try to cast my mind's eye over the vast
array of works of literary art from the
Book of Job to a poem by Mr. Eliot and
think of the numerous changes in taste
and attitude, the imense diversity of
works and of writers, and the vastly different conscious objectives which different artists have set themselves, I can see
how tentative and inadequate any answer
to the questions I have raised must be
even if I were much more of a polymath
than I can allow myself to claim. But in
the realm of critical ideas nothing significant can be achieved without boldness;
so, having listed the dangers, let me now
proceed to ignore them.

What does the loss of a common background of religious attitudes and symbols
mean to literature? The problem has
agitated poets for over a century. Nearly
a hundred years ago Matthew Arnold, in
his poem 'Dover Beach,' expressed a view
which is central to our present discon-
tents. Looking out over the Straits of
Dover on a calm, moonlit night he lis-
tened to the splash of the waves on the
shore and thought how Sophocles had
heard in that sound 'the turbid ebb and
flow of human misery.' He continued:

The Sea of Faith
Was once, too, at the full, and round
  earth's shore
Lay like the folds of a bright girdle furl'd.
But now I only hear
Its melancholy, long, withdrawing roar,

Retreating, to the breath
Of the night-wind down the vast edges
    drear
And naked shingles of the world.
Ah, love, let us be true
To one another! for the world, which
    seems
To lie before us like a land of dreams,
So various, so beautiful, so new,
Hath really neither joy, nor love, nor light,
Nor certitude, nor peace, nor help for
    pain;
And we are here as on a darkling plain
Swept with confused alarms of struggle
    and flight,
Where ignorant armies clash by night.

This mood of what Professor Trilling has called 'controlled self-pity,' this elegiac note which enables the poet to face a world without faith, represents a rather different use of poetic devices from that which we find at the conclusion of Job or even in Milton. The earlier writers, it is true, projected a mood, which is what Arnold is doing, but it was a mood which enabled man to achieve new equanimity and go about his business untroubled. In Job, in the older Greek dramatists, in Dante, in many of Shakespeare's tragedies, and in Milton, a 'katharsis' is achieved which frees writer and reader alike from inhibitive brooding. One might even venture a rash generalization and say that these older works freed man for action, while much romantic literature consigns man to perpetual introspection. In fact, this might be if not an adequate at least a workable definition of the two terms, 'classical' and 'romantic.' When Milton grows impatient with God and his destiny he writes a poem which resolves his doubts through projecting a mood of acceptance and preparation for action. Keats, concerned with the same fear that haunted Milton in 'Lycidas,' afraid, that is, lest he might die 'before my pen has gleaned my teeming brain,' found an answer in pure introspection:

When I behold upon the night's starred
    face
Huge cloudy symbols of a high romance,
And think that I may never live to trace
Their shadows with the magic hand of
    chance;
And when I feel, fair creature of an hour,
That I shall never look upon thee more,
Never have relish in the fairy power
Of unreflecting love—then on the shore
Of the wide world I stand alone, and
    think
Till love and fame to nothingness do sink.

How different this is from 'Tomorrow to fresh Woods, and Pastures new' or even 'They also serve who only stand and wait.'

Can we go so far as to say that an art with a religious background can achieve 'katharsis' more effectively than one without one? The Romantic poets, who substituted introspective plangency for religious assurance, often saw the function of art quite differently from the way in which Dante or Shakespeare saw it. Differences between Dante the mediaeval Catholic and Shakespeare the tolerant humanist are numerous and profound enough, but they are both religious in the sense in which I am using the term, a sense in which Keats and Tennyson and Matthew Arnold are not religious. The ending of *Hamlet* or *Macbeth*, with the reasserting of the norm and the preparation for daily activity is, in the largest symbolic sense, comparable to the ending of Dante's *Inferno*: *'e quindi uscimmo a riveder le stelle'* (And thence we came forth to see again the stars).

The release from troubled introspection into action is, however, very far from being the objective or the achievement of, say, Tennyson's 'Break, break, break,' Arnold's 'Dover Beach'—we can all add indefinitely to the list—which cultivate that very state from which the classical 'katharsis' (I am using the term now widely and symbolically) seeks to relieve writer and reader. The cultivation of this state is not, it should be added, peculiar to the English Romantic poets: there is, in fact, no more perfect example of it than in that remarkable sonnet *'L'Infinito'* by the Italian poet Leopardi in which a mood of complete surrender to trance-like contemplation is deliberately cultivated:

Cosi tra questa
Immensità s'annega il pensier mio:
E il naufragar m'e dolce in questo mare.

Thus amid this vastness my thought is
drowned,
And shipwreck is sweet to me in such a
sea.

The mood of 'Dover Beach' or 'Break, break, break' is not, of course, uniquely Romantic: it is not the mood so much as the use to which it is put in the poem that differentiates Arnold's description of the waves breaking on the lonely shore from similar descriptions in the classics— from say, the picture of Achilles in the twenty-third book of the *Iliad* mourning for his dead comrade Patroclus as he lay ἐν καθαρῷ ὅθι κύματ' ἐπ' ἠϊονος κλύζεσκον (in a lonely place where the waves splashed upon the shore). That is one of the most evocative—if you like, romantic —lines in Greek literature, but its purpose is not to exploit the temporary mood of plangent meditation but to prepare the way for the final 'katharsis' of Achilles' anger and grief.

Nevertheless, as Matthew Arnold saw as clearly as anybody, a mood of self-pity, however controlled and beautifully expressed, cannot for long remain a literary norm. In England, the mid and late nineteenth century poets played all possible variations on it and its potentialities were soon exhausted. A classical reaction set in in the second decade of the present century, with T. E. Hulme calling on the poets, in a misquoted line from the seven-

teenth century dramatist John Webster, to 'end your moan and come away.' Hulme advocated, and prophesied, a period of 'dry, hard, classical verse.' The cry was taken up by Eliot and others, and a revolution in poetic taste was achieved within a generation. 'The poet,' wrote Eliot in 1917, 'has not a "personality" to express, but a particular medium, which is only a medium and not a personality, in which impressions and experiences combine in peculiar and unexpected ways.' But in fact neither Eliot nor any other significant poet of our time was content to make of poetry the mere arranging of impressions and experiences in peculiar and unexpected ways. If the classical poets—again using the terms widely and symbolically—had created literature by exploiting the impact of personality on a religious tradition, and the Romantic poets had exploited personality by itself, what was the modern poet to do, who shared the Romantic poets' confusion about religion and at the same time repudiated their exploitation of personality? They could, of course, take Voltaire's position, and say that if God did not exist it would be necessary to create him, and some of the arguments brought forward by Mr. Eliot in his prose writing almost suggest that at times this is the line that he took. In his later poetry, however, from 'Ash Wednesday' on, Mr. Eliot has been concerned with the impact of personality on a religious tradition, and in the *Four Quartets* he has been remarkably successful in distilling a mood in the light of which the religious position becomes meaningful if not logically demonstrable. And that, as we have seen, is the way classical art works.

But Mr. Eliot's solution is not wholly satisfactory, and certainly not one that can be successfully employed by others, because, however sincerely his religious emotion is felt (and it is not for the literary critic to presume to judge that), the materials it works on are academic and its documents not central to any religious tradition. (Saint John of the Cross, for example, is a more fundamental source of imagery and structure in many of his poems than the Bible or the prayer book, and there is a curious air of coy connoisseurship about his handling of religious documents.) There is, in fact, however much Mr. Eliot may repudiate personality in poetry, a highly idiosyncratic personality at work here whose solutions of common problems are *not* really helpful to others, for all the influence of his merely technical procedures on younger poets.

The conflict between faith and reason, between religion and experience, is not the modern problem our contemporary writers have to solve. The more vital the religious tradition, the more real and fruitful has that conflict been: it is, as I have tried to show, in Job, the Greek dramatists, *Paradise Lost*, as well as in Dante and Shakespeare. The modern problem is to find a valid tradition with reference to which literary artists can pit their personality with poetic profit. There is always a gap between a traditional formulation of values and individual experience, and across that gap sparks the poetic insight. You can sometimes get away with making your own tradition, as in a sense Eliot has, for his Christian tradition is not, I venture to think, identical with any of the main forms of the Christian tradition in Western civilization, but there is something both artificial and dangerous about this: for how can there be tension between your personal experience and the impersonal tradition, when the impersonal tradition is something you have discovered or created for yourself? Yet there are ways out of this dilemma—dangerous ways, and not always imitable ways, but nevertheless ways which have on occasion been successfully taken. Let me glance

briefly at two of these, that taken by W. B. Yeats and that taken by Dylan Thomas.

There is a well-known statement of his early position made by Yeats in his autobiographical work, *The Trembling of the Veil:*

I am very religious, and deprived by Huxley and Tyndall, whom I detested, of the simpleminded religion of my childhood, I had made a new religion, almost an infallible church of poetic tradition, of a fardel of stories, and of personages, and of emotions, inseparable from their first expression, passed on from generation to generation by poets and painters with some help from philosophers and theologians. . . .

If this was all that Yeats had done, he would not have become the great poet we know him to have been. For to repudiate the religious tradition and to put in its place a tradition derived from the reflection of that repudiated tradition in art and philosophy is neither logical nor helpful. What is religion but the primary expression of those basic myths and values which in turn are used by artists in the way I have tried to suggest? The genuine agnostic can understand and appreciate a religious tradition in life and art, and understand how the tensions between that tradition and individual personality have helped to produce great art, but he certainly cannot go to that art and pick out from it a religious tradition unacceptable to him in its explicit form, though Yeats was not alone in thinking that this could be done. What makes Yeats's statement of his problem so interesting is not the solution he suggests but the awareness of the problem that it shows. He needed a religious tradition to work with, but he could not accept any tradition specifically denominated as religious.

We know, of course, what he eventually did. He built for himself out of the oddest and most miscellaneous material a symbolic system with reference to which he could organize his poetic expression. But if it was his own system, created by himself, how could he set himself over against it to develop those tensions between individual insight and impersonal system which I have suggested are the most significant way in which a poet can use a tradition? The answer is that the conflict in Yeats's poems is not between himself and the system, but between two aspects of the system, which, being a dialectical one, a balancing of opposites, afforded him all the tensions he could handle. The system itself, with its lunar phases and towers and spinning tops and spiral staircases, was based on the perpetual merging of opposites. As you climb the spiral staircase you move through all the points on the circumference of a circle, but when you reach the top of the spiral, which is a circle with an infinitely small circumference, you are at all points in the circumference simultaneously. Yeats's poetic imagery had been from the beginning dominated by a conflict of opposites; in his early poetry we find perpetually the human world contrasted with the supernatural world of faery, the familiar and domestic with the wild and strange, the tame with the heroic, the Christian with the pagan. Later on, his images seem to coalesce into a *tertium quid*, so that simple contrasts disappear and we find symbolic probings into the underlying affinity of apparent opposites. We have this implicitly in the 'Byzantium' poems, and quite explicitly in some of the 'Crazy Jane' poems:

A woman can be proud and stiff
When on love intent;
But Love has pitched his mansion in
The place of excrement;
For nothing can be sole or whole
That has not been rent.

Or consider:

Bodily decrepitude is wisdom: young
We loved each other and were ignorant.

Or this, from 'A Woman Young and Old':

How could passion run so deep
Had I never thought
That the crime of being born
Blackens all our lot?
But where the crime's committed
The crime can be forgot.

'Out of our quarrel with others we make rhetoric,' Yeats once remarked; 'out of our quarrel with ourselves, poetry.' Instead of the two poles being personality and tradition, they become opposing aspects of personality. A self-made tradition can only be of value to the literary artist when it contains self-contradictions.

My thesis has been, as will, I hope, be clear by now, that a religious tradition is of value to the literary artist as providing a challenge to individual experience out of which art may result. When that tradition disintegrates, the poet can take refuge in elegiac introspection or he can create or discover a tradition of his own. The former practice may produce much that is valuable, but in the nature of things it cannot be maintained for long, its potentialities being limited and its possibilities soon exhausted. The latter can only work when the created or discovered tradition is complex enough to contain within itself the tensions which the great artist needs; if it does not contain those tensions, then the artist is merely shadow boxing when he employs the tradition, since, being the product of his own imagination, it cannot at the same time be a challenge to his imagination.

Thus Yeats's dialectical symbolic system—if I may use such an ugly term for lack of a better—enabled him to organize the images and ideas in his poetry so as to achieve profound poetic statement. Instead of his own personality wrestling with the tradition, we find opposing elements of his own personality fighting it out and becoming reconciled within the tradition that he pieced together himself. This does not mean that we must understand—still less that we must agree with—the fantastic system which Yeats elaborated in *A Vision* before we can understand or appreciate his poems. Of his best poems it can be safely said that his system is a device to help him achieve the rich and significant patterning of image and idea out of which effective poetic expression is distilled. That significant patterning can be recognized, with all its rich overtones of meaning, in such a poem as 'Byzantium' without any reference to *A Vision*. Indeed, an attempt to interpret the poem too specifically in terms of Yeats's system narrows the meaning unduly and shuts off the reverberating meanings which give the poem its greatness. There are some poems of Yeats which do require the application of the system for their appreciation, but these are his less successful ones.

Dylan Thomas has achieved a very different kind of richly echoing poetic statement, but his success, too, is the result of his creation or discovery of a synthetic tradition in the light of which the proper tensions can be created and resolved. Christianity, Freudian psychology, Welsh folklore, are only some of the elements which he employs together in profound counterpoint to produce some of the most exciting poetry of our time. For a clearer understanding of what modern problem Thomas is solving by this counterpointing of apparently contradictory elements in our culture, let me quote from an author who, in an earlier phase of his career, was painfully aware of the problem, and who has since tried to solve it in a very different way from that chosen by Thomas. Aldous Huxley, in the opening

chapter of his novel *Antic Hay* (1923) makes Theodore Gumbril, the disillusioned school master, meditate in the school chapel as follows:

No, but seriously, Gumbril reminded himself, the problem was very troublesome indeed. God as a sense of warmth about the heart, God as exultation, God as tears in the eyes, God as a rush of power or thought—that was all right. But God as truth; God as 2 + 2 = 4—that wasn't so clearly all right. Was there any chance of their being the same? Were there bridges to join the two worlds?

Gumbril decided that there were not, and therein lay his dilemma. Or again, take the description of the string orchestra in the third chapter of *Point Counter Point* (1928):

Pongileoni's blowing and the scraping of the anonymous fiddlers had shaken the air in the great hall, had set the glass of the windows looking on to it vibrating; and this in turn had shaken the air in Lord Edward's apartment on the further side. The shaking air rattled Lord Edward's *membrana tympani*; the interlocked *malleus, incus,* and stirrup bones were set in motion so as to agitate the membrane of the oval window and raise an infinitesimal storm in the fluid of the labyrinth. The hairy endings of the auditory nerve shuddered like weeds in a rough sea; a vast number of obscure miracles were performed in the brain, and Lord Edward ecstatically whispered 'Bach!'

God as a sense of warmth about the heart as opposed to God as 2 plus 2 equals 4; music as a series of sound waves impinging on a physiological organism and music as something significant and moving—these are expressed as irreconcilable alternatives. Both explanations seem to be true, yet each seems to deny the other. If the dilemma is posed this way, the only solution would seem to be either complete scepticism or complete irrationality, and neither scepticism nor irrationality can provide a proper environment for great art. What the modern artist needs is some device which will enable him to hold these conflicting attitudes in suspension, as it were, or perhaps it could be better described as a state of tension, or of counterpoint, so that instead of being inhibitive of value they can increase and enrich value.

Huxley's observation about music is neither new nor original. Shakespeare's Benedick, in *Much Ado About Nothing*, remarks in an ironic moment: 'Is it not strange that sheeps' guts should hale souls out of men's bodies?' Unlike Huxley, Shakespeare was not tortured by this perception: he includes it dramatically as one element in the complex and paradoxical nature of things, so that it enriches rather than frustrates his picture of human values in action.

Returning now to Dylan Thomas, we note that his poetic technique enables him to handle in brilliant counterpoint all the different explanations of human situations given by religion, science, and folklore:

I, in my intricate image, stride on two
    levels,
Forged in man's minerals, the brassy
    orator
Laying my ghost in metal,
The scales of this twin world tread on the
    double,
My half ghost in armour hold hard in
    death's corridor,
To my man-iron sidle.

Beginning with doom in the bulb, the
    spring unravels
Bright as her spinning-wheels, the colic
    season
Worked on a world of petals;
She threads off the sap and needles, blood
    and bubble
Casts to the pine roots, raising man like a
    mountain
Out of the naked entrail.

Beginning with doom in the ghost, and
    the springing marvels,

Image of images, my metal phantom
Forcing forth through the harebell,
My man of leaves and the bronze root,
    mortal, unmortal,
I, in my fusion of rose and male motion,
Create this twin miracle.

What the modern artist needs is not so much a faith as a poetic principle to enable him to counterpoint against each other the different aspects of knowledge of which the modern world has made him aware. Consider this fact. We know, or we think we know, so much about psychological conditioning, about the psychosomatic aspects of illness, about the effect of childhood frustrations on adult vices, that we are in danger of being unable to pass any moral judgment on individuals. This man committed rape or murder, but we know that he saw something terrible in the woodshed when he was three, was brought up in a slum, was bullied by a drunken stepfather, had his emotions and instincts warped and frustrated in this way or that, so that we cannot really blame him for what he eventually was driven to do. *Tout comprendre, c'est tout pardonner*, to know all is to forgive all, says the French proverb; but to forgive all is to make it impossible to write the *Divine Comedy* or *Hamlet* or *Paradise Lost*. If we knew all about the inhibitions of King Claudius's childhood, we could not make him the villain in a tragedy. If we knew all Iago's psychological history we might be tempted to spend all our sympathy on him rather than on Othello. And it did not take even that much psychology to make the Romantics turn Milton's Satan into a hero. If our judgments of men are to be dissolved in psychological understanding, we can no longer pattern a tragedy or create any significant work of art with a human situation as its subject matter. Certainly a behaviourist psychology—and I use this term in its widest sense—leaves little room for an appraisal of personality as such, and without an appraisal of personality as such why should Hamlet's death be any more significant than that of Polonius?

Yet Hamlet's death, and all that leads up to it is significant because it is implicitly set against a tradition of what is valuable in human personality, and out of the implicit conflict with this tradition—which held, among other things, that a good man was doing right to punish an evil one—the tragedy emerges. Cannot we too acquire a double vision and set the fact of value in human personality beside the psychological knowledge that would seem to break down the basis of such value, and contemplate the subsequent tensions in art? Cannot the poet, at least, answer Huxley's question by accepting simultaneously both of his alternatives as each true in its own way and finding a richness of observation and expression in which the conflict can be resolved? Even in life, cannot we both forgive a man and pass judgment on him? All the more so, surely, should we be able to achieve this twofold attitude in art, which has so many devices for focusing multiple vision.

The problem of the modern literary artist, therefore, is not to find usable myths so much as to find ways of handling knowledge in a context of value. Knowledge should explain without ever explaining away; proof that Keats's genius flowered early because he had tuberculosis neither explains away the genius nor makes tuberculosis a desirable disease; a study of the nervous system can tell us all sorts of fascinating things about what makes us tick, but cannot alter the basic fact that we *do* tick and the conviction that in the last analysis that fact is mysterious and ineffable; neither physiology nor psychology nor sociology nor economic history, for all the valuable insights they give us into man's behaviour, can alter the fundamental mystery of the god in the machine—man being, as Molly

Bloom describes a character in Joyce's *Ulysses*, 'poached eyes on ghost.'

So I dissociate myself from the myth-hunters, who see the modern literary artist's basic need as new myths, as well as from those who deplore the lack of a common religious background in our civilization. I think cultural pluralism is a good thing. I think it is both wise and civilized to realize that no single religious creed represents either the final historical truth about what happened or the final theological truth about the nature of man and his relations with ultimate reality, but that any creed may have valuable insights to contribute. Any piece of faith which is destroyed by new knowledge is destroyed only in its formal expression, not in its fundamental reality—or if it is destroyed in its fundamental reality, then it clearly corresponds to no real need or perception and ought to be abandoned cheerfully. We need neither new knowledge nor new faith, but rather the ability to handle what we have. And that ability, since it involves the counterpointing of apparently contradictory insights, can best be given us by the artist, whose profession it is to distil rich significance out of such counterpointing.

There is then no inseparable gulf between the modern literary artist and his predecessors. If his predecessors enjoyed a more stable background of belief, they still needed to set their individual insights against that background before they could achieve the highest kind of art. We have more balls to juggle in the air, more conflicting claims to focus into a rich pattern of significance, more items of knowledge to organize into a profound and total vision of man's fate. That what should be regarded as an opportunity is often regarded as an inhibition is the result of social and other factors too complicated to be discussed here. Part of the trouble with the modern artist is that he has too many tools and a very indistinct notion of what he should do with them, with the result that he spends a great deal of time simply displaying them. If the artist would spend less time alternately bewailing his 'alienation' from society and flourishing his unemployed skills he might realize the exciting opportunity that awaits him. Everybody is so busy explaining everybody else's lack of success. To the chorus of breast-beaters, prophesiers of doom, *laudatores temporis acti*, be-raters of popular taste, deplorers of poets' obscurity, interpreters of the modern dilemma, and all the poetasters, critic-asters, and undertakers of the Muse who dance upon the grave of literature in the expectation of being hired to conduct the funeral, I can only say, as the Lord said to Job as he sat wailing among the ashes, 'Who is this that darkeneth counsel with words without knowledge? Gird up now thy loins like a man.'

Harry Levin

SYMBOLISM AND FICTION

Harry Levin, Irving Babbitt Professor of Comparative Literature at Harvard University, has written several books and many essays treating a variety of topics, authors, and periods in English, European, and American Literature, for example: *James Joyce: A Critical Introduction* (1941), *The Power of Blackness: Hawthorne, Poe, Melville* (1958), and the recent *The Gates of Horn: A Study of Five French Realists* (1963). "Symbolism and Fiction" was originally published as a monograph by the University of Virginia in 1956 and later included in Levin's collection of essays *Contexts of Criticism* (1958).

A few years ago we welcomed to our Department a colleague who had never before taught English literature. As a poet he had practiced it; as a lawyer he had once taught law; and as Assistant Secretary of State he may even have prepared himself to cope with the complexities of academic life. Why should I not mention the honored name of Archibald MacLeish? Mr. MacLeish was anxious to meet the minds of the college generation, and incidentally to test the observation that William Faulkner had supplanted Ernest Hemingway as their literary idol. His first assignment required his class, as a sort of touchstone, to read and report on Mr. Hemingways' "Big Two-Hearted River." They had not read it; but you have, and you remember that it is hardly a story at all; it is simply a sketch about a boy who goes fishing. Its striking quality is the purity of its feeling, its tangible grasp of sensuous immediacy, the physical sensation that Mr. Hemingway is so effective at putting into prose. The students did not seem to feel this quality. They liked the story; they wrote about it at length; but in their protocols, to a man, they allegorized it. Each of those fish that Nick Adams had jerked out of Big Two-Hearted River bore for them a mystical significance, which varied according to its interpreter—Freudian or Jungian, Kierkegaardian or Kafkaesque. May I leave these silvery, slippery trout dangling there in the water to incarnate the fascination and the elusiveness of our subject?

American literature would all be childishness, the innocent wonderment of the schoolroom—according to one of its most perceptive interpreters, D. H. Lawrence—if it did not invite us to look beneath its bland surface and to find a diabolic inner meaning. The reaction of Professor MacLeish's students might suggest that we do not enjoy the surfaces enough, that we

63

have become too morbidly preoccupied with the subliminal. In our restless search for universals, we may be losing sight of particulars: of the so-called quiddity, that "whatness" which characterizes a work of art, the truth of an object to its peculiar self. Literature is not a game of charades. Yet Lawrence's reinterpretation helped to rescue, out of the indiscriminate attic of children's books, the greatest classic in American literature; and *Moby-Dick* has plenty of deviltry at its core. When a lightning-rod man intruded upon Mark Twain, the upshot was a humoristic sketch. When a lightning-rod man intruded upon Herman Melville, the consequence became part of his lifelong quarrel with organized religion. It may now remain for some intrepid young allegorist to demonstrate, in some little magazine, that Mark Twain's sketch is nothing less than a cryptographic adumbration of a Rosicrucian tract.

At this juncture it may prove useful to be reminded that *Moby-Dick* itself, like "Big Two-Hearted River," is a simple story about a fishing trip. Basically, it is just another yarn about the big fish that got away. So is Mr. Hemingway's last book, *The Old Man and the Sea*, even though critics have seen themselves symbolized in the sharks that prey on the Old Man's gigantic catch. *Moby-Dick*, at all events, is a whopper; and, like all whoppers, it has the capacity to be expanded and elaborated *ad infinitum*. In the process of elaboration, Melville has introduced his linked analogies and dark similitudes, sometimes deliberately and— it would also seem—sometimes intuitively. He himself seemed scarcely conscious of certain implications which Nathaniel Hawthorne pointed out, and which thereupon fell into place—as Melville acknowledged—in "the part-and-parcel allegoricalness of the whole." (Or did he write "of the whale?" Melville's

handwriting, in his famous letter to Mrs. Hawthorne, is indeterminate at this crucial point.) One of his chapters, anatomizing the beached skeleton of a whale, tells us that some of its smaller vertebrae have been carried away to make children's rattles. And so, he goes on to moralize, almost anticipating the reception of his book, so the most momentous enterprises can taper off into child's play.

Mr. Faulkner, being our contemporary, has not suffered very much from the innocence of his readers. On the contrary, the title of his last novel, *A Fable*, proclaims his own ambition to universalize a message of some sort, impelled perhaps by the sense of international responsibility that seems to go along with the Nobel Prize. But let us revert to a more modest example of his story-telling skill, with which we may feel more at home, *The Bear*. This is another story about a hunting trip; it sticks to his region and it securely belongs, along with *The Adventures of Huckleberry Finn* and *The Red Badge of Courage*, among those wonderful American stories in which a boy reaches manhood through some rite of passage, some baptism of fire, an initiation into experience. We may not have noticed, and we should therefore be grateful for the critical comment that points it out, a possible resemblance between the youthful Ike McCaslin and the epic heroes of Homer and Vergil. But we may be less grateful than puzzled when the same Kenyon Critic informs us that *The Bear* is an allegory of "the transition from pagan to Christian culture, if not from the Old to the New Testament." We may even begin to suspect that the commentator lacks a sense of proportion, if not a sense of humor.

Needless to say, these lacks would not be considered serious enough to disqualify him from practicing criticism as it is frequently practiced today. Criticism is a child of the time, and it changes as times change. The catchwords of critics have tended to echo the ideals of their respective periods. Thus a whole epoch is summed up in the term "decorum," and another by the shibboleth "sublime." What is our key word? "Ambiguity" is not my own suggestion; it is an obvious recommendation from our contemporary masters of critical terminology. Their stronghold, be it Axel's castle or Kafka's, is not the old allegorical castle of love or war, of perseverance or indolence; it is a citadel of ambiguity. Since the numerous types of ambiguity presuppose as many levels of meaning, it might be more up-to-date to call this castle a skyscraper, and to call our typologists of ambiguity— borrowing a compendious adjective from *Finnegans Wake*—"hierarchitectitiptitoploftical." As an instance of such hier-architectitiptitoploftical criticism, without pretending to be citing at random, I might cite a recent interpretation of James Joyce's *Portrait of the Artist as a Young Man*. Here at the outset Cranly, the friend of the artist, is said to be not only John the Baptist but likewise Judas and Pilate—a wide and exacting and not exactly compatible range of roles for a secondary character.

Part of the difficulty would seem to spring from the critic's addiction to the copula. Some of our literary reviews, in this respect, might just as well be written in Basic English. Suggestive allusions tend to become flat assertions. Something, instead of suggesting some other thing, somehow *is* that other thing; it cannot mean, it must be. Everything must be stated as an equation, without recognizing degrees of relationship or the differences between allusion and fact. Now, as the name of his protagonist indicates, Joyce is fond of alluding to prototypes. Cranly is ironically linked with John the Baptist as a kind of predecessor; and to the extent

to which every betrayer of his friend is a Judas and every avoider of moral responsibility is a Pilate, he may be said to have momentarily figured in both of those positions. But what are we then to make of the Artist as a Young Man? A Jesus? There is a sense in which the life of every good Christian is, or should be, an imitation of Christ. But Stephen Dedalus expressly chooses to imitate Satan; "*Non serviam!*" The comment is therefore not an ambiguity nor an ambivalence nor a tension nor an irony nor a paradox. It is a contradiction or—to use a very old-fashioned term—an impertinence; and there are times when reason can do no more than imitate Dr. Johnson and kick the stone.

Such interpretations are dismissed as "cabalistics" by the introduction to one of the many current studies of Franz Kafka. But when we turn from this introduction to the study itself, having been all but convinced that its author is uniquely sane and that Kafka's other commentators are uniformly mad, we find that he too has a frenzied glint in his eye and a cabalistic theory of his own: all of Kafka is to be explained by the incidence of the number two. Two is an important number, of course, when we come to think about it; and when we start to look for it, it appears to be so ubiquitous that it explains not only Kafka but everything else. The only matter it does not explain is the difference between Kafka and everything else. And that, I fear, is the trouble with much that passes for psychoanalytic criticism: it reduces our vocabulary of symbols to a few which are so crudely fundamental and so monotonously recurrent that they cannot help the critic to perform his primary function, which is still—I take it—to discriminate. Nature abounds in protuberances and apertures. Convexities and concavities, like Sir Thomas Browne's quincunxes, are everywhere. The forms they compose are not always enhanced or illuminated by reading our sexual obsessions into them.

Isolating text from context in the name of "close reading," we can easily be led astray. So sensible a critic as Edmund Wilson has argued that Henry James's "Turn of the Screw" should be read as a psychological projection of its governess's frustrations. Subsequently it has been shown by Professor Robert L. Wolff—a professional historian on a Jamesian holiday—that the manifest content of the alleged fantasy came from a sentimental illustration in a Christmas annual to which James had also contributed. What is needed today perhaps, what readers and writers might well join together in forming, would be a Society for the Protection of Symbols from Critics. But I do not want to labor a point which is, indeed, that all too many points may have been labored already. Having labored a little in the symbolistic vineyard, I share the curiosities and admire the ingenuities of many of my fellow laborers. If these remarks have the intonation of a caveat, they should also have the overtones of a *mea culpa*. When, however, this hieratic tendency draws back upon itself the leveling criticism of the philistines who are always with us, thereby exacerbating the war of attrition between the quarterlies and the weeklies, we must all be concerned one way or another.

A primrose by a river's brim is, obviously, one thing to J. Donald Adams and quite another thing to Kenneth Burke. For the leveling critic the flower in the crannied wall may be simply that and nothing more. A rose itself, the emblem of romance and so much more, the *rosa sempiterna* of Dante, the *rosa mystica* of Hopkins or Yeats, the garden of T. S. Eliot's agony, the thorn of which Rilke may actually have died in aromatic pain— well, a rose is a rose is a rose. And *Moby-Dick* is a book which exists on a plane of comparison with the novels of Captain Marryat. Without capitulating to that simplistic view, we could well afford to concede that not every literary surface happens to mask a darker meaning. Every work of art may be a form of symbolic action, as Mr. Burke keeps patiently reminding us; and behind the reminder stands Coleridge's conception of the artist as a creator of symbols. When Hamlet could not accuse Claudius directly, he approached him by means of the play-within-the-play—"tropically." So Ernst Jünger, during the Nazi regime, was able to attack it symbolically in his fantastic tale, *From the Marble Cliffs*. But there are symbols and symbols. "My tropes are not tropes," says King Media to the philosopher Babbalanja in Melville's *Mardi*, "but yours are." That is the issue: when is a trope not a trope, and what is it then?

It should do us no harm to admit that art continues to have its simpler vehicles, such as love lyrics or works of sculpture, designed to convey feelings rather than ideas. When Mr. MacLeish's students dredged up such grimly subaqueous intimations from the limpid waters of the Big Two-Hearted River, they were essentially engaged in revealing themselves. Furthermore, they were reflecting the outlook of our age—an age which, as it looks back toward the nineteen-twenties from the vantage-point of a full generation afterward—seems to be looking across an enormous gulf. Writing at the end of that fabulous decade, Mr. Wilson terminated his *Axel's Castle* with a kind of farewell to the symbolists: to Yeats and Joyce and Proust and several other supreme individualists, and to those rare artificial worlds of their private creation. But symbolism proved much too deeply rooted to take the hint and retire. In the meanwhile, a call for a "science of symbolism" had been issued by C. K. Ogden and I. A. Richards. Exploring the personal and the collective unconscious, Freud and Jung had shown how primitive myths survive through oneiric fantasies. Furthermore, public events have intervened in our lives to strengthen the authority of symbols. Hence the movement, broadening its base, has been going forward—or is it backward? For symbolism, in the Hegelian worldview, characterizes the earliest phase of culture.

One of the signs of revival has been the popularity of Suzanne Langer's *Philosophy in a New Key*, with its stimulating argument that modern logic, semantics, metaphysics, and various schools of thought in the social sciences run parallel to the course of symbolism among the arts. But the key in which all this is pitched, by virtue of Mrs. Langer's synesthetic metaphor, is by no means new. It is so old that we might properly call it a "mode"; and it leads us back to other modes of thinking which are rather prelogical than logical, rather magical than scientific, rather transcendental than empirical. Mrs. Langer's two philosophical masters, Ernst Cassirer and Alfred North Whitehead, were both profoundly aware that symbolism is inherent in the very processes of language and thought. So was Quintilian: "*Paene quicquid loquimur figura est.*" We could hardly speak or think or vote without symbols; we live and die by them; we should hesitate to cross the street at a traffic intersection, were it not for their unambiguous accord. All art, in this sense, is more or less symbolic. More or less, and whether it is more symbolic or less may be determined by historical as well as by esthetic considerations.

Take an illustration which William Butler Yeats admired because it happened to be "out of nature," because it belonged to "the artifice of eternity." Take "such a form as Grecian goldsmiths make"—a Byzantine icon. Such a religious image had to be stylized and conventionalized along the lines that were sanctioned and prescribed by the Church of the East. Its style could be considered more symbolic than the painting of the West; for Western painters, freed from the conventions and prescriptions and restrictions of Iconoclastic dogma, could come closer and closer to life—even as material actuality was becoming secular and realistic. At the eastern extreme, the taboo of the Jewish and Mohammedan religions against the making of graven images sponsored an art which was decorative and functional but not precisely significant, as in a prayer-rug. "In a symbol," wrote Thomas Carlyle in his handbook for symbolists, *Sartor Resartus*, "there is both concealment and revelation." But if everything were revealed, then nothing would be symbolized; and if everything were concealed, then too nothing would be symbolized. Thus a symbol is a sort of excluded middle between what we know and what we do not know—or better, as Carlyle put it, a meeting point between the finite and the infinite.

Art is always an imitation, never quite the real thing. It cannot represent without symbolizing. By its devices of synecdoche or metonymy, it gives us the part for the whole or the attribute for the object. It never gives us a perfect replica; on the other hand, it never gives us a complete abstraction. What has been ineptly termed "nonobjective painting" proves—if nothing else—that there is really no such thing as pure design. In the dramatic moralities, Vanity is a highly feminine creature and the Vice is full of boyish mischief. Life itself is bound to be mixed up with any artistic representation of it; yet even the "slice of life" of the naturalists had to be framed by symbolic conceptions, as in the fiction of Emile Zola or his American disciple,

Frank Norris. Think of Norris' titles, *The Pit*, *The Octopus*—not to mention the monstrous tooth of McTeague. Banish the symbol, and it returns as a simile: the mine-shaft transformed by *Germinal* into a perpetually crouching beast. The London fog, with its natural aura of obfuscation, becomes a metaphorical vehicle for Dickens' critique of the law-courts in *Bleak House*. And Flaubert concentrates with such intensity on the details of materialistic circumstance that, in *A Simple Heart*, the stuffed parrot of his old servant-woman is apotheosized into the Paraclete.

Generally speaking, art seems to oscillate between two poles, the symbolistic and the realistic—or, we might say, the typical and the individual. In its westward movement it has kept pace with the development of human individuality. In its eastward purview it glances backward toward Byzantium, and toward an order of mind which derives its strength from the opposing principle of typicality. This polarity is recognized by philosophy in the habitual problem of the One and the Many, and it has innumerable repercussions in the political and sociocultural areas. Through some such oscillation, we have been moving—at least until lately—in the direction set by the Greeks. A humanistic literature, such as theirs, is not primarily regulated by symbolism. Homer and Sophocles made use of symbols, yes; but the *Odyssey* is a story about a man named Odysseus; it is not an ironic commentary upon a day in the life of a man named Leopold Bloom; while Oedipus, since he verily married his mother, was presumably the one recorded man who did not suffer from the frustrations of the Oedipus complex. The world of Odysseus and Oedipus was concrete; it was here and now as long as it lasted. Ages with less pride in the dignity of mankind would preach contempt for this world,

along with hope for another and better one hereafter. The visible things of this earth, in the doctrine of Saint Paul, shadow forth the invisible things of God. As Christopher Cranch, the transcendentalist poet, expressed it: "Nature is but a scroll,—God's handwriting thereon." It is held that the artist, like the prophet, should have the insight to read and translate these divine hieroglyphics. Such is the state of mind that makes for symbolism, both in creating and in interpreting a hermetic art.

The two points of view, the otherworldly and the humanistic, clashed in the conflict between Christian asceticism and the pagan classics, which Saint Augustine resolved by formulating a masterly distinction between the spirit and the letter. If the letter kills, the spirit brings new life; and if a text is literally profane, it may be read figuratively and endowed retrospectively with a spiritual significance. The Song of Songs reads suspiciously like an erotic poem; yet the Rabbis admitted it to the sacred canon by pronouncing it to be an allegory of God's love for Israel. Similarly the Fathers, for whom the Old Testament prefigured the New, accepted it as an expression of Christ's love for the Church. Following Augustine, through this retroactive procedure known as "figuration," the *Aeneid* could be taken as a pilgrimage of the soul adventuring among divers moral hazards. Thereafter Dante could take Vergil as his guide for a series of literal adventures through the next world. Dante, as he acknowledged, was also following Saint Thomas Aquinas, who—in answering the preliminary questions of his *Summa Theologica*—had sustained the doctrine that although the scriptures were literally true, they could be interpreted as figures on three ascending levels of spiritual meaning.

But though the *Divine Comedy* is

polysemous, as it is expounded in Dante's dedicatory letter to Can Grande della Scala, the poem cannot pretend to literal truth; the Florentine poet, after all, was making believe that he himself had journeyed through hell and purgatory and paradise; the "allegory of poets" is not the "allegory of theologians." The next step would be taken by the more worldly Boccaccio, who in his life of Dante supported the validity of poetic truth. Elsewhere he went even farther, with the affirmation that theology is God's poetry. It has remained for latter-day symbolists to round out the cycle by affirming that poetry is man's theology. With the humanism of the Renaissance and the Enlightenment, the other world seems gradually to recede. Nominalistic reality shifts to the foreground; things are valued for themselves, and not for what they may prefigure. The shift from the type to the individual has its protagonist in *Doctor Faustus,* Marlowe's early sketch for Goethe's portrayal of modernism in action. Faustus is one poet who is not content to compare his mistress with famous beauties. Metaphors will not do and symbols are not enough; he must attain the object of his comparison. He must have the one and only Helen of Troy, and he does so *in propria persona;* but the reality proves to be as elusive as the symbol.

Poetry with its metaphors, metaphysics with its analogies, bridge a gap between seen and unseen worlds. The breakdown of the bridge is that dissociation of which Mr. Eliot has written so feelingly; and it is more than a "dissociation of sensibility"; it is a break in the whole chain of being. Hume's critique of analogy might be regarded, under this aspect, as a philosophical counterpart of neoclassical poetic diction. A symbol, on the other hand, is a connecting link between two different spheres; for the original word in Greek meant throwing together, a violent fusion,

the very act of association. When man stands upon his own feet, proudly conscious of the achievements of his fellow men, he lives most fully and his art embodies the fullness of his life, his basic sense of reality. Then the *Aeneid* is not a *pélérinage de la vie humaine,* but the epic of a hero; the Song of Songs is not an allegory but a chant of love; and Shakespeare's tragedies are dramas of physical action and psychological conflict, not ballets of bloodless images or ceremonials for a dying god. In times which seem to be out of joint, when man is alienated from his environment, the heroic seems less immediately attainable and love itself may dim to a Platonic vision. A failure of nerve is accompanied by a retreat from reality.

Arthur Symons characterized the symbolistic movement of the nineteenth century as a perfervid effort to escape from materialism. It is much easier to comprehend what the symbolists were escaping from than what they were escaping to. Their problem was, and it certainly remains, to establish a viable set of intimate associations with another sphere. Some of them felt they had solved it personally through religious conversion; others frankly used their visionary imaginations, often abetted by stimulants and even by mental disorders. Whereas the traditional symbolist had abstracted objects into ideas, the self-proclaimed *symboliste*—as Jean Moréas announced in his manifesto of 1886—sought to invest the idea in concrete form. Hence his emphasis was on the object itself rather than its conceivable signification, on the denseness of the imagery rather than the pattern of the thought, on concealment rather than revelation in Carlyle's terms. But since the symbol was never clearly acknowledged as the key to any higher plane of existence, poets could not be blamed when it became a fetish cultivated for its own sake. Literature could not be expected to transcend itself by its own bootstraps; and yet, with Mallarmé, the esthetic process became the principal subject for symbolization. So it is with Proust; but when it is manifested in connoisseurship of ecclesiastical architecture, the symbols are already fraught with a transcendence of their own.

The unvoiced premise of *symbolisme*, which is not far from that of orthodox mysticism, had been handed on by the German idealists to the New England transcendentalists. For Baudelaire, moving out of the woods of naturalism back toward the church, nature was a temple with trees for pillars. Man walks through this forest of symbols which seem to know him better than he knows them, and the words he hears there are confused. *"Les parfums, les couleurs, et les sons se répondent."* Color and sound and other sensory impressions are linked together through correspondences, associative patterns whose final sanction is not discernible to the senses. Some of these were suggested by Rimbaud in his well-known sonnet on the vowels, but not everyone would accept his linkages. Different sounds would suggest different colors to different readers; and that is the essential dilemma of *symbolisme*. For all its efforts to reorder the universe, to categorize the diversity of experience, its influence has been unregenerately individualistic. Remy de Gourmont, the critical interpreter of the movement, aptly presents it as—among other things—the ultimate expression of individualism in art.

How far it stands apart from its medieval prototype might be measured by consulting the *Rationale* of Durandus, the thirteenth-century manual of Christian symbolism, as embodied in the sacramentalism of the Catholic church. Living tradition was—and is—practiced daily there, through the cruciform structure of the edifice, its orientation, ritual, and liturgy, the relation of the church year to the life of Christ, the reënactment of the last supper in the Eucharist. Through that rite of communion the paschal lamb, originally the sacrifice of the Jewish Passover, had become the commonest symbol for Jesus. The audience at fifteenth-century Wakefield, witnessing their *Second Shepherds' Play*, could not irreverently grasp a serio-comic parallel between the infant in the manger and the stolen sheep of the farcical underplot. This is an authoritative example of the technique of symbolic association. Conversely, we witness the effect of dissociation in *Madame Bovary*, when the great Cathedral of Rouen looks reprovingly down upon the lovers fleeing in their cab, and its disregarded sermons in stones exemplify all the values that Emma and Léon are flouting. It is a far cry from George Herbert's *Temple* to Baudelaire's.

"A symbol remains vital," the late Karl Vossler has written, "only when its representation is accompanied by faith." The number seven was no abstraction for Dante; behind it loomed the power of the Seven Sacraments, the Seven Deadly Sins, the Seven Gifts of the Holy Ghost. But when we turn away from the supernatural, in naturalistic suspension of belief, what —if anything—are we to make of Thomas Mann's conjurations with the same digit in *The Magic Mountain?* The seven chapters of the novel itself, the seven tables in the dining room of the Berghof sanitorium, which has seven letters in its name, as have its seven principal guests in their names, and all the recurrent multiples of seven—these are endowed with no more efficacy than the novelist's deliberate manipulation of coincidence. Whereas, if we now reconsider our fish, we find that it is alphabetically associated with the initial letters of the Greek words for "Jesus Christ, Son of God, the

Savior," which can be read acrostically as *ichthys*. As such it served in the catacombs, where overt symbols would have been dangerous, to conceal the Christian revelation. In the terms of Durandus, it was a positive rather than a natural symbol, or—as Yeats would say—arbitrary rather than inherent.

It is the inherent, the natural symbol that Coleridge seems to have in mind when he asserts that it always partakes of that reality which it renders intelligible. The cross of the lamb, as opposed to the fish, may well be termed an emblem, as distinguished from a sign. But Saint Augustine can transform a sign into an emblem, when he mystically envisions Jesus Christ as a fish swimming through the depths of mortality. This distinction between emblems and signs corresponds with that which has been drawn since Goethe, more broadly and often invidiously, between symbolism and allegory. The symbolic is the only possible expression of some essence, according to Yeats, whereas the allegorical may be one out of many. In the latter case, we are less engaged by the symbol itself than by what is arbitrarily symbolized. Yet when the fish is not a religious acrostic but Captain Ahab's whale, it is emblematic; and then, as W. H. Auden duly warns us, we must not expect a one-to-one correspondence. For what we then encounter is not an allegorical reference to something else in some particular respect, but a multiplicity of potential cross-references to other categories of experience.

These formulations could be tested by turning again to *Moby-Dick* and applying the polysemous method, the fourfold scheme of interpretation that Dante invited his readers to follow, which extends the meaning beyond the literal to the three figurative levels—allegorical, moral, and anagogical. Later allegories may not be as multileveled as the *Divine Comedy*; it is hard to discern more than three planes in the *Faerie Queene* or two in the *Pilgrim's Progress*. Under the subsequent impact of realism, the allegorical and the anagogical tend to wither away; the moral blends with the literal or drops out altogether, as writers turn from the Celestial City to Vanity Fair. But the Middle Ages maintained the sharp differentiation formulated in a Latin distich which can be conveniently paraphrased: the literal tells us what happens, the allegorical what to believe, the moral what to do, and the anagogical whither to strive. Thus, literally *Moby-Dick* is concerned with the voyage of the *Pequod*, the subject of whaling, the science of cetology; allegorically with society on shipboard, the parable of Ahab's "irresistible dictatorship"; morally with a series of object-lessons, such examples as the monkey-rope, the ligature of brotherhood that binds Ishmael to Queequeg; and anagogically . . . "*Quo tendas?* whither art thou striving?"

That is the question, and Melville offers no categorical answer. Dante knew, or believed he knew, the object of his journey; no traveler, to be sure, had returned to map out the topography of the next world; but Dante's account was based on the *terra firma* of assumptions universally shared, while Melville put out to sea in lone pursuit of "the ungraspable phantom of life." He was enough of a transcendentalist to ponder the meaning of this "great allegory, the world," enough of an iconoclast to strike through the pasteboard mask of outer appearances, and enough of a skeptic to respect the uncharted mystery beyond it. But the anagoge, which for Dante is the fulfillment of providential design, for Melville remains an ultimate question mark. His overwhelming whale has been identified with—among other concepts—nature, fate, sex, property, the father-image, God

Himself. It has meant various things to varying critics because it is Melville's enigma, like the doubloon nailed by Ahab to the mast, which signifies dollars to the Second Mate, the Zodiac to the First Mate, and the universe to the Captain. Shall we ever identify Moby-Dick? Yes, when we have sprinkled salt on the tail of the Absolute; but not before.

In one of his prophetic moments Melville even anticipated atomic fission, describing the tail of the whale as if it were a cyclotron. "Could annihilation occur to matter," Ishmael exclaims, "this were the thing to do it." However, the atomic is just as far beyond our scope as the cosmic; and we cannot necessarily count upon the rock of dogma for that firm foundation on which Durandus constructed his medieval symbology. Are we then at the mercy of sheer subjectivity, of the irresponsible caprice of the overingenious critic, making symbols mean what he wants them to mean? Or have we still some criteria at our disposal, technical means for determining the relevance—if not the truth—of any given comment? Here I would venture to suggest that students of literature might profitably emulate the researches now being carried on in the plastic arts under the heading of Iconology. Some of us have been collecting images, but not interpreting them very satisfactorily; others have been tracing the history of ideas, without paying much attention to formal context. Could we not hope for a discipline which would bring the tools of critical analysis to bear upon the materials of textual documentation, concentrating upon the thematic relationship between the idea and the image? Shall we ever discover the archetype behind them both except through comparative study of its most impressive manifestations?

This is more easily called for than provided. The leaders of the Iconological School are brilliantly conspicuous for their combination of discernment and learning. We shall not have literary iconologists in our Departments of English until our discerners have picked up a little learning and our learners have somehow acquired a little discernment. In the interim, are there not a few reasonable game laws, which we might undertake to observe whenever we go fishing? Or—to state the problem more pragmatically—could we not agree upon a code of fair-trade practices, which might conduce to a closer meeting of critical minds? Granted that divergence of opinion is salutary—indeed necessary—for the evaluation of a work of art, and that the very suggestiveness of some masterworks is most richly attested by the variety of interpretations accruing to them. Yet the work itself is always greater than the sum of its interpretations; and unless these are grounded within some frame of objective reference, we have no basis for differentiating between perception and deception. After all, criticism—in a Baconian phrase—is reason applied to imagination. Doubtless the fourfold method of exegesis, which Dante appealed to and Saint Thomas propounded, would be somewhat hierarchical for our day. Nevertheless, in more democratic terms, the common consent of educated readers might be gained at four descending levels of acceptance.

The first, which raises no questions, would be strictly conventional. No one has any doubt what Hawthorne intends by the accepted symbol of the eagle over the door of the Custom House in the introductory chapter of *The Scarlet Letter*; and Melville's eagle soaring over the Catskills, though less official, is a bird of the same feather. The second use of the symbol is explicit, as when Melville glosses the monkey-rope or moralizes up and down the deck in *Moby-Dick*; or, best of all, Hawthorne's scarlet letter itself—how similar in appearance, how different in connotation, from the "crowned A" of Chaucer's Prioress! Third, and here we cross an equatorial line, the implicit. "Thou too sail on, O ship of state!" is highly explicit, not to say conventional. But the good ship *Pequod*—like the frigate *Neversink* in *Whitejacket, or The World in a Man-of-War*—is a little world in itself; and when it goes down, what are we to make of the eagle that goes down with it or that rather sinister emblem, the hand with a hammer? Melville's "Tartarus of Maids" is explicitly a humanitarian sketch of a New England factory, and implicitly an obstetrical allegory of woman's fate. What is implied, in contrast to what is explicated by the author himself, can be possibly gaged by what are known in Shakespearean commentary as "fervors" and "recurrences."

These are patterns of repetition and emphasis, which in some fortunate cases can be reinforced by the facts of biography and the insights of psychology. Jay Leyda's *Melville Log* not only supplements the romances and tales, but fills in some missing segments of their imaginative configuration. Without such external evidence we could draw no sharp line between the implicit and, fourth, the conjectural level—or, for that matter, between the conjectural and the inadmissible. But once we admit degrees of plausibility, we may entertain, for whatever enhancement it may be worth, any conjecture likely to enrich our apprehension of the part-and-parcel allegoricalness of the whole. Does it enrich our apprehension of the later novels of Henry James if we construe them as Swedenborgian allegories? There is one tangential fact in support of this argument: the Swedenborgianism of the elder Henry James. And that is outweighed by the clearest expressions of intention, as well as by the internal consistency of the author's habits of thinking and writing. Therefore the purported symbolism is not conventional nor explicit nor implicit; it is, at best, conjectural; and since it obscures rather more than it illuminates, it should probably be discarded as inadmissible. Let us look for figures in the carpets, and not in the clouds.

And let us return, for the last time, to the whale. Surely no other literary symbol has invited and evaded so much conjecture; surely Melville intended to keep us guessing up to the bitter end and afterward. His book does not resemble life the less because it leaves us in a state of suspense. But just as insecurity seeks authority, just as complexity seeks simplification, just as pluralism seeks unity, so our critics long for the archetypal because they are bedeviled by the ambiguous. Groping amid ambiguities, they become increasingly hot for certainties; and symbols, they desperately hope, will provide the keys. So every hero may seem to have a thousand faces; every heroine may be a white goddess *incognita*; and every fishing trip turns out to be another quest for the Holy Grail. However, that boy of Hemingway's, fishing in Big Two-Hearted River, is not a type but an individual. He is not Everyman; he is Nick Adams; and, like every other single human being, he is unique. The river in which he fishes is neither the Nile nor the Liffey; it is a stream which runs through the Upper Peninsula of the state of Michigan. The sun that beats on his back is the same old planet that has generated myths since the world began. But the feeling it evokes is the existential conjunction of the scene, the moment, and human sensibility. Literature can give us many other things; but it gives us, first and last, a taste of reality.

II. *The Formalist Critic*

PAUL VALÉRY

CLEANTH BROOKS

WAYNE C. BOOTH

HOWARD NEMEROV

YVOR WINTERS

W. K. WIMSATT, JR.

INTRODUCTION

As its friends and enemies alike have agreed, formalist criticism has been the most influential and vigorous critical movement of the twentieth century in both England and the United States. It encompasses not only such diverse groups as the American New Critics, the Chicago Aristotelians, and the *Scrutiny* group in England (led by F. R. Leavis) but also such eminent individuals as R. P. Blackmur and Yvor Winters who follow no system but their own.

Formalism as a specific critical theory and practice has won few adherents in Germany and Italy, whereas in France the pedagogical method of *explication de texte*, which has some affinity with formalism, remains largely confined to the classroom. Between 1916 and 1930 there briefly flourished in Russia a special type of formalism whose influence spread to Poland and Czechoslovakia, but by 1930 it had expired as a unified movement and its exponents had scattered. Some of the men who came under its influence, for example, Roman Jakobson, later established important reputations as philologists.

Although formalism has been limited as a coherent movement largely to England and America, in these countries it has had tremendous impact—especially on American literary criticism and on the teaching of literature in American schools. Its fortunes comprise the other part of the story of what happened to the historical method: Formalism prospered as historicism waned, and, in fact, had much to do with historicism's decline. It arose in the 1920s, gathered strength in the 1930s, became supreme in the 1940s and early 1950s. It now seems at least temporarily to be suffering the fate of all successful revolutions—absorption into the culture it set out to reform, its goals largely achieved. Once thought radical, it now stands as a norm.

Because formalism as a modern critical movement has enlisted a variety of cohorts and has undergone numerous modifications, our purposes might be best served by concentrating upon that phase of the movement that has been perhaps the most fully articulated and influential, the American new criticism. The following discussion therefore will be especially, but not exclusively, pertinent to this phase. In order to avoid endless qualification I will take the liberty of using the terms *formalism* and *new criticism* almost synonymously.

In its fundamental aesthetic theory formalist criticism no doubt ultimately derives from Aristotle and from the Aristotelian emphasis upon the literary work's form, structure, style, and psychological effect (as opposed to Plato's emphasis on the work's content and social or moral effect). However, the immediate sources of formalism can be located in the late eighteenth century in Kant and in the nineteenth century in Coleridge. Although students of the development of modern formalism have demonstrated its indebtedness to such diverse sources as Poe, Bergson, Matthew Arnold, Bentham, the French symbolists, Remy de Gourmont, and T. E. Hulme, its major sources other than Kant and Coleridge have been Benedetto Croce, T. S. Eliot, and I. A. Richards.

From Kant's *The Critique of Aesthetic Judgment* came the inspiration for the formalist concept that art could stimulate a special kind of cognition, functioning symbolically, which was different from but no less important than cognition based wholly on logical reasoning. Kant thus both defined and dignified aesthetic judgment.

From Coleridge—the single greatest influence upon the new criticism—who assimilated the ideas of German transcendentalist philosophy and gave them literary application in his *Biographia Literaria,* came the emphasis upon the artist's imagination as the power to vivify experience and fuse discrete and seemingly incongruous combinations of materials into poetry. From Coleridge formalist critics have also drawn support for their view of literature as a mode of revelation and for their belief in the unique sort of truth and wisdom conveyed by literature, as opposed to the essentially different sort conveyed by science. From Croce came the analogous concept of the literary work as an inviolable fusion of images constituting a special form of knowledge.

In the 1920s T. S. Eliot and I. A. Richards launched the new criticism as an identifiable movement, although it did not receive its name (from John Crowe Ransom)[1] or manifest its significance until the next decade. Eliot, who had himself been influenced by de Gourmont, the French symbolists, and Ezra Pound, became one of the movement's most brilliant ornaments as well as one of its founders. Eliot's *The Sacred Wood* (1920), especially the essay "Tradition and the Individual Talent," is among the scriptures of twentieth-century formalism. The essay advances these three concepts basic to the formalist position:

1. Literary tradition—and, by implication, literary history—is not final and irrevocable but is constantly being rearranged by the appearance of new works; in effect, the past culminates in the present and is itself altered by the present.

2. The artist's experience, real or imagined, is finally concentrated in his work; thus, the work itself, not the man who made it, is the reader's proper concern.

3. The artist's emotion and personality are not important in themselves but disappear into the work of art; in this Eliot, together with Hulme, refuted the romantic notion of art as expression.

I. A. Richards, whose own views underwent considerable transition in a relatively short time, was perhaps the prime source for the scientism that paradoxically pervades formalist criticism in its vocabulary and method despite the movement's avowed opposition to science. In his two key works, *Principles of Literary Criticism* (1925) and *Practical Criticism* (1929), Richards made these important contributions: the concept of literature as the "completest mode of utterance," the method of close textual analysis as the basis for interpretation and judgment, and the concentration upon the language of the literary work. In *Practical Criticism* he also suggested the usefulness of precise and systematic analysis as a pedagogical technique, thereby anticipating the revolution in the classroom study of literature that formalist criticism soon accomplished.

As its several sources imply, formalism is not a single unified theory but, rather, a complex of related though not wholly consistent theories. In the versions articulated by some individuals and groups, for example, the Fugitives who gathered around John Crowe Ransom at Vanderbilt University in the late 1920s, formalism has even been advanced as a complete world-view: classical in its aesthetics, aristocratic in its social and political attitudes, and conservative in its religion. But regardless of the various factions and emphases of formalism, all who subscribe to it agree on one fundamental and inviolable principle: the primacy of the literary work itself. Indeed, the phrase *the work itself* recurs again and again in the writing of the formalist critic. Cleanth Brooks summarizes everything I have been saying:

> . . . it is possible to restate the history of criticism in our time thus: we have been witnessing a strenuous attempt to focus attention upon the poem rather

---

[1] The term *new criticism* was in use as early as 1910 by Joel E. Spingarn, but the sense and application it was given in the formalist movement derived from Ransom's employment of the term rather than Spingarn's.

than upon the poet or upon the reader. Along with this stress upon the poem as a structure in its own right, has come the attempt to fix the boundaries and limits of poetry. Modern critics have tried to see what was meant when one considered the poem as an artistic document. . . . Poetry has a characteristic structure and yields a characteristic knowledge. It does not compete with, but exists alongside of and complements, scientific knowledge and historical knowledge.

We discern that in Brooks' statement the word *poetry* denotes more than a particular genre or mode of literary expression; rather, it has assumed the same function given it by Aristotle and Coleridge: to encompass the whole of literature. This stress on the wholeness and integral identity of literature that pervades formalist criticism has also led to the development of a special vocabulary of terms or to the use of established terms in special ways. For example, the formalist uses such traditional terms as *irony* and *paradox* in a particular and delimited sense, although such other terms as *tension, ambiguity, complexity,* and *texture* have been made virtually anew and given greatly increased emphasis. The same stress on literature's unique properties can be observed even in some of the names that formalist criticism has been called, for example, *ontological criticism, contextual criticism,* and *intrinsic criticism. Ontological* suggests the formalistic view of the literary work as an objective structure of meanings with its own separate existence; *contextual* implies the belief in the work as a closed world, with language pointing inward, created as a total context; *intrinsic* conveys the conclusion that the work itself contains all the material and information necessary for its understanding and evaluation.

Although one could easily be lulled by the protestations of brotherly love and concord one hears today from the formalist and the historical critic alike, at least in its origins and basic precepts formalism remains hostile to the historical method. This hostility is displayed in Paul Valéry's "Problems of Poetry."* In 1936 Valéry wrote what other formalists were to assert repeatedly: "It will be time enough to deal with the poet's life, loves, and opinions, his friends and enemies, his birth and death, when we shall have advanced sufficiently in the *poetic knowledge* of his poem, that is, when we shall have made ourselves the instrument of what is written, so that our voice, our intelligence, and all the fibers of our sensibility are banded together to give life and powerful actuality to the author's act of creation." And in their enormously influential *Theory of Literature* René Wellek and Austin Warren declare, "The natural and sensible starting point for work in literary scholarship is the interpretation and analysis of the works of literature themselves. After all, only the works themselves justify all our interest in the life of the author, in his social environment and the whole process of literature. But, curiously enough, literary history has been so preoccupied with the setting of a work of literature that its attempts at an analysis of the works themselves have been slight in comparison with the enormous efforts expended on the study of environment."

In their reaction against the historical approach the formalists charged it with the commission of a number of fallacies, or errors in the conception of literature's true nature and the critic's proper role. In two widely read essays entitled "The Intentional Fallacy" and "The Affective Fallacy," W. K. Wimsatt, Jr. and Monroe C. Beardsley named and defined the most serious of the errors. The *intentional fallacy* was defined as the historical critic's tendency to accept the writer's intention or plan for this work—as this intention was studied externally of the work itself—as a reliable guide to the work's meaning and value. The *affective fallacy*, on the other hand, was defined as the historicist's tendency to equate the literary work's meaning and value with the intensity of the audience's emotional response to it. The names of these fallacies and the aesthetic arguments they embody have become part of our critical thought. They summarize both the formalist's major complaints against the historical criticism and the formalist credo that we must not confuse the nature of the work itself with either its origins or its effects.

Because the formalist critic refuses to give significant emphasis to the work's creator, genesis, historical relevance, place in literary tradition, or effect upon its readers, how then does he approach a particular work? What is his perspective and procedure? Here I will fall back on some advice by Kenneth Burke. Although Burke is actually an eclectic or pluralistic critic, he has often been identified as a formalist, and it is true that certain portions of his work could stand as exemplary illustrations of formalist methods. In *The Philosophy of Literary Form* Burke posits four crucial points of observation by which the critic can apprehend what Burke calls the *symbolic action* of a work. Note that all of these points stress elements within the work, that all comprise an intrinsic criticism:

1. The alignment of opposing principles or dramatic alignment in the work—what is versus what—for example, the violin versus the prize fight in Odets' *Golden Boy*, "into the night" imagery of one work and "to the bottom of the sea" imagery in another.

2. The situations by which a work opens, achieves its peripety or reversal, and closes; or, the route and stages of development of the work—from what through what to what—or, applied to character, the relationship of antagonist, protagonist, and mediating character or characters.

3. The critical points or "watershed moments" in a work—the entrance of a new element or a shift in medium—for example, the shift from verse to prose in *Murder in the Cathedral* or the transformation of the serpents in "The Rime of the Ancient Mariner" from loathsome to beautiful and blessed.

4. The underlying imagery or clusters of images that convey the work's conflict, for example, images of ice or fire, of growth or rot, of abyss or labyrinth, or of exile or return; or, the ways in which the images are differentiated: the pilgrimage as a quest for the Holy Grail, a pursuit of a creature, international travel, or a spiritualized journey of growth.

If Burke's suggestions are but one kind of application of the formalist approach, the example does make plain the axiom of the formalist critic that form and content, structure and meaning, are inseparable. Content or meaning exists only as it is integrated into form; without form, content remains the raw stuff of life, and life is not *art*. As Mark Schorer has put it, ". . . it is only when we speak of the *achieved* content, the form, the work of art as a work of art, that we speak as critics. The difference between content, or experience, and achieved content, or art, is technique. When we speak of technique, then, we speak of nearly everything."

Although the formalist critic might grant that a work's meaning can be extracted and stated or paraphrased as theme, he would remind us that in this process the aesthetic experience of the work itself has been destroyed, that the theme of the work cannot exist apart from the work itself in any sense as art. Even in so tacit and implicit a formalism as that in Howard Nemerov's "Composition and Fate in the Short Novel,"* with its emphasis on theme and its occasional use of both historical and mythopoeic approaches, the critic's underlying assumption is that the short novel has laws of its own and that it is organized according to the necessities of its intrinsic form. Accordingly, Nemerov's final definition of the short novel emphasizes neither its themes nor its characters, despite their importance, but rather its nature as an "ideal and primary form."

Yvor Winters, in "The Audible Reading of Poetry,"* carries the matter of form even to the insistence that poetry exists as poetry only if it is properly read, formally read, in accordance with what Winters perceives as its intrinsic nature. During this formal reading, in which the reader's own personality and histrionic tendencies to interpret the poem must be scrupulously restrained, subordinated wholly to the poem itself, each poem receives its "precise identity." And it is only with the identity of the poem that the critic is properly concerned. The critic's body itself becomes part of the instrumentality of poetry, in Winters' conception.

Other characteristically formalist approaches are aptly demonstrated in Cleanth Brooks' reading of Lovelace's "The Grasse-Hopper." Focusing on the poem's tone and applying the most careful attention to the nuances and ambiguities of its language, Brooks locates depth and richness of meaning in this seemingly shallow and pretty verse. The evidence and authority for Brooks' interpretation derive from two sources: first and most important, the critic's own knowledge of life and the functioning of language (that is, the critic's own sensibility); secondly— and Brooks' open admission of this documents the trend toward reconciliation between formalist and historicist—the critic's stock of historical information.

W. K. Wimsatt's treatment of Blake's "London," in the essay "What to Say About a Poem,"* likewise makes passing use of historical information, but Wimsatt, too, is primarily interested in the poem itself. He wishes to elucidate its implicit meanings by studying its pattern of images and by exploring the complex interrelationships and manifold possibilities of implication established by the poem's key words and phrases. Indeed, Wimsatt's essay both describes and demonstrates the formalist method and is itself virtually a synopsis of that method. It is also interesting to observe how Wimsatt's analysis inspires a normative response without overtly committing itself to normative statements and judgments, fulfilling Wimsatt's prediction that appreciation comes out of the other operations that the critic performs.

Wayne C. Booth's essay "Telling and Showing"* illustrates a special kind of formalism practiced by the so-called Chicago Critics, or Chicago Neo-Aristotelians, which arose at the University of Chicago in the late 1930s under the leadership of Richard McKeon and R. S. Crane. Although there has been a good deal of controversy between the new critics and the Chicago group—each accusing the other of being narrow, doctrinaire, and more interested in critical method than in literature—from the perspective of the entire Formalist movement, as it differs from other movements, the Chicagoans have much more in common with other formalists than with anyone else. They begin with the same focus, the work itself and the intrinsic study of literature as literature, but differ from the new critics in method and emphasis. The Chicagoans are pluralistic in their critical techniques; they subsume the activity of literary criticism within the broad context of what Crane calls *humanistic learning* (and thus tend to rely more heavily on overtly historical methods than the new critics); they concentrate on plot, composition, and genre rather than on language and symbolism; and they are deeply concerned with the Aristotelian concept of pleasure. Pleasure, from the Chicago standpoint, arises during the critic's reading of a work sequentially, in his discovery of its unifying principle and of its properties of wholeness. However, despite this indebtedness to Aristotelian thought, Crane has emphatically asserted the modern critic's obligation to use Aristotle only as a beginning. The critic must build upon Aristotle's system, combine it with other critical systems, or feel free to depart from it.

The Chicago school has been perhaps more influential in its critical theory than its applied criticism, yet it has also produced a number of able "practical" critics, among them Crane, Elder Olson, and most recently Wayne C. Booth. Booth's important book *The Rhetoric of Fiction*, which is the source for the essay here included, could well become the most significant demonstration of the Chicago method in this generation. Booth's fundamental concern is Aristotelian in the sense that he studies the work's effect on the reader not by speculation about the function of the creative imagination or by inquiry into reader psychology but by the focus upon the writer's technique, voice, and narrative strategy. Appropriately, Booth's major emphasis is upon the how of art, upon technique as rhetoric.

Booth's secondary purpose, one that illustrates the Chicago preference for greater pluralism in method than pure formalism tends to allow, is to free the writing and criticism of fiction from some of the strictures drawn around it by post-Jamesian critics, many of them formalistic. Throughout his entire book, as he does in his opening chapter "Telling and Showing,"* Booth reminds us that a story can be told in many ways and that its success or failure as a work of art does not wholly depend on the artist's use of certain approved narrative perspectives. Booth's work is representative of formalism, however, in the closeness and precision of his textual analysis and in his stress on the problem of point of view, which has preoccupied formalist critics during the past two decades.

Regardless of its lack of a single integrated aesthetic theory and the presence of such different and sometimes contending factions as the Chicago group and the group led by F. R. Leavis in England (whose bent is toward the sociocultural), formalist criticism has had incalculable effect upon the study of literature, at least in America. Indeed, most college and university teachers and a large proportion of secondary school teachers as well—and in turn their students—have been influenced by formalism to varying degrees. Even the critic not specifically trained in close textual analysis, explication of image and symbol, and concentration on the work's structure, often finds himself employing these and other essentially formalist methods either alone or in conjunction with other methods. We have absorbed them as if by osmosis. Both student and teacher have recognized the value of the formalist approach in posing and attempting to answer such pressing literary questions as these: How does this piece of writing work? What are its parts and how are they assembled? What is the central design of the work? How does it solve the problems its very design raises? How does its language function? What patterns of imagery and symbolism does it incorporate?

At this point it might be useful to offer a sketch, a brief example, of how the formalist might approach such a work as Whitman's superb short lyric "When I Heard the Learn'd Astronomer." It is the sort of analysis I have found helpful as a "way into" the poem:

WHEN I HEARD THE LEARN'D ASTRONOMER

When I heard the learn'd astronomer,
When the proofs, the figures, were ranged in columns before me,
When I was shown the charts and diagrams, to add, divide, and measure them,
When I sitting heard the astronomer where he lectured with much applause
    in the lecture-room,
How soon unaccountable I became tired and sick,
Till rising and gliding out I wander'd off by myself,
In the mystical moist night air, and from time to time,
Look'd up in perfect silence at the stars.

The organizing principle of the poem is that of problem-and-solution, or dilemma-resolution, with the first five lines advancing the problem, the last three the solution. The relationship of the separate elements of the problem, and thus the unity of the portion of the poem that states the problem, is emphasized by the repetition of *when* in the first four lines of the poem. This device of prepositional repetition also has the effect of portentousness, of creating what might be called a rhythm of suspense, which is culminated and released in *how soon, till,* and *from time to time,* in lines 5, 6, and 7. The poem pivots at line 5, preparing for the shift in tone and movement immediately to follow, for line 5 both describes the immediate effects of the problem upon the poem's persona and foreshadows its resolution. The word *unaccountable* in line 5 has an ambivalent function: It is sincere in its expression of the persona's conscious admiration of the astronomer's erudition and yet is ironic in its dismay, so that the speaker feels revulsion rather than exaltation in response to the erudition.

The poem's two-part structure is also perfectly appropriate to the duality conveyed in the poem's theme: the duality of different modes of experience or knowledge—"fact" and "truth," "head" and "heart." These crucial contrasts are further emphasized by the setting, action, and language of the poem. Note that the action of the first five lines of the poem takes place indoors, that of the last three out-of-doors. Note that the processes in the first part of the poem—adding, dividing, measuring, lecturing, hearing, being shown, and sitting—are all either passive, studied, or essentially intellectual states producing ennui; as opposed to rising, gliding, wandering, and looking up, which are spontaneous bodily or sensual actions producing a feeling of rejuvenation.

Similar patterns of contrast, antithesis, and duality operate in yet other aspects of the poem. Note that the first part of the poem is located in a single, fixed dimension, the same plane as that of the persona (suggesting the further paradox that results from the study of the stars in the lecture room), although in the second part of the poem the persona transcends this limitation by looking *up*. Note that in the first part, the persona is one of a crowd; in the second he is alone. The action of the first part is characterized by noise (lecturing, applause), the second by "perfect silence." The action of the first part can be described as dry, with all its symbolic implications; the second is moist. The action of the first part is measured, that of the second random and mystical. Note, finally, that the predominantly long lines of the first part, especially lines 2, 3, and 4, achieve the effect of droning, endless talk, although the terseness of the concluding lines reinforces the sense of fulfillment, resolution, and certainty that the words themselves connote.

Whatever the merit of this particular reading of the poem, I think it does serve to bring us closer to the work itself and to illustrate an apprehension of some aspects of Whitman's artistry. Certainly it suggests that on occasion Whitman sang in a voice other than a barbaric yawp.

Although it is commonly acknowledged that formalist criticism has been triumphant in its treatment of lyric poetry, even its loyal advocates admit less success in dealing with the novel. The formalist critic seems to be at his best with the shorter forms, whether of poetry or fiction. Formalism has also been quite selective in the authors and works it has treated, with the result that large bodies of formalist criticism have accumulated around particular writers and writings, with others slighted or ignored. For example, formalist critics have been strongly attracted to Donne, Marvell, Coleridge, and Yeats but have passed over Spenser, Milton's epics, Byron, and Browning. The Augustans and Victorians have generally received far less attention than the metaphysicals and moderns, and, as we have said, the works of many of the major novelists in all periods still await their due share of the formalists' concern. Even when the formalist critic has given abundant attention to a work, he may have stressed certain of its aspects, such as its language, imagery, or narrative method, to the exclusion of much else.

Indeed, this hyperselectivity frequent in formalist practice has been called *narrowness* by its opponents and repeatedly charged against it. René Wellek, a formalist in sympathy, concurs in this charge and admits that the principles of what he names the *new organistic formalism* remain valid for poetry but agrees that the movement has reached the point of exhaustion. Wellek proceeds to list other shortcomings: too limited a treatment of European literature, too short a historical perspective and too great a neglect of literary history, an insufficiently developed aesthetic foundation, and the failure to adapt modern linguistics to techniques for stylistic analysis.

Still other indictments of formalism have become commonplace during the past decade. Its opponents accuse it of promulgating its own fallacies, such as the objective fallacy, in which critic replaces author as the source of the work's meaning by omitting all consideration of the author's presence in such vital aesthetic elements as characteristic tone, use of language, or arrangement of experience for literary ends; or, the exhaustive fallacy, in which the critic proceeds to intensively analyze the separate parts of the work in the belief that this is the way to its wholeness.

However, by far the heaviest attack has been directed at the basic precept of formalist criticism: the principle that every work is complete in itself and that the critic must approach it without recourse to external information or extra-literary values. This, the attackers claim, is the ontological fallacy, for which I have found no more succinct description than Jacques Barzun's: "The pretense of remaining 'inside the work' is an illusion. . . . Either a work stands by itself, intelligible and potent, and then it needs no explaining; or else it requires explicating, and then something is brought to it from outside, were it only the beholder's experience of life and residue of education."

Such attacks, together with inevitable shifts of critical taste that are in part reactions to the very success of the formalist movement, as well as the movement's own deceleration after its tremendous momentum of a generation ago, have conjoined to put it now somewhat in disfavor and under the shadow of other critical approaches—some of them offshoots of formalism. However, as was once the case with historicism, we would undoubtedly be far too hasty at this point to compose either formalism's eulogy or epitaph. We suspect that it merely lies dormant, perhaps soon to emerge in new shapes and with renewed vitality.

SELECTED BIBLIOGRAPHY

Alvarez, A. "The Limits of Analysis," *American Scholar*, XXVIII (1958), 367–375.
Aubrun, Charles V. "On Literary Criticism," *Les Langues Modernes*, LII (1958), 22–30.

Barzun, Jacques. "The Scholar-Critic," in Lewis Leary, ed., *Contemporary Literary Scholarship* (New York, Appleton-Century-Crofts, Inc., 1958), pp. 3–8.

Bentley, Eric, ed., *The Importance of Scrutiny* (New York, New York University Press, 1964).

Bonnefoy, Yves. "Critics—English and French," *Encounter*, XI (1958), 39–45.

Brooks, Cleanth. "Implications of an Organic Theory of Poetry," in M. H. Abrams, ed., *Literature and Belief* (New York, Columbia University Press, 1958), pp. 53–79.

Calhoun, Richard C. "The New Criticism Ten Years After," *South Atlantic Bulletin*, XXVI (1960), 1–6.

Crane, R. S. *The Languages of Criticism and the Structure of Poetry* (Toronto, University of Toronto Press, 1953)

Crane, R. S., *et al.*, eds., *Critics and Criticism: Ancient and Modern* (Chicago, University of Chicago Press, 1957).

Daiches, David. *English Literature* (Englewood Cliffs, N.J., Prentice-Hall, Inc., 1964), pp. 90–110.

Davis, Robert Gorham. "The New Criticism and the Democratic Tradition," *American Scholar*, XIX (1949–1950), 9–20.

Erlich, Victor. *Russian Formalism: History, Doctrine* (The Hague, Mouton, 1965).

Foster, Richard. *The New Romantics* (Bloomington, Indiana University Press, 1962).

Hagopian, John V. "The New Writing and the Old and New Critics," *Intersection*, I (1953), 57–63.

Handy, William J. *Kant and the Southern New Critics* (Austin, Tex., University of Texas Press, 1963).

Holloway, John. *The Charted Mirror.* (New York, Horizon Press, Inc., 1962), pp. 164–226.

Holman, C. Hugh. "The Defense of Art: Criticism Since 1930," in Floyd Stovall, ed., *The Development of American Literary Criticism* (Chapel Hill, N.C., University of North Carolina Press, 1955), pp. 225–238.

Kahn, Sholom J. "Towards an Organic Criticism," *Journal of Aesthetics and Art Criticism*, XV (1956), 58–73.

Krieger, Murray. *The New Apologists for Poetry* (Minneapolis, University of Minnesota Press, 1956).

Krieger, Murray. "After the New Criticism," *Massachusetts Review*, IV (1962), 183–205.

Krieger, Murray. "Contextualism Was Ambitious," *Journal of Aesthetics and Art Criticism*, XXI (1962), 81–88.

Krieger, Murray. "Recent Criticism, 'Thematics,' and the Existential Dilemma," *Centennial Review of Arts and Sciences*, IV (1960), 32–50.

Marks, Emerson R. "The Achieve of, the Mastery . . . ," *Journal of Aesthetics and Art Criticism*, XVI (1957), 103–111.

Moorman, Charles. "The Vocabulary of the New Criticism," *American Quarterly*, IX (1957), 180–184.

O'Connor, William Van. *An Age of Criticism, 1900–1950* (Chicago, Henry Regnery Co., 1952), pp. 156–175.

Oxenhandler, Neal. "Ontological Criticism in America and France," *Modern Language Review*, LV (1960), 17–23.

Pizzorusso, Arnaldo. "Critique Formaliste et Critique Formelle: Problèmes et

Méthodes," *Cahiers de l'Association Internationale des Études Francaises*, No. 16 (1964), 143–155.

Pottle, F. A. "The New Critics and the Historical Method," *Yale Review*, XLIII (1954), 14–23.

Pritchard, J. P. *Criticism in America* (Norman, Okla., University of Oklahoma Press, 1956), pp. 231–265.

Raleigh, John Henry. "The New Criticism as a Historical Phenomenon," *Comparative Literature*, XI (1959), 21–28.

Sister Mary Janet. "Poetry as Knowledge in the New Criticism," *Western Humanities Review*, XVI (1962), 199–210.

Spilka, Mark. "The Necessary Stylist: A New Critical Revision," *Modern Fiction Studies*, VI (1960), 283–297.

Stallman, Robert Wooster. "The New Critics," in R. W. Stallman, ed. *Critiques and Essays in Criticism* (New York, The Ronald Press Company, 1949), pp. 488–506.

Straumann, Heinrich. "Cross Currents in Contemporary American Criticism," *English Studies*, XXXV (1954), 1–10.

Sutton, Walter. "The Contextualist Dilemma—or Fallacy?" *Journal of Aesthetics and Art Criticism*, XVII (1958), 219–229.

Sutton, Walter. "Contextualist Theory and Criticism as a Social Act," *Journal of Aesthetics and Art Criticism*, XIX (1961), 317–325.

Sutton, Walter. *Modern American Criticism* (Englewood Cliffs, N.J., Prentice-Hall, Inc., 1963), pp. 98–174.

Tate, Allen. "Is Literary Criticism Possible?" *Collected Essays* (Denver, Alan Swallow, Publisher, 1959), pp. 473–487.

Tindall, William York. "The Criticism of Fiction," *Texas Quarterly*, I (1958), 101–111.

Vivas, Eliseo. *Creation and Discovery* (New York, Noonday Press, 1955).

Waggoner, Hyatt H. "The Current Revolt Against the New Criticism," *Criticism*, I (1959), 211–225.

Warren, Austin. "The 'New Humanism' Twenty Years After," *Modern Age*, III (1958–1959), 81–87.

Wellek, René. *Concepts of Criticism*, Stephen G. Nichols, Jr., ed. (New Haven, Conn., Yale University Press, 1963), pp. 54–68, 353–360.

Wellek, René. "Some Principles of Criticism," in Anon., *The Critical Moment* (New York and Toronto, McGraw Hill, Inc., 1964), pp. 40–47.

Wellek, René, and Austin Warren. *Theory of Literature* (New York, Harcourt, Brace & World, Inc., 1956), pp. 127–145, 227–240.

Wimsatt, W. K., Jr. "The Chicago Critics," *Comparative Literature*, V (1953), 50–74.

Wimsatt, W. K., Jr., and Monroe C. Beardsley, "The Affective Fallacy," *Sewanee Review*, LVII (1949), 31–55.

Wimsatt, W. K., Jr., and Monroe C. Beardsley. "The Intentional Fallacy," *Sewanee Review*, LIV (1946), 455–488.

Wimsatt, W. K., Jr., and Cleanth Brooks. *Literary Criticism: A Short History* (New York, Alfred A. Knopf, Inc., 1964), pp. 610–680 *passim*.

Paul Valéry

PROBLEMS OF POETRY

Paul Valéry, critic, poet, philosopher, and academician, was until his death in 1945 one of the few eminent European formalist critics. Yet to such contemporaries as T. S. Eliot he was chiefly significant as a poet. Eliot considered Valéry a more representative poet of his time than either Yeats or Rilke. Valéry also wrote prolifically in such prose forms as the philosophical essay. "Questions de poésie" ("Problems of Poetry") was originally written as the preface to *Anthologie des Poetes de la N. R. F.* (1936), and appeared in English translation in Volume VII of *The Collected Works of Paul Valéry*, published by Bollingen Foundation, 1958.

In the course of some forty-five years I have seen Poetry subjected to many enterprises and very diverse experiments, seen it venture down entirely unknown paths, return at times to certain traditions; share, in fact, in the sudden fluctuations and in the regime of frequent change which seem characteristic of the world at present. Variety and fragility of combinations, instability of taste and rapid alteration of values, and, lastly, belief in extremes and the disappearance of what is enduring are features of this epoch, and they would be even more noticeable if they did not satisfy very exactly our own sensibility, which is becoming progressively more obtuse.

During this past half century a succession of poetic formulas or methods has been enunciated, from those of the "Parnassus," rigid and easily definable, to the loosest possible productions, and to experiments that are, in the truest sense,

free. It is useful, indeed necessary, to add to this sum of inventions certain revivals, often very felicitous: borrowings, from the sixteenth, seventeenth, and eighteenth centuries, of pure or learned forms, whose elegance is perhaps imprescriptible.

All these experiments were initiated in France, which is somewhat remarkable, as this country is considered to be not very poetic, although it has produced more than one famous poet. It is true that for about three hundred years the French have been taught to misunderstand the true nature of poetry and to follow, mistakenly, roads leading in a quite opposite direction from its home. I shall easily demonstrate this in a moment. It explains why the outbursts of poetry which have occurred among us from time to time have had to occur in the form of revolt or rebellion; or else, on the contrary, have been confined to a small number of ardent minds, jealous of their own secret certainties.

But, in this very nation which sings so little, an amazing richness of lyric invention appeared during the last quarter of the past century. Around 1875, when Victor Hugo was still living, and Leconte de Lisle and his followers were reaching fame, the names of Verlaine, Stéphane Mallarmé, and Arthur Rimbaud arose, those three Magi of modern poetics, bearers of such costly gifts and such rare spices that even the time that has elapsed since then has altered neither the glory nor the power of these extraordinary gifts.

The extreme diversity of their works, added to the variety of models offered by the poets of the preceding generation, has conduced, and conduces, to the conception, understanding, and practice of poetry in an admirable number of very different ways. There are some today, no doubt, who still follow Lamartine; others continue the work of Rimbaud. The same man may change his tastes and his style, burn at twenty what he adored at sixteen; some kind of inner transmutation shifts the power of seduction from one master to another. The lover of Musset becomes more *mature* and leaves him for Verlaine. Another, after being first nourished by Hugo, devotes himself completely to Mallarmé.

These spiritual changes generally operate in one particular *direction* rather than in the other, which is much less probable: it must be extremely rare for *Le Bateau ivre* to lead eventually to *Le Lac*. On the other hand, by loving the pure and hard *Hérodiade* one does not lose one's taste for the *Prière d'Esther*.

These defections, these sudden accesses of love or of grace, these conversions and substitutions, this possibility of being successively *sensitized* to the work of incompatible poets, are literary phenomena of the first importance. Therefore no one ever mentions them.

But—what are we talking about when we talk about "Poetry"?

It amazes me that in no other sphere of our curiosity is the observation of the *things themselves* more neglected.

I know that it is always the same when one has reason to fear that a truly searching look may dissolve its object or strip it of illusion. I was interested to notice the displeasure aroused by what I once wrote about History, and which consisted merely of simple observations that everyone can make. This little uproar was quite natural and easily foreseen, since it is less trouble to react than to reflect, and since in the majority of minds this minimum is bound to triumph. For myself, I always refrain from following that flight of ideas which shuns the observable *object* and, from sign to sign, hastens to stir up subjective impressions. . . . I believe that one should give up the practice of considering only what habit and the strongest of all habits, language, present for our consideration. One should try pondering other points than those suggested by *words*, that is to say, *by other people.*

I shall therefore try to show how Poetry is commonly treated, and turned into what it is not, at the expense of what it is.

One can scarcely say anything about "Poetry" which will not be exactly useless for *those in whose inner life* the strange power that causes Poetry to be sought after, or produced, is revealed as an inexplicable demand of their being, or as its purest answer.

These persons feel the need of something which in the ordinary way serves no purpose, and sometimes they perceive a kind of rightness in certain arrangements of *words*, which to other eyes appear quite arbitrary.

These people do not easily allow themselves to be taught to love what they do not love, nor not to love what they love—which used to be the chief aim of criticism.

For those who are not strongly aware either of the presence or the absence of Poetry, it is doubtless only an abstract and mysteriously acknowledged thing: something as empty as you please—though a tradition which it is proper to respect attaches to this entity some indeterminate value, of a kind that has a vague place in the public mind. The respect accorded to a title of nobility in a democratic country may be given as an example.

I consider that the essence of Poetry is, according to different types of minds, either quite worthless or of infinite importance: in which it is like God Himself.

Fate has arranged that among those men with no great appetite for Poetry, who feel no need for it and would not have invented it, there should be many whose task or destiny it is to judge it, to comment on it, to provoke and cultivate a taste for it: in short, to dispense something they do not possess. They often employ all their intelligence and zeal in this: which is why the results are to be feared.

Under the magnificent and discreet name of "Poetry," they are inevitably either led or forced to consider everything except the object with which they think they are occupied. Without realizing it, they make everything serve their turn for escaping or eluding what is essential. Everything serves their turn except that one thing.

For instance, they list what seem to be the methods used by poets: they note the frequency or absence of certain words in their vocabulary; remark their favorite images; point out borrowings, and resemblances between this one and that. Some try to reconstruct the poets' secret designs and, with deceptive clarity, read intentions and allusions into their works. With a complacency that shows where they go wrong, they like to study what is known (or thought to be known) about an author's life; as though one could ever know its true inner development, and moreover, as though the beauties of expression and the delightful harmony—always . . . *providential*—of terms and sounds were the more or less natural results of the charming or pathetic incidents of an existence. But everyone has been happy and unhappy; and the extremes of joy, like those of grief, have not been denied to the coarsest and least lyrical souls. *To perceive* does not imply *to make perceptible*—still less: *beautifully perceptible. . . .*

Is it not extraordinary that one should seek and find so many ways of treating a subject without ever touching on its principle, and that, by the methods one uses, the kind of attention one brings to it, and even the trouble one inflicts on oneself, one should reveal a complete and perfect misapprehension of the true *problem?*

Further: among the many scholarly works which, for centuries, have been devoted to Poetry, one finds amazingly few (and I say "few" to keep from saying "none") which do not imply a negation of its existence. The most perceptible characteristics and the very real problems of this most complex art are, as it were, perfectly obscured by the very type of glance turned on it.

What happens? The poem is treated as though it were (*and as though it ought to be*) divisible into a *discourse in prose* which is self-sufficient and self-contained and, on the other hand, a *piece of special music*, more or less allied to music proper, and such as the human voice can produce; but ours does not rise to song, which, in any case, scarcely preserves the *words*, being concerned only with the *syllables*.

As for the *discourse in prose*—that is, a discourse which if put into other words would answer the same purpose—this again is divided. It is thought that it can be broken up, on the one hand, into a short text (which can sometimes be reduced to one word, or to the title of the work) and, on the other, a certain amount of *accessory speech*: ornaments, images, figures, epithets, and "fine details," whose common characteristic is their capacity for being inserted, augmented, or deleted *ad libitum*. . . .

And as for the *music of poetry*, that *special music* I mentioned, it is imperceptible to some; unimportant for most; for others it is the object of abstract research, sometimes scientific and nearly always sterile. I know that honest efforts have been made to deal with the difficulties of this subject, but I fear that this energy has been misplaced. Nothing is more misleading than those so-called "scientific" methods (in particular, measurements and recordings) which always permit a "fact" to be given in answer to a question, even if it is absurd or badly put. Their value (like that of logic) lies in the way they are used. The statistics, the marks on wax, the chronometric observations which are used to solve entirely "subjective" problems of origin or trend, do indeed say *something*; but here, instead of resolving our difficulties and ending all controversy, the oracles merely introduce a naïvely disguised metaphysics under the forms and apparatus of the material of physics.

Even if we measure the footsteps of the goddess, note their frequency and *average* length, we are still far from the secret of her instantaneous grace. So far, we have not seen that the laudable curiosity which exerts itself in sifting the mysteries of the music of "articulated" language has produced anything of new and capital importance. There is the whole point. The only gauge of real knowledge is power: power to do or power to predict. "All the rest is Literature. . . ."

I must recognize, however, that these researches which I find not very fruitful have at least the merit of seeking precision. The intention is excellent. . . . Our epoch is easily satisfied by the *approximate*, wherever *material* things are not concerned. For this reason our epoch is at once more precise and more superficial than any other: in spite of itself, more precise; and of itself, more superficial. It values chance more than substance. It is amused by people and bored by man; and above all it dreads that happy boredom which, in more peaceful and so to speak emptier times, provided us with profound, critical, and desirable readers. Who would nowadays weigh his own lightest words, and for whom? And what Racine would ask his friend Boileau for permission to substitute the word *misérable* for the word *infortuné* in a certain line—a permission which was not granted?

Since I am undertaking to disengage Poetry a little from the prose and the prosaic mentality that overwhelm it, veiling it with kinds of knowledge quite unnecessary for a knowledge and possession of its nature, I may well observe the effect these labors produce on more than one mind of our time. It sometimes happens that the habit of extreme exactness developed in certain fields (and familiar to many, from its applications in practical life) tends to make useless, if not unbearable, many traditional speculations, many theses or theories which could doubtless still occupy us, spur our intellects a bit, and cause many an excellent book to be written—and even glanced through—but which, on the other hand, make us feel that a somewhat keener glance, or a few unexpected questions, would be enough to make these abstract mirages, arbitrary systems, and vague perspectives dissolve into mere verbal possibilities. Henceforward all *the sciences whose only assets are what they say* are "virtually" depreciated by the development of those sciences whose results are continually felt and used.

Imagine the judgments that can be formed by an intellect accustomed to some discipline, when confronted with certain "definitions" and "developments" purporting to initiate it into an understanding of Letters, and particularly of Poetry. What value can we attach to the arguments about "Classicism," "Romanticism," "Symbolism," etc., when we should have the greatest difficulty in linking the peculiar characteristics and qualities of execution which constitute the worth of a particular work, and have assured its preservation, *kept it alive*, with the so-called general ideas and "aesthetic" tendencies which these fine names are supposed to indicate? They are abstract and conventional terms: but conventions that are anything but "convenient," since the lack of agreement among authors about their meaning is somehow the rule; and since they appear to have been made in order to provoke this disagreement and to form a pretext for endless differences of opinion.

It is only too clear that all these classifications and cavalier judgments add nothing to the delight of a reader who is capable of love, nor do they increase a craftsman's understanding of the methods that the masters have used: they teach neither reading nor writing. Moreover, they sidetrack the mind and release it from the consideration of the real problems of art, while allowing many blind

men to discourse admirably on color. How many facile things have been written thanks to the word "Humanism," and how many stupidities in order to make people believe that Rousseau invented "Nature"! . . . It is true that once they have been adopted and absorbed by the public, with a thousand other useless phantasms that occupy its mind, these simulacra of thoughts take on a kind of existence and provide reason and substance for a mass of combinations of a certain scholarly *originality*. A *Boileau* is thus ingeniously discovered in *Victor Hugo*, a romantic in *Corneille*, a "psychologist" or a realist in *Racine*. . . . All these things are neither true nor false— in fact they could not possibly be either.

I agree that literature in general and poetry in particular may be held of no account. Beauty is a private affair; the impression one has of recognizing and experiencing it at a given moment is an accident that may be more or less frequent during one's existence, like that of sorrow and pleasure; but even more fortuitous. It is never certain that a particular object will delight us, nor that having once pleased (or displeased) us, it will please (or displease) us the next time. This uncertainty, which baffles all calculations and all forethought, and which permits combining all sorts of works with all sorts of individuals, permits every rejection and every idolatry, involves the fate of writings with the caprices, passions, and moods of anyone at all. If someone really savors a particular poem, the fact can be known by this: he speaks of it as of a personal affection—if he speaks of it at all. I have known men so jealous of what they passionately admired that they could hardly endure that others should be taken by it, or even acquainted with it, feeling their love spoilt by sharing. They preferred to hide rather than disseminate their favorite books, and treated them (to the detriment of the authors' general fame, but to the advancement of their worship) as the wise husbands of the East treat their wives, surrounding them with secrecy.

But if one wishes, as is customary, to make of Letters a kind of public utility, to associate with a nation's renown—which is, in fact, a *State security*—the titles of "masterpieces," which must needs be inscribed after the names of its victories; and if, by turning instruments of intellectual pleasure into means of education, one assigns to these creations an important place in the formation and classifying of young people—then one should take care not to corrupt thereby the true and proper sense of art. This corruption consists in substituting meaningless and external kinds of precision or agreed opinions, for the *absolute* precision of pleasure or direct interest aroused by a work, and in turning this work into a *reagent* for pedagogical control, a ground for parasitic developments, a pretext for absurd problems. . . .

All these aims lead to the same result: to avoiding the real problems and to forming a misconception. . . .

When I look at what is done to Poetry, at the questions asked and the answers given about it, the idea of it got in the classroom (and almost everywhere), my mind, which (no doubt because of the intimate nature of the mind) thinks itself the most simple of minds, is astonished "to the very limits of astonishment."

It says to itself: I see nothing in all this which helps me either to read this poem better—to *perform* it better for my own pleasure—or to understand its structure more clearly. I am being urged toward something quite different, and nothing is omitted that will lead me away from the *divine*. I am taught dates and biography,

I am told of quarrels and doctrines I care nothing about, when what is in question is the song and the subtle art of the voice transmitting ideas. . . . Where then is the essential matter of these remarks and theses? What has happened to the immediately perceptible part of a text, to the sensations that it was written to produce? It will be time enough to deal with the poet's life, loves, and opinions, his friends and enemies, his birth and death, when we shall have advanced sufficiently in the *poetic knowledge* of his poem, that is, when we shall have made ourselves the instrument of what is written, so that our voice, our intelligence, and all the fibers of our sensibility are banded together to give life and powerful actuality to the author's act of creation.

The superficial and fruitless character of the studies and teaching at which I have just been marveling appears at the slightest precise question. While I listen to these disquisitions which lack neither "documentation" nor subtlety, I cannot help thinking that I do not even know what a *Phrase* is. . . . I vary about what is meant by a *Verse*. I have read or invented twenty definitions of *Rhythm* and have adopted none of them. . . . Nay more! . . . If I merely stop to ask what a *Consonant* is, I begin to wonder; I search; and I find only the semblance of precise knowledge divided between twenty differing opinions. . . .

If I now decide to find out about those uses, or rather those abuses, of language which are grouped under the vague and general heading of "figures," I can discover no more than abandoned traces of the extremely imperfect analysis of these "rhetorical phenomena" which was attempted by the ancients. Now these figures, which are so neglected by modern criticism, play a role of the first importance not only in explicit and organized poetry, but also in that perpetually active

poetry which harasses the rigid vocabulary, expands or contracts the meaning of
words, works on them by symmetries or
conversions, constantly altering the values
of this legal tender—a poetry that, sometimes through the mouths of the people,
sometimes from the unforeseen needs of
technical expression, sometimes through
the writer's hesitant pen, engenders that
variation, in the language which insensibly changes it completely. No one seems
even to have attempted to resume this
analysis. No one tries, by a profound examination of these substitutions, these
abbreviated signs, these deliberate miscon-
ceptions, and these expedients (which
until now have been so vaguely defined
by the grammarians), to discover the particular qualities they imply, which cannot
be very different from those that are sometimes shown by the genius of geometry,
with its art of creating for itself instruments of thought progressively more flexible and penetrating. Without knowing it,
the Poet moves within an order of *possible* relationships and transformations, perceiving or pursuing only those passing and
special effects which are of use to him in a
particular phase of his inner activity.

I agree that researches of this kind are
terribly difficult and that their usefulness
can be apparent to only a limited number
of minds; and I grant that it is less abstract, more simple, more "human," more
"living" to develop observations on poetic
"sources," "influences," "psychology,"
"milieus," and "inspirations" than to devote oneself to the organic problems of
expression and its effects. I neither deny
the value nor contest the interest of a
literature that has Literature itself as a
décor, and authors for its characters; but I
must observe that I have never found
much there of any positive use to myself.
It is suitable for conversations, discus-
sions, lectures, examinations, or theses,
and all external matters of that kind—the

demands of which are very different from
those of the merciless confrontation of
someone's *purpose* with his *ability*. Poetry
is formed or communicated in the purest
abandon or in a state of profound attention: if one makes it an object of study, it
is in this direction that one must look:
into the living being and hardly at all at
his surroundings.

How surprising it is (my simple mind
runs on) that an age which, in the factory,
the workshop, the arena, the laboratory,
or the office, carries to incredible lengths
the division of labor, the economy and
efficacy of action, the purity and suitabil-
ity of procedures, should reject in the arts
the advantages of acquired experience
and refuse to invoke anything but im-
provisation, the bolt from the blue, or
dependence on chance under various flattering names! . . . At no other time has
contempt been more strongly marked, expressed, affirmed, and even proclaimed
for what ensures the true perfection of
works of art, and what, by linking their
different parts, gives them unity and consistency of form and all those qualities
which the happiest inspirations cannot
confer on them. But we are hasty. Too
many metamorphoses and revolutions of
every kind, too many rapid transmutations
of likes into dislikes and of things mocked
into things beyond price, too many and
too differing values presented simultaneously, have accustomed us to be content
with the first version of our impressions.
And how, nowadays, are we to think of
permanence, speculate on the future, and
desire to *bequeath?* It seems useless to us
to try to resist "time," and offer to unknown people who will live two hundred
years hence models capable of moving
them. We find it almost inexplicable that
so many great men should have thought
of us, and perhaps have become great
men for having so thought. In fact, every-

thing appears so precarious and so unstable in every way, so necessarily accidental, that we have ended by turning the accidents of sensation and unsustained consciousness into the substance of many works.

To sum up, the superstition of posterity having been abolished; concern for the day after tomorrow dissipated; composition, economy of means, elegance, and perfection having become imperceptible to a public less sensitive and more naïve than formerly, it is natural enough that the art of poetry and the understanding of that art should have declined (like so many other things) to the point of doing away with any forethought, and even any notion, of their immediate future. The fate of an art is linked, on the one hand, with that of its material means and, on the other, with that of the minds who are capable of being interested in it and who find in it the satisfaction of a real need. From the remotest antiquity to the present time, reading and writing have been the sole means of exchange and the only methods of developing and preserving expression through language. One can no longer answer for their future. As for minds, one already sees that they are wooed and captured by so much immediate magic, so many direct stimuli, which with no effort provide the most intense sensations and show them life itself and the whole of nature, that one may doubt whether our grandchildren will find the slightest savor in the outdated graces of our most extraordinary poets and of poetry in general.

My purpose being to show, by the way Poetry is generally considered, how it is generally unrecognized—the lamentable victim of intellects which are sometimes very powerful but which have no feeling for Poetry—I must go on with it and give some details.

I shall first quote the great d'Alembert: "Here, in my opinion," he wrote, "is the strict but just rule that our century imposes on poets: it now recognizes as good in verse only what it would find excellent in prose."

This pronouncement is one of those the reverse of which is exactly what we think should be thought. It would have sufficed for a reader in 1760 to state the contrary to discover what was going to be sought after and appreciated in the not too remote future. I do not say that either d'Alembert or his century was wrong. I say that he thought he was talking about Poetry, while he was thinking of something quite different under the same name.

Heaven knows that since the postulation of the "d'Alembert Theorem" poets have striven to contradict it! . . .

Some, moved by instinct, have fled in their works as far as possible from prose. They have even happily divested themselves of eloquence, ethics, history, philosophy, and everything in the intellect that can be developed only by expending *verbal currency*.

Others, a little more exacting, have tried, by a more and more subtle and precise analysis of poetic desire and delight, and of their workings, to construct a poetry that could never be reduced to the expression of a thought nor, consequently, be translated into other terms without perishing. They knew that the communication of a poetic state that involves the whole feeling organism is a different thing from the communication of an idea. They understood that the literal sense of a poem is not, and does not fulfill, its whole end; that the literal sense is therefore not necessarily *unique*.

However, in spite of some admirable researches and creations, our acquired habit of judging verse by the standard of prose and its function, of evaluating it, to a certain extent, *by the amount of prose it contains;* our national temperament, which has become more and more *prosaic* since the sixteenth century; the astonishing errors in the teaching of literature; the influence of the theater and of dramatic poetry (that is, of *action*, which is essentially *prose*): all these perpetuate many an absurdity and many a practice which show the most flagrant ignorance of the conditions of poetry.

It would be easy to draw up a table of "criteria" for the antipoetic mind. It would be a list of the ways of treating a poem, of judging and speaking of it, which constitute maneuvers directly contrary to the poet's efforts. Transferred to teaching, where they are the rule, these useless and barbarous operations tend to ruin the sense of poetry from childhood, together with any notion of the pleasure it could give.

To distinguish between form and content in poetry; between a subject and its treatment; between sound and sense; to consider rhythm, meter, and prosody as naturally and easily separable from the *verbal expression* itself, from the *words* themselves, and from the *syntax*; these are so many symptoms of noncomprehension or insensibility in poetic matters. *To turn a poem or to have it turned into prose, to make of a poem a matter for instruction or examinations:* these are no slight acts of heresy. It is a real perversion to insist on misconstruing the principles of an art in this way when, on the contrary, one

should initiate other minds into a universe of language that is not the common system of exchanging signs for acts or ideas. The poet's use of words is quite different from that of custom or need. The words are without doubt the same, but their values are not at all the same. It is indeed nonusage—the *not saying* "it is raining"—which is his business; and everything which shows that he is not speaking prose serves his turn. Rhymes, inversion, elaborated figures, symmetries, and images, all these, whether inventions or conventions, are so many means of setting himself in opposition to the prosaic leanings of the reader (just as the famous "rules" of the art of poetry have the effect of constantly reminding the poet of the *complex universe* of that art). The impossibility of reducing his work to prose, of *saying* it, or of *understanding it as prose* are imperious conditions of its existence, without which that work is *poetically* meaningless.

After so many negative propositions, I should now go on to the positive side of the subject; but I should think it hardly proper to preface a collection of poems, in which the most diverse tendencies and styles of execution appear, by an exposé of ideas that remain highly personal in spite of my efforts to preserve and produce only those observations and reasons which everyone can make for himself. Nothing is more difficult than not being oneself, or than being oneself only so far and no farther.

Cleanth Brooks

LITERARY CRITICISM: POET, POEM, AND READER

Cleanth Brooks has been identified with the new criticism since its beginnings in America and is regarded as one of its most able practitioners. He became associated with the Fugitive group at Vanderbilt University and was one of the founders of the *Southern Review*. His most important books are *Modern Poetry and the Tradition* (1939), *The Well-Wrought Urn* (1947), *Literary Criticism: A Short History* (with W. K. Wimsatt, Jr., 1957), and *William Faulkner: The Yoknapatawpha Country* (1963). He has also collaborated with Robert Penn Warren and others in editing a number of influential college textbooks. Mr. Brooks has taught at Yale University since 1947. The present essay was originally published in the 1962 collection edited by Stanley Burnshaw *Varieties of Literary Experience*.

The critical activity of the last forty years has created a sufficient stir. It has developed new methods for teaching literature; it has generated a new critical vocabulary, and, as might have been predicted, it has aroused a vigorous reaction. Undoubtedly there has been faddishness connected with some of its critical ideas and, like other kinds of faddishness, what is mere fad will die and will eventually be replaced, one supposes, by a newer fad. I dare say that aspects of recent criticism have been overpraised; but it is plain that other aspects have been overblamed. In any case the recent trend in criticism has been only partially understood even by some of its converts. The fact of misunderstanding helps account for the mechanization of certain of its critical "methods"—for example, heavy-handed and witless analyses of literary works,

often pushed to absurd limits and sometimes becoming an extravagant "symbolmongering."

These are general remarks. To become more specific: a typical misunderstanding interprets modern criticism as mere aestheticism. Our renewed interest in poetic form, in the eyes of some viewers, approaches dangerously near to a doctrine of art-for-art's sake in its apparent neglect of the great moral problems with which it is assumed that art ought to concern itself.

A few years ago, Professor Douglas Bush, in his presidential address to the Modern Language Association, put this case very forcibly. He scolded what he called the "new criticism" for its "preoccupation with technique, its aloof intellectuality, its fear of emotion and action, its avoidance of moral values, its dislike of 'impure' poetry (which includes," he went on to argue, "the greatest poetry we have)." He summed up the indictment of what he regards as "a timid aestheticism" by saying: "The common reader might go so far as to think that poetry deals with life, that for the serious poet life embraces morality and religion, and that it seems very strange for a serious critic to retreat into technical problems."

It may be amusing to reconsider, in the light of these strictures, the first great critical document of our Western tradition. Aristotle was certainly no timid aesthete. As a many-sided and healthy Greek of the great period, he took all knowledge to be his province. He was very much concerned with politics and morality as his *Nicomachean Ethics* and his treatise on politics testify. And what does he say about Greek tragedy? Does he praise Aeschylus for his profound insight into the human soul? Does he call attention to Sophocles' deep concern for moral problems? Well, hardly. Here is the sort of thing that Aristotle singles out for a comment in Sophocles' masterpiece, *Oedipus Rex:*

A Peripety is the change of the kind described from one state of things within the play to its opposite . . . as it is for instance in *Oedipus.* . . . A Discovery is, as the very word implies, a change from ignorance to knowledge, and thus to either love or hate, in the personages marked for good or evil fortune. The finest form of Discovery is one attended by Peripeties, like that which goes with the Discovery in *Oedipus.*

Aristotle made plot the soul of the drama, and since plot is concerned with action, his discussion of plot might seem to promise a consideration of moral problems. But when we turn to the text of the *Poetics,* we find that Aristotle is again back to technicalities, writing: "We assume that, for the finest form of Tragedy, the Plot must be not simple but complex. . . ." If the author were other than Aristotle, the moralistic critic might be tempted to argue that the sentence was written for the delectation of a coterie of aesthetes and that the critic had forgotten that the great Greek tragedies were presented before flesh-and-blood auditors, interested in and oppressed by, grave moral problems and the issues of life and death.

The *Poetics,* in sum, does not discuss the lives of the dramatists, nor their deep human experiences, nor the way in which their plays reveal their personalities. Even when Aristotle addresses himself directly to the moral issues encountered in a work of art, he scarcely writes in a fashion to satisfy the determined moralist. When he faces the specific question of whether something said in a poem is "morally right or not," the critic hot for certainties might find him evasive, for Aristotle counsels us to consider "not only the intrinsic quality of the actual word or deed, but also the person who says or does it, the time, the means, and the motive of the agent." Instead of making a strict interpretation of a given code, Aristotle seems to appeal to something like a principle of dramatic propriety. In asking us to judge a statement or action in terms of the total dramatic context he sounds suspiciously like the so-called (and badly named) "new critics."

Now my purpose in dragging Aristotle into this discussion is not to claim that the *Poetics* is the be-all and end-all of criticism. It is not even to claim that recent criticism is markedly Aristotelian. My point is a more modest one: I invoke Aristotle's example simply to suggest that a man who has a proper interest in politics, history, and morals may still find it useful to concern himself with the structure of literary works and with defining the nature and limits of aesthetic judgment.

In view of such considerations, it is possible to restate the history of criticism in our time thus: We have been witnessing a strenuous attempt to focus attention upon the poem rather than upon the poet or upon the reader. Along with this stress upon the poem as a structure in its own right, has come the attempt to fix the boundaries and limits of poetry. Modern critics have tried to see what was meant when one considered the poem as an artistic document.

I. A. Richards, some thirty years ago, argued that for the sake of the health of literature, we needed a spell of purer poetry and of purer criticism. The attempt at a purer criticism has been made. But in my more pessimistic moments, I wonder whether there has been much real clarification of the critical problem. The popular critics—in *Time* magazine, for example, or in the great metropolitan newspapers—continue to print their literary chitchat, their gossip, and their human interest notes on the author of the latest best-seller. And often out of the other side of their mouths, they go on to talk about the novelist's politics, his moral asseverations, and his affirmation or lack of affirmation of "life." To such people, the discussion of literary *form* is bound to seem empty. Ingrained habits of thinking make it hard for them to conceive of form as anything other than an empty container. On the other hand, when a critic like Allen Tate makes the point that form is *meaning*, he deliberately rejects any notion of form as a mere envelope for some valuable ethical or psychological content. Indeed, he rejects the whole implied dualism of a form-content poetics. To understand modern criticism, it is necessary to grasp this point. Some typical misunderstandings of this point may be avoided by remembering the example of Aristotle. A universal thinker, not a mere aesthete, a man who believed that art

"imitated" reality and that art could exert ethical and political pressure, could nevertheless find it profitable to deal with literature in formal terms on the assumption that it possessed a structure of a characteristic kind.

Poetry has a characteristic structure and yields a characteristic knowledge. It does not compete with, but exists alongside of, and complements scientific knowledge and historical knowledge. Since poetic knowledge is made available through poetic form, the attempt to assimilate poetic knowledge too directly and abruptly to other kinds of knowledge has its risks. We lose the value of poetic knowledge in losing the perspective that poetic form gives. It is surely quite proper to deal with Milton's *Paradise Lost*, for instance, as a reflection of a Puritan ethic. But we may learn more about its ethical content if we respect its own characteristic mode of statement as a poem and do not, in our anxiety to extract the ethical content, violate that mode.

My argument is not an esoteric one: it involves no mystical view of poetry. Rather it rests upon the evident fact that poetry does make use of certain characteristic devices and that if we ignore these devices we shall have badly misread the special kind of document that is the poem.

One of the simplest but surely the most essential of these devices is metaphor. (Robert Frost has made the point that poetry *is* fundamentally metaphor.) But the function of metaphor is often misconceived. Many readers still take its function to be that of mere illustration or decoration, with term A being "compared" to term B, or term B to term A. This misconception of metaphor as a kind of rhetorical glossing of the "facts" is one aspect of the form-content dualism which sees the poetic form as simply a superficial gilding of the content—not as something by which it is transformed. If, under the impression that we are somehow being "scientific" and thus more directly grasping reality, we do write off metaphor as mere decoration, we shall certainly lose what poetry has to give us. After all, we must not forget how much of our discovery of the truth—scientific as well as poetic—is gained through metaphor.

I confess that I once thought that the imagery in the second stanza of Wordsworth's "Solitary Reaper" was meant to be merely decorative, vaguely ennobling. Hence it is small wonder that I found the poem rather flat and dull. It was only when I stumbled upon the fact that the thinking of the poem was really being done through these images—that the poet had implicated a whole manifold of relations in associating the natural spontaneous songs of the nightingale and the cuckoo with the natural and spontaneous singing of the girl—it was only then that the poem came to be deeply meaningful to me. The Highland girl was not simply being complimented for the beauty of her song. Hers was presumably not a great voice; it was evidently an untrained voice —as "natural" as that of a bird. In effect, her song was wordless, for the girl was singing in an unknown tongue, Gaelic, as the nightingale sang in another unknown tongue, "nightingale." Like the birds, the girl was conscious of no audience and was singing for none, the song simply welling up out of the daily round of her activities, as the birds' welled up out of theirs. And like the birds, the girl sang "As if her song could have no ending." A work of art, Aristotle has told us, has a beginning, a middle, and an end; and the concert singer had better sing *her* song with a concern for its beginning, its middle, and its end. But the songs of the birds (and of the girl) are not the music of art, but of nature—they properly have no

ending. In sum, through the two bird images—and only through these images— the hearer indicates the special significance of the solitary reaper's song. It is as if the traveler had been allowed, through the utterly unself-conscious song of the solitary girl bending to her task, to overhear the "still, sad music of humanity" rising from hidden depths, plaintive, sweet, artless. Thus, the bird comparisons cannot be dismissed as mere decoration: what the poem "says" is said primarily through the imagery.

To refer to a point made earlier: the attempt to assimilate poetic knowledge too directly to other kinds of knowledge is dangerous. If we ignore the poetic form, we may hopelessly distort the meaning. One can illustrate the danger from another lyric by Wordsworth, one of the celebrated Lucy poems.

She dwelt among the untrodden ways
  Beside the springs of Dove,
A Maid whom there were none to praise
  And very few to love:

A violet by a mossy stone
  Half hidden from the eye!
—Fair as a star, when only one
  Is shining in the sky.

She lived unknown, and few could know
  When Lucy ceased to be:
But she is in her grave, and, oh,
  The difference to me!

A few years ago a critic and literary scholar insisted upon using the poem to make a sociological point. Knowing that the young Wordsworth sympathized with the common man and had been strongly affected by the French Revolution, our scholar was bent on showing how much this simple love poem actually reflected a transitional age and foreshadowed the modern age to come. Indeed, he found in the poem a number of remarkable reflections of the changing nineteenth-century social scheme. For one thing, the speaker was revealed to be conscious of his moral isolation in his choice of a love object—someone who "dwelt among the untrodden ways." Moreover, Lucy herself turned out to be a young woman of neurotic personality—and the speaker "modern" in choosing a neurotic. You may wonder how our scholar detected Lucy's neurosis. The answer is simple. He interpreted the lines "A Maid whom there were none to praise/And very few to love" with painful literalness. One had always assumed that the lines meant that in her remote, rural situation, none of the few simple people who knew the maiden and loved her was capable of singing her praises; that is, Lucy lacked the poet that her loveliness deserved. One had also supposed that the second stanza praised Lucy's modesty ("A violet by a mossy stone") and her sweet serenity ("Fair as a star, when only one/Is shining in the sky.") But our critic was convinced that her shyness concealed what he called "an unpleasant rejection of other people." Few loved her, and of those that did, none could honestly say a good word for her! Granted that the example just cited is an extreme case, there are plenty of misreadings conducted under the same auspices which are only somewhat less absurd.

I once knew a sociologist who delivered his judgment to the effect that Shakespeare's Cleopatra was simply a maladjusted girl. I dare say that in some sense she was. But his remark makes sufficiently plain the fact that he had missed the meaning of the play. One can, to be sure, treat *Antony and Cleopatra* sociologically, psychologically, historically, morally, etc., but the play is, after all, a work of art, and if we consider it to be a work of art we shall find ourselves talking about it necessarily in terms appropriate to aesthetic structure—whether terms like Aristotle's *peripeteia* and *anagnōrisis*, or those of recent criticism like *tension* and *ironic reversal*, or in still other terms. To treat the play in terms of aesthetic structure does *not* mean that we are denying ethical problems. There can certainly be no objection to making use of terms that have to do with human interests, human motives, and human emotions. Indeed, how can we avoid such references if we are to talk about the play in terms of its pattern of tensions, complications, and resolutions? For these are the things that are patterned, balanced, and resolved. But whatever the terminology we use, we will do well to keep the ethical problems at one remove, seeing them, that is, in the perspective which aesthetic structure affords and which the fictional nature of the play actually enjoins. Otherwise we shall find that our study of this play with its "maladjusted girl" and its adultery and double suicide threatens to turn into a clinical study or a police court inquest.

One could illustrate nearly everything about poetic structure and its relation to politics and morality from this complex and brilliant play. But present purposes call for an example that is smaller and more readily manageable. For that, one might go back to "The Solitary Reaper," which in spite of its apparent simplicity can tell us a great deal about poetic form. But it may be better to illustrate from a longer and more complicated poem, "The Grasse-hopper," by Richard Lovelace, one of the Cavalier poets of the seventeenth century.

THE GRASSE-HOPPER

To my Noble Friend, Mr. Charles Cotton

ODE

I.

O thou that swing'st upon the waving
    haire
Of some well-filled Oaten Beard,

Drunke ev'ry night with a Delicious teare
  Dropt thee from Heav'n, where now
    th'art reard.

II.

The Joyes of Earth and Ayre are thine
  intire,
    That with thy feet and wings dost hop
      and flye;
And when thy Poppy workes thou dost
  retire
    To thy Carv'd Acron-bed to lye.

III.

Up with the Day, the Sun thou welcomst
  then,
    Sportst in the guilt-plats of his Beames,
And all these merry dayes mak'st merry
  men,
    Thy selfe, and Melancholy streames.

IV.

But ah the Sickle! Golden Eares are
  Cropt;
    Ceres and Bacchus bid good night;
Sharpe frosty fingers all your Flowr's have
  topt,
    And what sithes spar'd, Winds shave
      off quite.

V.

Poore verdant foole! and now green Ice!
  thy Joys
    Large and as lasting, as thy Peirch of
      Grasse,
Bid us lay in 'gainst Winter Raine, and
  poize
    Their flouds, with an o'reflowing glasse.

VI.

Thou best of Men and Friends! we will
  create
    A Genuine Summer in each others
      breast;
And spite of this cold Time and frosen
  Fate
    Thaw us a warme seate to our rest.

VII.

Our sacred harthes shall burne eternally
  As Vestal Flames, the North-wind, he
Shall strike his frost-stretch'd Winges,
    dissolve and flye
  This Ætna in Epitome.

VIII.

Dropping December shall come weeping
  in,
    Bewayle th'usurping of his Raigne;
But when in show'rs of old Greeke we
  beginne,
    Shall crie, he hath his Crowne againe!

IX.

Night as cleare Hesper shall our Tapers
  whip
    From the light Casements where we
      play,
And the darke Hagge from her black mantle strip,
    And sticke there everlasting Day.

X.

Thus richer then untempted Kings are
  we,
    That asked nothing, nothing need:
Though Lord of all what Seas imbrace;
  yet he
    That wants himselfe, is poore indeed.

—The Poems of Richard Lovelace,
ed. C. H. Wilkinson (Oxford, 1925)

The poem is addressed by the poet "To my noble friend, Mr. Charles Cotton." It would be interesting to know more than we do about Lovelace's noble friend. The scholars do not agree as to his identity. C. H. Wilkinson thinks it was Charles Cotton, the son; C. H. Hartmann, Charles Cotton, the father. But even if we do not know the identity of the noble friend, we still can enjoy the poem and understand it.

There are, I grant, poems which do depend for their basic meaning upon some knowledge of the historical characters mentioned in them. Marvell's "Horatian Ode upon Cromwell's Return from Ireland" would be hopelessly obscure to a reader who knew absolutely nothing about Oliver Cromwell. Yet we can and must make a distinction between a poem as a personal document and as a poetic structure. For example, it is conceivable, though highly improbable, that some day a scholar may come upon a set of seventeenth-century letters which would tell us that Mr. Charles Cotton had performed several great services for our poet, and that this little poem had been written by Lovelace in grave apprehension as he received news that his friend had been stricken with a serious illness. While we are using our imaginations, let us suppose further that the letters showed that this poem was written in the hope of cheering his friend by suggesting that they had many more years of fine companionship before them. Such letters might very well enhance for us the meaning of the poem as a personal document of Lovelace's life. But if we may thus enhance a poem at will by importing into it all sorts of associations and meaning, then we can theoretically turn an obscure poem into a clear poem—and a poor poem into a good poem. Even the verse from the newspaper agony column beginning "It is now a year and a day/Since little Willie went away" might move us deeply if we actually knew little Willie and his sorrowing mother. But only the unwary would take the triggering of such an emotional response as proof of the goodness of the poem. In the hypothetical case just cited, the response comes not from the poem as poem but as personal document. What references and allusions are legitimate parts of a poem and what are merely adventitious associations? The distinction is not always obvious, and I do not care to try to fix here a doctrinaire limitation. But I think that we shall have to agree that some limits must exist.

The first part of Lovelace's poem derives from the Anacreontic poem "The Grasshopper." (I use Abraham Cowley's translation.)

Happy Insect *what can be*
In happiness compar'd to thee?
Fed with nourishment divine,

The dewy Mornings *gentle* Wine!
Nature *waits upon thee still,*
And thy verdant Cup *does fill;*
'Tis fill'd where ever thou does tread,
Natures selfe's *thy* Ganimed.
Thou does drink, and dance, and sing;
Happier than the happiest King! . . .

Lovelace evidently began his poem as a free translation of the Greek poem; but he went on to develop out of it a thoroughly different poem—different in theme and different in tone. The little Anacreontic poem becomes merely a starting point of the poem that Lovelace actually writes. Whereas the Greek poet contents himself with giving a charming account of the insect's life, Lovelace uses the account of the grasshopper's life to set up the contrast between the spurious summer of nature and the genuine summer to which men have access. If we are interested in the way in which the poem was composed, we shall certainly want to know what sources Lovelace used, and there may be a special delight in seeing how he has reshaped his sources to his own purpose. But a mere round-up of the sources will never in itself tell us what the poet has done with them. A bad poem may assimilate Anacreon as well as a good poem. The value of a poem as a work of art is not to be determined by an account of its sources.

In the same way, the history of ideas might tell us a great deal about this poem. The historian can trace the development of such concepts as that of the actual considered to be a dim and limited reflection of the ideal—specifically, the summer of the grasshopper in the natural world of the seasons viewed as a mere shadow of the genuine summer which transcends the seasonal world of nature. The historians of ideas can trace for us the development of the concept of richness based not upon the possession of goods but upon one's freedom from wants—that is, the notion of richness as completeness. The ideas that Lovelace is using here are familiar to most readers and can be taken for granted; but I concede that the reader who is not familiar with these concepts might have serious trouble with the poem. Even so, criticism has to be distinguished from the scholarship of the history of ideas, for the obvious reason that the historian of ideas may find just as much to explain in a poor and unsuccessful poem as in a good poem.

It is the critic of moralistic bias, as we have already noted, who is most likely to object sharply to modern critical procedure. The serious moralist finds it hard not to become impatient with a critic who seems to ignore the moral problems, and to concern himself merely with "form" and technique. Nor will he necessarily be satisfied with the critic's concession that wisdom is certainly to be found in poetry. Lovelace's poem, for example, says, among other things, that happiness is not dependent upon external circumstances but is an inward quality. But the moralist argues that this is surely the doctrine that ought to be emphasized in any critical account of the poem. For it may appear to him that it is this moral truth that gives the poem its value.

But the sternest moralist will have to concede that many poems that contain admirable doctrine—Longfellow's "Psalm of Life," for example—are very poor poems. Furthermore, if one tries to save the case by stipulating that the doctrine must not only be true, but must be rendered clearly, acceptably, and persuasively, he will have come perilously close to reducing the poet's art to that of the mere rhetorician.

Moralists as diverse as Marxists and the later Van Wyck Brooks are all for making the Muse a rewrite girl. But the Muse is willful and stubborn: a thesis presented eloquently and persuasively is not necessarily the same thing as a poem. "The Grasshopper" is, among other things, a document in the personal history of Lovelace, testifying to his relation with Charles Cotton. It is an instance of Lovelace's regard for the classics; it incorporates an amalgam of ideas inherited from the Christian-classical tradition of Western thought; it is an admonition to find happiness within oneself. The point is that it could be all of these things and yet be a very poor poem. It could be all of these things and not be a poem at all. It could be, for example, a letter from Lovelace to Charles Cotton, or an entry in Lovelace's commonplace book.

It happens to be a poem and a rather fine one. But defense of this judgment, if it were questioned, would involve an examination of the structure of the poem as poem. And with this kind of examination the so-called "new criticism" is concerned. I should be happy to drop the adjective "new" and simply say: with this kind of judgment, literary criticism is concerned.

Lovelace's poem is a little masterpiece in the management of tone. Lovelace makes the life of the insect thoroughly Lucullan. The grasshopper is "drunk ev'ry night": Lovelace provides him with a carved bed in which to sleep off his debauch. But actually the grasshopper is up with the dawn, for his tipple is a natural distillation, the free gift of heaven. The joys to which he abandons himself are all innocent and natural, and his merry-making makes men merry too.

The grasshopper's life, then, though described in terms that hint at the human world, is not used to symbolize a type of human experience to be avoided. We have here no fable of the ant and the grasshopper. Lovelace would not reform the little wastrel, but delights in him, so joyously and thoughtlessly at home in his world.

Stanzas V and VI define very delicately and precisely this attitude, one of humor and amusement, touched with the merest trace of pity. The grasshopper is happy because he cannot possibly foresee the harvest or the biting blasts of winter. "But ah the Sickle! Golden Eares are Cropt." Everything in the line conspires to place the emphasis upon the word *golden*, a word rich in every sort of association: wealth, ripeness, luxury, the Saturnian age of gold. But the full force of *golden* is perhaps not realized until we come to line 13: "Poore verdant foole! and now green Ice!" The clash of gold and green absorbs and carries within it the whole plight of the grasshopper. Green suggests not only the little insect's color but all that is growing, immature, unripe, and innocently simple. The oaten ears on which the grasshopper loves to swing change, by natural process, from green to gold; the grasshopper cannot change with them. The mature oaten ears may resemble the precious metal—one remembers Milton's "vegetable gold"—but greenness turned to something hard and stiff and cold—the sliver of green ice—is a pathetic absurdity.

I should not press the contrast so hard, had Lovelace not insisted on the color, and emphasized its connection with springing verdure by his phrase "Poore verdant foole!" And here it becomes proper to acknowledge the critic's debt to the lexicographer and to concede that my suggestion that *verdant* here means *gullible* has no specific dictionary warrant. The Oxford Dictionary's first entry for this sense of *verdant* is as late as 1824; the same dictionary, however, does indicate that *green* could carry these connotations as early as 1548. In the context of this poem, *verdant*, followed by the phrase "green ice," and associated as it is with "fool," must surely carry the meaning of inexperienced, thoughtless innocence.

The gentle and amused irony that suffuses "Poore verdant foole" continues through the lines that follow: the grasshopper's joys are measured by the instability of the insect's precarious perch—"Large and as lasting, as thy Peirch of Grasse." But the speaker soon turns from his contemplation of these ephemeral joys to man's perdurable joys—from the specious summer of nature to the genuine summer which he and his noble friend can create, each in the other's breast.

The poem pivots sharply in the fifth stanza, and the management of tone is so dextrous that we may be tempted to pass over the last half of the poem too easily. But these latter stanzas have their difficulties and if we want to understand the poem I think we shall want to find precisely what goes on. Moreover, these stanzas present their problem of tone also. The poem must not seem smug and sanctimonious; man's happiness must not seem too easily achieved. For if man rises superior to the animal kingdom, he is not, for all of that, a disembodied spirit. He is animal too, and he has to reckon with the "frost-stretch'd winges" of the North Wind and with the blackness of the winter night. Moreover, as man, he has his peculiar bugbears of a sort that the grasshopper does not have to contend with. There is at least a hint of this in the reference to "untempted Kings."

As a general comment, suffice it to say that in this poem the flesh is given its due: the warm hearth, the lighted casements, and showers of old Greek wine fortify the friends against the winter night and give a sense of real gaiety and mirth. If there is high thinking, the living is not so plain as to be unconvincing. And the sentiment on which the poem closes is none the less serious because it comes out of festivity and has been warmed by wine. He who "wants himselfe"—who owns things but has not mastered himself—is poor indeed. It is this full possession of himself, this lack of dependence upon things, which makes him richer than "untempted Kings."

The last phrase, however, is curious. In this context, Lovelace ought to be writing to his friend: "since we are untempted by material possessions, we are actually richer than kings." The force of the contrast depends upon the fact that kings are more than most men tempted by material possessions. Why then *untempted* kings? The solution is probably to be sought in the source of the poem. In the Anacreontic "Grasshopper" the insect is referred to as a king—the Greek text has Βασιλεύς—and Abraham Cowley, Lovelace's contemporary, uses the word *king* in his translation. Lovelace, then, for his fit audience who knew the Greek poem, is saying: we are like the grasshopper, that rare specimen, an untempted king; but we are richer than he, since our joys do not end with the natural summer, but last on through the genuine (and unending) summer of the heart.

But it is Stanzas VIII and IX that cause the real trouble. As C. H. Hartmann remarks: "Lovelace himself could on occasion become so involved as to be utterly incomprehensible even without the assistance of an eccentric printer." To deal first with Stanza IX: the drift of the argument is plain enough, but Lovelace's editor, Wilkinson, also confesses to difficulties here: the friends will whip night away from their casements. But what are we to make of the phrase "as clear Hesper"? Wilkinson writes "The meaning would seem to be that 'just as Hesperus shines clearer as the day draws to a close, so will our tapers whip night from the lighted casements of the room where we amuse ourselves. . . .'" But I fail to see the relevance of his argument that Hesper shines the brighter as the skies darken. Why not simply read "as clear Hesper" as an ellipsis for "as clear Hesper does"? Our tapers will whip away night as clear Hesper whips it away. Moreover, the poet chooses as the dispeller of gloom the modest light of the star just because it is modest. He is not claiming that he and his friend can abolish winter. "Dropping *December*" *shall* come weeping in. The friendly association with Cotton will not do away with the wintry night. What the human being can do is to rid the night of its horror—exorcise the hag—maintain a small circle of light amid the enveloping darkness. This is precisely what the evening star, clear Hesper, does, and all that he and his friend with their gleaming tapers propose to do. As with light, so with heat. Their hearth will be an Aetna, but an Aetna is epitome—a tiny volcano of heat. The poet is very careful not to claim too much.

Stanza VIII contains the most difficult passage in the poem, and Lovelace's editors have not supplied a note. "Dropping *December*" means *dripping*, or *rainy* December. But why will December lament the usurping of his reign? Does the warm fire and pleasant company maintained by the two friends constitute the usurpation against which he will protest? We may at first be inclined to think so, but the lines that follow make it plain that December is not crying out against, but rejoicing in, the two friends' festivities. Seeing them at their wine, December exclaims that he has "his Crowne againe." But what is December's crown? One looks for it throughout Greek and Roman mythology in vain.

We have here, I am convinced, a topical allusion. The crown of December is evidently the Christmas festivities, festivities actually more ancient than Christianity—the age-old feast of the winter solstice of which the Roman Saturnalia is an instance. December's crown is indeed a venerable one. And who has stolen December's crown—who has usurped his reign? The Puritans, by abolishing the celebration of Christmas. We remember that it is a Cavalier poet writing, and I suspect, if we care to venture at dating the poem, we shall have to put it at some time between the Puritan abolition of Christmas in 1642 and the publication of Lovelace's volume, *Lucasta*, in 1649. Line 23, then, "And spite of this cold Time and frosen Fate," is seen to refer to more than the mere winter season. It must allude to the Puritan domination—for Lovelace, a cold time and frozen fate indeed. I would not press the historical allusion. The poem is certainly not primarily an anti-Puritan poem. The basic contrast is made between animal life and the higher and more enduring joys to which man can attain. But a casual allusion to the troubled state of England would be a thoroughly natural one for the poet of "To Althea from Prison" to have written, and nowhere more appropriately than here, in a poem to a close friend.

The reader may not be convinced by this interpretation of the eighth stanza. Very frankly, my basic concern has been to read the poem, not to seek out historical allusions. But an honest concern with the text characterizes, or ought to characterize, the work of both scholar and critic. In view of the much advertised quarrel between scholarship and criticism, the point is worth stressing. The critic selects from scholarship those things which will help him understand the poem *qua* poem; in some matters the contribution of the scholar may be indispensable. Literary criticism and literary scholarship are therefore natural allies in their concern to understand the poem; they may at points coalesce. But if, because of unavoidable specialization, the scholar and critic cannot always be one and the same man, I think it a pity if, with short-sighted jealousy, they elbow each other as rivals and combatants.

Earlier in this paper, I said that recent criticism had attempted to focus atten-

tion on the poem rather than upon the poet or upon the reader. But there is no danger that people will cease to talk about the poet and his reader. Our basic human interest is most readily served when we talk about the reader's reactions —our own responses to the poem or the novel—the chill down our spine or perhaps it is the special sensation in the pit of the stomach that A. E. Housman claimed to experience when he encountered a genuine poem. Human interest may be almost as readily served if we talk about the personality of the author. Such talk may include everything from Lord Byron's amours to the possible effects of Keats's tuberculosis upon his personality —everything from Shakespeare's alleged Oedipus complex to Robert Frost's love for New Hampshire.

No one wants to forbid either the study of the author or the study of the reader. Both kinds of study are legitimate and have their own interest. In view of the present state of criticism, it may be somewhat more to the point to say a final word in justification of recent stress upon the poem as such.

A study of the reader's reactions may be most interesting and illuminating. But concentration on the reader's reactions tends to take us away from the work of art into the domain of reader-psychology. We ask why Keats's "Ode on a Grecian Urn" provokes the different responses that it does, and we find the answer in the differing psychological make-up of the various readers. Or we may ask why certain aspects of Shakespeare were praised in the eighteenth century and others in the nineteenth, and typically find our answer in the differing cultural climates of the two centuries. But even though a poem can be realized only through some reader's response to it, the proper study of the poem is the study of the poem.

A study of the poet's personality and intellectual background will almost certainly be rewarding. After all, the poem is an expression of the mind and sensibility of the man who wrote it, and may well reflect his cultural background and the time spirit of his age. Yet concentration upon these matters can also take us away from the poem—into author psychology or the history of ideas or cultural history. In any case, it is valuable to ponder the fact that we often know very little about the author's experience beyond what he has been able to catch and make permanent within the poem. We know, for example, very little about Richard Lovelace. About the greatest of our poets, Shakespeare, we know even less—if we exclude what we may surmise from the works themselves. Even where we know a great deal about the author's personality and ideas, *we rarely know as much as the poem itself can tell us about itself*; for the poem is no mere effusion of a personality. It is a construct—an articulation of ideas and emotions—a dramatization. It is not a slice of raw experience but a product of the poet's imagination—not merely something suffered by him but the result of his creative activity. As a work of art, it calls for a reciprocal imaginative activity on our part; and that involves seeing it for what it *is*.

Wayne C. Booth

TELLING AND SHOWING

Now Pullman Professor of English and Dean of the College at the University of Chicago, where he also received his M.A. and Ph.D. degrees, Wayne C. Booth has taught at Haverford and at Earlham College. He has held Ford and Guggenheim fellowships. Almost immediately after its publication in 1961, his book *The Rhetoric of Fiction* established itself as an indispensable work in the study of fictional technique. This selection is Chapter One of *The Rhetoric of Fiction.*

"Action, and tone, and gesture, the smile of the lover, the frown of the tyrant, the grimace of the buffoon,—all must be told [in the novel], for nothing can be shown. Thus, the very dialogue becomes mixed with the narration; for he must not only tell what the characters actually said, in which his task is the same as that of the dramatic author, but must also describe the tone, the look, the gesture, with which their speech was accompanied,—telling, in short, all which, in the drama, it becomes the province of the actor to express."
—Sir Walter Scott

"Authors like Thackeray, or Balzac, say, or H. G. Wells . . . are always *telling* the reader what happened instead of showing them the scene, telling them what to think of the characters rather than letting the reader judge for himself or letting the characters do the telling about one another. I like to distinguish between novelists that *tell* and those [like Henry James] that *show*."
—Joseph Warren Beach

"The only law that binds the novelist throughout, whatever course he is pursuing, is the need to be consistent on *some* plan, to follow the principle he has adopted."
—Percy Lubbock

"A novelist can shift his view point if it comes off, and it came off with Dickens and Tolstoy."
—E. M. Forster

AUTHORITATIVE "TELLING" IN EARLY NARRATION

One of the most obviously artificial devices of the storyteller is the trick of going beneath the surface of the action to obtain a reliable view of a character's mind and heart. Whatever our ideas may be about the natural way to tell a story, artifice is unmistakably present whenever the author tells us what no one in so-called real life could possibly know. In life we never know anyone but ourselves by thoroughly reliable internal signs, and most of us achieve an all too partial view even of ourselves. It is in a way strange, then, that in literature from the very beginning we have been told motives

108

directly and authoritatively without being forced to rely on those shaky inferences about other men which we cannot avoid in our own lives.

"There was a man in the land of Uz, whose name was Job; and that man was perfect and upright, one that feared God, and eschewed evil." With one stroke the unknown author has given us a kind of information never obtained about real people, even about our most intimate friends. Yet it is information that we must accept without question if we are to grasp the story that is to follow. In life if a friend confided his view that *his* friend was "perfect and upright," we would accept the information with qualifications imposed by our knowledge of the speaker's character or of the general fallibility of mankind. We could never trust even the most reliable of witnesses as completely as we trust the author of the opening statement about Job.

We move immediately in Job to two scenes presented with no privileged information whatever: Satan's temptation of God and Job's first losses and lamentations. But we conclude the first section with another judgment which no real event could provide for any observer: "In all this Job sinned not, nor charged God foolishly." How do we know that Job sinned not? Who is to pronounce on such a question? Only God himself could know with certainty whether Job charged God foolishly. Yet the author pronounces judgment, and we accept his judgment without question.

It might at first appear that the author does not require us to rely on his unsupported word, since he gives us the testimonial of God himself, conversing with Satan, to confirm his view of Job's moral perfection. And after Job has been pestered by his three friends and has given his own opinion about his experience, God is brought on stage again to confirm

the truth of Job's view. But clearly the reliability of God's statements ultimately depends on the author himself; it is he who names God and assures us that this voice is truly His.

This form of artificial authority has been present in most narrative until recent times. Though Aristotle praises Homer for speaking in his own voice less than other poets, even Homer writes scarcely a page without some kind of direct clarification of motives, of expectations, and of the relative importance of events. And though the gods themselves are often unreliable, Homer—the Homer we know—is not. What he tells us usually goes deeper and is more accurate than anything we are likely to learn about real people and events. In the opening lines of the *Iliad*, for example, we are told, under the half-pretense of an invocation, precisely what the tale is to be about: "the anger of Peleus' son Achilleus and its devastation."[1] We are told directly that we are to care more about the Greeks than the Trojans. We are told that they were "heroes" with "strong souls." We are told that it was the will of Zeus that they should be "the delicate feasting of dogs." And we learn that the particular conflict between Agamemnon, "the lord of men," and "brilliant" Achilles was set on by Apollo. We could never be sure of any of this information in real life, yet we are sure as we move through the *Iliad* with Homer constantly at our elbow, controlling rigorously our beliefs, our interests, and our sympathies. Though his commentary is generally brief and often disguised as simile, we learn from it the precise quality of every heart; we know who dies innocent and who guilty, who foolish and who wise. And we know, whenever there is any reason for us to

---

[1] Trans. Richmond Lattimore (Chicago, 1951). All quotations are from this translation.

know, what the characters are thinking: "the son of Tydeus pondered doubtfully/ .... Three times in his heart and spirit he pondered turning . . . (Book VIII, ll. 167–169).

In the *Odyssey* Homer works in the same explicit and systematic way to keep our judgments straight. Though E. V. Rieu is no doubt correct in calling Homer an "impersonal" and "objective" author, in the sense that the life of the real Homer cannot be discovered in his work,[2] Homer "intrudes" deliberately and obviously to insure that our judgment of the "heroic," "resourceful," "admirable," "wise" Odysseus will be sufficiently favorable. "Yet all the gods were sorry for him, except Poseidon, who pursued the heroic Odysseus with relentless malice till the day when he reached his own country."

Indeed, the major justification of the opening scene in the palace of Zeus is not as mere exposition of the facts of Odysseus' plight. What Homer requires of us is sympathetic involvement in that plight, and Athene's opening reply to Zeus provides authoritative judgment on what is to follow. "It is for Odysseus that my heart is wrung—the wise but unlucky Odysseus, who has been parted so long from all his friends and is pining on a lonely island far away in the middle of the seas." To her accusation of neglect, Zeus replies, "How could I ever forget the admirable Odysseus? He is not only the wisest man alive but has been the most generous in his offerings. . . . It is Poseidon . . . who is so implacable towards him. . . ."

When we come to Odysseus' enemies, the poet again does not hesitate either to speak in his own person or to give divine testimony. Penelope's suitors must look bad to us; Telemachus must be admired. Not only does Homer dwell on Athene's approval of Telemachus, he lays on his own direct judgments with bright colors. The "insolent," "swaggering," and "ruffianly" suitors are contrasted to the "wise" (though almost helplessly young) Telemachus and the "good" Mentor. "Telemachus now showed his good judgment." Mentor "showed his good will now by rising to admonish his compatriots." We seldom encounter the suitors without some explicit attack by the poet: "This was their boastful way, though it was they who little guessed how matters really stood." And whenever there might be some doubt about where a character stands, Homer sets us straight: " 'My Queen,' replied Medon, who was by no means a villain . . . ." Hundreds of pages later, when Medon is spared from Odysseus' slaughter, we can hardly be surprised.

The result of all this direct guidance, when it is joined with Athene's divine attestation that the gods "have no quarrel" with Telemachus and have settled that he "shall come home safe," is to leave us, as we enter upon Odysseus' first adventure in Book Five, perfectly clear about what we should hope for and what fear; we are unambiguously sympathetic toward the heroes and contemptuous of the suitors. It need hardly be said that another poet, working with the same episodes but treating them from the suitors' point of view, could easily have led us into the same adventures with radically different hopes and fears.[3]

---

[2] The *Odyssey*, trans. E. V. Rieu (Penguin ed., 1959), p. 10. The quotations that follow are from Rieu's translation, Books I–IV. Different translations give different emphases to Homer's moral judgments, and some use less forceful epithets than does Rieu. But no translator has been able to portray a neutral Homer.

[3] Some readers may fear at this point that I am stumbling blindfold into the "affective fallacy." I try to meet their legitimate concern in chaps. iii–v.

Direct and authoritative rhetoric of the kind we have seen in Job and in Homer's works has never completely disappeared from fiction. But as we all know, it is not what we are likely to find if we turn to a typical modern novel or short story.

Jim had a great trick that he used to play w'ile he was travelin'. For instance, he'd be ridin' on a train and they'd come to some little town like, well, like, we'll say, like Benton. Jim would look out of the train window and read the signs on the stores.

For instance, they'd be a sign, "Henry Smith, Dry Goods." Well, Jim would write down the name and the name of the town and when he got to wherever he was goin' he'd mail back a postal card to Henry Smith at Benton and not sign no name to it, but he'd write on the card, well, somethin' like "Ask your wife about that book agent that spent the afternoon last week," or "Ask your Missus who kept her from gettin' lonesome the last time you was in Carterville." And he'd sign the card, "A Friend."

Of course, he never knew what really come of none of these jokes, but he could picture what probably happened and that was enough. . . . Jim was a card.

Most readers of Lardner's "Haircut" (1926) have recognized that Lardner's opinion of Jim is radically different here from the speaker's. But no one in the story has said so. Lardner is not present to say so, not, at least, in the sense that Homer is present in his epics. Like many other modern authors, he has effaced himself, renounced the privilege of direct intervention, retreated to the wings and left his characters to work out their own fates upon the stage.

In sleep she knew she was in her bed, but not the bed she had lain down in a few hours since, and the room was not the same but it was a room she had known somewhere. Her heart was a stone lying upon her breast outside of her; her pulses lagged and paused, and she knew that something strange was going to hap-

pen, even as the early morning winds were cool through the lattice. . . .

Now I must get up and go while they are all quiet. Where are my things? Things have a will of their own in this place and hide where they like. . . . Now what horse shall I borrow for this journey I do not mean to take? . . . Come now, Graylie, she said, taking the bridle, we must outrun Death and the Devil. . . .

The relation between author and spokesman is more complex here. Katherine Anne Porter's Miranda ("Pale Horse, Pale Rider" [1936]) cannot be simply classified, like Lardner's barber, as morally and intellectually deficient; the ironies at work among character, author, and reader are considerably more difficult to describe. Yet the problem for the reader is essentially the same as in "Haircut." The story is presented without comment, leaving the reader without the guidance of explicit evaluation.

Since Flaubert, many authors and critics have been convinced that "objective" or "impersonal" or "dramatic" modes of narration are naturally superior to any mode that allows for direct appearances by the author or his reliable spokesman. Sometimes, as we shall see in the next three chapters, the complex issues involved in this shift have been reduced to a convenient distinction between "showing," which is artistic, and "telling," which is inartistic. "I shall not *tell* you anything," says a fine young novelist in defense of his art. "I shall allow you to eavesdrop on my people, and sometimes they will tell the truth and sometimes they will lie, and you must determine for yourself when they are doing which. You do this every day. Your butcher says, 'This is the best,' and you reply, 'That's *you* saying it.' Shall my people be less the captive of their desires than your butcher? I can *show* much, but show only. . . . You will no more expect the novelist to tell you precisely *how* something is said than you will expect him to stand by your chair and hold your book."[4]

But the changed attitudes toward the author's voice in fiction raise problems that go far deeper than this simplified version of point of view would suggest. Percy Lubbock taught us forty years ago to believe that "the art of fiction does not begin until the novelist thinks of his story as a matter to be *shown*, to be so exhibited that it will tell itself."[5] He may have been in some sense right—but to say so raises more questions than it answers.

Why is it that an episode "told" by Fielding can strike us as more fully realized than many of the scenes scrupulously "shown" by imitators of James or Hemingway? Why does some authorial commentary ruin the work in which it occurs, while the prolonged commentary of *Tristram Shandy* can still enthral us? What, after all, does an author do when he "intrudes" to "tell" us something about his story? Such questions force us to consider closely what happens when an author engages a reader fully with a work of fiction; they lead us to a view of fictional technique which necessarily goes far beyond the reductions that we have sometimes accepted under the concept of "point of view."

Two Stories from the "Decameron"

Our task will be simpler if we begin with some stories written long before anyone worried very much about cleaning out the rhetorical impurities from the house of fiction. The stories in Boccaccio's *Decameron*, for example, seem extremely simple—perhaps even simple-minded and

inept—if we ask of them the questions which many modern stories invite us to ask. It is bad enough that the characters are what we call two-dimensional, with no revealed depths of any kind; what is much worse, the "point of view" of the narrator shifts among them with a total disregard for the kind of technical focus or consistency generally admired today. But if we read these stories in their own terms, we soon discover a splendid and complex skill underlying the simplicity of the effect.

The material of the ninth story of the fifth day is in itself conventional and shallow indeed. There was once a young lover, Federigo, who impoverished himself courting a chaste married woman, Monna Giovanna. Rejected, he withdrew to a life of poverty, with only a beloved falcon remaining of all his former possessions. The woman's husband died. Her son, who had grown fond of Federigo's falcon, became seriously ill and asked Monna to obtain the falcon for his comfort. She reluctantly went to Federigo to request the falcon. Federigo was overwhelmed with excitement by her visit, and he was determined, in spite of his poverty, to entertain her properly. But his cupboard was bare, so he killed the falcon and served it to her. They discovered their misunderstanding, and the mother returned empty-handed to her boy, who soon died. But the childless widow, impressed by Federigo's generous gesture in offering his falcon, chose him for her second husband.

Such a story, reduced in this way to a bare outline, could have been made into any number of fully realized plots with radically different effects. It could have been a farce, stressing Federigo's foolish extravagance, his ridiculous antics in trying to think of something to serve his beloved for breakfast, and the absurdity of the surprise ending. It could have been

[4] Mark Harris, "Easy Does It Not," in *The Living Novel*, ed. Granville Hicks (New York, 1957), p. 117.

[5] *The Craft of Fiction* (London, 1921), p. 62.

a meditative or a comic piece on the ironical twists of fate, emphasizing the transformation in Monna from proud resistance to quick surrender—something on the order of Christopher Fry's *A Phoenix Too Frequent* as derived from Petronius. It could have been a sardonic tale written from the point of view of the husband and son who, like the falcon, must be killed off, as it were, to make the survivors happy. And so on.

As it is, every stroke is in a direction different from these. The finished tale is designed to give the reader the greatest possible pleasure in the sympathetic comedy of Monna's and Federigo's deserved good fortune, to make the reader delight in this instance of the announced theme for all the tales told on the fifth day: "good fortune befalling lovers after divers direful or disastrous adventures."[6] Though one never views these characters or their "direful or disastrous adventures" in anything like a tragic light, and though, in fact, one laughs at the excesses of Federigo's passion and at his willingness to pursue it even to poverty, our laughter must always be sympathetic. Much as Federigo deserves his disasters, in the finished tale he also deserves the supreme good fortune of winning Monna.

To insure our pleasure in such an outcome—a pleasure which might have been mild indeed considering that there are nine other tales attempting something like the same effect—the two main characters must be established with great precision. First the heroine, Monna Giovanna, must be felt to be thoroughly worthy of Federigo's "extravagant" love. In a longer, different kind of story, this might have been done by showing her in virtuous action; one could take whatever space were required for episodes drama-

tizing her as worthy of Federigo's fantastic devotion. But here economy is at least as important as precision. And the economical method of imposing her virtues on the reader is for the narrator to *tell* us about them, supporting his telling with some judiciously chosen, and by modern standards very brief and unrealistic, episodes. These can be of two kinds, either in the form of what James was later to call "going behind" to reveal the true workings of the heroine's mind and heart or in the form of overt action. Thus, the narrator begins by describing her as the "fairest" and "most elegant," and as "no less virtuous than fair." In a simple story of this kind, her beauty and elegance require for validation no more than Federigo's dramatized passion. Our belief in her virtue, however—certainly in Boccaccio a more unlikely gift than beauty and elegance—is supported both by her sustained chastity in the face of his courtship and, far more important, by the quality of what is revealed whenever we enter her thoughts.

Whereupon the lady was silent a while, bethinking her what she should do. She knew that Federigo had long loved her, and had never had so much as a single kind look from her: wherefore she said to herself:—How can I send or go to beg of him this falcon, which by what I hear is the best that ever flew, and moreover is his sole comfort? And how could I be so unfeeling as to seek to deprive a gentleman of the one solace that is now left him? And so, albeit she very well knew that she might have the falcon for the asking, she was perplexed, and knew not what to say, and gave her son no answer. At length, however, the love she bore the boy carried the day, and she made up her mind, for his contentment . . . to go herself and fetch him the falcon.

The interest in this passage lies of course in the moral choice that it presents and in the effect upon our sentiments that is implicit in that choice.

---

[6] Trans. J. M. Rigg (Everyman ed., 1930). All quotations are from this edition.

Though the choice is in one respect a relatively trivial one, it is far more important than most choices faced by the characters who people Boccaccio's world. Dramatized at greater length, it could in fact have been made into the central episode for the story—though the story that resulted would be a far different one from what we now have. As it is treated here, the choice is given precisely the degree of importance it should have in the whole. Because we experience Monna's thoughts and feelings at first hand, we are forced to agree with the narrator's assessment of her great worth. She is not simply virtuous in conventional matters like chastity, but she is also capable of moral delicacy in more fundamental matters: unlike the majority of Boccaccio's women, she is above any casual manipulation of her lover for her own purposes. Even this delicacy, admirable in itself, can be overridden by a more important value, "the love she bore the boy." Yet all this is kept strictly serviceable to our greater interest in Federigo and the falcon; there is never any question of our becoming sidetracked into deep psychological or sentimental involvement with her as a person.

Because the narrator has *told* us what to think of her, and then *shown* her briefly in support of his claims, all the while keeping our sympathy and admiration carefully subordinated to the comic effect of the whole, we can move to the most important episode with our expectations clear and—in their own kind—intense. We can move to Monna's relatively long and wonderfully delicate speech to Federigo requesting the falcon, with our hopes centered clearly on the "good fortune" of their ultimate union.

If all this skilful presentation of the admirable Monna is to succeed, we must see Federigo himself as an equally admirable, though not really heroic, figure. Too much moral stature will spoil the comedy; too little will destroy our desire for his success. It is not enough to show his virtues through his actions; his only admirable act is the gift of the falcon and that might be easily interpreted in itself as a further bit of foolish extravagance. Unless the story is to be lengthened unduly with episodes showing that he is worthy, in spite of his extravagance, the narrator must give us briefly and directly the necessary information about his true character. He is therefore described, unobtrusively but in terms that only an omniscient narrator could use with success, as "gallant," "full of courtesy," "patient," and most important of all, as "more in love than ever before"; the world of *his* desires is thus set off distinctly from the world of many of the other tales, where love is reduced for comic purposes to lust.

These completely straightforward statements of the narrator's opinions are supported by what we see of Federigo's own mind. His comic distress over not having anything to feed his beloved visitor, and his unflinching sacrifice of the bird, are rendered in intimate detail, with frequent —though by modern standards certainly shallow—inside views; his poverty "was brought home to him," he was "distressed beyond measure," he "inwardly" cursed "his evil fortune." "Sorely he longed that the lady might not leave his house altogether unhonoured, and yet to crave help of his own husbandman was more than his pride could brook." All this insures that the wonderful comedy of the breakfast will be the comedy of sympathetic laughter: we are throughout completely in favor of Federigo's suit. And our favor is heightened by the method of presenting the scene of discovery. "No sooner had Federigo apprehended what the lady wanted, than, *for grief that 'twas not in his power to serve her* . . . he fell a-weeping. . . ." At first Monna supposed that

" 'twas only because he was loath to part with the brave falcon that he wept." We might have made the same mistake but for the author's help provided in the clause I have italicized.

Once we have become assured of his character in this way, Federigo's speeches, like Monna Giovanna's, become the equivalent of inside views, because we know that everything he says is a trustworthy reflection of his true state of mind. His long speech of explanation about the falcon serves, as a result, to confirm all we have learned of him; when he concludes, "I doubt I shall never know peace of mind more," we believe in his sincerity, though of course we know with complete certainty, and have known from the beginning, that the story is to end with "good fortune."

Having seen this much, we need little more. To make Monna the heiress as provided in the will, her son must die in a passage only one or two lines longer than the one or two lines earlier given to the death of the husband. Her "inward commendation" of Federigo's "magnanimity" leads her to the decision to marry him rather than a wealthy suitor: "I had rather have a man without wealth than wealth without a man." Federigo is a man, as we know by now. Though his portrait is conventional, "flat," "two-dimensional," it includes everything we need. We can thus accept without irony the narrator's concluding judgment that married to such a wife he lived happily to the end of his days. Fiammetta's auditors all "praised God that He had worthily rewarded Federigo."

If we share in the pleasure of seeing the comic but worthy hero worthily rewarded, the reason is thus not to be found in any inherent quality of the materials but rather in the skilful construction of a living plot out of materials that might have been used in many different ways. The deaths of the husband and son, which in the finished version are merely conveniences for Federigo's exaltation, would in any truly impartial account occupy considerably more space than Federigo's anxiety over not having anything to serve his mistress. Treated impartially, the boy's death would certainly be dramatized as fully as the mother's hesitation about troubling Federigo for his falcon. But the demands of this plot are for a technique that wins us to Federigo's side.

Quite obviously this technique cannot be judged by modern standards of consistency; the story could not have been written from a consistent point of view without stretching it to three times its present length and thereby losing its taut comic force. To tell it entirely through Federigo's eyes would require a much longer introductory section, and the comedy of the visit to fetch the falcon would be partially lost if we did not see more of the preparation for it than Federigo can possibly be aware of. Yet since it is primarily Federigo's story, to see it through Monna's eyes would require a great deal of manipulation and extension. Such conjectural emendations are in a way absurd, since they almost certainly would never have occurred to Boccaccio. But they help to make emphatic the great gap that separates Boccaccio's technique from the more obviously rigorous methods we have come to look for. In this story there is no important revelation of truth, no intensity of illusion, no ironic complexity, no prophetic vision, no rich portrayal of moral ambiguities. There is some incidental irony, it is true, but the greatness of the whole resides in unequivocal intensity not of illusion but of comic delight produced in extraordinarily brief compass.

Any temptation we might have to attribute its success to unconscious or accidental primitivism can be dispelled by looking at the radically different experience offered by other tales. Since his different effects are based on different moral codes, Boccaccio can never assume that his readers will hold precisely the correct attitudes as they approach any one story. He certainly does not assume that his readers will approve of the license of his most licentious tales. Even Dioneo, the most lewd of all the ten narrators, must spend a good deal of energy manipulating us into the camp of those who can laugh with a clear conscience at his bawdy and often cruel stories. In the potentially distressing tale of how the holy man, Rustico, debauches the young and innocent Alibech by teaching her how to put the devil in hell (third day, tenth tale), great care is taken with the character and ultimate fate of the simple-minded girl in order to lead us to laugh at conduct that in most worlds, including the world in which Boccaccio lived, would be considered cruel and sacrilegious rather than comic.

If Dioneo, the lusty young courtier, must use care with his rhetoric in a bawdy tale, Fiammetta, the lovely lady, must use even more when she comes to praise infidelity. On the seventh day the subject is "the tricks which, either for love or for their deliverance from peril, ladies have heretofore played their husbands, and whether they were by the said husbands detected, or no." In "The Falcon" Fiammetta worked to build admiration for the virtue of Federigo and Monna Giovanna; she now (fifth tale) employs a different rhetoric. Since her task is to insure our delight in the punishment of a justifiably jealous husband, her commentary tells us directly what is borne out by our views of the husband's mind: he is "a poor creature, and of little sense" who deserves what he gets. More important, she prefaces the story

with a little oration, about one-seventh of the length of the whole story, setting our values straight: "For which reason, to sum up, I say that a wife is rather to be commended than censured, if she take her revenge upon a husband that is jealous without cause."

In support of this general argument, the whole tale is manipulated in such a way as to make the reader desire the comic punishment of the husband. Most of it is seen through the eyes of the woman, with great stress on her comic suffering at the hands of the great bullying fool. The climax is his full punishment, in the form of a clever, lashing speech from his wife. Few readers can feel that he has received anything but what he deserves when Fiammetta concludes that the cuckold's wife has now earned her "charter of indulgence."

These extremes by no means exhaust the variety of norms that we are led to accept by the shifting rhetoric as we move through the *Decameron*. The standards of judgment change so radically, in fact, that it is difficult to discern any figure in Boccaccio's carpet.[7] I shall try later on to deal with some of the

---

[7] Erich Auerbach, for example, complains that he can find no basic moral attitude and no clear approach to reality lying back of all the tales. So long as he considers what Boccaccio does "for the sake of the comic effect," he has nothing but praise for his "critical sense" of the world, "firm yet elastic in perspective, which, without abstract moralizing, allots phenomena their specific, carefully nuanced moral value" (*Mimesis: The Representation of Reality in Western Literature* [Berne, 1946], trans. Willard Trask [Anchor Books ed., 1957], p. 193). It is only on the level of the most general qualities, common to all the stories despite the differing needs of the moment, that Auerbach encounters difficulties and complains of the "vagueness and uncertainty" of Boccaccio's "early humanism" (p. 202). Auerbach's account is invaluable in showing how Boccaccio's style, in so far as it is common to all of the tales, serves as a kind of rhetoric convincing the reader of the reality of his world.

issues raised when an author heightens specific effects at the expense of his general notions of moral truth or reality. What is important here is to recognize the radical inadequacy of the telling-showing distinction in dealing with the practice of this one author. Boccaccio's artistry lies not in adherence to any one supreme manner of narration but rather in his ability to order various forms of telling in the service of various forms of showing.

THE AUTHOR'S MANY VOICES

In the next three chapters I shall look in detail at some of the more important arguments for authorial objectivity or impersonality. Most of these call for eliminating certain overt signs of the author's presence. As we might expect, however, one man's objectivity is another man's bête noire. If we are to have any degree of clarity as we make our way through attacks on the author's voice, we must have some preliminary notion of the variety of forms that voice can take, both in fiction and in attacks on fiction. What is it, in fact, that we might expunge if we attempted to drive the author from the house of fiction?

First, we must erase all direct addresses to the reader, all commentary in the author's own name. When the author of the *Decameron* speaks to us directly, in both the introduction and conclusion, whatever illusion we may have had that we are dealing immediately with Fiammetta and her friends is shattered. An astonishing number of authors and critics since Flaubert have agreed that such direct, unmediated commentary will not do. And even those authors who would allow it have often, like E. M. Forster, forbidden it except on certain limited subjects.[8]

But what, really, is "commentary"? If we agree to eliminate all personal intrusions of the kind used by Fielding, do we then agree to expunge less obtrusive comment? Is Flaubert violating his own principles of impersonality when he allows himself to tell us that in such and such a place one finds the worst Neufchatel cheeses of the entire district, or that Emma was "incapable of understanding what she didn't experience, or of recognizing anything that wasn't expressed in conventional terms"?[9]

Even if we eliminate all such explicit judgments, the author's presence will be obvious on every occasion when he moves into or out of a character's mind—when he "shifts his point of view," as we have come to put it. Flaubert tells us that Emma's little attentions to Charles were "never, as he believed, for his sake . . . but for her own, out of exasperated vanity" (p. 69). It is clearly Flaubert who constructs this juxtaposition of Emma's motive with Charles' belief about the motive, and the same obtrusive "voice" is evident whenever a new mind is introduced. When Emma's father bids farewell to Emma and Charles, he remembers "his own wedding, his own earlier days. . . . He, too, had been very happy. . . . He felt dismal, like a stripped and empty house" (pp. 34–35). This momentary shift to Rouault is Flaubert's way of providing us with an evaluation of the marriage and a sense of what is to come. If we are troubled by all reminders of the author's presence, we shall be troubled here.

But if we are to object to this, why not go the next step and object to all inside

---

[8] Forster would not allow the author to take "the reader into his confidence about his char-

acters," since "intimacy is gained but at the expense of illusion and nobility." But he allows the author to take the reader into his confidence "about the universe" (*Aspects of the Novel* [London, 1927], pp. 111–12).

[9] *Madame Bovary*, trans. Francis Steegmuller (New York, 1957), p. 80.

views, not simply those that require a shift in point of view. In life such views are not to be had. The act of providing them in fiction is itself an obtrusion by the author.[10]

For that matter, we must object to the reliable statements of any dramatized character, not just the author in his own voice, because the act of narration as performed by even the most highly dramatized narrator is itself the author's presentation of a prolonged "inside view" of a character. When Fiammetta says "the love she bore the boy carried the day," she is giving us a reliable inside view of Monna, and she is also giving a view of her own evaluation of events. Both are reminders of the author's controlling hand.

But why stop here? The author is present in every speech given by any character who has had conferred upon him, in whatever manner, the badge of reliability. Once we know that God is God in Job, once we know that Monna speaks only truth in "The Falcon," the authors speak whenever God and Monna speak. Introducing the great Doctor Larivière, Flaubert says:

He belonged to that great surgical school created by Bichat—that generation, now vanished, of philosopher-practitioners, who cherished their art with fanatical love and applied it with enthusiasm and sagacity. Everyone in his hospital trembled when he was angry; and his students so revered him that the moment they set up for themselves they imitated him as much as they could. . . . Disdainful of decorations . . . hospitable, generous, a father to the poor, practicing Christian virtues although an unbeliever, he might have been thought of as a saint if he hadn't been feared as a devil because of the keenness of his mind [pp. 363–364].

This unambiguous bestowal of authority contributes greatly to the power of the next few pages, in which Larivière judges for us everything that we see. But helpful as he is, he must go—if the author's voice is a fault.

Even here we cannot stop, though many of the critics of the author's voice have stopped here. We can go on and on, purging the work of every recognizably personal touch, every distinctive literary allusion or colorful metaphor, every pattern of myth or symbol; they all implicitly evaluate. Any discerning reader can recognize that they are imposed by the author.[11]

Finally, we might even follow Jean-Paul Sartre and object, in the name of "durational realism," to all evidences of the author's meddling with the natural sequence, proportion, or duration of events. Earlier authors, Sartre says, tried to justify "the foolish business of story-

---

[10] Such obtrusions are especially obvious in narration that purports to be historical. And yet intelligent men were until quite recently able to read ostensibly historical accounts, like the Bible, packed with such illicit entries into private minds, with no distress whatever. For us it may seem strange that the writers of the Gospels should claim so much knowledge of what Christ is feeling and thinking. "Moved with pity, he stretched out his hand and touched him" (Mark 1:41). "And Jesus, perceiving in himself that power had gone forth from him . . ." (5:30). Who reported to the authors these internal events? Who told them what occurs in the Garden, when everyone but Jesus is asleep? Who reported to them that Christ prays to God to "let this cup pass"? Such questions, like the question of how Moses could have written an account of his own death and burial, may be indispensable in historical criticism, but they can easily be overdone in literary criticism.

[11] Speaking of Joyce's *Ulysses*, Edmund Wilson once complained that as soon as "we are aware of Joyce himself systematically embroidering on his text," packing in puzzles, symbols, and puns, "the illusion of the dream is lost" ("James Joyce," *Axel's Castle* [New York, 1931], p. 235).

telling by ceaselessly bringing to the reader's attention, explicitly or by allusion, the existence of an author." The existentialist novels, in contrast, will be "toboggans, forgotten, unnoticed," hurling the reader "into the midst of a universe where there are no witnesses." Novels should "exist in the manner of things, of plants, of events, and not at first like products of man."[12] If this is so, the author must never summarize, never curtail a conversation, never telescope the events of three days into a paragraph. "If I pack six months into a single page, the reader jumps out of the book" (p. 229).

Sartre is certainly right in claiming that all these things are signs of the author's manipulating presence. In *The Brothers Karamazov*, for example, the story of Father Zossima's conversion could logically be placed anywhere. The events of Zossima's story took place long before the novel begins; unless they are to be placed at the beginning, which is out of the question, there is no natural reason for giving them in one place rather than another. Wherever they are placed, they will call attention to the author's selecting presence, just as Homer is glaringly present to us whenever the *Odyssey* takes one of its many leaps back and forth over a nineteen-year period. It is not accident but Dostoevski's careful choice that gives us Zossima's story as the sequel to Ivan's dream of the Grand Inquisitor. It is intended as a judgment on the values implied by that dream, just as everything that happens to Ivan afterward is an explicit criticism of his own ideas. Since the sequence is obviously not

dictated by anything other than the author's purposes, it betrays the author's voice, and according to Sartre, it presumably will not do.

But, as Sartre woefully admits (see chap. iii, below), even with all these forms of the author's voice expunged, what we have left will reveal to us a shameful artificiality. Unless the author contents himself with simply retelling The Three Bears or the story of Oedipus in the precise form in which they exist in popular accounts—and even so there must be some choice of *which* popular form to tell—his very choice of what he tells will betray him to the reader. He chooses to tell the tale of Odysseus rather than that of Circe or Polyphemus. He chooses to tell the cheerful tale of Monna and Federigo rather than a pathetic account of Monna's husband and son. He chooses to tell the story of Emma Bovary rather than the potentially heroic tale of Dr. Larivière. The author's voice is as passionately revealed in the decision to write the *Odyssey*, "The Falcon," or *Madame Bovary* as it is in the most obtrusive direct comment of the kind employed by Fielding, Dickens, or George Eliot. Everything he *shows* will serve to *tell*; the line between showing and telling is always to some degree an arbitrary one.

In short, the author's judgment is always present, always evident to anyone who knows how to look for it. Whether its particular forms are harmful or serviceable is always a complex question, a question that cannot be settled by any easy reference to abstract rules. As we begin now to deal with this question, we must never forget that though the author can to some extent choose his disguises, he can never choose to disappear.

[12] "Situation of the Writer in 1947," *What Is Literature?* trans. Bernard Frechtman (London, 1950), p. 169.

Howard Nemerov

COMPOSITION AND FATE IN THE SHORT NOVEL

Howard Nemerov is perhaps best known as poet and novelist (*The Homecoming Game*, 1957), although he has written enough criticism to comprise a volume, *Poetry and Fiction: Essays* (1963), in which this selection was included. He taught for many years at Bennington College and is now Professor of English at Brandeis University. "Composition and Fate in the Short Novel" was originally published in *The Graduate Journal* in 1963.

The writer attempting for the first time a short novel must face, I should think, nothing but problems, the first, though probably the least, of which is, What are short novels? For the writer who is by habit of mind a novelist they must represent not simply a compression but a corresponding rhythmic intensification, a more refined criterion of relevance than the one he usually enjoys, an austerity and economy perhaps somewhat compulsive in the intention itself. For the writer who habitually thinks in short stories—a bad habit, by the way—the challenge is probably greater: he will have to learn as never before about the interstices of his action; he will have to think about a fairly large space which must be filled, not with everything (his complaint against the novelist), but with something definite which must be made to yield in a quite explicit way its most reserved and recondite ranges of feeling; he will have to think, for once, of design and not merely of plot. To both writers

it must soon become apparent that a short novel is something in itself, neither a lengthily written short story nor the refurbished attempt at a novel sent out into the world with its hat clapped on at the eightieth page.

I am speaking, perhaps, ideally, and about the ideal; it is difficult not to. For quite apart from technical considerations, the tradition of the short novel—perhaps because for so long it was commercially useless and unacceptable—is a tradition of masterpieces; further than that, the composers of this tradition of masterpieces are almost without exception the composers of still greater works, such as *Moby Dick, War and Peace, The Possessed, The Magic Mountain,* and so on, from which their short novels differ, in fact, by a kind of intensification of art, by a closed and resonant style of composition suggestive of the demonstrations of mathematics or chess.

The writer proposing to himself a short novel probably ought not to scare him-

120

self with the thought that he is entering that kind of competition; once he begins, of course, he will resolutely forget all about those great men and their works, and pay his exclusive attention to the business in hand. Again, though, the game is scarcely worth playing without an acknowledgment of its specific difficulties; the specific difficulties, if they can be identified, are what define the form—without them it is not a form but only so and so many thousand words—and in a discussion like this one I see no way of approaching the matter at all except by attending to the ideal so far as it can be deduced from great examples.

The material economy of the short novel, and its strict analogical style of composition, seem to be functions one of the other. The epitome of the first point, material economy, I must fetch from far away; it seems brilliantly expressed in a discussion of variety in the creation, by Thomas Aquinas, who says that although an angel is a better thing, objectively considered, than a stone, yet a universe composed of two angels is inferior to a universe composed of one angel and one stone. A variousness so strictly limited and identified as that characterizes, as though by satiric exaggeration, the universe of the short novel. As to the strict and analogical style of composition, I shall quote a somewhat extended but very rewarding anecdote from the autobiography of a most admirable novelist, Vladimir Nabokov:

The place is . . . Abbazia, on the Adriatic. About the same time, at a cafe in nearby Fiume, my father happened to notice, just as we were being served, two Japanese officers at a table near us, and we immediately left—not without my hastily snatching a whole *bombe* of lemon sherbet, which I carried away secreted in my aching mouth. The year was 1904. I was five. Russia was fighting Japan. With hearty relish, the English illustrated weekly Miss Norcott subscribed to reproduced pictures by Japanese artists that showed how the Russian locomotives—made singularly toylike by the Japanese pictorial style—would drown if our Army tried to lay rails across the treacherous ice of Lake Baikal.

But let me see. I had an even earlier association with that war. One afternoon at the beginning of the same year, in our St. Petersburg house, I was led down from the nursery into my father's study to say how-do-you-do to a friend of the family, General Kuropatkin. To amuse me, he spread out a handful of matches on the divan where he was sitting, placed ten of them end to end to make a horizontal line and said, "This is the sea in calm weather." Then he tipped up each pair so as to turn the straight line into a zigzag—and that was "a stormy sea." He scrambled the matches and was about to do, I hoped, a better trick when we were interrupted. His aide-de-camp was shown in and said something to him. With a Russian, flustered grunt, Kuropatkin immediately rose from his seat, the loose matches jumping up on the divan as his weight left it. That day, he had been ordered to assume supreme command of the Russian Army in the Far East.

This incident had a special sequel fifteen years later, when at a certain point of my father's flight from Bolshevik-held St. Petersburg to southern Russia, he was accosted, while crossing a bridge, by an old man who looked like a grey-bearded peasant in his sheepskin coat. He asked my father for a light. The next moment each recognized the other. Whether or not old Kuropatkin, in his rustic disguise, managed to evade Soviet imprisonment, is immaterial. What pleases me is the evolution of the match theme; those magic ones he had shown me had been trifled with and mislaid, and his armies had also vanished, and everything had fallen through, like my toy trains that, in the winter of 1904–05, in Wiesbaden, I tried to run over the frozen puddles in the grounds of the Hotel Oranien. The following of such thematic designs through one's life should be, I think, the true purpose of autobiography.

—*Speak, Memory*, 1951, pp. 15–17.

A good deal that characterizes the composition of short novels is summed up and lightly demonstrated in this passage, even to a certain ruthlessness: "Whether or not old Kuropatkin . . . managed to evade Soviet imprisonment, is immaterial." And "the evolution of the match theme," with the problems attendant on it, is my proper subject here. But before going on to discuss examples I will try to suggest, without wasting time on attempts at unexceptionable definition, some of the things, other than length, which seem to set the novella apart from the short story and the novel. For the term "short novel" is descriptive only in the way that the term "Middle Ages" is descriptive—that is, not at all, except with reference to the territory on either side. And just as historians exaggerate the darkness of the Dark Ages and the brightness of the Renaissance, I shall exaggerate some elements of the short story and the novel, to make the middle term more visible.

The short story at present is a way of transacting one's fictional business which is shiny, efficient, and inexpensive; consequently it has become very attractive to non-artists. If publishers tell us despite this that collections of short stories rarely succeed, that is probably because everyone is too busy writing his own to be able to read anyone else's. To write a fine short story may be harder now than it has ever been, but there is no indication that large numbers of short story writers are aware of the fact. There are many honorable exceptions, perhaps, submerged in the flood of junk—commercial junk, high-literary junk, undergraduate junk, much of it competent and even attractive, but bearing too much the mark of the machine to give, even at the best, any deep pleasure. Short stories amount for the most part to parlor tricks, party favors with built-in snappers, gadgets for inducing recognitions and reversals: a small pump serves to build up the pressure, a tiny trigger releases it, there follow a puff and a flash as freedom and necessity combine; finally a Celluloid doll drops from the muzzle and descends by parachute to the floor. These things happen, but they happen to no one in particular.

Of many possible reasons why this fate has overtaken the short story, one must be the vast quantity of such stuff produced every day of every week and published in newspapers and magazines, on radio and television (for those "dramas" are either adapted from short stories or made up with the same requirements in mind). That so much of our experience, or the stereotype which passes for it, should be dealt with by means of the short story is perhaps the symptom, not unnoticeable elsewhere in the public domain, of an unlovely cynicism about human character, a propensity to see *individual* behavior as purely atmospheric—*colorful*, as they call it—and accordingly to require stereotyped behavior for everything having to do with the essential action. To invent an example: our hero is individual to the point of eccentricity, he is weirdly named Cyrus Pyracanth, he suffers from hemophilia, keeps pet snakes, and smokes a nargileh; but when it comes to the point, none of this has anything to do with the action his author requires him to perform, for the sake of which he might be called Mr. X and live in Bronxville on an average income and a moral equipment supplied by *Time* magazine or some other leading wholesaler. What has happened to him in the short story is not that he has lost his inwardness; only that for all practical purposes (the writer's purposes) it has ceased to matter.

It is natural that the mass production of short fiction should exert great pressure to bring the story down to its me- chanically imitable elements, so that it provides solutions at the expense of prob- lems, answers to which no one has asked the question; there is, indeed, a certain aesthetic pleasure to be gained from the contemplation of simple and pretty com- binations purified, as in the detective story, of human complication and human depth; but it is a pleasure easily ex- hausted. The story gets its power from a whole implied drama which it does not tell aloud; its neglect of that implication reduces it to clever trickery. There is much to be said for clever trickery as a contributing means to great works, nor do great novelists often neglect this part of art which is purely artifice—but when there is little or nothing else, and when in addition all the tricks have been played so many times . . . ?

This is not simply a question of length, but much rather a question of depth; when a short story's action comprises, by brilliant symbolic reflection, the whole of a life, it becomes novelistic. I think in this connection of two stories by Kay Boyle, "Keep Your Pity" and "Dear Mr. Walrus." Neither exceeds thirty pages, but those pages are written throughout with the kind of attention sometimes held to be proper only for poetry (I do not mean what is called "poetic prose," rather the reverse), whereas short stories such as I have been talking about usually betray themselves as having been written only with a view to the ending.

The word "novel" will cover a multi- tude of sins. I can think of an author "writing" a novella, but this simple term will not do for a novel, where I have to think of him "sitting down at his desk" and "addressing himself to the task." I think of lavish productions, casts of thousands, full technicolor, photographed against authentic backgrounds, and so on. Not all of this is accurate, or it need

not be, but I emphasize it for the sake of a contrast; besides, when faced with the need for a commanding generality on this topic, I find myself to have forgotten all the novels I have ever read. The contrast I want to bring out is this: for many novelists, all but the simplest element of compositional art (the plot) is destroyed by observation, by detail work, by reality which keeps poking its head in. The leisure, the "warm earthy humanity," of the novel owes itself to this considera- tion: people read novellas, but they tend to live in novels, and sometimes they live there very comfortably indeed: thus you have descriptions which are nothing but descriptions, thus you have philosophical excursions, set-pieces, summaries, double plot, and full orchestration, not to men- tion that all the chairs are heavily uphol- stered and even the walls padded. Sten- dhal provided benches for the reader to sit down on, but many novelists erect hotels for the same laudable accommoda- tion.

Let me try to bring this distinction back down to the ground. The master novelist is Shakespearean in combinative skill, if not in language: he handles actions which are long, complex, serious, and explicitly generalized through the social and political fabric, e.g., *The Pos- sessed, War and Peace, The Red and the Black, Remembrance of Things Past.* The authors of such works are masters in parable and reality simultaneously. Then there are masters in parable, and I would only indicate the range of this art by mentioning together the names of Jane Austen and Franz Kafka; if I say that *Emma* and *The Trial* are, for me, like short novels in spite of their length, that will suggest my feeling that the name "short novel" does not exactly discrimi- nate, and that some such terms as "sim- ple" and "complex" novels might be used instead. A few lesser examples may help here: Mrs. Compton-Burnett writes short novels at whatever length, as do Graham Greene and Henry Green and Virginia Woolf. I need hardly say that the distinction is not one of quality any more than it is one of length. *The Counterfeiters* means to be a novel, so does *Point Counter Point*, so does *Nostromo*, so does *Tender Is the Night*, but I do not prefer them before *Lafcadio's Adventures, After Many a Summer Dies the Swan, The Secret Agent*, or *The Great Gatsby*, which are examples of the other kind.

I favor this distinction of the simple and complex, the Greek drama and the Shakespearean, over the other which seems to be based purely on length. Simple novels will normally be shorter than complex ones anyhow, though not always—I notice for instance that Cyril Connolly refers to *Gatsby* and *The Spoils of Poynton* together as short novels, and I, sharing his feeling or mistaken memory as to the latter, was surprised to find it just twice as long as *Gatsby*. But I shall not insist on these terms, simple and complex, and will draw my illustrations in the following discussion from novels generally allowed to be *short* ones.

We have, after all, only two ways of thinking about literary composition. In one, general ideas are illustrated by appropriate particulars; in the other, the contemplation of particulars produces general ideas. Perhaps neither of these species can ever be seen in purity and isolation in any given work, especially since the work as we read it offers no certain guide to the means of its composition, so that all literary composition appears as a combination of these extremes, possibly to be characterized by the dominance of one or the other. The pure state of the first kind, in which the author determines first upon a more or less systematic arrangement of general notions, then devises particular appearances for them, would be allegory of the most rigorously scientific sort, like an equation; literary allegories can never be quite that rigid, because every particular does more than illustrate, it modifies the general idea. The pure state of the second kind would exist only if the contemplation of particulars quite failed to produce general ideas and systematic meanings, but produced only the intense view of particulars as themselves the *irrational* demonstration of the nature of things: symbolism is a way station on this road which runs further to expressionism, surrealism, dada, and the riddles of the Zen Koan.

It is fashionably believed at present that the artist belongs finally to the irrational, that his is the ecstasy of the unique, the individual and irreducible, the opaque detail existing in and for itself; conversely, that reason, construction, architecture of general ideas, will destroy him as an artist. It is a theme which I shall not develop at large in this place, but the tradition of the short novel offers a good deal of evidence for the opposite view. The most striking element shared by almost all the great pieces in this genre is their outright concentration upon traditional problems of philosophy, the boldness of their venture into generality, the evidence they give of direct and profound moral concern. We are not entitled to suppose, of course, that such works were composed from the point of view first of general ideas and philosophic problems and paradoxes, even though sometimes—as with the *Notes from the Underground*, for example—it is tempting so to suppose. What we may insist is that these works combine with their actions a most explicit awareness of themselves as parables, as philosophic myths, and almost invariably announce and demonstrate the intention of discursive profundity—the intention, it is not too much to say, of becoming sacred books: final instances, exhaustively analyzed, of a symbolic universe of whose truth we can be persuaded only by fictions. The result for composition is that problem becomes the center of the short novel, which with a peculiar purity dramatizes conflicts of appearance and reality (*Benito Cereno*), freedom and necessity (*Notes from the Underground*), madness and sanity (*Ward Number Six*); all these are of course forms of a single problem essential and not accidental to the genre, which I shall try to illustrate by describing and giving examples of one theme which is pervasive to the point of obsession in the short novel.

The theme is broadly speaking that of *identity*, and the action deriving from it may be generalized as follows: the mutual attachment or dependency between A and B has a mortal strength; its dissolution requires a crisis fatal to one or the other party; but this dissolution is represented as salvation.

It is clear from many examples that the story of the Passion itself, with its suffering and dying Redeemer, sin-eater, scapegoat, is explicitly thought of in connection with this theme, which may be told as a religious parable, an adventure story, a fantasy, a psychological novel, often with strong homosexual or narcissistic emphasis.

1. The most literal form of this attachment occurs in the conclusion of *St. Julian the Hospitaler*, which Flaubert adapted from the *Gesta Romanorum* (though the story embodies even older materials, such as the legends of St. Hubert and St. Christopher). Julian's final penance is to lie down in the embrace of the leper, who turns into a bright angelic being and takes him to heaven.

2. In *The Private Memoirs and Con-*fessions of a Justified Sinner, by James Hogg, the self-righteous man is seduced and destroyed by the Prince of Darkness who appears as his double; whether his repentance speaks much for self-knowledge may be doubtful enough, but there is a redemptive note in the circumstance that he ends his life in a manger, "a byre, or cowhouse . . . where, on a divot loft, my humble bedstead stood, and the cattle grunted and puffed below me."

3. Melville's short novels, those combinations of the most baldly stated symbolism with the most mysterious ambiguousness of resolution, explore this theme. Captain Delano in his benign unworldliness and innocence becomes responsible for Benito Cereno, through whose sufferings and death he is enabled to perceive, beneath appearances, how things really are. The Master in Chancery becomes liable personally, morally, religiously, and at one point legally, for Bartleby. His final phrase of sorrowful commiseration—"Ah, Bartleby! Ah, humanity!"—gains a certain force of revelation from being compared with some of his earlier statements, e.g., "I am a man who, from his youth upward, has been filled with a profound conviction that the easiest way of life is the best." *Billy Budd* is a somewhat more complex rendering. Billy and Claggart are represented as eternally fated to one another; beyond that it is Captain Vere who suffers the "mystery of iniquity" of this predestinated encounter. Billy suffers as Adam tempted and fallen, as Cain whose brother (Claggart) is preferred before him, as the Son of God whose death redeems to order an unruly people (the mutinous Navy), but who is publicly misrepresented in history (the newspaper article) and art (the ballad). Other, less religious interpretation is possible, but enough has been said for the present purpose.

4. In Conrad's *The Secret Sharer* the story is told with a particular purity as well as a rare optimism (in other examples where the disappearance of one party is allowed to do for his death, that disappearance is usually into an insane asylum). The young captain, irresolute and uncertain in his first command, comes face to face with his double: "It was, in the night, as though I had been faced by my own reflection in the depths of a somber and immense mirror." By protecting Leggatt (a legate from the darkness of the sea outside and the self within), by sharing his identity, by experiencing in homeopathic amounts the criminal element in his own nature, by at last liberating, or separating, this other self from his own at the risk of shipwreck, the young man gains a "perfect communion" with his first command.

Marlow says of Kurtz, "It was written I should be loyal to the nightmare of my choice," and he is loyal to the final extent of lying for him, though "there is a taint of death, a flavor of mortality, in lies." The view of Kurtz as scapegoat, as evil or fallen savior, is generalized throughout, notably in what Marlow says to his audience, those nameless masters of the world, the Director of Companies, the Lawyer, the Narrator: "You can't understand. How could you?—with solid pavement under your feet, surrounded by kind neighbors ready to cheer you or fall on you, stepping delicately between the butcher and the policeman, in the holy terror of scandal and gallows and lunatic asylums—how can you imagine what particular region of the first ages a man's untrammeled feet may take him into by the way of solitude—utter solitude without a policeman—by the way of silence —utter silence, where no warning voice of a kind neighbor can be heard whispering of public opinion. These little things make all the great difference." So Kurtz is an instance of absolute power corrupted absolutely, yes, but this power is further characterized as that of the impulsive, archaic life liberated, which no man can bear and live, which Marlow himself nearly died of the briefest and most homeopathic contact with, and which in some sense is the force that makes history and makes civilization.

5. The theme we are describing is of the first importance to Dostoevsky, who intensifies both the psychological penetration of the treatment and its ultimate religious or metaphysical expansions. The typical bond, between the worldly man and his sinister, underworld, epicene counterpart—his "poor relation," as the Devil is called in *The Brothers Karamazov*—occurs in the major novels in such double figures as Ivan and Smerdyakov, Ivan and the Devil, Christ and the Grand Inquisitor, Stavrogin and Pyotr Stepanovich, and, with a quite different tonality, Muishkin and Rogozhin. Two of the short novels concentrate exclusively on the development of this theme. *The Eternal Husband* ties together the seducer and the cuckold in a relation characterized as ambiguously homosexual and sadistic, a comedy agonizing enough but hardly more so than that of *The Double*, which relates how poor, stupid Mr. Golyadkin, portrayed from the outset as suffering symptoms of paranoia, comes face to face with his double, Golyadkin, Jr., who behaves insufferably, calls him "darling," pinches his cheek, embarrasses him in every way public and private, until the original Golyadkin, what remains of him, is driven off to the asylum. In this last scene several people run after the carriage, shouting, until they are left behind, and "Mr. Golyadkin's unworthy twin kept up longer than anyone . . . he ran on with a satisfied air, skipping first to one and then to the other side of the carriage . . . poking his head in at the window,

and throwing farewell kisses to Mr. Goly-adkin."

6. Without giving any further examples in detail I may merely mention a few more short novels in which this theme is developed: in Chekhov's *Ward Number Six*, Andrew Ephimich and the young man Ivan Dimitrich Gronov; the young soldier and his captain in Lawrence's *The Prussian Officer*; Aschenbach and Tadzio in Mann's *Death in Venice*, Mario and Cipolla in his *Mario and the Magician*; the condemned man and the officer in *In the Penal Colony* by Kafka; Howe and Tertan in Lionel Trilling's *Of This Time, of That Place*; Wilhelm and Dr. Tamkin in Saul Bellow's *Seize the Day*.

My intention is to discuss composition in the strict sense, rather than to consider the interpretation and historical placement of this thematic insistence. Yet it is worth pausing here to observe in how many of these stories the theme is employed to show the man of the middle class, rational, worldly, either rather stupid or of a somewhat dry intelligence and limited vision, plunged into the domain of the forbidden, extravagant, and illicit, the life of the impulses beneath or the life of compulsive and punitive authority above, both of them equally regions in which every detail gains fatal significance, every perception is excruciatingly intensified, and every decision for salvation or doom: so it happens in various ways, to Captain Delano, the Master in Chancery, Ivan Ilyich, Gustave Aschenbach, Velchaninov, Gregor Samsa, the Woman Who Rode Away, Andrew Ephimich. . . . And it is remarkable, too, how often, by the device of the double, the incubus as it were, their sufferings and perceptions seem to invade them ambiguously from the world outside and the self within. I am tempted to think that the characteristic economy of the short novel, its precisely defined space,

the peculiar lucidity and simplicity of its internal forms—two or three persons, a single action, equal tension among the persons, each of whom has a fate—tends to involve the artist more overtly than usual in trying to expound by fantasies what he himself is and what he is doing in his art. Indeed, this is perhaps cryptically hinted to us by Flaubert, when he makes his Félicité suffer the lash of a coachman's whip on the road between Honfleur and Pont l'Eveque, where he himself, riding in a carriage, suffered his first attack of epilepsy, or serious hysteria. And by Melville, who sees his scrivener —unwilling to copy the writings of others —as having had the previous job of handling dead letters "and assorting them for the flames"—this in the year after a fire at the publishing house had destroyed the plates for Melville's own works. Less cryptically by Mann, who sees his artist-heroes by turns as diseased aristocrats, confidence men, and monstrous tyrants (Savonarola, Cipolla). For the fullest meaning of the theme, most minutely expounded, we should have to refer to Proust, who by the most intricately woven analogies throughout his immense work characterizes the moral isolation of the poet as, on the one hand, that of the invalid, the pervert, the criminal, the Jew, the traitor, and, on the other hand, that of the hero, aristocrat, doctor or surgeon, and commander of armies in the field.

Whether what I have tried to describe is the product of a limited historical tradition or of a tragic circumstance as near eternal as that witnessed to in Greek tragedies or in the Book of Job I am unable to say certainly and must not stop to debate here. So far as the theme results in actions typical of the short novel —actions simple and decisive, generally mortal in fact, and involving few persons

—the following points of compositional interest arise.

Whereas the short story tends to rest upon action, a combination of circumstances to which the characters must very readily conform, while the novel, especially in English, goes toward the opposite pole and tends to produce "characters" as an independent value, the short novel strikes a very delicate and exact balance between motive and circumstance; its action generally speaking is the fate of the agonists, and this fate is regarded as flowing demonstrably and with some precision and in great detail from their individual natures, which accordingly are developed at considerable length. I need barely mention examples: the portraits, as distinct from the stories, of e.g., Aschenbach, Captain Delano, The Man from Underground, Gabriel Conroy, John Marcher . . . What happens to all these persons, and ever so many other protagonists of the short novel, happens expressly to them and because they are as they are; perhaps the simplest instance is that of Captain Delano, whose innocence is represented precisely as the condition of his survival in a naughty world: "a person of a singularly undistrustful good nature, not liable, except on extraordinary and repeated excitement, and hardly then, to indulge in personal alarms, any way involving the imputation of malign evil in man. Whether, in view of what humanity is capable, such a trait implies, along with a benevolent heart, more than ordinary quickness and accuracy of intellectual perception, may be left to the wise to determine."

The same balance is maintained by the authors of these compositions, in the exact division of their attention to the inside of things and the outside, between knowledge of the ordinary, undramatic world, and imagination of the drama which takes place under its exacting conditions. How this is so may be seen most simply from *Notes from the Underground*, where the argument and its dramatic equivalent are given separately; oftener, however, the two strands are concurrent, and occasionally, in very sophisticated and elegant works, they are identical; as in *Un Coeur Simple*, which may be read as the plain product of observation, as though a "sketch of provincial life," and read again, or simultaneously, as a structure of great intricacy and density, entirely musical and contrapuntal in the laws of its being, and consequently forming a world all its own, rhythmic, resonant, symmetrical, in which every detail balances another so as to produce great riches of meaning not so much symbolically in a direct sense as by constellation and patterning, the method James called the figure in the carpet. In this connection I would mention once again Kay Boyle as possibly the foremost modern practitioner of this subtle style, especially in two short novels, *The Crazy Hunter* and *The Bridegroom's Body*.

It is this balance, so like that of the poetic drama, the balance between the appearance and the motive, the observed world and the world of law, which I conceive to be more exactly drawn and maintained in the short novel than elsewhere, that gives to works in this genre the characteristic of ruthlessness I referred to before. The ideal, that every detail should at once seem freely chosen by probable observation, and be in fact the product of a developing inner necessity, confers on these tales something of the air of demonstrations; so that, for example, when Andrew Ephimich is first drawn to visit Gronov in the asylum it is as though the chess master announced mate in twelve—we neither doubt the result nor see at all how it is to be accomplished.

In this sense we sometimes feel the protagonists of short novels to be the victims not of fate or of the gods so much as of literary styles and laws of composition— that strict style of composition discussed by Adrian Leverkühn, himself such a victim, in Mann's *Dr. Faustus*.

This again is a subject I must be content to leave implicit: whether the idea itself of the "art work" any longer has anything to do with anything; whether, being based at last on religious valuations, magical sanctions, and the sense of a universe at once "real" and "symbolic," a universe of signatures, the work of art can continue to interpret human experience. I merely note that this theme is disturbingly *there*, and pass on to safer ground.

The characteristic balance I am speaking of reflects itself very distinctively in the treatment of detail in short novels; more so, or more perspicuously so, than in long ones. A few instances will serve to conclude this discussion.

There are two kinds of relevance in literary composition, and I think they are both readily observable in principle although it is doubtful whether they can always be distinguished in the work itself. One kind has to do with the temporal succession of events, as though the single point of the idea must be viewed in an added dimension as a straight line: in order to tell how a distinguished German author dies in Venice we must get him to Venice, keep him there, and supply a disease for him to die of. He will doubtless see many things, and think many things, on his journey—what things? We need another kind of relevance, having to do with association, symbol, metaphor, as well as with probable and realistic observation; while the distinguished author is in Venice it occurs to him, waking, that his situation is like that discussed in the *Phaedrus*, and, dreaming, that his situation is like that

of King Pentheus in *The Bacchae* of Euripedes.

The first kind of relevance you may call external, the second internal; or, better, the first is linear, and progresses in time, while the second is radical and comes at every instant from the central conception. The difference between them, practically speaking, is that the story could be told without the contribution of the symbolic details and could not be told without the succession of events. It will be objected, perhaps, that without the symbolic details, or with other symbolic details, it would be a different story and an inferior one, and that is true enough but for compositional purposes irrelevant. What is more important is that neither kind in itself accounts for the story, what makes it worth our while to hear that the distinguished German author went to Venice and died there— for that we require something that binds both sorts together, and makes the temporal and ideal situations the subject of the same decision: in this instance the figure of the boy Tadzio, who according to the first kind of relevance is the motive for Aschenbach's remaining in Venice long enough to contract his fatal disease, and according to the second kind plays Dionysus to his Pentheus, Phaedrus to his Socrates, inspires highly relevant reflections on love and morality, beauty and disease, form and corruption, aristocratic control and chaos, and so on.

The tensions of these two criteria of choice in the short novel tend to make the selection of details extraordinarily fateful; especially it seems that everything which is symbolic, associational, metaphorically relevant, is multiply determined, as the details of a dream are said to be, and thus gains a dramatic prominence and a kind of luminous quality. I will try to illustrate by a few examples.

When Aschenbach dies, there by the shore, we are told that the weather was autumnal, the beach deserted and not even very clean; suddenly we are given this: "A camera on a tripod stood at the edge of the water, apparently abandoned; its black cloth snapped in the freshening wind." That is all, our attention is given to Tadzio, Aschenbach's death soon follows, the camera is never mentioned again.

Crudely speaking, this camera is unnecessary and no one could possibly have noticed anything missing had the author decided against its inclusion; yet in a musical, compositional sense it exquisitely touches the center of the story and creates a resonance which makes us for a moment aware of the entire inner space of the action, of all things relevant and their relations to one another.

Our sense of this is mostly beyond exposition, as symbolic things have a way of being; but some of its elements may be mentioned. About the camera by the sea there is, first, a poignant desolation, the emptiness of vast spaces, and in its pictorial quality it resembles one of the earliest images in the story, when Aschenbach, standing by the cemetery, looks away down the empty streets: "not a wagon in sight, either on the paved Ungererstrasse, with its gleaming tramlines stretching off towards Schwabing, nor on the Föhring highway." Both pictures are by Di Chirico. The camera's black cloth reminds us of the gondola, "black as nothing else on earth except a coffin," and the repeated insistence on black in that description; also of the "labor in darkness" which brings forth the work of art. For we perceive that the camera stands to the sea as, throughout this story, the artist has stood to experience, in a morally heroic yet at the same time dubious or ridiculous or even impossible relation of form to all possibility,

and that at the summer's end, in the freshening wind, the camera is abandoned. It would be near forgivable, so full of Greek mysteries is this work, if we thought the tripod itself remotely Delphic.

Here is another example. At the beginning of *The Secret Sharer* Conrad gives us an image which at that time, perhaps, we cannot see as anything but pictorial: the young man, looking out across the sea, sees "lines of fishing stakes resembling a mysterious system of half-submerged bamboo fences." But when we have finished the story we may see even that image in the first sentence as compositionally resonant, as a cryptic emblem set up at the gateway of the action. This emblem suggests to us how the conscious distinctions, the property rights, of reason and society, extend also beneath the surface (of the sea, of the mind) and are in fact rooted down there: precisely what is learned by the narrator who before his adventure "rejoiced in the great security of the sea as compared with the unrest of the land, in my choice of that untempted life presenting no disquieting problems, invested with an elementary moral beauty by the absolute straightforwardness of its appeal and by the singleness of its purpose"—fine phrases, on which the story, like its opening image, comments in sympathetic, pedagogic irony.

Another example. In *The Death of Ivan Ilyich*, Tolstoy shows us the funeral service and a colleague of the dead man going in to visit the widow, who is under three several necessities which exclude one another: of showing terrible grief, of passing ashtrays to prevent the guest's spoiling the rug, of discussing the payment of her husband's pension. The visitor sits down "on a low pouffe, the springs of which yielded under his weight." The widow, however, catches her shawl on the edge of a table, so "Peter Ivanovich rose to detach it, and the springs of the pouffe, relieved of his weight, rose also and gave him a push. The widow began detaching her shawl herself, and Peter Ivanovich again sat down, suppressing the rebellious springs of the pouffe under him. But the widow had not quite freed herself, and Peter Ivanovich got up again, and again the pouffe rebelled and even creaked." A page later, as the widow approaches the subject of the pension, "Peter Ivanovich bowed, keeping control of the springs of the pouffe, which immediately began quivering under him."

This comically autonomous pouffe represents not merely the social obliquities of the interview, nor merely that inanimate objects continually mutter their comments to the detriment of human dignity and solemnity, but also how such objects may tend actively to push us where we do not wish to go, to represent some implacable hostility in the world of objects, especially those meant for our convenience. Death occurs with just the same independence of human volition, and we are emblematically informed— "As he sat down on the pouffe Peter Ivanovich recalled how Ivan Ilyich had arranged this room and had consulted him regarding this pink cretonne with green leaves"—of something we learn more explicitly later, that Ivan Ilyich's interest precisely in such things, in "decoration," caused his death: "when mounting a stepladder to show the upholsterer, who did not understand, how he wanted the hangings draped, he made a false step and slipped . . ."

This species of inner determination produces, in the short novel, not single details only but chains and clusters of iterative imagery also, such as we usually identify with the poetry of Shakespeare; and sometimes, as in Un Coeur Simple,

it is the elegant patterning and constatation of such groups of images which alone, implicitly, supply the meaning, or meanings: an interested reader may trace on his own, for example, the provenience of the parrot-paraclete Loulou, not in the action alone, but in the far-ranging associated imagery—how it is gradually prepared for before its appearance by much talk of jungles and far places, by the geography book given the children by M. Bourais, by Félicité's childish ideas of distant places and times, by Victor's voyages and death, by Mme. Auban's dream after the death of Virginie, and so on.

I have tried to describe the short novel, according to the examples I am most familiar with, not as a compromise between novel and short story, but as something like the ideal and primary form, suggestively allied in simplicity and even in length with the tragedies of antiquity, and dealing in effect with equivalent materials. No doubt in dealing with this subject I have slighted somewhat the complex novel and, even more, the short story; that has to do in part, as I said, with making the middle term visible, but perhaps in even greater part with my lasting delight in short novels, which I will even go so far as nearly to identify with tragic art in our fictional tradition. What is accomplished by the works I have been speaking of may be given the sanction of science as well as magic or religion in the following words of Sir D'Arcy Wentworth Thompson in the introductory chapter of his work On Growth and Form: "Like warp and woof, mechanism and teleology are interwoven together, and we must not cleave to the one nor despise the other; for their union is rooted in the very nature of totality. We may grow shy or weary of looking to a final cause for an explanation of our phenomena; but after we have accounted for these on the plainest principles of mechanical causation it may be useful and appropriate to see how the final cause would tally with the other, and lead towards the same conclusion." It is this double exploration which, I have contended, is undertaken in the short novel more than in other sorts of fiction. Even the matter of the length or brevity of such works ought not to be beneath discussion as "merely" mechanical; in the book I quoted from before, Vladimir Nabokov says something which I shall repeat for a conclusion to this matter. Discussing ways of seeing—the lantern slide, the microscope—he says, "There is, it would seem, in the dimensional scale of the world a kind of delicate meeting-place between imagination and knowledge, a point, arrived at by diminishing large things and enlarging small ones, that is intrinsically artistic."

Yvor Winters

THE AUDIBLE READING OF POETRY

Yvor Winters has combined an essentially formalistic approach with a continuing belief in the historical and moral aspects of literature, thus defying exact classification or affiliation with a particular group or method. Winters is Professor Emeritus at Stanford University, where he began teaching in 1928. "The Audible Reading of Poetry" appeared in a collection of Winters' essays *The Function of Criticism* (1957). He has also published several volumes of poetry. Some of his other important books are *Primitivism and Decadence* (1937), *Maule's Curse* (1938), and *In Defense of Reason* (1947).

My title may seem to have in it something of the jargon of the modern Educationist; if so, I am sorry, but I mean to indicate something more than the reading of poetry aloud. I mean to indicate the reading of poetry not merely for the sensual ear, but for the mind's ear as well; yet the mind's ear can be trained only by way of other, and the matter, practically considered, comes inescapably back to the reading of poetry aloud.

It is also important to learn to read prose aloud, and to hear the prose when one reads it silently. Melville, Gibbon, or Samuel Johnson about equally will be lost on us if we do not so hear it. Yet the readers are numerous who hear nothing when they read silently and who are helpless in their efforts to read aloud: some of them have defective sensibilities; some have merely never been trained; some have been trained by one or another of our psychological educationalists to read in this fashion in order that they may read more rapidly. That they can read more rapidly without hearing, I believe there is no doubt, especially if the matter with which they are dealing is trivial. The trouble is that the activity cannot properly be called reading. Such "readers" are barbarians; literature is closed to them, in spite of the fact that they may think otherwise. The scholar who appears to have read everything has commonly understood very little, and his failure to hear is one of the reasons.

My subject may seem a bit precious and tenuous, but it is neither; it is a matter of the utmost importance to the proper understanding of poetry, a matter fully as important as the philosophical speculation and learned paraphrasing of the New Critics, of whom I am sometimes reputed to be one. It is a matter of which there is almost no understanding at the present time.

Poetry, as nearly as I can understand it, is a statement in words about a human experience, whether the experience be real or hypothetical, major or minor; but it is a statement of a particular kind. Words are symbols for concepts, and the philosopher or scientist endeavors as far as may be to use them with reference to nothing save their conceptual content. Most words, however, connote feelings and perceptions, and the poet, like the writer of imaginative prose, endeavors to use them with reference not only to their denotations but to their connotations as well. Such writers endeavor to communicate not only concepts, arranged, presumably, either in rational order or in an order apprehensible by the rational mind, but the feeling or emotion which the rational content ought properly to arouse. The poet differs from the writer of any kind of prose in that he writes in metrical language. Any good prose is rhythmical up to a certain point: even purely expository prose should be rhythmical to the point that audible obstructions are minimized and meanings are emphasized; the prose of such a writer as Melville is far more elaborately rhythmical than this. But a rhythm which is not controlled by a definite measure will be relatively loose and lacking in subtlety. Poetry and music are based upon definite measure; in this they differ from all other forms of composition.

Rhythm and meter, it should be observed, are quite distinct from each other, in spite of the fact that many critics (myself among them) sometimes use the two words as if they meant the same thing. Meter is the arithmetical norm, the purely theoretic structure of the line; rhythm is controlled departure from that norm. The iambic pentameter norm, for example, proceeds as follows:

One *two*, one *two*, one *two*, one *two*, one *two*.

Yet no other line in the language corresponds exactly to the line just given; and to achieve another as regular one will have to resort to the same repetitive structure with a new pair of syllables. Every other line will depart from this one for these reasons: no two syllables ever have the same degree of accent—that is, so far as versification is concerned there is no such thing as an inherently accented or unaccented syllable, but syllables which count technically as accented can be recognized as such only with reference to the other syllable or syllables within the same foot; secondly, although quantity or syllable-length has no part in the measure, it is, like accent, infinitely variable and it affects the rhythm; and thirdly, feet of other types may be substituted for iambic feet, at least within reason. As I have said, rhythm results from the proper control and manipulation of these sources of variation.

Now rhythm is in a measure expressive of emotion. If the poet, then, is endeavoring to make a statement in which rational understanding and emotion are properly related to each other, metrical language will be of the greatest advantage to him, for it will provide him with a means of qualifying his emotion more precisely than he could otherwise do, of adjusting it more finely to the rational understanding which gives rise to it. The rational and emotional contents of the poem thus exist simultaneously, from moment to moment, in the poem; they are not distinct, but are separable only by analysis; the poet is not writing in language which was first conceptual and then emotionalized, nor in prose which has been metered; he is writing in poetical language. And the rhythm of the poem permeates the entire poem as pervasively as blood permeates the human body: remove it and you have a corpse. It is for this reason that the audible reading of poetry is quite as important as the philosophical understanding of poetry; without audible reading, and adequate audible reading, you simply do not have poetry.

We are thus confronted with the question of what constitutes adequate audible reading. From what I have just said, it should be obvious that adequate audible reading will be reading in which the rhythm of the poem is rendered intact, without the sacrifice of any other element. But what variety of reading will best achieve this end, and what are some of the problems which arise in connection with it?

Since I am defending an unpopular cause, I shall not scruple to avail myself of eminent support. In looking over the *Selected Writings* of Paul Valéry recently issued by New Directions, I found Valéry writing as follows:

. . . . in studying a piece of poetry one intends to recite, one should not take as source or point of departure ordinary conversation and common parlance, in order to rise from this level of prose to the desired poetic tone: but, on the contrary, I thought one should take song as a base, and should put oneself in the state of a singer; adjust one's voice to the plenitude of musical sound, and from there descend to the somewhat less resonant state suitable to verse. This, it seemed to me, was the only way to preserve the musical essence of poems. Above all, the voice must be placed quite away from prose, and the text studied from the point of view of necessary attack, modulation, sustained tone, little by little, lowering this musical disposition, which in the beginning one has exaggerated, to bring it down to the proportions of poetry. . . . above all do not be in a hurry to arrive at the meaning. Approach it without effort and, as it were, insensibly. And only in or by means of the

music attain to tenderness or to violence. . . . Remain in this pure musical state until such time as the meaning, appearing little by little, can no longer mar the musical form. You will introduce it at the end as the supreme nuance that will transfigure the passage without altering it.[1]

This appears to be a plea for a restrained but formal chant, in which a sustained tone and movement will serve as an impersonal but definite base for subtle variation. It is only by such a reading, for example, that *Le Cimetière Marin* can be rendered; it is only by a man who so read that such a poem could have been written.

A poem in the very nature of the case is a formal statement; and the reading of a poem is thus a formal occasion. A poem is not conversation; neither is it drama. Conversation is in general the least premeditated and least rhythmical of human utterance; and it depends very heavily upon intonations and even gestures and facial expressions which are not at the disposal of the poet. Dramatic speech is merely more or less formalized conversation. Dramatic poetry, of course, presents a special problem, and one with which I shall not at present concern myself, though it is closer to the kind of poetry with which I am dealing than it is to dramatic prose, and I agree with Valéry that it is commonly botched by the actors. I have never witnessed a performance of Shakespeare without more of pain than of profit or of pleasure. I have been repeatedly reminded of a story told by W. B. Yeats of the great Shakespearian actor of whom it was said that he read Shakespeare so beautifully that no one could tell it was poetry. In general I think

---

[1] *Extracts from* "A Discourse on the Declamation of Verse," by Paul Valéry, translated by Louise Varese. *Paul Valéry, Selected Writings,* New Directions, 1950.

the world would be well enough off without actors: they appear to be capable of any of three feats—of making the grossly vulgar appear acceptably mediocre; of making the acceptably mediocre appear what it is; and of making the distinguished appear acceptably mediocre. In any event, they cannot read poetry, for they try to make it appear to be something else, something, in brief, which they themselves can understand.

A poem calls for a formal reading, partly because the poem itself is of its own nature a formal statement, and partly because only such a reading will render the rhythm with precision. Furthermore, it is only with a formal tone as a basis that variations of tone within the poem can be rendered with precision: without such a formal tone to unify the poem, the poem becomes merely a loose assortment of details. The situation here is precisely analogous to that which I have described elsewhere[2] with regard to rhythm and meter: the firmer the metric structure, the more precise can be the rhythmic variations, and the greater the effect obtainable with a very slight variation; whereas if the structure is loose the variations lack significance.

A formal reading which avoids dramatic declamation will necessarily take on something of the nature of a chant. This kind of reading itself has dangers, however, for the reader may carry the procedure so far as to appear precious, and worse, he may deform syllables in the interests of what he considers musical intonation, much as a musical composer will draw syllables out or hurry over them in setting a poem to music. I never heard the late W. B. Yeats read aloud, but I

[2] The Influence of Meter on Poetic Convention, in *Primitivism and Decadence*, the essay on John Crowe Ransom, Section IX, in *The Anatomy of Nonsense*, both reprinted in *In Defense of Reason*.

have been told that he was guilty of both of these vices: if it is true that he was guilty of them, one has some reason to suspect that he never properly heard his own poems, a fact which may have been responsible for a number of curious rythmical mishaps which are scattered through his works. A poem should, on the contrary, be conceived as having a movement of its own, an autonomous movement, which should be rendered as purely and as impersonally as possible. The reader has no more right to revise the rhythms in the interest of what he considers an effective presentation than he has a right to revise any other aspects of the language. The poem, once set in motion, should appear to move of its own momentum.

A more or less recent poet who went farther than any other has gone in deforming the inherent rhythmic elements in our language and so rendering the structure of his poems indecipherable is Gerard Manley Hopkins. Hopkins held a theory of dramatic or declamatory reading, and I suspect from a few passages in his prose that he combined this with a theory of musical intonation. Hopkins was an eccentric and extremely egoistic man, and he worked in isolation. He apparently failed to realize that his own dramatic and musical deformations of language were not based on universal principles but were purely private. As a result one can often be only dumfounded when he indicates his intentions by metrical signs, and one can often be only baffled when he fails to do so. In *Spelt from Sibyl's Leaves*, for example, Hopkins uses an extremely long line, which, if it is read with normal accentuation, produces the effect of a loosely irregular but still readable verse. He does not provide us with many accent marks until he is about halfway through the poem; from there on he provides marks in abundance, frequently with strange results. The last two lines will serve as illustration:

But these two; ware of a world where but these / two tell, each off the other; of a rack

Where, selfwrung, selfstrung, sheathe- and shelterless, / thoughts against thoughts in groans grind.

We have here a kind of bad writing which is purely the result of bad reading; and even the best reading, if superimposed upon what the poet offers, can salvage the poem but very imperfectly.

In T. S. Eliot's reading of *The Waste Land*, as we have it on the recordings issued by The Library of Congress, we have another kind of dramatic reading, and conceivably a relationship between the way of reading and the way of writing. In those portions which exhibit a more or less definite rhythmic structure—for example, in *Death by Water*—Eliot reads more or less in the fashion which I am recommending, with a minimum of dramatic improvement on the text, and with a maximum of attention to movement. But in those portions of the poem —and they are the greater part of it—in which the rhythm does not cohere, in which the poem tends to fall apart in sandy fragments, Eliot reads dramatically; he does this with a good deal of skill, but most of what he puts into his voice is not in the poem—he descends to the practice of the actor who is salvaging a weak text. It would be interesting to know whether Eliot devised this mode of reading in order to rescue a weak poem, or whether the weak poem resulted in part from his having come gradually to employ such a mode of reading, so that he tended to see in his text as he was composing it something which he was not actually getting down on paper. This latter procedure in any event probably accounts for a good deal of the unrealized poetry of our time. For example, Randal Jarrell's reading of his poem *Lady Bates*, in The Library of Congress series, is very dramatic, very emotional, and very bad: I am unable to hear it without the conviction that Jarrell felt his emotions about his subject so readily and so uncritically that he did not trouble himself to write the poem. The poem itself is formless and dull.

The dependence upon superimposed rhythms or other effects which we get in a grotesque form in some of Hopkins and in a more skillful form in Eliot's reading of *The Waste Land* can lead to an astonishing degree of imperception on the part of critics (which is merely an impressive way of saying on the part of readers). In the volume entitled *Gerard Manley Hopkins*, by the Kenyon Critics, Mr. Harold Whitehall informs us that from about the year 1300 English poetry has become less and less amenable to being read aloud, because less and less rhythmical. And in another volume on Hopkins, edited by Norman Weyand, S.J., and written by a group of Jesuits, a volume entitled *Immortal Diamond*, Walter J. Ong arrives at similar conclusions. Both of these writers believe that there is no real rhythm without heavy stress; both believe that meter is based on declamatory rather than mechanical stress. Ong gives us no clue as to how we are to recognize our stressed syllables, and he fails to explain how Hopkins arrived at any of the stresses which he marked. Whitehall gives us his own system of stressing Hopkins, but it is quite as arbitrary as that of Hopkins, and when Whitehall's marked passages are finished we are left with no means of proceeding. Ong, convinced that there is no fine rhythm without heavy and obvious stress, is oblivious of the sensitivity of Sidney and the post-Sidneyan metrists, and equally of the structural principles of their verse; and his concept of reading aloud is indicated by the following passage: "If the poem calls for shouting, the shouting need not be kept imaginary for fear the beat of the rhythm will go. Shout, declaim, and you will only have thrust this rhythm home. So, too, if the shout should need to die to a whisper . . ." This clerical type of rendition strikes me as about equally impractical, insensitive, and indecorous.

Nevertheless, rhetorical stress has a certain relationship to the structure of meter, but it is not the relationship sought by Hopkins. As I have already said, the language does not divide itself evenly into accented and unaccented syllables, but there is almost infinite variation in degrees of accent. For this reason, the basic rule of English scansion is this: that the accented syllable can be determined only in relationship to the other syllable or syllables within the same foot. The accented syllable of a given foot, as we shall eventually see, may be one of the lightest syllables in its line. But with this rule as a reservation, we may go on to say that poetic meter must be constructed out of the inherent (or mechanical) accentual materials of the language, so that the accented syllable of a foot will be naturally heavier than the unaccented; and if the poet desires to indicate a rhetorical stress he should do it by a metrical stress, or if he is using two syllables either of which might receive heavier stress than the other, then the rhetorical stress should fall where the reader as a result of the previously established pattern will expect the metrical stress.

Keats neglects these considerations in the first line of his last sonnet. The inexpert reader who endeavors to render this line conversationally or dramatically will read it as if he were a sociable lady addressing another sociable lady at a party:

Bright star,   would I were steadfast
    as thou art,

and the rhythm is destroyed along with the possibility of a proper rhyme. The fault, however, lies largely with Keats. It is natural to stress the two contrasting pronouns somewhat, although one need not carry the stress all the way to the ridiculous. Furthermore, on the first pronoun the metrical stress indicates the rhetorical, so that the two are not in conflict. If we consider the words *Would I* in isolation, we shall see that so far as their mechanical properties are concerned, either can be stressed at the expense of the other; however, in this line the stressing of *would* would result in an inverted foot in the second position, and although inversion is possible in this position, it is difficult and generally unlikely, so that we naturally expect the stress to fall on *I*, which likewise is the natural recipient of the rhetorical stress. If we employ the four words *Would I were steadfast* in isolation, the stress may fall variously according to our meaning. If we are implying a contrast between steadfastness and our lack of it, the heaviest stress falls on *would*; if we are implying a contrast between steadfastness and another particular quality, a light stress falls on *would* and a heavy on *stead-*; if we are implying a contrast between our own lack of steadfastness and the steadfastness of another, the heavy stress falls on *I*, as in the actual line, but if, as in this line, the comparison is completed, an equal stress should fall on the second pronoun; but since this pronoun also is coupled with a verb which is mechanically its equal and on the basis of its inherent nature could as well take the accent, and since the foot ends the line, and a rhymed line at that, the accent must fall on *art*. This blunder by Keats could scarcely have occurred as a result of his reading poetry in a dramatic fashion, for he understood the structure of English poetry very well, and had he read the line dramatically he would have noticed the error. It probably occurred as a result of his reading with a somewhat mechanical scansion, so that he failed to observe that the meaning was struggling with the meter. One can read it, of course, by means of a more or less evasive glide, but it constitutes an unhappy moment.

One can observe a related difficulty in the sixth line of Wordsworth's sonnet *Upon Westminster Bridge:*

Ships, towers, domes, theatres, and temples lie.

The first four words of this line are coördinate in grammatical function and in importance, and in ordinary prose the first four syllables would be indistinguishable to the ear in the matter of accent. The average reader, if asked to mark the scansion of this poem, will indicate two spondees at the beginning of the line, but the first two feet are not spondaic—in spite of everything they are iambic. The truly spondaic foot is extremely rare in English; presently I shall have occasion to illustrate it, but for the present I shall merely describe it. It can occur as a variant in iambic verse, only if the accented syllables in the iambic feet are heavily accented and the unaccented are very light, and only if the cesural pause is heavily marked; and these conditions must prevail not merely in the line in question, but throughout much of the poem. The true spondee is a violent aberration—it is a form of what Hopkins calls sprung rhythm—and it is possible only where the rhythm is heavy and obvious. It can be found at least as early as Barnabe Googe and as late as the songbooks of John Dowland, and within these limits it may conceivably be found in as many as thirty poems, but I think it will be difficult to find it elsewhere except in the work of Gerard Hopkins, although something approaching it occurs occasionally in Henry Vaughan. In this sonnet by Wordsworth an extremely smooth iambic movement has been established in the first five lines, so effectively established that it dominates the sixth line, and almost any reader who is aware of rhythm at all will be forced to impose a very light iambic emphasis on the first two feet of the sixth line; to do otherwise will bring the poem apart in ruins. This can be done; but the difficulty indicates a defect in the poem, and a defect again which probably stems from faulty reading on the part of the poet. The difficulty is enhanced by the length of the syllables (a length increased by the commas) and by the all but insufferable series of dentals.

The relationship of rhetorical stress to metrical stress, and hence to reading, would appear, then, to be real, although the relationship can obviously be abused. Perhaps I should conclude the matter by offering these rules for poet and reader alike: (1) There should be no conflict between rhetorical stress and metrical stress, but insofar as it is possible the metrical stress should point the meaning; (2) where the mechanical potentialities of the language indicate the possibility of a stress in either of two directions, the grammatical structure should be so definite that a certain rhetorical stress will be unmistakable and will force the metrical interpretation in the right direction; and (3) the reader should deal with rhetorical stresses with the utmost restraint—he should indicate them as far as the occasion requires, but he should not become enthusiastic, undignified, or unmetrical about them. They are not to be superimposed upon the basic rhythm, nor can the basic rhythm be constructed from them.

I would like next to illustrate the importance of reading, by illustrating certain very marked differences in rhythm which may occur within the limits of the iambic pentameter line. English verse is predominantly iambic in structure, and although this fact has irritated certain poets and stirred them to curious experiments, the fact that so vast a number of eminent poets have found the iambic movement more useful than any other must have some kind of explanation. In the anapestic or dactyllic foot the accented syllable must be definitely heavy or the identity of the foot and of the line will disappear, and this necessity makes for monotony and a jingling obviousness:

I sprang to the stirrup, and Joris, and he;
I galloped, Dirck galloped, we galloped all
   three. . . .

The unequivocally trochaic line tends to exhibit some of the same heaviness (as in *Hiawatha*, for example) although the reason for this is less clear. The seven-syllable tetrameter line may be described as trochaic, with a monosyllabic foot in the last position, or as iambic with a monosyllabic foot in the first position; since it is frequently used as a variant on iambic tetrameter, the second classification would seem the better. When this line is used throughout a poem, the poem will be short, or else will become monotonous: the accents again are usually heavy most of the time, and although the meter may be used in a short poem for the purpose of obtaining a didactic or semi-songlike effect, it appears to have few other uses. The iambic movement, however, appears to be natural to the language; it asserts itself easily, and the poet does not have to hammer his accents out to maintain it. This situation allows

the poet to vary the degrees of his accents widely, to vary his cesuras, and to employ substitution with a certain freedom. Contrary to the views of Mr. Whitehall and of Father Ong, this type of meter lends itself very well to audible reading, but one must first know how to read. And when well written and well read it is far more flexible and perceptive than any other kind of English verse thus far devised.

My first example is by Barnabe Googe and was written early in the reign of Elizabeth, before the advent of Spenser and Sidney:

Give money me, take friendship who so
   list,
For friends are gone, come once adversity,
When money yet remaineth safe in chest
That quickly can thee bring from misery;
Fair face show friends, when riches do
   abound,
Come time of proof, farewell they must
   away;
Believe me well, they are not to be found,
If God but send thee once a lowering day.
Gold never starts aside, but in distress,
Finds ways enough to ease thine heaviness.

This poem has certain characteristics which one would expect to find in a period in which the pentameter line was new, when the misunderstandings of Wyatt had been only recently overcome: first of all there are no inverted feet and no trisyllabic feet; secondly the accented syllables are almost all heavy and of nearly the same weight—there are only two feet in the poem in which the accented syllables are noticeably light; thirdly the cesuras are all heavily marked, and in six of the ten lines they fall at the end of the second foot. The poem shows only one type of metrical variation; that is, the use of spondaic feet (or what I have elsewhere called syllabic sprung meter). The introduction of this variation into the newly acquired iambic pentameter line is Googe's principle contribution to the technique of English verse, and it is a contribution of no mean importance. There are two spondees at the beginning of line five; there is one at the beginning of six; there is one at the beginning of nine; and the first foot of the last line may be read with equal success as a spondee or as an iamb. All of these spondees can be forced into the iambic pattern, but they will have to be forced, and the poem will suffer. It is only in a poem such as this one, in which the rhythm is strongly and obviously marked by a great and regular distinction between accented and unaccented syllables that the true spondee can occur; in a smoother and subtler type of structure, such as my next example, two syllables of nearly the same degree of accent will be absorbed into the iambic pattern and will not stand out as approximately equal to each other; furthermore, any attempt to read them as spondees will destroy the movement of the poem.

My next example is from Shakespeare. Before this sonnet was written, Sidney and other early experimenters had rendered the line smoother, more varied, and more subtle:

When to the sessions of sweet silent
    thought
I summon up remembrance of things
    past,
I sigh the lack of many a thing I sought,
And with old woes new wail my dear
    time's waste:
Then can I drown an eye unused to flow,
For precious friends, hid in death's date-
    less night,
And weep afresh love's long-since-can-
    celled woe,
And moan th'expense of many a vanish'd
    sight:
Then can I grieve at grievances foregone,
And heavily from woe to woe tell o'er
The sad account of fore-bemoaned moan
Which I new pay as if not paid before.

But if the while I think on thee, dear
    friend,
All losses are restored and sorrows end.

The position of the cesura in this sonnet is less varied than in the poem by Googe; it falls after the second foot in eleven out of fourteen lines; but the cesura is much less noticeable, partly because it is not emphasized by heavy grammatical breaks, and partly because of other qualities of the rhythm. Aside from this difference in cesural value, the most considerable rhythmic difference between this poem and the poem by Googe resides in the fact that there are great differences in the degrees of accent to be found *among the syllables which count metrically as accented.* It will be remembered that I remarked earlier that the accented syllable can be recognized as such only with reference to the other syllable or syllables within the same foot, for no two syllables bear exactly the same degree of accent: it is this fact which gives the rhythm of the best English verse its extreme sensitivity. But rhythm, in poetry as in music, is controlled variation from an arithmetical norm; and the rhythm ceases to be rhythm, and becomes merely movement, whenever the norm itself is no longer discernible.

I will illustrate what I have been saying by two lines from the sonnet. The scansion of the first line gives us a trochee followed by four iambs. The third foot, however, which is composed of the second syllable of *sessions* followed by the preposition *of* (the accented syllable), is very lightly accented. In the following foot, which is composed of *sweet*, followed by the first syllable of *silent*, *sweet*, the unaccented syllable, is more heavily stressed than the accented syllable of the preceding foot, so that we have in effect a series of four degrees of accent within two successive feet. Furthermore, if the reader should suffer from the delusion (a common one) that the second of these feet is really a spondee, let him read it the way he is forced to read the true spondees in the poem by Googe, and he will discover that spondaic rhythm is a very different matter from what he has here, and that the attempt to introduce it into this poem will be disastrous. The same thing occurs in the fourth and fifth feet of line nine:

Then can I grieve at grievances foregone.

It occurs in the first two feet of Bryant's line:

Where thy pale form was laid with many tears.

It occurs in the last two feet of Ben Jonson's line:

Drink to me only with thine eyes.

It is, in fact, one of the commonest phenomena in English verse, yet I have seen a good many distinguished scholars and eminent poets interpret it wrongly.

I shall now quote a well known song from John Dowland's *Second Book of Aires:*

Fine knacks for ladies, cheap, choice, brave and new!
  Good pennyworths! but money cannot move.
I keep a fair but for the fair to view;
  A beggar may be liberal of love.
Though all my wares be trash, the heart is true.

Great gifts are guiles and look for gifts again;
  My trifles come as treasures from my mind.
It is a precious jewel to be plain;
  Sometimes in shell the Orient's pearls we find.
Of others take a sheaf, of me a grain.

Within this pack, pins, points, laces, and gloves,
  And divers toys, fitting a country fair.

But my heart lives where duty serves and loves,
  Turtles and twins, court's brood, a heavenly pair.
Happy the heart that thinks of no removes.

There are sprung, or spondaic, feet in the first, second, sixth, seventh, eleventh, thirteenth, and fourteenth lines of this poem. These feet represent the same kind of variant which we found in Googe, and for the most part we have the same strongly marked difference between accented and unaccented syllables and similarly strong cesural pauses, even in lines in which no spondees occur. Yet whereas the rhythm of Googe is hard, fast, and didactic, the rhythm of this poem is slower, more complicated, and very songlike. The result is partly due to more spondaic variants than we found in Googe, and to spondaic variants in other positions than the initial ones; it is partly due to the introduction at certain points of the type of line which we found in Shakespeare, such as the following:

It is a precious jewel to be plain.

a line in which the iambic fourth foot, composed of the second syllable of *jewel* and the preposition *to*, is extremely light and short and is followed by a final foot (*be plain*) in which the unaccented syllable is heavier than the accented syllable *to* before it; yet in this last foot the difference between *be* and *plain* is so marked that no one would be tempted to call the foot a spondee.

The author likewise does certain strange and ingenious things with his spondees. The first line, for example, goes as follows:

Fine knacks for ladies, cheap, choice, brave and new!

The first foot is spondaic, the second iambic; the third foot, consisting of the second syllable of *ladies* and of *cheap*, is likewise iambic, but the cesura, reinforced by the comma, in mid-foot, throws the accent onto *cheap* with unusual force, and *cheap* is then followed by the spondaic foot consisting of two syllables which are almost exactly equal to it, and which are likewise set off by commas, so that we have the illusion of a foot consisting of three accented syllables, or an English molossus. The author does something similar but almost more adventurous in the eleventh line, where the heavily iambic foot *this pack* is followed by the heavy spondee *pins, points*, which in turn is followed by the heavily inverted foot, *laces*, with the result that we get four strong accents in sequence, though only one spondee. Technically, this is one of the most brilliant poems in the language. Dowland (or his unknown poet) learned what he could from Googe and improved upon it; and he complicated the method (without destroying it—a difficult feat) by rhythms acquired from the refiners of the intervening period.

I shall now show the use of different types of iambic pentameter rhythm employed in a regular pattern. To do this, I shall employ a song by Campion. The song rhymes in couplets. The metric pattern begins with two lines of what one might call the primitive type, with heavy stresses and heavy cesuras, but with no spondees: in these two lines the first and third feet are inverted, the rest iambic, and the cesura falls after the second foot. The third and fifth lines are evenly iambic and are less heavily stressed, and the cesuras in these lines occur in different positions and are so light as to be all but imperceptible. The fourth and sixth lines are of the same type of iambic movement as the last lines mentioned, but contain seven feet instead of five. There are two stanzas, and the pattern in the two is as nearly identical as the inescapable variations of language permit:

Follow your saint, follow with accents
    sweet!
Haste you, sad notes, fall at her flying
    feet!
There, wrapt in cloud of sorrow, pity
    move,
And tell the ravisher of my soul I perish
    for her love:
But if she scorns my never ceasing pain,
Then burst with sighing in her sight, and
    ne'er return again.

All that I sung still to her praise did tend;
Still she was first, still she my songs did
    end;
Yet she my love and music both doth fly,
The music that her echo is and beauty's
    sympathy:
Then let my notes pursue her scornful
    flight!
It shall suffice that they were breathed
    and died for her delight.

I shall now quote a sonnet by Gerard Hopkins, which is basically iambic pentameter, but which employs every conceivable variant. I have marked and described the scansion of this sonnet in my essay on Hopkins, and at this time I shall make only a few general remarks about the structure. The poem contains iambic feet, trochees, spondees, one molossus (a foot of three accented syllables), monosyllabic feet, trisyllabic feet of one accent each, and one or two feet which must be considered either as containing more than three syllables or else as containing syllables which are extrametrical or elided. The poem is successful as regards structure and rhythm, and it offers a rhythmic departure from the norm about as extreme as anyone is likely to achieve:

No worst, there is none. Pitched past
    pitch of grief,
More pangs will, schooled at forepangs,
    wilder wring.
Comforter, where, where is your com-
    forting?
Mary, mother of us, where is your relief?
My cries heave, herds-long; huddle in a
    main, a chief

Woe, world sorrow; on an age-old anvil
  wince and sing—
Then lull, then leave off. Fury had
  shrieked 'No ling-
ering! Let me be fell: force I must be
  brief.'

O the mind, mind has mountains; cliffs
  of fall
Frightful, sheer, no-man-fathomed. Hold
  them cheap
May who ne'er hung there. Nor does long
  our small
Durance deal with that steep or deep.
  Here! creep,
Wretch under a comfort serves in a whirl-
  wind: all
Life death does end and each day dies
  with sleep.

By the use of five short poems I have
indicated a number of widely varying
rhythms all of which are measured by
iambic pentameter. So far as meter and
rhythm are concerned all five are masterpieces; and in spite of any faults which
may be found in them with regard to
other matters, all five are brilliant poems
and should be part of the literary experience of any man using the English language. Yet not one of these poems
amounts to anything if its rhythm is not
rendered with great precision; to read
the poem so that its rhythm does not
emerge in its totality and in every detail
is to reduce the poem to lifeless fragments. You cannot buy expert readings
of these poems on disks, as you can buy
expert renderings of Bach and Mozart;
nor can you go to a concert and hear
them—every man is his own performer.
It is important, therefore, that one read
properly. But to read properly one must
understand the principles both of English
meter and of English rhythm, and not in
a haphazard manner, but precisely; and
one must understand the use of one's
own voice; and after that one must practice.

I am at a disadvantage in dealing with
a subject of this kind before an audience
whom I cannot reach with my voice, for
I cannot demonstrate, but am forced to
try to describe. The nearest thing to a
demonstration that I can offer is my reading of my own poems in the Library of
Congress series. I do not consider myself
a finished performer, nor, I think, are
these readings the best of which I am
capable. But they are all I can offer, and
they will serve to indicate the method in
a general way.

I have been told that this method of
reading makes all poems sound alike, but
this can be true only for those persons to
whom all poems sound alike in any event,
or for whom essential differences are
meaningless. The virtue of the method,
on the contrary, is that it gives each poem
its precise identity, and no other method
will do this. If this precise identity does
not interest you, then you are not interested in poetry and you will in all likelihood never discover poetry. Some time
ago, when I was defending this method
of reading in public, a well-known scholar
objected to my theories with a good deal
of indignation, and he objected especially
to my reading of the Dowland poem
which I have quoted in these pages. He
said that it was a street song, or peddler's
song, and should be rendered as such. I
do not know exactly how Elizabethan
street songs were rendered, and I do not
believe that he knew; but any attempt so
to render it would be, I am sure, unfortunate, even if one had the necessary information. The poem is not a street song;
it is a poem on love and on the art of
poetry and on a relationship between the
two, and it is one of the most deeply
serious and deeply moving short poems in
the Elizabethan period—the peddler is
purely metaphorical, and his part in the
poem is both indicated and formalized by
the metrical structure and it should re-

main formal and no more than indicated in the reading. If the poet refers by way of metaphor to a cow, the reader is not, I trust, expected to moo. I refer the reader back to my quotations from Valéry, especially the last sentence. Of the "meaning" of the poem he says: "You will introduce it at the end as the supreme nuance that will transfigure the poem without altering it." By "the end," he means the end of the process of studying the poem and arriving at the proper rendering.

Bad reading and bad (or no) training in metrical theory are largely to blame, I believe, for the insensitive literary judgments by many critics who in other matters are very brilliant, and they are to blame also for a fair amount of bad academic work in literature. At Stanford University, at this writing, we have over one hundred graduate students in English, and about half of these are candidates for the doctorate. We are in a position to select our graduate students very carefully. We accept none who have not made excellent records here or elsewhere, and although some come to us from the smaller institutions (and incidentally some of our best), many come from places like Yale, Harvard, Chicago, Columbia, Princeton, and the better state universities. These people have made excellent records in the past, and most of them make excellent records here; yet almost none can read a line of poetry aloud so that one can discern the structure, and very few can mark the scansion from a line of Shakespeare's sonnets. These people are in these respects the products of their teaching, and the teaching should be improved. Most of our best critics and many of our best-known poets are not much better off. We have sunk into amateurism; and as a result we have in our time the meters of Eliot and of his imitators at the fifth remove, instead of meters comparable to those of the Elizabethans. And we have, worse still, a coherent (and fairly vocal) body of readers so ignorant that they prefer the incompetent to the expert.

If you answer that there are different kinds of poetry and hence we have different kinds of reading (this, of course, is the genteel answer which points to my lack of gentility), I am bound to reply that you are right: there are inferior kinds of poetry. By "inferior," I mean inferior in quality, not smaller in scope. The kind of reading which I defend is equally appropriate to a song by Campion or to an epic by Milton. Any poem which cannot endure the impersonal illumination of such a reading or which requires the assistance, whether expert or clumsy, of shouting, whispering, or other dramatic improvement, is to that extent bad poetry, though it may or may not be a good scenario for a vaudeville performance.

There will never be a first-rate poet or a first-rate critic who lacks a first-rate ear; and no one will ever acquire a first-rate ear without working for it and in the proper manner. Poetry, alas, like painting and music, is an art—it is not a form of happy self-indulgence; and to master an art or even understand it, one has to labor with all of one's mind and with at least a part of one's body.

W. K. Wimsatt, Jr.

WHAT TO SAY ABOUT A POEM

W. K. Wimsatt, Jr., has taught at Yale since 1939 and is the author of *The Prose Style of Samuel Johnson* (1941), *The Verbal Icon* (1954), and co-author (with Cleanth Brooks) of *Literary Criticism: A Short History*. He is a leading apologist and theoretician of formalistic criticism. "What To Say About a Poem" as presented here is taken from Wimsatt's *Hateful Contraries* (1965) but was originally delivered as a paper at the Eighth Yale Conference on the Teaching of English, April, 1962, and published in somewhat different versions in *College English Association Chapbook* (1963) and in *College English* (1963).

I

What to say about a poem. How to say something special about a poem, different from what is said by the ordinary reader, different quite likely from what would be said by the poet himself. Our professional preoccupation as teachers, scholars, critics, sometimes conceals from us the fact that our kind of interest in poems is after all a very special thing—a vocational or shop interest, somewhat strained perhaps at moments, even somewhat uncouth. Poems, a cultivated person might suppose, are made to be read and enjoyed. If I read a poem and enjoy it, why should I then proceed to dwell on it as an object about which something deliberate and elaborate has to be *said*—unless in a surreptitious effort to borrow or emulate some of the self-expression enjoyed by the poet? What a critic or a teacher does with a poem is not, certainly, the main thing the poem is intended for or fit for.

The poem is not the special property of these professionals. What they do with it in any deeper sense, what their purpose and methods are, we had better not try to say too quickly. It is the problem of this essay.

II

Many centuries of literary theory have equipped us with a large array of now more or less standard topics, handles or labels, for the analysis of poems. We are disciplined to speak of the *theme* (the most abstractive and assertive kind of meaning which the poem has), and we wish to distinguish this from its realization or more concrete definition in various expressive features conceived as denser, more real, than theme, and yet translucent with meaning. We speak of *diction, imagery, metaphor, symbol* (above all symbol); we sometimes resurrect such older terms as *personification*, *allegory, fable.* And in our most ambitious, or in our vaguer and more portentous, moments, we sum up such terms and magnify them into the name of *myth.* At the same time, we speak of the movement of the poem in time, its *rhythm,* and more precisely its *meter,* its *lines, stanzas, rhymes, alliteration* and *assonance,* its echoes, turns, agnominations, and puns, and also the more directly imitative qualities of its sound, the *onomatopoeia,* representative meter, and sound symbolism, the orchestration, and all that. Sound tangles with meaning. A whole poem has a *pattern,* both of meaning and of sound, interacting. It is an act of speech and hence a *dramatization* of a meaning; it is set in a landscape or a decor, an *atmosphere,* a world, a place full of flora and fauna, constellations, furniture, accoutrements, all "symbolic" of course. It is spoken by some person, fictitious, or fictive, if we rightly conceive him, a *persona,* a mask, a mouthpiece, and hence it has a point of view and a variety of emotive endowments, an attitude toward its materials, and toward the speaker himself, a self-consciousness, and a *tone* of voice towards you and me the readers or *audience.* And often we too, if we rightly conceive ourselves, are a part of the fiction of the poem. Or at least we read only over the shoulder of some person or group that is the immediate and fictive audience. The poem is furthermore (especially if we are historical critics) a poem of a certain type or *genre* (tragic, comic, epic, elegiac, satiric, or the like), and this conception implies certain *rules,* a tradition, a decorum, convention, or expectancy. The genre and its aspects are in truth a part of the language of the sophisticated poet, a backdrop of his gestures, a sounding board against which he plays off his effects. Often enough, or perhaps always, the exquisite poem presents a sort of finely blended or dramat-

ically structured opposition of attitudes and of the meanings which lie behind them—their *objective correlatives.* Hence the poem has *tension* (stress and distress), it lives in conflict; its materials are warped, its diction strained, dislocated. Catachresis is only normal. That is to say, the poem is *metaphoric.* The metaphoric quality of the meaning turns out to be the inevitable counterpart of the mixed feelings. Sometimes this situation is so far developed as to merit the name of *paradoxical, ambiguous, ironic.* The poem is subtle, elusive, tough, *witty.* Always it is an indirect stratagem of its finest or deepest meaning.

I have been running over some of the main terms of our inherited grammar of criticism and attempting just a hint at some of their relationships—the pattern, if not of the poem, at least of criticism itself. I hope it is evident that I am in no sense unfriendly to this grammar of criticism or to any one of the terms of which it is composed. I am all in favor of a grammar of criticism and of our making it as sober, tight, accurate, and technically useful as may be possible. The grammar, for instance, must be especially firm in the areas of syntax and prosody, where the poet himself has, at various times in various languages and poetic traditions, been compelled to be, or has allowed himself to be, most tight and technical. It is important, for instance, to know that *Paradise Lost* is written in iambic pentameter, and if we let ourselves be pushed around at the whim of random musical or linguistic theory into finding three, four, or seven or eight metrical beats in a Miltonic line of blank verse, we are making sad nonsense of literary history and of what this particular poet did and said. An analogous difficulty would be the enterprise of talking about the poet John Donne without the use of any such terms at all as paradox, metaphysical wit, irony.

On the other hand, grammar is grammar. And I will confess to a decided opinion that the kind of technical and quasi-technical matters which I have been naming ought to be discussed mainly at the level of generalization—they ought to be taken mainly as the preliminaries, the tuning-up exercises, the calisthenics of criticism. An essay on the theme of metaphor, of symbol, of lyrical dramatics, of irony, of meter, of rhyme or pun, is one sort of thing—it is likely to be extremely interesting and useful. But an interpretation or appreciation of a specific poem by the means mainly of an appeal to categories expressed by such terms is another sort of thing—this is likely in my opinion to be somewhat less interesting.

The purpose of any poem cannot be simply to be a work of art, to be artificial, or to embody devices of art. A critic or appreciator of a poem ought scarcely to be conceived as a person who has a commitment to go into the poem and bring out trophies under any of the grammatical heads, or to locate and award credits for such technicalities—for symbols, for ironies, for meter. These and similar terms will likely enough be useful in the course of the critic's going into and coming out of a given poem. But that is a different thing. To draw a crude analogy: It would be an awkward procedure to introduce one human being to another (one of our friends to another) with allusions to commonplaces of his anatomy, or labels of his race, creed, or type of neurosis. The analogy, as I have said, is crude. Poems are not persons. Still there may be a resemblance here sufficient to give us ground for reflection.

I am supposing that the specific thing we are discussing is what to say about a given poem—rather than how to make a survey of poetry in general in order to write a grammar of poetry. Not the most precisely definable and graded features of poems in general, the accepted grammar, but something in a sense even more generic, the basic activity of our own minds by which we examine a given individual—this is what I now wish to talk for a while about. This activity of our own in examining a poem, let me add immediately and firmly, does suppose that an object, with definable features, is there, independent of us, for us to examine.

III

Let us, for one thing, remember, and observe in passing, that as teachers, for instance, we are likely to put ourselves in a Socratic relation to our pupils—setting them exercises, asking them questions. So that our own first question, what to *say* about a poem, is likely enough to assume the shape: what to *ask* about a poem. This I think is a very special, intrinsic and difficult aspect of our professional problem. If we assume that we do know, roughly, the correct things to say about a poem, how can these be transposed into good questions? Sometimes the very attempt will reveal the emptiness of what we thought we had to say. This question about questions is obviously a matter of art and tact, our own personality and that of our pupils, and I believe that nobody ought to presume to write any manuals about it. But let me stay long enough to suggest that a good question about a poem should have at least two qualities—it should stand in a middle ground between two kinds of fault. That is, in the first place, it should have in mind an answer that is better than arbitrary or prescriptive. It should not mean in effect merely: "Guess what I am thinking about. Or, tell me what I ought to be thinking about." "How does the imagery, or the meter, in this poem accomplish its purpose?" We may look on such a question, if we like, as setting an exercise, a way of eliciting or demanding an overnight paper. It is scarcely a part of a Socratic discussion. But then in the second place, the question ought not be so good that it betrays or implies its own answer or the terms of its answer. "Is the imagery of the dead trees in this poem well suited to express the idea of mortality?" The answer that is being angled for ought to be more than simply *yes* or *no*—unless perhaps as a mere preliminary to some further and more real question. Sometimes, oddly enough, the two faults of question-making turn out to be the same thing—or at least some of our more careless questions will invite being taken in either of two ways, both empty. Rather accurate parodies of the world of discourse we teachers are capable of creating appear sometimes in the jokes, gags, or riddles (learned I suppose mostly over breakfast radio) which become the favorites of our youngest pupils. "What is large and red and eats rocks?" A certain father tried to be the ingenious pupil and answered, "A large poem by William Blake." But that of course was wrong. The answer was: "A large red rock-eater." A good question should have a definite answer—different from the question and yet entailed by it. Some questions the teacher will ask mainly for the sake of giving himself the occasion for reciting the answer. (I do not say that is always bad.) A good question about a poem will be less like the example I have already given than like this other from the same source—though not exactly like this either. "What is the difference between a lead pipe and an infatuated Dutchman? The father, though a teacher of poetry, gave up. The answer of course is that one is a hollow cylinder, the other is a silly Hollander.

IV

At the outset what can we be sure of? Mainly that a poem says or means some-thing, or ought to mean something (or ought to if we as teachers have any business with it—perhaps that is the safe minimum). The meaning of the poem may be quite obscure and difficult (rough, opaque and resistant to first glance), or it may be smooth and easy, perhaps deceptively smooth and easy, a nice surface and seemingly transparent. For either kind of poem, the simplest, but not the least important, kind of observation we can make, the simplest question we can ask, is the kind which relates to the dictionary. What does a certain word or phrase mean? We are lucky enough, I am assuming, to have a poem which contains some archaic, technical, or esoteric expression, which the class, without previous research, will not understand. If we are even luckier, the word has another, a modern, an easy and plausible meaning, which conceals the more difficult meaning. (Ambiguity, double or simultaneous meaning, our grammar instructs us, is a normal situation in poems.) In any case, we can put our question in two stages: "Are there any difficulties or questions with this stanza?" "Well, in that case, Miss Proudfit, what does the word *braw* mean?" "What does *kirkward* mean?" "When six braw gentlemen kirkward shall carry ye." We are lucky, I say, not simply that we have a chance to teach the class something—to earn our salary in a clear and measurable way. But of course because we hereby succeed in turning the attention of the class to the poem, to the surface, and then through the surface. They may begin to suspect the whole of this surface. They may ask a few questions of their own. This is success. A person who has been a teacher for a number of years masters the problem of knowing his lesson only to experience the more difficult problem of trying to remember what it is like not to know it.

v

The answers to the kind of questions we have just noticed lie in a clean, dictionary region of meaning. This kind of meaning is definitely, definably, and provably there—some of our pupils just did not happen to be aware of it. Let us call this *explicit* meaning. I believe it is important to give this kind of meaning a name and to keep it fixed. The act of expounding this meaning also needs a name. Let us call it *explanation*—explanation of the explicit.

Obviously, our talking about the poem will not go far at this level—not much farther than our translation of Caesar or Virgil in a Latin reading class.

And so we proceed, or most often we do, to another level of commentary on the poem—not necessarily second *in order* for every teacher or for every poem, but at least early and fundamental, or in part so. This level of commentary may usefully be called *description* of a poem —not explanation, just description. There is no way of describing the weather report, except to repeat what it says—describing the weather. A poem, on the other hand, not only says something, but *is* something. "A poem," we know, "should not mean but be." And so the poem itself especially invites description.

The meter of a poem, for instance, is of a certain kind, with certain kinds of variations and certain relations to the syntax; one kind of word rhymes with another kind (*Aristotle* with *bottle*, in Byron; *Adam* with *madam*, in Yeats); some conspicuous repetition or refrain in a poem shows partial variations ("On the Ecchoing Green. . . . On the darkening Green." "Could frame thy fearful symmetry. . . . Dare frame thy fearful symmetry"). Some unusual word is repeated several times in a short poem, or a word appears in some curious position. Some image (or "symbol") or cluster of images recurs in a tragedy or is played against some other image or cluster. Shakespeare's *Hamlet*, for instance, may be described as a dramatic poem which concerns the murder of a father and a son's burden of exacting revenge. At the same time it is a work which exhibits a remarkable number and variety of images relating to the expressive arts and to the criticism of the arts—music, poetry, the theater. "That's an ill phrase, a vile phrase; 'beautified' is a vile phrase." "Speak the speech, I pray you . . . trippingly on the tongue." "Govern these ventages with your finger and thumb . . . it will discourse most eloquent music."

Description in the most direct sense moves inside the poem, accenting the parts and showing their relations. It may also, however, look outside the poem. *Internal* and *external* are complementary. The external includes all the kinds of history in which the poem has its setting. A specially important kind of history, for example, is the literary tradition itself. The small neat squared-off quatrains of Andrew Marvell's *Horatian Ode* upon Oliver Cromwell go in a very exact way with the title and with the main statement of the poem. Both in ostensible theme and in prosody the poem is a kind of echo of Horatian alcaics in honor of Caesar Augustus. The blank verse of Milton's *Paradise Lost* and the couplets of Dryden's translation of the *Aeneid* are both attempts to find an equivalent for, or a vehicle of reference to, the hexameters of Greek and Latin epic poetry. A poem in William Blake's *Songs of Innocence* is written in simple quatrains, four rising feet or three to a line, with perhaps alternate rhymes. These are something like the stanzas of a folk ballad, but they are more like something else. A more immediate antecedent both of Blake's metric and of his vocabulary of childlike piety, virtues and vices, hopes and fears, is the popular religious poetry of the eighteenth century, the hymns sung at the evangelical chapels, written for children by authors like Isaac Watts or Christopher Smart.

VI

We can insist, then, on *description* of poems, both *internal* and *external,* as a moment of critical discourse which has its own identity and may be usefully recognized and defined. Let us hasten to add, however, that in making the effort to define this moment we are mainly concerned with setting up a platform for the accurate construction of something further.

The truth is that description of a poetic structure is never simply a report on appearances (as it might be, for instance, if the object were a painted wooden box). Description of a poetic structure is inevitably also an engagement with *meanings* which inhere in that structure. It is a necessary first part of the engagement with certain kinds of meaning. (*Certain kinds*—in the long run we shall want to lay some emphasis on that qualification. But for the moment the point is that there is meaning.) In the critic's discourse "pure description" will always have a hard time taking the "place of sense."

Perhaps we shall feel guilty of stretching the meaning of the word *meaning* slightly, but unless we are willing to leave many kinds of intimation out of our account of poetry, we shall have to say, for example, that Byron meant that criticism had fallen on evil days—and that it didn't matter very much. "Longinus o'er a bottle, Or, Every Poet his *own* Aristotle." We shall have to say, surely we shall wish to say, that Milton in the opening of his *Paradise Lost* means, "This is the language and style of epic, the greatest kind of poetry; and this is

the one theme that surpasses those of the greatest epics of antiquity." ("This" —in a sense—"is an epic to end all epics." As it did.) Alexander Pope in his *Epistle to Augustus* means, "This is a poem to the King of England which sounds curiously like the Epistle of Horace to the Emperor Augustus. Let anybody who cares or dares notice how curious it sounds." Shakespeare means that the action of *Hamlet* takes place on a stage, in a world, where relations between appearance and reality are manifold and some of them oddly warped.

Through description of poems, then, we move back to meaning—though scarcely to the same kind of meaning as that with which we were engaged in our initial and simple explanation of words. Through description, we arrive at a kind of meaning which ought to have its own special name. We can safely and usefully, I think, give it the simple name of the *implicit*. What we are doing with it had better too be given a special name. Perhaps *explication* is the best, though the harsher word *explicitation* may seem invited. The realms of the explicit and the implicit do not, of course, constitute sealed-off separate compartments. Still there will be some meanings which we can say are clearly explicit, and some which are clearly but implicit.

I believe that we ought to work to keep ourselves keenly aware of two things concerning the nature of implicit meaning. One of these is the strongly directive and selective power of such meaning—the power of the *pattern*, of the main formally controlling purpose in the well-written poem (in terms of Gestalt psychology, the principle of "closure"). It is this which is the altogether sufficient and compelling reason in many of our decisions about details of meaning which we proceed, during our discussion of the poem, to make quite explicit—though the dictionary cannot instruct us. In the third stanza of Marvell's *Garden:* "No white or red was ever seen / So am'rous as this lovely green." How do we know that the words *white* and *red* refer to the complexions of the British ladies?—and not, for instance, to white and red roses? The word *am'rous* gives a clue. The whole implicit pattern of meaning in the poem proves it. In these lines of this poem the words can mean nothing else. In Marvell's *Ode* on Cromwell: ". . . now the *Irish* are asham'd to see themselves in one Year tam'd. . . . They can affirm his Praises best, And have, though overcome, confest How good he is, how just, And fit for highest Trust." How do we show that these words do not express simply a complacent English report, for the year 1650, on the ruthless efficiency of Cromwell in Ireland? Only by appealing to the delicately managed intimations of the whole poem. The cruder reading, which might be unavoidable in some other context, will here reveal (in the interest of a supposedly stolid historical accuracy) a strange critical indifference to the extraordinary finesse of Marvell's poetic achievement. "Proud Maisie is in the wood, Walking so early. . . . 'Tell me, thou bonny bird, When shall I marry me?'—'When six braw gentlemen Kirkward shall carry ye.' " How do we know, how do we prove to our freshman class, that the word *proud* does not mean in the first place—does not necessarily mean at all—conceited, unlikable, nasty, unlovable, that Maisie does not suffer a fate more or less well deserved (withered and grown old as a spinster—an example of poetic justice)? Only, I think, by appealing to the whole contour and intent of this tiny but exquisitely complete poem.

"Who makes the bridal bed,
  Birdie, say truly?"—
"The gray-headed sexton
  That delves the grave duly.

"The glow-worm o'er grave and stone
  Shall light thee steady.
The owl from the steeple sing,
  'Welcome, proud lady.' "

The second thing concerning implicit meaning which I think we ought to stress is exactly its character as implicit—and this in reaction against certain confused modes of talk which sometimes prevail. It was a hard fight for criticism, at one time not so long past, to gain recognition of the formal and implicit at all as a kind of meaning. But that fight being in part won, perhaps a careless habit developed of talking about all sorts and levels of meaning as if they all were meaning in the same direct and simple way. And this has brought anguished bursts of protest from more sober and literal scholars. The critic seems all too gracefully and readily to move beyond mere explanation (Being a sophisticated man, he feels perhaps the need to do relatively little of this). He soars or plunges into descriptions of the colors and structures of the poem, with immense involvements of meaning, manifold explicitations—yet all perhaps in one level tone of confident and precise insistence, which scarcely advertises or even admits what is actually going on. The trouble with this kind of criticism is that it knows too much. Students, who of course know too little, will sometimes render back and magnify this kind of weakness in weird parodies, innocent sabotage. "I am overtired / Of the great harvest I myself desired," proclaims the man who lives on the farm with the orchard, the cellar bin, the drinking trough, and the woodchuck, in Robert Frost's *After Apple-Picking*. "This man," says the student in his homework paper, "is tired of life. He wants to go to sleep and die." This we mark with a red pencil. Then we set to work, somehow, in class, to retrieve the "symbolism." This monodrama of a tired applepicker, with the feel of the ladder rungs in his instep, bears nearly the same relation to the end of a country fair, the end of a victorious football season, of a long vacation, or of a full lifetime, as a doughnut bears to a Christmas wreath, a ferris wheel, or the rings of Saturn. *Nearly* the same relation, let us say. A poem is a kind of shape, a cunning and precise shape of words and human experience, which has something of the indeterminacy of a simpler physical shape, round or square, but which at the same time invites and justifies a very wide replication or reflection of itself in the field of our awareness.

Till the little ones, weary,
No more can be merry;
The sun does descend,
And our sports have an end.
Round the laps of their mothers
Many sisters and brothers,
Like birds in their nest,
Are ready for rest,
And sport no more seen
On the darkening Green.

What experience has any member of the class ever had, or what experiences can he think of or imagine, that are parallel to or concentric to that of the apple-picker? of the Ecchoing Green?—yet the words of the poem do not *mean* these other experiences in the same way that they mean the apples, the ladder, the man, the sport and the green. The kind of student interpretation which I have mentioned may be described as the fallacy of the literal feedback. Proud Maisie translated into conceited Maisie may be viewed as a miniature instance of the same. And this will illustrate the close relation between the two errors of implicit reading which I have just been trying to describe. The uncontrolled reading is very often the over-explicit reading.

VII

Explanation, then—of the explicit and clearly ascertainable but perhaps obscure or disguised meanings of words; description—of the poem's structure and parts, its shape and colors, and its historical relations; explication—the turning of such description as far as possible into meaning. These I believe are the teacher-critic's staple commitments—which we may sum up, if we wish, in some such generic term as *elucidation* or *interpretation.*

It is difficult to illustrate these matters evenly from any single short poem. Let me, nevertheless, make the effort. Not to show the originality of my own critical judgment, but to keep within the area of what is readily available and plausible, I choose the four quatrains of William Blake's *London* in his *Songs of Experience.*[1]

I wander thro' each charter'd street
Near where the charter'd Thames does
* flow,*
And mark in every face I meet
Marks of weakness, marks of woe.

In every cry of every Man,
In every infant's cry of fear,
In every voice, in every ban,
The mind-forg'd manacles I hear.

How the Chimney-sweeper's cry
Every black'ning Church Appalls;
And the hapless Soldier's sigh
Runs in blood down Palace walls.

But most thro' midnight streets I hear
How the youthful Harlot's curse
Blasts the new born Infant's tear,
And blights with plagues the Marriage
* hearse.*

Let me remark briefly that Blake engraved and printed and illuminated this poem as part of a pictorially designed

[1] For information about this poem, I have consulted mainly, though not exclusively, Joseph H. Wicksteed, *Blake's Innocence and Experience* (London, 1928) and *Selected Poems of William Blake,* ed. F. W. Bateson (New York, 1957).

page. But I believe that this poem (if perhaps not all of Blake's similarly illustrated poems) can be fully understood without any picture.

A further special remark is required by the fact that an early draft of this poem, which is available in Blake's notebook, the celebrated Rossetti manuscript, gives us several variant readings, even variants of key words in the poem. Such avenues of access to the poet's process of composition, a favorite kind of resort for the biographical detective, may also I believe be legitimately enough invoked by a teacher as an aid to exposition. Surely the variant reading, the fumbled and rejected inspiration, makes a convenient enough focus on the actual reading. We suppose that the poet did improve his composition, and usually he did. So if word A is worse, *why* is word B better, or best? Comparison opens inquiry, promotes realization. Sometimes the discovery of such an unravelled thread, in our learned edition of the poet, will save a classroom discussion which was otherwise moving toward vacuity. Nevertheless I choose here not to invoke the interesting variants to Blake's poem, because I believe the existence and the exhibition of such genetic vestiges is not intrinsic to the confrontation of our minds with the poem. Not that to invoke the variants would be unfair—it is simply unnecessary. If we really need inferior variants, we can make up some of our own. And perhaps we ought to.

Perhaps there is no single word in this poem which calls for the simple dictionary work which I have defined as the level of mere explanation. But the word *charter'd*, used twice in the first two lines, is nearly such a word. At any rate, its emphatic and reiterated assertion, its somewhat curious ring in its context, as well as its position at the start of the poem, make it a likely word to begin

with. How is a street chartered? How is the Thames chartered? A charter is a written document, delivered by a governmental authority, and granting privileges, recognizing rights, or creating corporate entities, boroughs, universities, trading companies, utilities. It is privilege, immunity, publicly conceded right. The Great Charter (*Magna Charta*) is a glorious instance of the concept in the history of men who speak English. I have been following, where it led me, the article under the word *Charter* in the *Oxford English Dictionary on Historical Principles*. But surely the great Dictionary is mistaken when under meaning 3.2 *figurative*. "Privileged, licensed," it quotes Shakespeare's *Henry the Fifth*, "When he speakes, The Ayre, a Charter'd Libertine, is still," and shortly after that, Blake, *Songs of Experience*, "Near where the charter'd Thames does flow." Surely the eminent Victorian person who compiled that entry was little given to the modern critical sin of looking for ironies in poetry. The force of that reiterated word in the first two lines of Blake's poem must have something to do with a tendency of the word, in the right context (and Blake's poem is that context), to mean nearly the opposite of those meanings of advantage listed in the Dictionary. For chartered privilege is a legalistic thing, which sounds less good when we call it vested interest, and which entails an inevitable obverse, that is, restriction or restraint. How indeed could the street or the river be chartered in any of the liberating senses listed in the Dictionary? It is the traffic on them or the right to build houses along them that is chartered in the sense of being conceded —to somebody. And this inevitably means that for somebody else—probably for you and me—the privilege is the restriction. Thus the strange twisted aptness, the happy catachresis, of the wanderer's calling so mobile and natural a force as the river chartered at all. The fact is that this meaning of the word *chartered* is not listed in the Oxford *Dictionary*.

We began with the Dictionary, but we have had to go beyond it, to correct it in a specific point, and even to reverse its general drift. Examples of dictionary explanation of words in poems almost always turn out to be not quite pure.

To turn away from the attempt at such explanation, then—what opportunities do we find for simply *describing* this poem— and first, with regard to its immediate historical contexts? Perhaps some note on the chimney sweeper will be needed for our twentieth-century American pupils. We can look a little to one side and see Blake's angry poem *The Chimney Sweeper* in the *Songs of Experience*: "A little black thing among the snow, Crying 'weep!' 'weep!' in notes of woe!" We can look back and see the companion *Chimney Sweeper,* tenderly comical, poignant, in the *Songs of Innocence*. ". . . I said 'Hush, Tom! never mind it, for when your head's bare You know that the soot cannot spoil your white hair.'" An Act of Parliament of 1788 had attempted to prohibit the employment of chimney sweeps until they were eight years old. In winter they began work at 7 a.m., in summer at 5. Their heads were shaved to reduce the risk of their hair catching fire from pockets of smouldering soot. An essay on the eighteenth-century London practice of chimney-sweeping would of course be an explication, *in extenso*, of the third stanza of this poem. We could add notes too for this stanza on the wars and armies of the period, on the condition of the London churches (the blackening of Portland limestone outside—suppositions about the failure of the ministry inside, priestly symbols of oppression in other lyrics by Blake), or for the fourth

stanza we could investigate harlots in eighteenth-century London. But I believe it is part of the power of this particular poem that it scarcely requires any very elaborate descriptive explications of this sort. "We can do pretty well with the poem," says one commentator, "in contexts of our own manufacture or out of our own experience."[2]

Another external point of reference, a part of Blake's immediate literary and religious tradition, has already been named—that is, when we alluded to the simple metrics and the innocent language of the eighteenth-century evangelical hymns. Blake's *Songs of Innocence and of Experience*, says one critic, are "almost a parody" of such popular earlier collections as the *Divine Songs Attempted in Easy Language for the Use of Children* by the nonconformist minister and logician Isaac Watts.[3] Blake knew that collection well. And thus, a certain *Song* entitled *Praise for Mercies Spiritual and Temporal*.

Whene'er I take my walks abroad,
　How many poor I see;
What shall I render to my God
　For all his gifts to me.

.　　.　　.　　.　　.　　.

How many children in the street,
　Half naked I behold!
While I am cloth'd from head to feet,
　And cover'd from the cold.

The echoes of such socially innocent hymnology in the minds and ears of Blake and his generation make, as I have suggested, a part of the meaning of his vocabulary and rhythm, part of a historic London sounding board, against which

----

[2] David V. Erdman, "Blake; The Historical Approach," *English Institute Essays 1950* (New York, 1951), p. 200.

[3] Cf. Mark Schorer, *William Blake, The Politics of Vision* (New York, 1946), pp. 406–407.

we too can enjoy a more resonant reading of the bitterness and irony of the wanderer in the chartered streets.

But to turn back to the words of our poem and to inquire whether any *internal* features of it deserve descriptive notice: For one thing, I should want a class to notice how the simple hymn-like stanzas of this poem are fortified or specialized in a remarkable way by a kind of phonemic tune, or prominent and stark, almost harsh, succession of similar emphatic syllables. This tune is announced in the opening verb *wander*, then immediately picked up and reiterated, doubly and triply:—*chartered* street, *chartered* Thames, "And *mark* in every face . . . *Marks* of Weakness, *marks* of woe." The word *mark* indeed, the inner mental act, the outer graven sign, is the very motif of this marking repetition. It was more than a semantic or dictionary triumph when Blake revising his poem hit on the word *chartered*—rejecting the other quite different-sounding word which we need not mention, which appears in the Rossetti manuscript.

The student of the poem will easily pick out the modulations of the theme through the rest of the poem: the rhyme words *man* and *ban*, the emphatic syllable of *man*acles, the *black*'ning Church, the *hap*less sigh, the *Pa*lace *Walls* . . . *Har*lot, *Blasts*, and *Marriage*. But what is the meaning of this phonetic pattern? A certain meaning, not in the sense necessarily of what Blake fully intended or would have confessed or defined if we had asked him, but in the sense of something which is actually conveyed if we will let it be conveyed, has been pretty much implied in the very description of the pattern. According to our temperaments and our experiences, and as our imagination is more auditory, eidetic, or kinesthetic, we will realize the force of this phonetic marking in images of insistently wandering, tramping feet, in a savage motion of the arms and head, in a bitter chanting, a dark repetition of indictments. Any one of these images, as I attempt to verbalize it, is perhaps excessive; no one is specifically necessary. But all of these and others are relevant.

We have said that the word *chartered* when applied to the street and even more when applied to the river is an anomaly. A close inspection of this poem will reveal a good many curiosities in its diction. Notice, for example, the word *cry*, which occurs three times in the course of stanzas two and three. Why do men cry in the streets of London? In addition to various random cries of confusion, hurry, and violence (which we are surely entitled to include in the meaning of the word), there is the more special and more continuous London street *cry*, the "proclamation," as the Dictionary has it, of wares or of services. If we had plenty of time for history we could read Addison's *Spectator* on "Street Cries." A more immediately critical interest is served when we notice that the steadily clamorous background of the London scene of charter and barter merges by a kind of metaphoric glide, in the next two lines, into a medley of other vocal sounds, "cries," in another sense, of fear, "voices," "bans"—that is to say, legal or official yells, proclamations, summonses, prohibitions, curses. Are the kinds of cries really separate, or are all much the same? In the next line the infant cry of fear merges literally with the cry of service—"sweep, sweep," or "weep, weep," as we learn the pronunciation from Blake's two Chimney Sweeper songs. The whole poem proceeds not only by pregnant repetitions but by a series of extraordinary conjunctions and compressions, by a pervasive emergence of metaphoric intimation from the literal details of the Hogarthian scene. Consider, for instance, how to *appall* is to dismay or terrify, and etymologically perhaps to make *pale*. Doubtless the syntax says here in the first place that the unconsciously accusing cry of the infant sweep strikes dismay, even a kind of pallor, into these irrelevant, mouldering, and darkening fabrics. At the same time the syntax does not forbid a hint of the complementary sense that the walls throw back the infant cry in ineffectual and appalled echoes. The strange assault of pitiful sounds upon the very color of the walls, which is managed in these first two lines by verbal intimation, erupts in the next two beyond verbalism into the bold, surrealistically asserted vision of the *sigh* which attaches itself as blood to place walls.

But most thro' midnight streets I hear
How the youthful Harlot's curse
Blasts the new born Infant's tear,
And blights with plagues the Marriage
  hearse.

The devotee of Blake may, by consulting the Rossetti manuscript, discover that the poet took extraordinary pains with this last stanza of the poem (which was an afterthought) : he wrote it and rewrote it, deleting words and squeezing alternatives onto his already used-up page. Clearly he intended that a lot of meaning should inhere in this densely contrived stanza—the climax, the *most* appalling instance, of the assault of the city sounds upon the citadels, the institutions, the persons of the chartered privilege. The new role of the infant in this stanza, lying between the harlot and the major target of her curse, and the impatient energy, the crowding of sense, from the harlot and her curse, through the blight, the plague, to the ghastly paradox of that final union of words—the marriage hearse —perhaps we had better leave this to a paper by our students, rather than attempt to exhaust the meaning in class.

I have perhaps already said too much about this one short poem. Yet I have certainly not said all that might be said. Relentless criticism of a poem, the technique of the lemon-squeezer, is not to my mind an ideal pedagogic procedure. It is not even a possibility. A descriptive explication of a poem is both more and less than a multiple and exhaustive précis. Our aim I think should be to say certain selected, intelligible things about a poem, enough to establish the main lines of its technical achievement, of its symbolic shape. When we have done that much, we understand the poem—even if there are grace notes and overtones which have escaped our conscious notice.

VIII

Let me back off then from the poem by William Blake and return once more, briefly, to my main argument. *Explanation, description,* and *explication:* we can recognize three phases of our interpretation of the poem, though they prove to be more closely entangled and merged with one another than we might have realized at the beginning. But are they all? Is there not another activity which has been going on in our minds, almost inevitably, all this while? The activity of *appreciation.* All this time, while reading the poem so carefully, have we not also been liking it or disliking it? Admiring it or despising it? Presumably we have. And presumably we ought now to ask ourselves this further question: Is there any connection between the things we have managed so far to say about the poem and the kind of response we experience toward it? Our liking it or our disliking it? Are we inclined to try to explain why we like the poem? Do we know how to do this? More precisely: Would a statement of our liking for the poem, an act of praise or appreciation, be something different from (even though perhaps dependent upon) the things we have already been saying? Or has the appreciation already been sufficiently implied or entailed by what we have been saying?

At the first level, that of simple dictionary explanation, very little, we will probably say, has been implied. And very little, we will most likely say, in many of our motions at the second level, the simply descriptive. It is not a merit in a poem, or surely not much of a merit, that it should contain any given vocabulary, say of striking or unusual words, or even that it should have metaphors, or that it should have meter or any certain kind of meter, or rhymes, as any of these entities may be purely conceived.

But that—as we have been seeing—is to put these matters of simple explanation and simple description more simply and more abstractly than they are really susceptible of being put. We pass imperceptibly and quickly beyond these matters. We are inevitably and soon caught up in the demands of explication—the realization of the vastly more rich and interesting implicit kinds of meaning. We are engaged with features of a poem which—given always other features too of the whole context—do tend to assert themselves as reasons for our pleasure in the poem and our admiration for it. We begin to talk about patterns of meaning; we encounter structures or forms which are radiant or resonant with meaning. Patterns and structures involve coherence (unity, coherence, and emphasis), and coherence is an aspect of truth and significance. I do not think that our evaluative intimations will often, if ever, advance to the firmness and completeness of a demonstration. Perhaps it is hardly conceivable that they should. But our discourse upon the poem will almost inevitably be charged with implications of its value. It will be more difficult to keep out these intimations than to let them in. Critics who have announced the most

resolute programs of neutrality have found this out. Take care of the weight, the color, the shape of the poem, be fair to the explanation and description, the indisputable parts of the formal explication—the appreciation will be there, and it will be difficult to avoid having expressed it.

Explicatory criticism (or explicatory evaluation) is an account of a poem which exhibits the relation between its form and its meaning. Only poems which are worth something are susceptible of this kind of account. It is something like a definition of poetry to say that whereas rhetoric—in the sense of mere persuasion or sophistic—is a kind of discourse the power of which diminishes in proportion as the artifice of it is understood or seen through—poetry, on the other hand, is a kind of discourse the power of which—or the satisfaction which we derive from it—is actually increased by an increase in our understanding of the artifice. In poetry the artifice is art. This comes close I think to the center of the aesthetic fact.

IX

One of the attempts at a standard of poetic value most often reiterated in past ages has been the doctrinal—the explicitly didactic. The aim of poetry, says the ancient Roman poet, is double, both to give pleasure and to teach some useful doctrine. You might get by with only one or the other, but it is much sounder to do both. Or, the aim of poetry is to teach some doctrine—and to do this convincingly and persuasively, by means of vividness and pleasure—as in effect the Elizabethan courtier and the eighteenth-century essayist would say. But in what does the pleasure consist? Why is the discourse pleasurable? Well, the aim of poetry is really to please us by means of or through the act of teaching us. The pleasure is a dramatized moral pleasure. Thus in effect some theories of drama in France during the seventeenth century. Or, the pleasure of poetry is a pleasure simply of tender and morally good feelings. Thus in effect the philosophers of the age of reason in England and France. And at length the date 1790 and Immanuel Kant's *Critique of Judgment:* which asserts that the end or effect of art is not teaching certainly, and not pleasure in anything like a simple sensuous way—rather it is something apart, a feeling, but precisely its own kind of feeling, the aesthetic. Art is autonomous—though related symbolically to the realm of moral values. Speaking from this nondidactic point of view, a critic ought to say, I should think, that the aesthetic merit of Blake's *London* does not come about because of the fact that London in that age witnessed evils which cried to Heaven for remedy, or because Blake was a Prophet Against Empire, or a Visionary Politician, or because at some time, perhaps a few years after he had written the poem, he may have come to view it as one article or moment in the development of an esoteric philosophy of imagination, a Fearful Symmetry of Vision, expanded gradually in allegorical glimpses during several phases of his life into a quasi-religious revelation or privilege which in some sense, at moments, he believed in. Blake's *London* is an achievement in words, a contained expression, a victory which resulted from some hours, or days, of artistic struggle, recorded by his pen on a page of the Rossetti manuscript.

Between the time of Immanuel Kant, however, and our own, some complications in the purity of the aesthetic view have developed. Through the romantic period and after, the poetic mind advanced pretty steadily in its own autonomous way, toward a claim to be in itself the creator. Today there is nothing that the literary theorist—at least in the British- and American-speaking world—will be more eager to repudiate than any hint of moral or religious didacticism, any least intimation that the poem is to measure its meaning or get its sanction from any kind of authority more abstract or more overtly legislative than itself. But on the other hand there has probably never been a generation of teachers of literature less willing to admit any lack of high seriousness, of implicit and embodied ethical content, even of normative vision in the object of their study. Despite our reiterated denials of didacticism, we live in an age, we help to make an age, of momentous claims for poetry—claims the most momentous conceivable, as they advance more and more under the sanction of an absolutely creative and autonomous visionary imagination. The Visionary imagination perforce repudiates all but the tautological commitment to itself. And thus, especially when it assumes (as now it begins to do) the form of what is called the "Tragic Vision" (not "The Vision of Tragedy"), it is the newest version of the *Everlasting No.* Vision *per se* is the vision of itself. "Tragic Vision" is the nearly identical vision of "Absurdity." (War-weariness and war-horror, the developing mind and studies of a generation that came out of the second War and has been living in expectation of the third may go far to explain the phenomenon, but will not justify it.) Antidoctrine is of course no less a didactic energy than doctrine itself. It is the reverse of doctrine. No more than doctrine itself, can it be located or even approached by a discussion of the relation between poetic form and poetic meaning. Antidoctrine is actually asserted by the poems of several English romantic poets, and notably, it would appear, though it is difficult to be sure, by the "prophecies" of William Blake. The idea of it may be hence a part of these poems, though never their achieved result or expression. Any more than an acceptable statement of Christian doctrine is Milton's achieved expression in *Paradise Lost*, or a statement of Aristotelian ethics is the real business of Spenser's *Faerie Queene*. Today I believe no prizes are being given for even the best doctrinal interpretation of poems. (The homiletic or parabolic interpretation of Shakespeare, for example, has hard going with the reviewer.) On the other hand, if you are willing to take a hand in the exploitation of the neuroses, the misgivings, the anxieties, the infidelities of the age—if you have talents for the attitudes of Titanism, the graces needed by an impresario of the nuptials of Heaven and Hell, you are likely to find yourself in some sense rewarded. It is obvious I hope that I myself do not believe the reward will consist in the achievement of a valid account of the relation between poetic form and poetic meaning.

III. The Sociocultural Critic

LIONEL TRILLING

STEPHEN SPENDER

GEORG LUKÁCS

IRVING HOWE

ERIC BENTLEY

INTRODUCTION

What I and others now call *sociocultural criticism,* Edmund Wilson described more than twenty years ago in a well-known essay entitled "The Historical Interpretation of Literature" as "the interpretation of literature in its social, economic, and political aspects." I happily accept Wilson's description but I balk at his rubric because it raises a certain confusion and because it merges two distinct bodies of criticism.[1] Although it is true that sociocultural criticism has close resemblances to the historical, and although it, like historical criticism—and in contrast to formalist criticism—views literature as a process rather than as an end in itself, in its origins, emphases, and practice sociocultural criticism asserts its separate identity.

Unlike the historical critic, the sociocultural critic is but passingly concerned with the literary work's text, linguistic condition, or transmission. He is, moreover, only tangentially involved with the writer's biography per se and with the literary

---

[1] The confusion between the terms *historical* and *sociocultural* is also in part one of semantics, for I believe Wilson used *historical* in its specifically Marxist sense.

work's place in a genre, convention, or tradition. His major and abiding concern, as Wilson's description accurately suggests, is in the literary work's interaction with life; and this interaction involves not only the work's social, economic, and political implications but also, in the largest sense, its moral and cultural implications. Indeed, the words *social, political, moral, cultural* or their cognates and synonyms occur again and again in the writing of the sociocultural critic. The sociocultural critic may at moments in his work be indistinguishable from the historical or even the psychological and the mythopoeic critic, but he will rarely be mistaken for the formalist.

The recognition that literature can have profound social importance and effect, an effect more urgent than its purely aesthetic quality, has existed since Plato's admonition in Book X of *The Republic.* There Plato warns, ". . . hymns to the gods and praises of famous men are the only poetry which ought to be admitted into our state." Historians of literary criticism have also suggested that the eighteenth-century theories of Vico and Herder were sources for sociocultural criticism. We might also include as part of its continuity the 1822–1823 lectures of Hegel, in which he viewed literature as expressive of its society and as the reflection of that society's dominant ideas.

For the direct sources of the contemporary sociocultural approach, however, we must look later in the nineteenth century to the writings of Taine, Marx and Engels, and Matthew Arnold. The sociocultural critic of the twentieth century builds his position on the foundations established by these men.

One of these foundations, the theories of Taine, also supported historical criticism. As noted earlier, Taine's 1863 *History of English Literature* postulated race, moment, and milieu (national character, epoch, and environment) as the three major determinants on literature. Taine's announced ambition was to use literature as a means to comprehend not only "the psychology of a people," but also to discover the wellsprings of human behavior. In the closing pages of the Introduction to his literary history he wrote:

> In this consists the importance of literary works: they are instructive because they are beautiful; their utility grows with their perfection; and if they furnish documents it is because they are monuments. The more a book brings sentiments into light, the more it is a work of literature; for the proper office of literature is to make sentiments visible. The more a book represents important sentiments, the higher is its place in literature; for it is by representing the mode of being of a whole nation and a whole age, that a writer rallies around him the sympathies of an entire age and an entire nation. . . . It is then chiefly by the study of literature that one may construct a moral history, and advance toward the knowledge of psychological laws, from which events spring.

It is significant of Taine's aesthetic theory that literature's beauty and moral value are inseparably intertwined and that in his conception of "psychological laws" he is undoubtedly closer to the Hegelian view of man than the Freudian.

Contrary to popular misunderstanding, the Marxist concept of literature as a factor in the revolutionary reconstruction of society originates not with Marx and Engels in the nineteenth century but with Lenin and Stalin in the twentieth. Marx and Engels made no unified or systematic pronouncements on literature; and if sociocultural criticism is or has been in part Marxist, it is no more purely and wholly a Marxist criticism than all formalist criticism is purely and wholly Coleridgean, psychological criticism Freudian, and mythopoeic criticism Jungian. Where sociocultural criticism does stand indebted to Marxist theory, it has been influenced not by a particular document or body of doctrine but by an essential attitude, expressed recurrently throughout the writing of Marx and Engels, that all of those human activities and institutions comprising what they call society's *superstructure* and including art, religion, and philosophy, follow upon and are shaped by man's material condition. However, Marx and Engels also allow that art need not mirror the exact material condition of the society in which it is made, that it may lag behind, anticipate, or in some periods even develop independently of the social condition. Nor is art wholly passive; it can itself help determine society's direction. Far from committing art to propagandistic purposes, Engels also wrote late in the century that art is socially most effective when its programmatic quality is least obvious and obtrusive.

But despite these qualifications and this permissiveness, the overwhelming drift of the Marxist attitude is toward the view that art is ultimately determined by the actualities of material existence. As Marx and Engels declared in *The German Ideology* (1846), "Men are the producers of their conceptions, ideas, etc.—real, active men, as they are conditioned by a definite development of their productive forces and of the intercourse corresponding to these, up to its furthest forms. . . . In direct contrast to German philosophy which descends from heaven to earth, here we ascend from earth to heaven. . . . The phantoms formed in the human brain are also, necessarily, sublimates of their material life-process, which is empirically verifiable and bound to material premises. Morality, religion, metaphysics, all the rest of ideology and their corresponding forms of consciousness, thus no longer retain the semblance of independence." From such a standpoint we can grasp something of the distance between the Marxist critic and the formalist, for the "German philosophy" here refuted is that of Kant, and therefore Coleridge and any theory of the autonomy of art that rests upon the power of separate aesthetic creation or cognition.

From Matthew Arnold the sociocultural critic derives much of his emphasis upon the moral, intellectual, and social aspects of literature and literary criticism. In this Arnold exerted almost as much influence upon twentieth-century criticism as Coleridge; it might be said that our conception of literature as educational comes largely from Arnold. Furthermore, Arnold declared that criticism took a crucial role in the creative process by providing the sort of intellectual climate in which literature flourishes. Criticism does not merely perform its function after the fact, i.e., after the artwork has come into existence; it can itself partake of the creative act. I believe that this is precisely the office for criticism Arnold claims in these statements from "The Function of Criticism at the Present Time" (1864): "It is the business of the critical power . . . to make an intellectual situation of which the creative power can profitably avail itself. It tends to establish an order of ideas, if not absolutely true, yet true by comparison with that which it displaces; to make the best ideas prevail. Presently these new ideas reach society, the touch of truth is the touch of life, and there is a stir and a growth everywhere; out of this stir and growth come the creative epochs of literature." Later in the same essay Arnold defined criticism as "*a disinterested endeavor to learn and propagate the best that is known and thought in the world*" and warned that the critic could not afford to limit himself to his own national literature but should approach the literature of all Europe as though it were one.

Elsewhere in his writing Arnold advanced equally ambitious definitions of culture and of literature as a vehicle for morality. Culture, Arnold asserted in "Sweetness and Light," was a "study of perfection" that should appeal to men of all classes and lead them to want more than merely material achievement. In this quest for what Arnold called *sweetness and light*, culture traveled the same road as poetry. The moral force of literature received even more emphatic statement in Arnold's introduction to his collection *Poems of Wordsworth* (1879), in which he wrote: "The question, *how to live*, is itself a moral idea; and it is the question which most interests every man, and with which, in some way or other, he is perpetually occupied. . . . If what distinguishes the greatest poets is their powerful and profound application of ideas to life, which surely no good critic will deny, then to prefix to the term *ideas* the term *moral* makes hardly any difference because human life itself is in so preponderating a degree moral. It is important, therefore, to hold to this: that poetry is at bottom a criticism of life; that the greatness of a poet lies in his powerful and beautiful application of ideas to life— to the question: How to live." Once again we must note that Arnold, like the other sources of the sociocultural criticism, does not ignore literature's formal and aesthetic aspects. An essential part of his definition is the phrase *powerful and beautiful application*—and these, power, beauty, and application, involve technique. Nevertheless, I think it is also clear that Arnold's concern for literature as belles-lettres is not all-consuming, that it partakes of a larger concern: life.

I have been at some pains to establish the background for sociocultural criticism and have quoted so liberally from a number of its major sources because the ideas we have treated still operate with peculiar force in the contemporary sociocultural approach. I will now summarize the basic precepts and most important considerations of that approach so that we may observe the sociocultural aesthetic as a whole, both as it reflects its sources and as it has expanded upon them in its current theory and practice. My summary takes the form of a series of assertions such as a sociocultural critic might make.

1. The literary work cannot be fully or truly understood apart from the milieu or culture or civilization in which it was produced. It must be studied in the widest possible context rather than by itself. Every literary work is the result of

a complex interaction of social and cultural factors and is itself a complex cultural object. It is, in any case, not an isolated phenomenon.

2. The ideas in the literary work are as important as its form and technique; form and technique are themselves in part determined or shaped by the work's ideas. Moreover, the quality of the work, the critical response it evokes, partakes of the quality of its ideas. No great and enduring work has ever been created on a basis of trivial, shallow, or vicious ideas. In this sense literature is serious.

3. Any literary work that endures is profoundly moral, both in its relation to the culture in which it appears and to the individual reader. The work is moral less in its advocacy of a particular code or system of behavior than in the sense that it is engrossed in life and presents an evaluative response to life. The work is, as L. C. Knights has called it, a *moral experiment*.

4. Society can impinge upon a work in two ways: either as a specific material factor or force or as tradition, that is, collective spiritual and cultural trends. These cultural trends may include purely literary traditions and conventions but are not limited to such conventions (note the distinction here between the emphasis of the historical and the sociocultural critic). Accordingly, form and content can reflect either sociological developments—for example, as the rise of the novel is influenced by the rise of the middle class—or subtle changes in the cultural temper; compare Trilling and Spender, who follow.

5. Literary criticism must be more than the disinterested aesthetic contemplation of the work itself; it must be engaged, committed. Criticism is a vital activity that can and should affect the very production of art, not by dictating the writer's choice of technique and material but by creating the kind of moment in which great art is engendered and by stimulating the sort of continuing critical discussion of art that carries over into the general culture and in turn invigorates both audience and artist.

6. The critic is responsible to the literature of both past and present. From the vast literature of the past the critic selects that which has especial pertinence to the present; his interest is never merely antiquarian or reconstructive (another sociocultural demarcation from the historical). Because the needs of each generation will demand different selections or a different emphasis, the critic's work of choice and reappraisal is simultaneously transient and unending. In this aspect of his role the critic is also a comparativist, ranging over several languages and literatures, choosing the pertinent works from them, and demonstrating the relationship of the selected works to each other, to the contemporary audience and to the contemporary production of art. In this role as mediator between art and its audience, the critic must heed the work of his own time. He considers the evaluation of contemporary work an integral and vital part of his critical function. Perhaps it is for this reason that many sociocultural critics are extremely active as reviewers, while other kinds of critics may consider reviewing a peripheral or secondary function.

Of the essays to follow, Lionel Trilling's "The Fate of Pleasure" is at once the broadest and most subtle demonstration of the principles I have defined. In Trilling's essay the interaction of literature with politics, morals, psychology, and religion is everywhere implicit but nowhere obtrusive. The key words, effective by their strategic placement rather than by their frequency, are *moral* and *culture*, used very much in the sense in which Arnold used them. To Trilling literature is an integral element of culture, both reflecting its changes and helping to produce them. Again and again Trilling suggests that what the writer perceives and sets down in his work as truth becomes true, either anticipating a significant change in the ways men respond to life, expressing a change already in effect but not yet verbalized, or bringing about a change desired although still unrealized. Literature becomes a social institution, like politics, in that it is combined with human wants and is compelled to take them into account. We also discern a Marxist element in Trilling's thought in his conception of cultural classes, that is, antagonistic forces in our civilization now divided not by money or social status but rather by artistic taste. The dominant, majority, and potentially fascistic class still believes in pleasure and in the arts that affirm the pursuit of pleasure; the minority, a morally stauncher group, denies pleasure and affirms the arts that attack it. Trilling's argument is made all the more persuasive by his erudition, his aptitude for synthesis, and the grace of his prose.

I wish to note two additional points in Trilling's essay. First, our culture's ambivalent response toward the principle of pleasure that Trilling sees as culminating in the "breach between politics and art," is somewhat reminiscent of the ambivalence of man's relationship to nature often recorded by the formalist critic, who interprets it as the "dissociation of sensibility." What I am really suggesting is the similarity or parallel between what the sociocultural critic views as a social event, the "breach between politics and art," and what the formalist sees as an aesthetic or psychological event. Secondly, Trilling argues that even the literature that in its violence and sordidness seems furthest removed from what is "moral," is at bottom the artist's mode for combating society's false values or "specious good."

Stephen Spender's essay, "The Visionary Individualists,"* as does Trilling's, ranges over the nineteenth and twentieth centuries and advances a thesis complementary to Trilling's but based on a different rationale. Spender also finds the artist's negation and social isolation significant of what was happening in the society at large, for in an age of cultural sterility the writer could preserve himself as an artist, and thus serve society, only by retreating inward.

Eric Bentley in "The Political Theatre Reconsidered"* affirms by means of negation. He begins his inquiry into the thesis-play and, by extension, into the entire question of art's social importance by stating that art deliberately produced as propaganda fails in its intended function. If it does succeed, it succeeds, paradoxically, as art and not as propaganda. Bentley also asserts that we tend to exaggerate the explicit social importance of art, that it has less effect upon events than we imagine. However, having said this, Bentley proceeds to characterize the artist as a man who will inevitably direct his work to what interests him, and what interests him is contained in his culture. This is an indirect way of reaffirming the relationship between art and society, thereby qualifying the essay's earlier statement.

This doubling-back on Bentley's part is deliberate. What he wants to correct is a simplistic view of art as either good or bad, significant or insignificant, based wholly on its politics and social impact. Bentley's argument has special emphasis in its application to Brecht, an artist who deliberately wrote politics into his plays but who increasingly compels our admiration as a playwright and not as a propagandist. However, even in Bentley's insistence that art cannot be justified on the grounds of its moral, political, or didactic functions or as a substitute for action but must be valued for itself and for its tonic effect on the individual, we perceive that Bentley continues to pay tribute to the emotional and intellectual appeal of art. Bentley's underlying premises are further visible in such statements as these: ". . . an artist cannot give up regarding himself as the conscience of mankind, even if mankind pays no attention," and "A leading playwright, I believe, might be expected to cope with *the* leading problem of the day. It will, of course, be of the highest interest *what* he considers that problem to be."

Irving Howe's "The Fiction of Anti-Utopia"* is a masterly analysis of Zamiatin's *We*, Orwell's *1984*, and Huxley's *Brave New World*, employing these books to define a subgenre or type of the novel, the anti-utopian novel. Although Howe deals with both technique and content, he gives fuller treatment to the latter, as we have come to expect in the sociocultural approach. His sociocultural perspective is revealed not only by his choice of subject but also by the unspoken assumptions that underlie his essay, especially the assumption that literature is compelling as much for its *weltanschauung* as for its form. Howe's essay takes on extraordinary interest in its attempt to relate literary form or type to particular sociopolitical developments, and in its argument that some kinds of literature can violate theoretical standards of aesthetic excellence and still succeed on their own terms. I think we must agree with Howe that the books he discusses are not literary masterpieces yet that they do have a strong grip upon our imagination.

Georg Lukács' essay "The Ideology of Modernism" demonstrates the sociocultural approach nearing its extreme limits. Beginning with questions of artistic form and within a philosophical context, Lukács' essay becomes more and more manifestly doctrinaire, at the end subordinating both form and philosophy to a political and economic thesis. To reduce Lukács' argument to its simplest terms, he finds modernism a betrayal of the artist's duty to involve himself with life (that is, the duty to help better the social condition). To Lukács, modernism constitutes both a sterile artistic movement and a futile sort of rebellion because it is largely subjective and introspective. What Lukács describes as the "psychopathology" typical of modernism he diagnoses as "a desire to escape from the reality of Capitalism."

But to leave Lukács' argument in this simplistic condition is to do it great injustice. It is not as simple as I have made it, nor so transparently political. What Lukács has to say about the relationship of form to content, of the philosophical background of modernism, and of the psychological perspective of the modern writer as it relates to his time and place is well worth hearing. Certainly no one has written more profoundly of realism than Lukács. It would be most instructive to compare the substance and quality of his thesis with the theses advanced by Daiches, Trilling, and Spender.

As learned and perceptive a critic as Lukács is, the programmatic element in his essay indicates one of the chief risks of the sociocultural criticism: its tendency toward excessive involvement in ideology at the expense of its integrity as literary criticism. It was precisely that danger that Arnold foresaw and warned against in "The Function of Criticism at the Present Time." The excesses of the sociocultural criticism are already a matter of record, for during the decade 1930–1940 it did too often lend itself to social and political purposes, accepting or rejecting works of art largely on the basis of their supposed social value. During this brief span, when the historic moment was right and when a great deal of literature was itself socially or politically obsessive, it was virtually dominant in America, England, and much of Europe. Then, weakened by its own errors and abuses and rendered anachronistic by rapid changes in world events, the sociocultural approach became an easy mark for emergent formalism. (Its fate parallels that of its relation, historical criticism.) Its opponents could draw up with considerable accuracy a long indictment of its sins: the neglect of literature as art; the narrowly prescriptive view of literature's proper function and content; the insistence that art mirror life, despite men's fundamental disagreement as to what life is; the tendency to become something other than literary criticism, that is, sociology or political science.

Except for Russia and her satellites, where sociocultural criticism continues to exist in its extreme form as the servant of an ideology—witness the critical response of Boris Pasternak's countrymen after the publication of his *Doctor Zhivago*— it is rarely guilty these days of subordinating literature to causes. Unfortunately, one still finds it attacked as perversely as though its current practice followed the radical and simplistic formulas of a generation ago.

The fact is that many of our best critics have exercised or in part adopted the sociocultural method and that in its present character it is a vital and instructive criticism. To the names represented in this collection we could add such others as Edmund Wilson, Alfred Kazin, L. C. Knights, Norman Podhoretz, Arnold Kettle, Richard Hoggart, Raymond Williams, Hans Meyer, Lucien Goldman, and Philip Rahv. Moreover, the sociocultural element is clearly visible in such diverse critics as W. H. Auden, Kenneth Burke, Leslie Fiedler, David Daiches, George Steiner, and Jean-Paul Sartre. Even the work of T. S. Eliot and F. R. Leavis, stalwarts of formalism, has at times reflected a keen awareness of literature's social and cultural values. The promising mythopoeic approach has much in common with the sociocultural in that myth always functions in a social setting and as a vehicle for community mores and beliefs. And, as we can see in the work of Trilling and others, there is close affinity between the sociocultural critic and the psychological.

Although sociocultural criticism has not been limited to any one period or literary type, it has made especially rich contributions to the study of nineteenth-century literature (of all nations), to realism and naturalism, and to modern writing. In two areas it has excelled where formalism has fallen short: in the treatment of comparative literature and in the criticism of the novel. The novel, with its penchant for the portrayal of material reality and with its sensitivity to social experience, has been perhaps the sociocultural critic's favorite genre.

The same paradox we have observed of other critical positions is equally true of the sociocultural: its strengths and weaknesses rest upon the same axis, with the crucial differences those of balance and proportion. That literature interacts with the larger life around it; that its medium, language, is a social construct; that its creator is a man affected by the economics, morality, and politics of his time and place; that it can on occasion produce social change or be itself produced by such change—these are all self-evident propositions to the sociocultural critic. In his attempt to hold these propositions before us, the sociocultural critic has the identical aims of all other critics: to arrive at an understanding of why men read, why some literary works live and others die, and why some move us and others do not. He wishes also to sharpen our apprehension of the material circumstances of literature, to study it as a whole human process.

Finally, he affirms with the utmost conviction the seriousness of literature because he is committted to the belief that books have consequences outside themselves. Above all, he has such faith in the power and beauty of literature that he believes it can be the source of grace to all who partake of it and to the civilization in which it appears.

SELECTED BIBLIOGRAPHY

Aaron, Daniel. *Writers on the Left* (New York, Harcourt, Brace & World, Inc., 1961).

Adler, Mortimer. *Poetry and Politics* (Pittsburgh, Duquesne University Press, 1966).

Brooks, Van Wyck. *The Writer in America* (New York, Avon Books, 1953).

Duncan, H. D. *Language and Literature in Society* (Chicago, University of Chicago Press, 1953).

Fischer, Ernst. *The Necessity of Art: A Marxist Approach* (Baltimore, Penguin Books, Inc., 1963).

Flores, Angel, ed. *Literature and Marxism* (New York, Critics Group, 1938).

Guérard, Albert. *Literature and Society* (Boston, Lothrop, Lee and Shepard Company, 1935).

Hardwick, Elizabeth. *A View of My Own* (New York, Farrar, Straus, & Giroux, Inc., 1962).

Hayward, Max, ed. *Literature and Revolution in Soviet Russia* (New York, Oxford University Press, 1963).

Hoggart, Richard. *The Uses of Literacy: Changing Patterns in English Mass Culture* (New York, Oxford University Press, 1957).

Kazin, Alfred. "The Function of Criticism Today," in *Contemporaries* (Boston, Little, Brown & Company, 1962), pp. 494–509.

Kern, A. C. "The Sociology of Knowledge in the Study of Literature," *Sewanee Review*, L (1942), 505–514.

Kettle, Arnold, ed. *Shakespeare in a Changing World* (New York and London, International Publishers, 1964).

Kott, Jan. *Shakespeare, Our Contemporary* (Garden City, Doubleday and Co., Inc., 1964).

Leavis, F. R. "Literature and Society," in *The Common Pursuit* (New York, New York University Press, 1952), pp. 82–94.

Lowenthal, Leo. *Literature, Popular Culture, and Society* (Englewood Cliffs, N.J., Prentice-Hall, Inc., 1961).

McCarthy, Mary. *On the Contrary* (New York, Farrar, Straus & Giroux, Inc., 1961).

Macdonald, Dwight. *Against the American Grain* (New York, Random House, Inc., 1962).

Mander, John. *The Writer and Commitment* (Philadelphia, Dufour Editions, 1962).

Marcus, Steven. *The Other Victorians* (New York, Basic Books, Inc., 1966).

Rahv, Philip. "Criticism and the Imagination of Alternatives," *Michigan Alumnus Quarterly Review*, LXIII (1956), 7–16.

Rahv, Philip. "Fiction and the Criticism of Fiction," *Kenyon Review*, XVIII (1956), 276–299.

Slote, Bernice, ed. *Literature and Society* (Lincoln, Neb., University of Nebraska Press, 1964).

Smith, Bernard. *Forces in American Criticism* (New York, Harcourt, Brace & World, Inc., 1939).

Steiner, George. "Humane Literacy," in Anon., *The Critical Moment* (New York and Toronto, McGraw Hill, Inc., 1964), pp. 21–30.

Steiner, George. "Marxism and the Literary Critic," *Encounter*, XI (1958), 33–43.

Sutton, Walter. *Modern American Criticism* (Englewood Cliffs, N.J., Prentice-Hall, Inc., 1963), pp. 51–97.

Wellek, René, and Austin Warren. *Theory of Literature* (New York, Harcourt, Brace & World, Inc., 1956), pp. 82–97.

Williams, Raymond. *Culture and Society, 1780–1950* (New York, Columbia University Press, 1958).

Williams, Raymond. *The Long Revolution* (New York, Columbia University Press, 1961).

Wilson, Edmund. *The Triple Thinkers* (New York, Oxford University Press, 1948), pp. 197–212, 257–270.

Wimsatt, W. K., Jr., and Cleanth Brooks. *Literary Criticism: A Short History* (New York, Alfred A. Knopf, Inc., 1964), pp. 455–734 *passim*.

Witte, W. "The Sociological Approach to Literature," *Modern Language Review*, XXXVI (1941), 86–94.

Lionel Trilling

THE FATE OF PLEASURE

Lionel Trilling has achieved recognition as one of the foremost critics of our generation. He has also written a distinguished novel, *The Middle of the Journey* (1947), and a number of frequently reprinted short stories. Among Trilling's critical writings are studies of Matthew Arnold and E. M. Forster and several collections of essays such as *The Liberal Imagination* and the recent *Beyond Culture* (1965), which is the source of this selection. Trilling has taught at Columbia University since 1931, and during 1963–1965 was Eastman Visiting Professor at Oxford University. "The Fate of Pleasure" was first printed in a somewhat different form in the *Partisan Review* in 1963.

Of all critical essays in the English language, there is none that has established itself so firmly in our minds as Wordsworth's Preface to *Lyrical Ballads*. Indeed, certain of the statements that the Preface makes about the nature of poetry have come to exist for us as something like proverbs of criticism. This is deplorable, for the famous utterances, in the form in which we hold them in memory, can only darken counsel. A large part of the literate world believes that Wordsworth defines poetry as the spontaneous overflow of powerful feelings. With such a definition we shall not get very far in our efforts to think about poetry, and in point of fact Wordsworth makes no such definition. Much less does he say, as many find it convenient to recall, that poetry is emotion recollected in tranquillity. Yet the tenacity with which we hold in mind our distortions of what Wordsworth ac-

tually does say suggests the peculiar power of the essay as a whole, its unique existence as a work of criticism. Its cogency in argument is notable, even if intermittent, but the Preface is not regarded by its readers only as an argument. By reason of its eloquence, and because of the impetuous spirit with which it engages the great questions of the nature and function of poetry, it presents itself to us not chiefly as a discourse, but rather as a dramatic action, and we are prepared to respond to its utterances less for their truth than for their happy boldness.

This being so, it should be a matter for surprise that one especially bold utterance of the Preface has not engaged us at all and is scarcely ever cited. I refer to the sentence in which Wordsworth speaks of what he calls "the grand elementary principle of pleasure," and says of it that it constitutes "the naked and native dignity of man," that it is the principle by which man "knows, and feels, and lives, and moves."

This is a statement which has great intrinsic interest, because, if we recognize that it is bold at all, we must also perceive that it is bold to the point of being shocking, for it echoes and controverts St. Paul's sentence which tells us that "we live, and move, and have our being" in God (Acts 17:28). And in addition to its intrinsic interest, it has great historical interest, not only because it sums up a characteristic tendency of eighteenth-century thought but also because it bears significantly upon a characteristic tendency of our contemporary culture. Its relation to that culture is chiefly a negative one—our present sense of life does not accommodate the idea of pleasure as something which constitutes the "naked and native dignity of man."

The word *pleasure* occurs frequently in the Preface. Like earlier writers on the subject, when Wordsworth undertakes to explain why we do, or should, value poetry, he bases his explanation upon the pleasure which poetry gives. Generally he uses the word in much the same sense that was intended by his predecessors. The pleasure which used commonly to be associated with poetry was morally unexceptionable and not very intense—it was generally understood that poetry might indeed sometimes excite the mind but only as a step toward composing it. But the word has, we know, two separate moral ambiences and two very different degrees of intensity. The pleasures of domestic life are virtuous; the pleasures of Imagination or Melancholy propose the idea of a cultivated delicacy of mind in those who experience them; the name of an English pipe-tobacco, "Parson's Pleasure," although derived from the place on the river at Oxford where men have traditionally bathed naked, is obviously

meant to suggest that the word readily consorts with ideas of mildness. None of these point to what Byron had in mind when he wrote, "O pleasure! you're indeed a pleasant thing, / Although one must be damn'd for you no doubt." The *Oxford English Dictionary* takes due note of what it calls an "unfavorable" sense of the word: "Sensuous enjoyment as a chief object of life, or end, in itself," and informs us that in this pejorative sense it is "sometimes personified as a female deity." The Oxford lexicographers do not stop there but go on to recognize what they call a "strictly physical" sense, which is even lower in the moral scale: "the indulgence of the appetites, sensual gratification." The "unfavorable" significations of the word are dramatized by the English career of the most usual Latin word for pleasure, *voluptas*. Although some Latin-English dictionaries, especially those of the nineteenth century, say that *voluptas* means "pleasure, enjoyment, or delight of body or mind in a good or a bad sense," the word as it was used in antiquity seems to have been on the whole morally neutral and not necessarily intense. But the English words derived from *voluptas* are charged with moral judgment and are rather excited. We understand that it is not really to the minds of men that a voluptuous woman holds out the promise of pleasure, enjoyment, or delight. We do not expect a voluptuary to seek his pleasures in domesticity, or in the Imagination or Melancholy, or in smoking a pipe.

It is obvious that any badness or unfavorableness of meaning that the word *pleasure* may have relates to the primitiveness of the enjoyment that is being referred to. Scarcely any moralist will object to pleasure as what we may call a secondary state of feeling, as a charm or grace added to the solid business of life. What does arouse strong adverse judgment is pleasure in its radical aspect, as it is the object of an essential and definitive energy of man's nature. It was because Bentham's moral theory represented pleasure in this way that Carlyle called it the Pig-philosophy. He meant, of course, that it impugned man's nature to associate it so immediately with pleasure. Yet this is just how Wordsworth asks us to conceive man's nature in the sentence I have spoken of—it is precisely pleasure in its primitive or radical aspect that he has in mind. He speaks of "the grand *elementary* principle of pleasure," which is to say, pleasure not as a mere charm or amenity but as the object of an instinct, of what Freud, whose complex exposition of the part that pleasure plays in life is of course much in point here, was later to call a *drive*. How little concerned was Wordsworth, at least in this one sentence, with pleasure in its mere secondary aspect is suggested by his speaking of it as constituting the *dignity* of man, not having in mind such dignity as is conferred by society but that which is *native* and *naked*.

When Carlyle denounced Bentham's assertion that pleasure is, and must be, a first consideration of the human being, it was exactly man's dignity that he was undertaking to defend. The traditional morality to which Carlyle subscribed was certainly under no illusion about the crude force of man's impulse to self-gratification, but it did not associate man's dignity with this force—on the contrary, dignity, so far as it was personal and moral, was thought to derive from the resistance which man offers to the impulse to pleasure.

For Wordsworth, however, pleasure was the defining attribute of life itself and of nature itself—pleasure is the "impulse from the vernal wood" which teaches us more of man and his moral being "than all the sages can." And the

fallen condition of humanity—"what man has made of man"—is comprised by the circumstance that man alone of natural beings does not experience the pleasure which, Wordsworth believes, moves the living world. It is of course a commonplace of Wordsworth criticism that, although the poet set the highest store by the idea of pleasure, the actual pleasures he represents are of a quite limited kind. Certainly he ruled out pleasures that are "strictly physical," those which derive from "the indulgence of the appetites" and "sensual gratification," more particularly erotic gratification. His living world of springtime is far removed from that of Lucretius: nothing in it is driven by the irresistible power of *alma Venus*. This is not to say that there is no erotic aspect to Wordsworth's mind; but the eroticism is very highly sublimated—Wordsworth's pleasure always tended toward *joy*, a purer and more nearly transcendent state. And yet our awareness of this significant limitation does not permit us to underrate the boldness of his statement in the Preface about the primacy of pleasure and the dignity which derives from the principle of pleasure, nor to ignore its intimate connection with certain radical aspects of the moral theory of the French Revolution.[1]

For an understanding of the era of the Revolution, there is, I think, much to be gained from one of the works of the German economic historian Werner Sombart, whose chief preoccupation was the origins

---

[1] And we ought not let go unheeded the explicit connection that Wordsworth makes between poetry and sexuality. Explaining the pleasure of metrical language, he says that it is "the pleasure which the mind derives from the perception of similitude in dissimilitude." And he goes on: "This principle is the great spring of the activity of our minds and their chief feeder. From this principle the direction of the sexual appetite, and all the passions connected with it, take their origin."

of capitalism. In his extensive monograph, *Luxury and Capitalism*, Sombart develops the thesis that the first great accumulations of capital were achieved by the luxury trades in consequence of that ever-increasing demand for the pleasures of the world, for comfort, sumptuousness, and elegance, which is observed in Western Europe between the end of the Middle Ages and the end of the eighteenth century. As a comprehensive explanation of the rise of capitalism, this theory, I gather, has been largely discredited. Yet the social and cultural data which Sombart accumulates are in themselves very interesting, and they are much to our point.

Sombart advances the view that the European preoccupation with luxury took its rise in the princely courts and in the influence of women which court life made possible; he represents luxury as being essentially an expression of eroticism, as the effort to refine and complicate the sexual life, to enhance, as it were, the quality of erotic pleasure. The courtly luxury that Sombart studies is scarcely a unique instance of the association of pleasure with power, of pleasure being thought of as one of the signs of power and therefore to be made not merely manifest but conspicuous in the objects that constitute the *décor* of the lives of powerful men—surely Egypt, Knossos, and Byzantium surpassed Renaissance Europe in elaborateness of luxury. But what would seem to be remarkable about the particular phenomenon that Sombart describes is the extent of its proliferation at a certain period—the sheer amount of luxury that got produced, its increasing availability to classes less than royal or noble, the overtness of the desire for it, and the fierceness of this desire. Sombart's data on these points are too numerous to be adduced here, but any tourist, having in mind what he has even casually seen of the secondary arts of Europe from the centuries in question, the ornaments, furniture, and garniture of certain stations of life, will know that Sombart does not exaggerate about the amount of luxury produced. And any reader of Balzac will recognize the intensity of the passions which at a somewhat later time attended the acquisition of elaborate and costly objects which were desired as the means or signs of pleasure.

What chiefly engages our interest is the influence that luxury may be discovered to have upon social and moral ideas. Such an influence is to be observed in the growing tendency of power to express itself mediately, by signs or indices, rather than directly, by the exercise of force. The richness and elaboration of the objects in a princely establishment were the indices of a power which was actual enough, but they indicated an actual power which had no need to avow itself in action. What a prince conceived of as his dignity might, more than ever before, be expressed by affluence, by the means of pleasure made overt and conspicuous.

And as the objects of luxury became more widely available, so did the dignity which luxury was meant to imply. The connection between dignity and a luxurious style of life was at first not self-evident —in France in 1670 the very phrase *bourgeois gentilhomme* was thought to be comical. In the contemporary English translation of the title of Molière's comedy, *The Cit Turned Gentleman*, it was funny too, but the English laugh was neither so loud nor so long as the French, with what good consequences for the English nation Tocqueville has made plain. Yet in France as in England, the downward spread of the idea of dignity, until it eventually became an idea that might be applied to man in general, was advanced by the increasing possibility of possessing the means or signs of pleasure.

That idea, it need scarcely be said, established itself at the very heart of the radical thought of the eighteenth century. And Diderot himself, the most uncompromising of materialists, as he was the most subtle and delicate, could not have wanted a more categorical statement of his own moral and intellectual theory than Wordsworth's assertion that the grand elementary principle of pleasure constitutes the native and naked dignity of man, and that it is by this principle that man knows, and lives, and breathes, and moves.

Nothing so much connects Keats with Wordsworth as the extent of his conscious commitment to the principle of pleasure. But of course nothing so much separates Keats from his great master as his characteristic way of exemplifying the principle. In the degree that for Wordsworth pleasure is abstract and austere, for Keats it is explicit and voluptuous. No poet ever gave so much credence to the idea of pleasure in the sense of "indulgence of the appetites, sensual gratification," as Keats did, and the phenomenon that Sombart describes, the complex of pleasure-sensuality-luxury, makes the very fabric of his thought.

Keats's preoccupation with the creature-pleasures, as it manifests itself in his early work, is commonly regarded, even by some of his warmest admirers, with an amused disdain. At best, it seems to derive from the kind of elegant minuscule imagination that used to design the charming erotic scenes for the lids of enameled snuff boxes. At worst, in the explicitness of its concern with luxury, it exposes itself to the charge of downright vulgarity that some readers have made. The word *luxury* had a charm for Keats, and in his use of it he seems on the point of reviving its older meaning, which is specifically erotic and nothing but erotic; for Chaucer and Shakespeare *luxury* meant lust and its indulgence. Women present themselves to Keats's imagination as luxuries: "All that soft luxury / that nestled in his arms." A poem is described as "a posy / Of luxuries, bright, milky, soft and rosy." Poetry itself is defined by reference to objects of luxury, and even in its highest nobility, its function is said to be that of comforting and soothing.

Nor is the vulgarity—if we consent to call it that—confined to the early works; we find it in an extreme form in a poem of Keats's maturity. The lover in *Lamia* is generally taken to be an innocent youth, yet the most corrupt young man of Balzac's scenes of Parisian life would scarcely have spoken to his mistress or his fiancée as Lycius speaks to Lamia when he insists that she display her beauty in public for the enhancement of his prestige. Tocqueville said that envy was the characteristic emotion of plutocratic democracy, and it is envy of a particularly ugly kind that Lycius wishes to excite. "Let my foes choke," he says, "and my friends shout afar, / While through the thronged streets your bridal car / Wheels round its dazzling spokes." I am not sure that we should be at pains to insist that this is wholly a dramatic utterance and not a personal one, that we ought entirely to dissociate Keats from Lycius. I am inclined to think that we should suppose Keats to have been involved in all aspects of the principle of pleasure, even the ones that are vulgar and ugly. Otherwise we miss the full complication of that dialectic of pleasure which is the characteristic intellectual activity of Keats's poetry.

The movement of this dialectic is indicated in two lines from an early poem in which Keats speaks of "the pillowy silkiness that rests / Full in the speculation of the stars"—it is the movement from the sensual to the transcendent, from pleasure to knowledge, and knowledge of an ultimate kind. Keats's intellect was brought into fullest play when the intensity of his affirmation of pleasure was met by the intensity of his skepticism about pleasure. The principle of pleasure is for Keats, as it is for Wordsworth, the principle of reality—by it, as Wordsworth said, we *know*. But for Keats it is also the principle of illusion. In *The Eve of St. Agnes*, to take the most obvious example, the moment of pleasure at the center of the poem, erotic pleasure expressed in the fullest possible imagination of the luxurious, is the very essence of reality: it is all we know on earth and all we need to know. And it is the more real as reality and it is the more comprehensive as knowledge exactly because in the poem it exists surrounded by what on earth denies it, by darkness, cold, and death, which make it transitory, which make the felt and proclaimed reality mere illusion.

But we must be aware that in Keats's dialectic of pleasure it is not only external circumstances that condition pleasure and bring it into question as the principle of reality, but also the very nature of pleasure itself. If for Keats erotic enjoyment is the peak and crown of all pleasures, it is also his prime instance of the way in which the desire for pleasure denies itself and produces the very opposite of itself.

Love in a hut, with water and a crust,
Is—Love, forgive us—cinders, ashes, dust;
Love in a palace is perhaps at last
More grievous torment than a hermit's fast.

This opening statement of the second part of *Lamia* is not, as it is often said to be, merely a rather disagreeable jaunty cynicism but one of Keats's boldest expressions of his sense that there is something perverse and self-negating in the erotic life, that it is quite in the course of nature that we should feel "Pleasure . . . turning to Poison as the bee-mouth sips." He insists on the seriousness of the statement in a way that should not be hard to interpret—referring to the lines I have just quoted, he says

That is a doubtful tale from faery land,
Hard for the non-elect to understand.

That faery land we know very well—in the Nightingale Ode, Keats's epithet for the region is *forlorn*; it is the country of La Belle Dame sans Merci, the scene of erotic pleasure which leads to devastation, of an erotic fulfillment which implies castration.

Keats, then, may be thought of as the poet who made the boldest affirmation of the principle of pleasure and also as the poet who brought the principle of pleasure into the greatest and *sincerest* doubt. He therefore has for us a peculiar cultural interest, for it would seem to be true that at some point in modern history the principle of pleasure came to be regarded with just such ambivalence.

This divided state of feeling may be expressed in terms of a breach between politics and art. Modern societies seek to fulfill themselves in affluence, which of course implies the possibility of pleasure. Our political morality is more than acquiescent to this intention. Its simple and on the whole efficient criterion is the extent to which affluence is distributed among individuals and nations. But another morality, which we may describe as being associated with art, regards with a stern and even minatory gaze all that is implied by affluence, and it takes a dim or at best a very complicated view of the principle of pleasure. If we speak not only of the two different modes of morality, the political and the artistic, but also of the people who are responsive to them, we can say that it is quite within the bounds of possibility, if not of consistency, for the same person to respond, and intensely, to both of the two moral modes: it is by no means uncommon for an educated person to base his judgment of politics on a simple affirmation of the principle of pleasure, and to base his judgment of art, and also his judgment of personal existence, on a complex antagonism to that principle. This dichotomy makes one of the most significant circumstances of our cultural situation.

A way of testing what I have said about the modern artistic attitude to pleasure is afforded by the conception of poetry which Keats formulates in "Sleep and Poetry." This poem does not express everything that Keats thought about the nature and function of poetry, but what it does express is undeniably central to his thought, and for the modern sensibility it is inadmissible and even repulsive. It tells us that poetry is gentle, soothing, cheerful, healthful, serene, smooth, regal; that the poet, in the natural course of his development, will first devote his art to the representation of the pleasures of appetite, of things that can be bitten and tasted, such as apples, strawberries, and the white shoulders of nymphs, and that he will give his attention to the details of erotic enticement amid grateful sights and odors, and to sexual fulfillment and sleep. The poem then goes on to say that, as the poet grows older, he will write a different kind of poetry, which is called nobler; this later kind of poetry is less derived from and directed to the sensuality of youth and is more fitted to the gravity of mature years, but it still ministers to pleasure and must therefore be strict in its avoidance of ugly themes; it must not deal with those distressing matters which are referred to as "the burrs and thorns of life"; the great end of poetry, we are told, is "to soothe the cares, and lift the thoughts of man."

Such doctrine from a great poet puzzles

and embarrasses us. It is, we say, the essence of Philistinism.

The conception of the nature and function of poetry which Keats propounds is, of course, by no means unique with him —it can be understood as a statement of the common assumptions about art which prevailed through the Renaissance up to some point in the nineteenth century, when they began to lose their force.[2] Especially in the eighteenth century, art is closely associated with luxury—with the pleasure or at least the comfort of the consumer, or with the quite direct flattery of his ego. The very idea of Beauty seems to imply considerations of this sort, which is perhaps why the eighteenth century was so much drawn to the idea of the Sublime, for that word would seem to indicate a kind of success in art which could not be called Beauty because it lacked the smoothness and serenity (to take two attributes from Keats's catalogue) and the immediacy of gratification which the idea of Beauty seems to propose. But the Sublime itself of course served the purposes of egoism—thus, that instance of the Sublime which was called the Grand Style, as it is described by its great English exponent in painting, Sir Joshua Reynolds, is said to be concerned with "some instance of heroic action or heroic suffering" and its proper effect, Reynolds explains, is to produce the emotion which Bouchardon reported he felt when he read

[2] One of the last significant exponents of the old assumptions was the young Yeats. He was "in all things pre-Raphaelite"—a partisan, that is, not of the early and austere pre-Raphaelite mode, but of the later sumptuous style, tinged with a sort of mystical eroticism —and he stubbornly resisted the realism of Carolus Duran and Bastien-Lepage, which was being brought back to England by the painters who had gone to study in Paris. His commitment to the "beautiful," as against truthful ugliness, was an issue of great moment between him and his father.

Homer: "His whole frame appeared to himself to be enlarged, and all nature which surrounded him diminished to atoms."[3]

In connection with the art of the eighteenth century I used the disagreeable modern word *consumer*, meaning thus to suggest the affinity that art was thought to have with luxury, its status as a commodity which is implied by the solicitude it felt for the pleasure and the comfort of the person who was to own and experience it. Certainly Wordsworth was preeminent in the movement to change this state of affairs,[4] yet Wordsworth locates the value of metrical language as lying in its ability to protect the reader from the discomfort of certain situations that poetry may wish to represent and he compares the effect of such situations in novels with their effect in Shakespeare, his point being that in novels they are "distressful" but in Shakespeare they are

not.[5] It was, we know, an explanation which did not satisfy Keats, who was left to puzzle out why it is that in *King Lear* "all disagreeables evaporate." He discovers that this effect is achieved by "intensity," and we of our day are just at the point of being comfortable with him when he disappoints our best hopes by hedging: he is constrained to say that the "disagreeables" evaporate not only by the operation of intensity but also by "their being in close connection with Beauty & Truth." But we do at last find ourselves at one with him when, in his sonnet "On Sitting Down to Read King Lear Once Again," he dismisses all thought of pleasure and prepares himself for the pain he is in duty bound to undergo:

> . . . Once again, the fierce dispute
> Betwixt damnation and impassion'd clay
> Must I burn through; once more humbly assay
> The bitter-sweet of this Shakespearian fruit.

He is by no means certain that the disagreeables really will evaporate and that he will emerge whole and sound from the experience, and he prays to Shakespeare and "the clouds of Albion" that they will guard him against wandering "in a barren

---

[3] All writers on the Sublime say in effect what Bouchardon says—that, although the sublime subject induces an overpowering emotion, even fear or terror, it does so in a way that permits us to rise superior to it and thus gives us occasion to have a good opinion of our power of intellect and of ourselves generally. The Sublime has this direct relation to comfort and luxury, that it induces us "to regard as small those things of which we are wont to be solicitous" (Kant, *Critique of Aesthetic Judgment*). A more ambitious treatment of my subject would require a much fuller exposition of the theory of the Sublime. Of this theory, which so much occupied the writers on art of the eighteenth century, it can be said that it has much more bearing upon our own literature than modern critics have recognized. The classic study in English is Samuel H. Monk's *The Sublime*, first published in 1935, recently reissued as an Ann Arbor Paperback.

[4] ". . . Men . . . who talk of Poetry as a matter of amusement and idle pleasure; who will converse with us as gravely about a *taste* for Poetry, as they express it, as if it were a thing as indifferent as a taste for rope-dancing, or Frontiniac, or Sherry."

[5] The strength of Wordsworth's impulse to suppress the "distressful" is suggested by the famous passage in *The Prelude* in which the poet explains how his childhood reading served to inure him to the terrors of actuality. He recounts the incident, which occurred when he was nine years old, of his seeing a drowned man brought up from the bottom of Esthwaite Lake. He was, he says, not overcome by fear of the "ghastly face," because his "inner eye" had seen such sights before in fairy tales and romances. And then he feels it necessary to go further, to go beyond the bounds of our ready credence, for he tells us that from his reading came "a spirit" which hallowed the awful sight

> With decoration and ideal grace
> A dignity, a smoothness, like the works
> Of Grecian Art, and purest poetry.

dream," and that, when he is "consumed in the fire," they will contrive his Phoenix-resurrection.

This we of our time can quite understand. We are repelled by the idea of an art that is consumer-directed and comfortable, let alone luxurious. Our typical experience of a work which will eventually have authority with us is to begin our relation to it at a conscious disadvantage, and to wrestle with it until it consents to bless us. We express our high esteem for such a work by supposing that it judges us. And when it no longer does seem to judge us, or when it no longer baffles and resists us, when we begin to feel that we *possess* it, we discover that its power is diminished. In our praise of it we are not likely to use the word *beauty*: we consented long ago—more than four decades ago—to the demonstration made by I. A. Richards in collaboration with Ogden and Wood that the concept of Beauty either could not be assigned any real meaning, or that it was frivolously derived from some assumed connection between works of art and our sexual preferences, quite conventional sexual preferences at that. "Beauty: it curves: curves are beauty," says Leopold Bloom, and we smile at so outmoded an aesthetic—how like him! With a similar amusement we read the language in which the young Yeats praised beauty in *The Secret Rose* (1896)—he speaks of those who are so fortunate as to be "heavy with the sleep / Men have named beauty."[6]

In short, our contemporary aesthetic culture does not set great store by the principle of pleasure in its simple and primitive meaning and it may even be said to maintain an antagonism to the principle of pleasure. Such a statement of course has its aspect of absurdity, but in logic only. There is no psychic fact more available to our modern comprehension than that there are human impulses which, in one degree or another, and sometimes in the very highest degree, repudiate pleasure and seek gratification in—to use Freud's word—unpleasure.

The repudiation of pleasure in favor of the gratification which may be found in unpleasure is a leading theme of Dostoevski's great *nouvelle, Notes from Underground*. Of this extraordinary work Thomas Mann has said that "its painful and scornful conclusions," its "radical frankness . . . ruthlessly transcending all novelistic and literary bounds" have "long become parts of our moral culture." Mann's statement is accurate but minimal—the painful and scornful conclusions of Dostoevski's story have established themselves not only as parts of our moral culture but as its essence, at least so far as that culture makes itself explicit in literature.

Notes from Underground is an account, given in the first person, of the temperament and speculations of a miserable clerk, disadvantaged in every possible way,

---

[6] Mr. Bloom's observation (which goes on to "shapely goddesses Venus, Juno: curves the world admires" and "lovely forms of women sculped Junonian") follows upon his lyrical recollection of his first sexual encounter with Molly; Yeats's phrase occurs in the course of a poem to Maud Gonne. I think it is true to say of Joyce (at least up through *Ulysses*) and of Yeats that they were among the last devotees of the European cult of Woman, of a Female Principle which, in one way or another, *ziegt uns hinein,* and that Molly and Maud are perhaps the last women in literature to be represented as having a transcendent and on the whole beneficent significance (although Lara in *Dr. Zhivago* should be mentioned—it is she who gives that novel much of its archaic quality). The radical change in our sexual mythos must surely be considered in any speculation about the status of pleasure in our culture. It is to the point, for example, that in Kafka's account of the spiritual life, which is touched on below, women play a part that is at best ambiguous.

who responds to his unfortunate plight by every device of bitterness and resentment, by hostility toward those of mankind who are more unfortunate than he is, and also by the fiercest contempt for his more fortunate fellow beings, and for the elements of good fortune. He hates all men of purposeful life, and reasonable men, and action, and happiness, and what he refers to as "the sublime and the beautiful," and pleasure. His mind is subtle, complex, and contradictory almost beyond credibility—we never know where to have him and in our exhaustion we are likely to explain his perversity in some simple way, such as that he hates because he is envious, that he despises what he cannot have: all quite natural. But we are not permitted to lay this flattering unction to our souls—for one thing, he himself beats us to that explanation. And although it is quite true, it is only a small part of the truth. It is also true that he does not have because he does not wish to have; he has arranged his own misery—arranged it in the interests of his dignity, which is to say, of his freedom. For to want what is commonly thought to be appropriate to men, to want whatever it is, high or low, that is believed to yield pleasure, to be active about securing it, to use common sense and prudence to the end of gaining it, this is to admit and consent to the *conditioned* nature of man. What a distance we have come in the six decades since Wordsworth wrote his Preface! To know and feel and live and move at the behest of the principle of pleasure—this, for the Underground Man, so far from constituting his native and naked dignity, constitutes his humiliation in bondage. It makes him, he believes, a mechanic thing, the puppet of whoever or whatever can offer him the means of pleasure. If pleasure is indeed the principle of his being, he is as *known* as the sum of 2 and 2; he is a mere

object of reason, of that rationality of the revolution which is established upon the primacy of the principle of pleasure.

At one point in his narrative, the protagonist of *Notes from Underground* speaks of himself as an "anti-hero." He is the eponymous ancestor of a now-numerous tribe. He stands as the antagonist opposite to all the qualities which are represented by that statue of Sophocles which Professor Margarete Bieber tells us we are to have in mind when we try to understand the Greek conception of the hero, the grave beauty of the countenance and physique expressing the strength and order of the soul; the Underground Man traces his line of descent back to Thersites. It is in his character of anti-hero that he addresses the "gentlemen," as he calls them, the men of action and reason, the lovers of "the sublime and the beautiful," and brags to them, "I have more life in me than you have."

More life: perhaps it was this boast of the Underground Man that Nietzsche recalled when he said, "Dostoevski's Underman and my Overman are the same person clawing his way out of the pit [of modern thought and feeling] into the sunlight." One understands what Nietzsche meant, but he is mistaken in the identification, for his own imagination is bounded on one side by that word *sunlight*, by the Mediterranean world which he loved: by the tradition of humanism with its recognition of the value of pleasure. He is ineluctably constrained by considerations of society and culture, however much he may despise his own society and culture, but the Underground Man is not. To be sure, the terms of the latter's experience are, in the first instance, social; he is preoccupied by questions of status and dignity, and he could not, we may suppose, have come into existence if the fates of the heroes of Balzac and Stendhal had not previously demonstrated that no object of desire or of the social will is anything but an illusion and a source of corruption, society being what it is. But it is the essence of the Underground Man's position that his antagonism to society arises not in response to the deficiencies of social life, but, rather, in response to the insult society offers his freedom by aspiring to be beneficent, to embody "the sublime and the beautiful" as elements of its being. The anger Dostoevski expresses in *Notes from Underground* was activated not by the bad social condition of Russia in 1864 but by the avowed hope of some people that a good social condition could be brought into being. A Utopian novel of the day, Chernyshevski's *What Is to Be Done?*, seemed to him an especially repugnant expression of this hope.[7] His disgust was aroused by this novel's assumption that man would be better for a rationally organized society, by which was meant, of course, a society organized in the service of pleasure. Dostoevski's reprobation of this idea, begun in *Notes from*

---

[7] "A Utopian novel of the day" does not, of course, give anything like an adequate notion of the book's importance in the political culture of Russia. Dostoevski chose his antagonist with the precision that was characteristic of him, for Chernyshevski, who thought of himself as the heir of the French Enlightenment, by his one novel exercised a decisive influence upon the Russian revolutionaries of the next two generations, most notably upon Lenin, who borrowed its title for one of his best-known pamphlets and whose moral style was much influenced by the character Rakhmétov. This paragon of revolutionists, although very fond of the luxury in which he was reared, embraces an extreme asceticism because, as he says, "We demand that men may have a complete enjoyment of their lives, and we must show by our example that we demand it, not to satisfy our personal passions, but for mankind in general; that what we say we say from principle and not from passion, from conviction and not from personal desire." Only one pleasure is proof against Rakhmétov's iron will —he cannot overcome his love of expensive cigars.

Underground, reached its climax in Ivan Karamazov's poem of the Grand Inquisitor, in which again, but this time without the brilliant perversities of the earlier work, the disgust with the specious good of pleasure serves as the ground for the affirmation of spiritual freedom.

I have taken the phrase "specious good" from a passage in Wallace Fowlie's little book on Rimbaud, in which Mr. Fowlie discusses what he calls "the modern seizure and comprehension of spirituality." Without evasion, Mr. Fowlie identifies a chief characteristic of our culture which critics must inevitably be conscious of and yet don't like to name. If we are to be aware of the spiritual intention of modern literature, we have to get rid of certain nineteenth-century connotations of the word *spiritual*, all that they may imply to us of an overrefined and even effeminate quality, and have chiefly in mind what Mr. Fowlie refers to when he speaks of a certain type of saint and a certain type of poet and says of them that "both the saint and the poet exist through some propagation of destructive violence." And Mr. Fowlie continues: "In order to discover what is the center of themselves, the saint has to destroy the world of evil, and the poet has to destroy the world of specious good."

The destruction of what is considered to be specious good is surely one of the chief literary enterprises of our age. Whenever in modern literature we find violence, whether of represented act or of expression, and an insistence upon the sordid and the disgusting, and an insult offered to the prevailing morality or habit of life, we may assume that we are in the presence of the intention to destroy specious good, that we are being confronted by that spirituality, or the aspiration toward it, which subsists upon violence against the specious good.

The most immediate specious good that a modern writer will seek to destroy is, of course, the habits, manners, and "values" of the bourgeois world, and not merely because these associate themselves with much that is bad, such as vulgarity, or the exploitation of the disadvantaged, but for other reasons as well, because they clog and hamper the movement of the individual spirit toward freedom, because they prevent the attainment of "more life." The particular systems and modes of thought of the bourgeois world are a natural first target for the modern spirituality. But it is not hard to believe that the impulse to destroy specious good would be as readily directed against the most benign socialist society, which, by modern definition, serves the principle of pleasure.

In the characteristically modern conception of the spiritual life, the influence of Dostoevski is definitive. By comparison with it, the influence of Nietzsche is marginal. The moral and personal qualities suggested by a particular class, the aristocracy, had great simple force with Nietzsche and proposed to his imagination a particular style of life. Despite the scorn he expressed for liberal democracy and socialist theory as he knew them, he was able to speak with sympathy of future democracies and possible socialisms, led to do so by that element of his thought which served to aerate his mind and keep it frank and generous—his awareness of the part played in human existence by the will to power, which, however it figures in the thought of his epigones and vulgarizers, was conceived by Nietzsche himself as comprising the whole range of the possibilities of human energy, creativity, libido. The claims of any social group to this human characteristic had weight with him. And he gave ready credence to the pleasure that attends one or another kind of power; if

he was quick to judge people by the pleasures they chose—and woe to those who preferred beer to wine and *Parsifal* to *Carmen!*—the principle of pleasure presented itself to him as constituting an element of the dignity of man. It is because of this humanism of his, this naturalistic acceptance of power and pleasure, that Nietzsche is held at a distance by the modern spiritual sensibility. And the converse of what explains Nietzsche's relative marginality explains Dostoevski's position at the very heart of the modern spiritual life.

If we speak of spirituality, we must note that it is not only humanism that is negated by the Underground Man but Christianity as well, or at least Christianity as Western Europe understands it. For not only humanism but the Christianity of the West bases reason upon pleasure, upon pleasure postponed and purified but analogous in kind to worldly pleasure. Dostoevski's clerk has had his way with us: it would seem to be true that, in the degree that the promises of the spiritual life are made in terms of pleasure—of comfort, rest, and beauty—they have no power over the modern imagination. If Kafka, perhaps more than any other writer of our time, lends the color of reality to the events of the spiritual life, his power to do so lies in his characterizing these events by unpleasure, by sordidness and disorder, even when, as in *The Castle*, the spiritual struggle seems to yield a measure of success. He understood that a divinity who, like Saint Augustine's, could be spoken of as gratifying all the senses, must nowadays be deficient in reality and that a heaven which is presented to us as well ordered, commodious, beautiful—as *luxurious*—cannot be an object of hope. Yeats tells us that "Berkeley in his youth described the summum bonum and the reality of Heaven as physical pleasure, and thought this conception made both more intelligible to simple men." To simple men perhaps, but who now is a simple man? How far from our imagination is the idea of "peace" as the crown of spiritual struggle! The idea of "bliss" is even further removed. The two words propose to us a state of virtually infantile passivity which is the negation of the "more life" that we crave, the "more life" of spiritual militancy. We dread Eden, and of all Christian concepts there is none we understand so well as the *felix culpa* and the "fortunate fall"; not, certainly, because we anticipate the salvation to which these Christian paradoxes point, but because by means of the sin and the fall we managed to escape the seductions of peace and bliss.

My first intention in trying to make explicit a change in the assumptions of literature which everybody is more or less aware of has been historical and objective. But it must be obvious that my account of the change has not been wholly objective in the sense of being wholly neutral. It asks a question which is inevitably adversary in some degree, if only by reason of the irony which is implicit in the historical approach to a fact of moral culture. It suggests that the modern spirituality, with its devaluation of the principle of pleasure, because it came into being at a particular time, may be regarded as a contingent and not a necessary mode of thought. This opens the way to regarding it as a mode of thought which is "received" or "established" and which is therefore, like any other received or established mode of thought, available to critical scrutiny.

And that possibility is by no means comfortable. We set great store by the unillusioned militancy of spirit which deals violently with the specious good. Upon it we base whatever self-esteem we can lay claim to—it gives us, as one of

D. H. Lawrence's characters says of it (or something very much like it), our "last distinction"; he feels that to question it is a "sort of vulgarity."[8] To what end, with what intention, is it to be questioned? Can an adversary scrutiny of it point away from it to anything else than an idiot literature, to "positive heroes" who know how to get the good out of life and who have "affirmative" emotions about their success in doing so? The energy, the consciousness, and the wit of modern literature derive from its violence against the specious good. We instinctively resent questions which suggest that there is fault to be found with the one saving force in our moral situation—that extruded "high" segment of our general culture which, with its exigent, violently subversive spirituality, has the power of arming us against, and setting us apart from, all in the general culture that we hate and fear.

Then what justification can there be for describing with any degree of adversary purpose the diminished status of the principle of pleasure which characterizes this segment of our culture?

Possibly one small justification can be brought to light by reference to a famous passage in the *Confessions* of Saint Augustine, the one in which Augustine speaks of an episode of his adolescence and asks why he entered that orchard and stole those pears. Of all the acts of his unregenerate days which he calls sinful and examines in his grim, brilliant way, there is none that he nags so persistently, none that seems to lie so far beyond the reach of his ready comprehension of sin. He did not steal the pears because he was hungry. He did not steal them because they were delicious—they were pears of rather poor quality, he had better at

---

[8] Gerald Crich, in chapter XXIX of *Women in Love*.

home. He did not steal them to win the admiration of the friends who were with him, although this comes close, for, as he says, he would not have stolen them if he had been alone. In all sin, he says, there is a patent motivating desire, some good to be gained, some pleasure for the sake of which the act was committed. But this sin of the stolen pears is, as it were, pure —he can discover no human reason for it. He speaks again of the presence of the companions, but although their being with him was a necessary condition of the act, it cannot be said to have motivated it. To the mature Augustine, the petty theft of his youth is horrifying not only because it seems to have been a sin committed solely for the sake of sinning, but because, in having no conceivable pleasure in view, it was a sort of negative transcendence—in effect, a negation—of his humanity. This is not strange to us—what I have called the extruded high segment of our general culture has for some time been engaged in an experiment in the negative transcendence of the human, a condition which is to be achieved by freeing the self from its thralldom to pleasure. Augustine's puzzling sin is the paradigm of the modern spiritual enterprise, and in his reprobation of it is to be found the reason why Dostoevski condemned and hated the Christianity of the West, which he denounced as, in effect, a vulgar humanism.

To be aware of this undertaking of negative transcendence is, surely, to admire the energy of its desperateness. And we can comprehend how, for the consumer of literature, for that highly developed person who must perforce live the bourgeois life in an affluent society, an aesthetic ethos based on the devaluation of pleasure can serve, and seem to save, one of the two souls which inhabit his breast. Nearly overcome as we are by the specious good, insulted as we are by

being forced to acquire it, we claim the right of the Underground Man to address the "gentlemen" with our assertion, "I have more life in me than you have," which consorts better with the refinement of our sensibility than other brags that men have made, such as, "I am stronger than you," or "I am holier than thou." Our high culture invites us to transfer our energies from the bourgeois competition to the spiritual competition. We find our "distinction"—last or penultimate— in our triumph over the miserable "gentlemen," whether they are others or ourselves, whether our cry be, "I have more life in me than you have" or "I have more life in me than I have."

Now and then it must occur to us that the life of competition for spiritual status is not without its own peculiar sordidness and absurdity. But this is a matter for the novelist—for that novelist we do not yet have but must surely have one day, who will take into serious and comic account the actualities of the spiritual career of our time.

More immediately available to our awareness and more substantive and simple in itself is the effect which the devaluation of pleasure has upon the relation between our high literature and our life in politics, taking that word in its largest possible sense. There was a time when literature assumed that the best ideals of politics were naturally in accord with its own essence, when poetry celebrated the qualities of social life which had their paradigmatic existence in poetry itself. Keats's *Poems* of 1817 takes for its epigraph two lines from Spenser which are intended to point up the political overtone of the volume: "What more felicity can fall to creature / Than to enjoy delight with liberty." Even when Wordsworth is deep in Toryism and Stoic Christianity, it is natural for him to assert the Utopian possibility.

> Paradise and groves
> Elysian, Fortunate Fields—like those of
>   old
> Sought in the Atlantic Main—why should
>   they be
> A history only of departed things,
> Or a mere fiction of what never was?

He goes on to say categorically that these imaginations may become, at the behest of rationality and good will, "a simple produce of the common day." But the old connection between literature and politics has been dissolved. For the typical modern literary personality, political life is likely to exist only as it makes an occasion for the disgust and rage which are essential to the state of modern spirituality, as one particular instance of the irrational, violent, and obscene fantasy which life in general is, as licensing the counter-fantasy of the poet.

In a recent essay,[9] William Phillips described in an accurate and telling way the division that has developed between modern literature and a rational and positive politics, and went on to explain why, for literature's sake, the separation must be maintained. "It now looks," Mr. Phillips said, "as though a radical literature and a radical politics must be kept apart. For radical politics of the modern variety has really served as an antidote to literature. The moral hygiene, the puritanism, the benevolence—all the virtues that sprout on the left—work like a cure for the perverse and morbid idealism of the modern writer. If writing is to be thought of as radical, it must be in a deeper sense, in the sense not simply of cutting across the grain of contemporary life but also of reaching for the connections between the real and the forbidden and the fantastic. The classic example is Dostoevski."

The situation that Mr. Phillips de-

scribes will scarcely be a matter of indifference to those of us who, while responding to the force of the perverse and morbid idealism of modern literature, are habituated to think of literature and politics as naturally having affinity with each other. We cannot but feel a discomfort of mind at the idea of their hostile separation, and we are led to ask whether the breach is as complete as Mr. Phillips says it is. His description, it seems to me, so far as it bears upon the situation of the moment, upon the situation as it presents itself to the practitioner of literature, needs no modification. But if we consider the matter in a more extended perspective, in the long view of the cultural historian, it must occur to us to speculate—even at the risk of being "hygienic"—whether the perverse and morbid idealism of modern literature is not to be thought of as being precisely political, whether it does not express a demand which in its own way is rational and positive and which may have to be taken into eventual account by a rational and positive politics.

If we do ask this question, we will be ready to remind ourselves that the devaluation of the pleasure principle, or, as perhaps we ought to put it, the imagination of going *beyond the pleasure principle* is, after all, not merely an event of a particular moment in culture. It is, as Freud made plain in his famous essay, a fact of the psychic life itself. The impulse to go beyond the pleasure principle is certainly to be observed not only in modern literature but in all literature, and of course not only in literature but in the emotional economy of at least some persons in all epochs. But what we can indeed call an event in culture is that at a particular moment in history, in our moment, this fact of the psychic life became a salient and dominant theme in literature, and also that it has been made

[9] "What Happened in the 30's," *Commentary*, September 1962.

explicit as a fact in the psychic life and forced upon our consciousness by Freud's momentous foray into metapsychology. And this cultural event may indeed be understood in political terms, as likely to have eventual political consequences, just as we understood in political terms and as having had political consequences the eighteenth-century assertion that the dignity of man was to be found in the principle of pleasure.

We deal with a change in quantity. It has always been true of some men that to pleasure they have preferred unpleasure. They imposed upon themselves difficult and painful tasks, they committed themselves to strange, "unnatural" modes of life, they sought out distressing emotions, in order to know psychic energies which are not to be summoned up in felicity. These psychic energies, even when they are experienced in self-destruction, are a means of self-definition and self-affirmation. As such, they have a social reference—the election of unpleasure, however isolate and private the act may be, must refer to society if only because the choice denies the valuation which society in general puts upon pleasure; and of course it often receives social approbation in the highest degree, even if at a remove of time: it is the choice of the hero, the saint and martyr, and, in some cultures, the artist. The quantitative change which we have to take account of is: what was once a mode of experience of a few has now become an ideal of experience of many. For reasons which, at least here, must defy speculation, the ideal of pleasure has exhausted itself, almost as if it had been actually realized and had issued in satiety and ennui. In its place, or, at least, beside it, there is developing—conceivably at the behest of literature!—an ideal of the experience of those psychic energies which

are linked with unpleasure and which are directed toward self-definition and self-affirmation. Such an ideal makes a demand upon society for its satisfaction: it is a political fact. It surely asks for gratification of a sort which is not within the purview of ordinary democratic progressivism.

What I have called the spirituality of modern literature can scarcely be immune to irony, and the less so as we see it advancing in the easy comprehension of increasing numbers of people, to the point of its becoming, through the medium of the stage and the cinema, the stuff of popular entertainment—how can irony be withheld from an accredited subversiveness, an established moral radicalism, a respectable violence? But although the anomalies of the culture of the educated middle class do indeed justify an adversary response, and perhaps a weightier one than that of irony, a response that is nothing but adversary will not be adequate.

We often hear it said nowadays, usually by psychoanalysts and by writers oriented toward psychoanalysis, that the very existence of civilization is threatened unless society can give credence to the principle of pleasure and learn how to implement it. We understand what is meant, that repressiveness and oppression will be lessened if the principle of pleasure is established in our social arrangements, and we readily assent. Yet secretly we know that the formula does not satisfy the condition it addresses itself to—it leaves out of account those psychic energies which press beyond the pleasure principle and even deny it.

It is possible to say that—whether for good or for bad—we confront a mutation in culture by which an old established proportion between the pleasure-seeking instincts and the ego instincts is being altered in favor of the latter.[10] If we follow Freud through the awesome paradoxes of *Beyond the Pleasure Principle*, we may understand why the indications of this change should present themselves as perverse and morbid, for the other name that Freud uses for the ego instincts is the death instincts. Freud's hav-

---

[10] See the remarks on tragedy in "On the Teaching of Modern Literature" (pp. 18 ff.) and also Lionel Abel's brilliant chapter on tragedy in *Metatheatre*. For a full and detailed account of the modern devaluation of that good fortune the destruction of which once pained us in tragedy, see Thomas Munro, "The Failure Story: A Study of Contemporary Pessimism," *The Journal of Aesthetics and Art Criticism*, vol. XVII, no. 2, December 1958.

ing made the ego instincts synonymous with the death instincts accounts, more than anything else in his dark and difficult essay, for the cloud of misunderstanding in which it exists. But before we conclude that *Beyond the Pleasure Principle* issues, as many believe, in an ultimate pessimism or "negation," and before we conclude that the tendencies in our literature which we have remarked on are nothing but perverse and morbid, let us recall that although Freud did indeed say that "the aim of all life is death," the course of his argument leads him to the statement that "the organism wishes to die only in its own fashion," only through the complex fullness of its appropriate life.

Stephen Spender

THE VISIONARY INDIVIDUALISTS

Stephen Spender is another of the rare men who attain distinction in more than one métier, for he is respected as poet, critic, translator, and editor (of *Encounter*). In the 1930s Spender, together with W. H. Auden, Louis MacNeice, and C. Day Lewis, founded the Oxford Group whose interests were directed to both poetry and politics. He is an extraordinarily productive writer and editor who has published more than thirty books in all genres, some of them collaborative works. A few of his critical books are *The Destructive Element* (1953), *The Creative Element* (1953), and *The Struggle of the Modern* (1963). Spender has also lectured at many universities in his native England and in the United States. "The Visionary Individualists" is the opening chapter of *The Creative Element*.

I

During the past hundred years many poets and novelists have attempted to construct a whole view of life upon their own individual vision. I call the vision individual because it has been cut off from orthodoxy, and when these writers have drawn on orthodox symbols and myths it has been to use them in an unorthodox way. Thus Rilke is at pains to point out that the central symbol of his *Duino Elegies*—the angel—has nothing to do with the angels of the Christian religion. James Joyce draws on the whole field of myths of all times and places, in order to create his own mythology. Yeats, in *A Vision*, created a system based on occultism and astrology which not only provided the framework of his later poetry, but also a private system of categories into which he could fit the char-

acters of all men living and dead and all the phases of Western civilization. An occultism constructed on premises surprisingly akin to Yeats' system told Rimbaud that he was a Magus, close to God and able in his poetry to transform existence.

Individualist vision was the result of the writers' rejection of—or rejection by—society and their endeavour to set up values of their own. A separation of the individualist values of the writer from the materialist ones of modern society is already noted in the pages of Baudelaire's *Journal*, written over a hundred years ago . . . The literature of individualist vision is really the writing of prophets in the desert who, having been driven out of society, cultivate their own visions and return to society with them. But this literature is representative of many

188

people besides the writer himself. Other men of taste and sensibility have also felt separated from the values of their time; and the visionary writer expresses their sense of isolation as well as his own. Since society is composed of individuals, theoretically it would be possible for everyone to feel outside the time in which he lives. The idea of society being redeemed by those who felt themselves to be outside it was common to a great many individuals.

The more separate the writers' vision of his world, the more it was expressed in terms of that separateness of his individuality. The deeper, too, the reader must go to enter into this isolated vision. Thus the more whole and explicit the vision of the writer in his work, the greater the demand it made upon the intelligence of the reader to understand the particular method, symbolism, and even the language of the writer.

The literature of the past two generations is littered with masterpieces which can only be entered into by readers acquiring special knowledge of the writers' imaginative worlds.

Someone is said to have protested to James Joyce that it would take him his lifetime to understand *Finnegans Wake*. 'That is the least I expect of my readers,' Joyce is supposed to have replied.

The impenetrability of this literature is one reason why writers may now have to turn back to orthodox views. The reaction today towards a less individualist kind of writing, and the endeavour of writers to relate their experience to more orthodox systems of thought, which are partly just a literary reaction, happens also to coincide with social changes which restrict the free development of individuality today.

All the same, the reasons which drove writers into the deserts of their own vision have not suddenly ceased. Writers went there on account of the decay of values in a materialist society. Society has not suddenly become less materialist, nor has religion suddenly started to influence its values, in a way in which it failed to do in the mid-nineteenth century. As for the *social* arguments which today tell us to abandon our excessive individualism and become responsible members of society, they are ones of political necessity. They are a re-statement, in different terms and circumstances, and within the new context of collectivized societies, of the idea of material progress. Progress, which today has a less optimistic air and is known as exigence, is the same materialism which drove the writers and artists of yesterday into spiritual isolation. Yesterday was the day of laissez-faire, when self-seeking individuals, pursuing their own interests, were supposed to distribute material benefits indirectly to all society. Today is the day of centralized bureaucracy, when governmental institutions are supposed to distribute material advantages, more directly perhaps, to all. The aims remain material and the religions which have recently enlisted the support of a great many writers show as little sign of influencing the new kind of materialism as they did the old.

If we accept the proposition that the isolated individualism of the great writers of the past hundred years has become untenable from the point of view of literature itself, we must none the less question the new Catholic and Anglican orthodoxies—and still more the political ones—and ask whether they really answer the protests of a generation of giant individualists who have preceded us against a materialist society: whether the new religious orthodoxy is not an exploration of 'Death's other kingdom' without there being any likelihood of its relating the values of religion to those of contemporary life.

We have just emerged from a great period in modern literature; a period of the isolated visions of the poetic imagination. These visions have more in common with Blake's Prophetic Books than with *The Divine Comedy*. They are the visions of writers with specialist or home-made philosophies and their own private interpretations of mythology. Nor are they confined to poets. For one of the features of modern poetic vision is that the creative writer with a large view of life may well use prose as a poetic medium, thinking the novel to be the form in our day which corresponds to the epic. The endlessly repeated variations in D. H. Lawrence's novels on the idea of a new relationship between men and women which could redeem the world by a revolution made for the sake of individual life is as much poetic vision as Rimbaud's *Les Illuminations*.

Poetic consciousness in this century, when it breaks beyond the very definite limits of the lyrical and becomes narrative or didactic, uses prose as much as poetry to express vision. The phrase 'the poetic novel' or its converse, the 'prose poem,' already acknowledges the endeavour of poetry to conquer the territory of prose, the felt need of prose to evoke the symbolism of poetry. The writer today lives in a world of prose: a world of weakened traditions, almost devoid of ritual, ceremony, and symbols within life which play more than an ornamental role in the community. It is a world where inventions, statistics, information, politics, advertising, and abstract ways of thinking about them, can hardly be digested and controlled within the traditional comparatively simple symbolism of poetry. There is not, within the traffic of facts, a sufficient quantity of living symbols to resist the flood of statistics.

Living therefore in an age of prose, prose may indeed be the medium most suited even to poetic imagination when it deals with the complexity and abstraction of modern life. Yet unless prose fiction is to be a mere reflection of prose life—as happens in the novels of writers like Upton Sinclair and John Dos Passos —it is also necessary that this prose should be poetic. These are perhaps the underlying considerations—working below the level where conscious decisions are made—which directed poetic talents like Henry James, James Joyce, and Virginia Woolf into the novel. Theirs was prose written for the sake of the poetic imagination. The ocean on which Conrad's ships sail, the English country houses which are the caskets holding the egg-shell sensibilities of Henry James, the landscape which becomes the language of Earwicker's sleep, assail us through a medium which has the effect of epic poetry.

What runs through the work of certain modern poets and novelists with such different and often opposed aims as those of Henry James, James Joyce, T. S. Eliot, Franz Kafka, Rainer Maria Rilke, and even the surrealists, is a modern poetic vision individual in each writer. Whether derived from past religious and traditionalist values or whether anti-religious and anti-traditional, this becomes so individual in each writer that it can only be explained in his particular terms. We have to find a key to his work in the history of his own development.

Dr. Erich Heller in his stimulating essays on German literature and thought, *The Disinherited Mind*, notes that in the 1820's Goethe was already conscious of his impulse to 'escape into the sphere of poetry':

It is this impulse (which Goethe hardly ever allows to get the better of him), this emphasis on the superiority of the inner vision as against a spiritually barren external world, that ever since has dominated European poetry.

This trend became more and more conspicuous with time, so that the Romantics whom Goethe rejected seem almost Realists compared with the later excesses of inwardness perpetuated by the Symbolists.

In the modern situation which Goethe already apprehended, it is important to look beyond this distinction between an external world which is 'real' and an inwardness supposedly 'unreal.' One has to ask what, in a world that is 'spiritually barren' can the real attitude of the inner life towards external things be? Significant reality is, surely, a balanced relationship between outer and inner worlds. The inner world of a writer may become incommunicable, but in a time when the external world has become 'spiritually barren' outer reality is only real in the sense of being factual. The result of that excessive outwardness of a 'spiritually barren external world' is the 'excessive inwardness' of poets who prefer losing themselves within themselves to losing themselves outside themselves in external reality.

We may deplore 'excessive inwardness' but we must not dismiss the literature of inner vision as escapism, just because it is not realism. We must ask whether writers, in creating their individual visions, did so to project inwardly their awareness of the external world, or whether they did so to escape from outer events. If they did maintain this awareness, then perhaps within their inner vision there is to be found the clue to new ways of relating inner life to outward reality.

In 1872, several months after Nietzsche (nursing German soldiers behind the lines at Metz) had been brooding over *The Birth of Tragedy*, Rimbaud wrote *Les Illuminations*, a high-water mark of the flooding-in of Inner Vision. Yet *Les Illuminations* can as little be dismissed as 'unreal' as can, say, the painting of Van Gogh. In its depiction of the desolation

of the modern city, its prophecy of disaster, and its affirmation of the Spirit, it is real as Ezekiel is real, and real as *The Birth of Tragedy* is real. Yet it is not at all Realist in the manner of a Zola or a Dos Passos. Hoelderlin, Nietzsche, Rimbaud, Van Gogh were all of them endowed with an excess of inner vision. Yet their names suggest that perhaps the artists of the inner visions become real when, in their lives, they are exposed to the most savage reality of their times. They are real in their art because they did not use the power of inner vision as a means of escaping from the reality of life.

Real, reality, Realism: these words have to be used with the utmost caution. But we can't at all avoid using them, because it is surely true that the values of the visionary writing of the last hundred years will ultimately be judged by the extent to which it is real: that is, to which it contains the felt experience of modern life. Does Joyce show a weaker grasp of reality in *Finnegans Wake* than in *Ulysses?* This is probably today an unanswerable question, but the position of *Finnegans Wake* will ultimately depend on the answer to it.

The balanced relationship of inner with outer world is extremely precarious, but it may be maintained by those whose awareness of the 'spiritual barrenness of the external world' forces them to create their own values within their inner lives. Rimbaud retains a balance between inner and outer even in his most hallucinated writing because—like Van Gogh—the weight of the real accompanied him like an illness. His delirium is that of the boy who froze and starved in the streets of Paris, not that of self-intoxication. But there is a danger with the Symbolists of the superior 'inner vision' becoming a kind of dug-out decked with flowers—or Ivory Tower, as it used to be called—in which the poet hides away from reality.

Writers on the Symbolists and Post-Symbolists (C. M. Bowra in *The Heritage of Symbolism* and Edmund Wilson in *Axel's Castle*) note the tendency of a creative impulse which begins with a religious intensity to deteriorate (as it did in the work of the poets of the 'eighties and 'nineties in England) into artificiality.

The modern individualist vision is characterized by its rejection of the orthodox, the operation which the poet has performed upon his imaginative life so as to separate it from materialism. Even when—as in the case of Baudelaire—it may be argued that the poet is orthodox —perhaps the one orthodox person in an unorthodox society—it should be pointed out that to penetrate into an orthodoxy which no one else can reach is paradoxical. Baudelaire was a Christian by virtue of being a Satanist, spiritual by virtue of regarding himself as qualifying to attain Christian damnation, and a citizen by virtue of despising the bourgeoisie.

In a world spiritually barren the opposite of what the traditional establishments regard to be the correct moral and aesthetic position may turn out as the only spiritually significant one. In the nineteenth century the only entrance to paradise might be through hell, and in the twentieth the writing which seems to the conventional minded to be entirely revolutionary may be that which has the greatest claim to belong to the tradition. The strangest reversals of roles take place: so that T. S. Eliot, who was long thought of as an innovator, has imperceptibly become a conservative force, and done so without any Wordsworthian renunciation of his early principles and without losing the respect of the 'advanced.' Indeed there is something deeply ambiguous about the position of Eliot, who introduced into English poetry the sensibility of French poets like Laforgue who were extremely 'original' talents; but who yet seems always to have had a profound distrust of originality and innovation.

In 'revolutionary traditionalism,' and in a concept of originality as that which is most profoundly unoriginal, there is an identification of opposite views, what W. B. Yeats would have called a meeting of the 'antinomies.' This might be dismissed as the affectation of writers who regard themselves as superior to a public they tend to despise, were it not for an underlying seriousness which makes it impossible to dismiss it. T. S. Eliot is both an original artist (probably outside the main stream of poetic development in English, because no other writer has been able to model a style effectively on his discoveries), and at the same time within his unique manner he has intensified our understanding of the role of tradition. Rimbaud, who raged against any religion but his own brand of occultism, provided Paul Claudel with proof of the reality of spiritual life which caused Claudel's conversion to catholicism. After reading *Les Illuminations* and *Une Saison en Enfer*, Claudel describes his almost physical impression of a supernatural existence ('l'impression vivante et presque physique du surnaturel'): 'It is Arthur Rimbaud who instructed and constructed me. I owe him all. He did not belong to this world.'[1]

His poetry did not belong to this world. That is the operative phrase which illuminates the paradox of the meeting of opposite views in much contemporary writing. Rimbaud created in these extraordinary medleys of prose and verse *Les Illuminations* and *Une Saison en Enfer* the vision of a sphere of poetic existence outside contemporary values. Yet it retains the balance between the 'inwardness' of his poetic life and the experience of the external world. The

---

[1] Quoted in Enid Starkie's Biography of Rimbaud, to which I am indebted throughout.

meeting of opposites takes place within this separate sphere of his inner life, disassociated from the values of his time. His real spiritual existence confronts the real materialism of external things.

The possibility of a dissociation of inner from outer realities was foreseen by Matthew Arnold, whose critical consciousness was perhaps in advance of his poetic achievement. Arnold looked to poetry to provide a 'substitute for religion,' which it could never be, though it could perhaps in its visions concentrate fragments of religion, broken away from the world. Yet Arnold understood the mechanism of modern society which might make poetry break off from religion, and perhaps even religion break away sometimes from religious institutions, floating off in fragments of poetry: 'Our religion has materialized itself in the fact, in the supposed fact; it has attached its emotion to the fact, and now the fact is failing it. But for poetry the idea is everything.'

The antinomies of the visionary writer arise from the separation of the values of his work from those of contemporary society. Already, even in this act of separation, there is contradiction. His antisocial isolation makes him valuable to society: what takes him away gives him back to society, in his work.

The necessity of such isolation is an idea common to writers as different as Baudelaire from Proust, as Henry James from the surrealist André Breton. In his attitude towards his responsibility as an artist Breton is only an extreme instance of the case of Henry James. In the first, rather famous, quotation here is Henry James defending himself against a parody of the writing of his last period in H. G. Wells's novel *Boon*. Wells held that the novel should be utilitarian like architecture, rather than aesthetic like painting.

Henry James:

I hold that interest may be, *must* be, exquisitely made and created, and that if we don't make it, we who undertake to, nobody and nothing will make it for us.

And in a second letter, returning to the fray:

It is art that *makes* life, makes interest, makes importance, for our consideration and application of these things, and I know of no substitute whatever for the force and beauty of its process.

And here is André Breton, in *What is Surrealism?* (translated by David Gascoyne):

In the domain of poetry, Lautréamont, Rimbaud and Mallarmé were the first to endow the human mind with what it lacked so much: I mean a truly *insolent grace*, which has enabled the mind, on finding itself withdrawn from all ideals, to begin to occupy itself with its own life. . . . It was they who really caused us to make up our minds to rely for our redemption here below upon ourselves alone, so that we have desperately to pursue their footsteps, animated by their feverish desire for conquest, total conquest, that will never leave us; so that our eyes, our precious eyes, have to reflect that which, while not existing, is yet as intense as that which does exist, and which has once more to consist of visual images, fully compensating us for what we have left behind.

Fundamentally, James and Breton agree on what is essential: each, that his art is the only surviving means of creating significant values. Where they part company, of course, is that for Henry James the operation severing him from the values of society has not been completed. Although he creates these values in his art, he takes them out of life, and then, as it were, makes them anew. It is an isolated re-making rather than an isolated making of everything in complete independence of values outside his writing.

If Breton went no further than to claim that 'our eyes have to reflect that which, while not existing, is yet as intense as that which does exist,' he might even have claimed Henry James as one of the band of premature surrealists. For in stories like *The Altar of the Dead, The Great Good Place,* and *The Middle Years* the writer is conceived of as one who can renew within his art a religious experience which has been lost in life. But James is a very conscious artist, creating conscious interest and significance out of the material of the unconscious, whereas the surrealists advocate a surrender to the automatism of the unconscious mind.

II

A vision is a panorama of a great extent of life—perhaps of all life—surrounding a central idea or image. Vision has both centre and circumference: its authority lies in the conviction that a central experience implies a circumference of much wider life. The vision may strike from the outside inwards to the centre or from the centre outwards. In either case the inference of the general application of a single particular insight is there.

In *Finnegans Wake* we are more aware of the circumference of the whole of history (and perhaps also of geography and humanity) than of the centre which is Earwicker himself. But in D. H. Lawrence it is the centre, the relationship between two people, which implies the circumference—society which might be saved by the multiplication of such a relationship. In Proust it is the little cake, the madeleine, which is the fusing centre of a whole vision of time redeemed within the sensation of a moment expanding in ever-widening circles.

The focusing point of vision is often to be found in one sentence, one phrase, one image. Thus in Dante, 'In His will is our peace'; in Blake, 'Damn braces. Bless relaxes.' And contemporaries abound in such central notes: 'In the destructive element immerse'; 'These fragments have I shored against my ruins'; 'Only connect.' Perhaps in Joyce's last work the key to the vision is the conjunctive 'and', or perhaps still more the idea of conjunction, in a sentence like the following: 'And it's old and old it's sad and old it's sad and weary, I go back to you, my cold father, my cold mad father, my cold mad feary father, till the near sight of the mere size of him, the moyles and moyles of it, moananoaning, makes me seasilt saltsick and I rush, my only, into your arms.'

Modern literature is characterized by this separation of the writer from all contemporary values, this search for a centre which implies a circumference. It is this search which the Victorians, with all their wish to understand contemporary ideas, to enter into current philosophical and theological debates, lack. With all their perceptiveness and their desire to express a *Weltanschauung,* they compromise with their age even when they most disapprove of it.

Among Victorian poets there was probably more serious effort to grapple with the scientific discoveries and the religious disputes of the age than there has been among poets of this century. Yet Tennyson, Browning, Arnold, and the others failed to create an idiom which could express these ideas, and perhaps this failure was utimately due to their compromising with their time. A true criticism of life could only have resulted from a separation of their values from the Victorian ones. Tennyson embarrasses us when he writes about Evolution and its effect on religious belief, or about Progress, in the idiom of Keats.

Tennyson's spirit of compromise makes

him a social prophet rather than a visionary. He is near to being a visionary only when he is at his very gloomiest. There are passages of *In Memoriam* which lead directly to the pessimistic vision of Hardy.

To compare a few lines from *Locksley Hall* with some from *Prometheus Unbound* will illustrate the distinction between social prophecy and what I mean by visionary writing:

For I dipt into the future, far as human
    eye could see,
Saw the Vision of the world and all the
    wonder that would be;

Saw the heavens fill with commerce, argo-
    sies of magic sails,
Pilots of the purple twilight, dropping
    down with costly bales;

Heard the heavens fill with shouting, and
    there rain'd a ghastly dew,
From the nations' airy navies grappling in
    the central blue. . . .

This is remarkable prophecy, by a poet who had thought about the developments implicit in the invention of the steam engine and dirigibles. Yet, as prophecy, it remains bound to the logic of material developments. If airships and bombers had never been invented, it would contain little which did not seem merely wrong; and as it is, one reflects that Tennyson was thinking of a battle of lighter-than-air dirigibles. The 'Federation of the world' which Tennyson anticipates in *Locksley Hall* is still relegated to the future, and his insight is into potential facts rather than into those impalpable truths which seem always to exist somewhere within the creative spirit of mankind. *Locksley Hall* does not provoke in us the reaction: 'This is a vision of human truth which must some day crystallize into the real!' We would admire the prophecy, for what it is worth,

still more if Tennyson had foreseen the gasoline engine.

The early Romantics were true visionaries, what Rimbaud called 'voyants'. In the Third Act of *Prometheus Unbound* Shelley prophesies a good many things which have not happened and are not likely to happen. Yet his vision—whether we approve or disapprove of it—still seems true of a conceivable future because it is true of man's feelings about his own nature. Today we are perhaps less likely than at any time since Shelley to believe that man when completely free will be wise and good. Yet Shelley's wrongness (if he is wrong) has qualities that can still trouble the imagination and raise hope. Shelley is preoccupied by a vision of man; not merely man who has shed oppressors, tyrants, and priests and Sir Timothy Shelley, but man who can create a new world after the image of himself without guilt or sense of sin:

The loathsome mask has fallen, the man
    remains
Sceptreless, free, uncircumscribed, but
    man
Equal, unclassed, tribeless, and nationless,
Exempt from awe, worship, degree, the
    king
Over himself; just, gentle, wise; but man
Passionless?—No, yet free from guilt or
    pain,
Which were, for his will made or suffered
    them,
Nor yet exempt, though ruling them like
    slaves,
From chance, and death, and mutability,
The clogs of that which else might over-
    soar
The loftiest star of unascended heaven,
Pinnacled dim in the intense inane.

Such a human being has not and may never be realized, yet he remains as it were among man's effective dreams, and his image might in a hundred or five hundred years still inspire peoples to action. He is real in the sense that we recognize in his image some potentiality that we passionately feel.

The distinction between visionary and non-visionary may be more subtly qualified by considering those lines from Matthew Arnold's *Dover Beach* which contain perhaps the profoundest statement in Victorian poetry of the human condition in the nineteenth century (if we leave aside the poems of Gerard Manley Hopkins):

The sea of faith
Was once, too, at the full, and round
*   earth's shore*
Lay like the folds of a bright girdle furl'd;
But now I only hear
Its melancholy, long, withdrawing roar,
Retreating, to the breath
Of the night-wind, down the vast edges
*   drear*
And naked shingles of the world.

Ah, love, let us be true
To one another! for the world, which
*   seems*
To lie before us like a land of dreams,
So various, so beautiful, so new,
Hath really neither joy, nor love, nor light,
Nor certitude, nor peace, nor help for
*   pain;*
And we are here as on a darkling plain
Swept with confused alarms of struggle
*   and flight,*
Where ignorant armies clash by night.

We all too easily recognize the force of this today. Arnold's poem has that intuition of an underlying future within contemporary events which we call prophecy. But it doesn't create those inner values which are yet related to the reality of the external world, that I call the modern vision.

Arnold draws a contrast between two worlds. One, an inner world of joyous anticipation—an image cast by an outer world supposedly various, beautiful, and new: the other, this outer world as it really is, without joy, love, light, certitude, peace, help for pain. The effect of this outer world being the real one is to overshadow and darken and expose as illusion the inner world of dreams. The inner world is only, as it were, the reflected anticipation of this external one, and therefore illusion.

So, the withdrawal of faith having extinguished the brightness of the inner world, all Arnold is left with is another person in his lightless, loveless world. 'Ah, love, let us be true / To one another!' This exclamation is the mutual recognition of two people that they have no world. For they have renounced the exterior world which has no sweetness and light, and the inner one is looked on only as an illusion produced by this. So far as two people can be dead within life these two are (and their situation anticipates situations in T. S. Eliot). They are lovers standing on the shore from which the sea of faith has receded, with their bodies and souls drained of flesh and dream, their reality reduced to a whisper of 'Ah, love, let us be true!' and there is no one else who is not conscripted into one or other of the 'ignorant armies'.

We now begin to understand where vision becomes real. It is when the real itself has ceased to appear real, to seem nothing but lovelessness and joylessness casting a shadow of unreality across the world of anticipation. The real in Arnold's poem belies life. Yet the reality we can make for ourselves in art is the result of an inter-relationship between objective and subjective worlds. If the spectacle of the outside world fails to have anything but a negative significance for us, then our inner minds which are filled through our senses with this outsideness either become negative also or we have to create a reality of inwardness to affirm our own existence in the face of the negation of the outer world.

Yet the outside world does not simply consist of the values of contemporary civilization. It also includes the whole universe, the unexplored or uncivilized, or pre-civilized areas of the map, and pasts of many civilizations which are not part of our own Western tradition and our own instinctual bodies and unconscious minds. When Matthew Arnold says that the world is not various nor beautiful nor new, he is obviously making an unobjective statement based on his own subjective view. Yet this view is important to him because it seems to him the only sincere view possible in a cultivated man living in his time. And, as such, *Dover Beach* expresses a general truth about the state of civilized consciousness among Europeans living in the latter half of the nineteenth century. It is the state of mind of men hypnotized by 'the spiritually barren external world'. Yet once the situation has been stated, other men must look elsewhere than through the exhausted channels of surviving tradition to establish their connection with life. Perhaps they should, as I say, create their own inner reality, or perhaps they should look to other traditions, other geographical and historical areas, in order to affirm the truth that the world is beautiful and various and new.

Arnold states a situation where the poet has become a ghost, banished from nature and history. This position, once stated, is seen to be unacceptable, because although it may be thought to be true by very civilized contemporaries like Arnold himself, it is not true of life. Man is forced on to another level of truth, outside society, outside contemporary history, where he rejects the idea that he is a ghost and reasserts the dream that the world is various and beautiful and new, and that it should have certitude and peace and help for pain. For this is the dream of his flesh as well as his spirit, and

it finds confirmation in geography as well as history. It is the dream which affirms life, and without such an affirmation life contradicts itself, denying its own existence, and men turn in on themselves, becoming mechanic ghosts moving in a machine-made society.

The inner vision which is the answer to *Dover Beach* must inevitably be tragic. For in refusing to accept the external evidence of the decline of civilization the individualist writers invented values of their own to set against the material forces of the age. What they rejected was not just the facts of materialism, but the faith in materialism expressed in the idea of Progress. The idea of Progress is optimistic, and therefore in rejecting Progress literature becomes pessimistic, and beyond pessimism the only possible triumph of the isolated spirit is in tragedy.

It is, indeed, the fatality of democratic industrialized societies to be progressive and optimistic. They cannot be anything else, because to justify the concentration of all the available forces of the society in the tasks of manufacturing consumer goods, people have to believe that they are going to benefit increasingly from this production. Even when things go badly, the faith in Progress remains; because it is always thought that without such a concentration on material aims, things would be worse.

The only literature of our time which is not tragic therefore is that which accepts the idea of Progress. The writers of romantic comedies are those, like Shaw and Wells, Galsworthy and Bennett, who do not contemplate the defeat of the spirit, because they think that social revolution, of a communist or socialist kind, will lead to greater happiness, more education, and therefore a new civilization of the Common Man. In the nineteen-thirties horror at fascism and unemployment led some young writers to think that they must, in their work, form an alliance with the forces resisting fascism and political reaction. But in doing so they joined what was inevitably a losing side, and their work was based rather on a kind of desperate hope than on faith in Progress.

During the war, in France at the time of the Resistance, there was a flaring up of patriotism which resulted in a literature of hope even more intense than that of the Spanish Civil War. These exceptions serve only to show that the modern writer in Europe generally tends to think of himself as outside society, and of society itself as entirely materialistic. Society has claims on his loyalty only when he feels it his duty to support the good it may accomplish, or when he feels bound to participate in a choice between greater and less social evil. When he is unable to support society for these reasons, he tends to drop out of it in his consciousness and to feel himself more a member of some past society, from which he is cut off by the tide of history, than of this materialist one. Therefore, like Matthew Arnold, he is aware of something ghostly about his own existence which, attached to the past, only haunts the present. The alternative to Arnold's position (which, although stated in a different idiom, is not far removed from that of Eliot) is to be an individualist rebel, tragically upholding his own passionately imagined values against the destructiveness of the present.

In a totalitarian society—communist or fascist—every artist is expected to believe in the theme of material progress (which may be renamed Exigence) and illustrate it in his work. The dictators are aware of the danger of artists not supporting the aims of their organized and directed communities. Failure to illustrate the theme of social optimism in their work means the tendency to create an inner world of vision which rejects these external values.

In Russia, shortly after the Second World War, certain poets were rebuked specifically for writing poems which were considered depressing.

It is revealing to compare *Dover Beach* with W. B. Yeats's famous poem *The Second Coming*. This has often been discussed, and my excuse for quoting it again is that I do not think that anyone has drawn the parallel of this poem with Arnold's. Yet *The Second Coming* could almost be described as the *Dover Beach* of the twentieth century.

Yeats begins—so to speak—where Arnold leaves off. The receding 'sea of faith' corresponds to the 'blood-dimmed tide' drowning 'the ceremony of innocence', while the 'ignorant armies that clash by night' parallel the 'best' who 'lack all conviction', and those who are 'full of passionate intensity'. I do not mean that Yeats was influenced by Arnold's poem, but he was writing out of a sense of the same situation half a century later.

But for Yeats, unlike Arnold, the answer to this situation is not to withdraw into personal isolation and appeal to the personal values of another who feels as he feels. It is to accept the situation and intensify it to a vision of tragic history in which our age will be superseded by the birth of a new age:

Surely some revelation is at hand;
Surely the Second Coming is at hand.
The Second Coming! Hardly are those
  words out
When a vast image out of Spiritus Mundi
Troubles my sight; somewhere in sands of
  the desert
A shape with lion body and the head of a
  man,
A gaze blank and pitiless as the sun,
Is moving its slow thighs, while all about it
Reel shadows of the indignant desert
  birds.

The darkness drops again; but now I know
That twenty centuries of stony sleep
Were vexed to nightmare by a rocking
* cradle,*
And what rough beast, its hour come
* round at last,*
Slouches towards Bethlehem to be born?

The difference between Arnold and Yeats is that in Yeats's poem an operation has been performed which separates his inner vision from the contemporary scene where 'mere anarchy' is 'loosed upon the world'. The situation of the external world of today enters into the vision he has worked out for himself of the whole of history. And according to the system of his book *A Vision*, to which this poem refers, our world is entering that phase of the moon where subjective values are completely blotted out, everyone wants to be like everyone else, and finally there is a complete darkening of human consciousness until a new phase of historic development begins.

Such an end of our civilization had already been envisaged by Baudelaire in the 1850's. Indeed, it reached English and American poetry by way of the French symbolists. We can follow in Baudelaire's *Intimate Journals* the development of an attitude towards his time which was the background to his poetry. Like Arnold he rejects the values of contemporary society and he sees no hope for the future. (I quote from the translation by Christopher Isherwood, published by the Blackmore Press.)

The world is about to end. Its sole reason for continuance is that it exists. What, under Heaven, has this world henceforth to do? Even supposing that it continued materially to exist would this existence be worthy of the name of the Historical Dictionary? . . . As a new example, as fresh victims of the inexorable laws, we shall perish by that which we have believed to be our means of existence. So far will machinery have Americanized us,

so far will Progress have atrophied in us all that is spiritual, that no dream of the Utopians, however bloody, sacrilegious or unnatural, will be comparable to the result. I appeal to every thinking man to show me what remains of Life. As for religion, I believe it useless to speak of it or to search for its relics.

The real degradation, though, is not of external civilization but of the man within:

It is not, however, specifically in political matters that the universal ruin or the universal progress—for the name matters little—will be manifested. That will appear in the degradation of the human heart. Need I describe how the last vestiges of statesmanship will struggle painfully in the last clutches of universal bestiality, how the governors will be forced—in maintaining themselves and erecting a phantom of order—to resort to measures which would make our men of today shudder, hardened as they are?

The whole passage is interesting in the light of later events. But it is even more valuable as a statement of the relationship of the modern poet to the external modern world. Baudelaire's positive views of what should be the purpose of life—individual life within the social framework—are also developed in the *Intimate Journals*:

There cannot be any Progress (true progress, that is to say, moral progress) except within the individual himself.

Theory of the true civilization. It is not to be found in gas or table-turning. It consists in the diminution of the traces of original sin.

The abolishers of the Soul (the materialists) are necessarily abolishers of Hell.

I have cultivated my hysteria with delight and horror.

Since Baudelaire's view is essentially Christian (despite the pagan elements in his poetry) why does he reject the Church? He does so because of its failure to interpret Christianity into terms which effectively criticize the values of modern civilization. Within the rituals of the Church man can still lead a moral existence; he can be damned, if not saved. But it is as an institution spiritualizing society that the Church has failed. Are not the politicians, the journalists, the bureaucrats, the society people whom Baudelaire detested all on the side of the Church? And what language does the Church speak which can be translated into terms of this materialistic life, penetrating it, criticizing it, condemning it? Faith can still exist, but it has ceased to act upon society objectively. This is, surely also Matthew Arnold's thought when he complains that the sea of faith is withdrawing. Why should it concern him that faith is not 'at the full'? Does its 'melancholy, long, withdrawing roar' provide him with any excuse for not believing in the truth, any reason for despair? If there are six Christians crucified by a populace of a million unbelievers, do the corpses of these martyrs prove that faith is a corpse?

With Matthew Arnold there was a lack of subjective faith, but all the same the real cause of his discouragement was akin to Baudelaire's, and the explanation is to be found in the memory of the martyrs. The city of the unbelievers is in a criticizing and criticized relationship to the martyrs. They crucify the martyrs because they fear them. But the modern situation is one in which the Church does not effectively criticize a materialist civilization; indeed, in many ways, it is a part of the general materialism, the spiritual death. This is what I mean by the difference between subjective and objective faith. You can—and many people do—lead spiritual lives within the Church, but the Church has no influence on the materialist values or lack of values of our society. It can be said that if there were

more churchgoers then, through them, faith would act objectively upon society. But this is not necessarily so. It is more probable that it would merely extend the split between inward and outward life which is so much a feature of modern society. Inwardly people would have faith, but outwardly they would continue to live in a world characterized by the lack of faith penetrating its tasks and productivity. The modern tragedy lies in the failure of the sea of faith to flood external things.

In the objective sense of flooding over society, a spiritual institution provides symbols which enable us to feel and think morally about the activities of external life. Thus, in the past, through the symbolism of the Church, people were able to think morally about power—the State and the Crown. Over the widest areas of life this symbolism provided what Yeats, in his private thinking, called the Mask: the projection of the personal into its opposite, the objective symbol. It is the failure of institutions of spiritual life to fulfil this function which has compelled poets to invent their own systems, which are substitutes for such institutions. The burden of spiritual existence has been thrown on to the inner poetic vision. The poets have endeavoured within their poetry to re-invent all values.

Today there is a reaction towards orthodoxy, and the most vital movement in literature in the West is religious. It is evident that the Christian orthodoxy of Eliot, Auden, Graham Greene, and Evelyn Waugh expresses more coherent and more accessible truths than the magic of Rimbaud and Yeats, the egalitarian socialism of Orwell. All the same, we have to bear in mind the reasons why for nearly a hundred years writers of genius forsook the ordering of their ideas which comes from conformity to institutions and went into deserts of their own isolation. They went there because the ortho-doxies failed to answer the question of how man could find significance in a modern world whose science and aims had no relationship to traditional values. They had to invent their own systems in order to discover their own kind of signifi-cance. And although the systems they improvised in the process were full of hocus-pocus, more important than the systems was the search, because it kept open the question which they asked. What we have to ask now is whether the new phase of returning to orthodoxy keeps open this question, or whether it simply is not a reaction from the unsatis-factory answers of home-made poetic philosophies and whether orthodoxy can connect us with the externally barren world any more today than it could a hundred years ago.

Georg Lukács

THE IDEOLOGY OF MODERNISM

Georg Lukács, a Hungarian who writes in German, has long been prominent in Europe as perhaps the leading Marxist critic of the mid-century. Although his collected works would run to thirty volumes, not including some fifty essays and articles, he has until recently been almost unknown to English-speaking audiences. Translations of three important books, *Studies in European Realism*, *The Historical Novel*, and *Realism in Our Time*, are now available in American editions. This essay is the opening chapter of *Realism in Our Time* (originally entitled *The Meaning of Contemporary Realism* in its 1962 British edition) as it appeared in the translation published in America in 1964.

It is in no way surprising that the most influential contemporary school of writing should still be committed to the dogmas of 'modernist' anti-realism. It is here that we must begin our investigation if we are to chart the possibilities of a bourgeois realism. We must compare the two main trends in contemporary bourgeois literature, and look at the answers they give to the major ideological and artistic questions of our time.

We shall concentrate on the underlying ideological basis of these trends (ideological in the above-defined, not in the strictly philosophical, sense). What must be avoided at all costs is the approach generally adopted by bourgeois-modernist critics themselves: that exaggerated concern with formal criteria, with questions of style and literary technique. This approach may appear to distinguish sharply between 'modern' and 'tradi-

tional' writing (i.e. contemporary writers who adhere to the styles of the last century). In fact it fails to locate the decisive formal problems and turns a blind eye to their inherent dialectic. We are presented with a false polarization which, by exaggerating the importance of stylistic differences, conceals the opposing principles actually underlying and determining contrasting styles.

To take an example: the *monologue intérieur*. Compare, for instance, Bloom's monologue in the lavatory or Molly's monologue in bed, at the beginning and at the end of *Ulysses*, with Goethe's early-morning monologue as conceived by Thomas Mann in his *Lotte in Weimar*. Plainly, the same stylistic technique is being employed. And certain of Thomas Mann's remarks about Joyce and his methods would appear to confirm this. Yet it is not easy to think of any two novels more basically dissimilar than *Ulysses* and *Lotte in Weimar*. This is true even of the superficially rather similar scenes I have indicated. I am not referring to the—to my mind—striking difference in intellectual quality. I refer to the fact that with Joyce the stream-of-consciousness technique is no mere stylistic device; it is itself the formative principle governing the narrative pattern and the presentation of character. Technique here is something absolute; it is part and parcel of the aesthetic ambition informing *Ulysses*. With Thomas Mann, on the other hand, the *monologue intérieur* is simply a technical device, allowing the author to explore aspects of Goethe's world which would not have been otherwise available. Goethe's experience is not presented as confined to momentary sense-impressions. The artist reaches down to the core of Goethe's personality, to the complexity of his relations with his own past, present, and even future experience. The stream of association is only apparently free. The monologue is composed with the utmost artistic rigour: it is a carefully plotted sequence gradually piercing to the core of Goethe's personality. Every person or event, emerging momentarily from the stream and vanishing again, is given a specific weight, a definite position, in the pattern of the whole. However unconventional the presentation, the compositional principle is that of the traditional epic; in the way the pace is controlled, and the transitions and climaxes are organized, the ancient rules of epic narration are faithfully observed.

It would be absurd, in view of Joyce's artistic ambitions and his manifest abilities, to qualify the exaggerated attention he gives to the detailed recording of sense-data, and his comparative neglect of ideas and emotions, as artistic failure. All this was in conformity with Joyce's artistic

intentions; and, by use of such techniques, he may be said to have achieved them satisfactorily. But between Joyce's intentions and those of Thomas Mann there is a total opposition. The perpetually oscillating patterns of sense- and memory-data, their powerfully charged—but aimless and directionless—fields of force, give rise to an epic structure which is *static*, reflecting a belief in the basically static character of events.

These opposed views of the world—dynamic and developmental on the one hand, static and sensational on the other—are of crucial importance in examining the two schools of literature I have mentioned. I shall return to the opposition later. Here, I want only to point out that an exclusive emphasis on formal matters can lead to serious misunderstanding of the character of an artist's work.

What determines the style of a given work of art? How does the intention determine the form? (We are concerned here, of course, with the intention realized in the work; it need not coincide with the writer's conscious intention). The distinctions that concern us are not those between stylistic 'techniques' in the formalistic sense. It is the view of the world, the ideology or *weltanschauung* underlying a writer's work, that counts. And it is the writer's attempt to reproduce this view of the world which constitutes his 'intention' and is the formative principle underlying the style of a given piece of writing. Looked at in this way, style ceases to be a formalistic category. Rather, it is rooted in content; it is the specific form of a specific content.

Content determines form. But there is no content of which Man himself is not the focal point. However various the *données* of literature (a particular experience, a didactic purpose), the basic question is, and will remain: what is Man?

Here is a point of division: if we put

the question in abstract, philosophical terms, leaving aside all formal considerations, we arrive—for the realist school—at the traditional Aristotelian dictum (which was also reached by other than purely aesthetic considerations): Man is *zoon politikon*, a social animal. The Aristotelian dictum is applicable to all great realistic literature. Achilles and Werther, Oedipus and Tom Jones, Antigone and Anna Karenina: their individual existence —their *Sein an sich*, in the Hegelian terminology; their 'ontological being,' as a more fashionable terminology has it—cannot be distinguished from their social and historical environment. Their human significance, their specific individuality cannot be separated from the context in which they were created.

The ontological view governing the image of man in the work of leading modernist writers is the exact opposite of this. Man, for these writers, is by nature solitary, asocial, unable to enter into relationships with other human beings. Thomas Wolfe once wrote: 'My view of the world is based on the firm conviction that solitariness is by no means a rare condition, something peculiar to myself or to a few specially solitary human beings, but the inescapable, central fact of human existence.' Man, thus imagined, may establish contact with other individuals, but only in a superficial, accidental manner; only, ontologically speaking, by retrospective reflection. For 'the others,' too, are basically solitary, beyond significant human relationship.

This basic solitariness of man must not be confused with that individual solitariness to be found in the literature of traditional realism. In the latter case, we are dealing with a particular situation in which a human being may be placed, due either to his character or to the circum-

stances of his life. Solitariness may be objectively conditioned, as with Sophocles' Philoctetes, put ashore on the bleak island of Lemnos. Or it may be subjective, the product of inner necessity, as with Tolstoy's Ivan Ilyitsch or Flaubert's Frédéric Moreau in the *Education Sentimentale*. But it is always merely a fragment, a phase, a climax or anti-climax, in the life of the community as a whole. The fate of such individuals is characteristic of certain human types in specific social or historical circumstances. Beside and beyond their solitariness, the common life, the strife and togetherness of other human beings, goes on as before. In a word, their solitariness is a specific social fate, not a universal *condition humaine*.

The latter, of course, is characteristic of the theory and practice of modernism. I would like, in the present study, to spare the reader tedious excursions into philosophy. But I cannot refrain from drawing the reader's attention to Heidegger's description of human existence as a thrownness-into-being' (*Geworfenheit ins Dasein*). A more graphic evocation of the ontological solitariness of the individual would be hard to imagine. Man is 'thrown-into-being.' This implies, not merely that man is constitutionally unable to establish relationships with things or persons outside himself; but also that it is impossible to determine theoretically the origin and goal of human existence.

Man, thus conceived, is an ahistorical being. (The fact that Heidegger does admit a form of 'authentic' historicity in his system is not really relevant. I have shown elsewhere that Heidegger tends to belittle historicity as 'vulgar'; and his 'authentic' historicity is not distinguishable from ahistoricity). This negation of history takes two different forms in modernist literature. First, the hero is strictly confined within the limits of his own experience. There is not for him—and apparently not for his creator—any pre-existent reality beyond his own self, acting upon him or being acted upon by him. Secondly, the hero himself is without personal history. He is 'thrown-into-the-world': meaninglessly, unfathomably. He does not develop through contact with the world; he neither forms nor is formed by it. The only 'development' in this literature is the gradual revelation of the human condition. Man is now what he has always been and always will be. The narrator, the examining subject, is in motion; the examined reality is static.

Of course, dogmas of this kind are only really viable in philosophical abstraction, and then only with a measure of sophistry. A gifted writer, however extreme his theoretical modernism, will in practice have to compromise with the demands of historicity and of social environment. Joyce uses Dublin, Kafka and Musil the Hapsburg Monarchy, as the locus of their masterpieces. But the locus they lovingly depict is little more than a backcloth; it is not basic to their artistic intention.

This view of human existence has specific literary consequences. Particularly in one category, of primary theoretical and practical importance, to which we must now give our attention: that of *potentiality*. Philosophy distinguishes between *abstract* and *concrete* (in Hegel, 'real') *potentiality*. These two categories, their interrelation and opposition, are rooted in life itself. *Potentiality*—seen abstractly or subjectively—is richer than actual life. Innumerable possibilities for man's development are imaginable, only a small percentage of which will be realized. Modern subjectivism, taking these imagined possibilities for actual complexity of life, oscillates between melancholy and fascination. When the world declines to realize these possibilities, this melancholy becomes tinged with contempt. Hofmannsthal's Sobeide expressed the reaction of the generation first exposed to this experience:

The burden of those endlessly pored-over
And now forever perished possibilities . . .

How far were those possibilities even concrete or 'real'? Plainly, they existed only in the imagination of the subject, as dreams or day-dreams. Faulkner, in whose work this subjective potentiality plays an important part, was evidently aware that reality must thereby be subjectivized and made to appear arbitrary. Consider this comment of his: 'They were all talking simultaneously, getting flushed and excited, quarrelling, making the unreal into a possibility, then into a probability, then into an irrefutable fact, as human beings do when they put their wishes into words.' The possibilities in a man's mind, the particular pattern, intensity and suggestiveness they assume, will of course be characteristic of that individual. In practice, their number will border on the infinite, even with the most unimaginative individual. It is thus a hopeless undertaking to define the contours of individuality, let alone to come to grips with a man's actual fate, by means of potentiality. The *abstract* character of potentiality is clear from the fact that it cannot determine development—subjective mental states, however permanent or profound, cannot here be decisive. Rather, the development of personality is determined by inherited gifts and qualities; by the factors, external or internal, which further or inhibit their growth.

But in life potentiality can, of course, become reality. Situations arise in which a man is confronted with a choice; and in the act of choice a man's character may reveal itself in a light that surprises even himself. In literature—and particularly in dramatic literature—the denouement often consists in the realization of just such a potentiality, which circumstances have kept from coming to the fore. These potentialities are, then, 'real' or concrete potentialities. The fate of the character depends upon the potentiality in question, even if it should condemn him to a tragic end. In advance, while still a subjective potentiality in the character's mind, there is no way of distinguishing it from the innumerable abstract potentialities in his mind. It may even be buried away so completely that, before the moment of decision, it has never entered his mind even as an abstract potentiality. The subject, after taking his decision, may be unconscious of his own motives. Thus Richard Dudgeon, Shaw's Devil's Disciple, having sacrificed himself as Pastor Andersen, confesses: 'I have often asked myself for the motive, but I find no good reason to explain why I acted as I did.'

Yet it is a decision which has altered the direction of his life. Of course, this is an extreme case. But the qualitative leap of the denouement, cancelling and at the same time renewing the continuity of individual consciousness, can never be predicted. The concrete potentiality cannot be isolated from the myriad abstract potentialities. Only actual decision reveals the distinction.

The literature of realism, aiming at a truthful reflection of reality, must demonstrate both the concrete and abstract potentialities of human beings in extreme situations of this kind. A character's concrete potentiality once revealed, his abstract potentialities will appear essentially inauthentic. Moravia, for instance, in his novel *The Indifferent Ones*, describes the young son of a decadent bourgeois family, Michel, who makes up his mind to kill his sister's seducer. While Michel, having made his decision, is planning the

murder, a large number of abstract—but highly suggestive—possibilities are laid before us. Unfortunately for Michel the murder is never actually carried out; and, from the sordid details of the action, Michel's character emerges as what it is—representative of that background from which, in subjective fantasy, he had imagined he could escape.

Abstract potentiality belongs wholly to the realm of subjectivity; whereas concrete potentiality is concerned with the dialectic between the individual's subjectivity and objective reality. The literary presentation of the latter thus implies a description of actual persons inhabiting a palpable, identifiable world. Only in the interaction of character and environment can the concrete potentiality of a particular individual be singled out from the 'bad infinity' of purely abstract potentialities, and emerge as the determining potentiality of just this individual at just this phase of his development. This principle alone enables the artist to distinguish concrete potentiality from a myriad abstractions.

But the ontology on which the image of man in modernist literature is based invalidates this principle. If the 'human condition'—man as a solitary being, incapable of meaningful relationships—is identified with reality itself, the distinction between abstract and concrete potentiality becomes null and void. The categories tend to merge. Thus Cesare Pavese notes with John Dos Passos, and his German contemporary, Alfred Doblin, a sharp oscillation between 'superficial *verisme*' and 'abstract Expressionist schematism.' Criticizing Dos Passos, Pavese writes that fictional characters 'ought to be created by deliberate selection and description of individual features'—implying that Dos Passos' characterizations are transferable from one individual to another. He describes the artistic consequences: by exalting man's subjectivity, at the expense of the objective reality of his environment, man's subjectivity itself is impoverished.

The problem, once again, is ideological. This is not to say that the ideology underlying modernist writings is identical in all cases. On the contrary: the ideology exists in extremely various, even contradictory forms. The rejection of narrative objectivity, the surrender to subjectivity, may take the form of Joyce's stream of consciousness, or of Musil's 'active passivity,' his 'existence without quality,' or of Gide's *action gratuite*,' where abstract potentiality achieves pseudo-realization. As individual character manifests itself in life's moments of decision, so too in literature. If the distinction between abstract and concrete potentiality vanishes, if man's inwardness is identified with an abstract subjectivity, human personality must necessarily disintegrate.

T. S. Eliot described this phenomenon, this mode of portraying human personality, as

Shape without form, shade without colour,
Paralysed force, gesture without motion.

The disintegration of personality is matched by a disintegration of the outer world. In one sense, this is simply a further consequence of our argument. For the identification of abstract and concrete human potentiality rests on the assumption that the objective world is inherently inexplicable. Certain leading modernist writers, attempting a theoretical apology, have admitted this quite frankly. Often this theoretical impossibility of understanding reality is the point of departure, rather than the exaltation of subjectivity. But in any case the connection between the two is plain. The German poet Gottfried Benn, for instance, informs us that 'there is no outer reality, there is only human consciousness, con-

stantly building, modifying, rebuilding new worlds out of its own creativity.' Musil, as always, gives a moral twist to this line of thought. Ulrich, the hero of his *The Man without Qualities*, when asked what he would do if he were in God's place, replies: 'I should be compelled to abolish reality.' Subjective existence 'without qualities' is the complement of the negation of outward reality.

The negation of outward reality is not always demanded with such theoretical rigour. But it is present in almost all modernist literature. In conversation, Musil once gave as the period of his great novel, 'between 1912 and 1914.' But he was quick to modify this statement by adding: 'I have not, I must insist, written a historical novel. I am not concerned with actual events. . . . Events, anyhow, are interchangeable. I am interested in what is typical, in what one might call the ghostly aspect of reality.' The word 'ghostly' is interesting. It points to a major tendency in modernist literature: the attenuation of actuality. In Kafka, the descriptive detail is of an extraordinary immediacy and authenticity. But Kafka's artistic ingenuity is really directed towards substituting his *angst*-ridden vision of the world for objective reality. The realistic detail is the expression of a ghostly unreality, of a nightmare world, whose function is to evoke *angst*. The same phenomenon can be seen in writers who attempt to combine Kafka's techniques with a critique of society—like the German writer, Wolfgang Koeppen, in his satirical novel about Bonn, *Das Treibhaus*. A similar attenuation of reality underlies Joyce's stream of consciousness. It is, of course, intensified where the stream of consciousness is itself the medium through which reality is presented. And it is carried *ad absurdum* where the stream of consciousness is that of an abnormal subject or of an idiot—

consider the first part of Faulkner's *Sound and Fury* or, a still more extreme case, Beckett's *Molloy*.

Attenuation of reality and dissolution of personality are thus interdependent: the stronger the one, the stronger the other. Underlying both is the lack of a consistent view of human nature. Man is reduced to a sequence of unrelated experiential fragments; he is as inexplicable to others as to himself. In Eliot's *Cocktail Party* the psychiatrist, who voices the opinions of the author, describes the phenomenon:

Ah, but we die to each other daily
What we know of other people
Is only our memory of the moments
During which we knew them. And they
  have changed since then.

To pretend that they and we are the same
Is a useful and convenient social convention
Which must sometimes be broken. We
  must also remember
That at every meeting we are meeting a
  stranger.

The dissolution of personality originally the unconscious product of the identification of concrete and abstract potentiality, is elevated to a deliberate principle in the light of consciousness. It is no accident that Gottfried Benn called one of his theoretical tracts 'Doppelleben.' For Benn, this dissolution of personality took the form of a schizophrenic dichotomy. According to him, there was in man's personality no coherent pattern of motivation or behaviour. Man's animal nature is opposed to his denaturized, sublimated thought-processes. The unity of thought and action is 'backwoods philosophy'; thought and being are 'quite separate entities.' Man must be either a moral or a thinking being—he cannot be both at once.

These are not, I think, purely private,

eccentric speculations. Of course, they are derived from Benn's specific experience. But there is an inner connection between these ideas and a certain tradition of bourgeois thought. It is more than a hundred years since Kierkegaard first attacked the Hegelian view that the inner and outer world form an objective dialectical unity, that they are indissolubly married in spite of their apparent opposition. Kierkegaard denied any such unity. According to Kierkegaard, the individual exists within an opaque, impenetrable 'incognito.'

This philosophy attained remarkable popularity after the Second World War —proof that even the most abstruse theories may reflect social reality. Men like Martin Heidegger, Ernst Jünger, the lawyer Carl Schmitt, Gottfried Benn and others passionately embraced this doctrine of the eternal incognito which implies that a man's external deeds are no guide to his motives. In this case, the deeds obscured behind the mysterious incognito were, needless to say, these intellectuals' participation in Nazism: Heidegger, as Rector of Freiburg University, had glorified Hitler's seizure of power at his Inauguration; Carl Schmitt had put his great legal gifts at Hitler's disposal. The facts were too well-known to be simply denied. But, if this impenetrable incognito were the true 'condition humaine', might not—concealed within their incognito—Heidegger or Schmitt have been secret opponents of Hitler all the time, only supporting him in the world of appearances? Ernst von Salomon's cynical frankness about his opportunism in *The Questionnaire* (keeping his reservations to himself or declaring them only in the presence of intimate friends) may be read as an ironic commentary on this ideology of the incognito as we find it, say, in the writings of Ernst Jünger.

This digression may serve to show,

taking an extreme example, what the social implications of such an ontology may be. In the literary field, this particular ideology was of cardinal importance; by destroying the complex tissue of man's relations with his environment, it furthered the dissolution of personality. For it is just the opposition between a man and his environment that determines the development of his personality. There is no great hero of fiction—from Homer's Achilles to Mann's Adrian Leverkühn or Sholochov's Grigory Melyekov—whose personality is not the product of such an opposition. I have shown how disastrous the denial of the distinction between abstract and concrete potentiality must be for the presentation of character. The destruction of the complex tissue of man's interaction with his environment likewise saps the vitality of this opposition. Certainly, some writers who adhere to this ideology have attempted, not unsuccessfully, to portray this opposition in concrete terms. But the underlying ideology deprives these contradictions of their dynamic, developmental significance. The contradictions co-exist, unresolved, contributing to the further dissolution of the personality in question.

It is to the credit of Robert Musil that he was quite conscious of the implications of his method. Of his hero Ulrich he remarked: 'One is faced with a simple choice: either one must run with the pack (when in Rome, do as the Romans do), or one becomes a neurotic.' Musil here introduces the problem, central to all modernist literature, of the significance of psychopathology.

This problem was first widely discussed in the Naturalist period. More than fifty years ago, that doyen of Berlin dramatic critics, Alfred Kerr, was writing: 'Morbidity is the legitimate poetry of Naturalism. For what is poetic in everyday life? Neurotic aberration, escape from life's dreary routine. Only in this way can a character be translated to a rarer clime and yet retain an air of reality.' Interesting, here, is the notion that the poetic necessity of the pathological derives from the prosaic quality of life under capitalism. I would maintain—we shall return to this point—that in modern writing there is a continuity from Naturalism to the Modernism of our day—a continuity restricted, admittedly, to underlying ideological principles. What at first was no more than dim anticipation of approaching catastrophe developed, after 1914, into an all-pervading obsession. And I would suggest that the ever-increasing part played by psychopathology, was one of the main features of the continuity. At each period—depending on the prevailing social and historical conditions—psychopathology was given a new emphasis, a different significance and artistic function. Kerr's description suggests that in naturalism the interest in psychopathology sprang from an aesthetic need; it was an attempt to escape from the dreariness of life under capitalism. The quotation from Musil shows that some years later the opposition acquired a moral slant. The obsession with morbidity had ceased to have a merely decorative function, bringing colour into the greyness of reality, and become a moral protest against capitalism.

With Musil—and with many other modernist writers—psychopathology became the goal, the *terminus ad quem*, of their artistic intention. But there is a double difficulty inherent in their intention, which follows from its underlying ideology. There is, first, a lack of definition. The protest expressed by this flight into psychopathology is an abstract gesture; its rejection of reality is wholesale and summary, containing no concrete criticism. It is a gesture, moreover, that is destined to lead nowhere; it is an escape into nothingness. Thus the propagators of this ideology are mistaken in thinking that such a protest could ever be fruitful in literature. In any protest against particular social conditions, these conditions themselves must have the central place. The bourgeois protest against feudal society, the proletarian against bourgeois society, made their point of departure a criticism of the old order. In both cases the protest—reaching out beyond the point of departure—was based on a concrete *terminus ad quem:* the establishment of a new order. However indefinite the structure and content of this new order, the will towards its more exact definition was not lacking.

How different the protest of writers like Musil! The *terminus a quo* (the corrupt society of our time) is inevitably the main source of energy, since the *terminus ad quem* (the escape into psychopathology) is a mere abstraction. The rejection of modern reality is purely subjective. Considered in terms of man's relation with his environment, it lacks both content and direction. And this lack is exaggerated still further by the character of the *terminus ad quem.* For the protest is an empty gesture, expressing nausea, or discomfort, or longing. Its content—or rather lack of content—derives from the fact that such a view of life cannot impart a sense of direction. These writers are not wholly wrong in believing that psychopathology is their surest refuge; it is the ideological complement of their historical position.

This obsession with the pathological is not only to be found in literature. Freudian psychoanalysis is its most obvious expression. The treatment of the subject is only superficially different from that in modern literature. As everybody knows, Freud's starting point was 'everyday life.' In order to explain 'slips' and daydreams, however, he had to have recourse to psychopathology. In his lectures, speaking of resistance and repression, he says: 'Our interest in the general psychology of symptom-formation increases as we understand to what extent the study of pathological conditions can shed light on the workings of the normal mind.' Freud believed he had found the key to the understanding of the normal personality in the psychology of the abnormal. This belief is still more evident in the typology of Kretschner, which also assumes that psychological abnormalities can explain normal psychology. It is only when we compare Freud's psychology with that of Pavlov, who takes the Hippocratic view that mental abnormality is a deviation from a norm, that we see it in its true light.

Clearly, this is not strictly a scientific or literary-critical problem. It is an ideological problem, deriving from the ontological dogma of the solitariness of man. The literature of realism, based on the Aristotelian concept of man as *zoon politikon,* is entitled to develop a new typology for each new phase in the evolution of a society. It displays the contradictions within society and within the individual in the context of a dialectical unity. Here, individuals embodying violent and extraordinary passions are still within the range of a socially normal typology (Shakespeare, Balzac, Stendhal). For, in this literature, the average man is simply a dimmer reflection of the contradictions always existing in man and society; eccentricity is a socially-conditioned distortion. Obviously, the passions of the great heroes must not be confused with 'eccentricity' in the colloquial sense: Christian Buddenbrook is an 'eccentric'; Adrian Leverkühn is not.

The ontology of *Geworfenheit* makes a true typology impossible; it is replaced by an abstract polarity of the eccentric and the socially-average. We have seen why this polarity—which in traditional realism serves to increase our understanding of social normality—leads in modernism to a fascination with morbid eccentricity. Eccentricity becomes the necessary complement of the average; and this polarity is held to exhaust human potentiality. The implications of this ideology are shown in another remark of Musil's: 'If humanity dreamt collectively, it would dream Moosbrugger.' Moosbrugger, you will remember, was a mentally-retarded sexual pervert with homicidal tendencies.

What served, with Musil, as the ideological basis of a new typology—escape into neurosis as a protest against the evils of society—becomes with other modernist writers an immutable *condition humaine*. Musil's statement loses its conditional 'if' and becomes a simple description of reality. Lack of objectivity in the description of the outer world finds its complement in the reduction of reality to a nightmare. Beckett's *Molloy* is perhaps the *ne plus ultra* of this development, although Joyce's vision of reality as an incoherent stream of consciousness had already assumed in Faulkner a nightmare quality. In Beckett's novel we have the same vision twice over. He presents us with an image of the utmost human degradation —an idiot's vegetative existence. Then, as help is imminent from a mysterious unspecified source, the rescuer himself sinks into idiocy. The story is told through the parallel streams of consciousness of the idiot and of his rescuer.

Along with the adoption of perversity and idiocy as types of the *condition humaine*, we find what amounts to frank glorification. Take Montherlant's *Pasiphae*, where sexual perversity—the heroine's infatuation with a bull—is presented as a triumphant return to nature, as the liberation of impulse from the slavery of convention. The chorus—i.e. the author —puts the following question (which,

though rhetorical, clearly expects an affirmative reply): 'Si l'absence de pensée et l'absence de morale ne contribuent pas beaucoup à la dignité des bêtes, des plantes et des eaux . . . ?' Montherlant expresses as plainly as Musil, though with different moral and emotional emphasis, the hidden—one might say repressed— social character of the protest underlying this obsession with psychopathology, its perverted Rousseauism, its anarchism. There are many illustrations of this in modernist writing. A poem of Benn's will serve to make the point:

O that we were our primal ancestors,
Small lumps of plasma in hot, sultry
    swamps;
Life, death, conception, parturition
Emerging from those juices soundlessly.

A frond of seaweed or a dune of sand,
Formed by the wind and heavy at the
    base;
A dragonfly or gull's wing—already, these
Would signify excessive suffering.

This is not overtly perverse in the manner of Beckett or Montherlant. Yet, in his primitivism, Benn is at one with them. The opposition of man as animal to man as social being (for instance, Heidegger's devaluation of the social as 'des Man,' Klages' assertion of the incompatibility of *Geist* and *Seele*, or Rosenberg's racial mythology) leads straight to a glorification of the abnormal and to an undisguised anti-humanism.

A typology limited in this way to the *homme moyen sensuel* and the idiot also opens the door to 'experimental' stylistic distortion. Distortion becomes as inseparable a part of the portrayal of reality as the recourse to the pathological. But literature must have a concept of the normal if it is to 'place' distortion correctly; that is to say, to see it *as* distortion. With such a typology this placing is impossible, since the normal is no longer a proper object of literary interest. Life under capitalism is, often rightly, presented as a distortion (a petrification or paralysis) of the human substance. But to present psychopathology as a way of escape from this distortion is itself a distortion. We are invited to measure one type of distortion against another and arrive, necessarily, at universal distortion. There is no principle to set against the general pattern, no standard by which the petty-bourgeois and the pathological can be seen in their social context. And these tendencies, far from being relativized with time, become even more absolute. Distortion becomes the normal condition of human existence; the proper study, the formative principle, of art and literature.

I have demonstrated some of the literary implications of this ideology. Let us now pursue the argument further. It is clear, I think, that modernism must deprive literature of a sense of *perspective*. This would not be surprising; rigorous modernists such as Kafka, Benn, and Musil have always indignantly refused to provide their readers with any such thing. I will return to the ideological implications of the idea of perspective later. Let me say here that, in any work of art, perspective is of overriding importance. It determines the course and content; it draws together the threads of the narration; it enables the artist to choose between the important and the superficial, the crucial and the episodic. The direction in which characters develop is determined by perspective, only those features being described which are material to their development. The more lucid the perspective—as in Molière or the Greeks —the more economical and striking the selection.

Modernism drops this selective principle. It asserts that it can dispense with it, or can replace it with its dogma of the *condition humaine*. A naturalistic style is bound to be the result. This state of affairs—which to my mind characterizes all modernist art of the past fifty years— is disguised by critics who systematically glorify the modernist movement. By concentrating on formal criteria, by isolating technique from content and exaggerating its importance, these critics refrain from judgment on the social or artistic significance of subject-matter. They are unable, in consequence, to make the aesthetic distinction between *realism* and *naturalism*. This distinction depends on the presence or absence in a work of art of a 'hierarchy of significance' in the situations and characters presented. Compared with this, formal categories are of secondary importance. That is why it is possible to speak of the basically *naturalistic* character of modernist literature—and to see here the literary expression of an ideological continuity. This is not to deny that variations in style reflect changes in society. But the particular form this principle of naturalistic arbitrariness, this lack of hierarchic structure, may take is not decisive. We encounter it in the all-determining 'social conditions' of Naturalism, in Symbolism's impressionist methods and its cultivation of the exotic, in the fragmentation of objective reality in Futurism and Constructivism and the German *Neue Sachlichkeit*, or, again, in Surrealism's stream of consciousness.

These schools have in common a basically static approach to reality. This is closely related to their lack of perspective. Characteristically, Gottfried Benn actually incorporated this in his artistic programme. One of his volumes bears the title, *Static Poems*. The denial of history, of development, and thus of perspective, becomes the mark of true insight into the nature of reality.

The wise man is ignorant
of change and development
his children and children's children
are no part of his world.

The rejection of any concept of the future is for Benn the criterion of wisdom. But even those modernist writers who are less extreme in their rejection of history tend to present social and historical phenomena as static. It is, then, of small importance whether this condition is 'eternal,' or only a transitional stage punctuated by sudden catastrophes (even in early Naturalism the static presentation was often broken up by these catastrophes, without altering its basic character). Musil, for instance, writes in his essay, *The Writer in our Age*: 'One knows just as little about the present. Partly, this is because we are, as always, too close to the present. But it is also because the present into which we were plunged some two decades ago is of a particularly all-embracing and inescapable character.' Whether or not Musil knew of Heidegger's philosophy, the idea of *Geworfenheit* is clearly at work here. And the following reveals plainly how, for Musil, this static state was upset by the catastrophe of 1914: 'All of a sudden, the world was full of violence. . . . In European civilization, there was a sudden rift. . . .' In short: thus static apprehension of reality in modernist literature is no passing fashion; it is rooted in the ideology of modernism.

To establish the basic distinction between modernism and that realism which, from Homer to Thomas Mann and Gorky, has assumed change and development to be the proper subject of literature, we must go deeper into the underlying ideological problem. In *The House of the Dead* Dostoevsky gave an interesting account of the convict's attitude to work. He described how the prisoners, in spite of brutal discipline, loafed about, working badly or merely going through the motions of works until a new overseer arrived and allotted them a new project, after which they were allowed to go home. 'The work was hard,' Dostoevsky continues, 'but, Christ, with what energy they threw themselves into it! Gone was all their former indolence and pretended incompetence!' Later in the book Dostoevsky sums up his experiences: 'If a man loses hope and has no aim in view, sheer boredom can turn him into a beast. . . .' I have said that the problem of perspective in literature is directly related to the principle of selection. Let me go further: underlying the problem is a profound ethical complex, reflected in the composition of the work itself. Every human action is based on a presupposition of its inherent meaningfulness, at least to the subject. Absence of meaning makes a mockery of action and reduces art to naturalistic description.

Clearly, there can be no literature without at least the appearance of change or development. This conclusion should not be interpreted in a narrowly metaphysical sense. We have already diagnosed the obsession with psychopathology in modernist literature as a desire to escape from the reality of capitalism. But this implies the absolute primacy of the *terminus a quo*, the condition from which it is desired to escape. Any movement towards a *terminus ad quem* is condemned to impotence. As the ideology of most modernist writers asserts the unalterability of outward reality (even if this is reduced to a mere state of consciousness) human activity is, *a priori*, rendered impotent and robbed of meaning.

The apprehension of reality to which this leads is most consistently and convincingly realized in the work of Kafka. Kafka remarks of Josef K., as he is being led to execution: 'He thought of flies, their tiny limbs breaking as they struggle away from the fly-paper.' This mood of total impotence, of paralysis in the face of the unintelligible power of circumstances, informs all his work. Though the action of *The Castle* takes a different, even an opposite, direction to that of *The Trial*, this view of the world, from the perspective of a trapped and struggling fly, is all-pervasive. This experience, this vision of a world dominated by *angst* and of man at the mercy of incomprehensible terrors, makes Kafka's work the very type of modernist art. Techniques, elsewhere of merely formal significance, are used here to evoke a primitive awe in the presence of an utterly strange and hostile reality. Kafka's *angst* is the experience *par excellence* of modernism.

Two instances from musical criticism —which can afford to be both franker and more theoretical than literary criticism—show that it is indeed a universal experience with which we are dealing. The composer, Hanns Eisler, says of Schönberg: 'Long before the invention of the bomber, he expressed what people were to feel in the air raid shelters.' Even more characteristic—though seen from a modernist point of view—is Theodor W. Adorno's analysis (in *The Aging of Modern Music*) of symptoms of decadence in modernist music: 'The sounds are still the same. But the experience of *angst*, which made their originals great, has vanished.' Modernist music, he continues, has lost touch with the truth that was its *raison d'être*. Composers are no longer equal to the emotional presuppositions of their modernism. And that is why modernist music has failed. The diminution of the original *angst*-obsessed vision of life (whether due, as Adorno thinks, to inability to respond to the magnitude of the horror or, as I believe, to the fact that this obsession with *angst* among bourgeois intellectuals has already begun to recede) has brought about a loss of substance in modern music, and destroyed its authenticity as a modernist art-form.

This is a shrewd analysis of the paradoxical situation of the modernist artist, particularly where he is trying to express deep and genuine experience. The deeper the experience, the greater the damage to the artistic whole. But this tendency towards disintegration, this loss of artistic unity, cannot be written off as a mere fashion, the product of experimental gimmicks. Modern philosophy, after all, encountered these problems long before modern literature, painting or music. A case in point is the problem of *time*. Subjective Idealism had already separated time, abstractly conceived, from historical change and particularity of place. As if this separation were insufficient for the new age of imperialism, Bergson widened it further. Experienced time, subjective time, now became identical with real time; the rift between this time and that of the objective world was complete. Bergson and other philosophers who took up and varied this theme claimed that their concept of time alone afforded insight into authentic, i.e. subjective, reality. The same tendency soon made its appearance in literature.

The German left-wing critic and essayist of the Twenties, Walter Benjamin, has well described Proust's vision and the techniques he uses to present it in his great novel: 'We all know that Proust does not describe a man's life as it actually happens, but as it is remembered by a man who has lived through it. Yet this puts it far too crudely. For it is not actual experience that is important, but the texture of reminiscence, the Penelope's tapestry of a man's memory.' The connection with Bergson's theories of time is obvious. But whereas with Bergson, in the abstraction of philosophy, the unity of perception is preserved, Benjamin shows that with Proust, as a result of the radical disintegration of the time sequence, objectivity is eliminated: 'A lived event is finite, concluded at least on the level of experience. But a remembered event is infinite, a possible key to everything that preceded it and to everything that will follow it.'

It is the distinction between a philosophical and an artistic vision of the world. However hard philosophy, under the influence of Idealism, tries to liberate the concepts of space and time from temporal and spatial particularity, literature continues to assume their unity. The fact that, nevertheless, the concept of subjective time cropped up in literature only shows how deeply subjectivism is rooted in the experience of the modern bourgeois intellectual. The individual, retreating into himself in despair at the cruelty of the age, may experience an intoxicated fascination with his forlorn condition. But then a new horror breaks through. If reality cannot be understood (or no effort is made to understand it), then the individual's subjectivity—alone in the universe, reflecting only itself—takes on an equally incomprehensible and horrific character. Hugo von Hofmannsthal was to experience this condition very early in his poetic career:

It is a thing that no man cares to think on,
And far too terrible for mere complaint,
That all things slip from us and pass away,

And that my ego, bound by no outward force—
Once a small child's before it became mine—
Should now be strange to me, like a strange dog.

By separating time from the outer world of objective reality, the inner world of the subject is transformed into a sinister, inexplicable flux and acquires—paradoxically, as it may seem—a static character.

On literature this tendency towards disintegration, of course, will have an even greater impact than on philosophy. When time is isolated in this way, the artist's world disintegrates into a multiplicity of partial worlds. The static view of the world, now combined with diminished objectivity, here rules unchallenged. The world of man—the only subject-matter of literature—is shattered if a single component is removed. I have shown the consequences of isolating time and reducing it to a subjective category. But time is by no means the only component whose removal can lead to such disintegration. Here, again, Hofmannsthal anticipated later developments. His imaginary 'Lord Chandos' reflects: 'I have lost the ability to concentrate my thoughts or set them out coherently.' The result is a condition of apathy, punctuated by manic fits. The development towards a definitely pathological protest is here anticipated—admittedly in glamorous, romantic guise. But it is the same disintegration that is at work.

Previous realistic literature, however violent its criticism of reality, had always assumed the unity of the world it described and seen it as a living whole inseparable from man himself. But the major realists of our time deliberately introduce elements of disintegration into their work—for instance, the subjectivizing of time—and use them to portray the contemporary world more exactly. In this way, the once natural unity becomes a conscious, constructed unity (I have shown elsewhere that the device of the two temporal planes in Thomas Mann's *Doctor Faustus* serves to emphasize its historicity). But in modernist literature the disintegration of the world of man— and consequently the disintegration of personality—coincides with the ideological intention. Thus *angst*, this basic modern experience, this by-product of *Geworfenheit*, has its emotional origin in the experience of a disintegrating society. But it attains its effects by evoking the disintegration of the world of man.

To complete our examination of modernist literature, we must consider for a moment the question of allegory. Allegory is that aesthetic genre which lends itself par excellence to a description of man's alienation from objective reality. Allegory is a problematic genre because it rejects that assumption of an imminent meaning to human existence which—however unconscious, however combined with religious concepts of transcendence —is the basis of traditional art. Thus in medieval art we observe a new secularity (in spite of the continued use of religious subjects) triumphing more and more, from the time of Giotto, over the allegorizing of an earlier period.

Certain reservations should be made at this point. First, we must distinguish between literature and the visual arts. In the latter, the limitations of allegory can be the more easily overcome in that transcendental, allegorical subjects can be clothed in an aesthetic immanence (even if of a merely decorative kind) and the rift in reality in some sense be eliminated—we have only to think of Byzantine mosaic art. This decorative element has no real equivalent in literature; it exists only in a figurative sense, and then only as a secondary component. Allegorical art of the quality of Byzantine mosaic is only rarely possible in literature. Secondly, we must bear in mind in examining allegory —and this is of great importance for our argument—a historical distinction: does the concept of transcendence in question contain within itself tendencies towards immanence (as in Byzantine art or Giotto), or is it the product precisely of a rejection of these tendencies?

Allegory, in modernist literature, is clearly of the latter kind. Transcendence implies here, more or less consciously, the negation of any meaning immanent in the world or the life of man. We have already examined the underlying ideological basis of this view and its stylistic consequences. To conclude our analysis,

and to establish the allegorical character of modernist literature, I must refer again to the work of one of the finest theoreticians of modernism—to Walter Benjamin. Benjamin's examination of allegory was a product of his researches into German Baroque drama. Benjamin made his analysis of these relatively minor plays the occasion for a general discussion of the aesthetics of allegory. He was asking, in effect, why it is that transcendence, which is the essence of allegory, cannot but destroy aesthetics itself.

Benjamin gives a very contemporary definition of allegory. He does not labour the analogies between modern art and the Baroque (such analogies are tenuous at best, and were much overdone by the fashionable criticism of the time). Rather, he uses the Baroque drama to criticize modernism, imputing the characteristics of the latter to the former. In so doing, Benjamin became the first critic to attempt a philosophical analysis of the aesthetic paradox underlying modernist art. He writes:

In Allegory, the *facies hippocratica* of history looks to the observer like a petrified primeval landscape. History, all the suffering and failure it contains, finds expression in the human face—or, rather, in the human skull. No sense of freedom, no classical proportion, no human emotion lives in its features—not only human existence in general, but the fate of every individual human being is symbolized in this most palpable token of mortality. This is the core of the allegorical vision, of the Baroque idea of history as the passion of the world; History is significant only in the stations of its corruption. Significance is a function of mortality—because it is death that marks the passage from corruptibility to meaningfulness.

Benjamin returns again and again to this link between allegory and the annihilation of history:

In the light of this vision history appears, not as the gradual realization of the eternal, but as a process of inevitable decay. Allegory thus goes beyond beauty. What ruins are in the physical world, allegories are in the world of the mind.

Benjamin points here to the aesthetic consequences of modernism—though projected into the Baroque drama—more shrewdly and consistently than any of his contemporaries. He sees that the notion of objective time is essential to any understanding of history, and that the notion of subjective time is a product of a period of decline. 'A thorough knowledge of the problematic nature of art' thus becomes for him—correctly, from his point of view —one of the hall-marks of allegory in Baroque drama. It is problematic, on the one hand, because it is an art intent on expressing absolute transcendence that fails to do so because of the means at its disposal. It is also problematic because it is an art reflecting the corruption of the world and bringing about its own dissolution in the process. Benjamin discovers 'an immense, anti-aesthetic subjectivity' in Baroque literature, associated with 'a theologically-determined subjectivity.' (We shall presently show—a point I have discussed elsewhere in relation to Heidegger's philosophy—how in literature a 're-ligious atheism' of this kind can acquire a theological character.) Romantic—and, on a higher plane, Baroque—writers were well aware of this problem, and gave their understanding, not only theoretical, but artistic—that is to say allegorical—expression. 'The image,' Benjamin remarks, 'becomes a rune in the sphere of allegorical intuition. When touched by the light of theology, its symbolic beauty is gone. The false appearance of totality vanishes. The image dies; the parable no longer holds true; the world it once contained disappears.'

The consequences for art are far-reaching, and Benjamin does not hesitate to point them out: 'Every person, every object, every relationship can stand for something else. This transferability constitutes a devastating, though just, judgment on the profane world—which is thereby branded as a world where such things are of small importance.' Benjamin knows, of course, that although details are 'transferable,' and thus insignificant, they are not banished from art altogether. On the contrary. Precisely in modern art, with which he is ultimately concerned, descriptive detail is often of an extraordinary sensuous, suggestive power—we think again of Kafka. But this, as we showed in the case of Musil (a writer who does not consciously aim at allegory) does not prevent the materiality of the world from undergoing permanent alteration, from becoming transferable and arbitrary. Just this, modernist writers maintain, is typical of their own apprehension of reality. Yet presented in this way, the world becomes, as Benjamin puts it, 'exalted and depreciated at the same time.' For the conviction that phenomena are *not* ultimately transferable is rooted in a belief in the world's rationality and in man's ability to penetrate its secrets. In realistic literature each descriptive detail is both *individual* and *typical*. Modern allegory, and modernist ideology, however, deny the *typical*. By destroying the coherence of the world, they reduce detail to the level of mere particularity (once again, the connection between modernism and naturalism is plain). Detail, in its allegorical transferability, though brought into a direct, if paradoxical connection with transcendence, becomes an abstract function of the transcendence to which it points. Modernist literature thus replaces concrete typicality with abstract particularity.

We are here applying Benjamin's paradox directly to aesthetics and criticism, and particularly to the aesthetics of modernism. And, though we have reversed his scale of values, we have not deviated from the course of his argument. Elsewhere, he speaks out even more plainly—as though the Baroque mask had fallen, revealing the modernist skull underneath:

Allegory is left empty-handed. The forces of evil, lurking in its depths, owe their very existence to allegory. Evil is, precisely, the non-existence of that which allegory purports to represent.

The paradox Benjamin arrives at—his investigation of the aesthetics of Baroque tragedy has culminated in a negation of aesthetics—sheds a good deal of light on modernist literature, and particularly on Kafka. In interpreting his writings allegorically I am not, of course, following Max Brod, who finds a specifically religious allegory in Kafka's works. Kafka refuted any such interpretation in a remark he is said to have made to Brod himself: 'We are nihilistic figments, all of us; suicidal notions forming in God's mind.' Kafka rejected, too, the gnostic concept of God as an evil demiurge: 'The world is a cruel whim of God, an evil day's work.' When Brod attempted to give this an optimistic slant, Kafka shrugged off the attempt ironically: 'Oh, hope enough, hope without end—but not, alas, for us.' These remarks, quoted by Benjamin in his brilliant essay on Kafka, point to the general spiritual climate of his work: 'His profoundest experience is of the hopelessness, the utter meaninglessness of man's world, and particularly that of present-day bourgeois man.' Kafka, whether he says so openly or not, is an atheist. An atheist, though, of that modern species who regard God's removal from the scene not as a liberation—as did Epicurus and the Encyclopedists—but as a token of the 'God-forsakenness' of the world, its utter desolation and futility. Jacobsen's *Niels Lyhne* was the first novel to describe this state of mind of the atheistic bourgeois intelligentsia. Modern religious atheism is characterized, on the one hand, by the fact that unbelief has lost its revolutionary *élan*—the empty heavens are the projection of a world beyond hope of redemption. On the other hand, religious atheism shows that the desire for salvation lives on with undiminished force in a world without God, worshipping the void created by God's absence.

The supreme judges in *The Trial*, the castle administration in *The Castle*, represent transcendence in Kafka's allegories: the transcendence of Nothingness. Everything points to them, and they could give meaning to everything. Everybody believes in their existence and omnipotence; but nobody knows them, nobody knows how they can be reached. If there is a God here, it can only be the God of religious atheism: *atheos absconditus*. We become acquainted with a repellent host of subordinate authorities; brutal, corrupt, pedantic—and, at the same time, unreliable and irresponsible. It is a portrait of the bourgeois society Kafka knew, with a dash of Prague local colouring. But it is also allegorical in that the doings of this bureaucracy and of those dependent on it, its impotent victims, are not concrete and realistic, but a reflection of that Nothingness which governs existence. The hidden, non-existent God of Kafka's world derives his spectral character from the fact that his own non-existence is the ground of all existence; and the portrayed reality, uncannily accurate as it is, is spectral in the shadow of that dependence. The only purpose of transcendence—the intangible *nichtendes Nichts*—is to reveal the *facies hippocratica* of the world.

That abstract particularity which we saw to be the aesthetic consequence of allegory reaches its high mark in Kafka. He is a marvellous observer; the spectral character of reality affects him so deeply that the simplest episodes have an oppressive, nightmarish immediacy. As an artist, he is not content to evoke the surface of life. He is aware that individual detail must point to general significance. But how does he go about the business of abstraction? He has emptied everyday life of meaning by using the allegorical method; he has allowed detail to be annihilated by his transcendental Nothingness. This allegorical transcendence bars Kafka's way to realism, prevents him from investing observed detail with typical significance. Kafka is not able, in spite of his extraordinary evocative power, in spite of his unique sensibility, to achieve that fusion of the particular and the general which is the essence of realistic art. His aim is to raise the individual detail in its immediate particularity (without generalizing its content) to the level of abstraction. Kafka's method is typical, here, of modernism's allegorical approach. Specific subject-matter and stylistic variation do not matter; what matters is the basic ideological determination of form and content. The particularity we find in Beckett and Joyce, in Musil and Benn, various as the treatment of it may be, is essentially of the same kind.

If we combine what we have up to now discussed separately we arrive at a consistent pattern. We see that modernism leads not only to the destruction of traditional literary forms; it leads to the destruction of literature as such. And this is true not only of Joyce, or of the literature of Expressionism and Surrealism. It was not André Gide's ambition, for instance, to bring about a revolution in literary style; it was his philosophy that compelled him to abandon conventional forms. He planned his *Faux-Monnayeurs* as a novel. But its structure suffered from a characteristically modernist schizophrenia: it was supposed to be written by the man who was also the hero of the novel. And, in practice, Gide was forced to admit that no novel, no work of literature could be constructed in that way. We have here a practical demonstration that —as Benjamin showed in another context —modernism means not the enrichment, but the negation of art.

Irving Howe

THE FICTION OF ANTI-UTOPIA

Irving Howe has written books on Sherwood Anderson and William Faulkner and on the political novel, as well as many essays. He is also an editor of *Dissent*. "The Fiction of Anti-Utopia" was included in Howe's collection *A World More Attractive* (1963). Howe has taught at Brandeis and at Stanford and is now Professor of English at Hunter College of the City University of New York. He contributes frequent reviews and articles to the *New Republic*, *Commentary*, *Partisan Review*, and other periodicals.

"I feel sometimes as though the whole modern world of capitalism and Communism and all were rushing toward some enormous efficient machine-made doom of the true values of life."

This sentence was written in 1922 by Max Eastman, then a prominent intellectual defender of the Russian Revolution. It contains the crux of what would later fill volumes of disenchantment; and the need to speak it constitutes one reason why the intellectual experience of our time has been so full of self-distrust and self-assault. For some decades there had already been present a tradition in which conservative thinkers assaulted the idea of utopia as an impious denial of the limitations of the human lot, or a symptom of political naïveté, or a fantasy both trivial and boring—this last view finding a curious echo in Wallace Stevens' dismissal of the utopia called heaven: "does ripe fruit never fall?" But the kind of fiction I have in mind and propose to call anti-utopian does not stem from the conservative tradition, even when wryly borrowing from it.

Eastman's sentence would not seem remarkable if spoken by G. K. Chesterton or Hilaire Belloc; its continuing power to shock depends upon our knowledge that it came from a man of the left. And anti-utopian fiction, as it seeks to embody the sentiments expressed by Eastman, also comes primarily from men of the left. Eugene Zamiatin (*We*) is a dissident from Communism; George Orwell (*1984*) a heterodox socialist; Aldous Huxley (*Brave New World*) a scion of liberalism. The peculiar intensity of such fiction derives from the writer's discovery that in facing the prospect of a future he had been trained to desire, he finds himself struck with horror. The work of these writers is a systematic release of trauma, a painful turning upon their own presuppositions. It is a fiction of urgent yet reluctant testimony, forced by profoundly serious men from their own resistance to fears they cannot evade.

What they fear is not, as liberals and radicals always have, that history will suffer a miscarriage; what they fear is that the long-awaited birth will prove to be a monster. Not many Americans are able to grasp this experience: few of us having ever cultivated the taste for utopia, fewer still have suffered the bitter aftertaste of anti-utopia. For Europeans, however, it all comes with the ferocity of shock. Behind the anti-utopian novel lies not merely the frightful vision of a totalitarian world, but something that seems still more alarming. To minds raised on the assumptions, whether liberal or Marxist, of 19th-Century philosophies of history—assumptions that the human enterprise has a purposive direction, or *telos*, and an upward rhythm, or *progress*—there is also the churning fear that history itself has proved to be a cheat. And a cheat not because it has turned away from our expectations, but because it betrays our hopes precisely through an inverted fulfillment of those expectations. Not progress denied but progress realized, is the nightmare haunting the anti-utopian novel. And behind this nightmare lies a crisis of thought quite as intense as that suffered by serious 19th-Century minds when they discovered that far more painful than doubting the existence of God was questioning the validity of his creation.

Whether to distinguish literary genres or sub-genres through purely formal characteristics or to insist upon the crucial relevance of subject, theme and intellectual content, is something of a problem for theorists of criticism. It is all the more so in regard to fiction, which is less a genre than a menagerie of genres. I am inclined to think that in regard to prose fiction strictly formal characteristics will never suffice, even while remaining necessary, for proper description; and so I shall note here some of the main intellectual premises shaping anti-utopian fiction and then a few of those formal properties by which it may be distinguished from the familiar kinds of novel.

The first of the intellectual premises I have already remarked upon: what might be called the disenchantment with history, history both as experience and idea. The second is closely related. It is the vision of a world foreseen by a character in Dostoevsky's *The Possessed* who declares his wish for a mode of existence in which "only the necessary is necessary." Zamiatin's *We*, the first and best of the anti-utopian novels, portrays a "glass paradise" in which all men live in principled unprivacy, without a self to hide or a mood to indulge. Zamiatin thus reflects, as Orwell later would in his "telescreen" and Charlie Chaplin in a sequence of *Modern Times*, the fear that the historical process, at break-neck speed and regardless of our will, is taking us toward a *transparent universe* in which all categories are fixed, the problematic has been banished, unhappiness is treason and the gratuitous act beyond imagining. In *Brave New World* docile human creatures are produced in a hatchery: the ideal of man's self-determination, so important to Western liberalism, becomes a mocking rationale for procreation by norm. One of the "disturbed" characters in *We* remarks to one of the well-adjusted: "You want to encircle the infinite with a wall" and shifting from the metaphysical to the psychological, adds: "We are the happy arithmetical mean. As you would put it, the integration from zero to infinity, from imbeciles to Shakespeare."

This world of total integration is deprived of accident, contingency and myth; it permits no shelter for surprise, no margin for novelty, no hope for adventure. The rational raised to an irrational power becomes its god. Reality, writes Orwell in *1984*, "is not external. Reality exists in the human mind and nowhere else . . . whatever the Party holds to be truth *is* truth." Reality is not an objective fact to be acknowledged or transformed or resisted; it is the culminating fabrication produced by the *hubris* of rationalism.

But a certain kind of rationalism, I must hasten to add; since none of the anti-utopian novelists, at least in their novels, has anything to do with invoked mysticism. The sociologist Karl Mannheim distinguishes between two kinds of rationality, "substantial" and "functional." Substantial rationality is "an act of thought which reveals intelligent insight into the interrelations of events in a given situation." Functional rationality, the parallel in conduct to the process of industrial rationalization, consists of

. . . a series of actions . . . organized in such a way that it leads to a previously defined goal, every element in this series of actions receiving a functional position and role. . . . It is by no means characteristic, however, of functional organization that . . . the goal itself be considered rational. . . . One may strive to attain an irrational eschatological goal, such as salvation, by so organizing one's ascetic behavior that it will lead to this goal. . . .

And Mannheim remarks:

The violent shocks of crises and revolutions have uncovered a tendency which has hitherto been working under the surface, namely the paralyzing effect of functional rationalization on the capacity for rational judgment.

In his abstract way Mannheim hits upon the nightmare-vision of the anti-utopian novelists: that what men do and what they are become unrelated; that a world is appearing in which technique and value have been split apart, so that technique spins forward with a mad fecundity while value becomes debased to a mere slogan of the state. This kind of "technicism,"

Spengler has remarked, is frequently visible in a society that has lost its self-assurance. And in his preface to *Brave New World* Huxley shows a keen awareness of the distinction between "substantial" and "functional rationality" when he remarks that "The people who govern the Brave New World may not be sane . . . but they are not madmen, and their aim is not anarchy but social stability." They live, that is, by the strict requirements of functional rationality.

All three of our writers have a lively appreciation of the need felt by modern men to drop the burden of freedom, that need crystalized in the remark of the 19th Century anarchist Michael Bakunin, "I do not want to be I, I want to be We." The schema of the anti-utopian novel requires that in one or two forlorn figures, sports from the perfection of adjustment, there arise once more a spontaneous appetite for individuality. In *Brave New World* it takes the form of historical nostalgia; in *1984*, a yearning for a personal relationship that will have no end other than its own fulfillment; and in *We*, a series of brilliant forays into self-consciousness. The narrator of *We* discloses the ethos of his world when he remarks that the half-forgotten Christians "knew that resignation is virtue and pride a vice; [and almost as if echoing Bakunin] that 'We' is from 'God,' and 'I' from the devil." But as a deviant from the deadening health of his society, he engages in a discovery of selfhood through a realization of how strange, how thoroughly artificial, the very notion of selfhood is:

Evening . . . the sky is covered with a milky-golden tissue, and one cannot see what is there, beyond, on the heights. The ancients "knew" that the greatest, bored skeptic— their god—lived there. We know that crystalline, blue, naked, indecent Nothing is there. . . . I had firm faith in myself; I believed that

I knew all about myself. But then . . . I look in the mirror. And for the first time in my life, yes, for the first time in my life, I see clearly, precisely, consciously and with surprise, I see myself as some "him!" I am "he." . . . And I know surely that "he" with his straight brows is a stranger. . . .

The idea of the personal self, which for us has become an indispensable assumption of existence, is seen by Zamiatin, Orwell and Huxley as a *cultural* idea. It is a fact within history, the product of the liberal era, and because it is susceptible to historical growth and decline, it may also be susceptible to historical destruction. All three of our anti-utopian novels are dominated by an overwhelming question: can human nature be manufactured? Not transformed or manipulated or debased, since these it obviously can be; but manufactured by will and decision.

When speaking about the historical determinants of human nature, one tacitly assumes that there *is* a human nature, and that for all of its plasticity it retains some indestructible core. If Zamiatin, Orwell and Huxley wrote simply from the premise of psychological relativism, they would deprive themselves of whatever possibilities for drama their theme allows, for then the very idea of a limit to the malleability of human nature would be hard to maintain. They must assume that there are strivings in men toward candor, freedom, truth and love which cannot be suppressed indefinitely; yet they have no choice but to recognize that at any particular historical moment these strivings can be suppressed effectively, surviving for men of intelligence less as realities to be counted on than as potentialities to be nurtured. Furthermore, in modern technology there appears a whole new apparatus for violating human nature: brainwashing and torture in *1984*, artificial biological selection in *Brave New World*, and an operation similar to a lobotomy in *We*. And not only can desire be suppressed and impulse denied; they can be transformed into their very opposites, so that people sincerely take slavery to be freedom and learn, in *Brave New World*, that "the secret of happiness and virtue is liking what you've got to like."

Ultimately the anti-utopian novel keeps returning to the choice posed by Dostoevsky's legend of the Grand Inquisitor in *The Brothers Karamazov*: the misery of the human being who must bear his burden of independence against the contentment of the human creature at rest in his obedience. But what now gives this counterposition of freedom and happiness a particularly sharp edge is the fact that through the refinements of technology Dostoevsky's speculation can be realized in social practice. In a number of intellectual and literary respects *Brave New World* is inferior to *1984* and *We*, but in confronting this central question it is bolder and keener, for Huxley sees that the problem first raised by Dostoevsky—will the satisfaction of material wants quench the appetite for freedom?—relates not only to totalitarian dictatorships but to the whole of industrial society. Like so many other manifestations of our culture, the anti-utopian novel keeps rehearsing the problems of the 19th Century: in this instance, not merely Dostoevsky's prophetic speculation but also the quieter fear of Alexis de Tocqueville that "a kind of virtuous materialism may ultimately be established in the world which would not corrupt but enervate the soul, and noiselessly unbend its springs of action."

The main literary problem regarding anti-utopian fiction is to learn to read it according to its own premises and limits, which is to say, in ways somewhat different from those by which we read ordinary novels.

Strictly speaking, anti-utopian fictions are not novels at all. Northrop Frye has usefully distinguished among kinds of fiction in order to remind us that we have lost in critical niceness by our habit of lumping all prose fiction under the heading of the novel. He is right of course, but I suspect that for common usage the effort to revive such distinctions is a lost cause, and that it may be better to teach readers to discriminate among kinds of novels. If we do for the moment accept Frye's categories it becomes clear that books like *We, 1984,* and *Brave New World* are not really novels portraying a familiar social world but what he calls Menippean satire, a kind of fiction that

. . . deals less with people as such than with mental attitudes. . . . The Menippean satire thus resembles the confession in its ability to handle abstract ideas and theories, and differs from the novel in its characterization, which is stylized rather than naturalistic, and presents people as mouthpieces of the ideas they represent. . . . At its most concentrated the Menippean satire presents us with a vision of the world in terms of a single intellectual pattern.

Accept this description and the usual complaints about the anti-utopian novel come to seem irrelevant. By its very nature the anti-utopian novel cannot satisfy the expectations we hold, often unreflectively, about the ordinary novel: expectations that are the heritage of 19th-Century romanticism with its stress upon individual consciousness, psychological analysis and the scrutiny of intimate relations. When the English critic Raymond Williams complains that the anti-utopian novel lacks "a substantial society and correspondingly substantial persons," he is offering a description but intends it as a depreciation, quite as if a critic complained that a sonnet lacks a complex

dramatic plot. For the very premise of anti-utopian fiction is that it projects a world in which such elements—"substantial society . . . substantial persons"— have largely been suppressed and must now be painfully recovered, if recovered at all.

One might even speculate that it would be a mistake for the author of an anti-utopian novel to provide the usual complement of three-dimensional characters such as we expect in ordinary fiction, or to venture an extended amount of psychological specification. For these books try to present a world in which individuality has become obsolete and personality a sign of subversion. The major figures of such books are necessarily grotesques: they resemble persons who have lost the power of speech and must struggle to regain it; Winston Smith and Julia in *1984* are finally engaged in an effort to salvage the idea of the human *as an idea*, which means to experiment with the possibilities of solitude and the risks of contemplation. The human relations which the ordinary novel takes as its premise, become the possibilities toward which the anti-utopian novel strains. What in the ordinary novel appears as the tacit assumption of the opening page is now, in the anti-utopian novel, a wistful hope usually unrealized by the concluding page. That the writer of anti-utopian fiction must deal with a world in which man has been absorbed by his function and society by the state, surely places upon him a considerable quota of difficulties. But this is the task he sets himself, and there can be no point in complaining that he fails to do what in the nature of things he cannot do.

The anti-utopian novel lacks almost all the usual advantages of fiction: it must confine itself to a rudimentary kind of characterization, it cannot provide much in the way of psychological nuance, it hardly pretends to a large accumulation of suspense. Yet, as we can all testify, the anti-utopian novel achieves its impact, and this it does through a variety of formal means:

1. *It posits a "flaw" in the perfection of the perfect.* This "flaw," the weakness of the remembered or yearned-for human, functions dramatically in the anti-utopian novel quite as the assumption of original sin or a socially-induced tendency toward evil does in the ordinary novel. The "law" provides the possibility and particulars of the conflict, while it simultaneously insures that the outcome will be catastrophic. Since the ending of the anti-utopian novel is predictable and contained, so to say, within its very beginning, the tension it creates depends less on a developed plot than on an overpowering conception. Leading to—

2. *It must be in the grip of an idea at once dramatically simple and historically complex: an idea that has become a commanding passion.* This idea consists, finally, in a catastrophic transmutation of values, a stoppage of history at the expense of its actors. In reading the anti-utopian novel we respond less to the world it projects than to the urgency of the projection. And since this involves the dangers of both monotony and monomania—

3. *It must be clear in the management of its substantiating detail.* Knowing all too well the inevitable direction of things, we can be surprised only by the ingenuity of local detail. And here arises a possible basis for comparative valuations among anti-utopian novels. Orwell's book is impressive for its motivating passion, less so for its local composition. Huxley's is notably clever, but too rationalistic and self-contained: he does not write like a man who feels himself imperilled by his own vision. Zamiatin is both passionate and

brilliant, clever and driven. His style, an astonishing mosaic of violent imagery, sustains his vision throughout the book in a way that a mere linear unfolding of his fable never could. But since the anti-utopian novel must satisfy the conflicting requirements of both a highly-charged central idea and cleverness in the management of detail, it becomes involved with special problems of verisimilitude. That is—

4. *It must strain our sense of the probable while not violating our attachment to the plausible.* To stay too close to the probable means, for the anti-utopian novel, to lose the very reason for its existence; to appear merely implausible means to surrender its power to shock. Our writers meet this difficulty by employing what I would call the dramatic strategy and the narrative psychology of "one more step." Their projected total state is one step beyond our known reality—not so much a picture of modern totalitarian society as an extension, by just one and no more than one step, of the essential pattern of the total state.

5. *In presenting the nightmare of history undone, it must depend upon the ability of its readers to engage in an act of historical recollection.* This means, above all, to remember the power that the idea of utopia has had in Western society. "The Golden Age," wrote Dostoevsky, "is the most unlikely of all the dreams that have been, but for it men have given up their life and all their strength. . . . Without it the people will not live and cannot die." Still dependent on this vision of the Golden Age, the anti-utopian novel thus shares an essential quality of all modern literature: it can realize its values only through images of their violation. The enchanted dream has become a nightmare, but a nightmare projected with such power as to validate the continuing urgency of the dream.

Eric Bentley

THE POLITICAL THEATRE RECONSIDERED

Eric Bentley, Brander Matthews Professor of Dramatic Literature at Columbia University since 1954, has been instrumental in making available the plays of Bertolt Brecht to English and American audiences. Bentley has aided Brecht's cause through his translations, productions, and cogent criticism of the playwright's work. Among Bentley's books are *The Playwright as Thinker* (1946), *In Search of Theatre* (1953), and *What Is Theatre?* (1956). This essay originally appeared in *Kenyon Review* in 1961.

One's thinking begins with the assumption that all the arts have a certain social importance. But do most members of most societies make this assumption? Probably not. So that, at the outset, the thinker finds himself in conflict with the world, and what he says will be polemic rather than philosophy. He is the champion of art against the philistines. And so it comes about that, in a world that doesn't believe in art at all, art is nearly always represented, in print, as having far more importance than it really possesses. A few great artists—Plato, for instance, and Tolstoy—have refused to swell the chorus of art worshippers, but every undergraduate learns to dismiss their opinions on the point as mere eccentricities.

If Plato and Tolstoy were mistaken, they are mistaken in the same way as most of their critics: they overestimated the influence of art. If the artist is not as dangerous as they thought, it is because

his work doesn't have that much effect one way or another.

When I speak of influence, I am speaking of tangible and overt influence—social influence. Didn't "good" works like *Uncle Tom's Cabin* have much less effect on history than Tolstoy thought? Isn't the same true of works he deplored, such as his own masterpieces?

Not that these questions are simple. The violent emotions that many experienced when reading Mrs. Stowe are certainly "effects." What I am questioning is whether such emotions played a decisive, or even a large, part in the freeing of the slaves. And if one followed up that discussion, one would have to ask to what extent these good emotions are truly good? The emancipation was itself highly ambiguous, and, if Mrs. Stowe had influence at all, we should also reckon with the way in which she antagonized the enemy and helped to create the present Southern intransigence. If her book is

226

useful today, it is useful chiefly, say, to Governor Faubus of Arkansas, who might justly cite it as an instance of Northern incomprehension. At that, I will stand by the position that literature is much less important, in the worldly sense, than it has usually been assumed to be. Governor Faubus can get along very nicely without Mrs. Stowe.

Let no one be misled by the fact that literature can *seem* to have a political importance much larger than it actually commands. Boris Pasternak, for instance, has truly become important politically. That is not to say that his writings have political influence. For one thing, they are profoundly unpolitical writings. What I have in mind is that Pasternak does not stand, in the eyes of the millions who know of him, as the author of words they have read, but as the author of words they have read *about*. The world is full of people who wept when they read in the paper of Pasternak's fate but who snored when they got to page ten of Pasternak's book. So what has this incident to do with the influence of literature?

I have had the lucky opportunity to observe at close range the most political of all dramatists, Bertolt Brecht. According to him, the drama was to be nothing if not social, and in an era like our own it was to do nothing if not contribute to social and revolutionary change. Brecht was a far more gifted writer than Mrs. Stowe. Yet can his contribution to history be considered any larger than hers?

As with Pasternak, we must distinguish between the writer as a name to conjure with, and the writer as mere writer. The name of Brecht was more valuable to the Communists than were the works of Brecht. Society's interest in art may be slight, yet society may at the same time accord prestige to the artist—just as one may revere a scientist like Einstein without having the least idea what he has

done that deserves revering. The sociology of art should deal with such factors as these.

The theme of drama and propaganda is full of paradox. Brecht's intention had been to take art down a peg and model his work on science. Ultimately, his error was the usual one made by artists and their critics: the over-estimation of art. For he attributed great political importance to the theatre, an institution that has very little effect on politics. Just as one can justifiably ask of someone who prefers Russia, why doesn't he go to Russia? so one can ask of someone who prefers science or politics, why doesn't he go in for science or politics? A playwright with a few notions about Galileo is never going to match the scientists on their own ground.

The sobering, and perhaps shocking, fact is that the artist has been and today remains a slave—or, if you like, a lackey. Communist critics have never tired of illustrating this fact with data from ancient, feudal, and capitalist society. There was always the patron, and there is still the patron today, even though his name be hidden behind that of a newspaper or a magazine or a publishing house. What we have become acutely aware of since 1930 is that Communist countries—except in the performing arts—have made matters worse rather than better. In Western society one can at least become the lackey of some rebel prince—let's say of a millionaire who supports a Communist magazine. The fate of Meyerhold and Eisenstein tells us what happens to rebels in Russia.

The rebel artist customarily plays just as subservient a role in rebellion as his brother plays in conservation. God help any regime—and God help any rebellion that depends heavily on its artists! They are, on the whole, not a dangerous lot, as Plato thought, but a useless lot. A brutal government might logically ship them off to forced labor—as one hears that the present Chinese government is doing.

The illusion that the artist is characteristically the master rather than the slave is the characteristic illusion of the artist himself—whom sheer powerlessness drives to dreams of power. The image of the artist as sublime and Promethean only holds for very great artists. The average artist is not a Prometheus but a Walter Mitty.

The phrase Propaganda and Drama will suggest different things to different people. To most it suggests a drama that furthers social change and particularly total change or revolution; but, after all, the "other side" has its propaganda too, and plays can be written in the interests of the status quo. Shakespeare's histories are a case in point.

I am thinking of works which directly champion the preservation of the status quo and implicitly recognize some threat to it. Works in which the status quo is merely accepted, and no alternative imagined, would not be propaganda unless we considerably extend the word's normal scope. In the past 50 years this has been proposed—chiefly by people influenced by Marxism. There is the slogan: Art Is a Weapon. And one used to hear people say—perhaps one still would everywhere except the United States—All Art Is Propaganda. Such a phrase has its utility in reminding us that even classic writers of wide academic acceptance had some ax to grind. It is still a little puerile to lump together Clifford Odets' *Waiting for Lefty* and Dante's *Divine Comedy*. So I will hold to the older understanding of the word as implying a direct effort at changing history, if, in some cases, only a little bit of history. For example, a work which seeks to convert you to a religion is propaganda; a work which merely presents that religion, or embodies its au-

thor's belief in it, is not. Admittedly, a person might be converted by the second type of work, and it has often been urged with some justice that propaganda is bad propaganda: the proselytizer makes fewest proselytes. But this is to remark on the limitations of propaganda, not to change the definition of it.

It is commonly assumed that propaganda is fundamentally offensive, not defensive. That is because only its offensives are visible. If one can generalize in this matter, I would say that the stance of the propagandist is a defensive one, and that, if he hits, it is only when he believes he is hitting back. The starting point is a threat, real or imagined. Hitler's plot to take over the world is the dream of a man who felt persecuted. His persecutions are at once a revenge for and a forestalling of persecutions to himself, more imagined, of course, than real. But the imagination is real.

It is common, in this connection, to give the origin of the word: *congregatio de propaganda fide*, a committee of cardinals who were charged with propagating the faith. If we stop here, we might make shift with the positive conception of the process and of the impulse that leads to it. The date when the congregation was set up tells us otherwise. It is 1622—at the height of the Counter Reformation. What brought this, the original propaganda, into being was the threat of Protestantism. From the Counter Reformation on, the word propaganda has kept the connotation of fanaticism, or at least zeal. It is the work of men in a tremendous hurry which they believe is imposed on them by events. Propaganda is a weapon, and it is an emergency weapon, one to use after police methods have failed. When literature won't work, so to say, you may be forced to try propaganda. One sees writers reaching this conclusion whenever there's a war on. And always with us are people who say there's already a war on, and so the time to use this heavy artillery is now. "It's later than you think!" "Act before it is too late!" These exclamations, which prompt propaganda in the first place, are nowadays its content too. And again one would have to point to the illusion of believing that literary propaganda makes very much difference.

Brecht said you don't paint a still life when the ship is going down. He seems not to have realized that you don't paint at all when the ship is going down. A few artists *have* voluntarily given up their art in view of the urgency of a social situation, but, if all artists were so consistent, propagandist art would be self-liquidating. At this point one sees that emergency art is based not only on an illusion but also on sophistry. The ship is going down and though one hasn't time to paint a still life one has time to paint a picture of ships that are going down because, no doubt, the shipowners want to collect the insurance. Such a picture is justified by its future utility, but actually it took as long to paint as a still life. If its utility is imaginary, the whole operation stands revealed as a double cheat. Meanwhile, the artist has brought painters of still lifes into disrepute, while securing automatic praise for his picture of a shipwreck on the grounds of its urgency, utility, rightmindedness, and so forth.

I have been talking as if a work were either pure propaganda or not propaganda at all. Yet the propaganda in Shakespeare's histories has lost all its urgency and some of its plausibility, while the plays remain alive because they have the virtues of good plays of the non-propagandist sort. An author may intend a piece of propaganda, and inadvertently produce a work of art. Or he may have two separate intentions, in conflict or in harmony. It is a mixed phenomenon.

One should distinguish between preaching to the converted and preaching to the heathen. The original Congregation of Propaganda was dedicated to the conversion of the heathen only. And a pattern of social drama that existed in the 1930s showed an irresolute person, characteristically a liberal, being forced into choosing between Communism and Fascism and choosing or failing to choose the former. Here the old reversal at the center of a dramatic plot is combined with a quasi-religious conversion. The real question—whether a person *is* forced into that particular dilemma—is begged. Propaganda was never strong on philosophy— "the point is not to understand the world but to change it." Dramaturgically, one might say that the skill in manipulating situations which is usually applied frivolously is in propaganda plays applied unscrupulously, as by a Machiavellian or Jesuitical extremist. Certainly the type of drama that is addressed to the task of converting people seldom tries to do it by reason. If you proceeded by pure reason, you wouldn't invoke the aid of theatre in the first place: another point overlooked by Bertolt Brecht, who thought of theatre as being as rational as a laboratory. But Brecht was consistent at least to the point of writing only one straight conversion play. Since his own more characteristic type of drama was devised to deal with our modern emergency, it is curious that he gives this emergency as his pretext for reverting to conventional drama in the play I am speaking of (*Die Gewehre der Frau Carrar*).

I suppose Bernard Shaw has come closer than anyone else to writing plays calculated to persuade. At least we think of him as such a playwright. Coming down to cases, we perhaps have only one case to come down to, and it is only part of a play at that: the Don Juan scene from *Man and Superman*. That is a piece of persuasion if there is a piece of persuasion in all of world drama. But is it actually persuasive? By this, I don't mean: was Shaw right? I mean: even assuming he was right, are the tactics of this masterpiece calculated to win over someone who disagrees? One assumes that Shaw agrees with Don Juan. Yet he also gives the Devil his due. Don Gonzalo and Ana do not argue, but they embody parts of human life not embraced by the Don. A favorable response to the play is not likely to take the form of feeling won over. Rather, we feel we have shared a noble vision of life. And that is another way of saying we have taken the scene to be not propaganda but drama.

There exists a series of works which are persuasive but are not quite dramas: Plato's dialogues. I go by fairly orthodox definitions. Shift the normal definitions, as Georg Kaiser did, and Plato's dialogues can be adjudged the quintessence of drama. They certainly have many of the obvious characteristics of the dramatic form, and the death of Socrates can be presented on stage as a tragedy with very little changing of the text. Are Plato's dialogues propaganda? Again, it is, in the first instance, purely a semantic question. I have suggested that urgency—a plan for immediate, overt change—belongs to the definition. That is why I couldn't include Plato among the propagandists. That is also why practical persons call him a Utopian.

Not very much writing actually tries to persuade, though quite a lot pretends it does. We are familiar with this kind of pretence from conversation and oratory. The motions of persuasion are gone through, but the audience actually envisaged is already persuaded. Before an audience of fellow Christians, a Christian gives his answer to the atheists—a different thing indeed from a Christian persuading an atheist to be a Christian.

Much drama that makes controversial points relies, without ever admitting it, on the audience's prior agreement. No Broadway play about Negroes tries to persuade a conservative Southerner he is wrong. Every such play seeks to confirm the anti-Southern Northerner in what he already feels. Hence, what is called the "boldness" in the presentation calls for no boldness in the author. On the contrary, it tempts him toward demagogic self-congratulation.

Is there a propagandist drama which is deliberately addressed to those who are already convinced? Certainly. Under this head comes religious drama addressed to a particular denomination, or political drama addressed to a particular party. Here the issue is not the truth or untruth of the cause, but only its celebration and its defense. Shakespeare put no case for nationalism in *Henry* V. He addressed his fellow nationals and fellow nationalists and called them to a feeling of solidarity —called them also to hatred of the French. The religious drama of the Middle Ages is not propagandist at all under the definition I am following, because it is not defensive. The religious drama of the Spaniards in the seventeenth century is often another matter: it is the literature of the Counter Reformation.

In most of the liberal and left-wing drama of our days there are ambiguities. Some of it might be read as an attempt by Communists to make converts of liberals. But often a double trick was played. The author didn't admit to his Communism. At the same time he strongly implied that the progressive view, as currently accepted by the Party, is already acknowledged as truth by any right-minded person—so no good man really needs any converting in the first place.

The equivocation invades even the writing of professed Marxists and fellow-travelers like Brecht. A certain amount of deliberate falsification was involved. For example, Brecht once wrote a scene to show that the Communists and Social Democrats continued to fight each other even when they were fellow prisoners in Nazi camps. On the advice of a better Communist than himself, he changed the scene to say just the opposite. The facts of the camps had not changed, but it was wartime and the policy was a united front against Hitler. A useful lie was told; but what, actually, was its usefulness? Not that very many people took Brecht's word for it and said: we can all sink our differences and fight Hitler. That is a supposed reason which few will accept as the real one. The actual effect was to give an impression that Marxist theory was softening in view of the fact that the Marxist poet no longer saw Social Democrats as the enemy. Many people did not see the dishonesty in the case.

If Brecht's plays are taken as argument, they can only be taken as arguing in a circle. What is proved at the end of *The Good Woman of Setzuan* is assumed at the beginning, and no fact is presented along the way except as exemplifying the initial assumptions. Brecht says: "These are the facts—and look what follows from them." Anyone is free to reply: "If those were the facts, those would be the consequences. But those are not the facts." In short, Brecht really had in mind an audience of people who wouldn't question his version of the facts. There is no exploration in any of his plays of what the facts are. The truth is something established before the first line is written. The questions that arise are questions like: will a person (his St. Joan) come to see this truth? Is a person strong enough (Galileo) to stand by this truth?

Brecht is said to have declared himself the last Catholic playwright, and certainly one remarks his tendency to write about martyrs of his faith. Doubts about the faith are seen not as possibly reasonable differences in opinion but as signs of personal inadequacy or outright cowardice. To make this point, Brecht attributes to Galileo views he could never possibly have held. The thesis is: Galileo held a modern progressive's view of history and even doubted the existence of God; if he didn't say so, it is because he was afraid of instruments of torture.

We have also seen in our time a revival of drama in the churches. Not much of it is propaganda in my definition, but I was surprised to hear T. S. Eliot say not long ago that *Murder in the Cathedral* was intended to be propaganda against the Nazis. His Becket was meant, apparently, as a sort of Pastor Niemöller in conflict with the state. Curious that such an intention should be revealed only years later, as in a note explaining an obscure line of *The Waste Land*. Anti-Nazi propaganda could scarcely be effective if kept such a closely-guarded secret.

How effective is *any* propaganda in the theatre? I have already expressed my scepticism about propaganda generally. I cannot waive it in this instance. What *Murder in the Cathedral* could have done against the Wehrmacht and the SS would in any event have been negligible. Persuasion, we have seen, is seldom attempted, seldom succeeds. With pretended persuasion, we come to propaganda drama that is really addressed to those already convinced. What can religion do for the converted—by theatrical means? and in the way of propaganda? The aim would be to fill with emotional content what may otherwise be a feebly "intellectual" tenet. You are made to feel strongly about a certain thing, and if the dose is repeated often enough your feeling will perhaps harden into a habit. One believes this; yet one cannot measure any of the factors involved. For example, the theatre might help to inculcate patriotism, but if a theatregoer is a patriot, how can you tell how much of his patriotism actually comes from the theatre? I cannot imagine any attitude becoming socially important unless many more people than the dramatists are fostering it.

I speak, of course, from a twentieth century background. The drama is now surrounded by radio, movies, and TV. Things were different in the days when the theatre was the principal source of entertainment. Yet even then the home, the church, and the school were more important training grounds. Our Puritan forebears thought the theatre more likely to be a place where wisdom is *un*learned. They had a good deal of evidence to go on.

We cast about for big claims to make. The arts seem to prompt people to grandiose pronouncements. Threatened, we make propaganda for theatre—as well as demand a theatre of propaganda. We even read in the papers that in asking some millionaire for money to build a theatre, a generous managing director has offered him in return all manner of high ideals. If a New York impresario wants to show us the Comédie Française, he starts to burble about international peace, and we have visions of general disarmament resulting from transatlantic crossings.

These big claims can, of course, be understood. I think they belong to a phase of history in which masses of people are having their first inkling that the arts might be a good thing and might even enter their lives. I myself come of unlettered parents who, when they gave me an education, had to interpret the arts I studied by making an analogy with religion. Their religion being evangelical, like most of the religion of England and America, they thought of the arts as being the way their son would do good to people, and perhaps abolish war, not to mention drunkenness. Then there is the guilt

we all feel, or have felt, at the fact that we are fiddling while Rome burns. The impulse to join Schweitzer in Africa, or Klaus Fuchs in East Germany, is felt by more people than actually do it. Many have tried to appease their guilt by saying: I will practise the kind of art that helps democracy, or that helps Stalin, or that helps God.

This making of excessive claims for art comes, oddly enough, from having too little faith in it. We search far afield for its purpose only because we cannot look it in the face. What worries us is the modesty, the intimacy, of art as it really is: its real effects are small, internal, personal, and hard to describe or even to observe. Hence, though the purpose of the *Ninth Symphony* may be to introduce universal brotherhood, the chilling fact is that it has failed to do so. Shall we join the Salvation Army, which undoubtedly has had more success in that direction? I would respect the man who drew such a conclusion more than the man who trumpets that our modern artists must strive to succeed where Beethoven failed.

There is a third possibility: to find what the *Ninth Symphony* can actually do for people—what it has done for some and will do for others. What actually happened to you when last you heard that work may seem rather a small incident compared with the invention of the atom bomb, but must you have an inferiority complex about this? The arts depend for their existence on our respect for such small incidents. I believe that we should start from respect, not for society, but for the individuals whom it comprises— and, in the first instance, for their private experience. Secondly, artistic activity must be taken as a good in itself and therefore not needing justification on grounds of its utility in other fields like religion and politics. Satisfying a natural and not unhealthy craving, it is part of the good life.

Not being suspect, it need not be on the defensive.

What conclusion can be drawn for the theatre of today and tomorrow? That propaganda, as I have defined it, falls far short of its objectives—and I have spoken throughout of the propaganda of artists, not of politicians and advertising men— is no reason why an artist should not be moral, or even didactic. It is not even a reason why he shouldn't write propaganda if that's what he wants to do—a comment I make uncynically, meaning thereby that, ultimately, artists do what they can't help doing, whether it works or not. In any event, an artist cannot give up regarding himself as the conscience of mankind, even if mankind pays no attention.

Will what we have all called the Social Drama have a future? First, perhaps, it should be established what we have—or should have—meant by the term. If, as is sometimes said, all drama is social, then the expression has indeed no value. Nor is there much more point in using the word "social" as an accolade and awarding it, as Arthur Miller does, to all the plays one approves of. It makes more sense to reserve it for its usual application—that is, to plays which are, in their main emphasis, political, sociological. The Germans have a term, Zeitstück, for a play that tries to cope with a problem of the day. A leading playwright, I believe, might be expected to cope with the leading problem of the day. It will, of course, be of the highest interest what he considers that problem to be.

There exists the possibility that the leading problem of the day cannot be coped with at all—at any rate by playwrights. One of our playwrights has, in fact, taken the position that it cannot. "The world of today," writes Friedrich Dürrenmatt, "cannot be envisioned because it is anonymous and bureaucratic.

. . . Creon's secretaries close Antigone's case." And yet Dürrenmatt writes plays, and these plays do present what the author quite evidently intends as an image of the characteristic reality of our time. The essay I have just quoted from also contains this avowal: "Any small-time crook, petty government official or cop better represents our world than a senator or president. Today art can only embrace the victims, if it can reach men at all. . . ."

A rejoinder to Dürrenmatt's essay was written by Brecht himself. Brecht said the world of today could be mirrored on stage if it was presented as alterable. Such was the softened version he gave in 1955 of the belief he had held since 1928 that a playwright could present life in our time only with the help of Marxism.

Both playwrights need the formula: Today art can only . . . Both make, in effect, the statement: "On the face of it, the world of today simply cannot be got on to a stage. And yet it can: with the help of my philosophy." Since both of these dramatists have written Social Drama of some distinction, one could argue that both are right—and that perhaps a third playwright could turn the trick with a third philosophy. Which amounts to saying that both are wrong, and that it was not the rightness of the philosophy in question that wrought the miracle. Mother Courage, to take an example, is one of the best social dramas of the century. Marxism enabled Brecht to state in this play that war is the continuation of capitalism by other means. But is it this statement that interests any admirer of the play? Is it this statement, even, that makes us feel the play is burningly relevant? On the contrary, it is the fact, admitted by all philosophers and non-philosophers, that war has become the supreme problem of our society. When the play urges that simple fact it speaks to the whole audience. When it links that fact to a particular sociological theory, it speaks to theorists—in the gray language of theory. Both Brecht and Dürrenmatt seem to tell us that it is as doctrinaires that they will survive. Their plays tell us another story.

The problem of poverty is now eclipsed by the problem of atomic war; nor can most of us agree that the two problems are one. A new orientation is called for; one can even see it coming. In its 1959 Christmas issue, the socialist *New Statesman* featured a cartoon in which the stable of Bethlehem cowered beneath a super-store selling TV sets and stream-lined cars with fins. A board read: We Never Had It So Good. Now when a radical cartoonist protests, not against poverty, but against prosperity, a landmark has been reached in the history of radicalism. At this point much of the old Social Drama becomes obsolete.

Not just the drama of the virtuous poor versus the wicked rich. Although war remains an issue, has in fact become *the* issue, many of the old war plays are obsolete. There is a theme in Brecht's war plays, including *Mother Courage*, that is as dead as a doornail: the theme of jingoism, the idea that what endangers the peace is the gleam of swords and the glamor of uniforms. The illusion that war is fun has gone. The only sword that now has symbolic value is the sword of Damocles.

And yet *Mother Courage* has a validity, which stems, not from "Das Lied vom Weib und dem Soldaten," but from the direct portrayal of a devastation distinctly similar to that of Hiroshima. Which is to say that the valid part of this "social drama" is not optimistic; but there is no need to describe it as pessimistic either. We have to do here with a vision of horror which is a vision of truth and there-fore necessary to any sane outlook, stormy or serene.

Atomic explosion: there will be plays about what it means to live under this particular mushroom. We must expect a literature of terror and defeat, which is to say, of nihilism. Insofar as the artist in our time simply sits and broods, he will write *Waiting for Godot* and *The Chairs*. Is sitting and brooding satisfactory? Is it even preferable to Stalinism? (The question, for Brecht for instance, was not a rhetorical one.) And yet: what else is possible? A few years ago men hoped to remake the world. Nothing short of that seemed worth exerting oneself for. Now we would be happy to stop the world from destroying itself. Do we think we can? And do we really want to?

To ask such questions is to realize that while war is the immediate problem, the ultimate problem is: what would we do with peace? A generation ago the liberal movement answered: "Feed the poor. Whatever is done about freedom, let the poor be fed." Sometimes the poor were fed; and always freedom was sacrificed. The reorientation that is at hand today will entail placing the question of slavery and freedom again at the center of liberal (radical, revolutionary) activity, especially intellectual activity. For, as Camus said in Stockholm, "the nobility of our calling will always be rooted in two commitments . . . the service of truth and the service of freedom."

The literature of freedom—our generation's literature of freedom, I mean—began as a response to a situation not unlike that of today. As the whole world now lives trembling beneath the shadow of a bomb, so Frenchmen of the Resistance lived from 1941–43 under what seemed the shadow of Nazi victory. The literature of what may then have seemed a special situation has now become the literature of the universal situation. As certain Frenchmen in 1942 had to regard the future as black, yet fought, regardless, against enslavement, so the writer today, unable to see through that mushroom cloud to the light of the sun, can proclaim his faith in that light, can struggle toward that light.

I am now indulging, I realize, in pure aspiration. There is little or no Social Drama of the kind I am talking about. Camus was attempting something of the sort but, I grant, Camus was not really a dramatist. Brecht gave up freedom long ago. Dürrenmatt seems to be a waiter for Godot. . . . But since my subject, for the moment, is the future, perhaps pure aspiration is in order.

IV. The Psychological Critic

NORMAN N. HOLLAND

KENNETH BURKE

HERBERT READ

GEORGES POULET

LESLIE A. FIEDLER

INTRODUCTION

Ours is indisputably an age of psychology, and there can be no doubt about the influence of psychology upon the creation and the criticism of modern literature. Most of the century's great writers, for example, Lawrence, Joyce, Eliot, Mann, Kafka, Hemingway, and O'Neill, either consciously make use of psychology in form, characterization, or theme, or take account of it indirectly. Such literary movements, trends, and techniques as surrealism, expressionism, the interior monologue and stream-of-consciousness, the Theatre of the Absurd, all demonstrate their indebtedness to certain psychological truths and discoveries. Even writing that is quite conventional in substance and method borrows heavily from psychology in its treatment of characters and in its construction of plot and situation.

Inevitably, literary criticism has been similarly influenced to the degree that not only has there arisen a specific psychological criticism but also that most of the other major critical approaches have also incorporated psychological information or insights in one fashion or another. These insights are employed most overtly in the mythopoeic approach, which is itself in part an offshoot of the psychological approach, and more covertly in the formalistic approach. The major psychological influence upon criticism has been Sigmund Freud and psychoanalysis; but what I have been loosely calling *psychology* would also include such systems as Gestalt psychology and the phenomenological-existential mode that has become prominent in Europe during the past generation, as well as various kinds of eclectic psychology.

Although the self-conscious use of the science or discipline of psychology by literary critics is uniquely a product of this century, psychology in the general sense has been a basic and recurrent element in criticism since Aristotle. Aristotle's pragmatic description of the workings of the mind in its aesthetic responses is based on the empirical observation of human behavior rather than deduced from metaphysical hypotheses. Because Aristotle was so keen a student of the psychology of perception, major portions of the *Poetics* can still accurately be described as psychological criticism, and it is noteworthy that, in the twentieth century, psychoanalysis has adapted Aristotle's term *katharsis* to its own clinical uses. In point of fact, just as the history of literary criticism begins with Aristotle, so most histories of psychology also name him as the founder of empirical psychology.

To continue briefly this sketch of origins, we find in Longinus' *On the Sublime* (first century A.D.) an essentially psychological concept; for the author pays tribute to the power of literature to transport its audience first by arousing and then by gratifying their emotions—a variation on Aristotle's doctrine. In the sixteenth century Sir Philip Sidney defended poetry with the argument that, because it can move men, it is a more effective teacher of truth and goodness than philosophy, which is another psychological perspective. Hume's eighteenth-century inquiry into the problem of how men take pleasure from tragedy's portrayal of suffering, likewise has a psychological basis (*Of Tragedy*, 1757). Coleridge's distinction between *reason* and *understanding* and his description of the role of the imagination in the creative process—concepts that have had far-reaching influence on modern criticism, especially formalism—are fundamentally psychological. In short, the relationship of psychology and literary criticism is as old as each of the separate disciplines.

But with Sigmund Freud and the founding of psychoanalysis, this relationship entered a new dimension. The history and development of Freudian thought as it impinged upon literature has been so thoroughly studied elsewhere, for example in Frederick J. Hoffman's definitive *Freudianism and the Literary Mind*, that I need not review it here. However, to further our own special purposes I will attempt to simplify the complex problem of the literary critic's use of psychoanalytic principles by describing what the critic does in dealing with each phase of the total literary process: the writer, the work, and the reader.

THE WRITER

In dealing with the writer, the psychological critic proceeds in much the same manner as the historical critic. That is, the critic either takes over directly or adapts to his own needs the method of psychoanalysis both to study the man behind the work—or, to phrase it differently, the work as a reflection and a projection of its creator—and to study the creative process itself. The critic may attempt to show how the writer's experiences and personality determine his style, choice of subject, and depiction of character. He may explain how and why a writer may have been motivated to create a particular work or even try to reconstruct the various stages of creation by which the raw materials of life are transformed into art. In so doing the critic tries to understand the processes by which the writer's private experience is made communicable and significant to others, the means by which the particular comes to stand for the general. Accordingly, scholars and critics who do not pay specific allegiance to the psychological approach have often used it (at times perhaps unwittingly) in their writing of literary biography or in adducing biographical evidence to support a critical argument. Many critics employ depth psychology deliberately and expertly. For example, Philip Young draws upon the psychoanalytic theory of the repetition-compulsion syndrome in his provocative study of Hemingway, and Newton Arvin explores Melville's relationship with his mother in order to illuminate certain aspects of his artistic development. In this connection we should note that one of Freud's few writings that concentrate wholly on literature, his essay "Dostoyevsky and Parricide," also sought to link the artist's work with the artist's human experience and to exhibit the parallels between the writer's emotional history and his handling of theme.

THE WORK

In dealing with the work, the psychological critic more closely resembles the formalist in his procedures. The critic may ignore any correspondence between the author's life and his creation but adapt the psychoanalytic method to the study of the characters in the literary work itself, treating them as self-complete entities wholly within the context of the work. Not only the characters of fiction and drama, but also the persona of the poem can constitute proper subjects for this kind of inquiry. Or, the critic may avoid psychography in any form and explore the literary work's symbolism. Because the psychological critic has learned from the psychoanalytic study of dreams that symbols are not logical or systematic formulations but products of emotion and the fusion of disguised, ambiguous, or even contradictory elements, the critic's approach can be as flexible and unorthodox as the materials he is considering. Although he might well benefit from the use of extrinsic facts in his interpretation, his success, like the formalist critic's, really depends on his own wisdom and perception directed to the work itself.

To take this matter one step further, the modern critic's preference for literary works that are complex and rich in texture, his awareness that in literary masterpieces meaning is piled upon meaning, and his commitment to the necessity of the most scrupulous explication may all be indebted to the Freudian view of the symbolic nature of most human acts and to the Freudian emphasis upon the difference between *manifest content* and *latent content*, or, simply, between what the work says and what it means. As Lionel Trilling has put it, Freud's contribution to literature consists less of a method than of an attitude, Freud's "whole conception of the mind." In Trilling's words: "... of all mental systems, the Freudian psychology is the one which makes poetry indigenous to the very constitution of the mind. Indeed, the mind, as Freud sees it, is in the greater part of its tendency exactly a poetry-making organ. . . . In the eighteenth century Vico spoke of the metaphorical, imagistic language of the early stages of culture; it was left to Freud to discover how, in a scientific age, we still feel and think in figurative formations, and to create what psychoanalysis is, a science of tropes, of metaphor and its variants, synecdoche and metonymy." We should also remark that although the psychological critic does not simply carry over the technical language or clinical methods of psychoanalysis to his treatment of imagery and symbolism, he has as a starting point the analyst's experience with dreams and with such psychic maneuvers as displacement, condensation, splitting, and projection, which have considerable analogy with aesthetic phenomena. What the critic must do is find literary equivalents for these specialized psychological data and render them in terms appropriate and coherent to the literary audience.

THE READER

Just as the psychological critic in his study of the creative process seeks to demonstrate how the personal testimony of one man, the writer, becomes meaningful to multitudes, so the psychological critic also inquires into the secret of the work's appeal to the individual reader. Here the critic intends to discover how the private experience that the reader brings to the work is wakened to respond to the work's special provocation, becoming at one with the experience conveyed in the work. At this point, because no man's experience is wholly unique but in part shared with others of his time and place, the psychological critic's concern is akin to that of the sociocultural critic.

Nor does the critic necessarily limit himself to the reader's conscious response. Few readers will insist that they find only intellectual and aesthetic satisfaction in literature; most are willing to admit that they are captivated by a magic in books beyond rational explanation. The quest to comprehend the nature and operation of this magic is one of the psychological critic's proper pursuits (a quest he shares with the mythopoeic critic), for he believes that literature takes hold over the reader by permitting the expression of deeply significant psychic material that has long been repressed. In this function as a release-mechanism, literature defends against or relieves profound tensions and anxieties.

As to the problem of aesthetics as it relates to this psychodynamic process, or, what we find beautiful in belles-lettres, a recent advocate of psychological criticism had this to say: "Freud's basic contribution to the understanding of art is the psychoanalytic insight that the pleasure which we unconsciously take in form, technique, and style is our acknowledged reward for having fulfilled our part of the compact with the artist and that our unacknowledged gain is the emotional release and enrichment a work of art affords us, a result which would not be possible without the relaxation of inhibition by aesthetic means." In other words, the psychological critic finds the aesthetic element interfused with the element of emotional appeal: the reader takes pleasure not only in the fact or achievement of release but also in the mode or process of release.

So far I have been stressing the psychoanalytic factor in psychological criticism, even to the point of using the term *psychological* as though it were synonymous with *psychoanalytic*. Now I must qualify the matter. Although the Freudian or psychoanalytic school—which in my broad usage is meant to include such "revisionists" as Jung,[1] Rank, and Adler—has unquestionably exerted the largest influence on the psychological critic's study of audience appeal as well as on the critic's study of the writer and the work, it has hardly been the only influence. I will outline briefly a few other systems pertinent to the contemporary psychological approach.

In such important early books as *Principles of Literary Criticism* (1924), *Science and Criticism* (1926), and *Practical Criticism* (1929), I. A. Richards employed an eclectic psychology that emphasized reader response and that drew upon behaviorism and Gestalt psychology, among others, although it borrowed relatively little from depth psychology. In *Practical Criticism* Richards declared that the critic's primary task was to establish the "experience, the *mental condition* relevant to the poem." As we have noted earlier, Richards' theories—often based on his own integration of various psychological concepts—became a wellspring for formalist criticism.

The Gestalt approach, founded soon after World War I by Max Wertheimer, Kurt Koffka, Wolfgang Kohler, and Kurt Lewin at the University of Berlin, has seemed in its basic precepts to be among the most promising systems for literary critics. The fundamental thesis of the Gestalt school[2] is that perceptions are not comprised of bundles or groups of sensations tied together by association or imagination but that all mental processes are dynamic structural units with unique properties that do not surrender to logical analysis. Applying this principle to art, the Gestaltist argues that both the creator and the audience of the artwork grasp the design or pattern of the *whole* work before they realize its details or constituent parts. And as his classic example of this mode of response the Gestaltist offers a fact discovered not in the laboratory or clinic but derived from man's experience of art: the axiom that we recognize a melody with greater ease and rapidity than we do a musical phrase. But despite its obvious congeniality to art and despite its emphasis upon structured wholes, the Gestalt system has

---

[1] I will discuss Jung separately and more appropriately in the next section, which deals with mythopoeic criticism.

[2] There is no exact English equivalent for *gestalt*. The closest would be *configuration* or *structural relationship*.

yet to attract adherents from the ranks of literary critics who would adapt its discoveries to their own uses, as critics have so eagerly adapted depth psychology.

The phenomenological-existential psychology, arising from and intimately connected to the dominant philosophy on the Continent during the past two decades, defies brief description. In my very pairing of the phenomenological and the existential, I am linking related but not identical things. But to offer a glimpse of the matter to those even less knowledgeable, I will characterize the phenomenological-existential psychology as subject-centered rather than method-centered and as the attempt to place men in a true and essential relationship with other men and the world. This psychology is profoundly concerned with what the individual experiences, with his response to things. The subjective experience therefore comprises the primary data of phenomenological-existential psychology, but before it can be categorized and explained or assume a status in reality it must be fully described. In this sense the belief of Freud and Jung that the content of abnormal mental processes must be wholly revealed and understood before diagnosis or therapy can begin was a phenomenological attitude.

Similarly, in the phenomenological-existential critic's description of an art object, the object gathers value and meaning only as experienced or communicated in its particular cultural context by members of that culture. Culture, in the phenomenological view, is a class of personal worlds. A man's *phenomenal field* includes everything he experiences at a given moment, including his awareness of self. If he thinks about an object not physically present, this object becomes a part of his phenomenal field; if he does not perceive an object physically present it is not part of his field. In short, to venture one final simplification on this point, we have here the fundamental emphasis of all psychological criticism, regardless of its particular variety: the emphasis upon subjective perception and emotional response as the *sine qua non* of the aesthetic experience.

The essays that follow exhibit the effects of the several psychologies upon literary criticism in accurate correspondence to the relative influence of each psychological approach. That is, the influence of depth psychology is most evident and pervasive, especially in the essays by Norman Holland, Leslie Fiedler, and Herbert Read. Read's essay also reflects the basic concept of Gestalt. Kenneth Burke employs an eclectic psychology not so much imitative of Richards as it is likewise individualistic. Georges Poulet illustrates the phenomenological-existential outlook.

Norman Holland's "Psychological Depths and 'Dover Beach' "* adapts the psychoanalytic concept of defenses or defense mechanisms to a reading of Arnold's famous poem and concludes that the poem's strategy brings into play a carefully disguised sexual symbolism that has been repressed and then transferred in such a way that painful experiences are made pleasurable. Holland goes on to find the same strategy of defense typical of Victorian culture at large. During the course of his analysis Holland also makes use of a close examination of the text, historical information, and a type of sociocultural argument to establish his major psychological point. The critic's point, as we have come to expect in psycho-analytic criticism, is to uncover the real motivation or situation, i.e., the latent meaning, of the literary work. The situation is the ubiquitous one propounded in the Freudian approach, the *family romance*. Although Holland concentrates on a special aspect of the family romance, the child's wish for sexually pure parents, we deduce that a similar analysis of a literature very different from Victorian literature might demonstrate some other aspect of this archetypal situation. In any case, Holland's deployment of a variety of techniques en route to his goal, his exploitation of the reader's subjective reaction, his exhaustive investigation of a single instance and then his projection of its implications to a broad cultural horizon, are all characteristic of the practice of the skilled psychological critic.

Leslie Fiedler's essay, which advances the major thesis of his provocative *Love and Death in the American Novel*, displays to advantage Fiedler's pluralistic method, a synthesis of the historical, mythopoeic, and sociocultural, resting on a foundation of depth psychology. That psychology is central, not peripheral, to Fiedler's method can be observed in his depiction of the romantic revolution (which he calls the *break-through*) as essentially a *psychic revolution* and in such statements as his conclusion: "The final horrors, as modern society has come to realize, are neither gods nor demons, but intimate aspects of our own minds." Fiedler's psychology is that of Freud, pointing back to the significance of child-hood experience, stressing the effects of the repression of love (in this instance one effect is the immaturity of the American novel), introducing biographical data to explain pertinent aspects of the writers' careers, and suggesting that the neurosis of one form of American art typifies a national neurosis.

In "The Creative Experience"* Sir Herbert Read performs a double task: first, he explicates a Coleridge poem that exists in two versions and assesses the relative merit of each version; secondly, he offers a hypothesis as to the source of poetic creativity. In his first function Read relies upon a psychological-historical method, working through the biographical circumstances of the poem to a psychologically oriented conclusion and speculating that the poem both grew out of and resolved certain conflicts in Coleridge. As Read interprets it, the act of poetic creation also becomes a therapeutic act by which tensions are sublimated. But Read then goes on—and in this he fulfills his second intention—to warn against reducing the magic of poetry to a mechanical formula soluble by quantitative analysis. In at-tempting to mediate between a mechanistic view of poetry as psychological process and a mystical depiction of it as some sort of ineffable spirituality, Read depends upon an argument derived from the Gestalt: the perception of significant struc-tured wholes that are more than the sum of their parts. In Read's words: "The poem is a sensuous unity, a totality of utterance, and meaningful as unity or totality. To break it down into image and idea is to ignore the fact that there are no internal sutures, no possibility of separating image from image, image from idea, or either from the language in which they are expressed." Thus we perceive that in his own kind of psychological criticism, a criticism that takes equally and without apparent contradiction from two psychological systems and yet that ultimately asserts the autonomy of the art object, Read leans toward formalism, while Holland and Fiedler tend more to the historical and sociocultural.

The psychology of Kenneth Burke's approach, as illustrated in "Catharsis: Second View,"* is even more eclectic than Read's. It is an underlying, implicit psychology and not that of any school or system, although, as I will shortly suggest, not without affinities and parallels to the Freudian. In the present essay, as elsewhere in his criticism, Burke draws analogies between the literary work's form, imagery, strategy, and effect, and common human experience, especially emotional experience. His frame of reference, his authority, depends as often on a familiar occurrence in life as it does a literary text. For example, he describes a complex relationship between love and anger or love and violence—a relationship important to his definition of catharsis—by posing the example of a little girl tussling with little boys. But such is Burke's method that he will reach out a moment later to Dante, Aristotle, and the Bible for further documentation.

Although Burke has the greatest respect for aesthetic form, we see here clearly that he conceives form not as an absolute or objective entity but as something dependent upon extrinsic factors, notably the audience's subjective experience of the work. Form cannot achieve its function unless it appeals to or embodies some common human experience, and we surmise from Burke's line of reasoning that this experience is fundamentally emotional, that is, psychological or psychophysical, rather than the purely intellectual or cognitive perception that is the ideal of some formalists.

Although Burke's psychology is indisputably his own, an integration of a number of diverse ingredients, if we apply a psychoanalytic approach to his essay we discover a type of latent Freudianism. By this I mean that in Burke's view of catharsis as pity and fear that are substituted for love because the world will not permit the naked display of love, we have a proposition like that of the interaction of the Freudian id-ego-superego complex and akin to the Freudian hypothesis of laughter or tears as a surrogate sexual fulfillment. We must further note that, although Burke's definition of cartharsis follows the Aristotelian pattern, Burke is also no doubt aware of the psychoanalytic sense of catharsis, which designates a stage in psychoanalytic therapy whereby tension and anxiety are released through the expression or the acting-out of past traumas.

The "psychology" of Georges Poulet's definition of comedy is such that only the critically sophisticated among Anglo-American readers will find its perspective familiar. Few have encountered its critical method in English. Although Poulet's juxtaposition of the normal or customary of the "serious" against the peculiar or temporary of the "comic" bears faint resemblance to the superego-id duality of depth psychology, Poulet's psychology is not that of Freud but rather of the phenomenological-existential mode that hews closer to metaphysics than it does to either biology or physiology. Nevertheless, that Poulet's criticism can at least in part be described as psychological is evident in his definition of the comic response as having its origin in our emotions. To quote Poulet: "If ridicule is indeed, as Molière says, the coldest of all our feelings, it is none the less authentically a feeling. It is at once judgment and feeling." Once more the personal response and the values formed from the direct confrontation with life are the dominant factors in the critic's conception of a type of art. For critics like Poulet, mood is an essential fact of aesthetic experience, a psychological fact, however intangible; and mood originates in man's perception of his relationship to reality and to other men—upon his existential predicament in a phenomenological world.

We have now arrived at the realization that, although of all critical approaches psychological criticism appears to depend most heavily upon a science, or a discipline that views itself as a science, it is in practice among the most various and eclectic of criticisms. Indeed, the vices of the psychological critic are manifested in direct ratio to his attempt to be scientific and on those occasions when he forgets, as R. M. Adams has said, that "Literature is not watered-down psychology; psychology is not methodized literature." Psychology, and especially the branch of psychoanalysis, has always found in literature rich support for its theories and has displayed a consistently more cordial attitude toward art and artists than have the other sciences. On his seventieth birthday, when Freud was honored as the discoverer of the unconscious, he disclaimed the honor and said that it rightfully belonged to the creative writers who had gone before him. But despite this cordiality, psychology has on occasions threatened to dominate literature, applying its methods to a literary text with the assumption that it would for once and all establish the truth about that text. Dr. Ernest Jones' brilliant reading of *Hamlet*, in what is perhaps the classic study of literature by a psychoanalyst, *Hamlet and Oedipus*, provides the keenest stimulation and insight to students of literature; nevertheless, we wonder whether this is ultimately literary criticism at all. Conversely, a good deal of the literary use of psychology and psychoanalysis has tended toward oversimplification, reduction, and the formation of stereotypes: *vide*, the rash of psychoanalytic biographies and critical studies of a generation ago, Van Wyck Brooks on Mark Twain, or Krutch on Poe, which concentrated on the writer's traumas or neuroses as the salient factor in his career. One still observes this predilection in some critical writing today.

The problem of art and neurosis is of the greatest interest to the psychological critic, as it is one of the few aesthetic problems that engages even the philistine. This problem has evoked continuing discussion, nowhere more than in America. But if art somehow is intertwined with neurosis or comes out of neurosis, a supposition for which there is much evidence, we must also consider it a superb kind of health. No doubt that writers and readers, as humans, have their problems, but these problems are transcended through the very agency of the literary work. At the same time, those who support the proposition of the neurotic basis of art —and they are by no means all enemies of literature—argue that the writer's neurosis may be at the very source of his authority, his authenticity, his genius.

The riddle still baffles us. As Freud wrote many years ago, "Unfortunately, be-

246 The Psychological Critic

fore the problem of the creative artist, analysis must lay down its arms." And as Ernst Kris has reminded us recently, we have not arrived at satisfactory answers to two vital questions: Why will one man with a particular pattern of experience become an artist, while another with a similar pattern will not? Why does one artist achieve greatness, and another never rise above mediocrity? To these queries we must add a third: How is literature beautiful?

In short, there are still mysteries to be plumbed about how literature is born, about how it works, and about how we react to it. It is with these matters that the psychological critic concerns himself. But psychological criticism need not only be genetic or explanatory, limiting itself to sources and processes. By helping us to perceive meaning where none seemingly existed before, it can also be evaluative. The critic who brings to his craft deep learning and skill both in psychology and literature can teach us much we are eager to know.

SELECTED BIBLIOGRAPHY

Adams, R. M., "Literature and Psychology: A Question of Significant Form," *Literature and Psychology*, V (1955), 67–72.

Basler, Roy P. *Sex, Symbolism, and Psychology in Literature* (New Brunswick, Rutgers University Press, 1948).

Bergler, Edmund. *The Writer and Psychoanalysis* (Garden City, Doubleday & Co., Inc., 1950).

Brown, Norman O. *Life Against Death* (Middletown, Conn., Wesleyan University Press, 1959), pp. 55–73.

Daiches, David. *Critical Approaches to Literature* (Englewood Cliffs, N.J., Prentice-Hall, Inc., 1956), pp. 340–357.

Edel, Leon. "Literature and Psychology," in N. P. Stallknecht and Horst Frenz, eds., *Comparative Literature: Method and Perspective* (Carbondale, Ill., Southern Illinois University Press, 1963), pp. 96–115.

Fraiberg, Louis. *Psychoanalysis and American Literary Criticism* (Detroit, Wayne State University Press, 1960).

Freud, Sigmund. *On Creativity and the Unconscious* (New York, Harper & Row, Publishers, Inc., 1958).

Fromm, Erich. *The Forgotten Language: An Introduction to the Understanding of Dreams, Myths and Fairy Tales* (New York, Holt, Rinehart & Winston, Inc., 1951).

Ghiselin, Brewster, ed. *The Creative Process* (Berkeley, University of California Press, 1952).

Hoffman, Frederick J. *Freudianism and the Literary Mind* (New York, Grove Press, Inc., 1959).

Hoffman, Frederick J. *The Mortal No: Death and the Modern Imagination* (Princeton, N.J., Princeton University Press, 1964).

Holman, C. Hugh. "The Defense of Art: Criticism Since 1930," in Floyd Stovall, ed. *The Development of American Literary Criticism* (Chapel Hill, N.C., University of North Carolina Press, 1955), pp. 216–225.

Hyman, Stanley Edgar. *The Armed Vision* (abridged ed.; New York, Vintage Books, 1955), pp. 142–160.

Hyman, Stanley Edgar. *The Tangled Bank: Darwin, Marx, Frazer and Freud as Imaginative Writers* (New York, Atheneum Publishers, 1962).

Jones, Ernest. *Hamlet and Oedipus* (Garden City, N.Y., Doubleday & Co., Inc., 1954).

Kris, Ernst. *Psychoanalytic Explorations in Art* (New York, International Universities Press, Inc., 1952).

Kubie, Lawrence. *Neurotic Distortion of the Creative Process* (Lawrence, Kansas, University of Kansas Press, 1958).

Langer, Susanne K. *Feeling and Form* (New York, Charles Scribner's Sons, 1953).

Lemon, Lee T. *The Partial Critics* (New York, Oxford University Press, 1965), pp. 91–95.

Lesser, Simon O. *Fiction and the Unconscious* (Boston, Beacon Press, 1957).

Lucas, F. L. *Literature and Psychology* (Ann Arbor, University of Michigan Press, 1957).

Maritain, Jacques. *Creative Intuition in Art and Poetry* (New York, Pantheon Books, 1960).

Muller, Herbert J. *Science and Criticism* (New York, George Braziller, Inc., 1956), pp. 130–172.

Phillips, William, ed. *Art and Psychoanalysis* (New York, Meridian Books, 1963).

Rieff, Philip. *Freud: The Mind of the Moralist* (New York, The Viking Press, Inc., 1959), pp. 118–147.

Sachs, Hanns. *Creative Unconscious* (Cambridge, Sci-Art Publishers, Mass., 1951).

Trilling, Lionel. "Freud and Literature," and "Art and Neurosis," in *The Liberal Imagination* (Garden City, N.Y., Doubleday & Co., Inc., 1953), pp. 44–64, 159–178.

Norman N. Holland

PSYCHOLOGICAL DEPTHS AND "DOVER BEACH"

Norman N. Holland has written extensively on the relationship between literature and psychology, for example, in his recent book *Psychoanalysis and Shakespeare* (1965). His other books are *The First Modern Comedies* (1959) and *The Shakespearean Imagination* (1964) Holland has taught at Harvard University and at the Massachusetts Institute of Technology and is now Chairman of the English Department at the State University of New York at Buffalo. This essay first appeared in *Victorian Studies* in 1965.

DOVER BEACH

The sea is calm to-night,
The tide is full, the moon lies fair
Upon the straits;—on the French coast the light
Gleams and is gone; the cliffs of England stand,
5 Glimmering and vast, out in the tranquil bay.
Come to the window, sweet is the night-air!
Only, from the long line of spray
Where the sea meets the moon-blanch'd land,
Listen! you hear the grating roar
10 Of pebbles which the waves draw back, and fling,
At their return, up the high strand,
Begin, and cease, and then again begin,
With tremulous cadence slow, and bring
The eternal note of sadness in.

15 Sophocles long ago
Heard it on the Ægæan, and it brought
Into his mind the turbid ebb and flow
Of human misery; we

Find also in the sound a thought,
Hearing it by this distant northern sea. 20

The Sea of Faith
Was once, too, at the full, and round earth's shore
Lay like the folds of a bright girdle furl'd.
But now I only hear
Its melancholy, long, withdrawing roar, 2
Retreating, to the breath
Of the night-wind, down the vast edges drear
And naked shingles of the world.

Ah, love, let us be true
To one another! for the world, which seems 3
To lie before us like a land of dreams,
So various, so beautiful, so new,
Hath really neither joy, nor love, nor light,
Nor certitude, nor peace, nor help for pain;
And we are here as on a darkling plain 3
Swept with confused alarms of struggle and flight,
Where ignorant armies clash by night.

Psychoanalysis and literary analysis have mingled uneasily ever since 15 October 1897, when Freud simultaneously found in himself and in Hamlet "love of the mother and jealousy of the father." Psychoanalysis, it turned out, could say many interesting things about plays and novels. Unfortunately, it did not do at all well with the analysis of poems. In the symbolistic psychoanalysis of 1915 or so, poems became simply assemblages of the masculine or feminine symbols into which psychoanalysis seemed then to divide the world. Poems, often, were reduced to mere dreams—for old-style psychoanalysis could look only at the content, not the form, of poetry.

Literary critics may fare better with new-style psychoanalysis—indeed, not so new, for one could date it from Anna Freud's The Ego and the Mechanisms of Defense in 1936. This later phase of psychoanalysis takes into account defenses or defense mechanisms—that is, ways of dealing with drives or impulses so as to ward off anxiety and to adapt drives to reality in a positive or useful way. A literary critic recognizes this concept of defense as something very like what Kenneth Burke would call a "strategy" or "trope." A psychology that can deal with defenses can deal with poems in terms of form as well as of content, for form is to content in literature as, in life, defense is to impulse. I would also like to suggest that because today's psychoanalysis can look at both literary form and literary content, we can from literary works frame a hypothesis as to the fundamental psychological patterns of drive and defense in a given culture. Such a psychological pattern should in turn tell us why some literary forms succeed in a given culture and others fail.

My test case is Victorian England. I would like to see, first, what an understanding of defenses can add to the conventional explication of a poem. Second, I would like to see what a knowledge of defenses can tell us for literary history— specifically, the literary history of Victorian England. Naturally, then, we should look at a Victorian poem, perhaps the Victorian poem.

"Dover Beach" (according to The Case for Poetry) is the most widely reprinted poem in the language. Certainly, it seems like the most widely explicated, once you begin researching it. Let me try to summarize in a few paragraphs what a dozen or so of the most useful explicators and annotators have to say.[1]

---

[1] Since explications necessarily overlap, it is hard to give credit where credit is due, but I will try. To avoid a cumbersome series of footnotes, I will simply give in parentheses after a given statement, what seems to me the most appropriate name or title, referring to the following list of explications: Paull F. Baum, Ten Studies in the Poetry of Matthew Arnold (Durham, N. C., 1958), pp. 85–97. Louis Bonnerot, Matthew Arnold, Poéte: Essai de biographie psychologique (Paris, 1947), p. 203. The Case for Poetry, eds. Frederick L. Gwynn, Ralph W. Condee, and Arthur O. Lewis, Jr. (Englewood Cliffs, 1954), pp. 17, 19, and "Teacher's Manual," pp. 14–15. Rodney Delasanta, The Explicator, XVIII (1959), 7. Elizabeth Drew, Poetry: A Modern Guide to its Understanding and Enjoyment (New York, 1959), pp. 221–223. Gerhard Friedrich, "A Teaching Approach to Poetry," English Journal, XLIX (1960), 75–81. Frederick L. Gwynn, Explicator, VIII (1960), 46. Wendell Stacy Johnson, "Matthew Arnold's Dialogue," University of Kansas City Review, XXVII (1960), 109–116. Wendell Stacy Johnson, The Voices of Matthew Arnold: An Essay in Criticism (New Haven, 1961), pp. 90–94. J. D. Jump, Matthew Arnold (London, 1955), pp. 67–68 and 81. J. P. Kirby, Explicator, I (1943), 42. Murray Krieger, " 'Dover Beach' and the Tragic Sense of Eternal Recurrence," University of Kansas City Review, XXIII (1956), 73–79. Gene Montague, "Arnold's 'Dover Beach' and 'The Scholar Gypsy,'" Explicator, XVIII (1959), 15. Frederick A. Pottle, Explicator, II (1944), 45. Norman C. Stageberg, Explicator, IX (1951), 34. C. B. Tinker and H. F.

First, the date. Arnold wrote a draft of the first three stanzas on notes for *Empedocles on Etna*. He had completed the poem, then, in the summer of 1850 (Tinker) or 1851 (Baum). Depending on which summer you settle for, the poem refers to some rendezvous with Marguerite or to Arnold's seaside honeymoon with Frances.

The reference to Sophocles in the second stanza is somewhat vague, but it seems quite clear that for the final image Arnold had in mind the episode in Book VII of Thucydides where, during the ill-fated Sicilian expedition, the Athenian troops became confused during the night battle at Epipolae. The enemy learned their password, and the Athenians went down to disastrous defeat (Tinker).

The poem itself moves from light to darkness, paralleling its thematic movement as a whole from faith to disillusionment (*Case for Poetry*), or from the wholly literal to the wholly metaphorical, from small abstractions to large ones, from past to present (Johnson, 1961). At the same time, the poem builds on a series of dualisms or contrasts. The most ironic of them is the contrast between the tranquil scene and the restless incertitude of the speaker (Kirby), but the most powerful is that between the land and the sea. The sea, in particular, evokes a rich variety of symbolic values: a sense of time and constant change, of vitality—the waters of baptism and birth—also a sense of blankness, formlessness, and mystery (Johnson, 1961). One could think of the land-sea conflict as one between man and nature or present and past (Krieger) or between the dry, critical mind (note the pun) and a natural, spontaneous, self-sufficient existence represented by the sea

---

Lowry, *The Poetry of Matthew Arnold: A Commentary* (London, 1940), pp. 173–178. I do not know of any psychoanalytic explications except that referred to in n. 7.

(Johnson, 1960). One could even think of the sea as a kind of Providence failing to master the Necessity represented by the eternal note of the pebbles (Delasanta). The sea is stable, as faith is; yet it has its ebb and flow and spray, turbid like human misery. Similarly, the land is itself solid and coherent, but its pebbles and shingles are atomistic and agitated (Gwynn), as though the point of misery and conflict were right at the edge or mingling of land and sea (*Case for Poetry*).

The dualism of the poem shows in its structure as well. Each of the four stanzas divides quite markedly into two parts. In stanzas one, three, and four, the first part is hopeful; the second undercuts illusion with reality (Krieger). In every case, illusion is presented in terms of sight, and reality in terms of sound (Delasanta). Thus, the poem moves back and forth from optimistic images of sight to pessimistic images of sound. We can perhaps think of hearing as "the more contiguous sense," the "more subtle sense" (Krieger), but the sounds that dominate the poem are alarms of battle and grating and withdrawing roars (Gwynn).

The poem builds on this manifold dualism, but at the same time it presses steadily forward, with each stanza referring to the one preceding (Krieger). There is a kind of five-part structure as the poem moves from a setting to a dramatic situation to a transitional passage (the second stanza) to an ethical, philosophical comment (the third stanza); finally, that philosophical comment converts to a seemingly unrelated image with a shock of abruptness and strangeness (Montague).

The first stanza gives us a scene so richly laden in values as to make us feel a kind of total satisfaction or utter completeness. Then, at the word "only" the scene lapses into the harsh sound and message of the pebbles (Krieger). Yet even in the first line, the word "to-night" hints at the transitory quality of this fullness and satisfaction (Friedrich), as do in the third and fourth lines the appearance and disappearance of the light from the French coast. The French lights, though, contrast with the stable cliffs of England which "stand,/Glimmering and vast" and so balance the French ebb and flow with permanency. The magnificent "Begin, and cease, and then again begin" also acts out in its rhythm the inexorable quality of the struggle (Krieger). The first stanza closes with the musical words "cadence" and "note," a humanistic overtone which bridges to Sophocles (Gwynn). But the first stanza also ends with the "grating roar," a harsh sound that shatters the calm of the opening and sends the poet more drastically off to the Ægæan (Drew).

The shift from the first stanza to the second represents a shift from the here and now to the everywhere and always (Krieger); the eternal note of sadness and the battle between sea and land merge past and present, we and they. The third stanza returns to the sea as complete and self-sufficient, then breaks at the "but" into a disillusionment expressed as sound (Krieger). The light fades as faith did (Stageberg) and leads us into the last half of the stanza whose falling rhythm and open vowels pour us relentlessly over into the final stanza (Jump).

That last stanza states the theme explicitly for the first time (Kirby), the contrast between seeming perfection and real chaos (Krieger), between the world as an illusion of beauty (Pottle) and the harsh reality of life (Drew). The last three lines give us a startlingly new image (Baum), harsh and surprising (Jump), one wholly metaphorical as against the otherwise wholly realistic setting of the poem (Johnson, 1961). Once we get over the shock of the image, though, we can see that it is not discontinuous, but progresses logically from what has gone before: the "darkling plain" continues the earlier contrast between the land and the sea (Kirby) and extends and enlarges the earlier image of the "naked shingles" (Kirby, Drew). The rhyme-word "light" halfway in the stanza and the subsequent "flight" and "night" take us back to the opening rhymes "to-night" and "light" (Kirby), giving us a sense of closure and completeness. Similarly, the first three stanzas mixed lines of five feet and less and used rhymes in an unpredictable way, though one that gave us a vague sense of recurrence. The last stanza, though, is rigorously rhymed *abba cddcc* with the break at the break in thought; and only the opening and closing lines have irregular lengths—the body of the stanza consists of seven five-foot lines (Krieger). Even so, within this heavy regularity, consonants clash to fill out in sound the sense of the final battle image (Drew).

The poem ends, thus, as it began, in duality. A sense of twoness runs through the various attempts by the explicators to state the idea that informs and pervades the poem: "the poet's melancholy awareness of the terrible incompatibility between illusion and reality" (Delasanta); "the repetitive inclusiveness of the human condition and its purposeless gyrations," "the tragic sense of eternal recurrence" (Krieger); "the sea-rhythm of the world in general and also of the poet's soul which finds itself mysteriously in accord with that cosmic pulse" (Bonnerot).

In general, the poem moves back and forth between here and there, past and present, land and sea, love and battle, but more importantly between sweet sight and disillusioning sound, between appearance and reality. What informs the poem, then, is an attempt to re-create in a personal relationship the sweet sight of stability and permanence which the harsh sound of the actual ebb and flow of reality negates.

Now, with all these explicatory riches, what can psychoanalysis add to a reading of the poem? Like all explications, these treat the poem as an objective fact, which it is—in part. The part we prize, though, is our subjective experience of the poem, the interaction of the poem with what we bring to the poem—our own habits of mind, character, past experience, and present feelings that act with the poem "out there" to make a total experience "in here." Psychoanalysis is that science that tries to speak objectively about subjective states; and, by the same token, the psychoanalytic critic tries to talk objectively about his subjective experience of the poem.

To me, "Dover Beach" is a tremendously peaceful and gently melancholy poem. And that is somewhat surprising, since, after all, it is a poem at least partly about disillusionment, loss of faith, despair—why should such a poem seem peaceful or satisfying? In effect I am asking the same question Aristotle (and indeed, Arnold himself) asked about tragedy: how is it that the most painful experiences can be felt as pleasurable in works of art?[2] A psychoanalyst would answer: "Because art imitates life." That is, we approach life through a series of interacting impulses and defenses, and a work of art offers us a ready-made interaction of impulses and defenses. When we take in Arnold's poem, experience it, we take in the drives the poem expresses. We also take in the poem's way of dealing with those drives, satisfying them and giving pleasure. And, further, the work of art typically transmutes patterns of impulse and defense into moral and intellectual meaning, a wholeness and completeness that our impulses and defenses do not have in everyday life.

Let us, then, talk about "Dover Beach" as a subjective experience. The poem gives me a tremendous feeling of pacification, tranquility, soothing peace.[3] Why? Be-

---

[2] "Though the objects themselves may be painful to see," notes Aristotle, "we delight to view the most realistic representations of them in art. . . . The explanation is to be found in a further fact: to be learning something is the greatest of pleasures not only to the philosopher but also to the rest of mankind, however small their capacity for it: the reason of the delight is that one is at the same time learning—gathering the meaning of things." And Arnold: "In presence of the most tragic circumstances, represented in a work of Art, the feeling of enjoyment, as is well known, may still subsist: the representation of the most utter calamity, of the liveliest anguish is not sufficient to destroy it. . . . What . . . are the situations, from the representation of which, though accurate, no poetical enjoyment can be derived? They are those in which the suffering finds no vent in action; in which a continuous state of mental distress is prolonged, unrelieved by incident, hope, or resistance; in which there is everything to be endured, nothing to be done. In such situations there is inevitably something morbid, in the description of them something monotonous" (Preface to *Poems*, 1853).

Neither Aristotle nor Arnold had a psychology adequate to the problem, but the insights of both are sound, as far as they go. Translated into modern terms, they are saying that painful events can give pleasure in tragedy because the work of art provides defensive ways of escaping the pain and turning it into meaningful pleasure. Aristotle, typically Greek, stresses intellectualization as a defense. Arnold, typically Victorian, stresses action. I, typically twentieth-century, would say you have to analyze the defenses and adaptations of particular tragedies, tragedy by tragedy, before generalizing.

[3] I realize that others find in the poem, not this sense of peace, but an ultimate feeling of failure and despair as, for example, in the explications of Delasanta and Krieger (though Bonnerot finds the pacification). Even so, if I can discover by analyzing my own reaction the drives the poem stirs up in me and the defenses the poem presents for dealing with those drives, then I can understand the different reactions of others for whom those defenses are less congenial or adequate.

cause, I think, the poem offers such a heavy, massive set of defenses. We begin with the exquisite description of the seascape in which everything is vast, tranquil, calm—any disturbance in that calmness, such as the word "to-night" in the first line, the appearance and disappearance of the light from France, is immediately balanced and corrected. Only after this strong reassurance does Arnold give us a stronger disturbance, the eternal note of sadness—and, immediately, he flees in space and time to Sophocles and the Ægæan; he turns the disturbing thought into literature—and far-off, ancient literature at that. And thus defended, he can permit the disturbance to come back again: "we/Find also in the sound a thought,'" but even as he returns to the here and now, he defends again. He turns the feeling of disturbance into an intellectual, symbolic, metaphorical statement, in a line that never fails to jar me by its severely schematic and allegorical quality: "The Sea of Faith." Defended again, he can again return to the disturbing sound, and in the most pathetic lines of the poem he lets it roll off the edge of the earth in long, slow vowels. In the last stanza, he brings in the major defense of the poem, "Ah, love, let us be true/To one another." He offers us as a defense a retreat into a personal relationship of constancy with another person; and so defended, he can give us the final, terrible image of the ignorant armies that clash by night. In short, the poem gives me—and others, too—this tremendous feeling of tranquillity because I am overprotected; because Arnold has offered me strong defenses against the disturbance the poem deals with—even before he reveals the disturbance itself in the final lines.

Further, that disturbance itself is never very clearly presented. It is described obliquely, by negatives. For example, the sea is calm "to-night"—and the "to-night" acts as a qualification: there are other nights when the sea is not calm, but we do not see them. The window in line six comes as something of a surprise—it is as though the poet were reaching back for his companion even as he reaches out to take in the seascape, a special form of the dualism that pervades the poem. But the disturbance is dim and oblique. We do not see the room or the person addressed, only the window facing away from them. The "grating roar" of the pebbles is humanized and softened into music: "cadence" and "note." "The turbid ebb and flow of human misery" seems metaphorized, distanced, more than a little vague. The world, we are told, seems like but is not a land of dreams, but what it is we are not told. We are told that faith is gone; and, while most critics seem to assume Arnold's "Faith" means religious faith, that, it seems to me, is only one of its meanings. The word "Faith" is not explained until the last stanza and is then only explained by what is missing: the ability to clothe the world with joy and love and light, to find in the world certitude, peace, and help for pain. But the poem does not tell us what the world is like without these things, except, metaphorically, in the image of the ignorant armies. In other words, the poem offers us not only massive defenses, but also a specific line of defense: we do not see the disturbance itself; we only see what it is not.

There is a second specific line of defense. The poem sees and hears intensely; it gives us pleasure through what we see and hear, but at the same time the seeing and hearing operate defensively. Often, in life, to see and hear one thing intensely may serve to avoid seeing and hearing something else.[4] In this poem, we look at

[4] Arnold's own psyche is no part of the present paper. It is interesting, though, to note how often the theme of seeing or being seen occurs in Arnold's writings. He praises, for ex-

and listen to the sea, the shingle, to Sophocles—what are we not looking at? What is being hidden from us that we are curious about, that we would like to see? I trust you will not think me irreverent if I remind you that this is a poem at least partly about a pair of lovers together at night. I cannot speak for everyone, but as for myself, I am curious as to what they are up to. The poem, however, tells me very little, for only six of its thirty-seven lines deal directly with the girl; and three of those six are so general they could refer to all mankind.

This is another case in which the poem shows us something indirectly, defensively, by showing us what it is not. The poet treats the particular here-and-now relationship between himself and the girl as the always-and-everywhere con-

ample, one "Who saw life steadily and saw it whole" ("To a Friend"). He spoke through Empedocles of "Gods we cannot see," and in "Self-Deception" of a parental "Power beyond our seeing." As suggested in the text, Arnold often looked intensely at one thing as a way of not seeing something else.

At the same time, though, this kind of intense seeing and hearing can operate defensively in another way. To say I am seeing can be a way of saying I am not being seen, and in Arnold's poetry the motif of not being seen or heard crops out repeatedly. Callicles, for example, must not be seen by Empedocles as the philosopher is about to jump into the burning crater. Neither Sohrab nor Merope recognizes (i.e., sees) his son. One can fairly guess, I think, at the poet's escaping the eyes of his parents, "He, who sees us through and through" ("A Farewell"), or a Mother Nature watching her struggling child ("Morality"). "I praise," he writes, "the life which slips away / Out of the light and mutely" ("Early Death and Fame"), such as the scholar-gypsy or Obermann. Thus, in "Dover Beach," Arnold treats the world, not as seeing himself and his love, but as indifferent, not caring, not offering help for pain: as *"ignorant armies."* One is reminded of the children in "Stanzas from the Grand Chartreuse," "secret from the eyes of all," watching distant soldiers march to war.

dition of all mankind. He defines the girl as a substitute for the world: let us be true to one another for the world proved false. He defines his wished-for relationship with the girl indirectly, obliquely, negatively, by stating what his relationship with the world at large is not.

What, then, is this world which the girl must replace? As the explicators point out, it is a world rather sharply divided into two aspects roughly corresponding to illusion and reality or, in the terms of the poem itself, the sight of a bright, calm seascape representing a world with faith, and the sound of agitated pebbles, one without faith.

The theme of sound reminds us of the importance of the sounds of the poem itself, and particularly the rhyme and rhythm so beautifully worked into the sense at three points: line twelve, "Begin, and cease, and then again begin"; the long withdrawal of the last four lines of stanza three; finally, the clotted consonants that accompany the image of the ignorant armies. It is worth noting that these points where the sound becomes particularly strong are all points of disillusionment in the poem. In general, strong rhyme seems linked in the poem to passages of expectation or trust or acceptance; strong rhythm seems linked to a sense of reality and solidity. Thus, the rhymes are strong in stanza two, the intellectual acceptance of disillusionment, and in stanza four, the emotional acceptance. Rhythm is strong at the opening of the poem with its great feeling of regularity, solidity, thereness.

In the first three stanzas of this poem of division and dualism, rhyme and rhythm tend to be divorced from each other. At points where we are strongly aware of the rhythm, the rhyme tends to disappear from consciousness or even from the poem. Conversely, at points of very regular rhyme, as in stanza two, the rhythm becomes irregular and tends to disintegrate. This sound pattern seems to be a part of the general defensive strategy of the poem—to divide the world and deal with it in parts, to show us things by showing us what they are not. Similarly, Arnold divides each of the lines from two to six halfway—and this, again, is part of the general strategy of division in the poem, but also, as all through the poem, a way of dealing with the world of the poem as he deals with the world described by the poem: dividing it in two to deal with it in parts. Finally, at the close of the poem, not only rhythm, but also rhyme becomes strong; there is a strengthening of defensive form as the poem comes to its moment of greatest stress and distress in content. Rhyme, rhythm, and sense all come together at the close to make us experience in ourselves the poem's final rhymed acceptance of a disturbing reality expressed as rhythmic sound.

Rhythmic sound itself seems to be the disillusioning influence which the poem struggles to accept. Obviously, we need to ask what the emotional significance of that rhythm is. Consider, for a moment, the two senses, sight and hearing. Why do we speak of "feasting" one's eyes or "devouring" with a look? Why do we speak of "the voice" of conscience or of God as "the word"?

"Dover Beach" taps our earliest experience of our two major senses. Sight, the child comes to first. As early as the third month of life, a baby can recognize a human face as such. By the fourth or fifth month, he can distinguish the face of the person who feeds and fondles him from other faces. Sight becomes linked in our minds to being fed, to a nurturing mother. Thus, for example, in "Dover Beach," the strong sight images of the first five lines lead into a demand that a woman come, a taste image ("sweet"),

and even, if we identify kinaesthetically with the poet, an inhaling of that sweet night air. In infancy, sight becomes associated with a taking in, specifically a taking in from a mother in whom we have faith, whom we expect to give us joy, love, light, certitude, peace, help for pain. Our first disillusionment in life comes as that nurturing figure fails to stand calm, full, fair, vast, tranquil, always there, but instead retreats, withdraws, ebbs and flows. And the poem makes us hear this withdrawal.

Our important experience with hearing comes later than seeing. Not until we begin to understand words does hearing begin to convey as much to us as sight does, and it seems to be in the nature of things that a good deal of what the one or two year old child hears is—"Don't." We experience sound as a distancing from a parent, often a corrective, not something we anticipate and expect, but something we must willy-nilly put up with, since we cannot shut our ears as we can our eyes. In "Dover Beach," then, what the poet wishes for from the world, but knows will not come, is the kind of fidelity, "Faith," or gratification a child associates with the sight of his mother, but the sound the poet hears routs his expectations. And the poem, by associating sight with the world as we wish and hope it would be, and sound as a corrector of that wish, finds in us a responsive note, for this has been part of our experience, too.

But what, specifically, does the harsh sound of grating pebbles bring to our minds, particularly as Arnold describes it in the poem? For one thing, as the explicators show, the point of misery and conflict seems to come right at the joining or mingling of land and sea. For another, the disturbance seems to lie in its very periodicity, its rhythm. Where the opening seascape is very solidly there, calm, full, tranquil—"the cliffs of England *stand*" (and the internal rhyme demands heavy stress)—the disturbance is an ebb and flow, a withdrawing, a retreat, a being drawn back and flung up; the waves "Begin, and cease, and then again begin." And slowly, what was simply a harsh, rhythmical sound gains other overtones. The "bright girdle" is withdrawn and we are left with "naked shingles." The world does not "lie before us like a land of dreams." Rather, the "Begin, and cease, and then again begin" has become a naked clash by night. There is a well-nigh universal sexual symbolism in this heard-but-not-seen naked fighting by night. The poem is evoking in me, at least, and perhaps in many readers, primitive feelings about "things that go bump in the night"—disturbing, frightening, but exciting at the same time, like a horror movie. This is one way Arnold's poem turns our experience of disillusionment or despair into a satisfying one, namely, through the covert gratification we get from this final image. A psychoanalyst would recognize a "primal scene fantasy." Arnold is talking about hearing a sexual "clash by night," just as children fantasy sex as fight.[5] At the same time, the image operates defensively as well. This poem tells about a pair of lovers in a sexual situation; as elsewhere in the poem, the image deflects our attention from that sexual situation and sublimates it into a distant, literary, and moral experience, a darkling plain from Thucydides.

The conventional explicators have found some logic underlying that final

startling image: a logical development from brightness to darkness, from the pebble beach to the darkling plain. Ordinary explication, however, offers little basis for the armies, while psychological explication offers considerable. The poem begins with a world which is very solidly there, a world which is seen, a world which is invested with a faith like a child's trust in the sight of his nurturing mother. The poem moves into sound, to the later, harsher sense, and with it to the sounds of withdrawal and retreat. Thus, the sound of the ocean shifts from the rhythm of waves to the more permanent, even geological withdrawal of the "Sea of Faith." The feeling is one of permanent decay, a sense of harsh reality akin to a child's growing knowledge that his mother does not exist for him alone, that she has a life of her own and wishes of her own which cause her to go away from him and come back, to retreat and withdraw. The final image brings in a still stronger feeling of rhythmic withdrawal, a feeling like that of a child's excited but frightened vague awareness of the naked, nighttime rhythmic sound of that other, separate adult life. It does not lie there like a land of dreams—rather, it is violent and brutal; the bright girdle is withdrawn and bodies clash by night. Roughly, we could say that the lovely appearances seen in the poem—the moonlight, the cliffs of England, the stillness—correspond to a faith in a mother. The harsh sounds of withdrawal heard in the poem correspond to the disillusioning knowledge of one's mother's relationship with father, the latter expressed perhaps as Sophocles or Thucydides (Arnold's father did edit Thucydides). In the manner of a dream, the two individuals hidden in the poem, a father and mother, are disguised as two multitudes, two "armies"; and they, usually all-seeing, all-wise, become in the violent moment of passion, "ignorant."

---

[5] In the discussion following the reading of this paper, it was suggested to me that the sexual symbolism is even more exact than stated in the text. The "darkling plain" may suggest to us, unconsciously, the nuptial bed, the "struggle" a man's activity and the "flight" a woman's passivity in the sexual situation.

But we still have not answered the question, How does the poem turn this disturbing awareness of withdrawal into a pleasurable experience? So far, we have talked only about the defenses the poem uses: the flight to Sophocles, symbolic disguise, intellectualization, most important, division, keeping a sharp difference between the seen appearance and the heard reality. But such defenses can only prevent unpleasure—how can the poem give us pleasure and create a rounded experience?

The pleasure lies in that aspect of the poem that the commentators almost without exception ignore (thus proving the strength and success of Arnold's defensive maneuvers). Let me remind you again that this is a poem that talks about a man and a woman in love and alone together. Yet how oddly and how brilliantly the poem handles this problem of stationing its speaker! For the first five lines we have only the vaguest inkling of where he is: looking at a seascape near Dover. Then, in line six, we suddenly learn, first, that he is indoors, second, that there is someone with him, someone whom he wishes to take in what he is taking in. Yet the poem does nothing more with this sudden placing. Instead, the curiosity it arouses, the faint feeling of disturbance, is displaced onto the sound heard in the lines after line six—another way of making us feel the sound as disturbing, and as complicating the scene.

The next two stanzas do little more with the problem of stationing. Stanza two places the speaker in space—by showing us where he is not, the Ægæan; then, it places him by "a distant northern sea." The "we" of line eighteen has all the ambiguities of the editorial we—it could be the poet as a public speaker, the poet and his companion, or the poet and all his contemporaries. Stanza three places the poet in time, again, negatively: not

"once" when the sea of faith was full, but "now"—again, something a bit vague and something we already know. Then, suddenly, line twenty-nine tells us something new again—that he is in love with his companion. Their relationship thus emerges from the rest of the poem like shadowy figures materializing,[6] until, at last, only two lines from the close, the poem firmly stations the poet and his love: "And we are here." Even here, though, there is some blurring, for the "we" could be the editorial we of stanza two as well as the we of you-and-I. And, further, we are no sooner "here" than we are there, metaphorically flown to the darkling plain swept by ignorant armies.

In short, the stationing of the poet and his love involves a good deal of shifting and ambiguity. As always in this poem, the poem is telling us what things are obliquely, by telling us what they are not. The ambiguity about where the poet and his love are suggests that we look to see where they are in another sense—and there, indeed, we can locate them quite precisely: they are right there in lines six, nine, eighteen, twenty-four, twenty-nine,

---

[6] This, too, is a recurring theme in Arnold's writing—a sense of the true state of affairs emerging like a human figure. Thus, the 1853 Preface to *Poems* speaks of a myth in the Greek spectator's mind "traced in its bare outlines . . . as a group of statuary, faintly seen, at the end of a long and dark vista: then came the Poet, embodying outlines. . . . the light deepened upon the group; more and more it revealed itself to the riveted gaze of the spectator: until at last, when the final words were spoken, it stood before him in broad sunlight, a model of immortal beauty." Similarly, at the opening of the 1869 Preface to *Essays in Criticism*, he describes Truth as a "mysterious Goddess" who, even if approached obliquely, can only be seen in outline, while, "He who will do nothing but fight impetuously towards her . . . is inevitably destined to run his head into the folds of the black robe in which she is wrapped." I am reminded of Empedocles' rushing into the crater.

and thirty-five. They occur precisely at the points of division in the poem where it moves from sight to sound, from appearance to reality, or, in stanza two, from a far-off, literary Sophocles to the here and now of "we" by the northern sea. To put it another way, the lovers come between the two kinds of experience the poem creates. This is the importance of the phrase, "And we are here," which makes us feel the closure and completeness of the poem. Read over the last lines with variant phrasings to see the importance of that clause:

... nor peace, nor help for pain;
And the world is, as on a darkling plain
Swept with confused alarms of struggle
    and flight,
Where ignorant armies clash by night.

... nor peace, nor help for pain;
And I am here, as on a darkling plain
Swept with confused alarms of struggle
    and flight,
Where ignorant armies clash by night.

The poem needs the finality both of being *here* and of being *we*, for this is the poem's ultimate defense.

Stanza one opened with sight, taken as reassuring, constant, full, and closed with sound sensed as a kind of corruption penetrating the fair sight. Stanzas two and three fled this conflict both in time and space, and fled it in another way through the poet's universalizing of his feelings, spreading them over all time, all space, all peoples. And yet this defense leaves him disillusioned, and he turns at the opening of stanza four to the girl as a way of dealing with the problem.

He begins by saying, "Ah, love, let us be true/To one another"; and "true" is the key word. He wants to re-create in his relationship with her the lost sense of faith; he wants her to be "true," not to withdraw as the earlier sight had done.

"True" also suggests that the relationship of the two, the poet and his love, will not be like the relationship of the two halves of the world as he sees them. The lovers will not corrupt or contradict one another as the two halves of the world do—rather, they will be "true/To one another."

The last stanza then moves into a series of lists that act out the poet's feeling toward the world that has failed him, that though it seems

So various, so beautiful, so new,
Hath really neither joy, nor love, nor light,
Nor certitude, nor peace, nor help for
    pain.

The lists give us a feeling of inclusiveness, of taking it all in, but the lists are negative, "neither," "nor," "nor"—so that it is precisely the inclusiveness that is rejected; precisely the fact that the world negates all the things the poet wants to take in that leads to the rejection of the world. Here is the first half of the poem's strategy: to try to take in joy, love, light, certitude, peace, help for pain; but, upon finding some one part of the world that negates these things, to reject all the world. A psychoanalyst would speak here of denial: the poet must deny whatever conflicts with his wish to be given joy, love, light, and the rest. In the key line, "And we are here," the poet turns back to the girl. "We are here," solidly, constantly, as the seascape was in stanza one; and we are quite distinctly separate from what conflicts with that solid, constant trust—the ignorant armies. They are quite distinctly not "we"; and they are distanced from "we" by "as," that is, by metaphor and literary reference. The fact that "we are here" stands between the first half of the stanza and the second, preventing the second half from penetrating the first. Paradoxically, as Theodore Morrison pointed out many years ago, the poem uses love precisely to prevent the disillusionment involved in a knowledge of sexuality.[7]

The strategy of the poem thus consists of four stages. First, the poet gives us a world felt as constant, nurturing, evoking faith. Second, he discovers a disillusioning sound. Third, he rejects the whole thing to get rid of that disillusioning sound. Fourth, he retreats from his global wishes and tries to re-create the earlier idyllic state in miniature, in a personal relationship. The poem defends by denial; it gets rid of the disillusioning sound by putting it metaphorically away from the poet. Then the poem gives pleasure by re-creating an adult world in terms of a child's wishes for constancy, trust, and faith in his parents.[8]

Notice, too, how the poet makes us

experience for ourselves the experience the poem describes. He gives us, first, the somewhat vague seascape, evoking in us both a wish to take in more, and a feeling of trust and security. Then he surprises us with the presence of another. We feel a disturbing influence, which the poem tells us is a sound. So it is—the sudden speaking voice of "Come to the window," and we want to know more, to take in more. Instead, the second and third stanzas try to intellectualize and distance the disturbing influence but fail and come back to it, thus building up tension in us. The fourth stanza abandons these earlier attempts to deal with the problem. First, it suddenly retreats from the external world to the smaller world of the lovers; second, it shifts in metaphor from the Dover seascape to the ignorant armies. The fourth stanza gives us the vague hope, "Let us be true"; and, as at the beginning of the poem, we feel trust, security, but also a desire to take in more. But now we learn that the danger, the moving back and forth, is elsewhere; we take a metaphorical flight in time and space to the plain of Epipolae. The efforts at flight that failed in stanzas two and three succeed in stanza four because "we are here." The phrase is almost parental; and thus, by the very acceptance of disillusionment, the poem gratifies us, because it does, ultimately, let us take in what we wished to take in: it lets us see two "true" lovers together with a glimpse of a "clash by night" elsewhere.

The poem makes us experience the experience described by the poem, and we can see it does in the various explications. We have spoken of the poem as a re-creating of the child's trust that he will be nurtured, that he will be able to take in and be taken into some comforting environment. Krieger speaks of the poem as "the repetitive *inclusiveness* of the human situation." We have spoken of the

<hr />

[7] "Dover Beach Revisited: A New Fable for Critics," *Harper's Magazine*, CLXXX (1940). "The ordinary degree of aggressiveness, the normal joy of conquest and possession, seemed to be wholly absent from him. The love he asked for was essentially a protective love, sisterly or motherly; in its unavoidable ingredient of passion he felt a constant danger, which repelled and unsettled him" (see pp. 240–241). Professor Morrison offers his insight in the whimsical spirit of a *Pooh Perplex*, but it seems to me sound nevertheless. This essay, by the way, contains the only other psychoanalytic explication of the poem I know.

[8] Like the theme of sight, the form of rejecting or giving up one thing so as to gain another (often a mollified version of the first) occurs over and over again in Arnold's writings. Among the poems that take this form are: "To a Republican Friend, 1848" (both poems), "Religious Isolation," "In Utrumque Paratus," "Absence," "Self-Dependence," "A Summer Night," "The Buried Life," "The Scholar-Gipsy," "Thyrsis," "Rugby Chapel"; and among the prose, "On Translating Homer," "The Function of Criticism at the Present Time," the rejection of Philistinism, anarchy, Hebraism, and so on. "I am fragments," Arnold wrote to "K," and the trope seems to represent a basic defense for him. "Dover Beach" is quintessential Arnold as well as quintessential Victorian.

poem as an attempt to re-create the world as it once was, in childhood. Krieger speaks of repetitiveness and "the tragic sense of *eternal recurrence*." We have spoken of the disturbing note in the poem as the sense of ebb and flow that cuts down a child's faith that the nurturing world will always be there. Bonnerot speaks of "the sea-rhythm of the world in general and also of the poet's soul which finds itself mysteriously in accord with that cosmic pulse,"[9] while Delasanta speaks of "terrible incompatibility"—the two sides of a child's trust.

In short, a psychological understanding of the poem as an interaction of impulses and defenses complements conventional explication because it reveals the emotional underpinnings to our objective understanding of the poem. It enables us to speak objectively about our subjective experience of the poem, even when those subjective experiences vary sharply. But what can this kind of awareness of the poem as impulse and defense contribute to literary history?

---

[9] Bonnerot offers a curious confirmation of the reading here suggested, that the sea in "Dover Beach" evokes feelings like those toward a nurturing mother. Immediately after the statement cited, he quotes (free associates to?) the following from *God and the Bible*: "Only when one is young and headstrong can one thus prefer bravado to experience, can one stand by the Sea of Time, and instead of listening to the solemn and rhythmical beat of its waves, choose to fill the air with one's own whoopings to start the echo." It is not too difficult to hear under Arnold's "whoopings" something like a child's anguished howls to prevent his mother's withdrawal or bring her back ("start the echo") or replace the void she leaves ("fill the air"). There is further confirmation in Arnold's letter to Clough of 29 Sept. 1848, where he describes himself as "one who looks upon water as the Mediator between the inanimate and man." See H. F. Lowry, ed., *The Letters of Matthew Arnold to Arthur Hugh Clough* (London, 1932), p. 92.

A preliminary question, though, must be: What do we mean by literary history? Once literary history moves beyond the mere chronicling of names and dates, as in a reference book, we ask, I think, that it be an attempt to understand literary events historically, that is, as having causes or meaningful relations to other events in time. Typically, though, when literary history moves from chronicle to history, it shades off into the history of ideas. Literary history, as such, ceases to be a separate discipline. The reason this happens, I think, is that we are accustomed to look at the content of literature when we are looking at literature historically. But content is not what is literary in literature—form is; the kind and quality of expression is. In psychoanalytic terms, form and mode of expression are defenses; and, therefore, to write literary history which is not merely a branch of the history of ideas, literary history which deals with what is literary in literature, we shall have to write about the defenses a particular culture uses. We shall have to think more like a cultural anthropologist than an intellectual historian.

Many critics have said "Dover Beach" is the representative, the quintessential Victorian poem, or, in Krieger's gentle pun, a "highly Victorian" poem. Mostly, however, the critics have said this because they see the poem as primarily about doubt and loss of faith—major themes in Victorian ideas. But "Dover Beach" is an emotional experience, not just an intellectual one. Further, to see the poem as only about doubt is not to see the form of the poem, for Arnold sets his doubt and despair against a sexual situation: this is a poem that tells about two lovers alone at night.[10]

---

[10] Thus, I think, Walter Houghton comes closer to the theme of doubt when he reminds us: "For the Victorians, the disagreeable facts

We have seen that "Dover Beach" defends against that situation and adapts it to moral and intellectual pleasure by employing three strategies. First, it avoids looking directly at the lovers by intensely looking at and listening to something else, the sea, the shingle, Sophocles, and so on. Second, the poem places its "you" and "I" between illusion and reality so as to keep up a division or dualism, to prevent certain things from mingling or penetrating. The feeling is that if the negative sound touches the positive sight, one must reject them both. One must either accept the world wholly or reject it wholly. Both these defenses the psychoanalyst would call forms of denial: denying the existence of forbidden things by seeing only what they are not; denying compromise or imperfection. Then, third, the poem tries to re-create in the relationship with the lover a simplified, more childish, but more satisfying version of an adult love for another person or the world as a whole.

In short, the psychoanalytic study of this quintessentially Victorian poem cues us to a particular hypothesis as to what makes it so "Victorian": a certain pattern of defenses, namely, the use of denial to re-create an adult world to meet a child's demand for perfection. Now, we need to ask, To what extent is this pattern characteristically Victorian? If it is characteristic, where did it come from? How did it sustain itself? And how is it expressed in literary forms?

Obviously, we cannot answer all these questions in a mere essay, but we can begin. We can begin with the way the

Victorian style itself began—with the rejection of the Regency and all the four Georges, the rejection of eighteenth-century club-life and other levities, the rejection of the aristocracy, and the rejection of Byronism and the excesses of Romanticism.[11] Psychologically, such a massive rejection of the past is, at some level of a man's being, a rejection of his parents, his forebears in a physical as well as an intellectual or historical sense. It is no accident, I think, that this age that so rejected immediate parenthood should also have been so preoccupied with the problem of evolution, parenthood distanced to a prehistoric past. Kenneth Burke suggests the characteristic mental habit of the nineteenth century was translating "essence" into "origin" so that the statement, "This is the essence of the situation," becomes "This is how it began."[12] And this strategy, too, I take it, is a way of looking for lost origins—parenthood—in areas safely distanced from real origins.

When the Victorians rejected their immediate past, what did they replace it with? Just as they stuffed and over-stuffed their rooms with furniture, they felt they were creating a new world themselves—and not without reason. "Your railroad," Thackeray could write, "starts the new era." "We are of the age of steam." "It

were primarily those of sex, and the terrifying truth the state of religion" (*The Victorian Frame of Mind, 1830–1870* [New Haven, 1957], pp. 413–414). In this section of my paper, I am relying very heavily on Professor Houghton's book. My feeling goes beyond mere indebtedness to sheer gratitude that such an encyclopedic and perceptive book exists.

[11] Houghton, pp. 45–53, 109, 300, and 342. Lionel Trilling, "The Fate of Pleasure: Wordsworth to Dostoevsky," in Northrop Frye, ed., *Romanticism Reconsidered: Selected Papers from the English Institute* (New York, 1963), pp. 73–106, particularly pp. 73–90 and 97–101. Professor Trilling's paper develops brilliantly the idea that Victorian moral and spiritual energy should be regarded as an effort to mask over—indeed, attack—pleasure erotic and gentlemanly. My own essay might well be regarded as the attempt to extend Professor Trilling's hypothesis to a particular poem and to literary forms.
[12] Cited by Stanley Edgar Hyman, *The Tangled Bank* (New York, 1962), p. 366.

was only yesterday, but what a gulf between now and then!" In a very real sense, the newly powerful middle class could claim to have created itself, psychologically, to have been its own parents or, in Clough's phrase, by its very success to have achieved "This keen supplanting of nearest kin."

But when we look to see how the Victorians thought of parents, we find that, if the Victorians were their own parents, they were a rather special kind of parent. Mother becomes Patmore's *Angel in the House*, or, as Tennyson's Prince describes her,

No angel, but a dearer being, all dipt
In angel instincts, breathing Paradise,
Interpreter between the gods and men . . .

As for the gods, we recognize the Victorian father: a man thought of primarily in terms of force and power and authority, a king or hero on Carlyle's model, a captain of industry, almost an Old Testament God. What such parents lack, of course, is adult sexuality, which is replaced by a kind of industrial force or household contentment.

We see the same denial in Victorian hero-worship, particularly of heroes who combined features of a father and a son: wild, primitive figures, but of impeccable moral stature. The favorite was the Galahad story, and it tells us the Victorian secret: the denial of sexuality leads to physical strength or, to put it another way, the Victorians looked at a man's strength as a way of not seeing a man's sexuality. Symbols for the denial are the baptismal images that recur in Victorian writing, of water or cleansing of the soiled self, as in *The Water Babies* or Kingsley's whole advice for life—"hard work and cold water."[13]

_____
[13] Jerome Buckley, *The Victorian Temper* (Cambridge, 1951), pp. 98–105.

What I am suggesting is that the Victorians in general, like Arnold in "Rugby Chapel," sought parents such as a child would wish, parents devoid of sexuality. What the Victorians rejected in their social parents, the eighteenth century, the Regency, they rejected in their actual parents: levity, libertinism, gentlemanly pleasures, sexuality. As Thackeray complained in the preface to *Pendennis,* his readers would not accept a virile man or a realistic woman. When the Victorians created their own new world, became parents themselves, they became parents on this infantile model. Thus, we find Beatrice Webb's father, though he was a railway tycoon, kneeling down morning and night to repeat the prayer he learned at his mother's lap—"Gentle Jesus, meek and mild, look upon a little child." Perhaps it is true of any age baffled by the complexities of rapid change that it regresses, tries to come to grips with its world in more primitive, childish terms; but the Victorians do seem to have done so more than most.

In this wish to re-create one's parents on the model of a child's wishes, we find an answer to what is to me the most puzzling problem of Victorian life: Why was it a stable society? After all, the Victorians tried to put down wit, levity, leisure, acceptance, and passivity, along with sex. It was a stately, solemn, perhaps dreary kind of culture. And yet it lasted fifty or so years. People must have found some sort of compensating pleasure in it. They found, I think, the granting of one of the strongest and deepest wishes of childhood, a wish that persists with great strength into adult life, namely, the desire to maintain the fantasy that one's parents be sexually pure.

Thus, obliquely, "Dover Beach" has led us to at least a hypothesis about the major Victorian modes of defense. In the terms of intellectual history, Walter Houghton describes them as "a process of deliberately ignoring whatever was unpleasant and pretending it did not exist." In psychoanalytic terms, these defenses are avoidance, denial, suppression, repression —all those defensive strategies summed up in Mr. Podsnap's formulaic, "I don't want to know about it; I don't choose to discuss it; I don't admit it!"

But these defenses have a positive side as well as the merely negative one. They lead to the Victorian effort to remodel the world, to earnestness, enthusiasm, the belief in the basic goodness of human nature, dogmatism, rigidity, an emphasis on doing (Arnold's "Hebraism"), the gospel of intellectual, moral, and social work, the drive and duty to succeed. All are ways of emulating a father conceived of as non-sexual industrial or moral drive; or of gratifying a mother conceived in terms of Ruskin's "Goddess of Getting-on," or what Arnold called "Mrs. Gooch's Golden Rule," her counsel to her son: "My dear Dan . . . you should look forward to being some day manager of that concern!" As for intellectual life, we find generally what Mill described as a "rather more demonstrative attitude of belief" than people thought necessary "when their personal conviction was more complete." We see the Victorian never-ending quest for truth, as though one were constantly trying to find some truth other than the one you have denied and left behind you. At the same time, we find an unwillingness to draw ultimate conclusions, to come to a stopping place lest the intellectual quest end. Thus, too, we find poems like "The Scholar-Gipsy" or Tennyson's "Ulysses" praising aspiration, movement, energy, force without aim or end, for if one came to an end, one might have to sit down and think about what

was left behind[14]—"The Buried Life," Arnold called it;

> our own only true, deep-buried selves,
> Being one with which we are one with the
> whole world.

For those with eyes less open than Arnold's, the buried life became the dark underside of Victorian optimism: the fear that what was denied might return, and the optimism founded on denial be upset. There might be a revolution from below, from the masses. There might come corruption from abroad, the pernicious writings of, say, Balzac or Flaubert, or even the local product, the "fleshly school of poetry." Abstract thought and contemplation are dangerous. Knowledge and love are antithetical, as in Browning's *Paracelsus*. Levity becomes the light treatment of evil. Leisure is thought of as the occasion of all evil. The devil finds work for idle hands—and we can guess at the fear of what idle hands might be doing. These are the anxieties, doubts, and pessimisms that gnaw underneath the superstructure of Victorian optimism, things that a Carlyle or even an Arnold would try to put down by force, George Eliot by a cult of obedience, or Macaulay by a trust in progress.

Doubt and despair followed by a commitment to work backed up by religious or philosophic principle—this is, of course, what Jerome Buckley (ch. v) has called "the pattern of Victorian conversion," and it is well known. What I am suggesting is a psychological paradigm

---

[14] "For the Victorians, intense activity was both a rational method of attacking the anxieties of the time, and an irrational method of escaping them" (Houghton, p. 262). See also Kristian Smidt, "The Intellectual Quest of the Victorian Poets," *English Studies*, XL (1959), 90–102.

for this Victorian life-style. We could put it this way: I reject my actual forebears (the eighteenth century and its attitudes). I create the world anew. I thus become my own parent, but—and this is the important point—I become a parent such as a child would wish. I deny the adult emotions, sexuality, but also easiness, indifference, the enjoyment of leisure, the tolerance of uncertainty. Instead, I work, I am enthusiastic, I am earnest. And the last steps carry out the first two. I deny the adult emotions and so continue the rejection of what went before. I busy myself and so I create the world anew. The system closes upon itself and becomes the stable, though uneasy, style of the long Victorian calm. It is uneasy because the whole circle rests on a denial that leaves a weak point at which Swinburne and Pater and Meredith and Hardy and Wilde will penetrate the system and break it down.

But what does this say about literary history? Obviously, much of the content of Victorian poetry expresses either the frantic affirmations or the covert doubts of Victorian culture. This is the content, however. What about defenses understood as giving rise to forms and modes of expression? "Dover Beach" cues us to look for three defenses. First, concentrating on one thing as a way of not seeing something else. Second, a tendency to try to keep things from mingling, to divide experience into total acceptance or total rejection, to avoid compromise or the acceptance of imperfection. Third, the re-creation of an adult world according to a child's wish for perfection, specifically, that his parents be sexually pure. If our hypothesis is correct, these defenses must give rise to at least some of the forms and styles of Victorian literature. And so, it seems to me, they do. Many critics have pointed to a kind of divided

allegiance in Victorian poetry: the poet as a public, social spokesman, but with a buried self; a pervasive dichotomy between social and moral subjects and personal ones. In psychoanalytic terms, we recognize one of the "Dover Beach" defenses, concentrating on one thing so as not to see another, or, as E. D. H. Johnson puts it, "The expressed content has a dark companion."[15] The same defense shows in the way the Victorian poet relies on a natural scene. "Arnold," notes Truss, "typically grafted an idea to a landscape, and he tried to make the landscape do his talking for him." Trilling's phrasing is kinder when he speaks of "Arnold's bold dramatic way of using great objects, often great geographical or topographical objects, in relation to which the subjective states of the poem organize themselves and seem themselves to acquire an objective actuality."[16] The massive landscape takes our attention away from the poet.

Another popular form of the period distances the same way: the dramatic monologue affirms an external reality at the expense of the poet's subjective state (though as Kristian Smidt has shown, the distancing often collapses into an "oblique" or "diagonal" point of view in which the poet blurs into his spokesman —the denial breaks down).[17] Along with the dramatic monologue, we find in criticism a tendency to look at the events described by a work of art rather than at

---

[15] E. D. H. Johnson, *The Alien Vision of Victorian Poetry* (Princeton, 1952), p. 217.

[16] Tom J. Truss, "Arnold's 'Shakespeare,' " *Explicator*, XIX (1961), 56. Lionel Trilling, ed., *The Portable Matthew Arnold* (New York, 1949), p. 39. See also Marshall McLuhan, "The Aesthetic Moment in Landscape Poetry," in Alan S. Downer, ed., *English Institute Essays 1951* (New York, 1952), pp. 168–181.

[17] Kristian Smidt, "Point of View in Victorian Poetry," *English Studies*, XXXVIII (1957), 1–12.

the work of art itself, to treat Shakespearean characters as real people, for example. This, too, enables the Victorian to concentrate on one thing as a way of not seeing something else—his own emotional reaction.

If "Dover Beach" is quintessentially Victorian, we should be able to find in Victorian forms generally the second of its defenses, namely, dividing the world into black and white, yea and nay. Thus, when the Victorian style began, poetic imagery shifted away from the growth and profusion of the Romantics, uniting with the world, to images of polarity and tension, dividing oneself from the world or dividing the world itself, as Arnold does in "Dover Beach" (Johnson, 1961, p. 2). In this sense, the pervasive dichotomy in Victorian poetry between social and moral subjects and personal ones becomes another way of polarizing the external world created from child-like optimism and the darker, more adult emotions within. Arnold, in particular, came increasingly to feel that a natural or general law proscribed the expression of his own deep feelings[18]—for "general law" we can read the pervasive defense of the man and his culture. Again, we find Victorian poetry heavily committed to poetic diction, a kind of fulfillment of Bentham's view of the arts. Poetic diction serves as a way of distinguishing poetry from normal adult speech, an optimizing of ordinary language, reconstructing it in terms of a wish for perfection—a kind of extremely adult baby-talk.

We can see both these "Dover Beach" defenses, for example, in the pre-Raphaelite style. Both the concentration on visual detail and the heavy use of emblem and allegory serve the Victorian denial much as Arnold's viewing of the seascape does. We look intensely at one thing, at one meaning or sight, and so we avoid seeing something else. Heavy symbolism and allegory; a retreat to Greek, Biblical, medieval, or exotic legend; the ample rendering of visual details—these are present to some extent in all Victorian poetry, but these various overstatements in the service of denial fuse in the pre-Raphaelite style to make it, too, quintessentially Victorian.

But poetry, of course, was not the greatest form in the period. The output may have been vast, but the quality was sharply limited, perhaps because poetry as the expression of personal feelings did not suit an age dedicated to the denial of certain key feelings. The "Spasmodic school" suggests the trouble poets got into when they tried to express feelings directly, unshielded by dramatic monologue or landscape. The novel expressed Victorian needs better, notably, the wish to concentrate on one thing as a way of not seeing another. Just as, on the stage, theatrical spectacle and declamatory acting shifted attention away from the lack of realistic emotion in the characters, so the great shift of the English novel from the eighteenth century to the nineteenth is a growing attention to the larger social environment surrounding the central characters. At the same time, the usual Victorian novel offered its readers adult emotions over-simplified and desexualized. The Victorian novel, like Victorian commerce, sought to order the complex adult world by the wishes of a child. As Joseph Schumpeter has shown, in Victorian commerce, the industrialist became paternalistic, a father; the colonial took on the burdens of his "little brown brother."[19] The larger political and eco-

---

[18] John M. Wallace, "Landscape and 'The General Law': The Poetry of Matthew Arnold," *Boston University Studies in English,* V (1961), 91–106.

[19] *Imperialism and Social Classes,* trans. Heinz Norden, ed. Paul M. Sweezy (New York, 1951), pp. 153–159, 169–170, 190–

nomic world was to be organized in terms of family responsibility. And so the novelist by the form of his novel often suggested—*Bleak House* is the obvious and best example—that the cure for the ills of the adult environment was simply to re-create the family world of a child in the world at large.

The Victorian novel polarized the world into a large environment and a family of central characters, just as Victorian drama polarized its world into elaborate visual spectacle and a star or two. Yet the novel thrived while the drama declined. I think we can understand the decline of the drama as a case in which a genre found itself caught between two Victorian modes of defense. On the one hand, there is avoidance of one thing by looking at another, giving rise to the interest in visual spectacle and declamatory acting as ways not to see the central characters too realistically. On the other hand, there was the wish to see adult emotions through a child's eyes. Thus, Hazlitt could say of Joanna Baillie, "She treats her grown men as little girls treat their dolls." We can accept what E. M. Forster calls "flat" characters in fiction; we can accept sentimentality, for the novelist can adjust the whole world of the novel to fit his myth, in this case, the re-creation through denial of a world to fit a child's wishes. But sentimentalism is harder to accept when physically set before us on a stage that so insists on physical realities and visual exactness as the Victorian theatre did, indeed as that whole age that invented photography did.

I have not yet mentioned the greatest

of all genres in the Victorian period: nonsense, which was the most admirably suited to the Victorian defensive strategy. Lear and Carroll offered a reassuring form of humor, one that did not "treat evil lightly," one that was not "levity, insincerity, and idle babble and play-acting" (to give Carlyle's list of sins). Rather, Lear and Carroll did the truly Victorian thing directly: they explicitly re-created the world of an adult through the eyes of a child.

So far, our hypothesis holds. "Dover Beach" cued us to look in Victorian culture and Victorian literary modes for a pattern of defense: the use of denial to re-create an adult world according to what a child wishes adults would be.[20] Allegory, poetic diction, dramatic monologue, landscape poetry, sentimentality in fiction and spectacle in drama, nonsense—all these forms and styles of Victorian literature we have looked at so far tend to confirm our hypothesis. Whether the hypothesis will stand further testing, time will tell. Obviously, one would have to have many, many more analyses of literary works to prove or disprove it finally. The more general point, though, the methodological one, stands. Psychoanalysis can offer the literary historian a hypothesis, at least,

---

205, and 220–221. Schumpeter's neo-Marxist analysis of the necessity for a family to do something de novo to break the class barrier and his concept of "patrimonialization" strikingly confirm, from the quite alien point of view of economics, the psychoanalytic hypothesis I am advancing about Victorian England.

[20] Obviously, throughout this essay, I have been using the term "Victorian" in a broad, attributive way, as if I were to look at a house or an attitude or a poem and say, "That's quite Victorian." The defensive pattern, then, explicates the word. Equally obviously, though, there are many particular Victorianisms: high and low, early, middle, and late, and so on. One could refine the technique developed in this essay by sketching out the kind of thing denoted by the more specific term "high Victorian" and then trying to analyze the kind of thing as analogous to psychological defenses. If this essay is correct, each specific Victorianism should turn out to be a narrower form of the general pattern of impulse and defense here suggested.

and perhaps even a full understanding of the way literary forms act analogously to defenses to meet the psychological needs of a culture.

I think psychoanalysis can add something else: sympathy. For example, in "Dover Beach" Arnold writes as though he actually expected the world to supply joy, love, light, certitude, peace, help for pain, and I—a creature of the twentieth century—am puzzled. My world has been the depression, World War II, Auschwitz, the cold war—frankly, I expect nothing from my world but trouble. In another sense, though, I can think back, experience back, to a time when my world was smaller and consisted of a mother and a father in a small apartment in New York. Then was a time when I, like Arnold, could expect—and get—joy, love, light, help for pain. And, therefore, despite what batterings that sense of basic trust may have taken, I can enter and experience Arnold's quite alien kind of world. I can love Arnold's poem.

In short, what psychoanalysis can bring to literary history is not only hypotheses about the uses of literary forms. It can also bring sympathy, an ability to call back to life in ourselves the feelings of writers and ages long gone. The message psychoanalysis sends the literary historian comes down simply to this: if you wish to write the literary history of Victorian England, do not simply seek the Victorian (like Carroll's snark) with forks and hope or names and dates back there. Look for the Victorian in yourself.

Kenneth Burke

CATHARSIS: SECOND VIEW

Kenneth Burke has been variously identified as a sociocultural, psychological, formalistic, and mythopoeic critic when, in fact, his work resists classification. It is his own unique synthesis. However, no perspective is more typical of Burke's criticism than that we might loosely term *psychological*. Burke's career as a man of letters spans forty years. He began as a poet, served as a music critic on the *Dial* and the *Nation*, then turned increasingly to criticism. A few of his important books are: *Permanence and Change* (1935), *The Philosophy of Literary Form* (1941), and *A Grammar of Motives* (1945). He also taught at Bennington College from 1943 to 1962. "Catharsis: Second View" was originally published in the *Centennial Review* in 1961.

In our first view of Catharsis,[1] because we were working primarily with Greek models we stressed the *civic* nature of the "pollution" for which tragedy concocts a remedy. But there is a sense in which even elations or sorrows shared by us as members of a collectivity are experienced by us as *individuals*, quite as each person at a public banquet derives a particular gratification from the particular food that is eaten by him in particular. The centrality of the nervous system is a *principium individuationis* whereby, no matter how collective the nature of our symbol-systems and of the socio-political structures that go with them, our pleasures and pains are our own naturally inalienable private property. And though

[1] [Mr. Burke's first essay on this topic, "On Catharsis, or Resolution," appeared in *Kenyon Review*, XXI (1959), 337–75.—Ed.]

all human animals go through the same general set of physiological and psychological processes, *universality* of that sort by no means removes the *individuality* intrinsic to the *centrality* of the nervous system. So our second view of Catharsis will shift the emphasis, though many of the observations in this second view might as well have been considered in the first. Also, the individuating nature of the nervous system will require us once more to consider the matter of "body-thinking," though this time from quite a different point of view.

So far as the body participates directly in the producing of catharsis by the organizing of symbol-systems, its two typical expressions are laughter and tears. The striking thing about both these modes of release is their nature as *completions, fulfillments*. Weeping or laughing are *end-products*. They have the finality of a ship coming into port. Also, although as responses to works of art they arise out of purely *symbolic* processes, at the same time they are both intensely *physical*. Thus, there is a sense in which they perfectly bridge the gap between man's nature as sheer animal and his nature as sheerly "rational" or "spiritual" (as symbol-user).

They differ in one notable respect: tears are a secretion, but laughter is not. To be perfectly symmetrical, we should match "laughter" not with "tears," but with "weeping." This alignment reminds us that *both* laughter and weeping can terminate in tears—but whereas mild weeping can cause tears, the same effect is produced only by intense, hysterical laughter, a distinction that must have a great deal to do with the relation between tragic catharsis and comic catharsis, though we're not quite sure what it might be. Nor are we quite sure just how the difference between tragedy and comedy is aligned with the difference between tears of sorrow and tears of joy.

But one thing is certain: though both pitiful weeping and mirthful laughter may be akin to love, they are not identical with it. And love has its own kind of bodily release (completion, fulfillment) different from the kinds of release natural to tragedy and comedy.

Surely the most "cathartic" experience possible would be the ability to love everything, without reservation, in such bodily spontaneity as attains its purely *verbal* counterpart in ejaculations of thanksgiving or praise. But besides the many situations which do not arouse in us the expansiveness of love, there are many others in which, even if we do feel so inclined, the social proprieties have inhibited the expressions natural to such an attitude.

Thus, whereas ideas of mirth readily attain natural bodily fulfillment in laughter, and ideas of pity lead similarly to tears, the codes of propriety that take shape in accordance with particular systems of property greatly restrict a corresponding naturalness of expression as regards the most cathartic emotion of all, the emotion of love.

We take it, then, that tragic catharsis through fear and pity operates as a *substitute* for catharsis through love. One's state of identification or communion with the object of one's pity is nearly like the kind of identification or communion one feels for a loved object—yet this slight deflection is enough to permit a natural bodily outlet which, under many conditions, is deemed permissible, whereas a corresponding expression of love in its direct form would not be. (Secondarily, of course, the restrictions on the expression of love may extend by contagion until they also greatly restrict the expression of *any* emotion. But in general there do remain available the subterfuges of imaginary pity.)

The total situation, then, would be as follows: perfect catharsis would arise from a sense of universal love. Insofar as such a condition is not attained, the next best thing is a sense of radical pity that lies on the slope of tearful release. Fear is not directly cathartic; but it is cathartic indirectly, insofar as it sets up the conditions for the feeling of pity. Wonder is cathartic in that, whereas it is in the same spectrum with fear, it is on the other edge of the spectrum, being itself a kind of "cleansed fear," like reverence. It in turn is aided by various devices such as heroic diction, that give magnitude to the action. Insofar as pity is employed to arouse our moral indignation, it is not wholly cathartic; but it may be employed secondarily to this end if the non-vindictive use of pity is primary. (Similarly, "derisive" laughter lacks the wholly cathartic function of "sympathetic" laughter, which comes close to pity. In *Don Quixote* the derisive becomes transformed into the sympathetic as the story proceeds.)

First, then, there is the fact that the expression of love, being greatly restricted by custom, attains as surrogate the expression of pity. Next, there is the fact that, even if the expression of love were not greatly restricted, we should ordinarily have great difficulty in loving our enemies. Pity solves this problem, too. For Aristotle observes that we pity undeserved suffering. And thus we could in imagination pity even our worst enemy, if we imagined him as undergoing heavier punishment than even we would wish on him. Finally, tragic catharsis by pity may provide a solution for a kind of universal or categorical love, "embracing all mankind," communing sympathetically with "everything," in an idealistic, depersonalized way that lacks body. Such "dialectical" kind of love, "loving in principle," puts a great strain on the imagination, if one would prevent the attitude from losing immediacy and becoming a mere edified "statement of policy" on mankind. For love is fullest only when immediately personal, whereas such a generalized attitude makes far too great diluting or abstracting of the emotion. And tragic pity, with its resources of *enargeia*, for bringing the person in his pitiableness before our very eyes, helps to correct even such caricatures of "positive thinking" as mark this kind of humanitarianism, or vague benevolence (which is, ironically, the counterpart of equally remote preparations for professional slaughter on the grand scale, when, as, and if the order is given).

II

Insofar as symbol-systems involve relationships and developments intrinsic to themselves and thus not strictly translatable into any kinds of bodily or social behavior, such purely symbolic sequences may possess modes of gratification or release not explainable by reference to physical hypotheses at all (except in the sense that the failure to solve a problem in physics or mathematics might impair a person's health, whereas success at finding a solution could have a good effect upon his attitude towards people and things in general).

When, in Poetics, we analyze the workings of a symbol-system, we require no reference to possible ways in which people might, by the complications of a plot, become in some sense physically charged and thus made ready to enjoy a corresponding physical state of discharge. Yet when asking about the possible relation between the symbol-using animal and his symbols, we do have to consider such "hypotheses," since the non-symbolic body is a necessary hypothesis of all symbol-systems.

So we must keep two different considerations in mind here. We must be on the look-out for possibilities of symbolic development that quite "transcend" the body (except insofar as physiological motions are a necessary ground of all empirical symbolic action). And we must be on the look-out for respects in which the body does figure, when we go from questions about comedy and tragedy as cathartic instruments to questions about laughter and tears as cathartic instruments. And as we should guard against seeking for too close a correlation between the body and its symbol-systems, so we should guard against a tendency to ignore the points at which the two realms do significantly correlate.

There is a relevant passage in the *Divine Comedy*, where Dante seems to indicate that, at least under certain conditions, tearfulness is analogous to going off half-cocked. The passage is in the *Purgatorio*, which should be watched with special care where questions of catharsis are concerned, particularly since Dante is exceptionally sensitive to analogies between ideas and their corresponding body-images.

In Canto XXX, Dante sees Beatrice for the first time, though her spirit has brooded over his entire climb, through Hell and up the Mount to Paradise—and in a sense every reference to blessings (as with the succession of Beatitudes, a different one of which is sung in each circle of Purgatory) indirectly bears upon her, the Woman Who Blesses. He says that she seems to him as *superba* as a mother seems to her child (*così la madre al figlio*). But in the next canto, a remark by Beatrice herself will remind us that this "child," with his head hanging bashfully, wears a *beard*. Lines 16–21 of this next canto describe how he bursts into a torrent of tears and sighs (*lagrime e sospiri*) that cause the voice of this bearded "child" to die away as he addresses his motherlike beloved.

Dante here employs the figure of a cross-bow that breaks from too great tension ("under this heavy charge"), whereat the bolt hits the mark "with lessened force." Later, Beatrice develops the figure of arrows being shot at birds; and she also refers to "the seed of weeping" (*il seme del piangere*) in connection with her rebukes to Dante for some unsavory amative adventures he had had since her death.

True, there is no explicit authorization at this point to interpret bows and arrows and seeds "venereally." In fact, there is even one notable sense in which we are strictly forbidden to do so. Though the nearest circle outside the realm of Paradisaic love is that where the lustful are diligently purging themselves by fire, the turn from lust to "innocent" love has been epitomized in Matilda's partial quotation from the first line of the Thirty-Second Psalm: "Blessed are those . . .

whose sins are covered" (the Old Testament usually speaking of forgiveness as a way of "covering" sin rather than as its cancellation or obliteration).

But the context of the cantos leaves no doubt that such images are "venereal" at least in a "transcendent" sense. Indeed, in an earlier canto Dante has been told that *all* motivation is reducible to terms of love and the perversions of that motive. But of course there still remains the question: just how specifically would you interpret the idea of the venereal (just how much sheerly "bodily" motivation would you assume to be lurking in these figures that are themselves a deflection of sexuality in the strictly physical sense, even while they suggest it)?[2]

---

[2] To review briefly the neat arrangement of the circles in Purgatory, with relation to the fact that all motivation has been reduced to terms of love:

Farthest down the Mount are the *perversions* of love (forms of ill-will towards one's neighbor). Lowest of all is Pride, the desire to excel by the abasement of others. Then comes Envy, resentment because the exalting of others implies the abasing of oneself. Then Wrath, the desire for vengeance, due to a sense of being wronged. The next higher circle, Sloth, occupies a midway position, a kind of dead center. It is a realm described by the word *accidia*, a term applied by the literature of mysticism to the state of "bitterness" or drought that arises when the mystic exaltation has flagged. Here the poet himself becomes so slothful that he closes the canto by rhyming *cerchi* with *cerchi*, though within this laziness there is a kind of enterprise, too, since the first *cerchi* is a plural form of the noun "circle," while the second *cerchi* is a second person, singular form of the verb "search." It is also notable that precisely here Dante has Virgil outline the logic of the whole canticle, and indeed give the motivational reduction of the poem as a whole. (Is he not thus in effect saying that, when we are stopped, precisely then we may start anew by pausing to *study* our situation?) The next higher circles are of *excessive* love: avarice, gluttony, and lust respectively—and as we pass through the purgative circle of the lustful we are not far from the loveliness of the Garden.

III

The simplest distortion of love, from the standpoint of catharsis, is the kind of art that would arouse sexual desire sheerly by the flaunting of sexual wares. Here is the burlesque of catharsis, as with the responses of the recondite roué who, after witnessing a lewd show, bought himself a steak, took it to his room, and pinched it unmercifully. Milder forms of such art are the specialty of Hollywood, which aims to have its stars appeal to their audiences as succubae and succubi.

A sufficiently mild and pleasant instance of pity as a subterfuge is the fantasy of the gallant coming to the aid of the Damsel in Distress. The lady, who would otherwise be aloof, is imagined as being placed in a situation that would justify the gentleman's advances. Without the assistance of her "pitiful" condition, he would be in the position of "forcing" his attentions upon her (attentions which the code would otherwise have demanded that she "repel," however much against her wishes).

Elsewhere we have considered how Wagner inclines towards the route that leads to love via pity. Othello touches upon the same connection in his way when saying of Desdemona (I,iii): "She lov'd me for the dangers I had pass'd/ And I lov'd her that she did pity them."

From there we might advance in another direction by considering the subtle disrelationship between *eros* (sexual, erotic love, *amor*) and *agape* (*charitas*, sheerly familial affection, shading into goodwill generally). Whatever the relation or disrelation between dramatic catharsis and love, the dissociation of erotic and agapetic motives must in itself raise problems that are never quite resolved. And insofar as a unitary principle underlies this dissociation, even the most thoroughgoing agapetic motives may be accompanied by erotic symptoms, as we learn from the writings of mystics such as Saint John of the Cross or St. Teresa of Avila.

Clearly the appeal of pity in Greek tragedy was agapetic. But we may expect it to have had erotic implications in the sense that, all tension having (within the terms of the fiction) been temporarily resolved, the individual members of the audience might well be in such a state of mind that erotic enjoyments could naturally follow, to cap the climax.

In sum, though pity is agapetic rather than erotic, it is on the slope of the erotic; and its tears imply such a letting-down of bars as can well culminate in a sheerly erotic act (albeit an act still somewhat edified by the spirit of the agapetic theme that led into it). However, since the arousing of pity requires the imitation of suffering, there are the deviations whereby the ambiguous relation between love and pity becomes rather an ambiguous relation between the erotic and cruelty. Here is an incident that provides a simple instance of such confusion, and in fact shows how the confusion can arise, as a kind of subterfuge. It is the "drama" of a young girl, of about ten or eleven, being "attacked" by two slightly older boys:

The scene: a playground near a school. The three children are on the way home. The two boys seize the girl, pull her to the ground, and aimlessly maul her in ways that could vaguely be classed under the head of "fighting." She makes such an outcry, demanding to be let alone, that they become frightened and release her. She rises and indignantly adjusts her clothing while the two boys stand back abashed. But at this point, instead of walking away as she could have done without being molested further, she gives one of the boys an angry shove—whereat the whole cycle begins anew, and is carried through to the same end, *da capo ad lib*. Here doubtlessly was a rudimentary kind of improvising, adapted to the fact that the code forbade such intimate bodily contacts if they were made in terms of affection. Accordingly, this state of intimacy, incipiently erotic, could be "properly" contrived only by the subterfuges of pugnacity and violence. In "defending" herself so stoutly, the girl would have nothing to "confess," though here surely were the makings of such "love" as could eventually express itself only by deviously sadistic or masochistic twists, ingredients that necessarily throw the ingredients of the recipe for tragedy out of proper proportion to one another.

Further, insofar as choice of sexual mate involves fighting among rivals, it is conceivable that the two essentially dissociated attitudes (of love and anger) could become merged into a simultaneity. For instance, if a dog is barking in rage at some distant threat, it may suddenly turn to snap at its master if its master happens to surprise it by a touch to which the dog spontaneously responds in terms of its rage-situation and before recognizing that there has also been introduced a "hand that feeds" situation. Thus, under certain condition, the turn from fighting with a rival to courting a mate might be so "telescoped into a simultaneity" that the motives of the fight situation become one with the motives of the courtship-situation—and thus in effect ingredients of rage proper to the rivalry could be directed against the loved object itself. At many points in this text we have come upon the notion that such telescoping is implicit in the nature of symbolic consistency. For insofar as the parts of a development are consistent, a single motivational principle must penetrate them all—and there is a sense in which such a principle obliterates its own distinctions.

Another common deflection involves a situation whereby dialectical resources lend themselves well to rhetorical self-deception. By such confusions, *hate* can be presented in terms of a "higher love." Thus on a radio program broadcasting a Sunday morning devotion, we heard this apt bit of militant sloganizing: "If you have a good religion, you must fight for it." Deceptions here could conceivably enter from two sources: (1) the "fighting" could be done in ways that are really a mockery of the "religion" that is supposedly being defended; (2) the "religion" could be but a covering for interests that are not only not religious, but essentially anti-religious.

As regards religion in general: its use to the ends of catharsis may often be at odds with its use as an administrative device, a means of "social control." The idea of Hell as a deterrent permits even threats of eternal torment to be equated with love, as when sinners are "lovingly" warned to mend their ways. But quite as "Mercy," which is a variant of "Pity," equals "Promise of Heaven," so "Justice," which is a variant of "Vengeance," equals "Threat of Hell." Thus, a theology as complex as the Christian is not intrinsically cathartic, though it can be manipulated to cathartic ends, by the stressing of some features and the slighting of others. The stories of mass conversion recited in the New Testament are obvious instances of the cathartic; but Paul's great administrative genius enabled him, even while placing great stress upon the cathartic principle, to build up the kind of ecclesiastical organization that would make the church an arm of government. Yet whatever might be one's difficulties when it came to loving troublesome neighbors, these problems might be lost sight of. For one could stress the love of God; and since God could be conceived of as a *universal* principle *personalized*, here would be dogmatic conditions favorable to catharsis.[3]

---

[3] As regards universalized love, a typical semi-secularized pattern (in a lyric related to outright religious thought somewhat as Greek

IV

One difficulty in trying to analyze catharsis as a process is due to what we might call "fragmentation." "Fragmentation" arises from the fact that the sacrificial motive can be broken into several moments, each of which has its own kind of universe.

For instance, insofar as the sacrifice is thought to purify, there may be rites whereby the persons who perform the sacrifice purify themselves as a way of preparing for their office. Thus the sacrificial principle will figure secondarily in regimens of penance, mortification, self-denial, study, etc.—and these in turn may allow for another kind of fragmentation, in the direction of "indulgences" which,

---

drama was to its origins in the Dionysian rites) would be Coleridge's lines in "The Eolian Harp":

And what if all of animated nature
Be but organic Harps diversely fram'd,
That tremble into thought, as o'er them
        sweeps
Plastic and vast, one intellectual breeze,
At once the Soul of each, and God of all?

And lyrics in the spirit of the lines just quoted from Coleridge can best be placed as Plato's method translated back again into poetry, with a greater stress upon imagery, though Plato's myth always had this, too.

The famous lines in "The Ancient Mariner," where the sufferer impulsively blesses the loathsome snakes, illustrates a similar semisecularization of the problem concerning the love of enemies:

O happy living things! no tongue
Their beauty might declare:
A spring of love gushed from my heart,
And I blessed them unaware.

Note that the curative moment here involves the personalizing of an animal species rather than the recognition of human personality; and the ethical shifts towards the aesthetic, in that these creatures are suddenly loved not for their "goodness" (as the book of Genesis might have required) but for their "beauty."

---

while reaffirming the sacrificial principle by taking for granted the assumptions that lie behind it, nonetheless at the same time introduce laxities that threaten it from another quarter. Or, when considering the details of a sacrificial ceremony, we may find some that are isolable like arias in an opera, or like the Stations of the Cross.

This matter of "fragmentation" is another aspect of the ambiguous relation between logical and temporal sequence. The cathartic process of a drama occurs in an irreversible temporal order. But its "moments" along the way are also related like a set of terms that mutually imply one another, without regard to any one temporal or narrative arrangement. Temporally, for instance, "infancy" may be one stage in a rebirth process—but when the Christians isolate the idea and image of the infant Jesus as a kind of summarizing moment to be depicted by itself, the moment can be so "dwelt on" that quite another kind of development takes place. And thus, since the idea of an infant implies the idea of a mother, pictures of Madonna and Child can be developed to the point where the stress shifts from Jesus to Mary. This development is *internal* to the moment; yet while it still remains related to the moment's place in the narrative as a whole, it can introduce an emphasis that some of the faithful will feel as a shift from "Christianity" towards "Mariolatry."

The dwelling upon moments makes possible a kind of development which threatens to obscure the functioning of that moment in the process as a whole. For instance, since a rite involving the use of a scapegoat has motives of murder and cruelty "implicit" in it, this confusion does not seem quite resolvable either by a sheerly humanitarian sympathy with the victim (through whose sacrifice the cleansing is expected to occur), or through whose sacrifice the cleansing is expected to occur), or through an over-eager emphasis upon the details of the suffering, or by such overly "rational" arrangements as the ancient Greeks finally hit upon, when keeping on reserve a supply of prisoners who had been con-demned to death for crimes but were used as sacrificial victims whenever the priests decided that a public purification was called for. Here also would figure the paradoxical scruples of one moment in the rites of Holy Week, when Adam's first disobedience is called "happy"; for by thus burdening all mankind with an in-heritance of "original sin," it led to Christ's coming in behalf of the Redemp-tion, a mission that, considered in itself, could be called "happy," though it cul-minated in a blood-offering. (See Herbert Weisinger's *Tragedy and the Paradox of the Fortunate Fall*, for examples of the way in which this moment can be dwelt upon and expanded by "cyclical" asso-ciations.) "Heretics" such as the Ophites and the Stercoranistae built their trouble-some doctrines by thus dwelling upon some one incidental moment in a system of interrelated terms until it became the "first" of the lot.

As regards the problem of drama in general, there is a troublesome moment of this sort which recurs too constantly to be treated merely as "incidental." This involves the relation between "sacrifice" and "the kill" (an ambiguity whereby Ernest Hemingway's somewhat repellent cult of the kill has acquired an almost nauseating popularity because it can im-part a sense of the sacrificial without hav-ing to negotiate the machinery of theol-ogy). The problem is reducible to these propositions:

Purgatives are divided into three kinds, de-pending on the intensity of their effects: laxa-tives, cathartics, and drastics. The word for the most intense variety comes from the same Greek root as the word for "drama." Insofar

as people like drama, they necessarily like victimage. For there can be no drama with-out the imitation of suffering in some form (ranging from comic embarrassment and be-wilderments through varying degrees of hard-ship to torture and death). In this sense, news stories of people in conflicts and catastrophes make the same appeal, but here the imitations are replaced by real victims.

Closely related to this cult of victimage implicit in the very nature of drama there is the act of *vicarage*, of *substitution*. The purgative effect of drama seems to require *vicarious* victimage, quite as in the case of the Christian drama built around the central moment of Christ as Media-tor. We should call substitution not a "fragmentary moment" of the cathartic motive, but the principle that underlies purgative victimage in general. (There is a certain paradoxical element with re-gard to suicide, however. Insofar as suicide is an attempt at catharsis, the purgand would seek to cleanse the self by using the self as purgative victim. This design becomes more obvious in its less drastic forms, as with people who deliberately "invite trouble." Popular speech recog-nizes the paradox in saying that such a person is "beside himself.")

v

A clear example of what we mean by "fragmentation" would be in Acts viii, 12: "But when they believed Philip preaching the things concerning the king-dom of God, and the name of Jesus Christ, they were baptized, both men and women." Note two different mo-ments here: (1) the kind of cleansing that went with the conversion, or change of belief itself; (2) the kind of cleansing that went with the rite of baptism. Theo-logians have called baptism a "regenera-tion," as distinct from "conversion"; but as seen from our formalistic point of view, either the change of belief or the "regenerative" bath of baptism could be considered as "fragments" of the cathartic principle in general.

There is an interesting fragmentation in Dante's *Purgatorio*, where the idea of a cleansing is figured in the image of a double stream, the waters on one side being called Lethe (because they had the power to cleanse by obliterating the memory of past sins), the waters on the other side being called Eunoë (because of their power to sharpen the memory of past good deeds). In her comic novel of split personality, *The Bird's Nest*, Shirley Jackson gets excellent burlesque by a fantastically efficient ritual cleansing, when all four of the heroine's personalities take baths in succession, without knowledge of one another, but all necessarily bathing the same body. Here fragmentation gets a new twist. Or we could cite K. Burke's piece, "The 'Anaesthetic Revelation' of Herone Liddell" (*Kenyon Review*, Autumn, 1957), in which the protagonist, a "word-man" recovering from the ill effects of surgery, becomes engrossed in studying the death of Keats, as revealed through Keats's letters. Here, by critically re-enacting the death of a "perfect" poet, the word-man in effect uses Keats as cathartic victim. But the cathartic principle is broken into other fragments also, as for instance, in shell-gathering, in speculations on the sea as life-giving charnel house, and in the change of scene, itself designed to be curative.

In Chapter XVIII of the *Poetics*, where Aristotle divides Attic tragedy into four species, the notion of "fragmentation" might be applied in a way that would make the alignment look slightly different. The species that Aristotle lists first (the Complex, or "entangled," *peplegmene*) could be treated as the paradigm; then the other three would be "fragmentations" of it. For insofar as tragedy involves suffering, a centering upon this element alone should lead to Aristotle's second species, the tragedy of suffering, the *pathetike*. (Plays about Ixion and Ajax, he says, are examples of the type.) The next important fragmentation would be the tragedy of character (*ethike*), presumably portraying tragic personality as such, though the examples mentioned have not survived. The lowest kind would stress spectacle (*opsis*). "All scenes laid in Hades" are examples of this emphasis—and by extension, this kind of fragmentation might cover the strictly "visionary" aspects of conversion. (The anchorite's choice of austere surroundings would thus be a "scenic fragmentation" of the cathartic motive.) In sum, type 1, the Complex kind of tragedy, would contain elements of suffering, character, and spectacle; but no one of these "fragments" would be isolated and given such special emphasis as make for the distinct literary species which Aristotle classes under the other three heads.

This approach might be carried further. Since, according to Aristotle, a Complex plot is distinguished by reversal and discovery, we note that the two taken together are the equivalent of "conversion," with the emergence of a new insight. In fact, "discovery" is but a special and sometimes attenuated instance of "reversal" (since the new bit of knowledge acquired by the characters or the audience notably changes the nature of the motivation).[4]

---

[4] As regards the six parts of tragedy named by Aristotle in Chapter VI of the *Poetics*: note that the *pathetike* could be said to stress one aspect of Plot, the *ethike* features Character, the *opsis*, Spectacle. "Discovery" (*anagnorisis*) can be considered a species of Thought (*dianoia*) insofar as it introduces a new perspective or point of view. We might say that it is Thought "implicitly" or "inchoately." For though the Discovery in itself may involve any change "from ignorance to knowledge" (xi), in the case of great dramas like Sopho-

Finally, as regards "fragmentation": just as each person undergoes experience in his own special way, meeting new conditions from the standpoint of a unique combination of past ones, hence with correspondingly unique bonds of association however great the range of attitudes he shares with other people, so each cathartic enterprise will involve developments peculiar to itself. Accordingly we cannot always be sure just which elements should be called essential to the catharsis, and which accidental. Thus, tentatively making an "existentialist" recipe for catharsis as contrived in Dante's *Purgatorio*, we might list "requirements" of this sort:

1. The purgand, to be purged, most contemplate, as an engaged observer, the

---

cles' *Oedipus Rex* it "speaks volumes." As regards the other two parts, Diction (*lexis*) and Song (*melopoiia*): passages of lamentation and rejoicing chanted by the Chorus and capable of isolation like arias in an opera or like Psalms could be treated as fragments of these two parts. However, such lyric passages are not featured to the extent of becoming distinct tragic species—and in fact, as Aristotle reminds us in *Poetics* IV, 16, tragedy developed precisely by the curtailing of the role alloted to the Chorus in the earlier Dionysian rites.

However, I feel a bit uneasy about my treatment of "thought" in this line-up. And I'd like to try again, along these lines: (1) The complex plot would embody the perfect stress upon act. (2) The *pathetike* would stress the passive side of action. (3) The *ethike* would stress character. (4) The *opsis* (and the oldest text is corrupt at this point) would stress spectacle. Diction and song are omitted because the overstress upon them would mark a turn from drama proper back to lyric, the kind of arias-with-dance which drama had necessarily subordinated in the very process of becoming drama. And you can't get a drama at all by an overstress upon sheer thought. That would mark the point at which drama would dissolve into exposition, homily, or dialectic (for instance, the dialogue form which Plato offered as a kind of medicine quite different from the sort provided by the playwrights).

sufferings, regrets, and efforts of other people.

2. He must proceed by orderly stages through the realms of the damned, the penitent, and the blessed, with each such stage divided into rationally distinguishable sub-stages.

3. He must have a male guide (a "father") whom he greatly admires, but behind this guide there must be a Madonna-like woman whom he had revered on earth, and whom he will see when he has been properly prepared.

4. All stages of the purgation proper must be under the sign of blessing (as with the singing of a Beatitude in each circle of the Purificatory Mount, while he proceeds towards the Woman Who Blesses).

5. The purgand's guide must generously keep him reminded that later there will be a change to a guide more highly qualified (an important point, because this arrangement in effect allows for a "transference" of allegiance without the need of "father-rejection").

6. About midway in his development, spurred by study precisely at a time when most threatened by sloth, the purgand must have all motivation authoritatively reduced for him to terms of a single impulse ("love"), with its corresponding problems and hierarchy.

7. He must accept a distinction in kind between a "natural" and a "spiritual" or "rational" order of motives. And maybe we should treat as cathartically essential the etymologically accidental fact that the root of the word for the "higher" kind of motive ("*d'animo*"—*Purg.* xvii, 93) also provides a generic terms for the lower kind: "animal."

8. He must have so strong a sense of wonder that references to wonder recur like an *idée fixe* throughout the text.

9. He must have confronted a basic conflict of authorities (spiritual and tem-

poral), where the spiritual authorities are in a state of corruption that he looks upon as infecting the temporal.

10. At stages along the way, the purgand must have dreams that foreshadow the course of his development.

11. He must accept it without question that people are cleansed by willingly undergoing hardships to make amends for previous laxities.

12. He must forever be pressing onwards and upwards, despite occasional lapses.

13. At every stage, there must be a language of imagery corresponding to a language of ideas—and these ideas must have their explicit expression, too, not being merely suggested through their imagistic counterparts.

VI

The principle of "fragmentation" ultimately involves a terministic situation we have already considered elsewhere, notably in connection with the "Cycle of Terms Implicit in the Idea of 'Order,'" in our essay on Genesis. If one term implies several others that are necessary to its meaning, there is no one sequence proper to such a family of terms. Thus, implicit in the idea of catharsis as cure there is the idea of disease, implicit in its meaning as an unburdening there is the idea of a load or charge, implicit in its meaning as a cleansing there is the idea of the unclean. And any such ideas would be translatable into corresponding images.

The spinning can be carried further: if there is a cleansing, there must be persons or things that do the cleansing, and there must be the offscourings that result from the cleansing. Implicit here, in turn, is the idea of the need to dispose of the offscourings, or in some way to neutralize their bad effects. And there is also the idea of so extending the cathartic principle that those persons who are entrusted

with the cleansing must themselves be cleansed in preparation for their office and perhaps also following the performance of the awful rites. Also, there must be situations marked by clean and unclean essences, with perhaps situations that are ambiguous and can thereby form transitional bridges between the opposite kinds of terms. Further, each of such moments along the way may be epitomized in some particular object or image that is the visible or tangible manifestation of a certain invisible, intangible essence, and thus secondarily a manifestation of the terministic reticulation which that essence in turn implies.

Or, reverting to a step already mentioned, we find implicit in the idea of offscourings the idea of substitution or vicarage whereby one thing becomes unclean as a result of the process whereby another is cleansed. (Thus, if the purifying bath is one kind of "fulfillment," the impure bath-water is another.) Here are the sheerly terministic makings of the "scapegoat principle"; for at the very least the vessel that bears these impurities must itself need purifying. And of course the principle of vicarage makes also for an accountancy whereby the victim designed to suffer vicariously for others may in turn be replaced by a substitute.

We could go on, "spinning" a whole world of implications from such a start (with cuts similar "in principle," but different in detail, according to the connotations uppermost in such pairs, half-idea, half-image, as sick vs. cured, burdened vs. unburdened, enslaved vs. free, lost vs. found, unclean vs. clean, tense vs. relaxed, etc.).

The subject of "fragmentation" also impinges upon a matter we have considered previously in another connection: the kind of "futurity" that is intensely experienceable as an intuition here and now, and that can be due purely to a terministic situation. We refer to the fact that one can feel a whole universe of terms vibrant in the key term he chooses as his point of departure. We mentioned the writings of a convert such as Paul, who spun his terminology from the essentially cathartic principle of Christ as Mediator by reason of His nature as Perfect Victim. We noted that, regardless of the intense conviction Paul derived from the circumstances of his conversion on the road to Damascus, there was the sheerly technical urgency of his nomenclature, as each term drives imperatively towards others implicit in it. In his writings one often finds sentences that transform such terministic spinning into the figure technically known as *gradatio,* or the ladder, thus: "But we glory in tribulation also: knowing that tribulation worketh patience; and patience, experience; and experience, hope." Or again: "Whom he did predestinate, them he also called: and whom he called, them he also justified: and whom he justified, them he also glorified." From the standpoint of terministic implications, this second sentence, for instance, would be a highly dramatized way of saying that the ideas of predestination, vocation, justification, and glorification mutually imply one another. Similarly, from the standpoint of terministic cyclicality, one should approach a play such as Sophocles' *Oedipus Rex* not by asking how King Oedipus' unconscious parricide and incest resulted in the condition of pollution under which the populace suffered and which could be alleviated only by his sacrifice, as brought about by such-and-such developments. Rather, one should ask how the ideas of kingship, parricide, incest, pollution, justice, and royal cathartic sacrifice all implied one another. Obviously, though the Freudian perspective would help us in making such an alignment, it could not wholly supply the answer.

So far as the paradigm of catharsis is concerned, if we center for a time upon its most common associations, we might say that it contains the "simultaneously present" ideas of these main moments: "unclean," "clean," "cleansing," "cleanser," and "cleansed." And though we might say that in catharsis as an *act* ("cleansing") there is implied a progression in one direction (from "unclean" to "clean"—or, similarly, from "burdened" to "unburdened," or from "enslaved" to "free," etc.) a closer look shows that this irreversibility is more apparent than real. For instance, insofar as the idea of catharsis is objectified in terms of offscourings (*katharmata*), there is a sense in which the cleaning has led to the unclean. Or, otherwise put: the unclean is either displaced, or "covered." And this principle of removal introduces in effect the principle of substitution, or vicarage, since the cleansing of one place incidentally involves the polluting of another.

Once this principle of vicarage is introduced, you have a terministic situation that makes possible a development in two directions at once: while the tragic protagonist may be proceeding from good fortune to bad, his simulated assumption of such a destiny may be so contrived formally and stylistically that the audience is proceeding from irresolution to resolution. (Or, if you will, the play embodies a counterpoint whereby these two strands work together.) And just at the stage where the victim is imitating the most intense suffering, the audience is cleansed by a bath of pitiful tears, a benign orgiastic downpour.

Partially as a result of the fact that the particular irreversible details of one cathartic drama are so different from those of another, some persons may contend that the catharsis of a drama is purely intrinsic to its form, and is not to be explained as borrowing part of its tensions from clearly or vaguely felt analogies to personal situations outside the play (the various individual "private dramas" which the members of the audience have in the back of their minds when they come to the theatre, and to which they will revert when the play is over). And unquestionably, whether or not the dramatist draws on such "unearned increment" for part of his effect, the drama must be analyzed first of all as a process intrinsically cathartic. But insofar as the cathartic process is purely intrinsic to the given drama, then that drama must somehow contrive within its own terms to establish a sense of the unclean—for how otherwise could there be a sense of cleansing? At the very least, insofar as the play begins by working up a tangle which must be untangled, this development from complication to dénouement must in some way set up a resolution to be resolved—and it must do so in accordance with norms of propriety that also prevail *outside* the given work, however unique the set of proprieties embodied *within* the work.

VII

But could we have a sufficiently comprehensive approach to the problem of catharsis if we treated it solely in such a purely formalistic manner? "Pity and fear and such emotions" are strongly personal, they do something to one personally—and we must consider not only the personalities of the *dramatis personae* but also the over-all "personality" of a given drama (for such "character" sums up the ways in which the tragic imitation itself can be said to *act*). Though a drama, to be successful, certainly need not allude to strictly local situations (as with "tendentious" plots that exploit our sympathies regarding social or political issues that happen at the time to be prominent in the news), surely its over-all enactment, and the roles by which such enactment is

made possible, are most effective when in some way they sum up human tensions prevailing "prior to" the particular circumstances of the particular tragedy that happens to be "cleansing" us. The sense of an "uncleanness" that needs "cleansing" can be suggested within the terms of a particular drama only insofar as we can somehow "meet it halfway," by responding with susceptibilities we have developed through experiences outside the drama.

In this way a dramatist's trickeries, while ostensibly resolving nothing but entanglements of his own making, may be *symbolically* or *metaphorically* resolving problems that are *literally* unresolvable, since they relate ultimately to motivational tangles that cannot be resolved, except insofar as we might class under "resolution" such blanket attitudes as piety, resignation, defiance, dissipation, and either outright sloth or the more common variants of sloth that conceal themselves beneath much show of activity. The character, or personality of a work may touch upon such ultimate discordancies natural to a given society; or it may to varying degrees transcend the culture in which it arose, and may "permanently" engage the human tribe in general (for in proportion as we perfect our understanding of these processes, surely we shall see how all great works are feeling their way through much the same astounding labyrinth).

People are "cleansed" in one respect when, after indecision, they hit upon a course of action. They are cleansed in another respect when they become so intensely "inside" to a symbol-system that a new quality or order of motives emerges from within it. And they are cleansed in still another respect when, the goal having been reached, fulfillment is complete. Each has its own kind of gratification, corresponding to the beginning, middle, and end of a project. They are purely formal aspects of catharsis that do not directly involve victimage. However, we need but think of the *Divine Comedy* to realize how readily the cathartic process, as given full body, comes to develop out of victimage.

The Inferno is the realm of hopelessness, as per the often quoted formula, III, 9: "Abandon all hope, ye who enter here" (*Lasciate ogni speranza, voi ch'entrate*). It is a region where the shrieks are "desperate" (I, 115). Thus, essentially, it would be a realm without direction. Yet, after the brief introduction, it is what gets the poem under way. There is thus a sense in which Dante is never really in Hell, since he is progressing towards Beatrice. His Hell is but a kind of Pre-Purgatory, as Beatrice says in effect when she tells him (*Purg.* XXX, 136–138): He had sunk so low, the only way of saving him was "to show him the lost people" (*mostrargli le perduti genti*). In effect, she was proposing that he become better acquainted with the eternal scapegoats that will match the saints eternally cleansed. And as regards the purely "formal" equivalent of Hell, Dante, the poet, had already passed beyond it, and into the motives of Purgatory (catharsis proper) once he had formed a clear idea of Hell's structure and of the stages through which Dante the pilgrim would proceed—or, more specifically, once he had hit upon that resonant first line (on being midway along life's journey, *Nel mezzo del camin di nostra vita*), a line that in itself suggests a peripety at the very start.

Quite as the region of Hell is in a sense *raised* to the level of catharsis by reason of the purpose or destination implicit in the realization that we are witnessing a guided tour *through* it, so by the same token there is a sense in which Heaven is *lowered* to the level of ca-

tharsis. For the Paradiso is not so much an ultimate consummation pure and simple as a kind of *Gradus ad Parnassum*, an educational progression through a series of steps each of which is a consummation in its own right, though all are mutually related in a kind of fixity quite unlike the temporal or narrative development Dante's journey imparts to them. It would be like saying that the squares on a checkerboard "go" from one to the next, as you move a checker across them. Even in Heaven, Dante is on the make. Thus, though the dialectic of Hell and Heaven is "frozen" in the sense that all relationships are permanently set, by the nature of his journey through them, Dante endows all three realms with the "progressive" quality of Purgatory.

However, within this qualification, we might say that Hell is indecision, Purgatory is decision, and Heaven is the arrival that follows decision persevered in. While the inmates of Purgatory (the realm that in effect has "catharsis" in its very name) are under great discomfiture, their sufferings have the satisfaction of being *purposive*. The shades in Purgatory are "contented in the fire" (*contenti nel fuoco*), for they "hope to come" eventually "among the blessed." In purgation as so conceived, the suffering must be *willed*. One is not "cleansed" when acting under duress; his engagements, however *necessary*, must also somehow be *free*.

VIII

To complete these pages on "fragmentation," we might recall another major moment, as regards the redemptive logic. We saw how, as one aspect of tragic dignification, there is the use of Wonder. Wonder is not directly related to either Love or Pity, though we noted how it could be related to Pity indirectly, by reason of its relation to Fear. (In *Permanence and Change*, Hermes Edition,

p. 145, we first tinkered with this notion, in linking Wonder, Reverence, Awe, Fear, and Dread, while ideas of Defense and Courage or Cowardice are in the offing). A related motive operates in the step from Wonder to Admiration. For the desire to build a character who is "good" for sacrifice as tragic hero can readily lead to the desire to make him "admirable." Next, a "moment" of this sort could build up requirements of its own, to the point where representative critics even questioned whether tragedy, as so conceived, really aimed at "catharsis." The Cornelian dramatist might so build up the appeal of this one moment in its own terms, that the direct relation to catharsis retreated behind the desire to be *imposing.* The shift is understandable sociologically, for though such drama was a State art, and thus to some extent like the Greek drama, it was a *court* art rather than a *civic* art. Or at least we could say that it was "on the slope" of court art. Might the effect, then, be more like that of witnessing a parade (a royal *cortège*) than like being made to feel that the interests of the high and the lowly were somehow one? Also, ironically enough, on looking back at the form in the light of what happened later, do we not see how it could be analyzed as implicitly containing the expression of emergent tendencies towards *revolt?* That is, these tendencies were present not as in Aeschylus, who seems deliberately to have sought ways to neutralize them, but rather as trends that were "creeping up" on the dramatists, and that thus got in by stealth (owing to the fact that drama requires a conflict, and insofar as the Cornelian drama became a *court* art, the enacting of conflict would involve, however roundabout, the introduction of motives *contrary to* the court).

In the introduction to the American Edition of *Les Chefs-d'Oeuvre de Corneille*, annotated by Georges Raeders, we are informed:

The audience and readers of the eighteenth century were much exercised for or against the political theories expressed by the characters in *Cinna.*

To one, *Cinna* was "fanaticism and demagogy crushed by the social and conservative spirit"; to another, it was "royalty made divine by mercy, the apotheosis of monarchy"; to a third, *Cinna* disclosed "both the secret of the building of the empire and the cause of its duration"; others reconciled all these views by showing that the piece "develops the republican idea in the early acts and the monarchic idea in the later ones."

Its version of imperial clemency is said to have been such a favorite with Louis XIV, that, on seeing it performed, he wanted to pardon a chevalier condemned to death, but his ministers insisted that such a policy would set a bad example.

All told, as catharsis it seems better designed to soften an absolute monarch than to mollify a disgruntled populace. From the standpoint of a cathartic "moment" that had developed sufficient independence as a motive all its own to lose direct relevance to catharsis (except perhaps for the King and the dramatist), we might state the case thus: Tragedy, to be most cathartically effective, builds "heroic" characters; Cornelian tragedy develops a cult of the heroic as such— and this makes for a theatre of "admiration" (while admiration could in turn be treated as a variant of the "wonder" that Aristotle considered helpful to the effectiveness of tragedy).

IX

This second view of catharsis derives partly from a shift of models (when we began, for instance, to ask about the cathartic ingredients in Pauline Christianity). But mainly it comes from a question that arose regarding Aristotle's own definition.

In the *Rhetoric* (II, iii) he observes that "it is impossible to be afraid and angry at the same time." He seems to mean that in proportion as we feel angry with someone, our fear drops away—and presumably if one were angry enough, one would attack in a rage, without thought of the consequences.

Thus, when considering Greek tragedy from the standpoint of a catharsis got by the symbolic cleansing of civic conflict, we saw that this formula of Aristotle's was quite relevant to our concerns. For it suggested that the tragedy might contrive to make us fear for the very class of citizen against whom we might otherwise feel angry (the socially superior).

At that point we noticed another twist: in II, iv, Aristotle distinguishes between anger and hate, by saying that we feel angry with individuals ("for instance Callias or Socrates"), whereas hatred applies to *classes* of people ("for instance, everyone hates a thief or an informer"). He next says that anger can be cured by time, but it is not so with hatred. He also says that anger is painful, but hatred is not.

The general picture suggested the thought that, insofar as civic conflict involved *class* conflicts, the modes of heroic personalization would first move the issue from the realm of hatred to the realm of anger. Next, the resources of fear would be so manipulated that tendencies to fear would replace the tendencies to anger. The dramatist would contrive this shift by depicting his heroes as the victims of greater misfortune than their misdeeds merited, and by bringing the intensity of their sufferings before our very eyes (*enargeia*), since the more remote a danger seems, the less it is feared. At this point we noted that both anger and hatred were on the slope opposite that of *love*. Here then, we thought, might be a deflection to provide for a problematical absence of love. And the next step was to observe how the arousing of pity might serve the same end, except in a more "positive" way.

Throughout the inquiry, the author has been tentatively asking himself just how to present the other two major cathartic devices, epitomized in Aristophanic comedy and Platonist dialectic (with the non-dramatic lyric, as distinguished from the tragic chorus, being in turn viewed as a variant of Platonic transcendence).

And now of a sudden the remainder of the task falls neatly into place. Aristophanes' priapic comedy was in its very essence vowed to peace (a variant of love, coming to a conclusion in a secularization of the sacred marriage and the lovefeast). And Plato's particular system of cure, which put him in direct competition with both tragic and comic playwrights, was based on the Socratic erotic, as propounded most directly in the *Phaedrus* and the *Symposium*: an ideological technique whereby bodily love would be transformed into love of wisdom, which in turn would be backed by knowledge derived and matured from the coquettish give and take of verbal intercourse.

Herbert Read

THE CREATIVE EXPERIENCE IN POETRY

Although Sir Herbert Read began his writing career in 1919 as a poet and has continued to publish verse, he has won an international reputation as a critic of art and literature and as an aesthetician. He has written more than two dozen books of essays and criticism. Some of his representative works are: *Phases of English Poetry* (1928), *Poetry and Anarchism* (1938), *The Philosophy of Modern Art* (1952), and *A Concise History of Modern Painting* (1959). The essay reprinted here was included in Sir Herbert's *The Forms of Things Unknown: Essays Toward an Aesthetic Philosophy* (1960).

In order to come close to the creative experience in poetry, it is necessary either to describe an experience of one's own, or to discover some revealing evidence among the manuscripts of an acknowledged poet. There are obvious disadvantages in relying on one's own experience. Time has not tested the products of that experience, and nothing is so deceitful as the poetic afflatus. Even if our poems were acknowledged by our contemporaries, we should still have the uneasy feeling that they might be no more than a manifestation of the Zeitgeist. I shall speak as a poet who is under the illusion that he has had authentic experiences of poetic creation; but I shall take as an example for analysis a poem that in England has had a high reputation for more than one hundred and fifty years, a poem that is complex enough to exhibit all aspects of poetry, whether intensive or extensive, and whose composition is fully documented: Coleridge's ode, which he called *Dejection*. It was first published in the London *Morning Post* on the 4th October 1802 but it had been written exactly six months earlier in a form very different from that given to the public. The full version was first published by Professor Ernest de Selincourt in 1937. It has been republished more recently,[1] but the poem in its completeness cannot be said to be well known. Yet not only is that original version a great and moving poem, but a comparison of the two versions, and a consideration of the reasons which led Coleridge to revise his original version before publication, raise problems of the greatest critical importance.

The original version is a continuous poem of 340 lines. What might be called the standard version, first published by

---

[1] Selincourt, Ernest de, *Wordsworthian and Other Studies*, Oxford, Clarendon Press, 1947, pp. 57–76.

284

Coleridge in 1817 in a collection of his poems called *Sibylline Leaves*, is merely 139 lines long, and the *Morning Post* version of 1802 is even shorter still. In its ruthlessly lopped state the poem is no longer a continuous train of thought, and is therefore divided into eight numbered and rearranged sections. Apart from these large structural changes, numerous small revisions have been made in the remaining text that completely disguise its origin and alter its tone. The considerations which Coleridge had in mind in making these alterations were partly personal and partly critical. But before we can discuss them we must take into account the circumstances in which the poem was composed.

Coleridge had married in haste and repented at leisure. For our present purposes it is not necessary to take sides in the quarrel, for we are only concerned with Coleridge's feelings in the matter, and of these there is no doubt. He gave full expression to them in a letter written in October of this same year 1802 to his friend and benefactor, Thomas Wedgwood. Here is a passage from this revealing document:

'After my return to Keswick, I was, if possible, more miserable than before. Scarce a day passed without such a scene of discord between me and Mrs. Coleridge, as quite incapacitated me from any worthy exertion of my faculties by degrading me in my own estimation. I found my temper injured, and daily more so; the good and pleasurable Thoughts, which had been the support of my moral character, departed from my solitude. I determined to go abroad—but alas! the less I loved my wife, the more dear and necessary did my children seem to me. I found no comfort except in the driest speculations . . . About two months ago after a violent quarrel I was taken suddenly ill with spasms in my stomach—I

expected to die—Mrs C. was, of course, shocked and frightened beyond measure —and two days after, I still being very weak and pale as death, she threw herself upon me and made a solemn promise of amendment—and she has kept her promise beyond any hope, I could have flattered myself with . . . If any woman wanted an exact and copious Recipe, "How to make a Husband compleatly miserable," I could furnish her with one —with a Probatum est, tacked to it. Ill-tempered Speeches sent after me when I went out of the House, ill-tempered Speeches on my return, my friends received with freezing looks, the least opposition or contradiction occasioning screams of passion, and the sentiments which I hold most base, ostentatiously avowed—all this added to the utter negation of all, which a Husband expects from a Wife—especially, living in retirement —and the consciousness that I was myself growing a worse man. O dear Sir! no one can tell what I have suffered. I can say with strict truth, that the happiest half-hours, I have had, were when all of a sudden, as I have been sitting alone in my Study, I have burst into Tears.'[2]

Such was Coleridge's state of mind when he wrote *Dejection*. But he did not tell Wedgwood the whole truth—he did not tell him that the passion he had once felt for Sarah Fricker, his wife, he now felt for Sara Hutchinson, the sister of Mary who was to become Wordsworth's wife.

All thoughts, all passions, all delights,
    Whatever stirs this mortal frame
All are but ministers of Love,
    And feed his sacred flame . . .

The beautiful ballad which opens with these lines had been inspired by this new

[2] *Collected Letters of Samuel Taylor Coleridge*, edited by Earl Leslie Griggs, Vol. II (1801–1806), Oxford, 1956, pp. 464–465.

and deep and hopeless passion and had been written three years before this letter to Wedgwood. That was in December, 1799, and the following summer, in order to be near the object of his new passion Coleridge had moved to the Lake District, and during the next few years they saw much of each other. During all this time Coleridge's health was rapidly deteriorating—apart from the spasms in the stomach mentioned to Wedgwood he suffered from giddiness and rheumatic pains, and it was then that he first had fatal recourse to opium. He was indeed a miserable man, but he was also a deeply religious man, and his convictions forbade any thought of divorce. He had three women to minister to him in his sickness, to sympathize with his misery—Mary and Sara Hutchinson, and Dorothy Wordsworth, who was as hopelessly in love with him as he was with Sara. It was in a mood induced by the tenderness of these ministering angels that he wrote the poem he called *Dejection.*

It is such an intimate poem, so self-revealing and so revealing of a complex passionate situation affecting others, that no other excuse would be necessary for the considerable excisions which Coleridge made in the published version. But there was another consideration to which I have already referred of a more theoretical nature. Coleridge held the view that the best poetry is not written out of what we might call private situations. The best poetry is *objective*, as we say—it is *aloof*. In the *Biographia Literaria* he praises Shakespeare for possessing this quality. A sign of his genius, he said, 'is the choice of subjects very remote from the private interest and circumstances of the writer himself. At least,' he adds, 'I have found, that where the subject is taken immediately from the author's personal sensations and experiences, the excellence of a particular poem is but an equivocal mark, and often a fallacious pledge, of genuine poetic power.'

I think there is no doubt that Coleridge had this particular poem of his own in mind when making such a statement. This general principle of objectivity or aloofness in art is not to be confused with the impersonality of primitive poetry: the 'objective correlative' is always correlated to a subjective state of mind. For the moment it is perhaps sufficient to note that objectivity, or 'aesthetic distance' as it is sometimes called, is a principle recognized by aestheticians in all the arts, and it is perhaps a distinguishing mark between certain schools of art—the classical artist, for example, accepting it as a matter of course, but the realist, and more particularly the expressionist artist, going to the opposite extreme to find the basis of his work in the immediacy of his personal emotions.

In the original version of Coleridge's poem there is no attempt to disguise the dramatis personae; Wordsworth appears as William, and Sara, Mary and Dorothy are mentioned by name. In the *Morning Post* versions, William became Edmund; in the final *Sibylline Leaves* version, all names whatsoever are suppressed, and only a vague 'virtuous Lady' is apostrophized—'O Lady! we receive but what we give,' instead of 'O Sara! we receive but what we give.' The process of depersonalization was complete.

Thanks to our knowledge of the circumstances in which it was composed, and to the evidence offered by two distinct versions, one immediate and spontaneous, the other pondered and selective, we are able to distinguish clearly between the intensive and extensive aspects of this particular poem. The two versions must be studied side by side before any conclusion about their respective merits can be reached. My own conclusions, after such a careful study, are not at all ambiguous. The original poem is a human document of great interest, essential to an understanding of the personality of a great poet; but the revised version which Coleridge published is an infinitely better work of art. Indeed, nearly all the specifically poetic lines in the poem are in the final version; the lines that have been sacrificed are almost without exception rhetorical or prosaic. It seems as though the poetic spirit in Coleridge soars aloft whenever he ceases to address Sara in person and descends to become sentimental in her presence. There are exceptions: for example, this description of a happy moment of domestic bliss:

Such joy I had, that I may truly say,
My spirit was awe-stricken with the excess
And trance-like depth of its brief happiness

And there is one longer passage which is very moving and essential to an understanding of the situation out of which the poem arose:

I speak not now of those habitual ills
That wear out life, when two unusual minds
Meet in one house and two discordant wills—
    This leaves me, where it finds,
Past cure, and past complaint,—a fate austere
Too fix'd and hopeless to partake of fear!

... Methinks to weep with you
Were better far than to rejoice alone—
But that my coarse domestic life has known
No habits of heart-nursing sympathy,
No griefs but such as dull and deaden me,
No mutual mild enjoyments of its own.
No hopes of its own vintage, none O! none—
Whence when I mourn'd for you, my heart might borrow
Fair forms and living motions for its sorrow.

But that is all. The great passages of the poem are in the public version, and are presented as direct utterances of the poet's own spirit, as a 'sudden flash of transcendental feeling'[3]:

There was a time when tho' my path was rough,
The joy within me dallied with distress;
And all misfortunes were but as the stuff
Whence fancy made me dreams of happiness;
For hope grew round me, like the climbing vine,
And leaves and fruitage, not my own, seem'd mine!
But now ill tidings bow me down to earth,
Nor care I that they rob me of my mirth—
But oh! each visitation
Suspends what nature gave me at my birth.
My shaping spirit of imagination!

My shaping spirit of imagination! It will perhaps now be evident why, of all poems that were possible, I have chosen for analysis this poem of Coleridge's. It contains within its lines an exact description of the problem we are discussing. Let me quote one more passage:

For not to think of what I needs must feel,
But to be still and patient all I can;
And haply by abstruse research to steal
From my own nature, all the natural man—
This was my sole resource, my only plan:
Till that, which suits a part, infects the whole,
And now is almost grown the habit of my soul ...

O Lady! We receive but what we give,
And in our life alone does Nature live

[3] An expression I take from a book which, though innocent of modern psychology, showed a deep understanding of the poetic process: The Myths of Plato, by J. A. Stewart, London, 1905.

Ours is her wedding garment, ours her
   shroud—
And would we aught behold of higher
   worth
Than that inanimate cold world allow'd
To the poor loveless ever anxious crowd,
Ah! from the soul itself must issue forth
A light, a glory, and a luminous cloud
Enveloping the earth!
And from the soul itself must there be
   sent
A sweet and potent voice of its own birth,
Of all sweet sounds, the life and element.

Coleridge proceeds to identify that
sweet and potent voice, this beautiful and
beauty-making power, with joy, with the
celebration and utterance of a feeling of
spiritual identity with the creative forces
of nature.

The poem, we see, proceeds quite
directly from a conflict in Coleridge's
mind, a moral and emotional embarrassment caused by his loss of love for his
wife, and his concurrent passion for a
woman not his wife. This personal conflict is seen by Coleridge as parallel to a
conflict between metaphysical speculation and poetic expression. The emotional conflict creates a tension which is
relieved by the act of poetic utterance; in
some way, or to some degree, the poetic
quality of the utterance is related to the
intensity of the conflict. There supervenes
in this emotional conflict an intellectual
conflict, a fear that he (Coleridge) may
be deprived of the capacity for poetic
utterance by an indulgence in 'abstruse
research,' that spontaneity may be en-
dangered by reflection.

Such is the personal equation implicit
in this one poem. But can we generalize
from this particular case? Not, of course,
with any scientific validity, but whenever
we uncover the springs of modern poetry
—and it should be remembered that I
am now discussing the post-Renaissance
subjective type of poetry—there we soon
detect a conflict of this nature. *Hamlet*

and *King Lear* are, at the beginning of
the period, the prototypes of such psychic
conflicts, resolved in poetry.

Twenty-five years ago, in 1934, a psychological study of these problems was
published by the Oxford University Press
—Maud Bodkin's *Archetypal Patterns in
Poetry*—a pioneering work which has not
had sufficient acknowledgment. The
archetypal pattern in poetry, according to
Miss Bodkin, is always one of conflict—
'The pattern consists of emotional tendencies of opposite character which are
liable to be excited by the same object
or situation, and, thus conflicting, produce an inner tension that seeks relief in
the activity either of fantasy, or of poetic
imagination, either originally or recep-
tively creative.' Miss Bodkin does not
presume to make any dogmatic assertion
about the nature of the opposed tendencies, but she suggests that they arise from
an ambivalent attitude towards the self—
'a certain organization of the tendencies
of self-assertion and submission' such as
we find in tragedy. 'The self which is
asserted is magnified by that same collective force to which finally submission
is made; and from the tension of the two
impulses and their reaction upon each
other, under the conditions of poetic
exaltation, the distinctive tragic attitude
and emotion appears to arise.'[4]

This description would apply to Coleridge's poem (and Miss Bodkin does
proceed to trace the same archetypal
pattern in Coleridge's *The Ancient
Mariner*, and in less detail in *Kubla
Khan*). The collective force is present in
Coleridge's acute sense of social morality,
his 'fate austere, Too fix'd and hopeless to
partake of fear!' His self is asserted in his
defiant love of Sara, friend devoutest of
his choice, and there is no possible reconciliation of those two contrary drives—
only the relief of poetic utterance, of a

---

[4] Op. cit., p. 23.

projection of the conflict into the objective form of poetry. The relief is all the greater the more objective that projection can be made. We also call the process sublimation. The poet in the end cannot get rid of the perilous conflict unless he forgets himself, and creates a symbolic conflict in which the hidden self, in tragic renunciation, submits to Fate, or Truth, or God—by whatever name we designate the collective wisdom of the race or group.

Such is the mechanism of the creative imagination, of the formative will in the unconscious of the poet. But have we forgotten the fact . . . that poetry does not consist wholly in an archetypal pattern of drama or action, that it is not only a form of art, but also a personal style? Whence comes the distinctive verbal magic of poetry, 'the sense of musical delight,' as Coleridge called it?

I believe that it comes from the same source—or at least, that only an inner conflict of sufficient intensity can elicit those magical images that contribute the sonorous intensive aspect of poetry. Ariel's Song is a crystal jet from the same imaginative fountain as *Hamlet* or *King Lear*, as *The Tempest* itself, in which the Song has its organic station and function. *The Tempest* is also a great poem about self-assertion and submission, and all its beauties, of expression, unity and intellect, proceed from its unique intensity. Ariel's Song is not an incidental beauty— it too is produced and modified by the predominant passion of the poetic drama. It is, indeed, a crystallization of the theme of the drama—the sea-change that reconciles youth and age, life and death, mortal man and immortal beauty. The words wait in the inchoate recesses of the poet's mind, ready to spring into active discourse whenever the intensity of the internal conflict calls for them.

Poeta nascitur non fit—that Latin tag has been repeated for two millennia as a confession of the defeat we experience if we try to explain the secret sources of poetry. I do not think that any modern philosopher or psychologist would be so rash as to claim that he had solved the age-long mystery. But I think he would claim that the concept of the unconscious, and more particularly the concept of the archetypes, have thrown much light, if not into the sources of poetry, at least on the mechanism of poetic experience, the formative process in the imagination. The psychologist has penetrated some distance into the recesses of the poet's subjectivity and found there, not darkness, but a clever piece of machinery.

The metaphysicians still maintain, of course, that it is not a piece of machinery at all, but is rather what Jacques Maritain calls a wholly mysterious 'divination of the spiritual in the things of sense.'[5]

Some kind of immateriality is, of course, intrinsic to the poetic process. Poetry is consistent only in its shadowiness, its indeterminacy, its intangibility. In writing poetry we have a sense of the inexhaustible depth of our subjectivity; and out of that depth, flowing as spontaneously as water from a spring, comes this sensuous utterance in rhythmic verse. Of course, it is spiritual or psychic, as water is earthy. Spirituality is generated by it, as 'a sudden flash of transcendental feeling,' but not added to it. Poetry creates its own potency, as Coleridge asserts in the poem we have examined:

O pure of heart! thou need'st not ask of me
What this strong music in the soul may be!
What, and wherein it doth exist,
This light, this glory, this fair luminous mist,
This beautiful and beauty-making power.

---

[5] *Creative Intuition in Art and Poetry*, New York and London, 1953, p. 3 *et passim*.

A light, a glory, a fair luminous mist— we cannot find more precise words to describe the experience of poetry. But what we have to insist on, against the theologians on the one side and the psychologists on the other side, is the originality and integrity of the process. There is no discernible reality, spiritual or otherwise, behind the process, no 'definite intellectual actuation' prompting the poetic flow. There is only within the total psyche a state of 'intrinsic indeterminacy.' This is Leone Vivante's phrase, and at this point I seek the support of his deeply sensitive, long considered philosophy. All art has as one of its distinctive features an intrinsic sensuous quality: it is sensuous at the moment of its origination, 'framed with senses of passions and affections,' to recall Vico's phrase. It is a sensuous process within the psyche, and any distinctions of spirit or matter are foreign to its innocent nature. To quote Vivante at some length:

'We cannot understand the importance of this factor, nor its full meaning, nor the possibility of its very existence, except through the conception . . . of a positivity implying indeterminacy, co-extensive with subjectivity, and containing— in embryo, *a parte subjecti*—the whole gamut of our psyche. We cannot, except through this conception, understand the union between sense and meaning nor the aptness of sense to express the highest values. Nor can we understand why, when we enter the realm of sensibility, we enter the realm of God—a world more sensible, richer, truer, less one-sided, at one and the same time more impersonal and more intimately personal, far more favoured by taste, and by grace, and wisdom, than the world of voluntary thought, which is that of external construction, and not of intimate growth.

'Philosophers have generally undervalued sensation, and (a most lamentable, in my opinion, and almost incredible error) they have put the principle of the synthesis outside it. They have considered sensation as entirely passive, a reality without problems and without mysteries. Poets have not followed the same way.

'The fact is that the fundamental problems—and the fundamental realities —of psychic activity are met in sensation no less than in sentiment, no less than in will, no less than in the cognitive activity. I mean, for instance, such problems as the unity, or inner transparency, of the psychic present; the problem of a cause not entirely derived; the reality, or else the illusion, of an actual origin of value (or quality); the degree of reality of mental activity.'[6]

We have to admit that the illumination cast by modern psychology on these 'fundamental problems' of creativity is almost nil. Myth and dream, symbol and image—all the paraphernalia of depth-psychology—are conceived as shadow play, and it is their analysable signification, and not their sensuous actuality, that attract the analyst. The depth-psychologist may claim that therapy is his only concern, and that the sensuous quality of works of art would merely distract him. That is to misunderstand the nature of art, and precisely its most intrinsic values. It is to disregard the unity of the psyche, which is not a unity of concepts, of spirit or intellect, or even of images, but of sensation. Thought in its deepest recesses is a sensuous, formative process: spontaneous, not controlled by any extrinsic will or consciousness. Though the psyche may be impelled to thought by conflict; though it may flow into channels that have been prepared by racial experience, as when the poet inno-

---

[6] Vivante, op. cit., p. 324f. [The reference is to Vivante's *English Poetry and Its Contribution to the Knowledge of a Creative Principle*, London, 1950.—Ed.]

cently repeats a fable or a myth that other poets in remote ages had invented —nevertheless, the thought of the poet is originally sensuous because it has its origins in physical perception and flows along the organs of sensation, and even as it flows, forms into determinate patterns of delight.

The sense of delight is, I think, the sense of illumination, of revelation, what Maritain calls specifically 'the poetic sense,' 'a meaning which is immanent in that object which is a poem or co-substantial with it.' And it follows, says Maritain, that 'the intelligible sense, through which the poet utters ideas, is entirely subordinate to the poetic sense, through which the poem exists.'[7] This poetic sense, which may be clear or obscure, analysable or unanalysable, is a self-sustaining reality, 'which is without comparison vaster and stronger, of a far greater spiritual breadth, than that of the planning will.'[8] The poem is a sensuous unity, a totality of utterance, and meaningful as unity or totality. To break it down into image and idea is to ignore the fact that there are no internal sutures, no possibility of separating image from image, image from idea, or either from the language in which they are expressed.

Do we then end with a mystery, and a veto on psychological attempts to explain it? Not exactly. We end with the reality of being or existence, and the experience of poetry is a proof of its intrinsic originality, of its ceaseless novelty, of its unpredictable form. There is a chain of cause and effect in our practical life, in our intercourse with the external world; but deep within man's subjectivity there is an effect which has no discernible cause, which is a process of discovery, of self-realization, a rending of the numi-

nous veil of consciousness. The immediate object of the poetic experience refuses to be identified: it is infinite and eternal, formless and uninformed. In so far as this poetic experience can be described, Francis Thompson described it in these paradoxical words:

O world invisible, we view thee,
O world intangible, we touch thee.
O world unknowable, we know thee,
Inapprehensible, we clutch thee!

View, touch, clutch—these are sensible modes of knowledge, and what we know by these means can be described only by the one simple but ambiguous word: Truth.

The experience I have been describing was described more eloquently and more subtly sixteen and a half centuries ago by the great Chinese poet, Lu Chi. In conclusion I will quote the last section of his Essay on Literature, the famous poem Wen Fu:

Such moments when Mind and Matter hold perfect communion,
And wide vistas open to regions hitherto entirely barred,
Will come with irresistible force,
And go, their departure none can hinder.
Hiding, they vanish like a flash of light;
Manifest, they are like sounds arising in mid air.

So acute is the mind in such instants of divine comprehension,
What chaos is there that it cannot marshal in miraculous order?
While winged thoughts, like quick breezes, soar from depths of heart,
Eloquent words, like a gushing spring, flow between lips and teeth.
No flower, or plant, or animal is too prodigal of splendour
To be recreated under the writer's pen.
Hence the most wondrous spectacle that ever whelmed the eye,
And notes of the loftiest music that rejoiced the ear!

---

[7] Maritain, op. cit., pp. 258–259.
[8] Vivante, op. cit., p. 328.

But there are other moments as though
the Six Senses were stranded,
When the heart seems lost, and the spirit
stagnant.
One stays motionless like a petrified log,
Dried up like an exhausted river bed.
The soul is indrawn to search the hidden
labyrinth;
Within oneself is sought where inner light
may be stored.

Behind a trembling veil Truth seems to
shimmer, yet ever more evasive,
And thought twists and twirls like silk
spun on a clogged wheel.
Therefore, all one's vital force may be dis-
persed in rueful failure;

Yet again, a free play of impulses may
achieve a feat without pitfall.
While the secret may be held within oneself,
It is none the less beyond one's power to
sway.
Oft I lay my hand on my empty chest,
Despairing to know how the barrier could
be removed.[9]

---

[9] Trans. by Shih-Hsiang Chen, The Antho-
ensen Press, Portland, Maine, 1952. A more
accessible translation (which, however, has
been drastically criticized) accompanied by a
full and interesting commentary, is given by
E. R. Hughes in *The Art of Letters*, Bollingen
Series, New York, 1951.

Georges Poulet

MOLIÈRE

Georges Poulet, a critic who has risen to eminence in France, is best known here through the translations of his books *Studies in Human Time* (1950, translated 1956) and *The Interior Distance* (1952, translated 1959). His most recent works are *Les Metamorphoses du Cercle* (1961), *L'espace Proustien* (1963), and *Le Point de Départ* (1964). Poulet teaches at the University of Zurich. His critical approach, a fusion of the philosophical and the psychological, has no exact counterpart in England and America. "Molière" is taken from *Studies in Human Time*.

"I find," says Molière, "that it is much easier to speak loftily of high feelings, to defy fate in verse, to reproach destiny and abuse the gods, than it is to enter properly into the ridicule of men. . . . It is a strange enterprise, that of making honest men laugh."[1] An enterprise strangely difficult, in fact, for the precise reason Molière gives us; for if, in tragedy, it is easier to speak loftily of high feelings, that is because such feelings are at one and the same time expressed and experienced. There is no separation between the author and his character; not even between the character and the spectator. When the hero "defies fate," his mood and his audacity are ours. There is established a kind of subjective identity which makes of the author, the character, and the public one single feeling being. The tragic moment is easy of achievement because it is a moment lived by a unique

person who expressly manifests what everyone feels.

All else is the comic moment. The difficulty which that implies is that it is not "given" to enter directly into the person of the character. Far from entering into his being, it is a matter of "entering into ridicule of him." And to enter upon ridicule is precisely the contrary of entering into a being; it is to withdraw from him: it is to put the person in the position of an object one sees, and not a being with whom one feels. It is to pose an object, instead of *being* a subject.

The "strange enterprise" which permits the creation of a comic moment is thus the very opposite of the unitive consciousness which forms the tragic moment. It has for its province the consciousness of a disunion between the author and his public, on one side, and the character in the play, on the other. On the one side, *us*; on the other, *him*. And whatever the

---

[1] *Critique de l'Ecole des Femmes.*

feelings of this *him*, they succeed in touching only our external senses and presenting manifestations of a person with whom it is impossible for us to identify ourselves, but with whom it is necessary to confront ourselves. The comic character is the triple object of our attention, our judgment, and our feeling.

II

And first of all it is the object before our senses. As such, it is only what it appears to be. It is a face, a voice, some gestures. It is its actions and nothing more. That is what Molière himself declares:

Let not anyone tell me that all the feelings which I attribute to men . . . are not felt as I describe them; for it is only in the occasion itself that it seems as if one has them or not; and not even then does anyone discover that he has them; it is just that one's actions make us suppose necessarily that one has them.[2]

These are words which can have been written only by someone who from instinct puts himself in the very situation in which the comic genius must put himself. It is not permissible in this situation to *feel oneself* experiencing the feelings of the character; one can only *attribute* them to him; and what is more, one can only attribute them to him on the *occasions* when he seems to have them; and their existence is perceived only because the character *acts* in such a way as to make one necessarily suppose that he has such feelings.

Thus the starting point of the comic art of Molière is situated in the *occasion*,

---

[2] In the *Lettre sur la comédie de l'Imposteur*. It is one of the most remarkable theoretical and critical essays of the seventeenth century; and if it was not written by Molière himself, it must have been written by someone of his circle, by dictation, or under his immediate inspiration. There is no document that better illuminates Molière's thought.

in which a being is comprehended only through his actions.

And, in fact, did not the theater of Molière begin by being exactly that, and nothing more than that? A comedy of actions and gestures which did not "imply" anything else: the *Médecin volant*; the *Jalousie du Barbouillé?*

But this starting point is only a point without duration. A deed, a gesture, is still not a complete action, it is not a thing that endures, it is an instantaneous manifestation. In the comic art of Molière there is first of all the actual presence of a certain demeanor which is immediately clear to the spectator.

But in the instant in which the demeanor of the object is understood by the spectator, the latter grants to the object the particular being which the object's demeanor makes the spectator necessarily suppose it possesses. He no longer sees only the object under the sensible appearance of its deeds, but as a being distinct from himself, which consequently requires a judgment on the part of his reason, and which provokes a reaction on the part of his sensibility.

III

Every object, every being distinct from us, is judged by us. And this judgment, says Molière, is a judgment of conformity. Our "essential reason" decides whether, in the moment in which it performs its deed, the performer fails to conform himself to the rules and order connected with a truth, which has a permanent value. Thus the judgment of reason implies a curious transfiguration of the object; for if, on the one hand, its nonconformity is situated in the instant in which it arises, on the other hand it is a nonconformity only in connection with what transcends all instants. From the point of view of the eternal reason, the instantaneous manifestation of an eternal nonconformity is itself eternal. It is *sub specie aeternitatis.* What is unreasonable is eternally unreasonable.

But with the judgment of reason there is associated another judgment which is at bottom that of our sensibility. Because, says Molière:

although Nature made us capable of knowing reason by following it, still, well aware that if there were not some visible mark attached to it which would render this knowledge easy, our frailty and our indolence would deprive us of the effect of so rare an advantage, she wished to give to reason some sort of exterior form recognizable from without. . . . Ridicule is the external and visible form which Providence has attached to all that is unreasonable. . . .[3]

This form is a "cause of joy," a "matter of pleasure." It is basically the immediate reaction of our being as we confront the deed which falls immediately under our senses. The instant it is perceived by our "essential reason" as incompatible with eternal principles, it is immediately felt by our "apparent reason" to be contrary to propriety. What is perceived as ridiculous is that which is perceived as an incongruous hiatus in the uninterrupted line of our customary experience. We say to ourselves: we are not accustomed to seeing gentlemen act like this.

This ridicule is the immediate perception of a sudden perturbation in the order of human duration. And, seen from this angle, it is no longer a permanent thing depending upon abstract reason alone. It presents itself in duration and appears there under the form of a moment which breaks up this duration. Ridicule is a moment of rupture.

IV

But rupture in the object, not in ourselves. It is because of this that the moment of rupture in Molière is so different from the moment of rupture in Corneille. Indeed, in Corneille the action by which the hero breaks with antecedent duration is a deed in which we adhere; it is an act of the will, a tragic act, to which we give consent. In Molière, on the contrary, the action by which the character is dissociated from the continuous duration of good usage is a deed by which he forces us simultaneously to dissociate ourselves from him. The instant he breaks with the order of things, we re-associate ourselves more closely with it. Thus the action of the character becomes absolutely isolated and, by consequence, inoffensive. It is a perturbation in the order which does not menace the order. The discontinuity it creates is localized in the single object which causes it. It is as if in following a well-defined path one saw someone stumble in it. Hence the simultaneous existence of two kinds of duration for the mind: the duration of the order in which one participates and which lasts; and the instant of disorder which is limited to the object and which interrupts time.

Thus the comic is the perception of an ephemeral and local fracture in the middle of a durable and normal world.

Let us imagine a seducer who one day is suddenly made to seem ridiculous: "These *first instants,*" says Molière, "are of important consideration in these matters; they produce almost the same effect as a long duration, because they always *break* the chain of passion and the course of the imagination, which ought to hold the soul attached, from beginning to end, to an amorous venture, in order for it to be successful. . . ."[4] But, in a certain sense, any relationship of a character to ourselves is a venture in seduction; any character, by the sole fact of his presence,

[3] *Lettre sur l'Imposteur.*

[4] Ibid.

tries to catch our sympathy. This is the case with the philosophy teacher when he praises moderation, or with Chrysale when he pretends to assert his authority. But when immediately afterward, in one of those "first instants which almost have the effect of a long duration," Chrysale yields before Philaminte, and the philosophy teacher to the impulse of anger, so in this precise moment the chain of our adherence finds itself broken. Our feeling is reversed. Suddenly we no longer feel *with* the character; we feel *against* him.

But we *feel* all the same. If ridicule is indeed, as Molière says, the coldest of all our feelings, it is none the less authentically a feeling. It is at once judgment and feeling. That is why Molière declares in the *Critique* that "the best way to judge is to abandon oneself to things." "Let us not consider in a comedy," he says, "what effect it is having on us. Let us abandon ourselves in good faith to the things that seize us by the entrails. . . ." And again: "When I see a comedy, I look only to see if things touch me."

But to abandon oneself to things, to let oneself be touched by them, is to react instantaneously in the order of sensibility. The comic genius operates, then, directly on the moment. Like the painter of frescoes, he knows his matter is "pressing" and wishes ". . . without compliance/That a painter come to terms with his impatience,/Treat it in his own way, and *with a sudden stroke/Seize the moment* it gives into his hand."

The comic spirit is a seizure of the instantaneous.

But then the question arises, the same question as for the theater of Corneille: how shall we make a comedy out of the comic instant? How shall we prolong our laughter? How shall we give a temporal value to a character whom our rational judgment has assigned to a kind of nega-

tive eternity, and who "touches" our judgment of sensibility only in the lightning flash of the instant?

There are two Molierean universes: the one of customs; the other of passions. The first is a durable universe. It is the universe of persons of good sense, of spectators, of gentlemen. A sort of connivance unites them and situates them in a constant duration which is not at all on trial and which is not at all in peril.

But there is another universe, that of the passions, which in itself is not less tragic in Molière than in Racine. It is a universe in which one is in incessant tension, in ceaseless agitation, in a perpetual renewing of the same desires. Such a mental universe inevitably recalls the conception of life held by the master of Molière, Gassendi. For him, in reality, nothing is more radically temporal than the life of the soul. Like the life of the body, to which it clings up to the point of becoming indistinguishable from it, like time itself, the life of the soul is "a flame which perpetually renews its form." Our imagination, our sensibility, our organism, exist and function only by virtue of a general effort of the whole being, an incessant effort which above all is a labor of substitution and equivalence. Compound perpetually changing, whose parts replace themselves, the human being feels this same rhythm of reproduction repeat itself in the generation and regeneration of the passions: "There ensues afresh in the component parts a new imagination, then a new motion, and thus always more and more."[5] And so passion can be described as "a hunger which returns, and from moment to moment is resumed anew."

There is the same rhythm of passion in

---

[5] Bernier, *Abrégé de la philosophie de Gassendi*, VI, 387.

Molière. A perpetual reincarnation of the hungry desire, the generation in a closed cycle of passion triumphant and passion frustrated—such is the essentially repetitive process by which Molière's characters continually manifest themselves in duration. For him, too, the life of the soul is a flame which perpetually renews its form. A precarious, spasmodic duration, always under the menace of an instantaneous explosion; a duration essentially tragic.

VI

But we do not experience this tragedy ourselves; we simply look at it from the outside; and in so doing, we make it undergo a transformation so radical that it renders the character unrecognizable. The continual generation of passion no longer seems to us like an interior drama experienced by a subject who suffers, but more like the comportment of an object which repeatedly strikes our attention and which, precisely by the force of this repetition, imprints its essential characteristics more clearly upon our mind. Thus, repetitive duration little by little takes on an exemplary value. Each new manifestation of the same passion becomes a new example of the same passion. By the repetition, the character is little by little dehumanized in our eyes; he becomes typical. For Molière does not take type as a starting point; he does not adopt the "realist" conception of an abstract being in more or less concrete finery. No, he comes to give his characters the value of types by the constant repetition of essential traits. The character becomes generalized as the play advances, by reason of the fact that, incessantly returning to strike our attention, the same traits are finally found to be retained at the expense of secondary traits; as if from an infinity of misers, one extracted little by little the idea of the exemplary miser, the paragon who represents them all.

An essentially nominalistic process, by which again Molière relates himself to Gassendi.

From this point of view there is no temporal movement in the plays of Molière. It is the same repetitive duration as in the drama of passion from which it eliminates the tragic. But in eliminating the tragic it eliminates movement also. It becomes a mere static repetition in which there is progress only in the pattern of the character and in the estimate we form of him. An historical progress, which has a place only in the order of knowledge, of abstraction even. In proportion as the character becomes more typical, he passes little by little from the actual to the absolute. He becomes the eternal example of an eternal unreasonableness.

Thus, if the resemblance, if the perceptible repetition were not there to reawaken within us in each instant the feeling of ridicule which those so decisive "first instants" had brought to birth there, the character would become completely detached from all temporality and all reality and would run the risk of falling into a schematic intemporality. There exists in this regard a veritably Proustian text of Molière's which marvelously lights up the subtle play of the "intermittences" of ridicule and of the "irregular progresses" of the comic. In the *Lettre de l'Imposteur*, speaking of Panulphe, that is to say of Tartuffe, he says this:

The excessive ridicule of the manners of Panulphe makes it certain that every time they are presented to the spectator on some other occasion they will assuredly seem to him ridiculous. . . . The soul, naturally avid of joy, will necessarily be delighted at the first sight of things that it once conceived as extremely ridiculous, and *will renew in itself the idea of the very lively pleasure it tasted that first time.*

Thus each time we notice a new comic manifestation of character, "we shall be first of all struck by the memory of that first time," and this memory, mingling itself with the present occasion, will "fuse the two occasions into one."

Thus to the objective repetition of the course of passion there is joined the subjective repetition of the feeling it provokes in us. The character repeats himself, and we begin to laugh again, and in beginning to laugh again we accord to him once more the freshness of actuality. The comic art of Molière is eternal in two ways: first in the manifestation of a reason, which makes an eternally valid judgment upon human deportment; and then in that of the sensibility, which never ceases to make us feel this deportment eternally present and living.

Leslie A. Fiedler

THE NOVEL AND AMERICA

Leslie A. Fiedler is among the boldest and most stimulating of contemporary American critics. Although his approach combines elements of the sociocultural, the mythopoeic, and the psychological, he is most consistently and fundamentally a psychological critic. "The Novel and America" is the opening chapter in Fiedler's most ambitious book, *Love and Death in the American Novel* (1960). Fiedler is Professor of English at the State University of New York at Buffalo. He has also written notable fiction, including two recent novels *The Second Stone* (1963) and *Back to China* (1965).

Between the novel and America there are peculiar and intimate connections. A new literary form and a new society, their beginnings coincide with the beginnings of the modern era and, indeed, help to define it. We are living not only in the Age of America but also in the Age of the Novel, at a moment when the literature of a country without a first-rate verse epic or a memorable verse tragedy has become the model of half the world. *The Age of the American Novel*, a French critic calls a book on contemporary writing; and everywhere in the West there are authors who quite deliberately turn from their own fictional traditions to pursue ours— or at least something they take for ours.

We have known for a long time, of course, that our national literary reputation depends largely upon the achievement of our novelists. The classical poetic genres revived by the Renaissance had lost their relevance to contemporary life be-fore America entered the cultural scene; and even the lyric has provided us with occasions for few, and limited, triumphs. Whitman, Poe, and Dickinson—beyond these three, there are no major American poets before the twentieth century; and even about their merits we continue to wrangle. It is Melville and Hawthorne and James (together with such latter-day figures as Faulkner and Hemingway) who possess the imagination of a Europe already committed to the novel as the pre-vailing modern form. Not only in the United States, though pre-eminently there, literature has become for most readers quite simply prose fiction; and our endemic fantasy of writing "the Great American Novel" is only a local instance of a more general obsession. The notions of greatness once associated with the heroic poem have been transferred to the novel; and the shift is a part of that "Americanization of culture" which some

299

European intellectuals continue ritually to deplore.

But is there, as certain continental critics have insisted, an "American novel," a specific sub-variety of the form? If we turn to these critics for a definition, we come on such terms as "neo-realist," "hard-boiled," "naive," and "anti-traditional"—terms derived from a standard view of America as an "anti-culture," an eternally maintained preserve of primitivism. This view (notoriously exemplified by André Gide) ends by finding in Dashiell Hammett the same values as in William Faulkner, and is more a symptom of European cultural malaise than a useful critical distinction. While America is, in a very real sense, a constantly recreated fact of the European imagination, it is not only, or even pre-eminently, that. It is tempting to insist on the pat rebuttal that, far from being an anti-culture, we are merely a branch of Western culture; and that there is no "American novel," only local variants of standard European kinds of fiction: American sentimental, American gothic, American historical romance, etc. Certainly no single sub-genre of the novel was invented in the United States. Yet the peculiarities of our variants seem more interesting and important than their resemblances to the parent forms.

There is a real sense in which our prose fiction is immediately distinguishable from that of Europe, though this is a fact that is difficult for Americans (oddly defensive and flustered in its presence) to confess. In this sense, our novels seem not primitive, perhaps, but innocent, unfallen in a disturbing way, almost juvenile. The great works of American fiction are notoriously at home in the children's section of the library, their level of sentimentality precisely that of a pre-adolescent. This is part of what we mean when we talk about the incapacity of the American novelist to

develop; in a compulsive way he returns to a limited world of experience, usually associated with his childhood, writing the same book over and over again until he lapses into silence or self-parody.

Merely finding a language, learning to talk in a land where there are no conventions of conversation, no special class idioms and no dialogue between classes, no continuing literary language—this exhausts the American writer. He is forever *beginning*, saying for the first time (without real tradition there can never be a second time) what it is like to stand alone before nature, or in a city as appallingly lonely as any virgin forest. He faces, moreover, another problem, which has resulted in a failure of feeling and imagination perceptible at the heart of even our most notable works. Our great novelists, though experts on indignity and assault, on loneliness and terror, tend to avoid treating the passionate encounter of a man and woman, which we expect at the center of a novel. Indeed, they rather shy away from permitting in their fictions the presence of any full-fledged, mature women, giving us instead monsters of virtue or bitchery, symbols of the rejection or fear of sexuality.

To be sure, the theme of "love" in so simple a sense is by no means necessary to all works of art. In the *Iliad*, for instance, and in much Greek tragedy, it is conspicuously absent; and in the heroic literature of the Middle Ages, it is peripheral where it exists at all. The *"belle Aude"* of the *Chanson de Roland* is a supernumerary, and the only female we remember from *Beowulf* is a terror emerging from the darkness at the bottom of the waters. The world of the epic is a world of war, and its reigning sentimental relationship is the loyalty of comrades in arms; but by the eighteenth century the notion of a heroic poem without romance had come to seem intolerable. The last pseudo-epics of the baroque had been obsessed with the subject of love, and the rococo had continued to elaborate that theme. Shakespeare himself appeared to the English Augustans too little concerned with the "reigning passion" to be quite interesting without revision. Why, after all, should Cordelia not survive to marry Edgar, they demanded of themselves—and they rewrote *King Lear* to prove that she should.

The novel, however, was precisely the product of the sentimentalizing taste of the eighteenth century; and a continuing tradition of prose fiction did not begin until the love affair of Lovelace and Clarissa (a demythicized Don Juan and a secularized goddess of Christian love) had been imagined. The subject par excellence of the novel is love or, more precisely—in its beginnings at least—seduction and marriage; and in France, Italy, Germany, and Russia, even in England, spiritually so close to America, love in one form or another has remained the novel's central theme, as necessary and as expected as battle in Homer or revenge in the Renaissance drama. When the Romantic impulse led in Germany to a technical recasting of the novel form, even the wildest experimentalists did not desert this traditional theme; Schiller's *Lucille* is a dialogue on freedom and restraint in passion. But our great Romantic *Unroman*, our typical anti-novel, is the womanless *Moby Dick*.

Where is our *Madame Bovary*, our *Anna Karenina*, our *Pride and Prejudice* or *Vanity Fair*? Among our classic novels, at least those before Henry James, who stands so oddly between our own traditions and the European ones we rejected or recast, the best attempt at dealing with love is *The Scarlet Letter*, in which the physical consummation of adultery has occurred and all passion burned away before the novel proper begins. Our

Madame Bovary is a novel about adultery with the adultery off-stage; and the child who is its product is so elfin and ethereal that it is hard to believe her engendered in the usual way. For the rest, there are *Moby Dick* and *Huckleberry Finn*, *The Last of the Mohicans*, *The Red Badge of Courage*, the stories of Edgar Allan Poe—books that turn from society to nature or nightmare out of a desperate need to avoid the facts of wooing, marriage, and child-bearing.

The figure of Rip Van Winkle presides over the birth of the American imagination; and it is fitting that our first successful home-grown legend should memorialize, however playfully, the flight of the dreamer from the shrew—into the mountains and out of time, away from the drab duties of home and town toward the good companions and the magic keg of beer. Ever since, the typical male protagonist of our fiction has been a man on the run, harried into the forest and out to sea, down the river or into combat—anywhere to avoid "civilization," which is to say, the confrontation of a man and woman which leads to the fall, to sex, marriage, and responsibility. One of the factors that determine theme and form in our great books is this strategy of evasion, this retreat to nature and childhood which makes our literature (and life!) so charmingly and infuriatingly "boyish."

The child's world is not only asexual, it is terrible: a world of fear and loneliness, a haunted world; and the American novel is pre-eminently a novel of terror. To "light out for the territory" or seek refuge in the forest seems easy and tempting from the vantage point of a chafing and restrictive home; but civilization once disavowed and Christianity disowned, the bulwark of woman left behind, the wanderer feels himself without protection, more motherless child than free man. To be sure, there is a substitute for wife or mother presumably waiting in the green heart of nature: the natural man, the good companion, pagan and unashamed —Queequeg or Chingachgook or Nigger Jim. But the figure of the natural man is ambiguous, a dream and a nightmare at once. The other face of Chingachgook is Injun Joe, the killer in the graveyard and the haunter of caves; Nigger Jim is also the Babo of Melville's "Benito Cereno," the humble servant whose name means "papa" holding the razor to his master's throat; and finally the dark-skinned companion becomes the "Black Man," which is a traditional American name for the Devil himself.

The enemy of society on the run toward "freedom" is also the pariah in flight from his guilt, the guilt of that very flight; and new phantoms arise to haunt him at every step. American literature likes to pretend, of course, that its bugaboos are all finally jokes: the headless horseman a hoax, every manifestation of the supernatural capable of rational explanation on the last page—but we are never quite convinced. *Huckleberry Finn*, that euphoric boys' book, begins with its protagonist holding off at gun point his father driven half mad by the D.T.'s and ends (after a lynching, a disinterment, and a series of violent deaths relieved by such humorous incidents as soaking a dog in kerosene and setting him on fire) with the revelation of that father's sordid death. Nothing is spared; Pap, horrible enough in life, is found murdered brutally, abandoned to float down the river in a decaying house scrawled with obscenities. But it is all "humor," of course, a last desperate attempt to convince us of the innocence of violence, the good clean fun of horror. Our literature as a whole at times seems a chamber of horrors disguised as an amusement park "fun house," where we pay to play at terror and are confronted in the innermost chamber with a series of inter-reflecting mirrors which present us with a thousand versions of our own face.

In our most enduring books, the cheapjack machinery of the gothic novel is called on to represent the hidden blackness of the human soul and human society. No wonder our authors mock themselves as they use such devices; no wonder Mistress Hibbins in *The Scarlet Letter* and Fedallah in *Moby Dick* are treated half jocularly, half melodramatically, though each represents in his book the Faustian pact, the bargain with the Devil, which our authors have always felt as the essence of the American experience. However shoddily or ironically treated, horror is essential to our literature. It is not merely a matter of terror filling the vacuum left by the suppression of sex in our novels, of Thanatos standing in for Eros. Through these gothic images are projected certain obsessive concerns of our national life: the ambiguity of our relationship with Indian and Negro, the ambiguity of our encounter with nature, the guilt of the revolutionist who feels himself a parricide—and, not least of all, the uneasiness of the writer who cannot help believing that the very act of composing a book is Satanic revolt. "Hellfired," Hawthorne called *The Scarlet Letter*, and Melville thought his own *Moby Dick* a "wicked book."

The American writer inhabits a country at once the dream of Europe and a fact of history; he lives on the last horizon of an endlessly retreating vision of innocence —on the "frontier," which is to say, the margin where the theory of original goodness and the fact of original sin come face to face. To express this "blackness ten times black" and to live by it in a society in which, since the decline of orthodox Puritanism, optimism has become the chief effective religion, is a complex and difficult task.

It was to the novel that the American writer turned most naturally, as the only *popular* form of sufficient magnitude for his vision. He was, perhaps, not sufficiently sophisticated to realize that such learned forms as epic and tragedy had already outlived their usefulness; but, working out of a cultural background at best sketchy and unsure, he felt insecure before them. His obligations urged him in the direction of tragedy, but traditional verse tragedy was forbidden him; indeed, a chief technical problem for American novelists has been the adaptation of nontragic forms to tragic ends. How could the dark vision of the American—his obsession with violence and his embarrassment before love—be expressed in the sentimental novel of analysis as developed by Samuel Richardson or the historical romance as practiced by Sir Walter Scott? These sub-genres of fiction, invented to satisfy the emotional needs of a merchant class in search of dignity or a Tory squirearchy consumed by nostalgia, could only by the most desperate expedients be tailored to fit American necessities. Throughout their writing lives, such writers as Charles Brockden Brown and James Fenimore Cooper devoted (with varying degrees of self-consciousness) all their ingenuity to this task, yet neither Brown nor Cooper finally proved capable of achieving high art; and the literary types invented by both have fallen since into the hands of mere entertainers—that is, novelists able and willing to attempt anything *except* the projection of the dark vision of America we have been describing. The Fielding novel, on the other hand, the pseudo-Shakespearean "comic epic" with its broad canvas, its emphasis upon reversals and recognitions, and its robust masculine sentimentality, turned out, oddly enough, to have no relevance to the American scene; in the United States it

has remained an exotic, eternally being discovered by the widest audience and raised to best-sellerdom in its latest imported form, but seldom home-produced for home consumption.

It is the gothic form that has been most fruitful in the hands of our best writers: the gothic *symbolically* understood, its machinery and décor translated into metaphors for a terror psychological, social, and metaphysical. Yet even treated as symbols, the machinery and décor of the gothic have continued to seem vulgar and contrived; symbolic gothicism threatens always to dissolve into its components, abstract morality and shoddy theater. A recurrent problem of our fiction has been the need of our novelists to find a mode of projecting their conflicts which would contain all the dusky horror of gothic romance and yet be palatable to discriminating readers, palatable first of all to themselves.

Such a mode can, of course, not be subsumed among any of those called "realism," and one of the chief confusions in our understanding of our own literature has arisen from our failure to recognize this fact clearly enough. Our fiction is essentially and at its best nonrealistic, even anti-realistic; long before *symbolisme* had been invented in France and exported to America, there was a full-fledged native tradition of symbolism. That tradition was born of the profound contradictions of our national life and sustained by the inheritance from Puritanism of a "typical" (even allegorical) way of regarding the sensible world—not as an ultimate reality but as a system of signs to be deciphered. For too long, historians of American fiction have mistakenly tried to impose on the course of a brief literary history a notion of artistic "progress" imported from France or, more precisely perhaps, from certain French literary critics. Such historians have been pleased to speak of "The Rise of Realism" or "The Triumph of Realism," as if the experiments of Hawthorne or Poe or Melville were half-misguided fumblings toward the final excellence of William Dean Howells!

But the moment at which Flaubert was dreaming *Madame Bovary* was the moment when Melville was finding *Moby Dick,* and considered as a "realistic" novel the latter is a scandalous botch. To speak of a counter-tradition to the novel, of the tradition of "the romance" as a force in our literature, is merely to repeat the rationalizations of our writers themselves; it is certainly to fail to be *specific* enough for real understanding. Our fiction is not merely in flight from the physical data of the actual world, in search of a (sexless and dim) Ideal; from Charles Brockden Brown to William Faulkner or Eudora Welty, Paul Bowles or John Hawkes, it is, bewilderingly and embarrassingly, a gothic fiction, nonrealistic and negative, sadist and melodramatic—a literature of darkness and the grotesque in a land of light and affirmation.

Moreover—and the final paradox is necessary to the full complexity of the case—ours is a literature of horror for boys. Truly shocking, frankly obscene authors we do not possess; Edgar Allan Poe is our closest approximation, a child playing at what Baudelaire was to live. A Baudelaire, a Marquis de Sade, a "Monk" Lewis, even a John Cleland is inconceivable in the United States. Our flowers of evil are culled for the small girl's bouquet, our novels of terror (*Moby Dick, The Scarlet Letter, Huckleberry Finn,* the tales of Poe) are placed on the approved book lists of Parents' Committees who nervously fuss over the latest comic books. If such censors do not flinch at necrophilia or shudder over the book whose secret motto is "I baptise you not in the name of the Father . . . but of the Devil," or fear the juvenile whose hero

at his greatest moment cries out, "All right, I'll *go* to Hell," it is only another irony of life in a land where the writers believe in hell and the official guardians of morality do not. As long as there's no *sex!*

Yet our authors are as responsible as the P.T.A.'s for the confusion about the true nature of their books; though they may have whispered their secret to friends, or confessed it in private letters, in their actual works they assumed what camouflage prudence dictated. They *wanted* to be misunderstood. *Huckleberry Finn* is only the supreme instance of a subterfuge typical of our classic novelists. To this very day, it is heresy in some quarters to insist that this is not finally the jolliest, the *cleanest* of books; Twain's ironical warning to significance hunters, posted just before the title page, is taken quite literally, and the irreverent critic who explicates the book's levels of terror and evasion is regarded as a busybody and scandal-monger. It is at last hard to say which is more remarkable, the eccentricity of American books or our critics' conspiracy of silence in this regard. (Or is it the critics' *unawareness* of the fact?) Why, one is driven to ask, why the distortion and why the ignorance? But the critics, after all, are children of the same culture as the novelists they discuss; and if we answer one question we will have answered both.

Perhaps the whole odd shape of American fiction arises simply (as simplifying Europeans are always ready to assure us) because there is no real sexuality in American life and therefore there cannot very well be any in American art. What we cannot achieve in our relations with each other it would be vain to ask our writers to portray or even our critics to miss. Certainly many of our novelists have themselves believed, or pretended to believe, this. Through *The Scarlet Letter,* there is a constant mournful undercurrent, a series of asides in which Hawthorne deplores the sexual diminution of American women. Mark Twain in *1601* somewhat similarly contrasts the vigor of Elizabethan Englishwomen with their American descendants; contrasting the sexual utopia of pre-colonial England with a fallen America where the men copulate "but once in seven yeeres"; and his pornographic sketch, written to amuse a clergyman friend (for men only!), ends on the comic-pathetic image of an old man's impotent lust that "would not stand again." Such pseudo-nostalgia cannot be taken too seriously, however; it may, indeed, be the projection of mere personal weakness and fantasy. Certainly, outside their books, Hawthorne and Twain seem to have fled rather than sought the imaginary full-breasted, fully sexed woman from whom American ladies had presumably declined. Both married, late in life, pale hypochondriac spinsters, intellectual invalids—as if to assert publicly that they sought in marriage not sex but culture!

Such considerations leave us trapped in the chicken-egg dilemma. How can one say whether the quality of passion in American life suffers because of a failure of the writer's imagination or vice versa? What is called "love" in literature is a rationalization, a way of coming to terms with the relationship between man and woman that does justice, on the one hand, to certain biological drives and, on the other, to certain generally accepted conventions of tenderness and courtesy; and literature, expressing and defining those conventions, tends to influence "real life" more than such life influences it. For better or for worse and for whatever reasons, the American novel is different from its European prototypes, and one of its essential differences arises from its chary treatment of woman and of sex.

To write, then, about the American novel is to write about the fate of certain European genres in a world of alien experience. It is not only a world where courtship and marriage have suffered a profound change, but also one in the process of losing the traditional distinctions of class; a world without a significant history or a substantial past; a world which had left behind the terror of Europe not for the innocence it dreamed of, but for new and special guilts associated with the rape of nature and the exploitation of dark-skinned people; a world doomed to play out the imaginary childhood of Europe. The American novel is only *finally* American; its appearance is an event in the history of the European spirit—as, indeed, is the very invention of America itself.

II

Though it is necessary, in understanding the fate of the American novel, to understand what European prototypes were available when American literature began, as well as which ones flourished and which ones disappeared on our soil, it is even more important to understand the meaning of that moment in the mid-eighteenth century which gave birth to Jeffersonian democracy and Richardsonian sentimentality alike: to the myth of revolution and the myth of seduction. When Charles Brockden Brown, the first professional American author, sent a copy of his *Wieland* to Thomas Jefferson in 1798, he must, beneath his modest disclaimers, have had some sense of his and the President's kinship as revolutionaries. "I am therefore obliged to hope," Brown wrote, "that . . . the train of eloquent and judicious reasoning . . . will be regarded by Thomas Jefferson with as much respect as . . . me." But if Jefferson ever found the time to read Brown's novel, he left no record; we know only that he expressed general approval of "works of the imagination" as being able, more than history, to "possess virtue in the best and

306 The Psychological Critic

vice in the worst forms possible." It is a chillingly rational approach to art and a perhaps sufficient indication of the hopelessness of Brown's attempting in those sensible years to live by his writing.

Yet despite the fact that no professional novelist of real seriousness was to find a supporting public in America for twenty-five or thirty years more, Brown's instincts had not deceived him. He and Jefferson *were* engaged in a common enterprise; the novel and America did not come into existence at the same time by accident. They are the two great inventions of the bourgeois, Protestant mind at the moment when it stood, on the one hand, between Rationalism and Sentimentalism, and on the other, between the drive for economic power and the need for cultural autonomy. The series of events which includes the American and the French Revolutions, the invention of the novel, the rise of modern psychology, and the triumph of the lyric in poetry, adds up to a psychic revolution as well as a social one—perhaps first of all to a psychic revolution. This revolution, viewed as an overturning of ideas and artistic forms, has traditionally been called "Romantic"; but the term is paralyzingly narrow, defining too little too precisely, and leading to further pointless distinctions between Romanticism proper, pre-Romanticism, *Stürm und Drang*, Sentimentalism, *Symbolisme*, etc. It seems preferable to call the whole continuing, complex event simply "the Breakthrough," thus emphasizing the dramatic entry of a new voice into the dialogue of Western man with his various selves.

The Break-through is characterized not only by the separation of psychology from philosophy, the displacement of the traditional leading genres by the personal lyric and analytic prose fiction (with the consequent subordination of plot to character); it is also marked by the promulga-

tion of a theory of revolution as a good in itself and, most notably perhaps, by a new concept of inwardness. One is almost tempted to say, by the invention of a new kind of self, a new level of mind; for what has been happening since the eighteenth century seems more like the development of a new organ than the mere finding of a new way to describe old experience. The triumph, for instance, of the theory that insanity is not possession by forces outside the psyche but a failure within the psyche itself is a representative aspect of the change-over.

It was Diderot who represented a first real awareness (as Freud represents a final one) that man is *double* to the final depths of his soul, the prey of conflicting psyches both equally himself. The conflict had, of course, always been felt, but had traditionally been described as occurring between man and devil, or flesh and spirit; that the parties to the dispute are both man and spirit was a revolutionary suggestion. In his demi-novel, *Rameau's Nephew*, Diderot projected the conflicting divisions within man's mind as the philosopher and the parasite, the rationalist and the underground man, debating endlessly the cause of the head versus that of the gut. And in his pornographic *Bijoux Indiscrets*, he proposed another version of the same dialogue: the enchanted (and indiscreet) genitals speak the truth which the mouth will not avow, thus comprising an allegorical defense of pornography in the guise of a pornographic work. In the same year in which Richardson's sentimental novel *Clarissa* was published, John Cleland's long-lived dirty book *The Memoirs of Fanny Hill* was making a stir. Pornography and obscenity are, indeed, hallmarks of the age of the Break-through. Not only pious novels but titillating ones show the emergence of the underground emotions (of what the period itself euphemistically called "the heart") into high culture. Quite as influential as Diderot (or Richardson or Rousseau) in the *bouleversement* of the eighteenth century is the Marquis de Sade, who stands almost emblematically at the crossroads of depth psychology and revolution.

Not only did de Sade shed new light on the ambivalence of the inner mind, revealing the true darkness and terror implicit in the drive which the neo-classical age (revolting against Christian notions of sin) had been content to celebrate as simple "pleasure" or polite "gallantry"; he may even have caused that symbolic storming of an almost empty prison with which the French Revolution begins. Himself a prisoner in the *Tour de la liberté* of the Bastille, de Sade, through an improvised loudspeaker made of a tube and funnel, screamed to bystanders to rescue his fellow inmates who were having their throats cut—and scattered handwritten leaflets complaining about jail conditions to the crowd he attracted. On July 3, 1789, he was finally transferred elsewhere to insure "the safety of the building," but not before he had started to write *Justine, or the Misfortunes of Virtue*, that perverse offshoot of the Richardsonian novel, and had thus begun to create the first example of revolutionary pornography. Maurice Blanchot, in an essay called *Lautréamont et Sade*, describes his method as follows: "What is striking is this: the language of de Sade is precisely opposite to the cheating language of hangmen; it is the language of the victim; he invented it in the Bastille. . . . He put on trial, reversing the process of his own judgment, the men who condemned him, God himself, and—in general—every limitation against which his frenzy clashed. . . ."

In the Marquis de Sade, the Breakthrough found its most stringent and spectacular spokesman: the condemned man judging his judges, the pervert mocking the normal, the advocate of destruction and death sneering at the defenders of love and life; but his *reductio* follows logically enough from assumptions shared by Jefferson and Rousseau, Richardson and Saint-Just. Whatever has been suspect, outcast, and denied is postulated as the source of good. Before the Breakthrough, no one, Christian or Humanist, had doubted the inferiority of passion to reason, of impulse to law; and though it is possible sophistically to justify all eighteenth-century reversals by quoting the verse which says the last shall be first, Christianity is dead from the moment such a justification is made. The Breakthrough, the triumphant intrusion of the libido into the place of virtue and reason, is profoundly anti-Christian though it is not always willing to appear so. There is a brief age of transition when the Enlightenment and Sentimentalism exist side by side, when it is still possible to pretend that true reason and true feeling, the urgings of passion and the dictates of virtue are identical—and that all are alike manifestations of the orthodox God. But Sentimentalism yields quickly to the full Romantic revolt; in a matter of months, Don Juan, enemy of Heaven and the family, has been transformed from villain to hero; and before the process is finished, audiences have learned to weep for Shylock rather than laugh him from the stage. The legendary rebels and outcasts, Prometheus and Cain, Judas and the Wandering Jew, Faust and Lucifer himself are one by one redeemed. The parricide becomes an object of veneration, and tourists (among them that good American abroad, Herman Melville) carry home as an icon Guido's picture of Beatrice Cenci, slayer of her father!

The process is continuous and nearly universal. Even the values of language change: "gothic" passes from a term of contempt to one of description and then of praise, while "baroque" makes more slowly the same transition; meanwhile terms once used honorifically to describe desired traits—"condescension," for example—become indicators of disapproval. The child is glorified over the man, the peasant over the courtier, the dark man over the white, the rude ballad over the polished sonnet, the weeper over the thinker, colony over mother country, the commoner over the king—nature over culture. At first, all this is a game: the ladies of the court in pastoral dress swing high into the air to show their legs with a self-consciousness quite unlike the abandon of children to which they are pretending. But in a little while, Jean-Jacques Rousseau has fainted on the road to Vincennes and awakened to find his waistcoat soaked with tears; and it is suddenly all in earnest. Whatever was down is now up, as the under-mind heaves up out of the darkness: barricades are erected and the novel becomes the reigning form; the Jew walks openly out of the ghetto, and otherwise sensible men hang on their walls pictures of trees and cattle. The conjunctions are comic in their unexpectedness and variety.

It is hard to say what was cause and what effect in the complex upheaval; everything seems the symptom of everything else. Yet deep within the nexus of causes (gods must die for new genres to be born) was that "death of God" that has not yet ceased to trouble our peace. Somewhere near the beginning of the eighteenth century, Christianity (more precisely, perhaps, that desperate compromise of the late Middle Ages and early Renaissance, Christian Humanism) began to wear out. It was not merely, or even primarily, a matter of the destruction of the political and social power of one Church or another, much less of the lapse of economic control by the priests.

The divisions within Christendom surely contributed to the final collapse, but they are perhaps better regarded as manifestations than as causes of the insecurity over dogma that was at work deep within. Institutionalized Christianity at any rate began to crumble when its God began to fail, that is to say, when its mythology no longer proved capable of controlling and revivifying the imagination of Europe.

The darker motive forces of the psyche refused any longer to accept the names and ranks by which they had been demeaned for almost two thousand years; once worshiped as "gods," they had been made demons by fiat, but now they stirred again in discontent. Especially the Great Mother—cast down by the most patriarchal of all religions (to the Hebrews, she was Lilith, the bride of darkness), ambiguously redeemed as the Blessed Virgin and denied once more by a Hebraizing Protestantism—clamored to be honored once more. The very distinction between God and Devil, on which the psychic balance of Europe had for so long been staked, was threatened. It did not matter that some people (chiefly women) continued to go to church, or even that there were revivals within the framework of surviving sects; fewer and fewer men lived by the legends of the church, and the images of saints represented not living myths but "mythology" in a literary sense, tales to be read for amusement or "analyzed" in the light of the teachings of anthropology or psychology. There remained only the job of carrying the news of God's death to those who had not yet heard the word.

The effect of the growing awareness (an awareness, to be sure, at first shared by only a handful of advanced thinkers) of this cosmic catastrophe was double: a sense of exhilaration and a spasm of terror, to which correspond the two initial and overlapping stages of the Breakthrough. There was first of all the conviction of the Age of Reason and its spokesmen, the *philosophes*, grave-diggers of the Christian God, that they—and all of mankind—were at last *free*, free of the superstition and ignorance so long sponsored by the priests for their own selfish ends. Those demons into which the early Christian apologists had translated the gods of antiquity seemed to the *philosophes* idle inventions of the Church itself: bugaboos to scare the pious into unquestioning subservience. Even the Christian God seemed to them such a contrivance, demonic and irrational. In the imagined universe presided over by their own "Author of Creation," there could be no place for mystery or blackness. Once "*l'infâme*," the scandalous Church, had been crushed, all monsters would be eliminated forever, and man could take up his long, baffled march toward perfection in a sweet, sunlit, orderly world. Just such a vision, however modified by circumstance, moved the Deist intellectuals who founded America, especially that Thomas Jefferson to whom C. B. Brown, himself a follower of the *philosophes*, proffered his gothic novel.

Insofar as America is legendary, a fact of the imagination as well as one of history, it has been shaped by the ideals of the Age of Reason. To be sure, the European mind had dreamed for centuries before the Enlightenment of an absolute West: Atlantis, Ultima Thule, the Western Isles—a place of refuge beyond the seas, to which the hero retreats to await rebirth, a source of new life in the direction of the setting sun which seems to stand for death. Dante, however, on the very brink of an age which was to turn the dream into the actualities of exploration, had prophetically sent to destruction in the West, Ulysses, the archetypal explorer. The direction of his westward journey through the great sea is identified with the sinister left hand; and Ulysses himself comes to stand for man's refusal to accept the simple limits of traditional duty: "not the sweetness of having a son, nor the pious claim of an old father, nor the licit love that should have made Penelope rejoice could quench in me the burning to become familiar with the vice of men and men's valor." It is a fitting enough epigraph to represent that lust for experience which made America. There is, indeed, something blasphemous in the very act by which America was established, a gesture of defiance that began with the symbolic breaching of the pillars of Hercules, long considered the divine signs of limit.

To be sure, the poets of later Catholicism made an effort to recast the dream of America in terms viable for their Counter-Reformation imaginations, to forge a myth that would subserve new political exigencies. It was not accident, they boasted, that the discoverer of America (sponsored by those most Catholic defenders of the Faith) had been called Cristoforo Colombo, "the Christ-bearing dove." Had he not carried orthodoxy into a world of unredeemed pagans, a reservoir of souls providentially kept in darkness until they were needed to replace the lapsed Christians of heretical northern Europe?

It is, however, the Enlightenment's vision of America rather than that of the Church that was written into our documents and has become the substance of our deepest sense of ourselves and our destiny. If North America had remained Latin, the story might have been different; but Jefferson himself presided over the purchase of the Louisiana Territory, which settled that question once and for all. History sometimes provides suitable symbolic occasions, and surely one of them is the scene that finds Jefferson and Napoleon, twin heirs of the Age of Reason, preparing the way for Lewis and Clark, that is to say, for the first actors in our own drama of a perpetually retreating West. Napoleon, it must be remembered, was the sponsor of the painter David and Jefferson the planner of Monticello; good neo-classicists both, they place the American myth firmly in the classicizing, neo-Roman tradition of the late eighteenth century. The New World is, of course, in one sense an older one than Europe, a preserve of the primitive, last refuge of antique virtue; indeed, the writers and artists of the Empire period could never quite tell the difference between Americans, red or white, and the inhabitants of the Roman Republic. The face of Washington, as rendered in bronze by Houdon, is that of the noblest Roman of them all, or, in Byron's phrase (already a cliché), "the Cincinnatus of the West."

But America is not exclusively the product of Reason—not even in the area of legend. Behind its neo-classical façade, ours is a nation sustained by a sentimental and Romantic dream, the dream of an escape from culture and a renewal of youth. Beside the *philosophes*, with whom he seemed at first to accord so well that they scarcely knew he was their profoundest enemy, stands Rousseau. It is his compelling vision of a society uncompromised by culture, of simple piety and virtue bred by "Nature," i.e., the untended landscape, that has left the deepest impress on the American mind. The heirs of Rousseau are Chateaubriand and Cooper, after whom the world of togas and marble brows and antique heroism is replaced by the sylvan scene, across which the melancholy refugee plods in search of the mysterious Niagara, or where Natty Bumppo, buckskinned savior, leans on his long rifle and listens for the sound of a cracking twig. The bronze face of a bewigged Washington gives way to the image of young Abe splitting logs in a Kentucky clearing.

The dream of the Republic is quite a different thing from that of the Revolution. The vision of blood and fire as ritual purification, the need to cast down what is up, to degrade the immemorial images of authority, to impose equality as the ultimate orthodoxy—these came from the *Encyclopédie*, perhaps, as abstract ideas; but the spirit in which they were lived was that of full-blown Romanticism. The Revolution of 1789 (for which ours was an ideological dress rehearsal) may have set up David as its official interpreter, but it left the world to Delacroix; and though it enthroned Reason as its goddess, it prepared for a more unruly Muse.

In Sentimentalism, the Age of Reason dissolves in a debauch of tearfulness; sensibility, seduction, and suicide haunt its art even before ghosts and graveyards take over—strange images of darkness to usher in an era of freedom from fear. And beneath them lurks the realization that the devils which had persisted from antiquity into Christianity were not dead but only driven inward; that the "tyranny of superstition," far from being the fabrication of a Machiavellian priesthood, was a projection of a profound inner insecurity and guilt, a hidden world of nightmare not abolished by manifestos or restrained by barricades. The final horrors, as modern society has come to realize, are neither gods nor demons, but intimate aspects of our own minds.

V. The Mythopoeic Critic

HERBERT WEISINGER

FRANCIS FERGUSSON

NORTHROP FRYE

PAUL GINESTIER

W. H. AUDEN

INTRODUCTION

Mythopoeic criticism is the most recent and the most ambitious of contemporary
critical approaches and perhaps the most provocative in its claims and possibilities.
Indeed, to accept it on its own terms is to endorse not only a critical method or
an aesthetic perspective but also a general humanistic theory that encompasses a
broad range of learning, that merges literature with disciplines from the sciences
and social sciences, and that ultimately offers an overview of human nature and
the human condition. The ideal mythopoeic critic would bring to literature materials drawn from such various bodies of knowledge as cultural anthropology, psychology, comparative religion, history, philosophy, and the fine arts. Furthermore,
he would use these materials not with any fear of subordinating literature to
"extrinsic" concerns but rather with the confidence of enhancing it, by demonstrating that in literature these very materials achieve their culmination in the
form of myth.

  Of all those critical perspectives we have examined, the mythopoeic critic
obviously feels himself least bound to a particular methodology. Nevertheless, he

can not accurately be described as an eclectic critic because he is committed to a fundamental thesis that his very flexibility of method is intended to serve. He can best be characterized as a pluralist in his techniques but a monist in his convictions. Because he is guided by a central principal that does not in itself dictate a specific method, the mythopoeic critic can comfortably and without fear of inconsistency bend the other critical approaches to his own purposes. Something of his catholicity can be seen in the work of Northrop Frye. Frye, the most eminent of contemporary mythopoeic critics (Frye himself would prefer the word *archetypal*), defines his positions as follows: "My general principle . . . is that in the history of civilization literature follows after a mythology. A myth is a simple and primitive effort of the imagination to identify the human with the nonhuman world, and its most typical result is a story about a god. Later on, mythology begins to merge into literature, and myth then becomes a structural principle of story-telling."

The mythopoeic critic can, therefore, take full advantage of whatever material seems pertinent to his inquiry. Like the historical critic he can make use of biographical information, intellectual history, literary convention, or patterns of influence in order to illustrate how mythic motifs and types vary from period to period or from writer to writer. For the mythopoeic critic literature exists simultaneously in two temporal dimensions: (1) It exists as a historical fact in particular moments of recorded time. (2) It exists as a continuum over and beyond historic time as the eternal and recurrent expression of archetypal characters, images, symbols, scenes, and plots. Like the historical critic the mythopoeist finds the facts garnered from his historic and quantitative research into myth to be the proper point of departure for his critical journey into literature.

In the manner of the formalist the mythopoeic critic will study the shapes and structures both of entire genres and types and of individual works, as these shapes and structures are determined by and expressive of archetypal patterns. Also, like the formalist critic, the mythopoeist insists that his interest is not in myth and ritual per se but in literature as the ultimate embodiment of myth and ritual in the form of art. Furthermore, the mythopoeic critic often engages in close textual analysis, especially in his explication of imagery and symbolism.

Since myth and ritual are engendered by communal experience and are themselves forms of communal activity, in turn giving rise to creeds, social practices, and institutions—and a literature that necessarily reflects these—the mythopoeic critic shares the sociocultural critic's concern with the interaction of literature and society. The mythopoeist has yet other beliefs in common with the socioculturalist: the belief that society and literature each depend on and affect the course of the other, and the belief that literature has an ethical function that is intrinsic to its very nature.

Finally, like a psychological critic the mythopoeist approaches literature as the vehicle for the expression of human emotion and experience and as a means of producing experience and emotion in its audience. In the mythopoeic critic's and the psychological critic's presumption of the close relationship between myth, literature, and dream, and in their conviction that the literary work always contains or is partly derived from the irrational element in man, they are virtually one. It follows that the mythopoeic critic is especially interested in depth psychology and often employs techniques of literary analysis that are inspired by those of psychoanalysis.

If the mythopoeic critic's own knowledge and skill permit, he may even exploit these methods concurrently in the same piece of criticism. For example, Northrop Frye in "The Drunken Boat: The Revolutionary Element in Romanticism"* proposes a historically oriented definition of *romanticism,* qualifies it and extends it by an argument based both on historical fact and a formalistic analysis of romantic imagery, and concludes with a detailed discussion of the romantic's relationship to his society and the psychological outlook of the romantic poet. However, we note that despite Frye's use of various critical methodologies he does not conclude that romanticism can be wholly explained as a historical phenomenon, aesthetic structure, socio-political position, or mental and emotional attitude, although it is in part all of these. What Frye is driving at in this essay, although less explicitly here than elsewhere in his work, is the *archetypal* basis of romanticism. Consequently, Frye suggests that, in romanticism's attempt to relate external nature to individual experience by means of intense concentration, it is akin to magic. He then offers this statement—which is also his thesis: "The sense of unity with a greater power is surely one of the reasons why so much of the best Romantic poetry is mythopoeic."

In short, the mythopoeic critic's resourcefulness in using techniques adapted from other critical systems may temporarily mislead us as to his real purpose, only later to discover that his final objective remains constant: to uncover the archetypal patterns in literature and to demonstrate how these pertain to the liberary work's form, substance, and effect.

That myth is fundamental to the nature of many literary works, for example, the Greek and Roman classics, the Bible, the ancient sagas and epics, and folk-literature, is now so familiar a truth that we seem to have always known it. However, the mythopoeic approach to literature as a distinct and self-conscious critical system has a relatively short history and one heavily influenced by extra-literary sources. I will reconstruct the most important of these, literary and otherwise.

Charles Darwin perhaps provided the original stimulus for the twentieth-century revival of scholarly and critical interest in myth by calling for evolutionary studies of human culture that would extend his own study of nature's organic development. Edward B. Tylor's *Primitive Culture* (1871) appeared as if in response to Darwin and advanced the thesis that our culture's institutions and artifacts repeated patterns derived from earlier societies. Tyler's evolutionary anthropology became dominant in British anthropological study, although it underwent some shift in focus and emphasis. James G. Frazer, the first great influence upon the mythopoeic approach and undoubtedly its immediate source, was himself influenced by Tylor in the earliest edition of *The Golden Bough* (1890).

The Golden Bough in its various editions had the important effect of making available to a large audience what had previously been a matter for specialists. It also culminated fifty years of intensive research into evolutionary anthropology. Furthermore, it generated enormous appeal for writers both because of the materials it contained and because of its own character as a quasi-literary work. A recent scholar, John B. Vickery, says: "*The Golden Bough* became central to twentieth century literature because it was grounded in the essential realism of anthropological research, informed with the romance quest of an ideal, and controlled by the irony in divine myth and human custom. Together these made it the discursive archetype and hence matrix of that literature."

The Golden Bough was, however, only one of many works that broadened our knowledge of myth and ritual; affected the creative artists who make our literature; demonstrated the affinity between ritual, myth, dream, and literature; and asserted the importance of myth to any larger understanding of human culture. At minimum, three other influential sources must be mentioned: the studies of the Cambridge anthropologists and classicists, the contributions of depth psychology—notably the work of Jung, and the philosophical essays of Ernst Cassirer.

Even as the several volumes and editions of *The Golden Bough* were appearing, Frazer's contemporaries Jane Ellen Harrison, F. M. Cornford, and A. B. Cook at Cambridge, together with Gilbert Murray at Oxford, explored ancient culture with the belief that ritual was prior to both myth and theology. In 1912 Miss Harrison published her important book *Themis*, which explored the chthonic origins of Greek myth and briefly treated the ritual forms behind Greek tragedy. *Themis* incorporated material by Cornford, Cook, and Murray and made three vital points, which are still generally accepted: (1) Myth derives from and is later than rite. (2) Myth is the spoken correlative of rite. (3) Myth is not a substitute for anything else but has its own identity and origin. With *Themis* a "Cambridge" or "ritual" approach to Greek culture became viable and applicable to nearly all its aspects. For literature the important document is probably Gilbert Murray's 1914 Shakespeare lecture "Hamlet and Orestes," which demonstrated the indebtedness of two historically distant plays to essentially the same myth and rite. Yet Murray also insisted on a point later to be reiterated by many other critics: that the plays themselves were neither myth nor rite but literature.

The writings of Freud, widely disseminated at the same time as Frazer's work and that of the Cambridge group, were also adapted by students of myth to support the growing body of mythopoeic data. For example, this data incorporated some of the major ideas of Freud's *Totem and Taboo* (1913), which set forth the hypothesis that the archetypal murder of the father by his sons became the basis for social organization. Even more important to the development of mythopoeic criticism than Freud's ideas, were a number of concepts taken from Carl Gustav Jung—although Jung's thought did not have its full impact until the

1930s. Because Jung's theories were less deterministic than Freud's, had wider cultural reference, and gave greater dignity to the artist than Freud's supposed view of him as a gifted neurotic, those writers and critics who were inclined toward myth embraced Jungian thought far more enthusiastically than they did the Freudian. Such Jungian concepts as that of the *persona*, the *anima-animus* duality, and the "shadow," were absorbed into literary discourse, while Jung's definition of the *archetype*, a term of key significance to his own work although his conception of it altered, became and still remains fundamental to the Mythopoeic interpretation of literature.

Contemporary scholars define archetypes as "basic age-old patterns of central human experience . . . [which] lie at the root of any poetry (or any other art) possessing special emotional significance" (Stanley Edgard Hyman); or, as Cleanth Brooks defines it: "Archetype . . . means a primordial image, a part of the collective unconscious, the psychic residue of numberless experiences of the same kind, and thus part of the inherited response-pattern of the race." Since the concept is so important to Mythopoeic Criticism, we should hear the final word on it from Jung himself. In *Psyche and Symbol* he writes: "The archetypes are by no means useless archaic survivals or relics. They are living entities, which cause the preformation of numinous ideas or dominant representations. . . . It is important to bear in mind that my concept of the 'archetypes' has been frequently misunderstood as denoting inherited patterns of thought or as a kind of philosophical speculation. In reality they belong to the realm of the activities of the instincts and in that sense they represent inherited forms of psychic behavior." Mythopoeic criticism is also indebted to Jung for the theory that much of the appeal of literature, especially its masterpieces, originates at the same level as dream or vision. To Jung the masterpiece gathers its materials from the collective unconscious and achieves its triumph by fusing individual experience with racial experience in such a form that it can be consciously and culturally apprehended.

Although a complete history and description of mythopoeic criticism would include a discussion of the contributions of such anthropologists as Malinowski and Lévy-Bruhl, I will conclude with a summary statement of the influence of the neo-Kantian philosopher Ernst Cassirer. In his writings, notably *The Philosophy of Symbolic Forms* and *Language and Myth*, Cassirer studied the structure of those mental images he called *symbolic forms* that he believed were essential to man's grasp of reality. Art was one of those forms man needed to augment his reason, using art to symbolically portray time, place, and social habit. Cassirer associated primordial language with intense emotional experience and particularly characterized the language of myth as the original form of man's intuition of reality, preceding his rational and scientific apprehension. Cassirer's influence amplified that of the anthropologists who studied primitive cultures, and we can observe this joint influence at work upon such mythopoeic theorists as Philip Wheelwright and Wayne Shumaker. Shumaker concludes his stimulating book *Literature and the Irrational* with this quotation from Cassirer: "Der Mensch sein eigenes Sein nur soweit erfasst und erkennt, als er es sich im Bilde seiner Götter sichtbar zu machen vermag." ("Man can only grasp and understand his nature insofar as he is able to mirror it in his representation of his Gods.") Cassirer's influence has also entered critical and aesthetic theory through the writings of such disciples as Susanne Langer.

Considering its varied sources, we could hardly expect unanimity among the practitioners of mythopoeic criticism either in their conception of how myth functions or in their specific application of myth to literature. Because the essays to follow will demonstrate several possibilities of methodology and application, I need say little more on that point. But because the term *myth*, as Francis Fergusson reminds us in " 'Myth' and the Literary Scruple"* has received such diverse definition, it would be well to restore the term to a usage which most Mythopoeic Critics would accept.

First, we can enumerate three widespread conceptions of myth that are not acceptable to professional mythopoeists and which would meet with the majority's vehement denunciation: (1) that myth is a form of captivating untruth, fairy tale, or allegory; (2) that it is a form of legendary history associated with real persons or events in the remote past (this is the so-called euhemerist view); (3) that it is a form of primitive proto-science, arising from the attempt to explain natural phenomena.

What, then, are the definitions that mythopoeists would endorse? There are several. (1) Myth is the verbal aspect of ritual and the means by which ritual is communicated. (2) It is the language by which the imagination links and orders basic mental images. (3) It is a mode of revelation and expression of ultimate reality and, as such, a statement not of fact but of value. (4) It is a construct analogous to literature and like literature an aesthetic creation mediating between the conscious and the unconscious in a way satisfying to both. (5) It is a story or narrative that is irrational and intuitive in its origins and nature and thus prior to and essentially different from the discursive, the logical, and the systematic.

As Herbert Weisinger suggests early in "The Myth and Ritual Approach to Shakespearean Tragedy"* most mythopoeic critics subscribe to the theory of a monomyth, an urmyth from which all others descend, although there is some disagreement about the precise nature and subject of the monomyth. Following the theory of Frazer, Joseph Campbell, and Lord Raglan, many critics subscribe to the original myth as that of a hero or god, a myth that incorporates the rites of passage—separation, initiation, return—and which repeats the life cycle and/or the cycle of the seasons. Northrop Frye endorses this cyclical view but argues that the monomyth is "the story of loss and regaining of identity." Robert Graves, on the other hand, believes the true urmyth to be that of the "White Goddess," or female principle associated with the moon. Others find the journey or quest of primary significance. However, this disagreement over the content of the basic myth seems to be neither very heated nor very decisive in the applied criticism of the mythopoeists.

The flexibility of the mythopoeic critic and his freedom to range over various historical periods and national literatures in his quest for mythic, ritualistic, and archetypal patterns, have given him potentially great scope and versatility. He has virtually equal access to all genres, and he is at liberty to treat popular and folk literature with the same seriousness he brings to acknowledged masterpieces. Some notion of his scope is implied in the essays reprinted here: Weisinger treats Shakespeare; Fergusson discusses Valéry, Wagner, and Dante; Frye considers the romantics and their successors; Ginestier works with a number of modern poets, some of them little known; Auden focuses on J. R. Tolkien.

However, mythopoeic criticism is still too recent in origin to have completely fulfilled its promise as an applied criticism. To date, its attention has not in fact been so widely bestowed as its capabilities would suggest. For example, it has exhibited continuing concern with the theory of tragedy (R. Y. Hathorn's *Tragedy, Myth, and Mystery*); it has illuminated the epic poem (I. G. MacCaffrey's *Paradise Lost as Myth*); it has amplified our understanding of Romanticism (Harold Bloom's *The Visionary Company*); it has inquired into the origin and efficacy of images and symbols (Philip Wheelwright's *The Burning Fountain* and *Myth and Metaphor*); it has produced any number of rich studies of such modern writers as Conrad, Yeats, Eliot, Mann, and Joyce, who themselves made significant use of myth (I pause to note that Eliot's 1923 review of Joyce's *Ulysses* was almost as important to the development of the mythopoeic approach as his "Tradition and the Individual Talent" was to the formalistic); it has resulted in provocative studies of basic patterns in national literatures (R. W. B. Lewis' *The American Adam*). On the other hand, mythopoeists have done relatively little with the Augustans and the Victorians, with the whole area of realism and naturalism, and with such subgenres as the novel of manners. We are tempted to speculate that the mythopoeic critic feels himself somewhat helpless before either highly "civilized" writing or any writing which has a strong element of verisimilitude. Douglas Bush's parody "Mrs. Bennett and the Dark Gods" (*Sewanee Review*, LXIV, 1965, pp. 591–596) supplies a horrific example of what might happen in an encounter between the mythopoeic critic and Jane Austen.

In the main the mythopoeic approach has so far proposed ideas of greater value to literary theory than to practical criticism. The mythopoeic perspective has been most impressively represented by Northrop Frye's *Anatomy of Criticism*, which stands as the *Poetics* of the entire mythopoeic movement. Frye argues that literary criticism has suffered from the lack of a central principle that would unite its scattered and often conflicting approaches and allow it to fulfill its vital role in the humanities. Archetypal criticism, Frye asserts, can best unify and integrate all the other perspectives because it alone assumes that all literature comprises one structure and one form, that literature itself is unified and integrated. To quote Frye: "In literary criticism myth ultimately means *mythos*, a structural organizing principle of literary form."

Anatomy of Criticism defies exact description. In conventional terms it might most accurately be characterized as theory of genre. Frye's quest is everywhere for synthesis, seeking to redefine and re-examine contradictory or inexact terminology and classification. For example, he argues persuasively that the amorphous genre we call the *novel* actually contains four distinct categories or types of narrative, each with its own features. He also defines comedy, romance, tragedy, and irony as aspects of a single unifying myth. He likewise attempts to place such specific forms as drama and the lyric in their appropriate mythopoeic context.

As might be expected, any book which makes such large claims will arouse resistance and skepticism. Indeed, in the several years since its publication it has come to occupy a curiously ambiguous position: it is at once universally respected and cited and repeatedly challenged. The majority praise its brilliance and erudition at the same time that many decry its ambitiousness and quarrel with its conclusions. I have yet to encounter a commentator who takes Frye's book lightly; but neither have I seen overwhelming evidence of miraculous conversion to its viewpoint. Whatever its final effect on our conception of literature, it seems at present a sound deduction that *Anatomy of Criticism* is among the most stimulating works of literary theory to appear in this generation and is certainly a work no contemporary critic can ignore.

The lofty ambition expressed in *Anatomy of Criticism* to exalt literary criticism to a supreme position as a humanistic study reappears in other forms in the writing of other mythopoeists. Frequently it takes the form of religious or ethical statement. For example, we find this passage in Maud Bodkin's pioneering study *Archetypal Patterns in English Poetry*, first published in England in 1934 but not readily available in America until 1958: "As in the exaltation of the bodily dance the faith of the tribesmen grew strong in the common life which should rise again exultant with the quickened earth and the new-born sun; so, in the rhythmic dance of words charged with meaning to which the stored secret powers of body and mind respond, our individual faith is renewed in the common life with its ideal interests and values which outlive the death of personal selves, and of personal affections and hopes." Miss Bodkin then suggests that in just this manner poetry may become a substitute for religion. We remark a similar suggestion in Philip Wheelwright's 1942 essay "Poetry, Myth, and Reality," which concludes with a lament that the modern imagination and modern literature have become impoverished by the twentieth-century man's incapacity to share in the vision of truth conveyed by myth: "This loss of myth-consciousness I believe to be the most devastating loss that humanity can suffer; for as I have argued, myth-consciousness is the bond that unites men both with one another and with the unplumbed Mystery from which Mankind is sprung and without reference to which the radical significance of things goes to pot."

The writings of the mythopoeic critics repeatedly advance these and related contentions: for example, that through his use of myth the writer can overleap his private, idiosyncratic experience and achieve universality; or, that because of its mythic basis, literature is primarily irrational in its appeal; or, that myth is the artist's best weapon in the struggle against domination by science and technology. Although mythopoeic critics are probably no more committed to religious belief than any other group, we do find an occasional mythopoeist who will enlist myth in the service of Christianity by asserting that Christianity is the ultimate myth— myth at its highest stage of development. *Anatomy of Criticism* is certainly not a book of Christian apologetics, yet some readers might so construe it in the light of Frye's insistence that our literary study should begin with the Bible. Frye conceives the Bible to be the central encyclopedic literary form in Western culture, a major source of literary imagery and symbolism, and a work that stands as "a definitive myth, a single archetypal structure extending from creation to apocalypse."

In short, as once said of formalism, mythopoeic criticism is ambitious. When mythopoeic criticism proposes itself as a way of mediating between individual and community and as a means of bettering man's spiritual condition, it runs the risk of becoming a kind of evangelism. The causes it espouses are admirable, but there is another cause, that of literary criticism, which it must not neglect. The ultimate cause of literary criticism, as the formalists helpfully reminded us, is literature itself.

Mythopoeic criticism is also subject to other abuses and hazards. I will summarize them briefly: (1) In its pursuit of the archetype, the monomyth, the ur-principle of literature, it can fall into a certain sameness and predictability; by stressing the basic mythopoeic patterns recurrent in literature, it often threatens to merge separate and distinctive literary works into a single work. (2) In its closer scrutiny of the materials and themes of the literary work rather than the work's technique or unique character as art, it has so far tended to be almost entirely analytical or descriptive but rarely evaluative; in fact, Northrop Frye argues that it is not the major function of criticism to evaluate literature but to interpret it. (3) In its attempt to return the literary work to its primal sources, mythopoeic criticism has sometimes reduced literature to a form of primitive expression and has depicted the artist as one with the child and the savage.

These points are highly controversial and worthy of lengthy discussion, but I will respond only to the last. It is true that the mythopoeic description of literature as having close kinship or analogy to primitive or irrational expression is meant to be a purely analytical statement and not a pejorative judgment. It is also true that the findings of depth psychology and cultural anthropology lend considerable authority to such a conclusion. Certainly such scholars as Wayne Shumaker have amassed impressive evidence that there is an intimate relationship between literature and the irrational. We must also hold in mind that the mythopoeist is apt to be an admirer of the noble savage, so that the comparison of the artist to the savage is implicitly complimentary rather than derogatory.

Nevertheless, for the modern reader who has been taught to believe that man is a rational being and that man's experience of art is a rational experience, any view of literature as a form of primitivism or as akin to the primitive will seem distasteful and debasing. It is the "art and neurosis" problem again, in another shape. Therefore, when the mythopoeist endorses the concept of literature as primitive expression, he not only irritates many of us but also strays close to the fallacious concept of literature as automatic writing, the product only of instinct, inspiration, dream, and vision, rather than the result of conscious craft, deliberation, discipline, and labor. If such a concept were carried to the extreme, it would be possible neither for the critic to study literature nor for the writer to learn anything beyond what his "gift" had bestowed upon him.

But if these and other dangers lurk in the mythopoeic approach, they are not the sort characteristic of a narrow or decadent system but rather the dangers attendant upon any dynamic, serious, and ambitious criticism. As we have seen, none of the types of contemporary criticism operates free of risk and immune to danger. For criticism to be worthy of literature itself, it must be willing to go beyond the safe, the known, the conventional, and the familiar. We want, at last, a critical perspective that is both broad and deep.

SELECTED BIBLIOGRAPHY

Bodkin, Maud. *Archetypal Patterns in Poetry* (New York, Vintage Books, 1958).

Calhoun, R. C. "Recent Literary Criticism," *South Atlantic Bulletin*, XXVII (1961), 1–6.

Campbell, Joseph. *The Hero with a Thousand Faces* (New York, Pantheon Books, 1949).

Chase, Richard. *Quest for Myth* (Baton Rouge, La., Louisiana State University Press, 1949).

Crane, R. S. *The Languages of Criticism and the Structure of Poetry* (Toronto, University of Toronto Press, 1953), pp. 128–138.

Douglas, W. W. "The Meanings of 'Myth' in Modern Criticism," *Modern Philology*, L (1953), 232–242.

Éliade, Mircea. *The Myth of the Eternal Return*, trans. by Willard R. Trask (New York, Pantheon Books, 1954).

Fiedler, Leslie A. *No! In Thunder* (Boston, Beacon Press, Inc., 1960), pp. 295–328.

Fromm, Erich. *The Forgotten Language: An Introduction to the Understanding of Dreams, Myths and Fairy Tales* (New York, Holt, Rinehart & Winston, Inc., 1951).

Frye, Northrop. *The Educated Imagination* (Bloomington, Ind., Indiana University Press, 1964).

Frye, Northrop. *Fables of Identity* (New York, Harcourt, Brace & World, Inc., 1963).

Gaster, Theodor. *Thespis: Ritual, Myth and Drama in the Ancient Near East* (Garden City, New York, Doubleday & Co., Inc., 1950).

Hyman, Stanley Edgar. *The Armed Vision* abridged ed.; (New York, Vintage Books, 1955), pp. 132–142.

Hyman, Stanley Edgar. *The Promised End* (Cleveland, World Publishing Co., 1963), pp. 278–294.

Jung, Carl Gustav. *Essays on Analytical Psychology* (New York, Pantheon Books, 1953).

Jung, Carl Gustav. *Modern Man in Search of a Soul* (New York, Harcourt, Brace & World, Inc., 1956).

Jung, Carl Gustav. *Psyche and Symbol* (Garden City, New York, Doubleday & Co., Inc., 1958).

Krieger, Murray. "After the New Criticism," *Massachusetts Review*, IV (1962), 183–205.

Langer, Susanne. *Philosophy in a New Key* (New York, New American Library, 1948).

Langer, Susanne. *Problems of Art* (New York, Charles Scribner's Sons, 1957).

O'Connor, William Van. *An Age of Criticism* (Chicago, Henry Regnery Co., 1952), pp. 151–155.

Ohmann, Richard, ed. *The Making of Myth* (New York, G. P. Putnam's Sons, 1962).

Raglan, Lord. *The Hero* (London, Watts, 1949).

Sebeok, Thomas A., ed. *Myth: A Symposium* (Bloomington, Ind., Indiana University Press, 1955).

Shumaker, Wayne. *Literature and the Irrational* (Englewood Cliffs, N.J., Prentice-Hall, Inc., 1960).

Sutton, Walter. *Modern American Criticism* (Englewood Cliffs, N. J., Prentice-Hall, Inc., 1963), pp. 175–191.

Thorp, Willard. "The Literary Scholar as Chameleon," in Carroll Camden, ed., *Literary Views: Critical and Historical Essays* (Chicago, University of Chicago Press, 1964), pp. 166–171.

Vickery, John B. "*The Golden Bough*: Impact and Archetype," *Virginia Quarterly Review*, XXXIX (1963), 37–57.

Waggoner, Hyatt. "The Current Revolt Against the New Criticism," *Criticism*, I (1959), 221–224.

Wellek, René, and Austin Warren. *Theory of Literature* (New York, Harcourt, Brace & World, Inc., 1956), pp. 179–183.

Whalley, George. *The Poetic Process* (London, Routledge & K. Paul, 1953).

Wheelwright, Philip. *The Burning Fountain* (Bloomington, Ind., Indiana University Press, 1954).

Wheelwright, Philip. *Metaphor and Reality* (Bloomington, Ind., Indiana University Press, 1962).

Wheelwright, Philip. "Poetry, Myth, and Reality," in G. J. and N. Goldberg, eds., *The Modern Critical Spectrum* (Englewood Cliffs, N.J., Prentice-Hall, Inc., 1962), pp. 306–320.

Wimsatt, W. K., Jr., and Cleanth Brooks. *Literary Criticism: A Short History* (New York, Alfred A. Knopf, Inc., 1957), pp. 708–720.

Herbert Weisinger

THE MYTH AND RITUAL APPROACH
TO SHAKESPEAREAN TRAGEDY

Herbert Weisinger's two books *Tragedy and the Paradox of the Fortunate Fall* (1953) and *The Agony and the Triumph* (1964) are often cited with admiration by students of literature and myth. The first book constitutes a profound theoretical inquiry; the second is comprised of perceptive essays that define and apply the mythopoeic approach. Weisinger taught at Michigan State University from 1942 to 1966 and is now Chairman of the English Department at the State University of New York at Stonybrook. This essay was included in *The Agony and the Triumph*.

The myth and ritual approach to literature is now one of the high gods in the pantheon of contemporary criticism and numbers among its devotees not a few eminently respectable names. This was not always so, however, and even as Zeus himself had laboriously to struggle up the ladder of divine acceptance, so the myth and ritual approach to literature now grows fat on quarterly hecatombs. So much so indeed, that the very word myth has acquired a mana of its own, and has been elevated into a substitute—less precise, less bold, and, if I may say so, less honest—for religion, though in this guise it has given many the courage of their conversion. As with other methods for the study of literature, the myth and ritual approach has its values, and they are distinctive and useful, but it also has its limitations, for it is certainly not a panacea concocted to cure all critical complaints.

What I want to do in this paper is to describe the myth and ritual approach to literature as I understand it and to show what new light it can throw on Shakespeare's tragedies, and presumably to illuminate them afresh. For the purposes of this analysis, I take the myth and ritual pattern as fundamental and anterior to tragedy and I pass Shakespeare's tragedies over this pattern, as tracings over the original drawing, in order to reveal his changes, modifications, and alterations of it; that is to say, I try to distinguish the uniquely Shakespearean from the generally tragic. I do not wish to be understood as suggesting that the myth and ritual pattern is either the *ur*-tragedy from which all others descend or the ideal tragedy toward which all others tend. But variation and difference cannot be separated except in terms of a fixed object arbitrarily put at rest, though it too is in motion and changes and is changed by the very process of observation.

Certainly I am not the first to suggest such a correlation; on the contrary, many critics have seen the connection and have in fact gone beyond the tragedies to the later plays in an effort to prove that the pattern of rebirth and reconciliation is fundamental to virtually the whole of Shakespeare's plays. "Birth, struggle, death, and revival," the late Theodore Spencer wrote, "these are not only the themes of the individual final plays, they are the themes which describe the course of Shakespeare's work as a whole, from his earliest plays through *King Lear* to *The Tempest*." E. M. W. Tillyard has said of the last plays: "Regeneration emerges dominant from the total tragic pattern" and he sums up this pattern as a ". . . general scheme of prosperity, destruction, and re-creation. The main character is a King. At the beginning he is in prosperity. He then does an evil or misguided deed. Great suffering follows, but during this suffering or at its height the seeds of something new to issue from it are germinating, usually in secret. In the end this new element assimilates and transforms the old evil. The King overcomes his evil instincts, joins himself to the new order by an act of forgiveness or repentance, and the play issues into a fairer prosperity than had first existed." And summing up nearly two decades of devotion to Shakespeare, G. Wilson Knight describes what he has found to be: ". . . the habitual design of Shakespearean tragedy: from normalcy and order, through violent conflict to a spiritualized music and then to the concluding ritual." So that if we add to this testimony the recent interpretations of the middle plays, particularly *Measure for Measure*, in the

light of the doctrine of atonement, we see that the bulk of Shakespeare's plays has been found to conform to the myth and ritual pattern.

While the myth and ritual pattern so used makes, if I may say so, a Christian Olympian out of Shakespeare, it does so only at the expense of the myth and ritual pattern and of the substance of the plays themselves. It is my contention that while the last plays of Shakespeare do indeed carry forward the tragic pattern established in *Hamlet, Othello, King Lear*, and *Macbeth*, they neither heighten nor deepen it but on the contrary reject and even destroy it. In fact, I would go so far as to argue that the tragic pattern in the tragedies themselves is scarcely maintained with equal strength over each of the plays. For, on the basis of a comparison between the myth and ritual pattern as I have described it in *Tragedy and the Paradox of the Fortunate Fall* and the tragedies, I think that Shakespeare's tragic vision, which he was able to sustain but tentatively in *Hamlet*, most fully in *Othello*, barely in *King Lear*, and hardly at all in *Macbeth*, failed him altogether in the last plays, and that this failure is manifested by the use of the elements of the myth and ritual pattern as mere machinery, virtually in burlesque fashion, and not as their informing and sustaining spirit. The instinct of the critics in applying the myth and ritual pattern to the plays has been sound but their superimposition of the pattern on the plays has been inexact and, I suspect, with the result that both the method and the plays have been falsified.

If I begin with some diffidence, it is because I am always acutely aware that the myth and ritual pattern, upon which the myth and ritual approach to literature must be founded, is as uncertain in its origins as it is unrealized in actuality. I have tried to account for the persistence and power of the myth and ritual pattern by retracing it generally to that initial impact of experience which produced the archetypes of belief, and specifically, to the archetype of rebirth as crystallized out of the archetype of belief. Unfortunately, no real proof of this process is possible, for the events which generated the primary shock of belief are now too deep and too dim in the racial memory of man to be exhumed by archaeological means, though the psychoanalytic probings of Freud have cleared a path through this labyrinth with reluctant confirmation coming from the anthropologists and classicists. Similarly, we must not forget that there is really no such thing as the myth and ritual pattern *per se*; at best, it is a probable reconstruction of many varieties and variations of a number of beliefs and actions so closely related to each other that it is reasonable to construct—reconstruct would be a misleading word here—an ideal form of the myth and ritual pattern more comprehensive and more realized than any variations of it which we actually possess.

The myth and ritual pattern of the ancient Near East, which is at least six thousand years old, centers in a divine king who was killed annually and who was reborn in the person of his successor. In its later development, the king was not killed, but went through an annual symbolic death and a symbolic rebirth or resurrection. Starting out as a magical rite designed to ensure the success of the crops in climates where the outcome of the struggle between water and drought meant literally the difference between life and death, the pattern was gradually transformed into a religious ritual, designed this time to promote man's salvation, and finally became an ethical conviction, freed now of both its magical and religious ritual practices, but still retaining in spiritualized and symbolic form

its ancient appeal and emotional certitude. Because it begins with the need to survive, the pattern never loses its force, for it is concerned always with survival, whether physical or spiritual. So far as can be ascertained at present, the pattern had a double growth, one along the lines of the ancient civilizations of the Near East, the Sumerian, the Egyptian, the Babylonian, both South and North, the Palestinian, first with the Canaanites, and then with the Hebrews and from thence into Christianity; the other along the lines of the island civilizations of the Aegean, from Crete to the mainland of Greece, from thence to Rome, and once more into Christianity, the two streams of development flowing into each other and reinforcing themselves at this crucial juncture.

Despite the differences between the religions of the ancient Near East, as, for example, between those of Egypt and Mesopotamia, and between that of the Hebrews and of the others, nevertheless they all possessed certain significant features of myth and ritual in common. These features, in their turn, stemmed from the common bond of ritual, characteristic in one form or another, of all together, though, as I have said, none possessed completely all the elements, which varied in some degree from religion to religion. In this single, idealized ritual scheme, the well-being of the community was secured by the regular performance of certain ritual actions in which the king or his equivalent took the leading role. Moreover, the king's importance for the community was incalculably increased by the almost universal conviction that the fortunes of the community or state and those of the king were inextricably intermingled; indeed, one may go so far as to say that on the well-being of the king depended the well-being of the community as a whole. On the basis of the evidence covering different peoples at different times, we know then that in the ancient Near East there existed a pattern of thought and action which gripped the minds and emotions of those who believed in it so strongly that it was made the basis on which they could apprehend and accept the universe in which they lived. It made possible man's conviction that he could control that universe for his own purposes; and it placed in his hands the lever whereby he could exercise that control.

From an analysis of the extant seasonal rituals, particularly the new year festivals, and from the coronation, initiation, and personal rituals of the ancient Near East, it is possible to make a reconstructed model of the basic ritual form. Essentially, the pattern contains these basic elements: 1) the indispensable role of the divine king; 2) the combat between the God and an opposing power; 3) the suffering of the God; 4) the death of the God; 5) the resurrection of the God; 6) the symbolic recreation of the myth of creation; 7) the sacred marriage; 8) the triumphal procession; and 9) the settling of destinies. We must remember, however, that the dying-rising of God theme constitutes but one illustration, so to speak, of the greater cycle of birth, death, and rebirth. The many and various rites connected with birth, with initiation, with marriage, and with death in the case of the individual, as well as the rites concerned with the planting, the harvesting, the new year celebrations, and with the installation ceremonies of the king in the case of the community, all these rites repeat, each in its own way, the deep-rooted and abiding cycle of death and rebirth. Not only do these rituals symbolize the passage from death to life, from one way of life to another, but they are the actual means of achieving the change-over; they mark the transition by which, through the processes of separation, regeneration, and the return on a higher level, both the individual and the community are assured their victory over the forces of chaos which are thereby kept under control.

The purpose of these rituals is by enaction to bring about a just order of existence in which God, nature, and man are placed in complete and final rapport with one another; they are both the defence against disorder and the guarantee of order. In the myth and ritual pattern, then, man has devised a mighty weapon by which he keeps at bay, and sometimes even seems to conquer, the hostile forces which endlessly threaten to overpower him. In the early stages of the development of the myth and ritual pattern, however, the best that man could hope for was an uneasy truce between himself and chaos, because the cycle merely returned to its beginnings; the God fought, was defeated, was resurrected, was momentarily triumphant, and thus ensured the well-being of the community for the coming year, but it was inevitable that in the course of the year he would again be defeated and would again have to go through his annual agony. Thus, nothing new could be expected nor was anticipated, and year after year man could hope for no more than a temporary gain which he was sure would soon be turned into an inevitable loss. To achieve genuine faith, therefore, was an act of courage difficult and infrequent to attain, and it is no wonder that we detect in the myth and ritual pattern of the ancient Near East before the Hebraic-Christian tradition takes over, too strong a reliance on the mere machinery of ritual, ultimately leading not to faith but to superstition, as well as the melancholy notes of despair and pessimism. But the Hebraic-Christian tradition in the very process of adapting the pattern, transformed it, for by virtue of its unique and tenacious insistence on the mercy and judgment of its transcendent God, it introduced a new and vital element to the pattern, that of the dialectical leap from out of the endless circle on to a different and higher stage of understanding. But the crucial moment in this transformation of the myth and ritual pattern comes when man, by himself, undertakes on his own to make the leap; to him remains the decision and his is the responsibility; by making the leap, he makes himself. The Hebraic-Christian tradition utilized the cycle of birth, life, death, and rebirth to conquer chaos and disorder, but it made its unique contribution to the pattern by giving man the possibility of defeating chaos and disorder by a single, supreme act of human will which could wipe them out at one stroke. In so doing, it preserved the potency of the pattern and retained its ancient appeal, and, at the same time, ensured its continued use by supplying the one element it had hitherto lacked to give it its permanent role as the means whereby man is enabled to live in an indifferent universe: it showed that man can, by himself, transcend that universe.

This, then, is the myth and ritual pattern as I understand it. What are its implications for tragedy? To start with, I would suggest that in the myth and ritual pattern we have the seedbed of tragedy, the stuff out of which it was ultimately formed. Both the form and content of tragedy, its architecture as well as its ideology, closely parallel the form and content of the myth and ritual pattern. But having said that, I must also say that the myth and ritual pattern and tragedy are not the same. Both share the same shape and the same intent but they differ significantly in the manner of their creation and in the methods of achieving their purposes. The myth and ritual pattern is the group product of many and

different minds groping on many and different levels over long and kaleidoscopic periods of time under the stimulus of motivations quite different from those which produce tragedy. I am not suggesting anything like the formerly accepted communal origin of the ballad for we know that myth in its form as the complement to ritual must have been devised by the priest-astrologer-magicians of the ancient world. The intent of the myth and ritual pattern is control, its method that of mimetically reproducing the rhythm of birth, death, and birth again to gain that control. But imitation here means, not acting alike, as we think of the term, a parallel and similar yet at the same time a distinct and different attitude and behavior toward the thing imitated, but rather the interpenetration of and union with the imitator, the thing imitated, and the imitation, all three being one and the same thing.

Tragedy, on the other hand, is a creation compounded of conscious craft and conviction. If we describe the myth and ritual pattern as the passage from ignorance to understanding through suffering mimetically and at first hand, then we must describe tragedy as the passage from ignorance to understanding through suffering symbolically and at a distance. To speak of symbolic meanings is already to have made the leap from myth to art. In the myth and ritual pattern, the dying-reborn God-king, the worshippers for whom he suffers, and the action of his agony are identical; in tragedy, the tragic protagonist undergoes his suffering at an aesthetic distance, and only vicariously in the minds of his audience. And for that reason does Aristotle tell us that tragedy is an imitation of an action. You participate in a ritual but you are a spectator of a play.

Moreover, tragedy reconstitutes the myth and ritual pattern in terms of its own needs. Of the nine elements which make up the myth and ritual pattern as I have described it, four have been virtually eliminated from tragedy, namely, the actual death of the God, the symbolic re-creation of the myth of creation, the sacred marriage, and the triumphal procession; two elements, the indispensable role of the divine king and the settling of destinies, are retained only by implication and play rather ambiguous roles in tragedy; while the remaining three, combat, suffering (with death subsumed), and resurrection, now give tragedy its structure and substance. I have already noted that one of the characteristics of the myth and ritual pattern is its adaptability, its ability to change shape while retaining its potency, and we should therefore not be surprised to find the same process at work in its relation to tragedy. What is revealing, however, is the direction of change for we find, first, that the theme of the settling of destinies which is the highest point in the myth and ritual pattern, the goal of the struggle, since without it the passion of the God would be in vain and chaos and disorder would be triumphant, this theme, so elaborately explicated in the ritual practices of the ancient Near East, is no more than implied in tragedy, just as the correspondence between the well-being of the king and the well-being of the community, again so detailed in ritual, is only shadowed forth, as a condition to be aimed at but not to be achieved in reality.

Second, we discover that even greater emphasis is placed on the small moment of doubt in tragedy than in the myth and ritual pattern itself. In the rituals of the ancient Near East, at the point between the death of the God and his resurrection, all action is arrested as the participants fearfully and anxiously wait for the God to be revived. After the din of combat, this quiet moment of doubt and indeci-sion is all the more awful for there is no assurance that the God will be reborn: "For a small moment have I forsaken thee." "But," continues Isaiah, "with great mercies will I gather thee." It is no wonder that the small moment is followed in the pattern by creation, the sacred marriage, and the triumphal procession as the peoples' expression of joy that the death of the God has not been in vain and that for another year at least "the earth remaineth, seedtime and harvest, and cold and heat, and summer and winter, and day and night shall not cease." And, clearly spelling out the implications of the second change made by tragedy in the myth and ritual pattern is the third, the freedom of choice of the tragic protagonist and the responsibility for the consequences of making that choice. For in that small moment of doubt and indecision, when victory and defeat are poised in the balance, only the moral force of man wills him on in action to success. The tragic protagonist acts in the conviction that his action is right and he accepts the responsibility for that action; for him to do less than that means the loss of his stature as a moral, responsible agent. The tragic occurs when by the fall of a man of strong character we are made aware of something greater than man or even mankind; we seem to see a new and truer vision of the universe.

But that vision cannot be bought cheaply. It cannot be bought by blind reliance on the mere machinery of the myth and ritual pattern and it cannot be bought by fixing the fight, as Handel's librettist fatuously puts it:

How vain is man who boasts in fight
The valour of gigantic might,
And dreams not that a hand unseen
Directs and guides this weak machine.

Better the indifferent Gods of Lucretius than the busybody *deus ex machina* of

Vine Street and Madison Avenue. Only the deliberate moral choice of the tragic protagonist confronted by two equal and opposite forces and fully aware of the consequences of his choice can bring off the victory, and then only at the expense of pain and suffering: "He was despised, and rejected of men; a man of sorrows, and acquainted with grief." But suffering can be made bearable only when at the same time it is made part of a rational world order into which it fits and which has an understandable place for it:

I called by reason of mine affliction unto
  the Lord,
And he answered me;
Out of the belly of hell cried I,
And thou heardest my voice.
For thou didst cast me into the depth, in
  the heart of the seas,
And the flood was round about me;
All thy waves and thy billows passed over
  me;
And I said, I am cast out from before
  thine eyes; ...
The waters compassed me about, even to
  the soul;
The deep was round about me;
The weeds were wrapped about my head.
I went down to the bottoms of the moun-
  tains;
The earth with her bars closed upon me
  for ever;
Yet hast thou brought up my life from
  the pit, O Lord my God . . .
They that regard lying vanities
Forsake their own mercy.
But I will sacrifice unto thee with the
  voice of thanksgiving;
I will pay that which I have vowed.
Salvation is of the Lord.

Salvation is indeed of the Lord, but Jonah must deliberately look to the holy temple and must remember the Lord of his own free will; *then* salvation is of the Lord.

Tragedy therefore occurs when the accepted order of things is fundamentally questioned only to be the more triumph-antly reaffirmed. It cannot exist where there is no faith; conversely, it cannot exist where there is no doubt; it can exist only in an atmosphere of sceptical faith. The protagonist must be free to choose, and though he chooses wrongly, yet the result of the wrong choice is our own escape and our enlightenment. Yet nothing less than this sacrifice will do, and only the symbolic sacrifice of one who is like us can make possible our atonement for the evil which is within us and for the sins which we are capable of committing. Nevertheless, in western thought, if man is free to choose, in the end he must choose rightly. He is free to choose his salvation, but he is punished for his wrong choice. Man is free, but he is free within the limits set for him by his condition as a man. So great is the emphasis placed on freedom of choice in tragedy that the settling of destinies, which in the myth and ritual pattern is the tangible reward of victory, recedes more and more into the background and the messianic vision implicit in the settling of destinies is personalized and humanized in tragedy in the form of heightened self-awareness as the end of the tragic agony. In short, what I have been saying is that the myth and ritual pattern pertains to religion which proceeds by assertion, tragedy to literature which proceeds by assessment.

To sum up, then, the structure of tragic form, as derived from the myth and ritual pattern, may be diagrammed in this way: the tragic protagonist, in whom is subsumed the well-being of the people and the welfare of the state, engages in conflict with a representation of darkness and evil; a temporary defeat is inflicted on the tragic protagonist but after shame and suffering he emerges triumphant as the symbol of the victory of light and good over darkness and evil, a victory sanctified by the covenant of the settling of destinies which reaffirms the well-being of the people and the welfare of the state. But in the course of the conflict there comes a point where the protagonist and the antagonist appear to merge into a single challenge against the order of God; the evil which the protagonist would not do, he does, and the good which he would, he does not; and in this moment we are made aware that the real protagonist of tragedy is the order of God against which the tragic hero has rebelled. In this manner is the pride, the presumption which is in all of us by virtue of our mixed state as man, symbolized and revealed, and it is this *hybris* which is vicariously purged from us by the suffering of the tragic protagonist. He commits the foul deed which is potentially in us, he challenges the order of God which we would but dare not, he expiates our sin, and what we had hitherto felt we had been forced to accept we now believe of our free will, namely, that the order of God is just and good. Therefore is the tragic protagonist vouchsafed the vision of victory but not its attainment:

But the Lord was wroth with me for your sakes, and would not hear me: and the Lord said unto me, Let it suffice thee; speak no more unto me of this matter.

Get thee up into the top of Pisgah, and lift up thine eyes westward, and northward, and southward, and eastward, and behold it with thine eyes: for thou shalt not go over this Jordan. (Deuteronomy 3: 26–27)

Seen from this point of view, *Hamlet* is a particularly fascinating example of the relationship between the myth and ritual pattern and tragedy because it shows within the action of the play itself the development of Shakespeare's awareness of tragedy as a heightened and secularized version of the pattern. Hamlet begins by crying for revenge which is personal and ends by seeking justice which is social.

Shakespeare deals with the problem of the play: how shall a son avenge the injustice done his father, by presenting it to us in four different yet related ways simultaneously, each consistent within its pattern of behavior, yet each overlapping and protruding beyond the other, like the successive superimpositions of the same face seen from different angles in a portrait by Picasso. First, there is Hamlet-Laertes who, incapable of seeking more than revenge, dies unchanged and unfulfilled, no better nor no worse than when he had begun. Then there is Hamlet the Prince, caught midway between revenge and justice, who passes from ignorance to understanding but too late. Third, there is Hamlet-Fortinbras who avenges his father's wrongs by joining the warring kingdoms into a single nation under his able rule. And finally, containing all these Hamlets, is Hamlet the King, idealized by his son into the perfect king whom he must replace. From this dynastic destiny stems Hamlet's ambivalence towards his father: he loves him for the man he wants to be himself and hates him for the King who stands in the way of the Prince and for the father who stands in the way of the son. Seeking his father's murderer, Hamlet finds himself. The same necessity holds Hal and Hamlet alike, but where Hal sees a straight line between his father and himself:

You won it, wore it, kept it, gave it me;
Then plain and right must my possession
    be. . . .
                    (II Henry IV. IV.v.222–23)

and is therefore sure of himself and of his actions, Hamlet finds himself in a labyrinth whose walls are lined with trick doors and distorting mirrors: "O cursed spite,/ That ever I was born to set it right!"

Hamlet's ambivalence is reflected in the fragmentation of his character; there are as many Hamlets as there are scenes in which he appears and each person in the play sees a different Hamlet before him. But of the contradictions in his character, two stand out as the major symptoms of his incompleteness. The first is Hamlet's yearning to be able to act, not for the sake of action alone, but rightly, in the clear cause of justice, for while no tragic protagonist acts more frequently and more vigorously than does Hamlet, he is more and more perplexed to discover that the more he would do good, that is, cleanse Denmark by avenging his father's death, the more evil he in fact accomplishes; hence his envy of Fortinbras' ability to act resolutely and without equivocation (IV.iv.). Second, though he is nominally a Christian, yet in the moments of sharpest crisis Hamlet turns instead to the consolations of Stoicism: "If it be now, 'tis not to come; if it be not to come, it will be now; if it be not now, yet it will come; the readiness is all. Since no man has aught of what he leaves, what is't to leave betimes?" (V.ii.231–35). And it is not enough: his mission succeeds only by mischance, his cause is still not understood, and with his dying breath he calls on Horatio, the true Stoic, to tell his story to the unsatisfied. Hamlet's vision is still clouded at his death: "Things standing thus unknown," Horatio's own version of the events is surprisingly but an advertisement for a tragedy by Seneca (V.ii.391–97), and there is something too cold and callous in the way Fortinbras embraces his fortune. In short, the myth and ritual elements have not been completely assimilated into the tragedy; the suffering of the tragic protagonist is neither altogether deserved nor altogether understood by him, the rebirth is not quite inevitable nor necessary, and the settling of destinies in the person of Fortinbras is somewhat forced and mechanical. The genuine sense of tragic loss

is somewhat vulgarized into regret: Hamlet has been too fascinating.

In *Othello*, Shakespeare mixed his most perfect amalgam of the myth and ritual elements with tragedy. Where in *Hamlet* he was almost too fecund and profusive in characterization, invention inundating integration, in *Othello* he ruthlessly simplified and organized; if *Hamlet* is linear, proceeding by the method of montage and multiple exposure, *Othello* is monolithic and nuclear: the opposites of good and evil in human nature are forcibly split and then fused together in the fire of suffering. By overvaluing human nature, Othello destroys the balance between good and bad which is the condition of man; by undervaluing human nature, Iago brings about the same destruction from the equal and opposite direction. Each in his own way is an incomplete man: where Othello responds emotionally, Iago reasons; where Othello feels that men are better than they are, Iago knows that they are worse; each, in short, believes only what he wants to, and they are alike only in that both lack tolerance and understanding. Othello must be made to realize that the perfect love which he demands: "My life upon her faith!" "And when I love thee not,/Chaos is come again," is nothing more than the perfect hate which Iago practices:

Othello.　Now art thou my lieutenant.
Iago.　　 I am your own for ever.
(III.iii.478–79)

If Iago is motivated by pride, will, and individualism, so then is Othello in his own way. Iago is the external symbol of the evil in Othello, for everything that Othello would stand for is negated and reversed in Iago: the subvertor of the order of God whose coming is after the working of Satan, the man who rejects principle, and who denies virtue, love, and reputation. To him, ideals are but a mask which conceals the sensuality, the brutality, and the greed for money, power, and sex, which he believes constitute man's true nature.

As the opposites of character in Othello and Iago meet and merge in Act III, scene iii, Othello becomes for the moment Iago: he reverts to paganism and calls on the stars for help, he orders his friend murdered, he spies on and humiliates and at the last repudiates his wife: "She's like a liar, gone to burning hell." But this is for him the bottom of the pit, and, by a supreme effort of will, he purges the Iago from within him; and in that awful moment of self-awareness, he re-creates himself as he might have been, he realizes his potential as a human being. Having by his rashness put the well-being of the people and the welfare of the state in jeopardy, as Brabantio had foretold, perhaps better than he knew:

Mine's not an idle cause: the duke himself,
Or any of my brothers of the state,
Cannot but feel this wrong as 'twere their own;
For if such actions may have passage free,
Bond slaves and pagans shall our statesmen be.
                                   (I.ii.95–99)

Othello is inevitably punished. And Iago is defeated by the one force which he is incapable of understanding, the power of principle. What he fails to see is that Othello's love for Desdemona is the symbol of Othello's faith in the goodness and justice of the world. What Othello seeks, therefore, when that faith is called into question, is not revenge, which is Iago's goal, but the cleansing of evil and the reaffirmation of goodness and justice: "It is the cause, my soul." From the depth of his self-awareness, bought at so dear a price, there emerges the theme of the settling of destinies, not embodied in the

person of a successor, but filling as it were with its vision the entire stage, the sign of evil purged and the good restored: the image of man in his full stature as responsible man: "Speak of me as I am." "And when man faces destiny," Malraux writes, "destiny ends and man comes into his own."

Both *Hamlet* and *Othello* possess three features in common which by contrast are not present in *Lear* and *Macbeth*. First, both *Hamlet* and *Othello* are, for the Elizabethan audience, contemporary plays laid in contemporary or nearly contemporary settings. No great historical distance separates them from their audience as it does in *Lear* and *Macbeth* which are laid in pre-Christian England and Scotland. Second, both *Hamlet* and *Othello* operate within the Christian framework, recognized and apprehended as such by the audience for which they were written. But in *Lear* and *Macbeth* the pagan background is insistent. From the depth of their suffering Lear and Gloucester can appeal no higher than to the heathen gods: "As flies to wanton boys, are we to th' gods, / They kill us for their sport" (IV.vi.80). In *Macbeth*, the witches play the same role as do the gods in *Lear*:

But 'tis strange;
And oftentimes, to win us to our harm,
The instruments of darkness tell us truths,
Win us with honest trifles, to betray 's
In deepest consequences.   (I.iii.122–26)

Finally, the theme of the settling of destinies, present directly in *Hamlet* and indirectly in *Othello*, fades away in *Lear* and disappears altogether in *Macbeth*. These changes reveal a significant shift in Shakespeare's use of the myth and ritual pattern and seem to be symptomatic of his increasing inability to bear the burden of the tragic vision. Having confronted the face of evil in *Othello* with an intensity unmatched even by the man staring at Death in Michelangelo's "Last Judgment" and having in the face of that evil been able to reassert the good, Shakespeare seems to have fallen back exhausted so to speak, the effort of holding off evil weakening with each successive play.

Lear begins with the abdication of responsibility already accomplished; that a king could even contemplate, let alone achieve, the division of his kingdom must have struck an Elizabethan audience with fear and horror. By his own act, Lear deliberately divests himself of power and retains only the trappings of power which in turn are one by one inexorably stripped from him until he stands naked on the heath in the rain. The waters of heaven give him wisdom but his insight into the hypocrisy of this great stage of fools comes to him only in his madness and he realizes at last that clothes—the symbols of his *hybris*—make neither the king nor the man. Having been purged of the pride of place, he sees himself as he is:

I am a very foolish fond old man,
Fourscore and upward, not an hour more
    nor less;
And to deal plainly,
I fear I am not in my perfect mind.
                              (IV.vii.60–63)

But this moment of illumination, of heightened self-awareness, so like Othello's, occurs not at the end of Act V where it would normally be expected but at the end of Act IV. Having said: "Pray you now, forget and forgive; I am old and foolish" (IV.vii.85), what is left for Lear to say? Yet Shakespeare forces the action on to the shambles of the Grand Guignol of Act V, completely cancelling the calming and cleansing effect of the tragic vision already attained with Lear's self-awareness. The play ends not with the hope that this suffering has not been in vain but with the defeatism of Kent's

"All's cheerless, dark, and deadly" and Edgar's "The oldest have borne most; we that are young shall never see so much, nor live so long." The order of nature has been turned topsy-turvy; the old who cannot bear suffering have endured too much of it; the young who should be able to bear it are too weak. But at least *Lear* gives us the consolation of the settling of destinies, mishandled and misplaced as it is; there is none in *Macbeth*.

The action of *Macbeth* begins with the figure of the bloody man and ends with the figure of the dead butcher, and nothing between mitigates the endless horrors of the progression from one to the other. Macbeth accepts the evil promise of the witches' prediction because they so neatly match the evil ambition already in him. Nor does his desire for the crown even pretend that it is for the well-being of the people and the welfare of the state, that excuse which gives some color to Bolingbroke's ambition: "I have no spurs/ To prick the sides of my intent," Macbeth confesses to himself, "but only/ Vaulting ambition." The country suffers under Macbeth's iron rule: "Things bad begun make strong themselves by ill" (III.iv.55) says Macbeth, and Malcolm confirms him:

I think our country sinks beneath the
    yoke;
It weeps, it bleeds; and each new day a
    gash
Is added to her wounds.   (IV.iii.39–41)

More—while Malcolm stands behind Macbeth as Fortinbras stands behind Hamlet, can we seriously accept him as the doctor who can:

    ... cast
The water of my land, find her disease,
And purge it to a sound and pristine
    health. ...
                              (V.iii.50–52)

What are we to make of a potential successor to the throne whose own ambivalence towards himself confounds even his strongest supporters? Is Macduff—are we —really persuaded that Malcolm is in fact capable of exhibiting "The king-becoming graces,/ As justice, verity, temp'rance, stableness,/ Bounty, perseverance, mercy, lowliness,/ Devotion, patience, courage, fortitude" (IV.iii.91–94)? Surely his black scruples, coupled with his innocence and inexperience, bode ill for Scotland, whatever the outcome, so that when at last Malcolm is hailed King of Scotland, and, like Hal and Fortinbras, emerges as the symbol of the settling of destinies, our eyes do not see the vision of peace rising from suffering and our ears hear only the echo of:

> . . . for, from this instant,
> Theres nothing serious in mortality.
> All is but toys; renown and grace is dead;
> The wine of life is drawn, and the mere
>   lees
> Is left this vault to brag of. (II.iii.96–101)

repeated in the dying close of Macbeth's reply to Seyton. The witches have indeed triumphed:

> He shall spurn fate, scorn death, and bear
> His hopes 'bove wisdom, grace, and fear;
> And, you all know, security
> Is mortals' chiefest enemy. (III.v.30–33)

Man's security, for which he has fought so feverishly, the guarantee of rebirth, has at the very last moment been snatched away from him. Tragedy may be much more and much different from what I have been suggesting here, but one thing it cannot be and that is a tale signifying nothing.

The disintegration of the tragic pattern which we have seen take place in the major tragedies is paralleled in the three middle comedies and comes to its culmination in the four last plays. In the period of eight years during which he was writing the tragedies from *Hamlet* to *Timon of Athens*, Shakespeare wrote three comedies: *Troilus and Cressida*, *All's Well That Ends Well*, and *Measure for Measure*. The latter two strike us immediately as being the only two ironic titles in the Shakespeare canon. "She knew her distance and did angle for me" —Bertram's protest well catches Helena's strategy and one may very well wonder how a marriage so described (V.iii.212), and in a bare one hundred lines later converted into "I'll love her dearly, ever, ever dearly" (V.iii.311), can indeed end well. It has always seemed to me that Shakespeare failed to write the best scene in the play in which Bertram and Helena, out of reach of the King's interference, and out of the public gaze, get down to brass tacks and have it out; I am sure that Helena would not under those circumstances second Katherina's fervent "Fie, fie" to headstrong women. Like *Lear*, *Measure for Measure* begins with the abdication of kingly responsibility: "It was a mad fantastical trick of him to steal from the state, and usurp the beggary he was never born to" (III.ii.98–100). Having allowed Vienna to go to the dogs for some fourteen years as he himself acknowledges, the Duke, who would eat his cake and have it too, puts on Angelo the burden of cleaning up the mess. Yet surely Angelo is the worst possible deputy to choose, for as the Duke himself observes of Angelo's character:

> Lord Angelo is precise,
> Stands at a guard with envy, scarce confesses
> That his blood flows, or that his appetite
> Is more to bread than stone; hence shall
>   we see,
> If power change purpose, what our seemers be.   (I.iii.50–54)

The extremes of licentiousness and rectitude clash with the expected results: the exemplar of rectitude is shown to have at least two feet of clay and the exemplar of licentiousness shows a tolerance— "Something too crabbed that way, friar" which the disguised Duke will not accept: "It is too general a vice, and severity must cure it" (III.ii.104–07). The Duke's reply shows how far a distance we have travelled from the cakes and ale of *Twelfth Night*. Nor does Isabella's defense of her chastity in the face of her brother's anguished appeal: "Sweet sister, let me live" strike me as exhibiting the quality of compassion so characteristic of the high comedies and tragedies; indeed, Emilia's realism stems from a deeper wisdom than the cloistered virtue of Isabella can plumb. And again, one cannot help wondering how the relationship between Angelo and Mariana, scarcely on a very firm footing at best, is going to be improved by the ducal decree: "Look that you love your wife." The Duke notes that Angelo perceives he is safe; he seems not to notice, however, that Angelo says nothing to Mariana. Nor can one help observing that in the midst of all the *brouhaha*, the Duke has managed to keep a sharp and steady eye on Isabella and rewards himself for his fine performance in the role of *deus ex machina* by snagging Isabella for himself. Since the Duke has suffered nothing and learned nothing, one can well imagine what the next fourteen years will be like in Vienna.

I am prepared to admit that the interpretation of these two plays as ironic commentaries on their own titles may, in the light of the most recent criticism of them, fail to carry conviction, but I cannot go along with the view, best summed up by Professor Coghill's declaration with reference to *Troilus and Cressida*, that "Knowledge of the medieval tradition behind Shakespeare has made rubbish of the recent sentimental view of his supposed disgust and disillusion with life." Certainly every artist works within tradition but it is what he does with it which distinguishes him from tradition and gives him his uniqueness and significance. *Troilus and Cressida* is Iago's *chef d'oeuvre* for it assumes the worst of human nature and proves it: ". . . our raging motions, our carnal stings, our unbitted lusts, whereof I take this that you call love to be a sect or scion . . . is merely a lust of the blood and a permission of the will." Professor Coghill has rightly called Ulysses the Machiavel, Ajax a braggart, Achilles a gangster, Thersites bastardly, and Cressida inconstant, but if Troilus stands for truth in love, his passion drives him to madness; and if Hector stands for chivalry in battle, he witlessly lets Troilus talk him to his death. When Diomedes gives the lie to Marlowe:

She's bitter to her country, Hear me, Paris:
For every false drop in her baudy veins
A Grecian's life hath sunk; for every scruple
Of her contaminated carrion weight,
A Trojan hath been slain   (IV.i.68–72),

Paris half-heatedly protests: "You are too bitter to your countrywoman," hardly the kind of reply we would expect from a man who has just been called a lecher and his mistress a whore. Aeneas winks an eye at Troilus' philandering, Calchas betrays his people, and like father like daughter, Cassandra cries in vain, and Pandarus bestows his name on the second oldest profession, and are these not Trojans too? Who can distinguish, as Professor Coghill suggests we can, which are the noble hearts who perish in contention with the scum of the earth; *Troilus and Cressida* is sonnet 129 realized on the stage. "Lechery, lechery; still wars and lechery; nothing else holds fashion"

(V.ii.196–97). Thersites' judgment holds; this is the way the world ends; unlike Eliot, Shakespeare does not sentimentalize.

From 1600 to 1608, then, Shakespeare seems to have swung from assertion to denial of the myth and ritual pattern and back again: first *Hamlet*, then *All's Well that Ends Well* and *Troilus and Cressida*, back to *Othello* and again to *Measure for Measure*, and from them to *Lear* and *Macbeth*. But as we watch the needle on the dial swing back and forth, we see that more and more it inclines toward the zero mark and in the end rests there. In no other plays of Shakespeare do the elements of the myth and ritual pattern occur so frequently as they do in the last four plays, but their very profusion is a sign of the breakup of the pattern in Shakespeare. Never does the sea storm so often and so violently, never is magic music heard so much, never do so many magicians practice their art, never are there so many mock deaths in so many guises followed by so many rebirths, never does the conflict between age and youth, between winter and summer, between the old and the new—"Thou met'st with things dying, I with things new-born"— break out so frequently and in so many different forms, never are there so many reconciliations, reformations, and marriages as take place in these plays. They remind me of nothing so much as Mozart's *Magic Flute* which abounds in much the same grotesque mockeries of the myth and ritual elements. But the measure of distance between *The Magic Flute* and *The Marriage of Figaro* is precisely the same as that between the high comedies and that late romances; the spirit is gone, leaving only the dry bones of stunning technique. If we look at the history of the myth and ritual pattern, we shall find that at those times when a breakdown of faith in the efficacy of the

pattern has occurred, and it has happened more than once, there is a corresponding preoccupation with the mere machinery of the pattern at the expense of its spirit. The less faith one has, the more desperately one relies on the exact and sterile performance of ritual for its own sake; superstition takes the place of belief. Mill's concluding remarks on the relation of liberty to the state apply here as well: ". . . a state which dwarfs its men, in order that they may be more docile instruments in its hands even for beneficial purposes will find that with small men no great things can really be accomplished; and that the perfection of machinery to which it has sacrificed everything will in the end avail it nothing, for want of the vital power which, in order that the machine might work more smoothly, it has preferred to banish." When the freedom of choice of the tragic protagonist is at the last coffined by the orthodoxy of conformity, the myth and ritual pattern is no longer operative, the small moment has run out, and he who dared confront Othello with Iago would have us content with:

*We are such stuff
As dreams are made on, and our little life
Is rounded with a sleep.*

The configuration of Shakespeare's thought was for the most part sympathetic to the shape of the myth and ritual pattern. But having raised the pattern to the heights of its most moving and significant expression, Shakespeare was unable to hold it there for long. But this does not mean that we must regard him as less than, say, Sophocles or Milton, neither of whom seems to have given way to doubt, nor does it mean that the myth and ritual pattern is inadequate either to its purposes or as a means of elucidating tragedy. On the contrary, the application of the pattern to Shakespeare's plays discriminates between them with nicety; it intensifies our awareness of the unique qualities of the individual plays, and it enables us to respond to Shakespeare on a most profound level of understanding. Recent critics of Shakespeare have enjoyed many a laugh at the expense of their predecessors who labored to box Shakespeare's plays under the neat labels in the workshop, in the world, out of the depths, and on the heights—to use Dowden's terms—but I cannot see that they themselves have done anything more than to say the same thing in perhaps more fashionable language. But the myth and ritual approach converts a Progress into a Calvary.

Shakespeare paid for the cost of the tragic vision by its loss. He looked long and directly into the face of evil; in the end, he shut his eyes. Writing of another artist who found himself in the same dilemma, Sir Kenneth Clark says: "The perfect union of Piero's forms, transcending calculation, rested on confidence in the harmony of creation; and at some point this confidence left him." As it seems to me, at some point Shakespeare too lost his confidence in the harmony of creation. I do not know when Shakespeare reached that point but I think that it perhaps came at the moment of his greatest expression of faith in the harmony of creation, in *Othello*, when he realized that he had left Iago standing alive on the stage. When in the bottommost circle of Hell, Virgil steps aside from Dante and reveals to him that creature fairest once of the sons of light: "Behold now Dis!" the poet is moved to cry out: "This was not life, and yet it was not death." So in the end Iago:

Demand me nothing; what you know, you know.
From this time forth I never will speak word.

The rest is silence.

Francis Fergusson

"MYTH" AND THE LITERARY SCRUPLE

Francis Fergusson's distinguished career includes experience as a drama critic and long service at Rutgers University as Professor of English. He is the author of three respected studies: *The Idea of a Theater* (1949), *Dante's Drama of the Mind* (1953), and *The Human Image in Dramatic Literature* (1957). "'Myth' and the Literary Scruple" was first published in the *Sewanee Review* in 1956 and reprinted in *The Human Image in Dramatic Literature*.

"Myth" is one of those words which it has become almost impossible to use without apologetic quotation marks. Ill-defined for centuries, it is now used in many senses and for many purposes: to mean nonsense or willful obscurantism in some contexts, the deepest wisdom of man in others. One would like to be able to banish it to that pale Hades where "irony" and "ambiguity" have their impotent but pretentious afterlife. But unfortunately the student of literature cannot get along without "Myth." It is too evident that poetry, to say nothing of religion, philosophy and history, are akin to mythopoeia. Drama, the lyric and fiction live symbolically with myths, nourished by them, and nourishing their flickering lives. Some of the inventions of poets—Kafka's *Metamorphosis*, Plato's tale of the charioteer with his white and his black horse—are modelled on myth. Some poetic works which we like—*Moby Dick*, Lorca's plays —have what we are pleased to call a "mythic" quality. Writers of all kinds use inherited myths in their own work. The student of literature cannot avoid talking about Myth; but how can he use the protean word with any decent rigor?

It was the early romantic poets and philosophers who started our modern cult of Myth. They sought in it some alternative to the narrow categories of modern rationalism, some defense of humane letters in a world created by applied science; often they felt it would replace formal religion. But in our time scientists and pseudo-scientists of every description— psychologists of several persuasions; archeologists, linguists, assorted varieties of anthropologists and sociologists—pronounce upon Myth with an imposing air of authority. And specialists in various fields have filled our books and our museums with countless mythic tales and mythic figures, not only from our own tradition but from every corner of the human time and space. In this welter of facts and theories the student of literature is in danger of losing his bearings

337

altogether. For he cannot simply disregard the labors of countless savants on Myth; he must use them for his own purposes when they strike him as illuminating. On the other hand, he lacks the knowledge and the training to join the debates of specialists on their own terms. What he needs, I think, is a renewed sense of his own stake in Myth, plus a firmer reliance on the evidences in literature and on the methods and the criteria of literary analysis. For the point at which Myth concerns the student of literature is the point at which it is brought to life again in poetry, drama or fiction.

From this point of view it is evident that it is not realistic to talk about Myth-in-general, as though we had a generally agreed upon definition which would apply to all the instances of Myth in art and letters. And if one makes the all-important distinction between the second-hand, merely reported or summarized mythic tale, as we find it in Bulfinch or *The Hero with a Thousand Faces*, and the mythic tale as it actually lives in poetry or drama, it appears that we lack an unmistakeable example of even *one* myth. For the myth of Oedipus is one thing in *Oedipus Rex*, and something quite different in the dramas of Seneca or Dryden. Giraudoux, clearly recognizing this point, called his play *Amphytrion 38*. One of the most striking properties of myths is that they generate new forms (like the differing children of one parent) in the imaginations of those who try to grasp them. Until some imagination, that of a poet or only a reader or auditor, is thus fecundated by a myth, the myth would seem to exist only potentially. And if we cannot lay hands on even one myth prior to its imaginative embodiments, how can we hope to pin down myth-in-general in *itself*?

We must, I think, adopt an extremely ascetic regimen in our dealings with Myth. We must abandon hope of reaching any very plausible generalizations, and pay close attention to some of the many ways in which myths actually live in our literature. Of course the evidence, even when thus arbitrarily reduced, is almost endless, and very diverse. How can we rule out any of the living works which the narrative in the Christian Creed at one extreme, the lightest tale of Ovid at the other, have generated in the imaginations of artists in thousands of years? All one could hope to do is to choose rather haphazardly a few examples, as illustrations of what a literary approach to Myth might be.

Let us begin with a rough preliminary classification of the kinds of myths to be found in literature. The classification I wish to propose is taken from Malinowski's study of the Trobriand Islanders. He found three types of myth in that culture: Legends, which he defined as stories about the past which were believed to be true of the past, and which served to give the Islanders some significant conception of their history; Folk or Fairy Tales, told only for fun, without reference to truth, on occasions when the tribe was gathered simply for entertainment; and Religious Myths, which represented basic elements in the creed, the morals, and the social structure of that people. Malinowski based this classification on his observations of the Trobrianders, but it looks as though he had understood them by analogy with our own culture, for we can recognize the three types (or the three attitudes to Myth) in our art and literature. Some scientific anthropologists mistrust Malinowski precisely because he feels the kinship between the Trobrianders and us; but for me his value lies in his sympathy and his sense of the humane analogies between cultures. Let us claim him for the Humanities, and see how his classification may help us to understand our own heritage.

I think we should have to go back to Dante's Christianized Vergilian Legend of Rome to find a fully developed Historic Legend in Malinowski's sense. But the Fairy Tales, Little Red Riding Hood, the innumerable Greek tales of Arcady, of nymphs and shepherds, charming stories whose truth we never enquire into, have been common since the early Renaissance. Readers of Professor Douglas Bush's studies of literary myths will think of countless examples. It is easy to see why the Fairy Tale conception of Myth is quite at home in times of the most intransigent rationalism. If the myth makes no claim to truth in itself, but at most serves as pleasing illustration of some moral or political concept, we may enjoy it with a clear conscience. But the romantic and post-romantic cult of Myth is not content with these neoclassic attitudes. It seeks the Religious Myth, or tries to attribute metaphysical meaning to the myths it invokes. Most of the contemporary debates about Myth assume this religious intention on the part of the lovers of Myth, and so we have many interesting attempts (like Wheelwright's in *The Burning Fountain* or Campbell's in *The Hero with a Thousand Faces*) to defend Myth as a mode of knowing.

But the most natural view of Myth in the modern world (by which I mean our tradition since Dante defined the "allegory of poets") has been the Fairy Tale conception. And in the hands of Paul Valéry this way with Myth has turned out to have new vitality. No one could accuse Valéry of underestimating Reason, the usual complaint of users of myths in our time. He is the champion of *l'intelligence*, the emancipated but scrupulous mind, Reason at its most ambitious and austere: the ultimate reliance of modernists, from Socrates through Da Vinci

to Valéry himself. And at the same time he is the high priest of pure poetry, "the representative poet of the first half of the 20th Century," as Eliot called him. His poetry should therefore be a crucial instance of the life of Myth in literature.

The first line of his *Fragments du Narcisse* announces the theme of that poem:

Que tu brilles enfin, terme pur de ma course!

We are to imagine Narcissus bending over the pool, addressing his own shining reflection as the pure goal, now recognized at last, of his life's course. Then come the beautiful music and the Arcadian imagery of the *Fragments*: the reeds, the water, the quiet evening, the echoes and reflections which echo and reflect the inward focus of thought and desire. The poem has the magic suggestiveness, or call it the abstract allusiveness, of the finest *symboliste* achievements, and I do not therefore attempt to analyse it in detail. Suffice it to say that as we let the poem sink in we come to see that the first line is to be understood in more senses than one. It is not only Narcissus' address to his reflection, it is the poet's address to Narcissus, who illustrates the paradoxical goal of pure reason and also of pure poetry. Thus it is also the poet's invocation of his own spirit at that creative center of life where thought and poetic intuition both have their source. When the life of reason attains its highest abstraction its pleasure lies in contemplating itself in the act of contemplation. And when poetry is pure enough—approaching the abstractness of music, freeing itself from all attachment, whether to persons, things, or transcendent moral or religious goals—it becomes its own object. The best poems in Valéry's *symboliste* tradition are based on the sad delectation of poetry's self-love.

It is easy to see why Narcissus is addressed by Valéry as the very image of his own goal. Narcissus aptly represents Valéry's lifelong study: the mind's creative or formative power when it turns inward in search of itself. The perversity of the mythic figure, the futility of introversion even when most subtle, is part of the poet's gloomy meaning. And yet the question of the reality of Narcissus himself never arises. The poet is not interested in exploring the mythic narrative itself. He does not present the thwarted nymphs who beseech Narcissus in vain (except in Narcissus' vague fear of their interruption) nor the fight, nor the transformation of Narcissus himself into that pretty specimen of vegetable life, the Narcissus flower, which seems so suggestive in any realistic reading of the story. The figure of Narcissus is perhaps the "inspiration" of the poem, as a metaphor or even a word may be; but its value remains strictly poetic. In all of this Valéry accepts the Fairy Tale notion of Myth, handling it lightly, almost playfully, as though for entertainment only. His use of his myth is basically a more sophisticated version of the neoclassic convention: as a language, closely analogous to the endlessly worked-over but still iridescent words of French. Hence the deflated exactitude of the Valérian taste, the crystalline hardness one feels beneath the shimmer of his effects.

Valéry as *symboliste* represents a culmination of the romantic movement, its "classic" moment of complete self-awareness, as he himself would put it. He is concerned with the unique essence of poetry and its absolute independence; in his hands Myth serves poetry, not vice versa. Though he is the heir of the romantic poets he does not have a trace of their religious attitude to Myth. This is Malinowski's description of the Religious Myth—the "myth proper" as he calls it— among the Trobrianders:

A special class of stories, regarded as sacred, embodied in ritual, morals and social organization. . . . These stories live not by idle interest . . . but are to the natives a statement of a primeval, greater and more relevant reality, by which the present life, fates and activities of mankind are determined, the knowledge of which supplies man with the motive for ritual and moral actions, as well as with indications how to perform them.

Valéry could accept none of this without betraying his faith in the independent formative power of the mind. But Malinowski's description applies by analogy to the narrative in the Christian Creed, the basis of European social and cultural order, and of much of European art, for a thousand years. And it applies also to what romantic poets seek vaguely, and more or less in vain, in the myths which they religiously invoke.

Wagner's *Tristan und Isolde* is the most perfect example I know of the romantic-religious cult of Myth. Thus Wagner opposes to Valéry's rationalist tradition, in which the mythic tales are told for fun or half-playfully allegorized, the Tristan narrative, in which he finds a "primeval, greater and more relevant reality" than that of reason and common sense. Valéry in *Narcisse* appeals to the individual intellect and its strictly poetic sensibility, but Wagner, basing all on the power of his music, reaches for a primitive, unindividualized mode of awareness in his hypnotized and mob-like audience. Valéry does not take the Narcissus story seriously except as metaphor or illustration, but Wagner makes the course of the Tristan narrative the very form, or "soul" of the opera. Each crucial episode: the drinking of the love-potion, the single night of love, the final *Liebestodt*: has a ritual significance which perhaps reflects (as De Rougemont suggests) the rites of the half-forgotten cult of the Cathars. Valéry expects no result from his poem but the refined pleasures of the mind and the sensibility, but Wagner wants to effect an initation or change of heart, and the final love-death seems to demand a momentary faith, at least, in a greater, unseen reality. We know that there is, in fact, a Wagnerian cult, which helped to nourish Hitler's attempt to create a German *Volk* by magic. One may even see in Schopenhauer, in Nietzsche's *Birth of Tragedy*, and in Freud, with his death-wish and his boundless libido, a kind of theology for the gloomy-religious action of *Tristan*.

Wagner's treatment of the Tristan myth fulfills the requirements of Malinowski's definition of the Religious Myth. It also agrees with what Maritain has to say of "metaphysical myths" in his *Creative Intuition*: "The metaphysical myths are the organic signs and symbols of some faith actually lived. . . . They are forms through which a conviction of the entire soul nourishes and quickens from within the very power of creative imagination. Such myths have no force except through the faith man has in them." Wagner must, I think, have worked upon *Tristan* with the faith which Maritain describes, for the creative power of the opera is unmistakeable. But unfortunately a faith may be desperate and deluded when one sees in "myth a source of higher teaching and ultra-spiritual insights, converting it into a magic mirror that reflects the heart's desire," as Philip Rahv says of the romantic cult of Myth. Wagner's religious acceptance of the Tristan myth is possible only at too great an expense: the rejection of the contemporary world along with all the achievements of reason, from morality to science. Those who see in the cult of Myth only willful obscurantism would find much in Wagner to support their thesis. And such reflections as these must throw some doubt on the faith which Wagner himself had in the "greater and more relevant reality" symbolized by *Tristan;* we know that he changed his mind about it later in his life.

The fact is that we are here in that dim and treacherous realm between firm religious belief on one side and make-believe on the other. Belief and make-believe have similar fertilizing effects upon human creativity. An actor must make-believe his role very deeply and with full concentration if he is to give more than a superficial performance, yet we do not attribute religious faith to him, even when we in the audience "believe" in the character he is presenting. And in our time we are more at home with make-believe than we are with belief—or perhaps we have simply lost the sense of the distinction. Even the truths of science begin to look like partial metaphors: necessary (though sometimes contradictory) hypotheses, which guide and nourish the scientific imagination for a time, not adequate and final truth. Thus the whole problem of the Religious Myth is on the edge of an even darker mystery: that of the nature, even the possibility, of real faith in our time.

That is one important reason why, in our attempt to collect the crucial evidences of poetry as it reincarnates myths, we must at this point remember Dante. For in the *Divine Comedy* we unmistakeably encounter the solidity of real belief. That poem, based on the Christian Creed, celebrates the faith and the moral, philosophic, and liturgical order which regulated Europe from the Dark Ages to the threshold of modern times: that "primeval, greater and more relevant reality" which Malinowski says the Religious Myth, the "myth proper," is supposed to embody. The *Divine Comedy* would, for this reason alone, be required reading for the study of the life of Myth in poetry.

Moreover the *Divine Comedy* contains all the kinds of Myth, and all the attitudes to Myth, which Malinowski describes, all in significant relation to each other and to the enlightened Reason of Dante's time. Thus Malinowski's "historic legend" is built into the framework of the poem: Virgil's legendary interpretation of Rome, which Dante combines with the historic drama of the Old Testament and places in the perspective of the Incarnation, wherein both the Hebrew and the Pagan traditions are fulfilled. This historical legend serves exactly the purpose Malinowski describes: based on the known facts of the past, which are accepted as true of the past, it gives Dante's generation its bearings in the historic sequence. What Malinowski calls Fairy Tales—the loot of Ovid and Lucan, more obscure tales from Arabic or Celtic sources—are alive again in every part of the *Comedy*. Dante takes them in a spirit akin to Valéry's: "my not-false errors" he calls them, when they inspire his imagination on the purgatorial stair. They provide much of the great poem's sensuous movement and variety; and when we look more closely we see that each has also its tropological meaning: they are visionary embodiments of the momentary experiences of the pilgrim spirit as the moral life unfolds. The ultimate meaning of the moral life, like that of the life of the race in history, is seen in the Incarnation and Sacrifice of Christ. It is that narrative, of course, which commands Dante's real belief and provides (quite apart from the question of *our* belief) the very pattern of the Religious Myth.

A real study of Dante's masterful way with his vast heritage of myths would require not minutes but years; and it would require a combination of erudition and tact which is not available. But one may get some slight sense of his virtuosity from almost any detail of the poem. Consider, for instance, what he does with the Siren in the dream which forms the opening sequence of *Purgatorio* XIX:

Nell'ora che non può il calor diurno intiepidar più il freddo della luna, vinto da terra o talor da Saturno;
quando i geomanti lor maggior fortuna veggiono in oriente, inanzi all'alba, surger per via che poco le sta bruna:
mi venne in sogno una femmina balba, negli occhi guercia e sopra i piè distorta, con le man monche, e di colore scialba.
Io la mirava: e come il sol conforta le fredde membra che la notte aggrava, così lo sguardo mio le facea scorta
la lingua, e poscia tutta la drizzava in poco d'ora, e lo smarrito volto, come amor vuol, così le colorava.
Poi ch'ell'avea il parlar così disciolto, cominciava a cantar sì che con pena da lei avrei mio intento rivolto.
"Io son," cantava, "io son dolce Sirena, che i marinari in mezzo mar dismago: tanto son i piacere a sentir piena.
Io volsi Ulisse del suo cammin vago col canto mio; e qual meco si ausa rado sen parte, sì tutto l'appago."
Ancor non era sua bocca richiusa, quando una donna apparve santa e presta lunghesso me per far colei confusa.
"O Virgilio, o Virgilio, chi è questa?" fieramente diceva; ed ei venia con gli occhi fitti pure in quella onesta.
L'altra prendeva, e dinanzi l'apria fendendo i drappi, e mostravami il ventre; quel mi svegliò col puzzo che n'uscia.

(At the hour when the heat of the day can no longer warm the cold of the moon, being overcome by earth or perhaps by Saturn;
When the geomancers see their *fortuna major* in the east, just before dawn, rising along a path which will not be dark for long:
There came to me in dream a stuttering woman, squint-eyed, twisted on her feet, with stunted hands, yellow in color. I gazed upon her, and as the sun comforts cold limbs which night weighs down, so my gaze made ready
Her tongue, and then in a short time set her all straight, and her pale face, just as love wills, it colored.
As soon as her speech was loosened she began to sing, so that with difficulty I should have

turned my attention from her. "I am," she sang, "I am that sweet Siren who bemuses sailors in the midst of the sea, so full I am of pleasure for them to feel.

"I turned Ulysses from his wandering way to this my song; whoever risks himself with me rarely departs, I satiate him so fully."

Her mouth was hardly closed when there appeared beside me a woman, alert and holy, to make that one confused.

"O Virgil, Virgil, who is this?" she was saying proudly, and he was coming, with his eyes fixed only on that honest one. He seized the other and opened her in front, ripping the clothes, and showed me the belly, which waked me with the stench that issued from it.)

Dante's treatment of the Siren in this passage is similar in several ways to Valéry's treatment of Narcissus: it is an example of Dante's "allegory of poets." Thus, like Valéry, he is more interested in the mythic figure than in her whole traditional story, and he uses her to get the sensuous immediacy and the subtle complexity of poetry. But she seems to have more reality than Valéry's conventional figure: if not a metaphysical entity in her own right, she is at least an ineluctable trope, the embodiment of one eternally-recurrent human experience. That is because the Siren has her place in a vaster vision which includes the perspectives of ethics and faith. Valéry's Narcissus, on the other hand, is presented as "pure" poetry.

Dante establishes the being and the meanings of his Siren by means of the context in which she appears: a certain point in the Pilgrim's spiritual growth, at a certain place on the Mountain, and toward the end of the second night of the purgatorial journey. By showing us the psyche in whose imagination the Siren appears, Dante includes several dimensions of mythopoeia which Valéry omits. We *see* the dreamer see his mythic enchantress, an image which at first says nothing to him. We then see him "be-

lieve" the image, and focus his attention and his unsatisfied desire upon it. Under that warmth and light the ancient myth, "colored as love wills," reveals some of the meanings she had held only potentially: in short, she is "brought to life." But the night in which she appears also helps us to understand her. In all three nights of the purgatorial journey the Pilgrim can rely neither upon his direct perception of the world, his moral will, or his reason. In the solitude and passivity of sleep he knows the call of many forms of love, including that irrational brute weight of desire which pulls, like gravitation, toward the bottom of the universe. In this passage the nocturnal chill that weighs limbs down presents this pull: the occasion for the Siren's appearance. The direction of love's movement thus indicated (night against reason and the day, the ambiguity of love and death) reminds one strongly of the motivation and the nocturnal imagery of *Tristan*. Dante may have seen at this point the object of Wagner's desperate faith.

But this is the *second* night of the purgatorial journey, and the Pilgrim has by this time acquired a certain moral awareness. After the Siren is warmed into beauty and song, at the very moment of pleasurable yielding, Virgil appears by that Grace which hovers over this region, and reveals the Siren's deathly aspect once more. Virgil represents reason and the accumulated wisdom of experience in the real world, and by this time his voice and presence are in a sense *within* the Pilgrim's spirit. In the dream he plays a role like that of the orthodox Freudian "superego," representative of moral truth. At this point in his development the Pilgrim (and the reader) can understand the mythic Siren from a moral point of view, and that suffices for escape.

But because of the sturdy realism which underlies the whole conception of the

Divine Comedy the Siren, for all her moral meaning, is not reduced to the status of a moral allegory only. She retains some sort of being in her own right; she does not forfeit her status as one of the amoral figures of Myth, and that is characteristic of Dante's way with myths. Their visionary being is established first, their possible philosophical meaning for the Pilgrim, second; and when they disappear we do not feel that they have been rationalized out of all existence. The Siren first looks strange and evil, then she appears as infinitely attractive, then as dismaying and disgusting, but in all of these metamorphoses we never lose the sense that she was somehow *there*; and her power and mystery remain when we leave her.

If Dante can handle the figures of Myth with such subtle and flexible realism—that is, with respect both for the reality of the imagination in which they appear, and for the different reality of the figures themselves—it is because he understands them, not in conceptual terms, but by analogy with the Incarnation. The process whereby a myth is brought to life in a human imagination corresponds to that by which Christ lives again in the spirits of the faithful, through belief, concentration, love, and an imitative movement of spirit. The mythic forms which tempt the human spirit may in Dante's scheme be childish or deceptive. But their meaning for us, and the process whereby we reincarnate them in our own beings, are to be understood by analogy with the human figure, and the imitation, of Christ. Even Hell, where Dante endows so many evil forms with

his own life and love, was made by Divine Power, Highest Wisdom and Primal Love. It is because Dante believes so completely in the reality of this basic Analogue that he can both share in the lives of many kinds of myths, and yet also pass beyond them, to consider their meaning in other terms and in relation to each other. His belief in the "primeval, greater and more relevant reality" of the Christian Narrative gives him a key to the heritage of Myth, makes him a master (probably *the* master) of the mythic modes of understanding.

The view of the world which Dante inherited, formed by the converging and age-long labors of Hebrew and Greek, has dissolved long since. His *modus vivendi* between Reason and Mythopoeia is no longer accessible to us. But if we are to consider the life of Myth in the poetry of our tradition, I do not see how we can continue to neglect the vast lore in the *Divine Comedy.*

One can sympathize with those numerous writers who use "Myth" to mean only wishful thinking or Machiavellian obscurantism. It would be nice to get rid of the term and its puzzles so simply. But that recourse is not available to those who stubbornly continue to be interested in Poetry, or indeed in any form of the Humanities. We cannot get rid of "Myth," but we can beware of it. We can remember some of the countless ways in which myths live in our literature from Homer to Faulkner. And we can study some of the forms this life takes with the respect for the unique individuality of play or poem which the masters of literature have taught us.

Northrop Frye

THE DRUNKEN BOAT:
THE REVOLUTIONARY ELEMENT IN ROMANTICISM

From 1959 to 1966 Principal of Victoria College at the University of Toronto and now Toronto's first University Professor, Northrop Frye is the leading advocate of mythopoeic criticism in this generation. His book *Anatomy of Criticism,* published in 1957, has already become one of the few critical works that no contemporary student of literature can ignore. Frye's other writings are impressive in scope; he has written eight books, edited twelve others, and published more than a hundred essays, articles, and reviews. "The Drunken Boat" originally appeared in *Romanticism Reconsidered* (1963), a collection of Columbia University English Institute Papers edited by Frye.

Any such conception as "Romanticism" is at one or more removes from actual literary experience, in an inner world where ten thousand different things flash upon the inward eye with all the bliss of oversimplification. Some things about it, however, are generally accepted, and we may start with them. First, Romanticism has a historical center of gravity, which falls somewhere around the 1790–1830 period. This gets us at once out of the fallacy of timeless characterization, where we say that Romanticism has certain qualities, not found in the age of Pope, of sympathy with nature or what not, only to have someone produce a poem of Propertius or Kalidasa, or, eventually, Pope himself, and demand to know if the same qualities are not there. Second, Romanticism is not a general historical term like "medieval": it appears to have another center of gravity in the creative arts. We speak most naturally of Romantic literature, painting, and music. We do, it is true, speak of Romantic philosophy, but what seems to us most clearly Romantic in that are such things as the existential ethic of Fichte or the analogical constructs of Schelling; both of them, in different ways, examples of philosophy produced by an essentially literary mind, like the philosophies of Sartre or Maritain in our day. So at least they seemed to Kant, if one may judge from Kant's letter to Fichte suggesting that Fichte abandon philosophy, as a subject too difficult for him, and confine himself to lively popularizations.

Third, even in its application to the creative arts Romanticism is a selective

345

term, more selective even than "Baroque" appears to be becoming. We think of it as including Keats, but not, on the whole, Crabbe; Scott, but not, in general, Jane Austen; Wordsworth, but not, on any account, James Mill. As generally used, "Romantic" is contrasted with two other terms, "classical" and "realistic." Neither contrast seems satisfactory. We could hardly call Wordsworth's preface to the *Lyrical Ballads* anti-realistic, or ignore the fact that Shelley was a better classical scholar than, say, Dryden, who, according to Samuel Johnson, translated the first book of the *Iliad* without knowing what was in the second. Still, the pairings exist, and we shall have to examine them. And yet, fourth, though selective, Romanticism is not a voluntary category. It does not see Byron as the successor to Pope or Wordsworth as the successor to Milton, which would have been acceptable enough to both poets: it associates Byron and Wordsworth, to their mutual disgust, with each other.

Accepting all this, we must also avoid the two traps in the phrase "history of ideas." First, an idea, as such, is independent of time and can be argued about; an historical event is not and cannot be. If Romanticism is in part an historical event, as it clearly is, then to say with T. E. Hulme: "I object to even the best of the Romantics" is much like saying: "I object to even the best battles of the Napoleonic War." Most general value-judgments on Romanticism as a whole are rationalizations of an agreement or disagreement with some belief of which Romantic poetry is supposed to form the objective correlative.

This latter is the second or Hegelian trap in the history of ideas, which we fall into when we assume that around 1790 or earlier some kind of thesis arose in history and embodied itself in the Romantic movement. Such an assumption leads us to examining all the cultural products we call Romantic as allegories of that thesis. Theses have a way of disagreeing with each other, and if we try to think of Romanticism as some kind of single "idea," all we can do with it is what Lovejoy did: break it down into a number of contradictory ideas with nothing significant in common. In literature, and more particularly poetry, ideas are subordinated to imagery, to a language more "simple, sensuous, and passionate" than the language of philosophy. Hence it may be possible for two poets to be related by common qualities of imagery even when they do not agree on a single thesis in religion, politics, or the theory of art itself.

The history of imagery, unlike the history of ideas, appears to be for the most part a domain where, in the words of a fictional Canadian poetess, "the hand of man hath never trod." Yet we seem inexorably led to it by our own argument, and perhaps the defects in what follows may be in part excused by the novelty of the subject, to me at least. After making every allowance for a prodigious variety of technique and approach, it is still possible to see a consistent framework (I wish the English language had a better equivalent for the French word *cadre*) in the imagery of both medieval and Renaissance poetry. The most remarkable and obvious feature of this framework is the division of being into four levels. The highest level is heaven, the place of the presence of God. Next come the two levels of the order of nature, the human level and the physical level. The order of human nature, or man's proper home, is represented by the story of the Garden of Eden in the Bible and the myth of the Golden Age in Boethius and elsewhere. Man is no longer in it, but the end of all his religious, moral, and social cultivation is to raise him into something resembling it.

Physical nature, the world of animals and plants, is the world man is now in, but unlike the animals and plants he is not adjusted to it. He is confronted from birth with a moral dialectic, and must either rise above it to his proper human home or sink below it into the fourth level of sin, death, and hell. This last level is not part of the order of nature, but its existence is what at present corrupts nature. A very similar framework can be found in classical poetry, and the alliance of the two, in what is so often called Christian humanism, accounts for the sense of an antagonism between the Romantic movement and the classical tradition, in spite of its many and remarkable affinities with that tradition.

Such a framework of images, however closely related in practice to belief, is not in itself a belief or an expression of belief: it is in itself simply a way of arranging images and providing for metaphors. At the same time the word "framework" itself is a spatial metaphor, and any framework is likely to be projected in space, even confused or identified with its spatial projection. In Dante Eden is a long way up, on top of the mountain of purgatory; heaven is much further up, and hell is down, at the center of the earth. We may know that such conceptions as heaven and hell do not depend on spatial metaphors of up and down, but a cosmological poet, dealing with them as images, has to put them somewhere. To Dante it was simple enough to put them at the top and bottom of the natural order, because he knew of no alternative to the Ptolemaic picture of the world. To Milton, who did know of an alternative, the problem was more complex, and Milton's heaven and hell are outside the cosmos, in a kind of absolute up and down. After Milton comes Newton, and after Newton ups and downs become hopelessly confused.

What I see first of all in Romanticism is the effect of a profound change, not primarily in belief, but in the spatial projection of reality. This in turn leads to a different localizing of the various levels of that reality. Such a change in the localizing of images is bound to be accompanied by, or even cause, changes in belief and attitude, and changes of this latter sort are exhibited by the Romantic poets. But the change itself is not in belief or attitude, and may be found in, or at least affecting, poets of a great variety of beliefs.

In the earlier framework, the disorder of sin, death, and corruption was restricted to the sublunary world of four elements. Above the moon was all that was left of nature as God had originally planned it before the fall. The planets, with their angel-guided spheres, are images of a divinely sanctioned order of nature which is also the true home of man. Hence there was no poetic incongruity in Dante's locating his Paradiso in the planetary spheres, nor in Milton's associating the music of the spheres with the song of the angels in the *Nativity Ode*, nor in using the same word "heaven" for both the kingdom of God and the sky. A post-Newtonian poet has to think of gravitation and the solar system. Newton, Miss Nicolson has reminded us, demanded the muse, but the appropriate muse was Urania, and Urania had already been requested by Milton to descend to a safer position on earth for the second half of *Paradise Lost*.

Let us turn to Blake's poem *Europe*, engraved in 1794. *Europe* surveys the history of the Western world from the birth of Christ to the beginning of the French Revolution, and in its opening lines parodies the *Nativity Ode*. For Blake all the deities associated with the planets and the starry skies, of whom the chief is Enitharmon, the Queen of

Heaven, are projections of a human will to tyranny, rationalized as eternal necessity and order. Christianity, according to this poem, had not abolished but confirmed the natural religion in the classical culture which had deified the star-gods. The doom of tyranny is sealed by the French Revolution, and the angel who blows the last trumpet as the sign of the final awakening of liberty is Isaac Newton. The frontispiece of *Europe* is the famous vision of the sky-god Urizen generally called the Ancient of Days, holding a compass in his left hand, and this picture is closely related to Blake's portrait of Newton, similarly preoccupied with a compass and oblivious of the heavens he is supposed to be studying.

Blake's view, in short, is that the universe of modern astronomy, as revealed in Newton, exhibits only a blind, mechanical, subhuman order, not the personal presence of a deity. Newton himself tended to think of God still as "up there," even to the extent of suggesting that space was the divine sensorium; but *what* was up there, according to Blake, is only a set of interlocking geometrical diagrams, and God, Blake says, is not a mathematical diagram. Newtonism leads to what for Blake are intellectual errors, such as a sense of the superiority of abstractions to actual things and the notion that the real world is a measurable but invisible world of primary qualities. But Blake's main point is that admiring the mechanisms of the sky leads to establishing human life in mechanical patterns too. In other words, Blake's myth of Urizen is a fuller and more sophisticated version of the myth of Frankenstein.

Blake's evil, sinister, or merely complacent sky-gods, Urizen, Nobodaddy, Enitharmon, Satan, remind us of similar beings in other Romantics: Shelley's Jupiter, Byron's Arimanes, the Lord in the Prologue to *Faust*. They in their turn beget later Romantic gods and goddesses, such as Baudelaire's female "froide majesté," Hardy's Immanent Will, or the God of Housman's "The chestnut casts his flambeaux," who is a brute and blackguard because he is a sky-god in control of the weather, and sends his rain on the just and on the unjust. The association of sinister or unconscious mechanism with what we now call outer space is a commonplace of popular literature today which is a Romantic inheritance. Perhaps Orwell's *1984*, a vision of a mechanical tyranny informed by the shadow of a Big Brother who can never die, is the terminal point of a development of imagery that began with Blake's Ancient of Days. Not every poet, naturally, associates mechanism with the movements of the stars as Blake does, or sees it as a human imitation of the wrong kind of divine creativity. But the contrast between the mechanical and the organic is deeply rooted in Romantic thinking, and the tendency is to associate the mechanical with ordinary consciousness, as we see in the account of the associative fancy in Coleridge's *Biographia* or of discursive thought in Shelley's *Defence of Poetry*. This is in striking contrast to the Cartesian tradition, where the mechanical is of course associated with the subconscious. The mechanical being characteristic of ordinary experience, it is found particularly in the world "outside"; the superior or organic world is consequently "inside," and although it is still called superior or higher, the natural metaphorical direction of the inside world is downward, into the profounder depths of consciousness.

If a Romantic poet, therefore, wishes to write of God, he has more difficulty in finding a place to put him than Dante or even Milton had, and on the whole he prefers to do without a place, or finds "within" metaphors more reassuring than "up there" metaphors. When Wordsworth speaks, in *The Prelude* and elsewhere, of feeling the presence of deity through a sense of interpenetration of the human mind and natural powers, one feels that his huge and mighty forms, like the spirits of Yeats, have come to bring him the right metaphors for his poetry. In the second book of *The Excursion* we have a remarkable vision of what has been called the heavenly city of the eighteenth-century philosophers, cast in the form of an ascent up a mountain, where the city is seen at the top. The symbolism, I think, is modeled on the vision of Cleopolis in the first book of *The Faerie Queene*, and its technique is admirably controlled and precise. Yet surely this is not the real Wordsworth. The spirits have brought him the wrong metaphors; metaphors that Spenser used with full imaginative conviction, but which affect only the surface of Wordsworth's mind.

The second level of the older construct was the world of original human nature, now a lost paradise or golden age. It is conceived as a better and more appropriate home for man than his present environment, whether man can regain it or not. But in the older construct this world was ordinarily not thought of as human in origin or conception. Adam awoke in a garden not of his planting, in a fresh-air suburb of the City of God, and when the descendants of Cain began to build cities on earth, they were building to models already existing in both heaven and hell. In the Middle Ages and the Renaissance the agencies which helped to raise man from the physical to the human world were such things as the sacraments of religion, the moral law, and the habit of virtue, none of them strictly human inventions. These were the safe and unquestioned agencies, the genuinely educational media. Whether the human arts of poetry and painting

and music were genuinely educational in this sense could be and was disputed or denied; and the poets themselves, when they wrote apologies for poetry, seldom claimed equality with religion or law, beyond pointing out that the earliest major poets were prophets and lawgivers.

For the modern mind there are two poles of mental activity. One may be described as sense, by which I mean the recognition of what is presented by experience: the empirical, observant habit of mind in which, among other things, the inductive sciences begin. In this attitude reality is, first of all, "out there," whatever happens to it afterwards. The other pole is the purely formalizing or constructive aspect of the mind, where reality is something brought into being by the act of construction. It is obvious that in pre-Romantic poetry there is a strong affinity with the attitude that we have called sense. The poet, in all ages and cultures, prefers images to abstractions, the sensational to the conceptual. But the pre-Romantic structure of imagery belonged to a nature which was the work of God; the design in nature was, as Sir Thomas Browne calls it, the art of God; nature is thus an objective structure or system for the poet to follow. The appropriate metaphors of imitation are visual and physical ones, and the creative powers of the poet have models outside him.

It is generally recognized that Rousseau represents, and to some extent made, a revolutionary change in the modern attitude. The primary reason for his impact was, I think, not in his political or educational views as such, but in his assumption that civilization was a purely human artifact, something that man had made, could unmake, could subject to his own criticism, and was at all times entirely responsible for. Above all, it was something for which the only known model was in the human mind. This kind of assumption is so penetrating that it affects those who detest Rousseau, or have never heard of him, equally with the small minority of his admirers. Also, it gets into the mind at once, whereas the fading out of such counter assumptions as the literal and historical nature of the Garden of Eden story is very gradual. The effect of such an assumption is twofold. First, it puts the arts in the center of civilization. The basis of civilization is now the creative power of man; its model is the human vision revealed in the arts. Second, this model, as well as the sources of creative power, are now located in the mind's internal heaven, the external world being seen as a mirror reflecting and making visible what is within. Thus the "outside" world, most of which is "up there," yields importance and priority to the inner world, in fact derives its poetic significance at least from it. "In looking at objects of Nature," says Coleridge in the Notebooks, "I seem rather to be seeking, as it were *asking* for, a symbolical language for something within me that already and forever exists, than observing anything new." This principle extends both to the immediate surrounding world which is the emblem of the music of humanity in Wordsworth and to the starry heavens on which Keats read "Huge cloudy symbols of a high romance."

Hence in Romantic poetry the emphasis is not on what we have called sense, but on the constructive power of the mind, where reality is brought into being by experience. There is a contrast in popular speech between the romantic and the realist, where the word "romantic" implies a sentimentalized or rose-colored view of reality. This vulgar sense of the word may throw some light on the intensity with which the Romantic poets sought to defy external reality by creating a uniformity of tone and mood. The establishing of this uniformity, and the careful excluding of anything that would dispel it, is one of the constant and typical features of the best Romantic poetry, though we may call it a dissociation of sensibility if we happen not to like it. Such a poetic technique is, psychologically, akin to magic, which also aims at bringing spiritual forces into reality through concentration on a certain type of experience. Such words as "charm" or "spell" suggest uniformity of mood as well as a magician's repertoire. Historically and generically, it is akin to romance, with its effort to maintain a self-consistent idealized world without the intrusions of realism or irony.

For these reasons Romanticism is difficult to adapt to the novel, which demands an empirical and observant attitude; its contribution to prose fiction is rather, appropriately enough, a form of romance. In the romance the characters tend to become psychological projections, and the setting a period in a past just remote enough to be re-created rather than empirically studied. We think of Scott as within the Romantic movement; Jane Austen as related to it chiefly by her parodies of the kind of sensibility that tries to live in a self-created world instead of adapting to the one that is there. Marianne in *Sense and Sensibility*, Catherine in *Northanger Abbey*, and of course everybody in *Love and Friendship*, are examples. Crabbe's naturalistic manifesto in the opening of *The Village* expresses an attitude which in itself is not far from Wordsworth's. But Crabbe is a metrical novelist in a way that Wordsworth is not. The soldier in *The Prelude* and the leech-gatherer in *Resolution and Independence* are purely romantic characters in the sense just given of psychological projections: that is, they become temporary or epiphanic myths. We should also notice that the internalizing of reality in Romanticism proper develops a contrast between it and a contemporary realism which descends from the pre-Romantic tradition but acquires a more purely empirical attitude to the external world.

The third level of the older construct was the physical world, theologically fallen, which man is born into but which is not the real world of human nature. Man's primary attitude to external physical nature is thus one of detachment. The kind of temptation represented by Spenser's Bower of Bliss or Milton's Comus is based on the false suggestion that physical nature, with its relatively innocent moral freedom, can be the model for human nature. The resemblances between the poetic techniques used in the Bower of Bliss episode and some of the techniques of the Romantics are superficial: Spenser, unlike the Romantics, is consciously producing a rhetorical set piece, designed to show that the Bower of Bliss is not natural but artificial in the modern sense. Man for pre-Romantic poets is not a child of Nature in the sense that he was originally a primitive. Milton's Adam becomes a noble savage immediately after his fall; but that is not his original nature. In Romanticism the cult of the primitive is a by-product of the internalizing of the creative impulse. The poet has always been supposed to be imitating nature, but if the model of his creative power is in his mind, the nature that he is to imitate is now inside him, even if it is also outside.

The original form of human society also is hidden "within." Keats refers to this hidden society when he says in a letter to Reynolds: "Man should not dispute or assert but whisper results to his neighbour . . . and Humanity . . . would become a grand democracy of Forest Trees!" Coleridge refers to it in the *Biographia* when he says: "The

medium, by which spirits understand each other, is not the surrounding air; but the *freedom* which they possess in common." Whether the Romantic poet is revolutionary or conservative depends on whether he regards this original society as concealed by or as manifested in existing society. If the former, he will think of true society as a primitive structure of nature and reason, and will admire the popular, simple, or even the barbaric more than the sophisticated. If the latter, he will find his true inner society manifested by a sacramental church or by the instinctive manners of an aristocracy. The search for a visible ideal society in history leads to a good deal of admiration for the Middle Ages, which on the Continent was sometimes regarded as the essential feature of Romanticism. The affinity between the more extreme Romantic conservatism and the subversive revolutionary movements of fascism and nazism in our day has been often pointed out. The present significance for us of this fact is that the notion of the inwardness of creative power is inherently revolutionary, just as the pre-Romantic construct was inherently conservative, even for poets as revolutionary as Milton. The self-identifying admiration which so many Romantics expressed for Napoleon has much to do with the association of natural force, creative power, and revolutionary outbreak. As Carlyle says, in an uncharacteristically cautious assessment of Napoleon: "What Napoleon *did* will in the long-run amount to what he did *justly*; what Nature with her laws will sanction."

Further, the Romantic poet is a part of a total process, engaged with and united to a creative power greater than his own because it includes his own. This greater creative power has a relation to him which we may call, adapting a term of Blake's, his vehicular form. The sense of identity

352   *The Mythopoeic Critic*

with a larger power of creative energy meets us everywhere in Romantic culture, I think even in the crowded excited canvases of Delacroix and the tremendous will-to-power finales of Beethoven. The symbolism of it in literature has been too thoroughly studied in Professor Abrams's *The Mirror and the Lamp* and in Professor Wasserman's *The Subtler Language* for me to add more than a footnote or two at this point. Sometimes the greater power of this vehicular form is a rushing wind, as in Shelley's Ode and in the figure of the "correspondent breeze" studied by Professor Abrams. The image of the Aeolian harp, or lyre—Romantic poets are apt to be sketchy in their orchestration—belongs here. Sometimes it is a boat driven by a breeze or current, or by more efficient magical forces in the *Ancient Mariner*. This image occurs so often in Shelley that it has helped to suggest my title; the introduction to Wordsworth's *Peter Bell* has a flying boat closely associated with the moon. Those poems of Wordsworth in which we feel driven along by a propelling metrical energy, *Peter Bell*, *The Idiot Boy*, *The Waggoner*, and others, seem to me to be among Wordsworth's most central poems. Sometimes the vehicular form is a heightened state of consciousness in which we feel that we are greater than we know, or an intense feeling of communion, as in the sacramental corn-and-wine images of the great Keats odes.

The sense of unity with a greater power is surely one of the reasons why so much of the best Romantic poetry is mythopoeic. The myth is typically the story of the god, whose form and character are human but who is also a sun-god or tree-god or ocean-god. It identifies the human with the nonhuman world, an identification which is also one of the major functions of poetry itself. Coleridge makes it a part of the primary as well as the sec-

ondary imagination. "This I call *I*," he says in the Notebooks, "identifying the percipient and the perceived." The "Giant Forms" of Blake's prophecies are states of being and feeling in which we have our own being and feeling; the huge and mighty forms of Wordsworth's *Prelude* have similar affinities; even the dreams of De Quincey seem vehicular in the same sense. It is curious that there seems to be so little mythopoeic theory in Romantic poets, considering that the more expendable critics of the time complained as much about the obscurity of myth as their counterparts of today do now.

One striking feature of the Romantic poets is their resistance to fragmentation: their compulsion, almost, to express themselves in long continuous poems is quite as remarkable as their lyrical gifts. I have remarked elsewhere that the romance, in its most naive and primitive form, is an endless sequence of adventures, terminated only by the author's death or disgust. In Romanticism something of this inherently endless romance form recurs. *Childe Harold* and *Don Juan* are Byron to such an extent that the poems about them can be finished only by Byron's death or boredom with the *persona*. *The Prelude*, and still more the gigantic scheme of which it formed part, has a similar relation to Wordsworth, and something parallel is beginning to show its head at once in Keats's *Sleep and Poetry* and Shelley's *Queen Mab*. We touch here on the problem of the Romantic unfinished poem, which has been studied by Professor Bostetter. My present interest, however, is rather in the feature of unlimited continuity, which seems to me connected with the sense of vehicular energy, of being carried along by a greater force, the quality which outside literature, according to Keats, makes a man's life a continual allegory.

We have found, then, that the metaphorical structure of Romantic poetry tends to move inside and downward instead of outside and upward, hence the creative world is deep within, and so is heaven or the place of the presence of God. Blake's Orc and Shelley's Prometheus are Titans imprisoned underneath experience; the Gardens of Adonis are down in *Endymion*, whereas they are up in *The Faerie Queene* and *Comus*; in *Prometheus Unbound* everything that aids mankind comes from below, associated with volcanoes and fountains. In *The Revolt of Islam* there is a curious collision with an older habit of metaphor when Shelley speaks of

A power, a thirst, a knowledge . . . below
All thoughts, like light beyond the atmosphere.

The *Kubla Khan* geography of caves and underground streams haunts all of Shelley's language about creative processes: in *Speculations on Metaphysics*, for instance, he says: "But thought can with difficulty visit the intricate and winding chambers which it inhabits. It is like a river whose rapid and perpetual stream flows outwards. . . . The caverns of the mind are obscure, and shadowy, or pervaded with a lustre, beautifully bright indeed, but shining not beyond their portals."

In pre-Romantic poetry heaven is the order of grace, and grace is normally thought of as descending from above into the soul. In the Romantic construct there is a center where inward and outward manifestations of a common motion and spirit are unified, where the ego is identified as itself because it is also identified with something which is not itself. In Blake this world at the deep center is Jerusalem, the City of God that mankind, or Albion, has sought all

through history without success because he has been looking in the wrong direction, outside. Jerusalem is also the garden of Eden where the Holy Word walked among the ancient trees; Eden in the unfallen world would be the same place as England's green and pleasant land where Christ also walked; and England's green and pleasant land is also Atlantis, the sunken island kingdom which we can rediscover by draining the "Sea of Time and Space" off the top of the mind. In *Prometheus Unbound* Atlantis reappears when Prometheus is liberated, and the one great flash of vision which is all that is left to us of Wordsworth's *Recluse* uses the same imagery.

Paradise, and groves
Elysian, Fortunate Fields—like those of old
Sought in the Atlantic Main—why should they be
A history of departed things,
Or a mere fiction of what never was? . . .
—I, long before the blissful hour arrives,
Would chant, in lonely peace, the spousal verse
Of this great consummation.

The Atlantis theme is in many other Romantic myths: in the Glaucus episode of *Endymion* and in De Quincey's *Savannah-la-Mar*, which speaks of "human life still subsisting in submarine asylums sacred from the storms that torment our upper air." The theme of land reclaimed from the ocean plays also a somewhat curious role in Goethe's *Faust*. We find the same imagery in later writers who continue the Romantic tradition, such as D. H. Lawrence in the "Song of a Man Who Has Come Through":

If only I am keen and hard like the sheer tip of a wedge
Driven by invisible blows,
The rock will split, we shall come at the wonder, we shall find the Hesperides.

In *The Pilgrim's Progress* Ignorance is sent to hell from the very gates of heaven. The inference seems to be that only Ignorance knows the precise location of both kingdoms. For knowledge, and still more for imagination, the journey within to the happy island garden or the city of light is a perilous quest, equally likely to terminate in the blasted ruin of Byron's *Darkness* or Beddoes's *Subterranean City*. In many Romantic poems, including Keats's nightingale ode, it is suggested that the final identification of and with reality may be or at least include death. The suggestion that death may lead to the highest knowledge, dropped by Lucifer in Byron's *Cain*, haunts Shelley continually. A famous passage in *Prometheus Unbound* associates the worlds of creation and death in the same inner area, where Zoroaster meets his image in a garden. Just as the sun is the means but not a tolerable object of sight, so the attempt to turn around and see the source of one's vision may be destructive, as the Lady of Shalott found when she turned away from the mirror. Thus the world of the deep interior in Romantic poetry is morally ambivalent, retaining some of the demonic qualities that the corresponding pre-Romantic lowest level had.

This sense that the source of genius is beyond good and evil, that the possession of genius may be a curse, that the only real knowledge given to Adam in Paradise, however disastrous, came to him from the devil—all this is part of the contribution of Byron to modern sensibility, and part of the irrevocable change that he made in it. Of his Lara Byron says:

> He stood a stranger in this breathing world,
> An erring spirit from another hurl'd;
> A thing of dark imaginings, that shaped
> By choice the perils he by chance escaped;
> But 'scaped in vain, for in their memory yet

> His mind would half exult and half regret . . .
> But haughty still and loth himself to blame,
> He call'd on Nature's self to share the shame,
> And charged all faults upon the fleshly form
> She gave to clog the soul, and feast the worm;
> Till he at last confounded good and ill,
> And half mistook for fate the acts of will.

It would be wrong to regard this as Byronic hokum, for the wording is very precise. Lara looks demonic to a nervous and conforming society, as the dragon does to the tame villatic fowl in Milton. But there is a genuinely demonic quality in him which arises from his being nearer than other men to the unity of subjective and objective worlds. To be in such a place might make a poet more creative; it makes other types of superior beings, including Lara, more destructive.

We said earlier that the Romantic poet's political views would depend partly on whether he saw his inner society as concealed by or as manifested in actual society. A Romantic poet's moral attitude depends on a similar ambivalence in the conception of nature. Nature to Wordsworth is a mother-goddess who teaches the soul serenity and joy, and never betrays the heart that loves her; to the Marquis de Sade nature is the source of all the perverse pleasures that an earlier age had classified as "unnatural." For Wordsworth the reality of Nature is manifested by its reflection of moral values; for De Sade the reality is concealed by that reflection. It is this ambivalent sense (for it is ambivalent, and not simply ambiguous) of appearance as at the same time revealing and concealing reality, as clothes simultaneously reveal and conceal the naked body, that makes *Sartor Resartus* so central a document of the Romantic movement. We spoke of Wordsworth's Nature as a mother-goddess, and her psychological descent from mother-figures is clearly traced in *The Prelude*. The corn-goddess in Keats's *To Autumn*, the parallel figure identified with Ruth in the *Ode to a Nightingale*, the still unravished bride of the Grecian urn, Psyche, even the veiled Melancholy, are all emblems of a revealed Nature. Elusive nymphs or teasing and mocking female figures who refuse to take definite form, like the figure in *Alastor* or Blake's "female will" types; terrible and sinister white goddesses like La Belle Dame sans Merci, or females associated with something forbidden or demonic, like the sister-lovers of Byron and Shelley, belong to the concealed aspect.

For Wordsworth, who still has a good deal of the pre-Romantic sense of nature as an objective order, nature is a landscape nature, and from it, as in Baudelaire's *Correspondances*, mysterious oracles seep into the mind through eye or ear, even a bird with so predictable a song as the cuckoo being an oracular wandering voice. This landscape is a veil dropped over the naked nature of screaming rabbits and gasping stags, the nature red in tooth and claw which haunted a later generation. Even the episode of the dog and the hedgehog in *The Prelude* is told from the point of view of the dog and not of the hedgehog. But the more pessimistic, and perhaps more realistic, conception of nature in which it can be a source of evil or suffering as well as good is the one that gains ascendancy in the later period of Romanticism, and its later period extends to our own day.

The major constructs which our own culture has inherited from its Romantic ancestry are also of the "drunken boat" shape, but represent a later and a different conception of it from the "vehicular form" described above. Here the boat is usually in the position of Noah's ark, a fragile container of sensitive and imaginative values threatened by a chaotic and unconscious power below it. In Schopenhauer, the world as idea rides precariously on top of a "world as will" which engulfs practically the whole of existence in its moral indifference. In Darwin, who readily combines with Schopenhauer, as the later work of Hardy illustrates, consciousness and morality are accidental sports from a ruthlessly competitive revolutionary force. In Freud, who has noted the resemblance of his mythical structure to Schopenhauer's, the conscious ego struggles to keep afloat on a sea of libidinous impulse. In Kierkegaard, all the "higher" impulses of fallen man pitch and roll on the surface of a huge and shapeless "dread." In some versions of this construct the antithesis of the symbol of consciousness and the destructive element in which it is immersed can be overcome or transcended: there is an Atlantis under the sea which becomes an Ararat for the beleaguered boat to rest on.

I give an example from Auden, partly because he is prominently featured in this session of the Institute, and partly to show that the Romantic structures of symbolism are still ours. In Freud, when the conscious mind feels threatened by the subconscious, it tries to repress it, and so develops a neurosis. In Marx, the liberal elements in an ascendant class, when they feel threatened by a revolutionary situation, develop a police state. In both cases the effort is to intensify the antithesis between the two, but this effort is mistaken, and when the barriers are broken down we reach the balanced mind and the classless society respectively. *For the Time Being* develops a religious construct out of Kierkegaard on the analogy of those of Marx and Freud. The liberal or rational elements represented by Herod feel threatened by the revival of superstition in the Incarnation, and try to repress it. Their failure means that the effort to come to terms with a nature outside the mind, the primary effort of reason, has to be abandoned, and this enables the Paradise or divine presence which is locked up inside the human mind to manifest itself after the reason has searched the whole of objective nature in vain to find it. The attitude is that of a relatively orthodox Christianity; the imagery and the structure of symbolism is that of *Prometheus Unbound* and *The Marriage of Heaven and Hell*.

In Romanticism proper a prominent place in sense experience is given to the ear, an excellent receiver of oracles but poor in locating things accurately in space. This latter power, which is primarily visual, is associated with the fancy in Wordsworth's 1815 preface, and given the subordinate position appropriate to fancy. In later poetry, beginning with *symbolisme* in France, when there is a good deal of reaction against earlier Romanticism, more emphasis is thrown on vision. In Rimbaud, though his *Bateau Ivre* has given me my title, the poet is to *se faire voyant*, the *illuminations* are thought of pictorially; even the vowels must be visually colored. Such an emphasis has nothing to do with the pre-Romantic sense of an objective structure in nature: on the contrary, the purpose of it is to intensify the Romantic sense of oracular significance into a kind of autohypnosis. (The association of autohypnosis and the visual sense is discussed in Professor Marshall McLuhan's new book, *The Gutenberg Galaxy*.) Such an emphasis leads to a technique of fragmentation. Poe's attack on the long poem is not a Romantic but an anti-Romantic manifesto, as the direction of its influence indicates. The tradition of *symbolisme* is present in imagism, where the primacy of visual values is so strongly stated in theory and so cheerfully ignored in practice, in

Pound's emphasis on the spatial juxtaposing of metaphor, in Eliot's insistence on the superiority of poets who present the "clear visual images" of Dante. T. E. Hulme's attack on the Romantic tradition is consistent in preferring fancy to imagination and in stressing the objectivity of the nature to be imitated; less so in his primitivism and his use of Bergson. The technique of fragmentation is perhaps intended to reach its limit in Pound's publication of the complete poetical works of Hulme on a single page.

As I have tried to indicate by my reference to Auden, what this anti-Romantic movement did not do was to create a third framework of imagery. Nor did it return to the older construct, though Eliot, by sticking closely to Dante and by deprecating the importance of the prophetic element in art, gives some illusion of doing so. The charge of subjectivity, brought against the Romantics by Arnold and often repeated later, assumes that objectivity is a higher attribute of poetry, but this is itself a Romantic conception, and came into English criticism with Coleridge. Anti-Romanticism, in short, had no resources for becoming anything more than a post-Romantic movement. The first phase of the "reconsideration" of Romanticism discussed by this group is to understand its continuity with modern literature, and this phase is now well developed in the work of Professor Kermode and others. All we need do to complete it is to examine Romanticism by its own standards and canons. We should not look for precision where vagueness is wanted; not extol the virtues of constipation when the Romantics were exuberant; not insist on visual values when the poet listens darkling to a nightingale. Then, perhaps, we may seen in Romanticism also the quality that Melville found in Greek architecture:

Not innovating wilfulness,
But reverence for the Archetype.

Paul Ginestier

HOMO FABER AND POETRY

Although the French poet and critic Paul Ginestier has written and edited several volumes, including books on Camus and the contemporary theater, he is virtually unknown in the United States. He follows in and extends the mode of psychoanalytic-philosophical-archetypal criticism best exemplified by Gaston Bachelard, a type of work whose special character is not duplicated in Anglo-American criticism. This essay is a chapter from Ginestier's *The Poet and the Machine*, published in English translation in 1961.

The machine age has not fundamentally changed the study of human character. There are many superficial changes, to be sure. Progress has had repercussions on our psychic life; but behind that, the essential nature of the "homo faber" and the "homo sapiens" remains unchanged. The conquest of nature still constitutes the dominant task, and this conquest becomes more efficient as man masters more energy. Here we have our first vicious circle: the more energy man has at his disposal, the more energy he draws out of nature. To this simple fact is due the hallucinating acceleration of progress. Then again, the transformation of raw material into energy or into an industrial product always requires the intervention of fire, one of the four elements, as indispensable to the human race as to the imagination. It seems that we have here the privileged point where "homo sapiens" and "homo faber" meet; fire is a power essential to industry, and it is the most important element in the forming of the imagination. The factory, according to a definition as famous as it is grand, is "the Iron Kingdom where His Majesty Fire reigns."[1] There is much more than a connection; there is a relationship of cause and effect. The curve of the exploitation of fuel resources is in general directly proportional to the curve of a country's industrialization. The necessity of developing and utilizing natural resources results in technical progress which, in turn, augments the productivity of all industry.

In the form of fuel and electricity, fire is as important to us as it was to the fabulous Oulhamr described by J. H. Rosny in his strange novel set one hundred thousand years ago: "All joy dwelled near it. It brought out the savory odor of

---

[1] Guy de Maupassant, "Au soleil et la vie errante" in *Oeuvres Complètes IX* (Paris: Librairie de France, 1935), p. 328.

357

meats, hardened the spear points, burst hard rocks; the limbs derived comfort and strength from it. . . . It was the Father, the Guardian, the Savior, more ferocious however, more terrible than Mammoths when it escaped from its cage and devoured the trees."[2] Naturally so versatile an element, whose utility is of such prime importance, had to have a profoundly marked effect on the dialectic of the imagination. Fire is not only simple combustion or one of the four elements; it constitutes first of all a bit of the sun, symbol of the whole. For this reason, it plays a large role in primitive religions, a role admirably described in *The Golden Bough*.[3] Consequently fire, in addition to having great material utility, expresses at one and the same time on the spiritual plane both life ("anima") and intelligence (e.g., Prometheus in Greek mythology, the tongues of flame of the Holy Spirit in Christianity, etc.).

However, modern man, like Vulcan, does not keep his fire pure, and as a result, our world is characterized by *Smoke and Steel,* to adopt the title of Carl Sandburg's volume of poetry.[4] This industrial inferno and the sort of curse which seems to hover over the workers-with-fire correspond to Vulcan's fall from Olympus.

Nevertheless, the worker is not characterized as "homo faber" because of a transitory activity, but because of the result he produces. The unknown bard who wrote the eighth-century epic *Beowulf* was aware of this when he systematically utilized the following locutions to name the sword: *fela laf* ("produced or 'left' by files"), *hamere gepruen* ("beaten by

hammers"), and *homera lafe* ("produced or 'left' by hammers"). Today the product of the fire's controlled energies is the machine, and this results in a withering repetition likely to brutalize humanity.

TO IRON-FOUNDERS AND OTHERS

Your worship is your furnaces,
Which like old idols, lost obscenes,
Have molten bowels; your vision is
Machines for making more machines.[5]

This introduces us to the third sociological significance of fire, its role as purifier, which gives meaning to all those human sacrifices of which the most famous in literature is the horrifying scene in *Salammbô* in which children are burned to death inside a glowing statue of Moloch.

Fire burns away impurities, and consequently combustible fuel is burdened with the kind of curse recurrent in all extracting industries, and from which the most recent, the oil industry, is not exempt.

Le pétrole comme les cheveux d'Eléonore
Bouillonne au-dessus des continents
Et dans sa noix transparente
A perte de vue il y a des armées qui s'observent.[6]

[*Petroleum like Eleonore's hair*
Bubbles above continents
And in its transparent shell
As far as the eye can reach, armies are on guard.]

But the most spectacular infernal conquest is undoubtedly that of the mine. Geographically, this victory is dearly

---

[2] *La Guerre du feu* (Paris: Le Club du Livre, 1948), p. 2.
[3] Chaps. LXII, "The Fire Festivals of Europe," and LXII, "The Interpretations of Fire Festivals."
[4] In *Complete Poems* (New York: Harcourt, Brace, 1950).

[5] Gordon Bottomley, "To Iron Founders and Others" in *Poems of Thirty Years* (London: Constable, 1925).
[6] André Breton, "Cours-les toutes" in *Poètes d'aujourd'hui*, Vol. 18 (Paris: Editions Pierre Seghers, n.d.).

bought. The coal-bearing regions have cut themselves off from the ancient boundary gods of the country and from the regenerating spiritual power of history. Kenneth Ashley develops these themes in a poem whose title alone is a whole program.

NORMAN CHURCH:
NEW COALFIELD

New corn shone harsh and green, but new
  brick's harsher red
Showed that down there more coal than
  corn was won.
Tall chimneys flew their smoke as masts
  fly flags;
Great wheels on headstocks spun, and
  stopt, and spun again.[7]

In France, Dornier replies in corresponding lines:

C'est un noir pays foré de puits, qui fume
Par ses lourds hauts-fourneaux, par ses
  larges corons,
Ses trains dont les sifflets vrillent de trous
  la brume
Et cassent le ciel bas que l'air houilleux
  corrompt.[8]

[It's a black country drilled with coal pits,
  smoking
From its ponderous blast furnaces, from
  its big coal towns,
Its trains whose whistles puncture the fog
And crack the low sky tainted by coal
  smoke.]

So sinister an atmosphere must overcloud a wretched and tragic society. The mine-shaft has become Moloch, thus closing the infernal circle. Purification by sacrifice takes place at the level of the fuel itself, without the intervention of

fire, and within the mystery of the subterranean struggle. J. P. Fletcher, who was himself a miner, describes the pit-shaft thus:

The low galleries pressed
The wide air's freedom to a little thing
Obscured and soon forgotten. To the
  breast
Gaped infants for their birthright hunger-
  ing

And took the taste of poverty. Son after
  son
Gaunt women sacrificed at the dark pit-
  head
—It was their devil-god which, late or
  soon,
Would have them kneeling by their broken dead.[9]

Further on, in Book XIII of this long poem, the author leads us to the bottom of the gallery. There the theme of the rape of nature is drawn; the miner finds himself at the very heart of the enemy, struggling with the strongest of the four elements, earth, that which—as Bachelard points out—initiates the Reveries of the Will. Reading these lines, do we not recall the Titans, damned by Uranus, howling in the unfathomable gulfs of Tartarus?

Sweat.
Sweat.
Sweat.
Dust—thick, treacling out
The roof-scarred heads, down
  unbelievable faces
Into blood-circled eyes
He
despairs   Stench of naked torsos, acrid,
  human,
Grease glistening, scribbled
  with coiling rivulets—
Of coal-dust sweat
Smoking the sotted air.

[7] *Up Hill and Down Dale* (London: J. Lane, 1924).

[8] Charles Dornier, "Aube sanglante" in *L'Ombre d l'homme* (Paris: Société de Librairie, 1905).

[9] "Unprofitable Journey?" in *Tally 300* (Aldington, Kent: The Hand and Flowers Press, 1956).

Men curled like vermin gnawing
At the world's long gut, like animals growling,
Winning a white loaf from hell-darkness

This last tercet especially illustrates the profound sense of malediction. The miner, driven on by greed, reaches the bowels of the earth to plunder. Here are the cardinal sins of theft and rape, as Milton expounded them in *Paradise Lost*:

Men also, and by his [Mammon's] suggestion taught,
Ransack'd the Center, and with impious hands
Rifl'd the bowels of their mother Earth
For Treasures better hid. . . .[10]

Indeed, the earth, because it is the maternal symbol par excellence, is also taboo.[11] For these reasons, work underground has an immense and monstrous brutalizing power. The man who violates such a great taboo is both subjected and possessed by it. Witness the miners of Verhaeren:

Le corps rampant, avec la lampe entre vos dents
Jusqu'à la veine étroite où le charbon branlant
Cède sous votre effort obscur et solitaire. . . .[12]

[Your body groveling with the lamp between your teeth,
Up to the narrow vein where the loose coal
Yields to your dark and lonely labor. . . .]

And the perfectly sinister atmosphere which Dornier depicts:

Seul l'echo mat que fait dans l'air la pioche
Comme un tic-tac d'horloge au loin coupe la nuit,
Et le labeur plus long se compte sous la roche
Par l'eau qui coule goutte à goutte au fond du puits.[13]

[Only the thudding echo the pickaxe makes in the air,
Like the ticking of a distant clock, breaks the night,
And the long labor beneath the bedrock is measured
By water falling drop by drop to the bottom of the pit.]

Here we are plunged into the sinister rivers of the mythological Inferno, from which the ordinary man never returns. This explains too why the poet proposes no solution other than total overwhelming destruction:

La mort allume enfin un soleil dans leurs yeux.[14]

[Death at last kindles a sun in their eyes.]

This is accomplished, as inevitably in reality as in the dialectic of the imagination, by fire. Thus the privileged instant of death appears, that cosmic point from which there is a view over two worlds, one on this side of the grave and one beyond. Fire—like the ceremonial sacred fires lit by primitive tribes[15] which were supposed to help the sun move at the time of the solstice, that is, when the sun appears to come to a stop in its progress north or south—guarantees the eternal progress of the sun on its course beyond time. The sun, principle of life, gives the earth its fecundity, especially if it has been purified by the sacred fire, and thus

---

[10] Book I, lines 685–688.
[11] Frazer, "Not to touch the earth," *op. cit.*, p. 592.
[12] Emile Verhaeren, "L'Effort" in *La Multiple splendeur* (Paris: Mercure de Farnce, 1926).
[13] Dornier, *op. cit.*
[14] *Ibid.*
[15] Frazer, *op. cit.*, p. 641.

the miner in the depths of the earth can be seen in a third perspective, as a midwife.

Hands
Waiting to dig deep into pregnant earth
And aid its childbirth. . . .[16]

We know that psychically the notions of birth and death are very close. Death is often envisaged as a return to the mother. The mine is therefore in essence a modern form of the myth of Antaeus, son of Gaea, and of his return to the womb of the earth. Psychically, as in reality, the earth is a crust covering a sun. Tristan Tzara rediscovers the zodiac in the mine:

Les lampes hypnotisées de la mine de sel
Font pâlir le crachat dans la bouche vigilante
Les wagons figés dans le zodiaque
Un monstre montre son cerveau de terre calcinée. . . .[17]

[The hypnotized lamps of the salt mine
Make pale the spittle in the vigilant mouth
Trucks frozen in the zodiac
A monster displays his brain of calcined earth. . . .]

which naturally corresponds to the Phlegethon in Hades.

It is remarkable that each of the texts cited above exhibits a measure of disgust, serving as a kind of psychic bridge between the myths of earth and fire, which are solidly linked deep in our consciousness. It is by virtue of this equivalence that the poet assures the contribution, and even the complicity, of our reason, which is indispensable to a complete aesthetic gratification. Thus the rational implications are united with the subliminal activity of the mind to produce the poetic spark. Beyond this aesthetic conditioning, of which he is usually unaware, the reader knows—or rather used to know twenty years ago—that coal is the source of all mechanical power, that is, of all civilization based on the efforts of industry. Thus the circle is closed completely; the machine age springs from coal and returns under its domination. It is Koundalini, the coiled serpent swallowing its own tail, of ancient Sanskrit. There is a myth of the miner because the modern reader knows how much he depends on him, and its symbolic importance is demonstrated by its extension from the coal miner to a miner extracting any other material, such as salt, from the earth. We are presented with a triangular aesthetic: man, nature, and industry. And this is a transposition of that other famous trinity: man, nature, and war, which can be found, for example, in the legend of the death of Roland taken up by Vigny in "Le Cor." It is analogous to the most primitive of all triangles: father, mother, and child, in the sense that the child results from a sort of fertile fight between the sexes. The industrial effort, moreover, is a struggle which seems to be without solution; man can wrest nature's treasures from her heart only at the risk of his life. On the individual level the struggle is hopeless, but the mere fact that it is continued confers a semblance of epic grandeur upon the origins of mechanical civilization. This rape is not despicable because it is fructifying and full of danger.

In studying the problem of fire, there is another step of the industrial revolution to consider. Thanks to fire, a purifying and dangerous ally, man has attained domination over the world. In the transformation of matter by fire there is a magnificent theme which brings forth violent and ardent poetical sentiments in Verhaeren.

[16] Julius Lipton, "Hands" in *Poems of Strife* (London: Lawrence & Wishart, 1936).
[17] *Cinéma calendrier du coeur abstrait* (Paris: Au Sans Pareil, 1920).

Et vous enfin, batteurs de fer, forgeurs
    d'airain,
Visages d'encre et d'or trouant l'ombre et
    la brume,
Dos musculeux tendus ou ramassés, sou-
    dain,
Autour de grands brasiers et d'énormes
    enclumes, . . .[18]

[And finally you, hammerers of iron, forg-
    ers of brass,
Faces of ink and gold breaching the sha-
    dow and fog,
Brawny backs stretched or crouched, sud-
    den,
Around great coal fires and huge an-
    vils, . . .]

And in Victor Hugo:

Et lui, poussant du pied tout ce métal
    sonore,
Il courait à la cuve où bouillonnait encore
        Le monument promis.
Le moule en était fait d'une de ses
    pensées.
Dans la fournaise ardente il jetait à bras-
    sées
        Les canons ennemis![19]

[And he, kicking aside all that sonorous
    metal,
Ran to the vat where the promised monu-
    ment was still seething.
Its matrix was made of one of his thoughts.
Into the furnace he flung armfuls of
    enemy cannons!]

Still, the second text, more fluid than the first, lays the emphasis on the origin rather than on the execution. The mysterious effect remains unchanged, but it is obtained by different means. On the one hand there is color and concrete solidity, and on the other, the fluidity of abstraction. In a description similar to the last, Luc Durtain presents the glass-blowers, and underlines too the aspect of mystery by calling up in us the complex of the Alchemist in dizzying imagery. But the poetry lies entirely in the idea, and it is skillfully worked.

Les halls obscurs où, élevant de fours,
    soleils carrés,
Leurs boules rouges, les souffleurs, noirs et
    splendides dieux planétaires,
Tournent lentement et s'évitent, puis la
    canne prudente entre au moule
L'anse ou la tige soudée, le recuit, muet
    enfer de flammes bleues. . . .[20]

[Sombre halls where, lifting from fur-
    naces, square suns,
Their glowing balls, the glass-blowers,
    splendid black planetary gods,
Slowly turn and avoid each other; then
    the careful blowing-iron puts into the
    matrix
The handle or fused stem, bakes it again,
    mute inferno of blue flames. . . .]

We feel ourselves quivering before this evocation as before the mysterious beauty of a primitive painting.

Here the cosmic has entered the factory, but the opposite procedure is possible, and it is curious to see it embody itself in a poem composed on the romantic model which Musset had already parodied in his "Ballade à la lune."

The Moon's an open furnace door
Where all can see the blast,
We shovel in our blackest griefs,
Upon that grate are cast

Our aching burdens, loves and fears
And underneath them wait
Paper and tar and pitch and pine
Called strife and blood and hate.[21]

This allegory is far from being the inexplicable result of chance. Otto Rank,

---

[18] Verhaeren, *op. cit.*
[19] "A la colonne" in *Les Chants du crépuscule.*
[20] "Lise à la verrerie" in *Lise* (Paris: Crès, 1918).
[21] Vachel Lindsay, "What the Coal-Heaver Said" in *Collected Poems* (New York: Macmillan, 1923).

in his book *The Trauma of Birth*,[22] includes a psychoanalytic study of Egyptian sun-worship which elucidates the meaning of the two stanzas above. The moon (Isis) is the mother, sister, and wife of the sun (Osiris). This relationship explains the metaphor of the furnace door which, superficially, would seem better adapted to the sun than to the moon. The moon, linked to the night, is pre-eminently a symbol of the mother and will later be dethroned by the sun, symbol of the father. This is justified because every night Osiris goes to the kingdom of the dead, and thus satisfies the original desire for union with the mother, a desire which psychically compensates for all our sufferings and rids us of them—exactly as the purifying fire of primitive religions has the power to banish pain. We have here a kind of industrial catharsis through which our age tries to adapt itself to the civilization of the machine. These efforts are still pathetic because the catharsis, as always, is dearly bought. This is Carl Sandburg's description:

A bar of steel—it is only
Smoke at the heart of it, smoke and the blood of a man.
A runner of fire ran in it, ran out, ran somewhere else,
And left—smoke and the blood of a man
And the finished steel, chilled and blue.[23]

Still, if man left nothing but his blood, he would come off cheap. But in the machine age he seems to lose even his intellectual integrity, which he sacrifices on the altar of the new god. He renounces thought, as in Paul Morand's feverish and labored hymn to "Business."

5,000 dollars
à qui prouvera

qu'on peut faire entendre un mot dans
    l'usine
à l'heure où l'on forge les chaudières tubu-
    laires.
Les châssis s'envolent, suspendus;
le crâne éclate
sur les marteaux-pilons.
J'aime ça.[24]

[$5000
To whoever can prove
That a word can be heard in the factory
When they are forging copper-tube boil-
    ers.
The hanging chassis take flight,
The skull bursts upon the power ham-
    mers.
I like that.]

We could hardly judge better the decline of human values expressed in the poem than by putting it beside these lines of Boileau:

. . . un affreux serrurier, laborieux Vulcain,
Qu'éveillera bientôt l'ardente soif du gain,
Avec un fer maudit, qu'à grand bruit il
    apprête,
De cent coups de marteau me va fendre
    la tête.[25]

[. . . a frightful locksmith, a laborious
    Vulcan,
Whom the burning thirst for profit will
    soon awaken,
With an accursed iron prepared in a great
    din,
Will split my head with a hundred ham-
    mer-blows.]

There is a greater difference between these two poems than that which separates the acceptance from the refusal. There is also manifest a psychical opposition. Boileau aspires after solitude in order to converse with himself, while the typical American described by Morand

---

[22] (New York: Harcourt, Brace, 1929).
[23] "Smoke and Steel" in *op. cit.*

[24] *Feuilles de température* (Paris: Au Sans Pareil, 1920).
[25] Satire VI.

utilizes the rhythm of the machine to avoid this tête-à-tête which would be unendurable to him. It is understandable that a humanist like Jules Romains should revolt and attack the progressive White Man, unmasking his inexpiable sin.

Tes forces mal à toi, mechantes filles du feu roux,
Tes forces qu'un fil conduit et que moulinent des roues,
Tes forces de dieu voleur dont tu n'as jamais assez![26]

[Woe to your baneful powers, wicked daughters of red fire,
Your powers conducted by wire and milled by wheels,
Your robber god's powers which are never enough for you!]

Erasmus Darwin reveals to us in a curious poem the origin of this mechanical force, the transformation of caloric energy into motive power, of fire into movement through the instrumentality of steam.

Nymphs! You. . .
Bade round the youth explosive steam aspire,
In gathering clouds, and wing'd the wave with fire;
Bade with cold streams the quick expansion stop,
And sunk the immense of vapour to a drop.—
Press'd by the ponderous air the Piston falls
Resistless, sliding through its iron walls;
Quick moves the balanced beam, of giant birth,
Wields its large limbs, and nodding shakes the earth.[27]

---

[26] Jules Romains, "Cinquième chant" in *L'Homme blanc* (Paris: Flammarion, 1937).
[27] "Canto I, vi" of *Botanic Garden*, quoted by Dr. Francis D. Klingender in *Art and the Industrial Revolution* (London: N. Carrington, 1947), p. 32.

But it is to Rudyard Kipling that we really owe the saga of the machine in all its fullness. Unfortunately, it is impossible for us to quote in its entirety the long poem entitled "The Secret of the Machines," which is in itself a complete history of machines from their material and spiritual conception (the stages of mineral extraction and the engineer's plan) up to the moment when, simply nourished on water, coal, and oil, they come to life and move with precision to a thousandth of an inch . . . and immediately become the absolute slave of man, ready to serve him twenty-four hours a day! And what power!

We can print and plough and weave and heat and light,
We can run and jump and swim and fly and dive,
We can see and hear and count and read and write!

This is the marvel: semi-divine man, power, the epic of conquest . . . are we going to lose our heads? We must be very careful not to do so, and Kipling, a moralist like every self-respecting Englishman, draws the following conclusion, which is unfortunately true:

But remember, please, the Law by which we live,
We are not built to comprehend a lie,
We can neither love nor pity nor forgive.
If you make a slip in handling us you die![28]

Thus the modern age tends to be inhuman, tends to reintroduce into our lives that notion of "fatum" which characterized the ancient world, which we find in the Wotan of Scandanavian mythology, "the god of driving force." One slip means death. But it is this very idea

---

[28] *Rudyard Kipling's Verse* (New York: Doubleday, 1944).

which provides so much poetry for mythologies and sagas. It is Laius who, in spite of the oracle, has a son. It is Athalie who worries over a dream. It is Clytemnestra taking Aegisthus as her lover. . . . This perpetual and obscure menace gives a poetic uncertainty to life at the very moment when the disparity between the initial fault and the final punishment excites our pity. This is accentuated when the punishment, unjust by all human standards, is executed with a cold, mechanical precision. The machine often plays a role analogous to the wicked giant of the myths. Is it not a sort of Minotaur which Julius Lipton presents in "Rhythm"?

Roar on, Machine, roar on, roar on,
  Drown the workers' moaning;
Louder, Machine, louder, louder,
  Drown our feeble groaning.
Eat, eat, Machine, eat, eat, eat, eat,
  Our limbs are for your meal. . . .[29]

Thus the poet experiences the tragedy of the industrial age. In humanity's great effort to snatch its well-being from nature, human blood must pay the price. If once the sacrifice of Iphigenia was necessary to drive forth the Greek fleet, today our ships' engines are built in factories where workers have been sacrificed, and coal is dug from pits where miners have died. Perhaps oil and atomic power are yet more murderous than coal. The machine age has not exempted man from the tribute he owes to the mysterious forces of the beyond. There is, however, one notable difference in the present age. If ancient and modern man both feel themselves to be the playthings of a power beyond themselves, modern man has, in addition, the feeling of having created this power, of being physically capable of ridding himself of it, but of not

having the moral strength to do so. We inflict upon ourselves a sort of perpetual punishment from which springs the latent masochism of our age, analogous to that of the flagellant monks of the Middle Ages; but we do not even have any more the prospect of gaining salvation through our sufferings. In this revenge of the material world, the order of which has been upset by the industrial movement, lies a source of irremediable despair.

Consequently many poets turn toward the masses to see how they react, and they interpret the common man according to the tendency of their own psychological make-up. Some, seized by an epico-lyrical fever, exalt the masses. Among these is the bard of the machine age, Verhaeren:

Groupes de travailleurs, fiévreux et haletants,
Qui vous dressez et qui passez au long des temps
Avec le rêve au front des utiles victoires . . .
Quelles lignes fières de vaillance et de gloire
Vous inscrivez tragiquement dans ma mémoire![30]

[Bands of workers, feverish and panting,
Rising up and passing through time
With the dream of useful victories on your brows . . .
What proud lines of courage and glory
You inscribe tragically in my memory!]

Across the Atlantic, Walt Whitman also exults:

Of Life immense in passion, pulse, and power,
Cheerful, for freest action form'd under the laws divine,
The Modern Man I sing.[31]

But always, behind the grandeur of the effort, we have the spectre of inhuman

---

[29] Lipton, op. cit.

[30] Verhaeren, "L'Effort" in op. cit.
[31] "One's-Self I Sing" in Leaves of Grass.

weariness and sordid misery. Another American, Trumbull Stickney, having evoked the shrill call of a siren on a cold evening, shows us a wretched flock of workers returning to their humble dwellings, and continues:

I love you, human labourers. Good-night!
Good-night to all the blackened arms that
  ache![32]

And finally, above everything else, hovers the theme of great tragedy, the mechanical Nemesis indefatigably pursuing man with her greatest threat, that of making him useless. Driven out by the productive machine, the individual ceases to be able to justify his existence. Stephen Spender in England and Carl Sandburg in America have drawn poignant variations upon this theme. We will cite the latter since he develops simultaneously the cause and the result—without, however, being able to explain the connection, which remains mysterious in this mechanical universe, where machines which produce riches also produce poverty through unemployment.

    The man in the street is fed
Here and there a man in the street
is young, hard as nails,
cold with questions he asks
from his burning insides.
    Bred in a motorized world of trial
        and error
    He measures by millionths of an
        inch,
    Knows ball bearings from spiral
        gearings,
    Chain transmission, heat treat-
        ment of steel,
    Speeds and feeds of automatic
        screw machines,
    Having handled electric tools
    With pistol grip and trigger
        switch.

Yet he can't connect and he can name
    thousands
Like himself idle amid plants also idle.[33]

Thus through science man has forged his own calamity. Now the greatest imaginable offense is done to him. The technical progress to which he has devoted his life supplants him. The great human effort ends nowhere. Paradise barely glimpsed remains as far off as ever, and knowledge is as maleficent as it was in Adam's time. We may say that from the human point of view the poetry of industrial progress is the saga of a gigantic failure and of the relentlessly growing disparity between the creator and his creation. Man cannot seek to become God with impunity. The more he understands nature and dominates matter, the greater becomes the gap between his knowledge and his moral evolution. Retributive justice, the poetic justice par excellence, is always there, immanent, punishing man's body and his heart for daring too much.

It is most curious to observe that American poets have arrived at a stage where they no longer seem to dare envisage the future, or, wherever any such vision exists, it discloses a return to a blind, termite-like civilization. The French poets are still probably not so much engaged in the mesh of machine age collectivity that they cannot wriggle out in a sort of pirouette, like this by Max Jacob.

Un peu de modernisme en manière de
conclusion

Dans la nuit d'encre, la moitié de l'Exposition universelle de 1900, illuminée en diamants, recule de la Seine et se renverse d'un seul bloc parce qu'une tête folle de poète au ciel de l'école mord une étoile de diamants.[34]

---

[32] "Six O'Clock" in *The Oxford Book of American Verse* (New York: Oxford University Press, 1950).

[33] Carl Sandburg, *op. cit.*
[34] *Le Cornet à dés* (Paris: Stock, 1923).

[*A little modernism by way of concluding*

In the inky night, half of the World's
Fair of 1900, lighted with diamonds,
steps back from the Seine and overturns
all of a piece, because the mad head of a
poet in the sky of the school is chewing
on a diamond star.]

Among the English, on the other hand, we find the question of the future clearly posed and a painful unanimity of pessimism developing. To John Betjeman it seems that a soulless, insectile collectivity awaits us, as in "The Planester's Vision."

I have a Vision of the Future, chum,
    The workers' flats in fields of soya beans
        Tower up like silver pencils, score on
        score:
And Surging Millions hear the Challenge
    come
    From microphones in communal can-
        teens
        "No Right! No Wrong! All's perfect,
        evermore."[35]

For Stephen Spender "The Human Situation" is simply, cleanly, mechanically stamped out in six lines.

This I is one of
The human machines
So common on the gray plains—
Yet being built into flesh
My single pair of eyes
Contain the universe they see....[36]

That is the terrible vengeance of things, the punishment of pride for wanting to transform everything into machines. Man has accomplished his process of mechanization but now he cannot stop, and he runs the risk of being mechanized himself. Elsewhere this same poet emphasizes the tragedy of modern man who has a clear

apprehension of all that he is capable of, but which he never attains, borne astray by his own intelligence. This torment, recalling the agony of Tantalus, is inflicted on the lucid and sensitive modern thinker.

... I will confess to you.
At night I'm flooded by a sense of future,
The bursting tide of an unharnessed
    power
Drowning the contours of the present....
But beyond windows of this waking dream
Facts do their hundred miles an hour
Snorting in circles round the plain;
The bikes and track are real; and yet the
    riders lose
All sense of place; they're ridden by
Their speed; the men are the machines.[37]

These sorcerer's apprentices have become the slaves of the forces they have unleashed. Modern poetry is fully conscious of the upheaval caused by the machine all over the face of the earth. There are sentimental souls who, confronted by the reality of mass-production in impersonal assembly lines, prefer to look back and celebrate the antiquated charm of crafts which are passing from the scene. Just as progress was associated with intelligence, this poetic regression is founded on a simplicity which borders on naïveté. What calm we find in these lines by Francis Jammes:

Il y a un petit cordonnier naïf et bossu
qui travaille devant de douces vitres ver-
    tes.
Le dimanche il se lève et se lave et met sur
lui du linge propre et laisse la fenêtre ou-
    verte.[38]

[*There is a simple, little hunchbacked*
shoemaker

[35] *New Bats in Old Belfries* (London: J. Murray, 1945).
[36] *The Still Centre* (London: Faber & Faber, 1939).

[37] "The Uncreating Chaos" in *ibid*.
[38] "Il y a un petit cordonnier" in *De l'angélus de l'aube à l'angélus du soir* (Paris: Mercure de France, 1898).

Who works in front of soft green windows.
On Sundays he gets up and washes and
   puts on
Clean linen and leaves the window open.]

André Salmon writes with equal gentle-
ness (although, as we shall see later, he
finds violent tones to describe Antwerp).

Le travail est venu chez toi faire une fête,
Les beaux métiers d'autrui sont de jolis
   métiers,
Le menuisier portait trois planches sur sa
   tête,
Ainsi que des miroirs endormis par l'été.[39]

[Work is having a holiday at your place,
The trades of others are fine trades,
The carpenter carried three boards on his
   head,
Like mirrors made drowsy by summer.]

So we see that normally the tranquillity
of the artisan's craft, by a kind of osmosis,
pervades the town. Since modernism is so
eminently a social characteristic, if a few
individuals succeed in preserving their
personalities, the example must inevitably spread. In Marianne Moore's "The
Steeple-Jack" there is more than a mere
description. There is a message.

It scarcely could be dangerous to be living in a town like this, of simple people
who have a steeple-jack placing danger-
   signs by the church
when he is gilding the solid-
   pointed star, which on a steeple
stands for hope.[40]

But there is another kind of peace, that
of devitalization, and another silence,
that of "towns which the enemy is ready

to surround," to use Montesquieu's fine
phrase. The precision of our mechanical
civilization has imprisoned man so narrowly that he has lost even his spiritual
independence, and for the most part, it
has been accomplished so insidiously that
he is not even aware of it. W. H. Auden
writes a poem entitled "The Unknown
Citizen" which he dedicates to identification number JS/07/M/378. The number
certainly makes immediate classification
possible as it is always based on a code
and it renders human contact superfluous,
as each of us has with those around him
the relationship of a cog wheel to the
rest of the machinery.

He worked in a factory and never got fired,
But satisfied his employers, Fudge Motors
   Inc.
Yet he wasn't a scab or odd in his views,
For his Union reports that he paid his
   dues,
(Our report on his Union shows it was
   sound) . . .
Was he free? Was he happy? The ques-
   tion is absurd:
Had anything been wrong, we certainly
   should have heard.[41]

The subject here is the dedication engraved on a marble monument erected by
the State. T. S. Eliot envisages the drama
from the other extremity, at the moment
when the young man enters modern society to be slowly crushed by the machine. The pure and simple transcription
of the statement of working conditions,
such as can be seen every day in the help-
wanted sections of the classified adver-
tisements, is heavy with tragedy like a
death sentence. With consummate skill
the poet allows pathos to emerge from
the commonplace:

[39] "Anvers" in *Les féeries* (Paris: Vers et
Prose, 1907).
[40] *Collected Poems* (New York: Macmillan,
1951).
[41] Auden, *op. cit.*

What shall I cry?
Arthur Edward Cyril Parker is appointed
    telephone operator
At a salary of one pound ten a week rising
    by annual increments of five shillings
To two pounds ten a week; with a bonus
    of thirty shillings at Christmas
And one week's leave a year.[42]

In France, Saint-Exupéry lyrically ana-
lyzes the psychological cause for this new
edition of the myth of the man who has
lost his soul, so common among primitive
peoples: "Old bureaucrat, my comrade,
it is not you who are to blame. No one
ever helped you to escape. You, like a
termite, built your peace by blocking up
with cement every chink and cranny
through which light might pierce."[43]
Bureaucratic organization is the quintessence of mechanization on the social
plane. If we admit, with Freud, that the
appearance of the machine in dreams
symbolizes the male genital organs, mechanization involves an imaginary suppression of the mother with the punitive
retribution of an Electra complex. Thus
we are heading for disaster psychically as
well as socially. We have a hint of the
failure of civilization in the transfer of
individual worth to a deification of the
community, a kind of supreme and hidden being to whom we are valued only in
proportion to our mechanical output.
If there is something grandiose in such an
apocalyptic vision, it is still possible to stir
our feelings by evoking the purely human
aspect, by describing this idea of matern-
ity so gravely threatened in its very essence, as does this poem by Louis Mac-
Neice.

PRAYER BEFORE BIRTH

I am not yet born; O fill me
With strength against those who would
                            freeze my
    humanity, would dragoon me into a
                            lethal auto-
    maton, would make me a cog in a
                            machine, a
    thing with one face, a thing, and
                            against all
        those who would dissipate my
                            entirety,
        would blow me like thistle-
                    down hither and
        thither or hither and thither
                        like water
        held in the hands would
                        spill me
Let them not make me a stone and let
    them not spill me.
Otherwise kill me.[44]

We are struck, first of all, by the success of this typographical presentation
which fully attains its purpose, conveying
the idea of a slow gliding followed by a
sudden stop. The text also reveals the
aesthetic method employed; on the one
hand man, represented by the weakest
and most pitiful being imaginable, the
unborn child, and on the other, the
gigantic forces of the mechanical world
which await him, menacing, ready to
mold that innocent living material into
all their inhuman forms. At the center, as
arbiter and an ever-possible refuge, is
death. This death soon will be man's only
possibility of escape from a mechanical
civilization.[45] To die is, in fact, an attribute of life. The body is the only machine
which is, so far at least, irreparable.

---

[42] "Coriolan, II" in The Complete Poems
and Plays (New York: Harcourt, Brace, 1952).
[43] Antoine de Saint-Exupéry, Wind, Sand
and Stars (New York: Harcourt, Brace, 1939),
p. 23.

[44] Collected Poems: 1925–1948 (London:
Faber & Faber, 1951).
[45] Is not this the significance which ought
to be attached to the "gratuitous" suicide (in
the Gidean sense) of the surrealist poet
Jacques Vaché just after the end of World
War I?

W. H. Auden

THE QUEST HERO

The distinction of W. H. Auden's verse has overshadowed the excellence of his prose, which includes three volumes, *The Enchafèd Flood* (1950), *Making, Knowing, and Judging* (1956), and *The Dyer's Hand* (1962), as well as many essays. Auden has also been active as a dramatist, editor, translator, and librettist. He became an American citizen in 1946 and has taught at several American universities. From 1956 to 1961 he was Professor of Poetry at Oxford University. Among his numerous honors are a Pulitzer Prize, a Bollingen Prize, and a National Book Award. "The Quest Hero" appeared in the *Texas Quarterly* in 1961.

To look for a lost collar button is not a true quest: to go in quest means to look for something of which one has, as yet, no experience; one can imagine what it will be like but whether one's picture is true or false will be known only when one has found it.

Animals, therefore, do not go on quests. They hunt for food or drink or a mate, but the object of their search is determined by what they already are and its purpose is to restore a disturbed equilibrium; they have no choice in the matter.

But man is a history-making creature for whom the future is always open; human "nature" is a nature continually in quest of itself, obliged at every moment to transcend what it was a moment before. For man the present is not real but valuable. He can neither repeat the past exactly—every moment is unique—nor leave it behind—at every moment he adds to and thereby modifies all that has previously happened to him.

Hence the impossibility of expressing his kind of existence in a single image. If one concentrates upon his ever open future, the natural image is of a road stretching ahead into unexplored country, but if one concentrates upon his unforgettable past, then the natural image is of a city, which is built in every style of architecture, and in which the physically dead are as active citizens as the living. The only characteristic common to both images is a sense of purpose; a road, even if its destination is invisible, runs in a certain direction; a city is built to endure and be a home.

The animals who really live in the present have neither roads nor cities and do not miss them. They are at home in the wilderness and, at most, if they are social, set up camps for a generation. But man requires both. The image of a city with no roads leading from it suggests a prison; the image of a road that starts from nowhere in particular suggests, not a true road, but an animal spoor.

A similar difficulty arises if one tries to describe simultaneously our experience of our own lives and our experience of the lives of others. Subjectively, I am a unique ego set over against a self; my body, desires, feelings, and thoughts seem distinct from the *I* that is aware of them. But I cannot know the Ego of another person directly, only his self, which is not unique but comparable with the selves of others, including my own. Thus, if I am a good observer and a good mimic, it is conceivable that I could imitate another so accurately as to deceive his best friends, but it would still be I imitating him; I can never know what it would feel like to be someone else. The social relation of my Ego to my Self is of a fundamentally different kind from all my other social relations to persons or things.

Again, I am conscious of myself as becoming, of every moment being new, whether or not I show any outward sign of change, but in others I can only perceive the passage of time when it manifests itself objectively; So-and-so looks older or fatter or behaves differently from the way he used to behave. Further, though we all know that all men must die, dying is not an experience that we can share; I cannot take part in the deaths of others nor they in mine.

Lastly, my subjective experience of living is one of having continually to make a choice between given alternatives, and it is this experience of doubt and temptation that seems more important and memorable to me than the actions I take when I have made my choice. But when I observe others, I cannot see them making choices; I can only see their actions; compared with myself, others seem at once

less free and more stable in character, good or bad.

The Quest is one of the oldest, hardiest, and most popular of all literary genres. In some instances it may be founded on historical fact—the Quest of the Golden Fleece may have its origin in the search of seafaring traders for amber—and certain themes, like the theme of the enchanted cruel Princess whose heart can be melted only by the predestined lover, may be distorted recollections of religious rites, but the persistent appeal of the Quest as a literary form is due, I believe, to its validity as a symbolic description of our subjective personal experience of existence as historical.

As a typical example of the traditional Quest, let us look at the tale in the Grimm collection called *The Waters of Life*. A King has fallen sick. Each of his three sons sets out in turn to find and bring back the water of life which will restore him to health. The motive of the two elder sons is not love of their father but the hope of reward; only the youngest really cares about his father as a person. All three encounter a dwarf who asks them where they are going. The first two rudely refuse to answer and are punished by the dwarf, who imprisons them in a ravine. The youngest answers courteously and truthfully, and the dwarf not only directs him to the castle where the Fountain of the Waters of Life is situated but also gives him a magic wand to open the castle gate and two loaves of bread to appease the lions who guard the Fountain. Furthermore, the dwarf warns him that he must leave before the clock strikes twelve or he will find himself imprisoned. Following these instructions and using the magic gifts, the youngest brother obtains the Water of Life, meets a beautiful Princess who promises to marry him if he will return in a year, and carries away with him a magic sword which can slay whole armies and a magic loaf of bread which will never come to an end. However, he almost fails because, forgetting the dwarf's advice, he lies down on a bed and falls asleep, awakening only just in time as the clock is striking twelve; the closing door takes a piece off his heel.

On his way home he meets the dwarf again and learns what has happened to his brothers; at his entreaty the dwarf reluctantly releases them, warning him that they have evil hearts.

The three brothers continue their homeward journey and, thanks to the sword and the loaf, the youngest is able to deliver three kingdoms from war and famine. The last stretch is by sea. While the hero is asleep, his older brothers steal the Water of Life from his bottle and substitute sea water. When they arrive home, their sick father tries the water offered by the youngest and, naturally, is made worse; then the elder brothers offer him the water they have stolen and cure him.

In consequence the King believes their allegation that the youngest was trying to poison him and orders his huntsman to take the hero into the forest and shoot him in secret. When it comes to the point, however, the huntsman cannot bring himself to do this, and the hero remains in hiding in the forest.

Presently wagons of gold and jewels begin arriving at the palace for the hero, gifts from the grateful kings whose lands he had delivered from war and famine, and his father becomes convinced of his innocence. Meanwhile the Princess, in preparation for her wedding, has built a golden road to her castle and given orders that only he who comes riding straight along it shall be admitted.

Again the two elder brother attempt to cheat the hero by going to woo her themselves, but, when they come to the golden road, they are afraid of spoiling it; one rides to the left of it, one to the right, and both are refused admission to the castle. When the hero comes to the road he is so preoccupied with thinking about the Princess that he does not notice that it is made of gold and rides straight up it. He is admitted, weds the Princess, returns home with her, and is reconciled to his father. The two wicked brothers put to sea, never to be heard of again, and all ends happily.

The essential elements in this typical Quest story are six.

1. A precious Object and/or Person to be found and possessed or married.

2. A long journey to find it, for its whereabouts are not originally known to the seekers.

3. A hero. The precious Object cannot be found by anybody, but only by the one person who possesses the right qualities of breeding or character.

4. A Test or series of Tests by which the unworthy are screened out, and the hero revealed.

5. The Guardians of the Object who must be overcome before it can be won. They may be simply a further test of the hero's *arete*, or they may be malignant in themselves.

6. The Helpers who with their knowledge and magical powers assist the hero and but for whom he would never succeed. They may appear in human or in animal form.

Does not each of these elements correspond to an aspect of our subjective experience of life?

1. Many of my actions are purposive; the *telos* towards which they are directed may be a short-term one, like trying to write a sentence which shall express my

present thoughts accurately, or a lifelong one, the search to find true happiness or authenticity of being, to become what I wish or God intends me to become. What more natural image for such a *telos* than a beautiful Princess or the Waters of Life?

2. I am conscious of time as a continuous irreversible process of change. Translated into spatial terms, this process becomes, naturally enough, a journey.

3. I am conscious of myself as unique —my goal is for me only—and as confronting an unknown future—I cannot be certain in advance whether I shall succeed or fail in achieving my goal. The sense of uniqueness produces the image of the unique hero; the sense of uncertainty, the images of the unsuccessful rivals.

4. I am conscious of contradictory forces in myself, some of which I judge to be good and others evil, which are continually trying to sway my will this way or that. The existence of these forces is given. I can choose to yield to a desire or to resist it, but I cannot by choice desire or not desire.

Any image of this experience must be dualistic, a contest between two sides, friends and enemies.

On the other hand, the Quest provides no image of our objective experience of social life. If I exclude my own feelings and try to look at the world as if I were the lens of a camera, I observe that the vast majority of people have to earn their living in a fixed place, and that journeys are confined to people on holiday or with independent means. I observe that, though there may be some wars which can be called just, there are none in which one side is absolutely good and the other absolutely evil, though it is all too common for both sides to persuade themselves that this is so. As for struggles between man and the forces of nature or wild beasts, I can see that nature is unaware of being destructive and that, though there are animals which attack men out of hunger or fear, no animal does so out of malice.

In many versions of the Quest, both ancient and modern, the winning or recovery of the Precious Object is for the common good of the society to which the hero belongs. Even when the goal of his quest is marriage, it is not any girl he is after but a Princess. Their personal happiness is incidental to the happiness of the City; now the Kingdom will be well governed, and there will soon be an heir.

But there are other versions in which success is of importance only to the individual who achieves it. The Holy Grail, for example, will never again become visible to all men; only the exceptionally noble and chaste can be allowed to see it.

Again, there are two types of Quest Hero. One resembles the hero of Epic; his superior *arete* is manifest to all. Jason, for example, is instantly recognizable as the kind of man who can win the Golden Fleece if anybody can. The other type, so common in fairy tales, is the hero whose *arete* is concealed. The youngest son, the weakest, the least clever, the one whom everybody would judge as least likely to succeed, turns out to be the hero when his manifest betters have failed. He owes his success, not to his own powers, but to the fairies, magicians, and animals who help him, and he is able to enlist their help because, unlike his betters, he is humble enough to take advice, and kind enough to give assistance to strangers who, like himself, appear to be nobody in particular.

Though the subject of this essay is the Quest in its traditional form, it is worth while, perhaps, to mention, very briefly, some variants.

A) The Detective Story. Here the goal is not an object or a person but the answer to a question—Who committed the murder? Consequently, not only is there no journey, but also the more closed the society, the more restricted the locale, the better. There are two sides, but one side has only one member, the murderer, for the division is not between the Evil and the Good but between the Guilty and the Innocent. The hero, the Detective, is a third party who belongs to neither side.

B) The Adventure Story. Here the journey and the goal are identical, for the Quest is for more and more adventures. A classic example is Poe's *Gordon Pym*. More sophisticated and subtler examples are Goethe's *Faust* and the *Don Juan* legend.

The condition laid down in his pact with Mephisto is that Faust shall never ask that the flow of time be arrested at an ideal moment, that he shall never say, "Now, I have reached the goal of my quest." Don Juan's Quest can never come to an end because there will always remain girls whom he has not yet seduced. His is also one of the rare cases of an Evil Quest which ought not to be undertaken and in which, therefore, the hero is the villain.

C) *Moby Dick*. Here the Precious Object and the Malevolent Guardian are combined and the object of the Quest is not possession but destruction. Another example of a Quest which should not have been undertaken, but it is tragic rather than evil. Captain Ahab belongs in the company of Othello, not of Iago.

D) The Kafka novels. In these the hero fails to achieve his goal, in *The Trial* either to prove himself innocent or learn of what he is guilty, in *The Castle* to obtain official recognition as a land surveyor; and he fails, not because he is unworthy, but because success is humanly impossible. The Guardians are too strong and, though Kafka avoids saying so I think one can add, too malevolent. What makes K a hero is that, despite the evidence that Evil is more powerful than Good in the world, he never gives up the struggle to worship the Prince of this world. By all the rules he ought to despair; yet he doesn't.

Any literary mimesis of the subjective experience of becoming is confronted by problems of form and limitations of subject matter. Like a man's life which has a beginning, birth, and an end, death, the Quest story has two fixed points, the starting out and the final achievement, but the number of adventures in the interval cannot but be arbitrary, for, since the flow of time is continuous, it can be infinitely divided and subdivided into moments. One solution is the imposition of a numerical pattern, analogous to the use of metre in poetry. Thus, in *The Waters of Life* there are three brothers, three kingdoms to be delivered from war and famine, and three ways of approaching the Princess's castle. There are two tests, the dwarf and the golden road, but the right and wrong behaviour are symmetrically opposed; it is right to take notice of the dwarf but wrong to take notice of the road.

The hero twice nearly comes to disaster by falling asleep, on the first occasion in direct disobedience of the dwarf's instructions, on the second in neglect of the warning that his brothers are evil men.

To take a man on a journey is to cut him off from his everyday social relations to women, neighbours, and fellow-workers. The only sustained relation which the Quest Hero can enjoy is with those who accompany him on his journey, that is to say, either the democratic relation between equal comrades-in-arms, or the feudal relation between Knight and

Squire. Aside from these, his social life is limited to chance and brief encounters. Even when his motive for understanding the Quest is erotic, the lady has to remain in wait for him either at the start or the end of the road. Partly for this reason and partly because it deals with adventures, that is, situations of crisis in which a man behaves either well or badly, the Quest tale is ill adapted to subtle portrayals of character; its personages are almost bound to be Archetypes rather than idiosyncratic individuals.

So much for general observations. I shall devote the rest of this essay to an examination of a single work, Mr. J. R. R. Tolkien's trilogy, *The Lord of the Rings*.

THE SETTING

Many Quest tales are set in a dreamland, that is to say, in no definite place or time. This has the advantage of allowing the use of all the wealth of dream imagery, monsters, magical transformations and translations, which are absent from our waking life, but at the cost of aggravating the tendency of the genre to divorce itself from social and historical reality. A dream is at most capable of allegorical interpretation, but such interpretations are apt to be mechanical and shallow. There are other Quest tales, a thriller like *The Thirty-Nine Steps*, for example, which are set in places which we can find in the atlas and in times we can read of in history books. This gives the Quest a social significance, but the moral ambiguities of real history clash with the presupposition which is essential to the genre, that one side is good and the other bad.

Even in wartime, the sensitive reader cannot quite believe this of the two sides which the writer of thrillers takes from real life. He cannot help knowing that, at the same time that John Buchan is mak-

ing the heroes English and American and the enemies German, some German author may be writing an equally convincing thriller in which the roles are reversed.

Mr. Tolkien sets his story neither in a dream world nor in the actual world but in an imaginary world. An imaginary world can be so constructed as to make credible any landscape, inhabitants, and events which its maker wishes to introduce, and since he himself has invented its history, there can be only one correct interpretation of events, his own. What takes place and why is, necessarily, what he says it is.

But the construction of a convincing imaginary world makes formidable demands upon the imagination of its creator. There must be no question which, according to our interests, we ask about the real world to which he cannot give a convincing answer, and any writer who, like Mr. Tolkien, sets out to create an imaginary world in the twentieth century has to meet a higher standard of concreteness than, say his medieval predecessor, for he has to reckon with readers who have been exposed to the realistic novel and scientific historical research.

A dream world may be full of inexplicable gaps and logical inconsistencies; an imaginary world may not, for it is a world of law, not of wish. Its laws may be different from those which govern our own, but they must be as intelligible and inviolable. Its history may be unusual but it must not contradict our notion of what history is, an interplay of Fate, Choice, and Chance. Lastly, it must not violate our moral experience. If, as the Quest generally requires, Good and Evil are to be incarnated in individuals and societies, we must be convinced that the Evil side is what every sane man, irrespective of his nationality or culture, would acknowledge as evil. The triumph of Good over Evil which the successful achievement of the

Quest implies must appear historically possible, not a daydream. Physical and, to a considerable extent, intellectual power must be shown as what we know them to be, morally neutral and effectively real: battles are won by the stronger side, be it good or evil.

To indicate the magnitude of the task Mr. Tolkien set himself, let me give a few figures. The area of his world measures some thirteen hundred miles from east (the Gulf of Lune) to west (the Iron Hills) and twelve hundred miles from north (the Bay of Farochel) to south (the mouth of the River Anduin). In our world there is only one species, man, who is capable of speech and has a real history; in Mr. Tolkien's there are at least seven. The actual events of the story cover the last twenty years of the Third Historical Epoch of this world. The First Age is treated as legendary so that its duration is unknown, and its history is only vaguely recalled, but for the 3441 years of the Second Age and the 3021 years of the Third, he has to provide a continuous and credible history.

The first task of the maker of an imaginary world is the same as that of Adam in Eden; he has to find names for everyone and everything in it and if, as in Mr. Tolkien's world, there is more than one language, he has to invent as many series of names as there are tongues.

In the nominative gift, Mr. Tolkien surpasses any writer, living or dead, whom I have ever read; to find the "right" names is hard enough in a comic world; in a serious one success seems almost magical. Moreover, he shows himself capable of inventing not only names but whole languages which reflect the nature of those who speak them. The Ents, for example, are trees which have acquired movement, consciousness, and speech, but continue to live at the tempo of trees. In consequence their language is "slow, sonorous, agglomerated, repetitive, indeed long-winded." Here is only a part of the Entish word for *hill*:

a-lalla-lalla-rumba-kamanda-lind-or-buruma.

The extremes of good and evil in the story are represented by the Elves and Sauron, respectively. Here is a verse from a poem in Elfish:

A Elbereth Gilthoniel,
silivren penna míriel
o menel alglar elenath!
Na-chaered palan díriel.
o galadhremmin ennorath,
Fanuilos, le linnathon
nef aer, sí nef aearon.

And here is an evil spell in the Black Speech invented by Sauron:

Ash nazg durbatulûk, ash nazg gimbatul, ash nazg thrakatalûk, agh burzum-ishi-krimpatul.

An imaginary world must be as real to the senses of the reader as the actual world. For him to find an imaginary journey convincing, he must feel that he is seeing the landscape through which it passes as, given his mode of locomotion and the circumstances of his errand, the fictional traveler himself saw it. Fortunately, Mr. Tolkien's gift for topographical description is equal to his gift for naming and his fertility in inventing incidents. His hero, Frodo Baggins, is on the road, excluding rests, for eighty days and covers over 1800 miles, much of it on foot, and with his senses kept perpetually sharp by fear, watching every inch of the way for signs of his pursuers, yet Mr. Tolkien succeeds in convincing us that there is nothing Frodo noticed which he has forgotten to describe.

Technologically, his world is preindustrial. The arts of mining, metallurgy, architecture, road and bridge building, are highly developed, but there are no firearms and no mechanical means of transport. It is, however, a world that has seen better days. Lands that were once cultivated and fertile have gone back to the wilderness, roads have become impassable, once famous cities are now ruins. (There is one puzzling discrepancy. Both Sauron and Saruman seem to have installed heavy machinery in their fortresses. Why, in that case, are they limited to waging untechnological warfare?) Though without machines, some people in this world possess powers which our civilisation would call magical because it lacks them; telepathic communication and vision are possible, verbal spells are effective, weather can be controlled, rings confer invisibility, etc.

Politically, the commonest form of society is a benevolent monarchy, but the Shire of the hobbits is a kind of small-town democracy and Sauron's kingdom of Mordor is, of course, a totalitarian and slave-owning dictatorship.

Though the unstated presuppositions of the whole work are Christian, we are not told that any of the inhabitants practise a religious cult.

The Elves, the Wizards, and Sauron, certainly, and perhaps some others, believe in the existence of the One the Valas, to whom He has entrusted the guardianship of Middle Earth, and a Land in the Uttermost West which I take to be an image of Paradise.

The Quest Hero

In our subjective experience, of which the Quest is, I have suggested, a literary mimesis, what we ought to become is usually dependent upon what we are; it is idle and cowardly of me if I fail to make the fullest use of any talent with which I have been endowed, but it is presumptuous of me to attempt a task for which I lack the talent it requires. That is why, in the traditional Quest story, the hero desires to undertake the quest and, even when to others he appears lacking in power, he is confident of success. This problem of vocation is specifically dealt with in one Quest tale, *The Magic Flute*. Prince Tamino is the typical hero, who must dare the trials by Fire and Water to attain wisdom and win the hand of the Princess Pamina.

But beside him stands Papageno, who is, in his own way, a hero too. He is asked whether he is prepared to endure the trials like his master and he answers, no, such dangers are not for the likes of him. "But," says the priest, "if you don't, you will never win a girl." "In that case," he replies, "I'll remain single." This answer reveals his humility, and he is rewarded with his mirror image, Papagena. In contrast to him stands the villain Monostatos. Like Papageno, he is incapable of enduring the trials but, unlike him, he lacks the humility to forego the rewards of heroism; he is even unwilling to accept an equivalent of Papagena and demands nothing less than the Princess.

But there is another kind of vocation which may be called religious. Not everybody experiences it, and even for those who do, it may concern only moments of their life. What characterises the religious vocation is that it comes from outside the self and, generally to the self's terror and dismay, as when God calls Abraham out of the land of Ur, or when a man, by nature physically timid, is called to enter a burning building to rescue a child because there is no one else around to do it.

Some of the characters in *The Lord of the Rings*, Gandalf and Aragorn, for instance, are expressions of the natural vocation of talent. It is for Gandalf to plan the strategy of the War against Sauron because he is a very wise man; it is for Aragorn to lead the armies of Gondor because he is a great warrior and the rightful heir to the throne. Whatever they may have to risk and suffer, they are, in a sense, doing what they want to do. But the situation of the real hero, Frodo Baggins, is quite different. When the decision has been taken to send the Ring to the Fire, his *feelings* are those of Papageno: "such dangerous exploits are not for a little hobbit like me. I would much rather stay at home than risk my life on the very slight chance of winning glory." But his conscience tells him: "You may be nobody in particular in your self, yet, for some inexplicable reasons, through no choice of your own, the Ring has come into your keeping, so that it is on you and not on Gandalf or Aragorn that the task falls of destroying it."

Because the decision has nothing to do with his talents, nobody else can or should try to help him make up his mind. When he stands up at the Council of Elrond and says: "I will take the Ring though I know not the Way," Elrond replies: "It is a heavy burden. So heavy that none could lay it on another. I do not lay it on you. But if you take it freely, I will say that your choice is right."

Once he has chosen, Frodo is absolutely committed; the others who set out with him are not.

The Ring Bearer is setting out on the Quest of Mount Doom: on him alone is any charge laid—neither to cast away the Ring nor to deliver it to any servant of the Enemy, nor indeed to let any handle it, save members of the Company and the Council, and only then in gravest need. The others go with him as free companions to help him on his way. You may tarry, or come back, or turn aside to other paths as chance allows. The further you go, the less easy it will be to withdraw; yet no oath or bond is laid upon you to go further than you will. For you do not yet know the strength of your hearts and you cannot foresee what each may meet on the road.

"Faithless is he who says farewell when the road darkens," said Gimli.

"Maybe," said Elrond, "but let him not vow to walk in the dark who has not seen the nightfall."

"Yet sworn vow may strengthen quaking heart," said Gimli.

"Or break it," said Elrond. "Look not too far ahead. But go now with good hearts."

THE CONFLICT OF GOOD AND EVIL

If it is a defect in the usual Quest tale that Good triumphs over Evil simply because Good is more powerful, this is not a defect that can be avoided by giving Good no power at all. Quite rightly, Mr. Tolkien makes the elves, dwarfs, wizards, and men who are Sauron's opponents a formidable lot indeed, but in sheer strength, Sauron is, even without his Ring, the stronger. Yet their power has its part to play, as Gandalf points out.

Victory cannot be achieved by arms. I still hope for victory but not by arms. For into the midst of all these policies comes the Ring of Power, the foundation of Barad-dûr and the hope of Sauron. If he regains it, your valour is vain, and his victory will be swift and complete; so complete that none can foresee the end of it while this world lasts. If it is destroyed, then he will fall; and his fall will be so low that none can foresee his arising ever again. . . . This, then, is my counsel. We have not the Ring. In wisdom or great folly, it has been sent away to be destroyed lest it destroy us. Without it we cannot by force defeat his force. But we must at all costs keep his eye from his true peril. We cannot achieve victory by arms, but by arms we can give the Ring Bearer his only chance, frail though it be.

The Quest is successful and Sauron is overthrown. One of Mr. Tolkien's most impressive achievements is that he convinces the reader that the mistakes which Sauron makes to his undoing are the kind of mistakes which Evil, however powerful, cannot help making just because it is Evil. His primary weakness is a lack of imagination, for, while Good can imagine what it would be like to be Evil, Evil cannot imagine what it would be like to be Good. Elrond, Gandalf, Galadriel, Aragorn are able to imagine themselves as Sauron and therefore can resist the temptation to use the Ring themselves, but Sauron cannot imagine that anyone who knows what the Ring can accomplish, his own destruction among other things, will not use it, let alone try to destroy it. Had he been capable of imagining this, he had only to sit waiting and watching in Mordor for the Ring Bearer to arrive, and he was bound to catch him and recover the Ring. Instead, he assumes that the Ring has been taken to Gondor where the strongest of his enemies are gathered, which is what he would have done had he been in their place, and launches an attack on that city, neglecting the watch on his own borders.

Secondly, the kind of Evil which Sauron embodies, the lust for domination, will always be irrationally cruel since it is not satisfied if another does what it wants; he must be made to do it against his will. When Pippin looked into the Palantír of Orthanc and so revealed himself to Sauron, the latter had only to question him in order to learn who had the Ring and what he intended to do with it. But, as Gandalf says: "He was too eager. He did not want information only: he wanted *you* quickly, so that he could deal with you in the Dark Tower, slowly."

Thirdly, all alliances of Evil with Evil are necessarily unstable and untrustworthy since, by definition, Evil loves only itself and its alliances are based on fear or hope of profit, not on affection. Sauron's greatest triumph has been his seduction of the great wizard Saruman but, though he has succeeded in making him a traitor to the cause of Good, he has not yet completely enslaved him, so that Saruman tries to seize the Ring for himself.

Lastly, unforeseeable by either side, is the role played by Sméagol-Gollum. When Frodo first hears about him from Gandalf, he exclaims:

—What a pity Bilbo did not stab that vile creature when he had the chance!
—Pity? It was pity that stayed his hand. Pity and Mercy: not to strike without need. And he has been well rewarded, Frodo. Be sure that he took so little hurt from the evil, and escaped in the end, because he began his ownership of the Ring so. With Pity.
—I cannot understand you. Do you mean to say that you and the Elves have let him live on after all those horrible deeds? He deserves death.
—Deserves it? I daresay he does. But do not be eager to deal out death in judgment. For even the wise cannot see all ends. I have not much hope that Gollum can be cured before he dies, but there is a chance of it. And he is bound up with the fate of the Ring. My heart tells me that he has some part to play yet, for good or ill, before the end; and when that comes, the pity of Bilbo may rule the fate of many, yours not least.

Gollum picks up Frodo's trail in the Mines of Moria and follows him. When Frodo manages to catch him, he remembers Gandalf's words and spares his life. This turns out to his immediate advantage for, without Gollum's help, Frodo and Sam would never have found their way through the Dead Marshes or to the pass of Cirith Ungol. Gollum's motives in guiding them are not wholly evil; one part of him, of course, is waiting for an opportunity to steal the Ring, but another part feels gratitude and genuine affection for Frodo.

Gandalf was right, however, in fearing that there was little hope of his being cured; in the end his evil side triumphs. He leads Frodo and Sam into Shelob's lair and, after their escape, pursues them to Mount Doom and attacks them. Once again they spare his life. And then the unexpected happens.

. . . there on the brink of the chasm, at the very Crack of Doom, stood Frodo, black against the glare, tense, erect, but still as if he had been turned to stone.

"Master!" cried Sam.

Then Frodo stirred and spoke with a clear voice . . . it rose above the throb and turmoil of Mount Doom, ringing in the roofs and walls.

"I have come," he said. "But I do not choose now to do what I came to do. I will not do this deed. The Ring is mine!" And suddenly, as he set it on his finger, he vanished from Sam's sight . . . Something struck Sam violently in the back, his legs were knocked from under him and he was flung aside, striking his head against the stony floor, as a dark shape sprang over him. . . .

Sam got up. He was dazed, and blood streaming from his head dripped in his eyes. He groped forward, and then he saw a strange and terrible thing. Gollum on the edge of the abyss was fighting like a mad thing with an unseen foe. . . . The fires below awoke in anger, the red light blazed, and all the cavern was filled with a great glare and heat. Suddenly Sam saw Gollum's long hands draw upwards to his mouth; his white fangs gleamed, and then snapped as they bit. Frodo gave a cry, and there he was, fallen upon his knees at the chasm's edge. But Gollum, dancing like a mad thing, held aloft the Ring, a finger still thrust within its circle.

"Precious, precious, precious!" Gollum cried. "My Precious! O my Precious!" And with that, even as his eyes were lifted up to gloat on his prize, he stepped too far, toppled, wavered for a moment on the brink, and then with a shriek he fell. . . .

"Well, this is the end, Sam Gamgee," said a voice by his side. And there was Frodo, pale and worn, and yet himself again; and in his eyes there was peace now, neither strain of will, nor madness, nor any fear. His burden was taken away. . . .

"Yes," said Frodo. "Do you remember Gandalf's words: '*Even Gollum may have something yet to do?*' But for him, Sam, I could not have destroyed the Ring. The

Quest would have been in vain, even at the bitter end."

THE FRUITS OF VICTORY

"And so they lived happily ever after" is a conventional formula for concluding a fairy tale. Alas, it is false and we know it, for it suggests that, once Good has triumphed over Evil, man is translated out of his historical existence into eternity. Mr. Tolkien is much too honest to end with such a pious fiction. Good has triumphed over Evil so far as the Third Age of Middle Earth is concerned, but there is no certainty that this triumph is final. There was Morgoth before Sauron and, before the Fourth Age ends, who can be sure that no successor to Sauron will appear? Victory does not mean the restoration of the Earthly Paradise or the advent of the New Jerusalem. In our historical existence even the best solution involves loss as well as gain. With the destruction of the Ruling Ring the three Elven Rings lose their power, as Galadriel foresaw.

Do you not see now wherefore your coming to us is as the footsteps of Doom? For if you fail, we are laid bare to the Enemy. Yet if you succeed, then our power is diminished, and Lothlórien will fade, and the tide of time will sweep it away. We must depart into the West or dwindle to a rustic folk of dell and cave, slowly to forget and be forgotten.

Even Frodo, the Quest Hero, has to pay for his success.

"But," said Sam, and tears started from his eyes, "I thought you were going to enjoy the Shire for years and years after all you've done."

"I thought so, too, once. But I have been too deeply hurt, Sam. I tried to save the Shire, and it has been saved, but not for me. It must often be so, Sam, when things are in danger:

someone has to give them up, lose them, so that others may keep them."

If there is any Quest Tale which, while primarily concerned with the subjective life of the individual person as all such stories must be, manages to do more justice to our experience of social-historical realities than *The Lord of the Rings*, I should be glad to hear of it.

Index

Abel, Lionel, 187
 Metatheatre, 187
Abrams, M. H., 10
 Mirror and the Lamp, The, 352
Adams, J. Donald, 66
Adams, Robert Martin, 245
Adler, Alfred, 241
Adorno, Theodor W., 214
 Aging of Modern Music, The, 214
Aeschylus, 7, 33, 54, 282
 Eumenides, 33
 Oresteia, 33, 36
 Prometheus, 36, 51
Alembert, Jean le Rond d', 94
Anacreon, 102
Aristotle, 33, 40, 54, 78, 81, 97, 98, 100, 204,
 238, 244, 252 n., 270, 276, 283
 Nicomachean Ethics, 97
 Poetics, 31, 39, 40, 97, 238, 276
 Rhetoric, 283
Arnold, Matthew, 54, 55, 76, 162, 163–164,
 166, 193, 194, 196–197, 198, 200, 250,
 252, 253–267, 356
 Buried Life, The, 263
 Dover Beach, 54, 55, 56, 196–197, 242–
 243, 249–267
 Early Death and Fame, 254 n.
 Empedocles on Etna, 250
 Essays in Criticism (1869), 257 n.
 Farewell, A, 254 n.
 To a Friend, 254 n.
 Function of Criticism at the Present Time,
 The, 164, 168
 God and the Bible, 260 n.
 Morality, 254 n.
 Poems (1853), 252 n., 257 n.
 Poems of Wordsworth, 164
 Rugby Chapel, 262
 Scholar Gypsy, The, 263
 Self-Deception, 254 n.
 Sweetness and Light, 164
Arvin, Newton, 239
Ashley, Kenneth, 359
 Norman Church: New Coalfield, 359
Asselineau, Roger, 10
Auden, W. H., 71, 168, 200, 317, 355, 356,
 370
 For the Time Being, 355–356

Auden, W. H. (Continued)
 Unknown Citizen, The, 368
Auerbach, Erich, xii, 5, 7, 8, 9, 12, 116 n.
 Mimesis, 116 n.
Austen, Jane, 123, 317, 346, 350
 Emma, 123
 Love and Friendship, 350
 Northanger Abbey, 350
 Pride and Prejudice, 301
 Sense and Sensibility, 350

Baillie, Joanna, 266
Bakunin, Michael, 222
Balzac, Honoré de, 108, 174, 180, 210, 263
Barzun, Jacques, 84
Bateson, F. W., 9
 Selected Poems of William Blake, 153 n.
Baudelaire, Pierre Charles, 70, 188, 192, 193,
 199–200, 304, 348
 Correspondances, 355
 Intimate Journals, 188, 199–200
Baum, Paull F., 249 n., 251
Beardsley, Monroe C., 79
 Intentional Fallacy, The, 79
Beckett, Samuel, 208, 211
 Molloy, 208, 211, 219
 Waiting for Godot, 234
Beddoes, Thomas Lovell, 354
 Subterranean City, 354
Beethoven, Ludwig von, 232, 352
 Ninth Symphony, 232
Belloc, Hillaire, 220
Bellow, Saul, 127
 Seize the Day, 127
Benjamin, Walter, 214, 216–219
Benn, Gottfried, 208, 211, 212–213, 219
 Doppelleben, 208
Bennett, Arnold, 197
Bentham, Jeremy, 76, 173, 265
Bentley, Eric, 166–167, 226
Beowulf, 300, 358
Berdyaev, Nicholas, 43, 47, 48
Bergson, Henri, 43, 76, 214
Betjeman, John, 367
 Planester's Vision, The, 367
Bible, The Holy, 16–27, 273, 279, 319, 342
 Acts, 275
 Deuteronomy, 329

Bible, The Holy (*Continued*)
  Genesis, 16–27, 274 n.
  Job, 51, 52, 54, 55, 57, 62, 109, 111, 118, 127
  Jonah, 328
  Mark, 118
  Samuel, II, 19
  Song of Solomon, 68, 69
Bieber, Margate, 180
Blackmur, R. P., xii, 75
Blake, William, 149, 153–157, 159, 190, 194, 351, 352, 353, 355
  Chimney Sweeper, The, 155
  Europe, 347
  London, 153–157, 159
  Marriage of Heaven and Hell, The, 356
  Songs of Experience, 153, 154, 155
  Songs of Innocence, 150–151
Bloom, Harold, 317
  Visionary Company, The, 317
Boccaccio, Giovanni, 69, 112–119
  Decameron, 112–119
Böckh, August, 2
Bodkin, Maud, 318
  Archetypal Patterns in English Poetry, 288, 318
Boethius, 346
Boileau-Despréaux, Nicolas, 40, 91, 363
Bonnerot, Louis, 249 n., 251, 252 n., 260 n.
Booth, Wayne C., 81–82, 108
Bostetter, Edward E., 352
Bowra, C. M., 10
  Heritage of Symbolism, The, 192
Boyle, Kay, 123
  Bridegroom's Body, The, 128
  Crazy Hunter, The, 128
  Dear Mr. Walrus, 123
  Keep Your Pity, 123
Brecht, Bertolt, 38, 39, 167, 226–235
  Good Woman of Setzuan, The, 231
  Mother Courage and Her Children, 229, 233, 234
Breton, André, 193, 194
  What Is Surrealism?, 193
Brod, Max, 218
Brooks, Cleanth, 77–78, 80, 96, 315
Brooks, Van Wyck, 103, 245
Brown, Charles Brockden, 303, 304, 305–306, 309, 349
  Wieland, 305
Browne, Sir Thomas, 65, 349
Browning, Robert, 83, 194

Browning, Robert (*Continued*)
  Paracelsus, 263
Buckley, Jerome, 263
  Victorian Temper, The, 262 n.
Bulfinch, Thomas, 338
Bunyan, John, 71, 354
  Pilgrim's Progress, 71, 354
Burke, Kenneth, xiii, 66, 79, 168, 242, 244, 249, 261, 268, 276
  Philosophy of Literary Form, The, 79
Bush, Douglas, xii, 9, 54, 96, 317, 339
Byron, George Gordon, Lord, 35, 83, 150, 151, 310, 346, 348
  Cain, 354
  Childe Harolde's Pilgrimage, 352
  Darkness, 354
  Don Juan, 352
  Lara, 354
  Sardanapalus, 35

Calvin, John, 30
Campbell, Joseph, 316
  Hero with a Thousand Faces, The, 338, 339
Campion, Thomas, 143, 145
Camus, Albert, 235
Carlyle, Thomas, 69, 173, 262, 263, 266, 351
  Sartor Resartus, 354–355
Carroll, Lewis (C. L. Dodgson), 266, 267
Cassirer, Ernst, 67, 314, 315–316
  Language and Myth, 315
  Philosophy of Symbolic Forms, The, 315
Castelvetro, Lodovico, 31
  Poetica d'Aristotele vulgarizata, 31
Cervantes Saavedra, Miguel de, 42
  Don Quixote, 49, 270
Chapman, George, 32, 35, 36
  Bussy d'Ambois, 35
  Tragedy of Chabot, Admiral of France, The, 35
Chateaubriand, François René, 310
Chaucer, Geoffrey, 7, 28, 30, 73, 175
  Canterbury Tales, 28–29
Chekhov, Anton, 37
  Ward Number Six, 125, 127
Chernyshevski, Nicholas, 181
  What Is to Be Done?, 181
Chesterton, G. K., 220
Churchyard, Thomas, 30
  Mirror for Magistrates, 30
Cintio, Giraldo, 33
Clark, Sir Kenneth, 336
Claudel, Paul, 31, 39, 192

Cleland, John, 304, 306
  Memoirs of Fanny Hill, The, 306
Clough, Arthur Hugh, 260 n., 262
Cocteau, Jean, 33
  Machine infernale, 40
Coghill, Neville, 334
Coleridge, Samuel Taylor, 66, 76, 78, 83, 163, 238, 243, 274 n., 284–289, 350, 352, 356
  Biographia Literaria, 76, 286, 348
  Dejection: an Ode, 284–289
  Eolian Harp, The, 274 n.
  Kubla Khan, 288, 353
  Rime of the Ancient Mariner, The, 79, 274 n., 288, 352
  Sibylline Leaves, 285, 286
Compton-Burnett, Ivy, 124
Connolly, Cyril, 124
Conrad, Joseph, 44, 317
  Heart of Darkness, 126
  Nostromo, 124
  Secret Agent, The, 124
  Secret Sharer, The, 126, 130
Cook, A. B., 314
Cooper, James Fenimore, 303, 310
  Last of the Mohicans, The, 301
Corneille, Pierre, 34, 39, 40, 91, 295, 296
Cornford, F. M., 314
Cotton, Charles, 101, 102, 103
Cowley, Abraham, 102, 105
Crabbe, George, 346, 350
  Village, The, 350
Cranch, Christopher, 68
Crane, R. S., xii, 81
Crane, Stephen, 64, 301
  Red Badge of Courage, The, 64, 301
Croce, Benedetto, 76
Cromwell, Oliver, 101
Cunningham, J. V., 8
Curtius, Ernst Robert, 9

Daiches, David, 6, 7, 8, 9, 50, 168
Daniel, Samuel, 35
Dante Alighieri, 28, 32, 54, 55, 57, 66, 68, 71, 72, 194, 270–271, 309, 336, 339, 341–344, 347, 348, 356
  Divine Comedy, 55, 60, 68–69, 71, 190, 228, 270–271, 276–278, 281, 339, 341–344
Darwin, Charles, 313
Darwin, Erasmus, 364
  Botanic Garden, 364
Delacroix, Ferdinand, 352

Delasanta, Rodney, 249 n., 250, 251, 252 n.
DeQuincy, Thomas, 352
  Savannah-la-Mar, 353
Dickens, Charles, 44, 45, 46, 47, 108, 119
Dickinson, Emily, 299
Diderot, Denis, 39, 306–307
  Rameau's Nephew, 306
  Bijoux Indiscrets, 306
Doblin, Alfred, 206
Donne, John, 83, 147
Dornier, Charles, 359, 360
  Aube sanglante, 359
Dos Passos, John, 190, 191, 206–207
Dostoevsky, Fyodor, 119, 179–182, 184, 213, 223, 225, 239
  Brothers Karamazov, The, 119, 126, 181, 223
  Double, The, 126
  Eternal Husband, The, 126
  House of the Dead, The, 213
  Notes from Underground, 124, 125, 128, 179–181
  Possessed, The, 120, 123, 221
Dowden, Edward, 336
Dowland, John, 139, 143, 144
  Second Book of Aires, 142
Drew, Elizabeth, 249 n., 251
Dryden, John, 35, 38, 39, 40–41, 150, 338, 346
  All for Love, 40, 41
  Aureng-Zebe, 40
  Essay of Dramatic Poesy, An, 1, 40
  Iliad (translation), 346
  Marriage à la Mode, 40
  Troilus and Cressida, 40
Durandus (Guillume Durand), 70, 71, 72
  Rationale, 70
Dürrenmatt, Friedrich, 233, 234, 235
Durtain, Luc, 362
  Lise à la verrerie, 362

Eastman, Max, 220
Eliot, George, 44, 119, 263
  Daniel Deronda, 44
Eliot, T. S., xii, 8, 31, 39, 54, 56, 57, 69, 76–77, 137, 168, 190, 192, 196, 200, 207, 208, 231, 237, 356, 368
  Ash Wednesday, 56
  Cocktail Party, The, 208
  Coriolan II, 369
  Four Quartets, 56
  Murder in the Cathedral, 79, 231

Eliot, T. S. (*Continued*)
  Tradition and the Individual Talent, 77, 317
  Waste Land, The, 137, 231
Empson, William, xii
Engels, Friedrich, 162, 163
  German Ideology, The, 163
Erasmus, Desiderius, *Adagia*, 28
Erdman, David V., 155 n.
Euripedes, 33

Faulkner, William, 6, 47, 64, 205, 299, 300, 304, 344
  Bear, The, 64
  Fable, A, 64
  Sound and the Fury, The, 208
Fergusson, Francis, 316, 317, 337
Fichte, Johann Gottlieb, 345
Fiedler, Leslie A., xiii, 168, 242–243, 299
  Love and Death in the American Novel, 243
Fielding, Henry, 112, 119, 303
Fitzgerald, F. Scott, 6
  Great Gatsby, The, 124
  Tender Is the Night, 124
Flaubert, Gustave, 68, 70, 111, 117, 118, 127, 263
  Legend of St. Julian the Hospitaler, 125
  Madame Bovary, 70, 117, 118, 119, 301, 304
  Salammbo, 358
  Simple Heart, A, 68, 128, 131
Flecknoe, Richard, *Short Discourse of the English Stage*, 37
Fletcher, J. P., 359
  Unprofitable Journey?, 359–360
Ford, Ford Madox, 44
Ford, John, 33
Forster, E. M., 177, 266
  Aspects of the Novel, 117 n.
Fowlie, Wallace, 181
Frazer, Sir James G., 313–314, 316
  Golden Bough, The, 314, 358, 360 n.
Freud, Anna, *Ego and the Mechanisms of Defense, The*, 249
Freud, Sigmund, 67, 173, 179, 185, 186, 187, 210, 238–245, 249, 306, 341, 355
  Beyond the Pleasure Principle, 185, 187
  Dostoyevsky and Parricide, 239
  Totem and Taboo, 314
Fricker, Sara, 285, 286
Friedrich, Gerhard, 249 n., 251

Frost, Robert, 98, 106, 152
  After Apple-Picking, 152
Fry, Christopher, *A Phoenix Too Frequent*, 113
Frye, Northrop, 224, 312, 313, 316, 317–318, 319, 345
  Anatomy of Criticism, 317–319
Furnivall, F. J., 2

Galsworthy, John, 197
Gardner, Helen, 5
Garnier, Robert, 33, 35
  Marc-Antoine, 34, 35
Gassendi, Pierre, 296, 297
Gibbon, Edward, 133
Gide, André, 207, 219, 300
  Counterfeiters, The, 124, 319
  Lafcadio's Adventures, 124
Ginestier, Paul, xii, 317, 357
Giraudoux, Jean, *Amphytrion 38*, 338
Goethe, Johann Wolfgang von, 13–14, 33, 69, 190, 191, 202
  Faust, 348, 353, 374
Goldmann, Lucien, 168
Googe, Barnabe, 139, 140–143
Gorki, Maxim, 213
Gourmont, Remy de, 70, 76, 77
Graves, Robert, 36, 316
Green, Henry, 124
Greene, Graham, 124, 200
Greville, Fulke, 35
  Alaham, 35
  Mustapha, 35
Grimm, Jakob and Wilhelm (brothers), 2
  Waters of Life, The, 371–372, 374
Gwynn, Frederick L., 249 n., 250, 251
  Case for Poetry, The, 249 n., 250

Hagopian, John V., 4
Hammett, Dashiell, 300
Handel, George Frederick, 327
Hardy, Thomas, 44–48, 195, 264, 348
  Return of the Native, The, 47
Harris, Mark, 111–112
Harrison, Jane Ellen, 314
  Themis, 314
Hartmann, C. H., 101, 105
Hassan, Ihab, 8
Hathorn, R. Y., *Tragedy, Myth, and Mystery*, 317
Hawthorne, Nathaniel, 64, 72, 299
  Scarlet Letter, The, 72, 301, 302, 304

Hazlitt, William, 266
Hegel, Georg Wilhelm Friedrich, 162, 204, 208
Heidigger, Martin, 204, 208, 211, 213, 217
Heller, Erich, 190
   Disinherited Mind, The, 190–191
Hemingway, Ernest, 6, 63, 73, 112, 237, 239, 275, 299
   Big Two-Hearted River, 63
   Clean, Well-Lighted Place, A, 4
Herbert, George, 70
   Temple, The, 70
Herder, Johann Gottfried von, 162
Hicks, Granville, *Living Novel, The,* 112 n.
Hitler, Adolf, 208, 228, 231, 341
Hoffman, Fredrick J., *Freudianism and the Literary Mind,* 238
Hofmannsthal, Hugo von, 215
Hogg, James, *Private Memoirs and Confessions of a Justified Sinner,* 125
Hoggart, Richard, 168
Hölderlin, Johann Friedrich, 33, 191
Holland, Norman N., xii, 242–243, 248
Homer, 12–27, 64, 68, 109, 178, 213, 301, 344
   Iliad, 14, 22, 56, 109, 300
   Odyssey, 12–15, 68, 110–111, 119
Hopkins, Gerard Manley, 66, 136, 196
   Spelt from Sibyl's Leaves, 136–144 *passim*
Horace, 35
Houghton, Walter, 260–261 n., 263
   Victorian Frame of Mind, The, 261 n.
Housman, A. E., 348
Howard, Sir Robert, 39
Howe, Irving, 167, 220
Howells, William Dean, 304
Hugo, Victor, 88, 91
   À la colonne, 362
   Prière d'Esther, 88
Hulme, T. E., 56, 76, 346, 356
Hume, David, 238
   Of Tragedy, 238
Hutchinson, Sara, 285, 286, 287, 288
Huxley, Aldous, 59, 60, 220
   After Many a Summer Dies the Swan, 124
   Antic Hay, 59
   Brave New World, 167, 220–225
   Point Counter Point, 59, 124
Hyman, Stanley Edgar, 261 n., 315
   Tangled Bank, The, 261 n.

Ibsen, Henrik, 30, 31, 37, 39, 41

Ionesco, Eugene, *Chairs, The,* 234
Isherwood, Christopher, 199

Jackson, Shirley, *Bird's Nest, The,* 276
Jacob, Max, *Le Cornet à dés,* 366
Jacobsen, Jens Peter, *Niels Lyhne,* 218
Jakobson, Roman, 75
James, Henry, Jr., 44, 45–46, 47, 49, 66, 73, 108, 112, 113, 128, 190, 193, 299, 301
   Altar of the Dead, The, 45, 194
   Great Good Place, The, 194
   Jolly Corner, The, 45
   Middle Years, The, 194
   Portrait of a Lady, 45
   Sense of the Past, The, 45, 47
   Spoils of Poynton, The, 124
   Turn of the Screw, The, 66
James, Henry, Sr., 73
Jammes, Francis, *Il y a un petit cordonnier,* 367
Jarrell, Randall, 137
   Lady Bates, 137
Jefferson, Thomas, 305–306, 309
Jocasta, 29, 30
Jodelle, Étienne, 33
   Cléopatre captive, 34
Johns Hopkins University, The, 2
Johnson, E. D. H., 264
Johnson, Samuel, 1, 133, 346
Johnson, Wendell Stacy, 249 n., 250, 251, 265
Jones, Ernest, *Hamlet and Oedipus,* 245
Jonson, Ben, 32, 33, 35–36, 37, 40
   Catiline's Conspiracy, 35–36
   Sejanus, 30–31, 35
   Silent Woman, The, 35
   Volpone, 35, 36
Joyce, James, 42, 44, 47, 61, 66, 188, 189, 190, 191, 194, 202–203, 205, 207, 219, 237
   Finnegan's Wake, 42, 43, 47, 48, 49, 65, 189, 191, 194
   Portrait of the Artist as a Young Man, 64
   Ulysses, 47, 48, 61, 179, 191, 202–203, 317
Jump, J. D., 249 n., 251
Jung, Carl Gustav, 67, 241, 242, 314–315
   Psyche and Symbol, 315
Jünger, Ernst, 208

Kafka, Franz, 65, 179 n., 182, 190, 205, 207, 212, 213–214, 217, 218–219, 237, 374
   Castle, The, 182, 213, 218, 374

Kafka, Franz (*Continued*)
  Metamorphosis, 337
  In the Penal Colony, 127
  Trial, The, 213–214, 218, 374
Kaiser, Georg, 230
Kalidasa, 345
Kant, Immanuel, 76, 163, 345
  Critique of Aesthetic Judgment, 76, 178
  Critique of Judgment, 159
Kazin, Alfred, 168
Keats, John, 55, 60, 138–139, 175–178, 276, 346, 350, 351, 352
  To Autumn, 355
  Endymion, 353
  Eve of St. Agnes, The, 176
  Lamia, 175, 176
  Ode to a Grecian Urn, 106
  Ode to a Nightingale, 355
  On Sitting Down to Read King Lear Once Again, 178
  Poems (1817), 184
  Sleep and Poetry, 177, 352
Kermode, Frank, 356
Kerr, Alfred, 209
Kettle, Arnold, 168
Kierkegaard, Soren, 208, 355
Kipling, Rudyard, *Secret of the Machines, The*, 364
Kirby, J. P., 249 n., 250, 251
Knight, G. Wilson, 323
Knights, L. C., 165, 168
Koeppen, Wolfgang, *Das Treibhaus*, 207
Koffka, Kurt, 241
Kohler, Wolfgang, 241
Krieger, Murray, 249 n., 250, 251, 252 n., 259, 260
Kris, Ernst, 246
Krutch, Joseph Wood, 245
Kyd, Thomas, 32

Laforgue, Jules, 192
Lamartine, Alphonse Marie Louis de, 88
  Le Lac, 88
Langer, Susanne, 67, 316
  Philosophy in a New Key, 67
Lardner, Ring, *Haircut*, 111
Lattimore, Richmond, 109 n.
Lawrence, D. H., 63, 64, 183, 190, 237
  Prussian Officer, The, 127
  Song of a Man Who Has Come Through, 353
  Women in Love, 183 n.

Lear, Edward, 266
Leavis, F. R., 75, 82, 168
Lenin, Nikolai, 163, 181
Leopardi, Count Giacomo, *L'Infinito*, 56
Levin, Harry, 6, 8, 9, 63
Lévy-Bruhl, Lucien, 315
Lewin, Kurt, 241
Lewis, Matthew Gregory ("Monk"), 304
Lewis, R. W. B., *American Adam, The*, 317
Lewis, Sinclair, 2
Lewis, Wynham, 47
Leyda, Jay, *Melville Log, The*, 73
Lindsay, Vachel, *What the Coal-Heaver Said*, 362
Lipton, Julius, *Hands*, 361 n.
  Rhythm, 365
Livy, 28
Longfellow, Henry Wadsworth, *Hiawatha*, 140
  Psalm of Life, The, 103
Longinus, *On the Sublime*, 238
Lorca, Frederico Garcia, 337
Lovejoy, Arthur O., 346
  Great Chain of Being, The, 8
Lovelace, Richard, 100–107
  Grasse-hopper, The, 100–106
  Lucasta, 106
Lowes, John Livingston, *Road to Xanadu, The*, 8
Lowry, H. F., 250 n.
  Letters of Matthew Arnold to Arthur Hugh Clough, The, 260 n.
Lubbock, Percy, 112
  Craft of Fiction, The, 112 n.
Lu Chi, *Wen Fu*, 291–292
Lucan, 342
Lucretius, 327
Lukács, Georg, xii, 167–168, 202
Lydgate, John, 30

Macaulay, Thomas Babington, 263
MacCaffrey, I. G., *Paradise Lost as Myth*, 317
McKeon, Richard, 81
MacLeish, Archibald, 63, 66
McLuhan, Marshall, *Gutenberg Galaxy, The*, 356
MacNeice, Louis, 369
  Prayer Before Birth, 369
Malinowski, Bronislau, 315, 338–339, 340, 341, 342
Mallarmé, Stéphane, 70, 88

Mallarmé, Stéphane (*Continued*)
  Hérodiade, 88
Mann, Thomas, 44, 49, 70, 209, 210, 213, 215, 237, 317
  Death in Venice, 127, 129–130
  Dr. Faustus, 129, 215
  Lotte in Weimar, 202–203
  Magic Mountain, The, 70, 120
  Mario and the Magician, 127
Mannheim, Karl, 222
Maritain, Jacques, 289, 291, 341, 345
  Creative Intuition in Art and Poetry, 289, 341
Marlowe, Christopher, 32, 33, 69
  Tragedy of Edward the Second, The, 29
  Tragical History of Doctor Faustus, The, 30, 32, 69
Marvell, Andrew, 83, 150
  Garden, The, 152
  Horatian Ode upon Cromwell's Return from Ireland, 101
Marx, Karl, 162, 163, 355
  German Ideology, The, 163
Maupassant, Guy de, 357 n.
Melville, Herman, 64, 71, 72, 73, 127, 133, 239, 299, 307, 356
  Bartleby the Scrivener, 125, 127
  Benito Cereno, 125, 302
  Billy Budd, 125
  Mardi, 66
  Moby Dick, 6, 64, 71–72, 120, 301, 302, 304, 337, 374
  Tartarus of Maids, 73
  Whitejacket, 73
Meredith, George, 264
Meyer, Hans, 168
Middleton, Thomas, 33
Mill, John Stuart, 263, 335
Milton, John, 6, 8, 33, 50–55, 60, 83, 104, 145, 147, 151, 160, 335, 346, 347, 348, 351, 354
  Comus, 351
  Lycidas, 51, 55
  Nativity Ode, 347
  Paradise Lost, 51, 52–53, 57, 60, 98, 147, 150, 151, 160, 347, 351, 360
  Samson Agonistes, 36–37, 50–51, 53–54
Mirandola, Pico della, 30
Molière, 212, 245, 293–298
  Bourgeois Gentilhomme, 174
  Critique de l'École des Femmes, 293 n., 296

Molière (*Continued*)
  Jalousie du Barbouille, 294
  Lettre sur la comédie de l'Imposteur, 294, 295, 297
  Médecin volant, 294
Monk, Samuel H., *Sublime, The*, 178 n.
Montague, Gene, 249 n., 250
Montherlant, Henri de, 211
  Pasiphae, 211
Moore, Marianne, *Steeple-Jack, The*, 368
Morand, Paul, 363
  Feuilles de température, 363
Moravia, Alberto, 206
  Indifferent Ones, The, 206
Moréas, Jean, 69
Morrison, Theodore, 258–259
Mozart, Wolfgang Amadeus, 335
  Magic Flute, The, 335, 377
  Marriage of Figaro, The, 335
Munro, Thomas, 187 n.
Murray, Gilbert, 314
  Hamlet and Orestes, 314
Musil, Robert, 205, 207, 209, 210, 211, 212, 217, 219
  Man Without Qualities, The, 207
  Writer in Our Age, The, 213
Musset, Alfred de, 88
  Ballade à la lune, 362

Nabokov, Vladimir, 121, 132
  Speak, Memory, 121
Napoleon Bonaparte, 309–310, 351
Nemerov, Howard, 80, 120
Newton, Sir Isaac, 347, 348
Nicolson, Marjorie, 347
Nietzsche, Friedrich Wilhelm, 180, 182, 191
  Birth of Tragedy, The, 191, 341
Norris, Frank, 6, 68
  Octopus, The, 6, 68
  Pit, The, 68

Odets, Clifford, 79, 228
  Golden Boy, 79
  Waiting for Lefty, 228
Ogden, C. K., 66
Olson, Elder, 81
O'Neill, Eugene, 237
  Mourning Becomes Electra, 41
Ong, Walter J., 137, 140
Orwell, George, 46, 200, 220, 221
  1984, 167, 220–225, 348
Ovid, 342

Oxford English Dictionary, 104, 154, 155, 172

Pasternak, Boris, 168, 227
  Dr. Zhivago, 168, 179 n.
Pater, Walter, 264
Patmore, Coventry, *Angel in the House*, 262
Pavese, Cesare, 206–207
Pavlov, Ivan Petrovich, 210
Pearce, Roy Harvey, 5
Phillips, William, 185
Pirandello, Luigi, 39
Plato, 162, 226, 227, 230, 274 n., 283
  Phaedrus, 283
  Republic, The, 162
  Symposium, 283
Podhoretz, Norman, 168
Poe, Edgar Allan, 6, 76, 299, 301, 304, 356
  Arthur Gordon Pym, 374
Pope, Alexander, 151, 345, 346
  Epistle to Augustus, 151
Porter, Katherine Anne, 111
  Pale Horse, Pale Rider, 111
Pottle, Frederick A., 249 n.
Poulet, Georges, xii, 242, 244–245, 293
Pound, Ezra, 77, 356
Prior, Matthew, 36
Propertius, 345
Proust, Marcel, 44, 66, 127, 193, 194, 214
  Remembrance of Things Past, 123

Quintilian, 67

Racine, Jean Baptiste, 30, 33, 34, 38, 39, 91
Raeders, Georges, *Les Chefs d'Oeuvre de Corneille*, 282
Raglan, Lord, 316
Rahv, Philip, 168
Raleigh, John Henry, xii, 7, 8, 10, 42
Rank, Otto, 241, 362
  Trauma of Birth, The, 363
Ransom, John Crowe, xii, 77
Read, Sir Herbert, 242, 243–244, 284
Richards, I. A., 66, 76–77, 98, 241
  Practical Criticism, 77, 241
  Principles of Literary Criticism, 77, 241
  Science and Criticism, 241
Richardson, Samuel, 303, 305, 307
  Clarissa, 301, 306
Rieu, E. V., 110
Rigg, J. M., 113
Rilke, Ranier Maria, 66, 188
  Duino Elegies, 188
Rimbaud, Arthur, 70, 88, 188, 191, 192, 200, 356

Rimbaud, Arthur (*Continued*)
  Le Bateau Ivre, 88, 356
  Les Illuminations, 190, 191, 192
  Une Saison en Enfer, 192
Roland, Chanson de, 300
Romains, Jules, 364
  Cinquième chant, 364
Rosny, J. H., 358
  La Guerre du feu, 358
Rougemont, Denis de, 340
Rousseau, Jean-Jacques, 307, 308, 310, 349
Ruskin, John, 263
Rymer, Thomas, 38–39, 40
  Tragedies of the Last Age, The, 38

Sade, Marquis de, 304, 307, 354
  Justine, 307
Saint Augustine, 68, 71, 183–184
  Confessions, 183–184
Saint-Exupéry, Antoine de, 369
  Wind, Sand and Stars, 369
Saint John of the Cross, 57, 272
Saint Teresa of Avila, 272
Saint Thomas Aquinas, 68, 72, 121
  Summa Theologica, 68
Sainte-Beuve, Charles Augustin, 1, 2
Saintsbury, George, 41
Salmon, André, 368
  Anvers, 368
Salomon, Ernst von, 208
  Questionnaire, The, 208
Sandburg, Carl, 358, 363, 366
  Smoke and Steel, 358, 363, 366
Santayana, George, 42
Sartre, Jean-Paul, 118, 119, 168, 345
  What Is Literature?, 119 n.
Scaliger, Julius Caesar, 31
Schiller, Johann Christoph Friedrich von, 13–14, 18, 39
  Lucille, 301
Schopenhauer, Arthur, 341, 355
Schorer, Mark, 80
  William Blake, The Politics of Vision, 155 n.
Schumpeter, Joseph, 265
  Imperialism and Social Classes, 265–266 n.
Scott, Sir Walter, 303, 346, 350
Selincourt, Ernest de, 284 n.
Seneca, 28, 32, 33, 35, 330, 338
Shakespeare, William, 4, 30, 31, 32, 33, 36, 37, 38, 39, 55, 57, 69, 106, 107, 131, 135, 141, 142, 151, 154, 160, 175, 178, 210, 230, 301, 322–323, 329–336

Shakespeare, William (*Continued*)
  All's Well That Ends Well, 333, 335
  Antony and Cleopatra, 100
  Hamlet, 5, 31, 33, 37, 60, 61, 150, 151, 245, 288, 289, 323, 329–330, 331, 335
  Henry IV (II), 329
  Henry V, 154, 230
  King Lear, 178, 288, 289, 301, 323, 331–332, 335
  Macbeth, 323, 331-333, 335
  Measure for Measure, 323, 333-334
  Much Ado About Nothing, 60
  Othello, 272, 323, 330–331, 334, 335, 336
  Richard II, 32
  Tempest, The, 289, 323
  Timon of Athens, 333
  Troilus and Cressida, 333, 334–335
  Twelfth Night, 334
  Winter's Tale, The, 32
Shaw, George Bernard, 38, 39, 197, 206, 229–230
  Devil's Disciple, The, 206
  Man and Superman, 229–230
Shelley, Percy Bysshe, 195, 346, 348, 353
  Alastor, 355
  Defence of Poetry, A, 348
  Prometheus Unbound, 195, 353, 354, 356
  Queen Mab, 352
  Revolt of Islam, The, 353
  Speculations on Metaphysics, 353
Sheridan, Richard Brinsley, 40
Shumaker, Wayne, 315–316
  Literature and the Irrational, 315–316
Sidney, Sir Philip, 33, 36, 138, 140, 141, 238
  Apology for Poetry, An, 31–32
Sinclair, Lipton, 190
Skeat, W. W., 2
Smart, Christopher, 151
Smidt, Kristian, 263 n., 264
Sombart, Werner, 173–174
  Luxury and Capitalism, 174
Sophocles, 39, 68, 77, 204, 335
  Oedipus at Colonus, 36
  Oedipus Rex, 37, 68, 97, 277 n., 279, 338
Spender, Stephen, 165, 166, 168, 188, 366, 367
  Human Situation, The, 367
  Uncreating Chaos, The, 367
Spengler, Oswald, 43
Spenser, Edmund, 83, 140, 184, 351
  Faerie Queene, The, 160, 349, 351, 353
Spingarn, Joel E., 76 n.

Stageberg, Norman C., 249 n., 251
Stalin, Joseph, 163
Starkie, Enid, 192
Steiner, George, 6, 8, 9, 28, 168
Stendhal, 180, 210
  Red and the Black, The, 123
Sterne, Laurence, *Tristram Shandy*, 112
Stewart, J. A., *Myths of Plato, The*, 287 n.
Stickney, Trumbull, 366
  Six O'Clock, 366
Stowe, Harriet Beecher, 226, 227
  Uncle Tom's Cabin, 226
Strauss, Richard, 39
Strindberg, August, 37
Swinburne, Algernon Charles, 264
Symons, Arthur, 69

Tacitus, 35
Taine, Hippolyte-Adolphe, 1, 162
  History of English Literature, 2, 162
Tasso, Torquato, 40
  Torrismondo, 33
Tate, Allen, xii, 98
Tennyson, Alfred Lord, 55, 56, 194–195, 262, 263
  Break, Break, Break, 55, 56
  In Memoriam, 195
  Locksley Hall, 195
  Ulysses, 263
Terence, 28
Thackeray, William Makepeace, 44, 45, 108
  Pendennis, 262
  Vanity Fair, 301
Thomas, Dylan, 8, 57, 59, 60
Thompson, Sir D'Arcy Wentworth, 131
  On Growth and Form, 131–132
Thucydides, 256
Tillyard, E. M. W., 9, 323
Time magazine, 98, 122
Tinker, C. B., 249 n., 250
Tocqueville, Alexis de, 174, 175, 223
Tolkien, J. R. R., 375–381
  Lord of the Rings, The, 375–381
Tolstoy, Leo, 108, 226
  Anna Karenina, 301
  Death of Ivan Ilyich, The, 130–131
  War and Peace, 120, 123
Tourneur, Cyril, 33
Trilling, Lionel, xii, 7, 165–166, 168, 171, 240, 261 n., 264
  Of This Time, of That Place, 127
Trissino, Giovan Giorgio, 33
Trollope, Anthony, 44, 46

Trollope, Anthony (*Continued*)
  Eustace Diamonds, The, 44
Truss, Tom J., 264
Twain, Mark, 64
  Adventures of Huckleberry Finn, The, 64,
    301, 302
  1601, 305
Tylor, Edward B., 313, 314
  Primitive Culture, 313
Tzara, Tristan, 361
  Cinéma calendrier du coeur abstrait, 361

Vaché, Jacques, 369 n.
Valéry, Paul, 78, 87, 135, 145, 339–340, 342,
    343
  Le Cimitière Marin, 135
  Fragments du Narcisse, 339–340
  Selected Writings, 135
Van Gogh, Vincent, 191
Vaughan, Henry, 139
Verhaeren, Emile, 360, 365
  L'Effort, 360, 361–362, 365
Verlaine, Paul, 88
Vickery, John B., 314
Vico, J. B., 162, 290
Vigny, Alfred Victor de, *Le Cor*, 361
Virgil, 64, 68, 150, 336, 342, 343
  Aeneid, 68, 150
Vivante, Leone, 290
  *English Poetry and Its Contribution to the
    Knowledge of a Creative Principle*, 290 n.
Voltaire, François Marie Arouet de, 38
Vossler, Karl, 70

Wagner, Richard, 30, 39, 272, 340–341
  Tannhäuser, 29
  Tristan und Isolde, 340–341
Wallace, John M., 265 n.
Warren, Austin, *Theory of Literature*, 78
Warren, Robert Penn, 96
Wasserman, Earl, *Subtler Language, The*, 352
Watts, Isaac, 151, 155
  Praise for Mercies Spiritual and Temporal,
    155
Waugh, Evelyn, 200
Webb, Beatrice, 262
Webster, John, 33, 56
  White Devil, The, 31
Wedgwood, Thomas, 285, 286
Weisinger, Herbert, xii, 316, 317, 322
  *Tragedy and the Paradox of the Fortunate
    Fall*, 275, 323

Wellek, René, 78, 84
  Theory of Literature, 78
Wells, H. G., 108, 197
  Boon, 193
Wertheimer, Max, 241
Weyand, Norman, *Immortal Diamond*, 137
Wheelwright, Philip, 315
  Burning Fountain, The, 317, 339
  Myth and Metaphor, 317
  Poetry, Myth, and Reality, 318
Whitehall, Harold, 137, 140
Whitehead, Alfred North, 67
Whitman, Walt, 82, 83, 299, 365
  One's-Self I Sing, 365
  When I Heard the Learn'd Astronomer,
    82–83
Wicksteed, Joseph H., *Blake's Innocence and
    Experience*, 153, n.
Wilde, Oscar, 264
Wilkinson, C. H., 101, 105
Williams, Raymond, 168, 224
Wilson, Edmund, xii, 66, 118 n., 161, 168
  Axel's Castle, 66, 118 n., 192
Wimsatt, W. K., Jr., 79, 80–81, 146
  Intentional Fallacy, The, 79, 80
Winters, Yvor, xiii, 75, 80, 133
Wolfe, Thomas, 204
Woolf, Virginia, 124, 190
Wordsworth, Dorothy, 286
Wordsworth, Mary (Hutchinson), 285, 286
Wordsworth, William, 99, 139, 171–173,
    175, 176, 178, 180, 184, 285, 286, 346,
    350, 352, 354–355, 356
  Idiot Boy, The, 352
  Peter Bell, 352
  Preface to *Lyrical Ballads*, 171–173, 349,
    350, 352, 355
  Prelude, The, 178
  Recluse, The, 353
  Resolution and Independence, 350
  She Dwelt Among the Untrodden Ways,
    99–100
  Solitary Reaper, The, 99, 100
  Upon Westminster Bridge, 139
  Waggoner, The, 352

Yeats, William Butler, 6, 8, 39, 57–59, 66,
    67, 71, 83, 135, 136, 150, 177, 179, 182,
    188, 192, 198–199, 200, 317
  Byzantium, 58, 59
  Second Coming, The, 198–199
  Secret Rose, The, 179

Yeats, William Butler (*Continued*)
  Trembling of the Veil, The, 57
  Vision, A, 59
Young, Philip, 239

Zamiatin, Eugene, W*e,* 167, 220–225
Zola, Emile, 6, 67, 191
  Germinal, 6, 67

68 69 70   7 6 5 4 3 2 1